New York's Forts
in the Revolution

New York's Forts in the Revolution

Robert B. Roberts

Rutherford • Madison • Teaneck
Fairleigh Dickinson University Press
London and Toronto: Associated University Presses

© 1980 by Associated University Presses, Inc.

Associated University Presses, Inc.
Cranbury, New Jersey 08512

Associated University Presses
Magdalen House
136-148 Tooley Street
London SE1 2TT, England

Library of Congress Cataloging in Publication Data

Roberts, Robert B.
  New York's forts in the Revolution.

  Bibliography: p.
  Includes index.
  1. New York (State)—History—Revolution, 1775-1783.
2. Fortification—New York (State) 3. Historic sites—
New York (State) I. Title.
E263.N6R6   974.7'03   77-64395
ISBN 0-8386-2063-9

PRINTED IN THE UNITED STATES OF AMERICA

**Dedicated to the Memory
of our Colonial Forebears
for Completing a Successful Revolution**

Contents

Preface

Although the present posterity of our Revolutionary forebears have been celebrating the recent Bicentennial of their national independence, some measure of our American heritage still remains uncomprehended or almost wholly unrecognized by the general populace. Many locales deserving of greater remembrance, many people caught in the throes of a bloody struggle, and many events—small by themselves perhaps, but in aggregate of world-shaking significance—have almost vanished into the mists of history.

However it was termed—*Revolution* by the Americans or *Rebellion* by the British—the first war for American independence consisted of approximately three hundred battles, nearly a third of them fought on New York soil. The all-important New York frontier, bordering on the Continental Army's critical granaries, was the most bitterly contested. Though ravaged by war and pestilence, this colony supplied more men and money than any other to the cause of freedom. Continentals and militia battled British and Hessians from Brooklyn to Canada, and Tories and Indians in the verdant hinterlands.

Chapter 1, "Frontier War," the narrative section of the book, relates the harrowing experiences of Mohawk Valley and Schoharie settlers—their homes and fields devastated by Indian and Tory torches, driven to seek refuge in larger fortified settlements, and leaving behind them blackened ruins. The longer second chapter, "New York's Revolutionary Forts," delineates in separate sections the history of each of that colony's bulwarks of defense—forts, blockhouses, stockades, and fortified dwellings.

The author, having depended on many historical sources and generous assistance from American history specialists, is solely responsible for the factual content of the book. Traditions, legends, and unverified hearsay have been almost totally eliminated; what is set forth in the following pages constitutes the fascinating military history of Revolutionary New York.

Acknowledgments

Much of the material in this book is a product of many years' research for an encyclopedic history of all American fortifications. Additional data to complete this work were obtained through the generous cooperation of various historical repositories, too many to list here. The author, however, feels that special honorable mention may indicate his deep appreciation to the following:

USMA Library at West Point: Alan C. Aimone, Military History librarian; Lieut. Col. John H. Bradley, Director, Bicentennial Activities; Mrs. Marie T. Capps, Map and Manuscript Librarian; Mrs. Johanna de Onis, Reference Librarian; Robert E. Schnare, Chief, Special Collections Division; Egon Weiss, Librarian.

American Antiquarian Society; Center of Military History, Department of the Army; Constitution Island Association; Fort Plain Museum; Fort Ticonderoga Museum; Herkimer County Historical Society; Library of Congress; Long Island Historical Society; Montgomery County Department of History and Archives; National Archives; New-York Historical Society; New York Public Library; Office of Chief of Military History, Department of Defense; Public Archives of Canada; Old Fort Niagara Association; Royal Archives, Windsor Castle; St. Lawrence County History Center; and Wallace F. Workmaster, Central New York State Parks Commission.

The author's gratitude is due the following for authorization to use material verbatim from their respective publications:

American Enterprise Institute for Public Policy Research for permission to quote material from "The American Revolution as a Successful Revolution" by Irving Kristol (Distinguished Lecture Series on the Bicentennial).

Lt. Col. John H. Bradley, USMA, West Point, New York, for permission to quote in entirety his history chart "Revolutionary War Fortifications" (1976), appearing in *Notes*.

British Library Board, London, for permission to reproduce and quote Joseph Brant Letters, Add. MSS. 21785, folios 32-33 v. and Add. MSS. 21775, folios 49-50.

Citadel Press (division of Lyle Stuart, Inc.) for permission to quote material from *League of the Iroquois* by Lewis Henry Morgan. Copyright 1962 by Corinth Books.

Constitution Island Association for permission to quote material from "The Fort That Never Was" by Merle G. Sheffield; "Constitution Island and West Point in the Revolutionary War" by Alexander C. Flick; and "Constitution Island—Historical Sketch" by Adam E. Potts. Copyright 1965 by Constitution Island Association.

Constitution Island Association for permission to quote material from "History Beneath Our Feet," an address by John H. Mead, September 28, 1969. Copyright 1969 by Constitution Island Association.

Dodd, Mead and Company for permission to quote material from *An Old Frontier of France* by Frank Severance. Copyright 1917.

Dutchess County Historical Society for permission to quote material from the Society's *Year Book,* 1935.

Fort Ticonderoga Museum for permission to quote material from "The French Colonial Forts at Crown Point Strait" by Edward P. Hamilton. Fort Ticonderoga *Bulletin,* October 1970.

Harvard University Press for permission to quote material from *Timothy Dwight's Travels in New England and New York.* Copyright 1969.

Holt, Rinehart and Winston, Inc. for permission to quote material from *The Revolutionary Frontier, 1763-1783* by Jack Sosin. Published by the Dryden Press; copyright 1967.

J. B. Lippincott Company, Publishers, for permission to quote material from *Quaint and Historic Forts of North America* by John Martin Hammond. Copyright 1915.

Long Island Newsday, Garden City, New York, for permission to quote material from "The British Were Here! The British Were Here!" by Robert B. Roberts (July 1, 1973). Copyright 1973 by Newsday, Inc.

Massachusetts Historical Society for permission to quote material from the Society's *Proceedings* 12: 89-90: "John Burgoyne's Proclamation."

William Morrow and Company, New York, and The Penguin Press,

London, for permission to quote material from *Britain and Her Army, 1509-1970* by Correlli Barnett. Copyright 1970.

National Park Service for permission to quote material from *Colonials and Patriots: Historic Places Commemorating Our Forebears, 1700-1783* by Frank B. Sarles, Jr., and Charles E. Shedd. Washington, D.C., 1964.

New Hampshire Historical Society for permission to quote material from *Journal* by Samuel Lane. Copyright 1937.

New-York Historical Society for its courtesy in permitting use of Horatio Gates Letter, September 2, 1777.

Dave Richard Palmer for permission to quote material from his *The River and the Rock: The History of Fortress West Point, 1775-1783*. Published by Greenwood Press; copyright 1969 by Dave Richard Palmer.

Royal Archives, Windsor Castle, England, and Mrs. Stanley Pargellis for permission to quote material from *Military Affairs in North America, 1748-1765,* edited by Stanley Pargellis. Copyright 1964 by Stanley Pargellis.

Royal Historical Manuscripts Commission, London, for permission to quote material from *Report on the Manuscripts of the Late Reginald Rawdon Hastings*. Copyright London, 1930-1947, H.M. Stationery Office.

Rutgers University Press for permission to quote material from *The Revolutionary War in the Hackensack Valley: The Jersey Dutch and the Neutral Ground, 1775-1783* by Adrian Coulter Leiby. Copyright 1962.

United States Military Academy Library for permission to quote material from "Archaeological Excavations at Constitution Island, 1971" by Edward Jelks.

William L. Clements Library, University of Michigan, for permission to quote material from *Lexington to Fallen Timbers, 1775-1794* by Randolph G. Adams and Howard H. Peckham. Copyright 1942.

University of North Carolina Press and the Institute of Early American History and Culture for permission to quote material from *Travels in North America in the Years 1780, 1781 and 1782* by the Marquis de Chastellux. Edited, with revised translation, Introduction and Notes by Howard C. Rice, Jr. Copyright 1963.

Viking Press, Inc. for permission to quote material from *Secret History of the American Revolution* by Carl Van Doren. Copyright 1941 by Carl Van Doren; copyright 1969 by Margaret Van Doren Bevans, Barbara Van Doren Klaw, and Anne Van Doren Ross.

Yale University Press for permission to quote material from *The American Rebellion: Sir Henry Clinton's Narrative of His Campaigns, 1775-1782,* edited by William B. Willcox. Copyright 1954.

GEORGE WASHINGTON
Courtesy of West Point Museum Collections
Painting by Polk

New York's Forts
in the Revolution

If Historiographers should be hardly enough to fill the page of History with the advantages that have been gained with unequal numbers (on the part of America) in the course of this contest, and attempt to relate the distressing circumstances under which they have been obtained, it is more than probable that Posterity will bestow on their labors the epithet and marks of fiction; for it will not be believed that such a force as Great Britain has employed for eight years in this Country could be baffled in their plan of Subjugating it by numbers infinitely less, composed of Men oftentimes half starved; always in Rags, without pay, and experiencing, at times, every species of distress which human nature is capable of undergoing.

General George Washington to Major General Nathanael Greene, Newburgh, February 6, 1783.

1
Frontier War

Rebellion? or Revolution?

The American Revolution had its beginnings in the change of Britain's policies toward her American Colonies soon after the great victory over the French on the Plains of Abraham in 1759, coincident with the accession of George III in 1760. But victory over France on land and sea, resulting in the acquisition of vast new territories, brought almost overwhelming responsibilities. Britain was confronted with problems of organization and administration, the integration of conquests into her colonial empire, and the mounting of additional defenses on new frontiers. Magnifying the governmental headaches was the huge national debt she had amassed.

During her perpetual troubles with France, England had avoided any repressive actions that might weaken the loyalty of the colonies, and so left them, for the most part, to their own devices. For one hundred years the general administration of the Colonies was in the hands of a standing committee of the Privy Council, called the Lords of the Committee of Trade and Plantations, familiarly abbreviated as the Lords of Trade.

To the Council in the mother country went a steady flow of reports from the governors, detailing the proceedings of the colonial legislatures, the manner in which public monies were spent, the amount of revenues, and the status of trade and agriculture. The accounts sent to London constantly complained of the feuds between the royal governors and the popular independent assemblies that controlled the purse strings, representing "the Americans as a factious and turbulent people, with their heads turned by queer political crotchets, unwilling to obey the laws and eager to break off their connection with the British Empire."[1]

The colonial governors thus created in London the idea that America's people were lawlessly unrestrained and greatly in need of a strong hand on the reins of their provincial governments. As a consequence, the Lords of Trade began to send out an ever-increasing flow of instructions, restrictions, and impositions of taxes, some ridiculously arbitrary. In addition, the original charters and grants accorded the provinces had been contravened by the Fort Stanwix Treaty of 1768, which erected a barrier to westward expansion and imprisoned the growing provincial populations in their Atlantic seacoast milieus.[2]

The British authorities considered the Boston Tea Party (December 16, 1773) an act of open defiance. George III's demand that Massachusetts be punished resulted in Parliament's enactment, in the spring of 1774, of five bills—the Quebec Act, the Quartering Act, and three others that specifically applied to Massachusetts. The Americans called these laws the "Intolerable Acts."

Concerted action by all the Colonies was a primary requisite since there was no central government in America. The militant Sons of Liberty in New York first proposed a Continental Congress. Their suggestion was immediately seconded by the members of the Virginia House of Burgesses, which was thereupon arbitrarily dissolved by Virginia's governor. The First Continental Congress convened at Carpenter's Hall in Philadelphia on September 5, 1774, with delegates from every province but Georgia. The Congress adopted the historic Declaration of Resolves on October 14 and created the Continental Association four days later.

The Quebec Act's sanction of the free exercise of Catholicism throughout Canada offended very little the prejudices of the colonials south of the St. Lawrence. What turned the white-hot screw of repression even deeper into the vitals of the Colonies was the provision of the Act to expand the boundaries of Canada southward to the Ohio River, a direct contravention of the territorial claims of Massachusetts, Connecticut, New York, and Virginia.

The general colonial uproar over the acts of repression stimulated movements and forces that materialized into a war of revolution; the British throughout the conflict called the armed protest a "rebellion." In 1777 Benjamin Franklin, in answer to a critical lady correspondent, rebuked her with "You are too early, *Hussy,* as well as too saucy, in

KING GEORGE III
Courtesy of Royal Library, Windsor Castle.
Reproduced by gracious permission of Her Majesty, Queen Elizabeth II.
Copyright reserved.
Painting by Beechey H. Gilder

calling me Rebel; you should wait for the event, which will determine whether it is a *rebellion* or only a *revolution*."[3]

Irving Kirstol's lecture on the war as "a successful revolution" discusses its intellectuality and the differences between a *rebellion* and a *revolution:*

All revolutions unleash tides of passion, and the American Revolution was no exception. But it *was* exceptional in the degree to which it was able to subordinate these passions to serious and nuanced thinking about fundamental problems of political philosophy. The pamphlets, sermons, and newspaper essays of the revolutionary period—only now being reprinted and carefully studied—were extraordinarily "academic", in the best sense of that term. Which is to say, they were learned and thoughtful and generally sober in tone. This was a revolution infused by *mind* to a degree never approximated since, and perhaps never approximated before. By mind, not by dogma. The most fascinating aspect of the American Revolution is the severe way it kept questioning itself about the meaning of what it was

doing. Enthusiasm there certainly was—a revolution is impossible without enthusiasm—but this enthusiasm was tempered by doubt, introspection, anxiety, skepticism. This may strike us as a very strange state of mind in which to make a revolution; and yet it is evidently the right state of mind for making a successful revolution.
. . .

Only the American Revolution is worthy of the name. A rebellion . . . is a meta-political event, emerging out of a radical dissatisfaction with the human condition as experienced by the mass of the people, demanding instant "liberation" from this condition, an immediate transformation of all social and economic circumstance, a prompt achievement of an altogether "better life" in an altogether "better world". The spirit of rebellion is a spirit of desperation. . . .

A revolution, in contrast, is a political phenomenon. It aims to revise and reorder the political arrangements of a society. . . . It requires an attentive prudence, a careful calculation of means and ends, a spirit of sobriety—the kind of spirit exemplified by that calm, legalistic document, the Declaration of Independence. . . .

The present-day student of revolutions will look in vain for any familiar kind of "revolutionary situation" in the American colonies prior to '76. The American people at that moment were the most prosperous in the world and lived under the freest institutions to be found anywhere in the world. They knew this well enough and boasted of it often enough. Their quarrel with the British crown was, in its origins, merely over the scope of colonial self-government, and hardly anyone saw any good reason why this quarrel should erupt into a war of independence. It was only after the war got under way that the American people decided that this was a good opportunity to make a revolution as well—that is, to establish a republican form of government.

The document that precipitated the beginning of the war at Lexington and Concord (April 19, 1775) was the order by Thomas Gage, Commander-in-Chief of His Majesty's forces in America, to Lieut. Col. Francis Smith:

Sir, A Quantity of Ammunition and Provision together as Number of Cannon and small Arms having been collected at Concord for the avowed Purpose of asserting a Rebellion against His Majesty's Government, You will march with the Corps of Grenadiers and Light Infantry put under your command with the utmost expedition and secrecy to Concord, where you will seize and destroy all the Artillery and Ammunition, provisions, Tents & all other military stores you can find.[5]

Three weeks later, on May 10, the Second Continental Congress met at the State House (Independence Hall) in Philadelphia, by coincidence the same day Fort Ticonderoga was flamboyantly captured by Ethan Allen and Benedict Arnold. This was indeed a working congress: May

24, on the resignation of Peyton Randolph, elected John Hancock to the presidency; May 29, adopted a memorial to Canadians, pleading with them to enter the war, and voted to raise forces in Pennsylvania, Maryland, and Virginia to support the Continental Army in Boston; June 15, elected George Washington as commander-in-chief of the new army, and adopted a general plan and voted $2 million in bills of credit to prosecute and finance the war.

The choice of George Washington of Virginia was determined by political, geographical, and military judgments. The northern delegates, particularly those from New England, had decided that, in order to secure the support of the southern colonies, a southerner should be selected. Washington's eligibility was enhanced by his scrupulous character, charisma, and a dignified demeanor that exuded a steadfast confidence in his conviction that the American cause was a righteous one. His military experience during the French and Indian War, though restricted entirely to frontier warfare, was probably greater than that of any other man in the South. Washington acknowledged his ignorance of the management of a large army of men, but this lack of experience was more than adequately compensated by his ability for leadership and his business acumen.[6]

GENERAL HORATIO GATES
Courtesy of USMA Library

On July 3 Washington took formal command of a new army, which he described as "a mixed multitude of people . . . under very little discipline, order or government." He stipulated that "discipline is the soul of an army. It makes small numbers formidable; procures success to the weak and esteem to all." He selected experienced Horatio Gates as his adjutant general (with the rank of brigadier general) and gave him the onerous task of working up regulations and orders to instill discipline into the army's rank and file. Both officers and men were imbued with the spirit of rebellion, a feeling transmuted into loathing for any form of regimentation. Vigorous efforts were made to put a stop to the disrupting comings and goings of officers and men and to put into effect uniform roll calls and post returns. Washington instituted strict rules of distinction to obviate the camaraderie between officers and enlistees. To stress the new regimen or code of conduct, a varied assortment of punishments was meted out to inculcate discipline: castigations included the lash, wooden horse, pillory, and drumming out of camp, with courts-martial being regular day-to-day affairs.[7]

In 1775 the American Colonies had a total population of about 2,500,000 people (exclusive of Indians), a number ordinarily large enough to furnish the manpower for a sizable army for those times. Not all the male members of this colonial society, however, could be considered eligible for military service, in particular the black slaves, who constituted about twenty percent of the potential. A very small percentage of male blacks did serve with distinction in the cause of the Revolution and were not segregated into special battalions.

> Perhaps one-third of the "politically active" Americans remained loyal to the British Government. As in any society there were also the apathetic and indifferent who swayed with the tide. The genuine patriots still provided a far larger potential of military manpower than the British could possibly transport and supply across the Atlantic, but most of the men of military age were farmers who married young and immediately started large families. Whatever their patriotic sentiments, few were ready to undertake long terms of military service, fearing that if they did their farms and families at home would suffer. Accustomed to the tradition of short-term service under local commanders, they infinitely preferred it to long-term service in the Continental Army.[8]

The plan for the new Continental Army called for "26 regiments of infantry of 728 men each, plus one regiment of riflemen and one of artillery, 20,372 men in all, to be uniformly paid, supplied, and administered by the Continental Congress and enlisted to the end of 1776."

It looked good on paper, but the commander-in-chief very soon learned to his exasperation that the plan could not be implemented:

> Both officers and men resisted a reorganization that cut across the lines of the locally organized units in which they were accustomed to serve. The men saw as their very first obligation their families and farms at home, and they were reluctant to re-enlist for another year's service. On December 10 [1775], despite pressures and patriotic appeals, most of the Connecticut men went home and militia from New Hampshire and Massachusetts had to be brought in to fill their places in the line.[9]

On New Year's Day 1776, instead of the planned strength of twenty thousand men, Washington found that he had only eight thousand enlistees. With innumerable gaps in his regiments, he had to rely on short-term militia to fill the openings, and this chaotic process was repetitive throughout the war. The patriotic view in 1775 foresaw a short struggle, with the result that the colonial tradition of short-term enlistments took precedence over the for-the-duration needs of the Continental Army, committed to the winning of total independence.

From the beginning the war had gone beyond the semblance of a civil war; it had progressed to the status of fratricidal warfare. Kinships were sundered by divided familial loyalties. Sons turned against fathers, and brothers ruptured their fraternal regard for each other. The Six Nations of the Iroquois were likewise divided, their more astute leaders faced with the dilemma of whether to maintain their alliance with the British or to adopt a stand of strict neutrality.

The audacious two-pronged Continental invasion of Canada had been made possible by the capture of Ticonderoga in May. Congress resolved in June not to attempt such an expensive and hazardous expedition, but three weeks later it reversed itself, apparently captivated by the optimistic possibility of conquering lightly held Canada and making it the fourteenth colony or state.

Benedict Arnold's decimated army just about survived the harrowing march through the Maine wilderness. Gen. Richard Montgomery, after a successful siege of St. Johns, captured Montreal. Leaving a garrison to hold that prize, Montgomery joined Arnold before Quebec. Minus siege artillery and confronted by year-end expiring enlistments, their only hope was to assault the old citadel and overwhelm its defenses in one great burst of patriotic energy. The attack was launched during a raging blizzard on the night of December 31/January 1. Montgomery was killed while leading an advance against a fortified position at Point Diamond; Arnold suffered a severe leg injury during the fierce fighting in Quebec's Lower Town.

The Americans, stricken with morale paralysis, sick and hungry, lingered outside the walls of Quebec. Confined to his hospital bed, Arnold was still obsessed with taking Quebec. The St. Lawrence ice pack began to break up with the spring thaw and, just as inevitable, was the entry into the river of fifteen British transports from Europe, loaded to the gunwales with more than ten thousand reinforcements, a sizable portion of whom encamped at Three Rivers. Guy Carleton emerged from Quebec with nine hundred men and four guns to rout the Continentals under Maj. Gen. John Thomas, who retreated precipitately with his men to the Sorel River.

Arnold was relieved of his command before Quebec by seventy-year-old Gen. Thomas in early April and sent to Montreal to hold that town, establishing his headquarters in the Chateau de Ramezay.[10] He had already sent out frantic appeals for more men. Congress was embroiled in discussions about a document called the Declaration of Independence[11] and Gen. Washington was involved in defense plans to deal with the probable invasion of New York. In May Congress belatedly issued orders to Generals John Sullivan and William Thompson to reinforce the remnants of the Canadian expedition and return to the siege lines around Quebec.

At the American-held fortified post at The Cedars, situated on a tongue of land jutting into the St. Lawrence about thirty miles west of Montreal, the Patriot force of 390 men capitulated to an enemy column of some 600 British regulars, Canadians, and Indians. Originally under the direction of Col. Timothy Bedel (veteran of the French and Indian War and commander of the New Hampshire Ranger brigade), the command devolved on Maj. Isaac Butterfield when Bedel set out for Montreal to procure reinforcements. Maj. Butterfield, from the very first, offered to surrender the post, continually refusing for two days to allow his men to fight it out. Bedel and Butterfield were later castigated by Congress for their cowardly dereliction of duty. A relief force of about 120 men, marching from Montreal, was ambushed about four miles from The Cedars on May 20 and compelled to surrender. That evening two prisoners were executed by the British and four or five others tortured to death by the Indians. The Mohawk war leader, Joseph Brant, was not present at The Cedars, as was erroneously reported by some historians; Brant was, at the time, in England and did not return to America until the end of July.[12]

Thompson's assault with two thousand men on heavily garrisoned Three Rivers turned into an American debacle, in which the general and two hundred men were taken prisoner. Gen. Sullivan, beset by additional reverses and finding his army seriously depleted by sickness, desertions, and deaths, determined to quit Canada. He therefore, on the 14th of June, abandoned his position at the mouth of the Richelieu River and slowly moved south in the direction of St. Johns. Arnold and his occupation army departed from Montreal on the 15th and joined Sullivan at Chambly, north of St. Johns.

The beaten army reached St. Johns during the last week of June. The desperately sick, stricken with smallpox and severe dysentery, were at once sent by boat to Point au Fer, Isle aux Noix, and Isle La Motte. When the boats returned, the remainder of the troops went to Isle aux Noix where they waited for eight days while the sick were transported to Crown Point. The last of the Arnold-Montgomery expedition, leaving a trail of fresh graves behind them, reached Crown Point on July 3rd. The troops stayed about ten days and, when they departed for Ticonderoga, left behind them an additional three hundred new graves.

In June Gen. Philip Schuyler, commander of the Northern Department, ordered, with the approval of Congress, the seizure and restoration of the abandoned and ruined British Fort Stanwix at the Oneida Carrying Place (today's Rome, New York). The work, started by Col. Dayton, was brought to near completion in 1777 by Col. Gansevoort of Albany with his Third New York Continentals. American foresight in establishing a strong garrison here, at the headwaters of the Mohawk River, put the British on the Niagara Frontier on the defensive.

Early in 1776 Congress had ordered Gen. Schuyler to arrest Sir John Johnson, son of the late Sir William Johnson. Because his wife obstinately refused to leave manorial Johnson Hall at Johnstown, Sir John gave his pledge to be beholden to the orders of Congress. In May, however, the baronet violated his parole and fled to Fort Niagara. Burning with hatred for the rebels, who had mistreated his wife and seized his Mohawk Valley estate, Sir John urged the formation of a British expeditionary army to invade the valley and organize the Loyalists there into an effective auxiliary force.

British Gen. Carleton accomplished wonders when he assembled an army of thirteen thousand troops, including five thousand Hessians, and a fleet of gunboats and transports at St. Johns. He began operations on September 10, with his armada ready to sail during the first week of October. But the impetuously brilliant Benedict Arnold, in suicidal desperation, ruined the British timetable on the eleventh at Lake Champlain's Valcour Island in the war's greatest "sea" battle. Sir John's revenge had to wait another year.

Gentleman Johnny Burgoyne spent the winter of 1776-77 in England, where he promoted the military campaign for 1777 (the Year of the Hangman for superstitious Patriots), which incorporated Sir John

Johnson's proposal. Guy Johnson promised "swarms of Six Nations warriors." The ambitious three-pronged invasion plan called for Burgoyne and a great army to descend from Montreal and capture Forts Crown Point and Ticonderoga to gain the upper Hudson Valley; St. Leger and a smaller force were to leave from Oswego, descend to the Oneida Carrying Place, thence to capture Fort Stanwix and penetrate the Mohawk Valley; and, at the same time, Lord Howe and his land and sea forces were to ascend the Hudson from New York City to capture the Highlands forts. All three expeditions, if successful in their separate ventures, would meet at Albany, thus divide the Colonies, and possibly end the war.

St. Leger's diversionary expedition into the Mohawk Valley ended at its gateway during the last week of August. After a long frustrating siege before the ramparts of Fort Stanwix, during which part of his army engaged Gen. Herkimer's relief force in a bloody battle at Oriskany six miles away, he was routed into frantic retreat by the exaggerated news of the approach of Benedict Arnold's eight hundred-man relief force. Almost two months later, on October 17, Burgoyne surrendered his British and Riesdesel's Hessian forces to the Continentals at Saratoga. Sir Henry Clinton, replacing William Howe (who had sailed south with a major share of the New York forces for the Philadelphia campaign) as commander of the Hudson Highlands invasion force, captured Forts Clinton and Montgomery, routed the small garrison on Constitution Island, burned Esopus (Kingston), then retreated on Howe's orders and request for reinforcements in Pennsylvania.

The British failure to capture the Hudson Valley and take Albany dispersed the Tories and Indians into the northern hinterland. Barry St. Leger and the harried remnants of his force made all haste for Oswego and, eventually, to Carleton Island; Sir John Johnson and his Royal Greens returned to their haven at Montreal; and John Butler led hundreds of Tories and Loyalists back to the sanctuary at Niagara. Gen. Carleton fell in with the plan to initiate frontier raids and gave his approval for the recruitment of a Loyalist Ranger regiment, with Butler as colonel and guiding genius of the murderous marauders. The winter of 1777-78 saw Washington and his Continentals, ousted from Philadephia by Howe, settled miserably at Valley Forge and Germantown, huddled around warming fires and subsisting on meager rations.

1778 and 1779

The year 1778 witnessed unprecedented bloody assaults by Tory auxiliaries and Six Nations Indians, mostly Seneca and Mohawk, against the northern settlements. The forays were carefully planned and successfully executed raids to destroy the bountiful granaries that fed Washington's Continental Army biding its time in New Jersey.

The enemy auxiliaries, vengeful in their ferocity to wipe out the insults and indignities suffered by their kin at the hands of the Patriots, very often attired themselves in Indian garb and war-painted their faces. Despite their disguises, they were often recognized for what they were—''blue-eyed Indians.'' In the British view, the simplest and most direct method to cripple Washington's army was to reduce into oblivion the golden wheat and fat herds in the verdant Mohawk, Schoharie, and Wyoming valleys, and to so demoralize the farmers that they could neither sow nor harvest the crops nor tend their livestock. Since the farmers themselves constituted the militia and could not both fight the enemy and work the fields, Washington would be compelled to send Continentals to garrison the pioneer frontier forts, thus depleting his already thin ranks to protect his army's breadbaskets.

John Fiske, while admitting to the inevitability of Indian war against the encroaching white, condemned the devilish British war office design to put to use the savagery of the Indians:

> The barbarous border fighting of the Revolutionary War was largely due to the fact that powerful tribes of wild Indians still confronted us on every part of our steadily advancing frontier. They would have tortured and scalped our backwoodsmen even if we had no quarrel with George III, there could be no lasting peace until they were crushed completely. When the war broke out, their alliance with the British was natural, but the truculent spirit which sought to put that savage alliance to the worst uses was something which it would be fair to ascribe to the British commanders in general; it must be charged to the account of Lord George German [British Secretary of State for American Colonies] and a few unworthy men who were willing to be his tools.[13]

The Burgoyne and St. Leger defeats, major victories for the Patriots, had no effect on the British occupation of Canada, the Old Northwest, or their strongholds in western New York and on Lake Champlain. The colonial settlements closest to the vulnerable long frontier were easy prey for Tory-Indian raiding parties. In the Old Northwest, Detroit was the British base for forays against settlements on the Ohio River, ranging down into present-day Kentucky. Major attacks against communities in northern New York and upper Pennsylvania emanated from Fort Niagara and Oswego, with minor raiding parties using Crown Point and Carleton Island as bases. The Iroquois towns of Unadilla (a settlement with stone and frame houses deserted by the whites in June 1777) on the Susquehanna River, about forty miles south of Lake Otsego, and

Oquaga (present-day Ouaquaga), twenty miles below Unadilla, Joseph Brant's main base during St. Leger's expedition, were Indian assembly points for assaults against the settlements in the Mohawk Valley.

The calendar of Tory and Indian raids spells out now memorialized dates on which male Patriots were either taken prisoner or killed—in most cases, women and children were not harmed—and their homes leveled by fire. The first town to be hit was Fairfield, eight miles north of German Flats (Herkimer) and located on Sir William Johnson's original grant. In the middle of March 1778, a small raiding party of Tories and Indians, led by a former resident of the community, quietly crossed the snow-covered fields and surprised the town. One boy was reportedly killed and scalped, a dozen or more men were taken prisoner, and Patriots' homes burned down. On April 30 a small band of perhaps twenty-five Indians, "blue-eyed" men among them, appeared at Ephratah, about ten miles to the west of Johnstown, and methodically set fire to every home, barn, and mill.

Late in May there occurred a bloody incident that illustrated the cleverness of Indian leadership. The prosperous farming settlement of Cobleskill, at the gateway to the beautiful Schoharie Valley, was invaded by Brant and a sizable mixed force of Indians and Tories. An urgent message had been sent to the authorities, citing Cobleskill's fears of a raid because some Indians had been seen scouting the area. The warning was taken seriously and a detachment of thirty to forty Continentals and fifteen militiamen was dispatched. On May 30 a score of Indians appeared in the immediate neighborhood of the house where the militiamen were billeted. The entire Patriot contingent, to a man, turned out in pursuit. They were skillfully led into an ambush set by some three hundred of the enemy. There was a short but fierce skirmish, terminating when the Americans, about to be completely encircled, precipitately retreated. They left fourteen of their comrades dead on the field. The Cobleskill residents, following on the heels of the defeated militia, made for Schoharie and safety, leaving their homes and barns to the Indian torch.

The early spring raids against the settlements on the Mohawk Valley's northern slopes successfully forced the badly frightened farmers to desert their homes and fields to seek shelter and protection afforded by the American forts along the Mohawk. Joseph Brant, with his Indians and Tories, returned to Oquaga. His preparations for major raids began with orders to foraging Indian parties to obtain large stockpiles of provisions from the Patriot farming communities and the Tory sympathizers in the Unadilla region, not neglecting to recruit partisans for Butler's Rangers.

Brant's first major raid was against Springfield on June 18. The town was situated at the head of Lake Otsego, about seven miles west of Cherry Valley and ten miles south of Fort Herkimer. Apparently the Mohawk chief had issued strict orders not to harm the women and children, for he had them all put in one house and applied the torch to all the other structures, even taking the time to burn wagons, wooden farming implements, and haystacks in the fields. The men were taken prisoner. Leading provision-loaded horses and herding more than two hundred head of cattle and horses before them, the Indians headed down the Susquehanna to Tioga Point, where John Butler's force was encamped. Brant relinquished most of his marauding army to the Tory leader. Keeping about sixty of his faithful Mohawks and a score of Tories, Brant began raiding activities along the Delaware and into the Minisink settlements.

John Butler selected one of Washington's critical granaries, the fertile twenty-five-mile-long Wyoming Valley in northeastern Pennsylvania, to suffer the enemy's initial major assault of the frontier war. Originally occupied by the Shawnees, who were dispossessed by the Delawares, who then suffered the same fate at the hands of the Iroquois, Wyoming became the battleground of conflicting royal grants. A six-year internecine war was waged between the Connecticut Yankees and the Pennsylvania Pennamites, the latter attempting to oust the former, with the last battle occuring in 1775. Inhabited by nearly five thousand Yankees, mostly Patriots, the prosperous valley was isolated from the nearest white settlements sixty miles away, with the Iroquois bases at Oquaga and Old Tioga, northeast and northwest respectively, only fifty miles distant. Two important factors aggravated the settlement's isolation: the Pennsylvanians, bitterly remembering their losses in the Wyoming war, would be loath to come to the aid of the valley; Wyoming's contribution of two companies of able-bodied men for Washington's Continental Army left mostly untried local militia and a small contingent of Continentals to garrison Forty Fort, the strongest bastion in the valley.[14]

In his fiftieth year, in "uncertain health, fat, short of breath, but bristling with determination," Butler left Niagara in early May with a party of his Rangers. They proceeded east to Lake Seneca, then south to Tioga Point (now Athens, Pennsylvania), at the confluence of the Susquehanna and Chemung rivers. There Butler was joined by a large contingent of Indians, mostly Senecas and Cayugas under the leadership of Sayenqueraghta (Old King).[15] The strong force lingered at Tioga Point while a fleet of rafts and boats was constructed to carry the men down the Susquehanna. June 30 found the invasion force establishing temporary camp on a high hill overlooking Wyoming. Butler's reports of the campaign do not specifically reveal the exact strength of his small army. Patriot inflated estimates ran as high as 1,100 men while the journal kept by Richard Cartwright,[16] a Tory with Butler, reports that the expedition consisted of only 110 Rangers and 464 Indians.[17]

Butler, counseled by William Caldwell, a former inhabitant of the valley exiled for his Tory machinations,[18] took his time advancing. Scouts were sent out to estimate the strength of each fort in the valley. On July 1 Butler moved forward cautiously but with resolution. Two stockaded defenses, Wintermoot's Fort and Jenkin's Fort, surrendered without a fight and were put to the torch. Two days later the defenders of Forty Fort were enticed out of the ramparts and drawn into a craftily contrived ambuscade. Nearly three hundred Patriots lost their lives on the bloody field. The next day, July 4, the fort was surrendered by the surviving garrison and the hundreds of people who had sought refuge within its walls. Guarantees were exchanged. The defenders marched out without fear of molestation and were paroled on their word not to participate in the war's future hostilities.

Contrary to lurid contemporary reports, born of the hysteria and fear of the many hundreds who fled the valley to other white settlements in Pennsylvania, there was no Indian massacre of noncombatants. Witnesses testified that Joseph Brant was among the leaders of the Indians, but the Mohawk leader at the time was many miles away, between Unadilla and the Minisink settlements. Butler's Tories and Indians leisurely completed the devastation of Wyoming and left the valley a blackened ruin. The work of rebuilding began in August when Gen. Lachlan McIntosh ordered Colonels Daniel Brodhead and Zebulon Butler to reoccupy the valley with four hundred troops.[19]

Two weeks later, on July 18, Brant and a large party of his Indians struck Andrustown (Andrew's Town), inhabited by fewer than ten families, eight miles south of German Flats and north of the town of Warren. Four men were slain and the rest of the inhabitants, with all their personal possessions and provisions, taken prisoner and escorted to either Unadilla or Oquaga.[20]

On September 13 Brant struck again, this time at German Flats itself, a settlement of about seventy-five homes on both sides of the Mohawk. Two miles to the west was Fort Dayton, a dilapidated relic of the French and Indian War. The surprise raid planned by the Mohawk war leader, with 150 of his Indians and 300 Tories led by Capt. Caldwell, was spoiled by the bravery and perseverance of one of four scouts dispatched from the fort to scour the country toward Unadilla. Adam Helmer outsped Indian pursuers for many miles and spread the alarm. The warning no doubt saved many lives as the settlers hurriedly left their homes to find refuge in two forts and a church. The invaders had to be content with only wreaking complete destruction of the Mohawk Valley settlement. On September 19, after a survey had been made of the stricken settlement, Col. Peter Bellinger, commandant of Fort Dayton, wrote his report to Gen. Stark at Albany that the enemy had put the torch to sixty-three houses, with nearly as many barns filled with grain and fodder, three mills, and a sawmill, driving off a large number of horses, cattle and sheep, and leaving behind in the blackened ruins two white men and one black man killed.[21]

Brant's devastating raids led Col. Peter Livingston to investigate the state of the stricken settlements in both the Mohawk and Schoharie valleys. He reported that unless a sufficient number of Continental troops were posted in the endangered areas, the whole region would be deserted by the fearful inhabitants. In desperation the Continental authorities ordered the destruction of the Indian strongholds on the Susquehanna. Col. William Butler, with a force of five hundred men, mostly Fourth Pennsylvania Continentals, left the Schoharie on October 2 and in the next two weeks made a sweep of the country about Unadilla and Oquaga. The two enemy bases were burned, more than four thousand bushels of corn destroyed, and all the livestock slaughtered. At the time, Brant and his marauders were on the Delaware on a series of raids, and their towns were amost deserted. Butler caused much material damage, but not one casualty was inflicted against the Indians. The American foray, as it turned out, was a useless exercise and influenced the Indians and Tories to take frightful revenge on Cherry Valley the following month.

Exposed and vulnerable Cherry Valley, several miles directly east of Otsego Lake, had no refuge for its inhabitants until 1777, when a palisade and earthworks were constructed around the home of Col. Samuel Campbell. After solicitations were made to the Marquis de Lafayette at Johnstown in the spring of 1778, a strong fort was built at Cherry Valley and named Fort Alden for its first commander, Col. Ichabod Alden, who arrived there in July with about 250 Continentals.

Despite persistent intelligence reports of an impending Indian and Tory attack, Alden refused to take proper precautions; he even neglected to protect his own person and the lives of his officers by having them billeted outside the fort. When settlers sought to enter the fort after strong rumors of an assault had been aired, Alden scoffed at their alarm and refused them entrance. The Continental officer's obstinacy cost him his life in the very first minutes of the attack.

In keeping with the plan to knock out the back settlements. Col.

Butler, obtaining the necessary authorization, delegated his son, Capt. Walter Butler, to undertake from Fort Niagara the hazardous venture of destroying Cherry Valley and its fort. While the Continentals were burning the Indian bases on the Susquehanna, young Butler and two hundred of his father's Rangers had to sit on the sidelines at Chemung, just south of the New York-Pennsylvania border, about 45 miles west of Oquaga. While he remained quiescent in his camp, Butler and Brant kept up a long-distance exchange of intelligence in efforts to arrange a joining of their forces. Although the threat of meeting up with the American retaliatory force had dissipated by the middle of October, when the Patriots had returned to Middle Fort in the Schoharie Valley, Butler, for unknown reasons, still tarried at Chemung. Prolonging the beginning of the operation until late in the season certainly aggravated the Tory and Indian retreat from Cherry Valley to Niagara, a distance of about 280 miles through snow-covered country, with a dearth of wild game for sustenance and the enemy at their heels in pursuit.

Walter Butler, with his two hundred Rangers and Brant with more than five hundred Mohawks and Senecas, finally joined forces on the Susquehanna during the first week of November. One of Col. Alden's very few precautions, the dispatching of a party of four men to scout downstream along the river's banks, ended when they were captured on the morning of November 10 as they slept around their campfire. Under pressure the scouts divulged the news that Fort Alden's officers were billeted outside of the fort's walls, and they even located the houses where they were quartered. The Tory and Indian leaders thereupon completed their plan of attack.

The weather during the night and early morning of November 10/11 proved ideal for initiating the attack. Several inches of fresh snow on the ground and a thick winter haze silenced and covered the enemy approach on the sleeping settlement. The fort was the ultimate objective of the attackers, but their primary concern was to eliminate the fort's officers billeted in several houses. While identification of the dwellings was passed from Tory to Indian, one of Cherry Valley's inhabitants rode across their path on his way to the fort. The Rangers fired and wounded him but he escaped to sound the alarm. A party of Senecas, in advance of the main body, attacked the Wells home four hundred yards from the fort. Alden was one of several officers, along with about twenty-five men, billeted in the house. He and a few of his officers and men were killed trying to make the fort on the run.

Tories and Indians raced for the fort in an effort to overwhelm its defenders in one furious assault, but the garrison, with only a few moments warning, managed to close the gate in the face of the enemy.

Butler and Brant kept at it for three-and-a-half hours, but in mid-afternoon they finally withdrew in defeat. Indians were historically noted for their reluctance to storm a strongly fortified position, and the Mohawks and Senecas that day were no exceptions. They stole away in small parties during the action to vent their fury on the inhabitants. When Butler realized their design, he at once dispatched a squad of Rangers to shield the people. Before the Rangers could disperse among the dwellings to offer their protection, the Indians had killed thirty-two noncombatants, thirteen of them at the Wells house and the remainder in six other houses, several women and children among the victims.

Chroniclers for a century thereafter maligned Butler and Brant, picturing them as devils incarnate. The lurid tales of these writers, all based on wildly exaggerated hearsay, narrated in horrible detail how babies were snatched from the arms of their mothers and brained against tree trunks. At odds, biographers of Walter Butler and Joseph Brant verbalized on the culpability of these men in the massacre. John Butler was quoted by one writer as alleging that Brant "secretly incited the Indians in this massacre in order to stigmatize his son" Walter, an accusation never confirmed by archival evidence. Brant's biographer refutes accusations that the Mohawk chief had inflamed his Indians to murder and says he "did all in his power to prevent the shedding of innocent blood."

The military history of North America is abundant with instances of the unreliability of Indians as military adjuncts. Their innate reliance on individual action caused them to reject regimentation and military discipline. The loss of their homes and personal possessions when Unadilla and Oquaga were destroyed enraged the Mohawks and Senecas and their revenge taken in blood-letting should not have been unexpected. Until the raid on Cherry Valley, the Patriots had not reported any instances of atrocities against noncombatants or the killing of women and children.

The raiders took with them at least seventy men, women, and children, and camped for the night in the village's vicinity. Over Indian objections, Butler released all of the prisoners under a strong Ranger guard the next day, except for two women and their seven children, kept as hostages for the Tory commander's mother, aunt and several Tory officers' wives held as Continental prisoners in Albany. Furious with the Indians for their shocking behavior, Butler sent the majority of them away in disgrace. Expecting an early arrival of American reinforcements, Butler gave the order to retreat and began the long, strenuous trek through the early-winter snow to the British base at Fort Niagara.[22]

The Cherry Valley raid was a brilliantly executed psychological stroke. Militarily, however, the British mission was a failure—Fort Alden remained as a guard and haven. The partial success of the enemy can be attributed to the arrogant obstinacy of the American military commander.

At Quebec, Governor General Frederick Haldimand became livid with anger on hearing the news of the atrocities and reiterated orders that a strict restraint be put on their Indian allies. Indeed, when Walter Butler returned to Fort Niagara, he vowed that never again would he command a mission where Indians far outnumbered the Tories. It is to his credit that he not once faltered in that resolution.

In spite of Continental support of the patriotic farming communities, however inadequate it might prove to protect the long frontier, the Tory and Indian penetration into the settlements of New York and Pennsylvania demanded a retributive offensive against the Iroquois. Washington ruled out any direct campaign against Canada because of the lack of transportation and the short supply of provisions. He instead concentrated on the immediate urgency of destroying the Indian villages, burning their stores of foodstuffs, devastating their bountiful fields and orchards and, hopefully, capturing Fort Niagara and the Oswego fortifications. Granted the possibility of only a partial success, the destruction of the Iroquois granary would still oblige the Indian warriors and their families to seek succor at the British forts already suffering from inadequate lines of supply. A radical weakening of the British-Indian ability to mount strikes against the frontier would bring relief to the beleaguered settlements, releasing the protective Continental and militia forces to strengthen the American hold on the Hudson Highlands.

When Gen. Horatio Gates declined the command of the three-pronged expedition on the plea that he was too old at the age of fifty-two to undertake such a hazardous campaign, Washington offered it to Maj. Gen. John Sullivan, a singularly militarily inept and luckless thirty-nine-year-old Maine-born lawyer who was a New Hampshire resident. According to one biographer, this Gen. Sullivan, who was then in Rhode Island, hesitated to accept for several reasons: his health was precarious; he was beset by financial problems; and he was loath to be separated from his family for a comparatively long period of time.[23] Though Sullivan was being seriously attacked in Congress for his past inadequacies in Canada, on Long Island, at Brandywine, and in Rhode Island, Washington, oddly enough, still retained a modicum of faith in him despite his truculence and overweening ambition.[24]

With the northern theater of war at a stalemate, Washington could afford to release an appreciable number of Continental regulars to Sullivan, even furnishing scouts and a contingent of Daniel Morgan's famed riflemen. Washington wisely kept the employment of under-trained militia to an absolute minimum. His orders were specific: he sought "the total destruction and devastation" of the Iroquois villages, which were not to be "merely overrun but destroyed," with "the capture of as many prisoners of every age and sex as possible" to be held as security for the Indians' future conduct.

The opening of the campaign, destined to become one of the largest and best-planned actions of the war, was scheduled for the spring of 1779, with Gen. James Clinton, brother of New York's governor, George Clinton, leading an expedition from the upper waters of the Mohawk River and Fort Stanwix into the Onondaga country. The second phase would have Clinton assemble his column at Canajoharie on the Mohawk, then push obliquely through New York in a southwesterly direction, burning Indian towns, cornfields and orchards, as he took the path of the Susquehanna River down to Tioga where he was to rendezvous with Gen. Sullivan's column.

At approximately the same time, Col. Daniel Brodhead was to leave from Fort Pitt in western Pennsylvania, proceed up the Allegheny River, overcome the Indians and destroy their settlements. His instructions were to exchange intelligence with Sullivan and to traverse western New York to form a union with him somewhere in the Seneca country.

Gen. Sullivan was to start from Easton, Pennsylvania, with the main body of the expedition and cross the state to Tioga and, after combining with Clinton's column, to penetrate the territory of the Cayugas and Senecas. Subsequent to depriving these Indians of their power to continue participation in the war and defeating the British and Tories with them, the Americans had every hope of capturing Fort Niagara and the Oswego stronghold.

Almost from the outset, logistical problems caused long delays, and there were petulant differences among the commanders of the three pincers. Continental regulars had begun to assemble at Easton when Sullivan arrived there on May 7. It took exactly six more weeks to get his column on the road. While his troops camped in the Wyoming Valley for an additional five weeks (June 23 to July 31), many miles to the south Joseph Brant, apparently on his own initiative to either fatten his commissary or throw a spoke into Sullivan's army machinery, launched a surprise raid into the Minisink settlements.

The Mohawk chief headed a sizable party down the Delaware River from Oquaga to a place called Grassy Brook on the east shore of the river, a couple of miles above the mouth of Lackawaxen Creek. Leaving most of his force there, he led eighty-seven Indians and Tories to the sleeping village of Minisink (now Port Jervis in Orange County) on the night of July 19/20. The raiders plundered and burned what they could in the few hours Brant allocated, knowing full well that it would not be long before an American militia force appeared on the scene. Martinus Decker's Fort and Van Auken's Fort were among the stockades attacked. Killing four men and leaving the settlement engulfed in flames, they carried off a considerable stock of provisions and several prisoners, driving before them a large herd of cattle back over the same route to the rendezvous.

A force of about 150 militiamen, most of them from the Goshen area, met at Minisink, now a ruination, on the morning of the 21st to take up the pursuit of Brant's Indians and Tories. By the next morning they had caught up with the raiders, slowed by the consequence of transporting their considerable booty, within sight of the Delaware and the mouth of Lackawaxen Creek. The main body of Brant's force had by this time rejoined the Minisink village raiders and they set up an envelopment of the militia's rear. The Americans retreated to high ground where they held out till dusk, at which time their position was penetrated by the enemy. The day-long battle became a massacre. The Americans suffered at least forty-five men killed. The Goshen monument, commemorating the battle, lists only forty-five names. Minisink did not see the last of Brant: he revisited the village on April 4, 1780.[25]

Gen. Sullivan reached Tioga on August 10, the same day Col. Brodhead left Fort Pitt. Brodhead led six hundred Continentals and volunteers up the Allegheny River from the British-built fort, but the Seneca and Delaware villages in northwestern Pennsylvania were almost completely deserted. Misled by incompetent guides, Brodhead got no farther than a point some miles south of present-day Salamanca in New York. Aborting his rendezvous with Sullivan somewhere in the Genesee region, he turned about and returned to Fort Pitt by another route, creating additional havoc in other Indian communities along the line of retreat. Except for a brief skirmish with a party of about forty Indians, Brodhead's column saw no action, but it captured large stores of provisions and supplies, burned many Indian houses, and devastated more than five hundred acres of vegetables.[26]

The other columns fared better. On April 19, from Fort Stanwix, Cols. Gose Van Schaick and Marinus Willett commanded more than 550 men on a memorable one-hundred-eighty-mile five-and-a-half-day preliminary raid against the Onondaga villages between Fort Stanwix and Oswego. Without the loss of a single man killed or wounded, they destroyed between forty and fifty houses, took thirty-seven prisoners (mostly women and children held as hostages), killed more than twenty Indian warriors, and captured one hundred muskets.[27]

Clinton's column of sixteen hundred men worked heroically. The general at Albany issued orders to the selected military contingents to meet at Canajoharie on the Mohawk River. More than two hundred flat-bottomed boats were constructed at Schenectady, loaded with provisions and supplies for both his and Sullivan's armies, and taken up the river to Canajoharie. From June 17 until early July, the boats were portaged twenty miles by wagon to the head of Lake Otsego and floated to the foot of the lake, where the troops reassembled.

While Clinton waited more than a month for orders to proceed to Tioga, he gave much thought to the problem of getting the boats down the creek from the lake to the Susquehanna River. He came up with the ingenious scheme of damming the lake's outlet after the boats were pushed through the narrow opening; on receipt of orders on August 9 to proceed to the rendezvous with Sullivan, he destroyed the dam and floated the boats down to Tioga on the lake's outpouring, arriving there on August 19.

On August 26, a week after the union of the two columns, the troops left Tioga and slowly proceeded up the east bank of the Chemung River. Sullivan's entourage consisted of nearly four thousand men, ten pieces of artillery, and a cumbersome train of twelve hundred packhorses. On the other hand, before Sullivan had gone a dozen miles, his forces became engaged in the only battle of the campaign.

Uncertainty over the American objective led Governor General Haldimand in Canada to take measures that were much too weak and too late. He finally dispatched Sir John Johnson with reinforcements, but they never got any farther than British-held Oswego. Meanwhile, John Butler rendezvoused with his son Walter not far from Tioga. They took their 250 Rangers and 15 British regulars to Chemung (destroyed by the Americans on August 13), where they combined forces with Joseph Brant and his 800 Indians and Tories. The Butlers and Brant were in favor of mounting harassments against Sullivan's army, but the Indians vociferously demanded that they make a stand against the Americans, selecting a place near New Town, six miles southeast of today's Elmira. They erected a long, camouflaged log breastwork on a rise of ground parallel with the Chemung, and there the Battle of New Town, August 29, was joined. The enemy's presence, however, had been revealed hours earlier, as evidenced by a letter dated "New Town, 5 miles above Chemung, August 30th 1770," from Clinton to his brother:

> Sunday the army was put in motion about nine o'clock with the greatest circumspection and Caution. Our Scouts had brought intelligence the preceding Evening that the Enemy were discovered at about five miles distance, supposed to be at or near New Town, & from the

magnitude of their Fires, appeared to be in Considerable force; that the sound of their axes were heard distinctly which induced us to believe they intended either to throw up works or obstruct the march of the army, until they could form a Plan to attack our Flanks or rear.

. . .

About ten O'clock a scattering Fire commenced between some of their Scouts and a few of our Rifle men & Volunteers when the former gave way, and the latter proceeded untill they plainly discouvered their Works which were very extensive, tho' not impregnable. . . . About one O'clock Col. Proctor commenced a very warm Cannonade upon their Works, which continued near two hours. . . . The Enemy finding their Situation in their Lines rather uncomfortable and finding we did not intend to storm them, abandoned them. . . .

During the action which lasted from the first to the last near six hours, we had three privates killed, and forty wounded, among whom were three officers, Major Titcomb, Capt. Clause & Lt. McCauly, who is since dead of his wounds; there are few of the wounded dangerous.

The Enemy's loss must be considerable; nine of them were found dead on the field, and many of them must have been wounded, as they were tracked some three miles by the Blood, while others were seen sent off in canoes.[28]

John Butler's account of the battle was in a report dated "Catherine's Town August 31st 1779." It corroborates the Indians' fear of artillery ("thunder trees"):

After remaining here exposed to the heat of the Sun without refreshment of any kind, till 2 o'Clock PM. a few of the Enemy made their appearance at the skirt of the Wood in our Front & amused us with some scattering shot from their Rifles, while under the cover of the Wood they were planting their Artillery and fetching a compass round the mountain to our left in order to surround us and gain the Passes by which we must retreat. I suspected their Design & endeavored to prevail upon the Indians to retire and gain the mountain; Joseph Brant also and the Cahouga [Cayuga] Chief came up from our Right to point out the necessity of this step, as it was evident the Enemy had discovered us & knew our situation; but the Indians were obstinately bent upon staying in the Lines. After a little while they began to play their Artillery consisting of six pieces of Cannon & Cohorns against our breast-work, discharging shells, round & grape shot, Iron Spikes, &c. incessantly which soon obliged us to leave it. I retreated with the Rangers & a number of the Indians to the Hill, which I found the Enemy had gained before us, as I foresaw they intended. The shells bursting beyond us, made the Indians imagine the Enemy had got their Artillery all round us, & so startled & confounded them that great part of them run off. . . . Many of the Indians made no halt, but preceded [sic] immediately to their respective Villages. . . . Our loss in men, considering everything, is much less than could be expected; of the Rangers we have five men killed or taken and three wounded, & of the Indians five killed and nine wounded.[29]

An officer, possibly on Sullivan's staff, wrote the following to a friend in Boston:

Yesterday a general action ensued, in which the Indians and Tories got compleately routed. The conflict was long, and I believe on their part was bloody, though only 11 dead bodies were found upon the field, and they, I suppose, would not have been left, if our troops had not pushed them at the point of the bayonet. Our loss was but trifling, I think five or six were killed, and between 40 and 50 wounded. The cannonade on our part was elegant, and gave the Indians such a panic, that they fled with great precipitation from the field. One Tory and one negro were taken prisoners.[30]

The Indian country in central and western New York was abundantly dotted with cornfields, vegetable gardens, and fruit orchards, constituting the primary granary for the British at Fort Niagara and in Canada. Now this region was at the mercy of Sullivan's army. More important, however, was Sullivan's recurrent defect of not capitalizing on the enemy's weaknesses. His blunders were the flamboyant use of artillery, which demoralized the Indians into flight, and then failing to pursue the panicked enemy. Possessing a Patriot superiority of four to one, the enemy at New Town should have been either annihilated or captured, thus removing forever the Butlers and Brant from the New York-Pennsylvania theater of war.

Sullivan's army resumed the business of devastation, applying the torch liberally to every Indian habitation. The troops proceeded up the east side of Seneca Lake to Kanadaseagea (modern Geneva), a Seneca castle of eighty houses, then westward through Canandaigua, Honeoye, and Kanagha, arriving on the twelfth at the Indian village of Conesus, the home of Seneca Chief Big Tree, a former influential friend of the Americans.

Lieut. Boyd and twenty-six riflemen were sent to reconnoiter an Indian town seven miles to the west (today's Groveland). Four men went into the village and "found it abandoned" except for a few Indians, one of whom was killed and scalped. The lieutenant sent several men ahead to report to Sullivan while he and the rest of the men moved slowly back toward camp. They ran into an ambush of Indians and Tories. A few of the men escaped to carry the news to Sullivan. All the rest were killed except Boyd and a private, who were captured. The ambush was the only engagement after the Battle of New Town that could be considered a skirmish.[31]

Tory chief John Butler's report of the Groveland ambush was dated "Buffaloe Creek 14th September 1779":

A Lieut. who commanded the Party and a Private were taken. The Officer who is a very intelligent Person Says, their Army consists of near 5000 Continental Troops. . . . They have but a month's Provisions, and intend, according to his account, to come no further than Genessee. . . . I am now on my march to Niagara, and all the Indians with their Families are moving in, as their Villages & Corn are Destroyed, and they have nothing left to support themselves upon. The Indians say, that after they have moved their Families to a Place of Safety, they will then go and take Revenge of the Enemy.[32]

The Americans entered the Seneca stronghold of Little Beard's Town at Genesee Castle, a village of 130 houses about twenty miles south of today's Rochester and the farthest point of the expedition, arriving there on the afternoon of September 14, not quite three weeks after leaving Tioga. There they found the bodies of the two prisoners, "mangled in a most horrid manner." After questioning them, the Butlers had apparently given the two men to the Indians.

On the same day, Gen. Haldimand wrote to Lord George Germain, warning him that if the Continentals captured Fort Niagara, the rich fur trade would be lost, the western Indians would be enlisted to war against the British, and a rebel fleet would be free to cruise the St. Lawrence River. But Fort Niagara, the optimistic ultimate of the Patriot expedition, had to remain out of the reach of the Americans because they ran short of supplies by the middle of the month. On the 17th Sullivan's troops turned about to return by the same route to Easton, where they were demobilized on October 15; James Clinton took his men homeward through the Mohawk country.

"The Hard Winter"

The Niagara Frontier and the Northwest would have been invaluable prizes for the Continental Congress to savor had the Sullivan-Clinton expedition received appreciable logistical support at the time it penetrated the Finger Lakes region. The immediate results of its work was the destruction of more than forty Indian villages and 160,000 bushels of corn. The burned towns remained ruinations throughout the exceptionally hard winter that followed. Indians by the thousands sought assistance at Fort Niagara, where Guy Johnson scraped the bottom of the commissary barrel to feed and clothe them.

Two centuries of Iroquois League power and influence were fire-blasted into oblivion in five months by the Americans. The Six Nations never recovered from the disaster. The dispossessed warriors, however, were not tamed into submission: as soon as the relative quiet of the bitter winter was over, the Indians were abroad again, in even greater numbers.

No one could forsee the tragic link of the autumn's war and the winter's weather, but now it was plain that it was folly to have injured the Indians as Sullivan did, and then leave Niagara unscathed for them to refit, and strike back. To have injured them so dreadfully and not to have wiped them out was a colossal blunder.[33]

Resentful of British restraint, the Indians took their terrible revenge in almost continuous raids. The augmented Iroquois onslaught against the frontier settlements influenced Guy Johnson to write in July 1780:

The Number of Men of the Six Nation Confederacy is about sixteen hundred, about twelve hundred of who are Warriors, and of the latter, eight hundred and thirty are now on service agst the frontiers, and more in readiness to follow them, which far exceeds that had ever been out at one time without the army, few, or none remaining, but those necessary to assist in planting, and providing for their families.[34]

The winter of 1779/80 was the most bitter in the memories of the people, white and Indian; in retrospect, it seems to have been the coldest on record. For many weeks a half dozen feet of snow blanketed the whole Northeast. The severe cold penetrated all the Colonies from Maine to Georgia, and from Detroit in the Old Northwest to New Orleans. Indeed, climatologists agree that a "Little Ice Age" started in America about the year 1750 and continued for some one hundred years. Remarkable evidence, amassed by David M. Ludlum and presented in his fascinating two-volume study of early American winters, points out that 1779/80 was the extreme winter of the "cool hundred years" and earned the contemporary designation of "The Hard Winter."[35]

Samuel Lane of Stratham, New Hampshire, kept a sixty-four-year chronology of the winters he had endured. His comments on the monumental freeze of 1779/80 are worth repeating:

This year has been Remarkable on Many Accounts, which as they are of a Publick Nature I think worthy to be observ'd.

We had the Most hard Difficult Winter, by reason of Violent cold weather, beginning Early in the year; tedious Storms of Deep Drifted Snows, and Difficult passing, even from Neighbour to Neighbour, in Case of Sickness or otherwise, ('tis Said) that ever was known by any Person now Living. The violent weather began about the 13th of Dec.

1779, and Continued about Nine weeks; in all which time there was not more than Day or two, So moderate as to thaw on the Suney Side of a House: and the Snow So Deep & Drifted, that People could not possibly keep the Roads open; tho' it was a Considerable part of their Business to break them with oxen and Shoveling by men, untill they were quite Discouraged, and gave up the point; and Endeavoured to pass (tho' with great Difficulty) on the top of the Snow, and through fields, on Rivers, and any where that they could get along. Many Suffered for want of Wood; and were obliged to cut down Apple trees, and other Trees that Stood near the path, for firewood. Many oblig'd to hall Wood, & go to Mill on handsleds &c. . . .

The Cold weather so froze up the Water, that People were put to great Difficulty for want of Meal in most of our Towns far and Near. . . . The Roads were so Block'd up with Snow, that the Members of the General Court, as well as other People, were oblig'd to travel on the River, the greatest part of the way, from Portsmouth to Exeter, for a long time. The bad traveling held in many places, till the latter end of March: and the beginning of April it was so cold, that there was Some pretty good Sleding on the top of the Snow banks.[36]

Recorded American history cites only one winter during which all the waters encompassing New York City froze over and prevented passage of navigation for many days. This phenomenon occurred during The Hard Winter of 1779/80. While Washington was encamping his near-frozen, starving Continentals at Morristown, New Jersey, just twenty miles to the eastward, the British were much more comfortably ensconced in New York City, but fearing a cross-the-ice assault by Patriot troops.

On January 2, a Sunday, the wintry blast caught West Point unaware and paralyzed the Hudson River bastion's garrison.[37] Gen. Washington had kept a weather diary for most of his adult life. On January 6, 1780, he noted that "the snow which in general is eighteen inches deep is much drifted—roads impassable." James Thacher, Washington's surgeon-general, noted at the same time that the snow accumulation had reached a depth of four feet. Writing the commander-in-chief from Fort Pitt, Col. Daniel Brodhead noted that "such a deep snow and such ice has not been known at this place in the memory of the eldest natives; Deer & Turkies die by hundreds for want of food. . . ."[38]

It was not highly unusual two centuries ago for New York City's Hudson and East Rivers to freeze over, allowing pedestrian traffic to New Jersey and Long Island. But recorded history cites no instance, except during that Hard Winter, when the great harbor's Upper Bay iced deep enough to permit sleighs and pedestrians to cross the five miles between Manhattan's Battery and Staten Island and to traverse the Narrows to Brooklyn. One contemporary historian related that the

Bristish even dragged large cannon across the ice to reinforce their positions on Staten Island, which had been a target for Patriot raids from New Jersey. He reported that on February 6 about eighty-six sleighs loaded with provisions and war material skimmed across the ice to Staten Island.[39]

Well-below-zero temperatures solidly froze briny, deepwater, coastal seas and bays from Chesapeake Bay to Boston Harbor, preventing communication with the rest of the world. Lakes George and Champlain were congealed so deep that through-the-ice fishing was an impossibility. Deer, elk, and other denizens of the forest, unable to feed through the deep snow, died by the thousands. Already deprived of their crops destroyed by Sullivan's army, the Iroquois were in extremely dire straits, unable to find enough game to feed their families; an unknown number of them died of starvation and the cold. Most of the settlers' livestock—cattle, hogs, horses—died of the severe cold in the Mohawk, Schoharie, and Wyoming valleys. Because of the unusually early visitation of winter, the farmers lost most of their produce, thus seriously aggravating the already near-starvation condition of Washington's Continental Army. Governor Clinton, rueing the calamities that had befallen the Patriots, was moved to write the President of the Continental Congress: "Bending under a load of Debt, and groaning under the accumulation of Distress We entered the year 1780 with universal Dismay, as the Hand of God had been upon us in blasting our crops the preceding Harvest."[40]

Historians have assigned varying dates, ranging from The Hard Winter of 1779/80 to the following October, for the destruction of the Oneida and Tuscarora villages in retribution for their years of neutrality and subsequent alliance with the Americans late in the war. Assiduous research reveals that gradual desertion of their villages, instigated by threats in the spring of 1780, preceded their ultimate destruction in July by Joseph Brant and his army of warriors and Tories. The refugee Indians eventually were forced to seek safety in squalid hovels at Schenectady, where they suffered extreme poverty, disease, disillusionment, and even prejudice. The tragic history of the Oneidas' persevering idealistic neutrality and the dissolution of the Iroquois Confederacy as a political entity were important influences on events in the northern frontier war.

The Oneidas occupied a band of territory west of Herkimer and east of Oneida Lake, from Ogdensburg in the north to Binghamton in the south, with a large segment of them residing at Ganowalohale,[41] the center of the Oneida Nation, southeast of the lake. Their homeland, which included the vital portage between the lake and the Mohawk River and the fertile central valley on both sides of the waterway, formed a protective buffer for the Americans against forays from the Tory strongholds at Niagara and Oswego.[42]

For years Sir William Johnson had encouraged missionaries to go into the Iroquois nations to further Christianize the Indians. He did not foresee the possibility of the alienation of any Indian loyalties to the Crown. Most of the missionaries belonged to non-Anglican denominations and were principally Presbyterian, proponents of either absolute pacifism or complete alliance with the Patriots. The Oneidas were the most susceptible to religious instruction. Historically, these Indians were the most looked up to for advice in negotiations regarding matters of importance within the Confederacy. Furthermore, they were, more than any other Iroquois people, personally mild and disposed to peace. Samuel Kirkland, Congregational minister and former friend and associate of Joseph Brant at the Indian School at Lebanon, Connecticut, influenced the Oneida Nation to maintain a position of neutrality, thereby disrupting forever the unanimity of the Iroquois League. Caught in the squeeze between the warring parties and threatened with destruction by other Iroquois, the Oneidas finally threw in their lot with the Patriots and performed their assigned military duties with remarkable, even heroic determination.[43]

Threatened with death for his influence over the Oneidas, Samuel Kirkland was obliged to remove his family to Stockbridge, Massachusetts, but he still continued to labor among his Oneidas. The Continental Congress on July 18, 1775, had recommended to the Indian commissioners of the northern department to employ the minister to insure the neutrality of the Iroquois. Kirkland, in his role of Patriot ambassador to the Iroquois, made long, tiring journeys to the various tribal villages, and attended many councils at Albany, German Flats (Herkimer), Oneida, and Onondaga. In appreciation for his efforts, the Congress appointed Kirkland chaplain to the garrison at Fort Stanwix and other forts, with the rank and pay of Brigade Chaplain.[44]

Kirkland's most loyal disciple was Skenandoa (known to the whites as John Skenando), a celebrated Oneida chief and former father-in-law of Joseph Brant. The old sachem, dying at Oneida Castle at the age of 110 years on March 11, 1816, was a strong friend of the Patriots and was the most devout supporter of the Oneida church. He had often expressed his desire to be interred beside the remains of his friend and minister, so that he might take hold of the skirt of his cloak and go up with him to Heaven. In 1856, when Kirkland's remains were transferred to the cemetery at Hamilton College, Skenandoa's body was also taken there, and the Christian minister and the Indian warrior-chief now repose side by side in their tombs.[45]

Of all the Confederacy peoples, the Oneidas resided closest to the white frontier and were influenced by the proximity. Though militarily neutral during the early years of the conflict, they were pro-American politically, professing on numerous occasions their amicable disposition toward the Americans. At the council held at German Flats on June 28, 1775, the Oneidas did offer a suggestion of military significance, urging that old Fort Stanwix be rebuilt and fully garrisoned. The renovation, however, of the French and Indian War fortification, guarding the western portal of the frontier, did not take place for another year.[46]

After his return from London in the summer of 1776, Brant spent the remainder of the year visiting Six Nations' villages, establishing his winter residence among the Cayugas. His propaganda found interested audiences wherever he went, except at the castles where the Oneidas and Tuscaroras resided. But he found, too, among the Cayugas, Onondagas, and Senecas, large cliques of warriors who were more inclined to remain at peace. At the Tuscarora town of Ganaghsaraga (modern Canaseraga, near Chittenango), the Mohawk chief and a delegation of Oneida sachems met in angry conference. The Oneidas steadfastly declared their neutrality, vowing that they would not be partisan to the cause of either the British or the Americans. To impress the Oneidas, Brant told them how the Crown's soldiers were everywhere overcoming the Americans, capturing their fortifications, and putting them to flight. No doubt he had in mind the debacle of the Patriots in the Battle of Brooklyn, at which he was an entranced spectator. In rebuttal, the Oneidas stated that if such was the case, then there was no need of their arms.[47]

Propaganda, offers of gifts (declined), and threats by the British and their Iroquois allies failed to influence the Oneidas. The neutrals were warned, time and again, that affiliation with the Americans would bring them only deprivation and great sorrow. The Oneidas' involvement in the bloody action at Oriskany served to sever their already-damaged ties to the Iroquois League.

In the fall of 1779 a plan to wipe out the principal Oneida castle was adopted by Sir John Johnson. He had arrived at Fort Niagara on October 5 with a force of his Royal Greens, a company of German mercenaries, and a contingent of Canadian Indians, with the intention of launching an expedition against Sullivan's fort at Tioga (Fort Sullivan at today's Athens). Talked out of taking the hazardous three-hundred-mile journey because of the lateness of the season and the insufficiency of provisions and supplies to fuel such an undertaking, Johnson then decided to attack the Oneidas. With an added complement of 150 Butler's Rangers, he sailed his army to Oswego, arriving there on October 13. John Butler, accompanied by a large detachment of Cayugas and Senecas, and Brant, with his Mohawks, traveling overland, showed up at Oswego a few days later to combine with Johnson's force. When the British-allied Indians, particularly those from Canada, learned of their destination, they vehemently disapproved of the planned assault against their kin, and the expedition was thereupon abandoned. The British terminated their 1779 campaign and left Oswego the last week of October for winter quarters.[48]

During the spring of 1780 the Oneidas were increasingly harassed, then threatened with imminent destruction by the pro-British Iroquois if they did not leave their villages and proceed to Niagara. Canaseraga, occupied by neutral Tuscaroras and Onondagas, was left almost completely uninhabited when the occupants, under duress, packed up and moved to Niagara.

Several Oneida chiefs went to Fort Stanwix and implored Col. Cornelius Van Dyck, the commandant, to assist with the removal of their people to a place of safety among the Americans, in return for which the Oneida warriors would volunteer their services in the Patriot army. Before anything could be done to alleviate the plight of the Oneidas, a force of Butler's Rangers and Mohawk warriors appeared at Ganowalohale on June 24 to enforce the threat of destruction should the Oneida chiefs still refuse to proceed to Fort Niagara.

In the evening of the same day, the Oneida chiefs conferred among themselves on how best to avoid a showdown. The decision was made for them the next day when a war party of Senecas entered the village. Surrounded as they were by truculent warriors and menacing Rangers, the Oneida chiefs acquiesced to their demands. Eleven Oneida warriors accompanied the war parties back to Niagara, with the promise that once the dependents of the chiefs and the other warriors were provided for, the remainder would follow. Military coercion and the absence of promised American protection gave Kirkland's Oneidas no alternative than to preserve their families from bloodshed and their property from the torch.[49]

Continued threats of death and destruction had the desired effect: by July 2 nearly 300 neutrals had come into Fort Niagara—184 Onondagas, 78 Tuscaroras, and 32 Oneidas from their principal village. On July 11 Brant departed from Niagara with an undetermined number of men, up to 600 warriors and 200 Tories. Accompanying the strong war party were three-score Oneida, Onondaga, and Tuscarora penitents, members of the migration to Fort Niagara less than two weeks earlier. Ruthless in his determination to prevent the return of the Oneidas to their castle, Brant had Ganowalohale put to the torch. During the last week of the month, his army completed the work of devastation by burning the other Oneida and Tuscarora villages, not neglecting the Oneida church and old Skenandoa's house; whatever livestock they did not appropriate for themselves, they slaughtered. A small number of Oneidas and Tuscaroras, known to have done service for the Americans, were prevailed upon to go to Fort Niagara, probably under guard. The majority, however, of the dispossessed Oneidas and Tuscaroras, with some Mahican (Stockbridge) and Caughnawaga Indians who lived with them, took flight from their flaming homes and blackened fields, and made all haste for Fort Stanwix, pursued by a large detachment of Brant's Indians.[50]

GENERAL PHILIP SCHUYLER
Painting by John Trumbull
Courtesy of National Archives

In the fall the survivors of the fragmented neutral Indian nations went east to the American sanctuary of Schenectady and there erected wretched makeshift shelters on the eastern outskirts of the town. Informed by disturbed Patriots that the miserable huts could not possibly safeguard the refugees throughout the coming winter, Gen. Philip Schuyler, then a member of the Board of Commissioners for Indian Affairs, made numerous sincere efforts to assist the Indians. He directed that the Indians be accommodated at once in the Schenectady barracks.[51] In his letter of November 6 to Henry Glen, agent for Indian affairs at Schenectady and deputy assistant quartermaster general, he made no bones about the need to billet the Indians in proper quarters:

If the barracks are occupied by the french people, they must go to Albany to the barracks there, or into the country into peoples houses where they can get. It is in vain for them to make any representations on this subject; *they must comply* for it is of vast Consequence to this state in particular and all the states in general that these faithful Indians should be as well provided as the distressed circumstances we are in will permit.[52]

The Marquis de Chastellux, French war veteran, writer, and aide to Gen. Rochambeau, paid a visit to Schenectady in December. Accompanied by Henry Glen, he inspected the squalid camp where many of the Oneidas and Tuscaroras were pathetically trying to cope with starvation rations and the rigors of winter. The marquis described the Indians' miserable living quarters:

These huts are like our barracks in time of war, or like those built in vineyards or orchards, when the fruit is ripe and has to be watched at night. The framework consists only of two uprights and one cross-pole; this is covered with a matted roof, but is well lined within by a quantity of bark. The inner space is rather below the level of the ground, and the entrance by a little side-door; in the middle of the hut is the fireplace, from which the smoke ascends by an opening in the roof. On each side of the fire are raised two platforms, which run the length of the hut and serve as beds; these are covered with skins and bark.[53]

The poverty-stricken, refugee Indian village was occupied by 406 Indians—93 men, 54 women, and 259 children. Charitable contributions from the generally destitute Schenectady populace could not offer them even the barest subsistence. A few of the Indians died of malnutrition. Through Schuyler's influence, the Board of War and Ordnance on November 10 requested from Congress an appropriation of $6,464 in severely depreciated Continental bills of credit to buy essential clothing for the Indians. One month later the clothing order had not been filled; the area's merchants would not cooperate until they had been paid in hard money rather than in almost worthless currency.[54]

With the onset of winter, rather than submit passively to slow starvation, many of the Indians made a thirty-mile northward move in the late fall of 1780. They established a hunting camp nearly Palmerstown, a pioneer village now incorporated in the town of Wilton, Saratoga County.[55] Many times more men were killed by smallpox than by the bullet, and now the scourge made its deathly appearance at the refugee camp and accompanied those Indians who went north in a desperate search for food.

Furious with a dilatory Congress, which he felt was honor bound to support a homeless, maligned, and suffering people allied to the Patriots, Schuyler sent off three urgent letters to Philadelphia between December 2 and January 18. His first letter listed the absolute minimum in clothing the Indians required to withstand the rigors of winter; on December 26 he sent off an inquiry, probing the whereabouts of the clothing; his letter of January 18 delineated, in no uncertain terms, the sufferings of the Indian allies. Schuyler had been making small requisitions from the army's lean stores and commissary to alleviate their misery, but in February the larder was bare. On February 24 he turned to the New York State Legislature as his only alternative, offering his personal credit as collateral. The state body authorized the purchase of 200 blankets, followed by an approval on March 8 to purchase a quantity of cloth. But with the end of winter in sight, only 185 blankets and no cloth were provided and distributed among the desperate Indians.

When the party of Indians left Schenectady to hunt, Schuyler moved the remaining Oneidas and Tuscaroras into the barracks occupied by soldiers. Their short sojourn in the barracks proved to be a disaster. The white frontier's hatred of Indians was reflected in the contempt and physical injury that the soldiers inflicted on their allies. Beatings were a daily occurrence until one of the Indians was murdered in cold blood. Schuyler, almost at wit's end in his attempts to provide for the Indians, had them moved out and returned to their miserable hovels. The general managed to scare up a stack of lumber, which the Indians used to board up the huts.

But Brant was not satisfied to devastate the neutral villages; he still sought to further avenge the indignities suffered by his kin when the Oneidas, in retribution for Molly Brant's spying activities that precipitated the Battle of Oriskany, looted the Mohawk chief's ancestral home during their destruction of Canajoharie. Learning of the hunting camp near Palmerstown, Brant planned to attack it in March. The Oneidas, however, unaware of impending disaster, had decided to break camp and return to Schenectady to rejoin their suffering brethren.

Because of their alliance with the Patriots, the Oneidas were homeless and without any means to sustain themselves, but still maintaining their affinity with the Americans. Without a doubt, had the Oneidas quit their support of the rebellious colonists, Fort Niagara would have proved to be a beneficent haven, offering them a much more amenable refuge, sustenance from a much more provident commissary, and immunity from insult.

Deprivation and tragedy stalked the Oneidas throughout the war, just as the British and their Iroquois allies had predicted. Even in the postwar years the Oneidas had no peace, for they were hounded by land-hungry Yankees. In 1785 the Oneidas and Tuscaroras, bowing before pressures, sold the first piece of their ancestral land; four years later New York State bought the remainder, containing the Indians on a small reservation in return for a paltry annuity. Later the Oneidas were awarded additional small annuities as rewards for their heroic loyalty to the United States.[56]

Spring 1780

On March 21, 1780, the Skenesborough garrison, consisting of only thirteen men instead of the forty assigned to the post, was captured in a surprise attack by a sizable party of Indians. In April Mohawks and Tories under Brant, once again operating from Unadilla, revisited settlements where they had scored earlier successes and made initial raids on other communities.

On April 2 the Mohawk chief struck Harpersfield, twenty miles south of Cherry Valley and only fifteen miles from Schoharie's fortifications. The settlement, already deserted by most of its inhabitants, was utterly destroyed, with several of the remaining people killed and Capt. Alexander Harper and eighteen others taken prisoner. Brant had planned to attack Schoharie's Upper Fort at Fultonham, but was dissuaded by Harper's deliberate misinformation that the place was strongly defended by three hundred Continental regulars. Instead, Brant took his marauders eastward and on April 14 again raided Minisink.[57]

On April 3 a small party of Indians unsuccessfully attacked the blockhouse at Sacandaga, about twenty miles north of Johnstown. Loitering in the neighborhood, the raiders were surprised three days later by a militia detachment and all were killed. On the day of the Sacandaga attack, between sixty and eighty Indians and Tories attacked Snyder's Bush (near today's Dolgeville), the site of Rheimensnyder's blockhouse, about six miles north of Little Falls. For unknown reasons, not one person was killed, nor were any houses burned, but nineteen men were taken prisoner and a mill set afire.[58]

Ephratah was again attacked; the houses left untouched in the earlier raid were burned, with some of the people either killed or taken prisoner. Numerous small bands of Mohawks, seeking to restock their depleted leaders, took eight people prisoner when they raided the settlement of New Darloch (today's Sharon), about five miles east of Cherry Valley. The roving bands struck the Schoharie Valley, German Flats, and the

Catskill area. On April 24 Cherry Valley was again raided, this time by seventy-nine Indians and several Tories, who killed a few inhabitants, destroyed the unmanned fort, and burned the church; now Cherry Valley was a complete ruin. The new series of savage forays drove hundreds of settlers to the forts, where their fears were only partially dissipated by the dubious protection afforded by too few Continentals and weak-hearted militiamen.[59]

May brought more havoc to the Mohawk River settlements as the first of several carefully organized Tory-Indian invasions struck the northern frontier. Intelligence reports gave the British in Canada knowledge of rebel intentions to imprison the Loyalists still residing in the Johnstown settlement where the manorial home of the Johnsons was located. Governor Haldimand provided Sir John Johnson with the authorization to assemble a strong force to succor their kin and friends. The expedition, four hundred of Johnson's Greens and two hundred Mohawks under Brant, came down by way of Lake Champlain, Crown Point, and the Sacandaga River. When they stealthily entered the northern limits of Johnstown late in the evening of Sunday, May 21, Brant took his Indians, circled the settlement and, at dawn on the twenty-second, invaded Caughnawaga (modern Fonda) on the Mohawk, a few miles to the south. He sent detachments to the east and west along the river, killing and burning, while Sir John and his Tories cut a swath of terror through the heart of Johnstown. Loyalist homes and their occupants were in all instances carefully left unharmed.

Johnson headed straight for Johnson Hall, where he lingered for a short time. Then he proceeded with his men to Caughnawaga, where Brant rejoined him. The reunited force, after burning all the houses and barns there, leaving only the church, returned to Johnson Hall where Sir John unearthed two barrels of family silverware, secretly interred when he escaped to Canada. For the remainder of the day Johnson played host as Tory sympathizers in the neighborhood came to visit their relatives and friends in the expedition's force. Many of the settlement's Loyalists, having gathered what possessions they could carry, accompanied Johnson back to Canada, where the physically fit among them took up arms in the British cause. Early on the morning of the twenty-third, having heard that a large militia force was assembling at Fort Johnstown, Johnson began his retreat north through the settlement, taking about forty Patriots as prisoners.

Sir John apparently took his time, lingering in the neighborhood of Mayfield, less than ten miles to the northeast, where he waited for a militia attack that never came. Finally, on the 27th, the expedition took its leave and headed north for Lake Champlain and Canada. New York's

Governor Clinton and troops departed from Albany in an effort to cut off Johnson at Ticonderoga, but the enemy outdistanced the Americans and arrived unscathed at Montreal by way of St. Johns.[60]

Brant's remarkable generalship and keen sense of strategy were once again demonstrated as he lured the American military in the Mohawk Valley into sending aid to Fort Stanwix. During the last days of July, when the dispossessed Oneidas and Tuscaroras were pursued right up to the ramparts of the fort, Brant established a temporary siege around its walls and waited. As usual, the fort's garrison was undermanned and short of critical supplies. Rumors, purposely broadcast by Brant, of the imminent fall of this bastion at the valley's western portal, initiated immediate preparations for a strong relief force.

Col. Peter Gansevoort and his regiment were garrisoning Fort Plank, a three-story blockhouse at present-day Fort Plain, the strongest fortification in that sector of the valley. When news of Fort Stanwix's danger arrived, the colonel began to draw all available military personnel from the surrounding settlements to escort a convoy to reinforce the fort. As soon as the Patriots were on their way, with all their attention focused on the apparent peril confronting Fort Stanwix, the Mohawk war leader took his four hundred Indians (mostly Senecas) and Tories on a phenomenal sixty-mile, round-about, night-and-day march through the wilderness. His southeasterly route, by way of Otsego Lake, Van Hornesville, and Starkville, allowed him to enter Canajoharie from the east on August 1. Brant divided up his force into small detachments and sent them on a two-day series of kill-and-destroy raids throughout the well-settled townships of Minden and Stark. Fort Plank, now manned by little more than a skeleton of a garrison, boomed a cannon over the countryside, alerting the settlers to come within its walls for refuge. Brant did not attack the fort, and its defenders did not come out to do battle with the enemy.

Brant applied more than his usual ruthlessness in the devastation of Canajoharie, the pre-Revolutionary War principal Mohawk castle and ancestral home of his antecedents, leaving the settlement a blackened desolation. The only structure in Fort Plain left untouched by fire was the fort, from which surviving settlers viewed with horror the eradication of all their possessions.

The army of destructives burned fifty-three homes, a like number of barns, a mill, two minor forts, and the Canajoharie church in which Brant had prayed as a youth and occasionally led services for the Mohawk congregation. The raiders killed sixteen settlers who were unable to flee with the rest of the inhabitants to Fort Plank, Fort Clyde (about two miles southwest of Fort Plain at today's village of Freysbush), or other fortified havens. Between fifty and sixty others were carried off as prisoners, and about three hundred head of cattle were either slaughtered or taken with them by the raiders in the retreat. As soon as the first news of Brant's raid reached Schenectady, that town's militia was dispatched up the valley. But, as was usual with Indian hit-and-run incursions, the soldiers arrived too late, only to stay a bit to assist with burying the dead. Brant's people had been driven from their ancestral castles into the hinterland, but he made certain that their usurpers would be left, at least for a time, equally homeless.[61]

On August 9, one week after his work of devastation along the Mohawk, Brant led about eighty Indians and six Tories in a raid on the Schoharie settlement around Middle Fort (Middleburg), known locally as Vrooman's Land. The entire region was set afire. Eleven members of the prominent Vrooman family were carried off, with three others, the mother, father, and an eight-year-old son, killed. There were some other wanton killings, not ascribed to Brant himself. Fourteen captives in all were taken, but most of them—women and children—were released by Brant on the second day of the retreat toward Niagara. Subsequent to this bloody foray, the garrisons of all the Schoharie forts were strengthened.[62]

By this time it had become painfully obvious to the American military commanders that New York's frontier could not be guarded against Indian-Tory penetration by the impotent militia, principally involved in the continuance of the forts and stockades as havens for the beleaguered inhabitants. The frontier's security could be obtained only by the posting of appreciable numbers of Continental regulars. In less than a year the American strategy had changed drastically. Whereas in 1779 Washington had no compunction about supporting with sixteen Continental regiments John Sullivan's expedition against the Iroquois, he now could not spare a single detachment for the protection of the frontier.

Washington was devoting all his energies to solving other monumental problems: the task of keeping his decimated army from starving; joint action with the first French expeditionary force landing at Newport, Rhode Island, on July 11; and the pressing necessity of dispatching assistance to the endangered South. Confronted by these enigmas, bitterly acknowledging all the while that the enemy was ruining his granaries, Washington had no choice but to leave the New York frontier to its own devices. There was, however, one compensatory reward: the defeat of the British scheme to force Washington to diminish his major operations by relinquishing Continental troops for the defense of the bloodied northern frontier.

Then, suddenly, Washington's iron steadfastness received a terrible jolt. Possibly the most devastating personal affront to the commander-in-chief, spawning a short-lived crisis within the high echelons of the army, was the overwhelming treason of Benedict Arnold. Seriously deficient in character and disposition, the turncoat was nevertheless the most talented field commander in the Revolution. The revelation of the conspiracy to betray the citadel of West Point came as a thunderbolt during the last week of September. Washington immediately strengthened his garrisons in the Highlands. Though the attempted betrayal was his bitterest disappointment, he was confronted by a much greater menace: mutiny within the ranks. His immediate concern was the subjugation of mutineers who contaminated some of his best regiments (the Pennsylvania Line, for instance) by citing pay many months in arrears, scanty food, clothing shortages, and termination of enlistments.[63]

The most damaging assault of the year came in October. Not yet content with the devastation already wrought in human life and property, the British authorized another three-winged invasion from the north. Though not of the magnitude of Burgoyne's expedition, it was much more destructive and had the determination to push the frontier back to Schenectady. Sir John Johnson left Montreal with a force in excess of six hundred men, consisting of his Royal Greens, Butler's Rangers, German mercenaries, and British regulars, armed with three light pieces of artillery, two small mortars, and a brass three-pounder grasshopper. He proceeded to Carleton Island at the head of the St. Lawrence, a couple of miles from ruined Fort Frontenac, and sailed across Lake Ontario to Oswego. From this old British stronghold he marched his army through the blackened Iroquois country to Unadilla on the Susquehanna, where he joined up with several hundred Iroquois, mostly Mohawks captained by Brant and Senecas under Cornplanter, the half-blood Seneca war chief.

At approximately the same time, the second arm of the assault had Maj. Christopher Carleton lead an army of six hundred regulars, auxiliaries, and two hundred Canadian Indians down Lake Champlain and Lake George to scour the region toward Schenectady and Albany. The mysterious Carleton, a romantic figure dressed and painted as an Indian in the role of an erstwhile Mohawk Valley spy with a never-claimed price on his head, also had the distinction of being doubly related, nephew and brother-in-law, to the former governor of Canada, Sir Guy Carleton.[64]

Johnson's and Carleton's expeditions were planned to synchronize with Arnold's treasonable surrender of West Point, the accomplishment of which would have been taken in hand by Sir Henry Clinton marching up the Hudson with a very powerful force of regulars. The ultimate of this triumvirate of military might was identical with Burgoyne's: to split east and west the northern rebellious Colonies. With the accidental capture of the unfortunate John André and the subsequent explosive revelation of the plot, Sir Henry remained in New York and the invasion's main purpose was defeated.

In rapid succession, starting on October 11, Carleton took Fort George (one mile from the ruins of Fort William Henry), Fort Anne, and Fort Edward. The rendezvous with Johnson and Clinton having been aborted, he turned back after getting as far south as the Saratoga County village of Ballston, only a dozen miles above Schenectady, which he pillaged.

Proceeding up the east branch of the Susquehanna (Charlotte River), Johnson led his army into the Schoharie Valley on the evening of October 16, landing three miles from the Upper Fort (Fultonham). After camping for several hours, still preserving intact the element of surprise, Sir John deliberately bypassed the fort in predawn darkness. His army, however, was discovered by Peter Feeck, a farmer living near the fort, on his way to retrieve his cows from their pasture. Feeck ran to the fort at top speed and raised the alarm. Capt. Hager, commander, ordered the firing of the warning cannon, which was answered in turn by the Middle and Lower Forts to the north. The valley having been alerted, Sir John at once began a three-day reign of terror and devastation, Brant's Mohawks and Cornplanter's Senecas burning down all dwellings, barns, and crops in his path as he approached Middle Fort (Middleburg) in the first light of October 17.

Pandemonium was everywhere in the valley. Inhabitants rushed for safety to the forts, which sent out scouting detachments to assess the strength of the enemy. Several boxes of ammunition were hurried from the Lower Fort to the Middle Fort. On arrival there, Sir John ordered the destruction of the Dutch Reformed Church and the surrounding settlement. He immediately instituted siege lines around the fort. As the flames spread from the near environs of the fort into the countryside, his light artillery pieces were unloaded and set up to begin a relatively harmless bombardment of the defense, the strongest of the three in the valley. At the time, the Indians were deployed in small bands throughout the surrounding country to complete the work of destruction.

Garrisoned by 150 short-term Continentals and 50 militiamen under the command of weak-kneed Maj. Melancthon Woolsey, the fort found itself besieged by a vastly superior enemy. In response to a white flag, Woolsey was all too willing to participate in a parley leading to capitulation. But Timothy Murphy, militiaman, scout, and sharpshooter

THE OLD STONE FORT (LOWER FORT), Schoharie
Courtesy of New York State Department of Commerce

with his long rifle, differed with the fort's commander. He fired a shot
over the heads of the white-flag team, driving it back in haste. The major
was furious at this breach of military etiquette. Twice more the enemy's
parley team was driven back by Timothy's rifle. Woolsey was at the
point of arresting Murphy, but vociferous support by other militiamen
and some Continental officers changed his mind. He then ordered the
white flag of surrender run up the flagpole. Murphy offered to kill any
soldier who moved to obey the command. Maj. Woolsey, unable to cope
with a near-mutinous garrison, relinquished the command of the fort to
Col. Peter Vrooman, who directed a good show of resistance though the
fort's ammunition was almost depleted. Assisting with the defense was
Vrooman's young daughter, Angelica, who molded bullets for the fort's
rifles. Toward the middle of the afternoon, unaware of what had
transpired within the fort and committed to withdrawal, Sir John
decided to lift the siege.

Johnson's destructives marched up the valley five miles to Schoharie
and the Lower Fort, a stockaded stone church with two bastions, called

locally the Old Stone Fort. Maj. Joseph Becker's garrison consisted of two hundred men. He posted a corps of skilled riflemen in the tower of the church. The cannon in the north and south blockhouses were primed and manned. The militiamen were readied within the stockade to repel an expected assault. Johnson remained for about an hour and a half, during which time he attempted a half-hearted rush on the stockade and lodged a cannon ball in the fort's wall near the roof. There were no injuries to the defenders. Sir John then moved his force north to Sloansville on Schoharie Creek, where camp was made for the night. No sooner had the enemy disappeared than a large group of incensed Patriots left their refuges, stormed through the valley, and destroyed those Loyalist dwellings which the British and Indians had taken care to leave intact.

By nightfall, except for the valley's three forts, not a house or a grain-stuffed barn stood untouched by fire in the valley south of Sloansville. The Patriots reported that at least one hundred thousand bushels of wheat were destroyed by the torch (the Schoharie that year had had a better-than-usual harvest). The loss of life at the military posts were trifling—only two killed at the Middle Fort. A greatly exaggerated estimate states that at least one hundred noncombatants were killed while their homes were attacked.

At dawn on October 18 Sir John's army broke their undisturbed camp and proceeded north. He laid waste the remainder of the Schoharie Valley, a twenty-mile-long strip of prosperous farmland between Sloansville and old Fort Hunter on the other side of the Mohawk, being careful to avoid the immediate environs of the fort. With detachments of Indians and Tories working the north side of the river, Sir John took his main force up the south bank. They made camp that night near the present town of Randall. The next morning the remorseless march of destruction was resumed. At the village of Sprakers, Sir John arrived at the eastern edge of the sphere of country that Brant had desolated during his August forays against Canajoharie and Fort Plain. The Tory leader took his main army across the river ford at Sprakers, joined up with his destructives on the far side, and turned north for Stone Arabia.

Patriotic efforts to pursue the enemy, trap, and then destroy them, proved to be a disastrous fiasco, contributed to in large measure by the criminal negligence, dereliction of duty, and military ineptitude of a field commander. When the first startling news of the Schoharie invasion reached Albany, Gen. Robert Van Rensselaer assembled the Albany and Schenectady militia units and started westward in search of the enemy, with Governor Clinton following at his heels.

At Fort Hunter, Van Rensselaer's army was augmented by Col. Peter

Vrooman's Schoharie contingents collected from the valley's three forts and by a band of Oneidas brought by Col. John Harper from Fort Plain. When scouts informed Van Rensselaer that Johnson was headed for Stone Arabia, the general sent orders to Col. John Brown,[65] commander of Fort Paris at that village, to march out the next morning at 9 A.M. and engage the enemy. Van Rensselaer assured Col. Brown that he would arrive in time to attack Johnson's rear.

At ten o'clock on the morning of October 19, Col. Brown with about 150 men met Sir John's whole army on the road near ruined Fort Keyser, about a mile and a half north of the Mohawk River. Outnumbered almost ten to one, the Patriot force within minutes faced complete encirclement and had to retreat precipitately. Brown and between thirty and forty of his men were killed.

When Van Rensselaer's army, now aggregating almost twice the number of the enemy, reached Sprakers, they heard the sounds of battle in the direction of Stone Arabia. Forsaking his promise to Col. Brown, the general refused to cross the river at that point despite the entreaties of subordinate officers, and instead continued almost to Fort Plain. Leaving his army on the south side of the river, he proceeded to the village of Fort Plain to dine with Governor Clinton. At about four o'clock he returned, to find his army waiting impatiently on the north side of the Mohawk, having ingeniously bridged the river with baggage wagons.

Immediately following the rout of Col. Brown's column, Sir John's army commenced the destruction of Stone Arabia. The booty-laden destructives passed to the south of Ephratah and headed east for St. Johnsville on the river. The Patriots belatedly took up the chase and caught up with the enemy's rear guard. No alternative offering, Sir John had a rude breastwork thrown up and deployed his forces for the imminent battle, selecting for his stand Klock's Field (Fox's Mills) on the eastern edge of St. Johnsville near Fort Klock. The Indians and Hessians were secreted in a clump of scrub oaks on Johnson's left flank.

With sunset fast approaching, the Americans at once launched a strong attack, with Col. Morgan Lewis in the vanguard of the assault; the rear and main American lines were commanded by Col. Abraham Cuyler on the left and by Col. Lewis Dubois on the right, which included sixty Oneida volunteers. The initial attack panicked the British auxiliaries out of their cover into seeking escape across the river, Sir John fleeing with them. While attempting to rally his Indians, Brant was wounded in the heel. The leaderless bulk of the enemy force found itself hemmed in on three sides by Patriots and on the fourth by the Mohawk River.

Their position hopelessly untenable, the surrounded British regulars and Tories were apparently at the point of surrendering, when suddenly, to their stupefied astonishment, the whole American army wheeled about and paraded along the river. Van Rensselaer's subordinate officers had urged the storming of the breastwork to overrun the enemy, but he refused to issue an order to that effect, and even objected to any pursuit of the fleeing Indians and Hessians. With nightfall at hand, the American commander decided to call it a day, marched his men about three miles east to old Palatine, and there bedded down for the night.

Morning found the enemy, still amazed at their good fortune, many miles away and headed for Onondaga, where they had hidden their boats. Two detachments of Americans took up the chase, with the main body of the army trailing as far as German Flats. Some advance units of the pursuing Patriots finally caught up with Sir John's destructives. But with their main force so far to the rear, the Americans wisely refrained from risking an attack and the pursuit was dropped.

Already having done irreparable damage to a potentially successful attempt to destroy the enemy force, Van Rensselaer sent word to Fort Stanwix, ordering its commander to speed a detachment to Onondaga before Sir John arrived there, to burn the British watercraft. The force of one hundred men that left the fort for the Onondaga landing place had a traitorous soldier in its midst; feigning sickness, he dropped out of the column, found the British, and informed Sir John of the expedition's purpose. The Tory leader immediately dispatched Indians and Rangers ahead. The Americans from Fort Stanwix were captured while camped and eating their dinner. Sir John's force arrived at Fort Niagara by way of Oswego without further incident.

Gen. Van Rensselaer and his militia army never got any farther than German Flats. On October 21 he marched his men back to Albany. The officer was later court-martialed and, though the testimony was overpowering in its condemnation of his behavior, he was vindicated by the military court. There is no doubt that the Van Rensselaer name, the family's wealth, and its social prominence influenced the court.[66]

The expedition was one of the most rigorous forays of the war. There were never enough provisions to go around for so large a number of men. Sir John's traveling commissary department had constantly to depend on a corps of hunters to bring in game, and their catches were considerable. In the course of the army's depredations, the primary prize was food, often eaten with one hand while applying the torch with the other. On more than one occasion, the Tories, Indians, and German mercenaries were reduced to eating the horses they had taken in their raids. Though great hardships were endured, not one man suffered the extremity of death from starvation.[67]

Governor Clinton assessed the losses in Washington's New York granaries at more than 150,000 bushels of grain; more than two hundred dwellings went up in flames during this last enemy assault of the season. The country west of Schenectady was a smoking, desolated ruin, with its occupants homeless and hungry, dependent upon charitable handouts by straitened compatriots at Schenectady and Albany. Clinton had a fit epitaph for the Patriots' disastrous year: "Schenectady may now be said to become the limits of our western frontier."[68]

The catastrophic year of 1780 on the New York frontier came to an end. The toll in lives, property, livestock, and military installations was the heaviest of the war. At least three hundred persons, military and civilian, were killed or taken as prisoners to Canada; more than seven hundred dwellings, barns, and mills were burned; and seven hundred head of cattle were driven off and six forts destroyed. The loss in grain and produce was immense, signifying even leaner Continental Army larders. Once-prosperous settlements were nearly depopulated, most of the terrorized inhabitants having fled to strongly garrisoned havens far removed from family hearths.[69]

The ruined condition of "the most fertile Part of the State" influenced Governor Clinton to write an appeal to the President of the Congress, Samuel Huntington of Connecticut:

> We are now arrived at the year 1781, deprived of a great Portion of our most valuable and well inhabited Territory, numbers of our Citizens have been barbarously butchered by the ruthless Hand of the Savages, many are carried away into Captivity, vast numbers entirely ruined, and those with their Families become a heavy Burthen to the distressed Remainder; the frequent Calls of the Militia has capitally diminished our Agriculture in every Part of the State. . . . We are not in a Condition to raise Troops for the Defence of our Frontier, and if we were, our Exertions for the common cause have so effectually drained and exhausted us, that we should not have it in our Power to pay and subsist them. In short, Sir, without correspondent Exertions in other States and without Aid from those for whom we have not hesitated to sacrifice all, we shall soon approach to the Verge of Ruin.[70]

1781

The worst was yet to come. The year 1781 had hardly begun when raids were resumed despite the cold January weather, by no means as severe as the previous winter, and continued through the spring and summer into early fall. The populations in Washington's New York granaries were reduced to barely a third of their former numbers, with homeless and ruined inhabitants jammed into two-dozen forts. The expulsion of the Oneidas the previous spring and summer had deprived the Mohawk Valley of its buffer and source of warning. The destructives now had a clear, direct passage through the Oneidas' desolated homeland to the valley, and their former route by way of the Chemung and Susquehanna Rivers was rendered obsolete.

Fort Stanwix, at the valley's western gate, was utterly useless; Brant, completely recovered from his wound received at Klock's Field, was besieging it with many Indians. The garrison's soldiers stood little chance of escaping death or capture if they left the fort's confines. During the early days of March, a detachment of fifteen men—wood foragers and their guards—were ambushed only a half mile from the fort; one man was killed, another miraculously escaped, and the rest were captured and marched off to Niagara.

The forces of nature accomplished what Brant could not: the destruction of Fort Stanwix. In May a rampaging Mohawk River, followed a few days later by a devastating fire, destroyed the historic fort, and the troops evacuated the post. Now the door to the Oswego portage was wide open, with Fort Dayton assuming the role of the frontier's westernmost bulwark of defense.[71]

During the first several months of the year, the paralysis of the American military was evidenced by the ability of the enemy to invade any settlement in central and eastern New York State. The Tories and Indians were hard put to find a dwelling, barn, or mill to set afire that had not already been destroyed. Fort Plain, Canajoharie, German Flats, Cherry Valley, the Schoharie Valley, Saratoga, and Ulster County were revisited, with one party of marauders raiding the Esopus (Kingston) area.

In the face of these depredations and the constant threat of death, those who lived in the forts came out, planted crops, and harvested them while militiamen stood nervous guard in the fields. Albany and Schenectady were in a perpetual state of anxiety, as reports and rumors combined to suggest planned massive-invasion thrusts from Niagara, Oswego, Carleton Island, and Montreal. So unhindered were their movements that Tories invaded large towns and villages and attempted abduction of prominent citizens. Col. Peter Gansevoort narrowly escaped being seized while he was at Saratoga. In a bolder foray, Philip Schuyler's home in Albany's suburbs was assaulted, but the general evaded capture by a ruse that dispersed the British partisans, who were loaded with some of the Schuyler family's silver plate.[72]

A development in late June, a product of American military desperation, served to give new life and soaring hopes to the beleaguered inhabitants on the frontier. Irrepressible Son of Liberty during the years leading up to the war and already a legendary hero by reason of his courageous exploits, Col. Marinus Willett succumbed to Governor Clinton's entreaties and was assigned the unenviable task of mounting a frontier defense. Clinton's order, dated Poughkeepsie, April 28, 1781, specified as follows:

> Sir, The Regiment of Levies for the Defence of the State which you are appointed to command, is to be composed of those raised in the Counties of Albany, Tryon, Charlotte and Part of Dutchess, and when collected & embodied they are to be so disposed of as to give the best Security to the Frontier Settlements of the three first above mentioned Counties. In making the Distribution for this Purpose, you are to have Regard to the Aid to be derived from the Continental Troops & Militia, and as your Regiment is subject to the order of the Commander in Chief of the army, you are to be governed by the advice of the Commanding Officer of the Northern Department.[73]

The forty-one-year-old great-grandson of an English sea captain and an émigré to Plymouth Colony, Willett possessed military expertise born of his inestimable services at Ticonderoga (Abercromby's Expedition, 1758), Fort Frontenac (Bradstreet's Expedition, 1758), Quebec (Canada Invasion, 1775/76), Fort Stanwix (St. Leger's Siege, 1777), and New Town (Sullivan's Expedition, 1779). With four hundred Continentals he took over the command of the frontier forts, then ineffectively protecting some five thousand settlers in an area of approximately two thousand square miles, with posts at German Flats (Fort Herkimer), Ballston, and Catskill constituting a triangle.

Willett established his command post with a nucleus of 150 veteran Continentals and volunteers in the centrally located Canajoharie Settlement (which included the village of Fort Plain) at Fort Rensselaer, from which place he could spring out and leap upon enemy marauding parties.[74] The remainder of his minuscule army was apportioned among the widely separated settlement posts. In his July 6, 1781, eight-page report to Washington, dated "German Flatts, Fort Herkimer," Willett delineated the almost insurmountable difficulties facing him and the steps he proposed to take to deal with the task at hand. The colonel estimated that at the beginning of the conflict Tryon County's militia numbered 2,500 men, but two-thirds of them had disappeared by death or capture, desertion to the enemy, or self-imposed transfer to less-perilous precincts. Now, in the sixth year of the war, there were only 800 militiamen, many of them shoeless and clothed in tattered remnants of uniforms, garrisoning the forts. From German Flats in the west to Schenectady and Albany in the east, from Saratoga in the north to Schoharie and the Catskills in the south, there were only 250 Continentals to aid in the defense.[75]

Willett was hardly settled in his new responsibility when, on the afternoon of July 9, a strong party of Tories and Indians, numbering between 200 and 350 men, commanded by John Doxtader (a former Tryon County resident), descended on Currytown, a small settlement about eleven miles southeast of Fort Plain.[76] Most of the community's people, in the fields when the attack came, ran for the woods or Fort Lewis, a fortified dwelling, which successfully repelled the enemy. The destructives burned a dozen houses, exempting only the fort and a dwelling occupied by a Tory family, and killing or capturing a small number of the people.

A few days after Willett assumed his frontier command, he had sent a detachment of thirty-five men under Capt. Gross to New Darloch (today's Sharon, about eleven miles southeast of Canajoharie) to investigate suspected Tory activities in that area. Shortly after the contingent left, Willett and his Continentals saw smoke rising from the direction of Currytown. A messenger was sent scurrying after Capt. Gross directing him to investigate immediately. Simultaneously, Willett dispatched Capt. Robert McKean with a detachment of sixteen men to the blazing settlement; McKean's party arrived only in time to assist with the dousing of the fires.

After assembling all available militia, Willett with about two hundred men, including Fort Clyde's militia, set off in pursuit of the enemy. The colonel received intelligence from Capt. Gross that Doxtader's destructives were planning to camp at New Darloch. Willett and his aggregation of Continentals, militia, and a few volunteers made an eighteen-mile night march, but lost their way for a time in a dense cedar swamp and arrived too late at break of day to effect a surprise attack. At the edge of Sharon Springs Swamp, where the battle took place, Willett's two advance detachments rejoined his force. Doxtader and his raiders were ready and waiting for the Patriots.

Outnumbered almost two to one but determined to make a fight of it, Willett outmaneuvered the enemy in the thick woods by deploying his force in a crescent. He ordered Lieut. Jacob Scammons and his unit to advance as though to assault the enemy line but to retreat after an initial firing of their weapons. Doxtader, eager to annihilate his pursuers, was drawn with his men into the trap and were met by a hail of bullets. The two arms of the crescent, Capt. McKean on the left flank and Col. Willett on the right, closed in on the raiders. The fighting, often at close quarters, raged for an hour and a half. The Tories and Indians finally gave way despite their numerical superiority, and took flight in the direction of the Susquehanna River, discarding all their plunder and leaving at least ninety dead among the trees. The Patriots reported a loss of only five men killed and nine wounded or missing. Capt. McKean received multiple wounds and died a few days later. He was buried near the Fort Plain blockhouse, which was renamed Fort McKean in his memory.[77]

On the afternoon of August 6, Donald McDonald (not to be confused with the North Carolinian Loyalist general), a refugee Scotch Loyalist leader from Johnstown, at the head of a party of more than sixty Tories and Indians, made a surprise raid on Schell's Bush, a German community about five miles north of Herkimer. Most of the inhabitants, in the fields tending to their crops, fled to Fort Dayton. But an affluent farmer, John Christian Schell (anglicized to Shell), with his wife and eight sons, two of whom were captured by the raiders, ran from the fields to their blockhouse. The family put up a heroic defense until dusk without suffering any additional casualties. Mrs. Schell frantically reloaded muskets while her menfolk stood resolutely at their loopholes and held off the enemy.

When the Indians were unsuccessful in their efforts to fire the blockhouse, McDonald attempted to force the refuge's door with an iron lever, but he was shot and pulled inside by the defenders. As daylight waned the attackers broke off the siege and withdrew. McDonald was taken to Herkimer the next day but he died within a few hours after his shattered leg was amputated. The enemy's casualties were extremely heavy, considering the number involved—eleven killed, with the two captured Schell boys later reporting that nine more died of wounds on the retreat to Canada. A week or so later the settlement was again hit when a small party of Indians caught the elder Schell and one son in the fields and killed them.[78]

On August 22 Ulster County, far to the south of the Mohawk, was raided by about four hundred Tories and Indians under Capt. William Caldwell, one of Butler's Ranger officers. Great destruction was caused to the isolated settlements before a sizable militia force, led by Col. Albert Pawling, made a forced march and engaged Caldwell's marauders. During the running battle, with the main action taking place at Wawarsing (named for an ancient Indian tribe) in the southern foothills of the Catskills about twenty miles west of the Hudson, the determined militia forced the enemy to retire after suffering considerable casualties. The hero who led the Patriots in the action at Wawarsing was Capt. J. L. Hardenbergh.[79]

During the next two months an Indian ambuscade near Fort Plain and several forays of little consequence by small hit-and-run parties of Indians were made in the Stone Arabia and Palatine Church areas, and against Cobleskill and German Flats. On September 7, near Fort Plain, an ambush by a war party of about one hundred Indians caught Lieut. Solomon Woodworth's company of fifty militia scouts and slaughtered more than half of the detachment, the lieutenant among the victims. Fifteen Patriot rangers escaped; the remaining survivors were marched off to Niagara.[80] Among the more fortunate militiamen was Daniel Frederick Bakeman, who lived to be the last surviving soldier of the Revolution.[81]

The stimulating presence of Col. Willett in the Mohawk Valley spread an aura of comparative serenity and security, much more than the inhabitants had experienced for several years. The militia now had a leader whom they respected and admired. Even Joseph Brant, returning from his unrewarding summer campaign on the Ohio, deferred to Willett's astute generalship of his swift-moving, tiny army and made no incursions into the frontier settlements. But in October the valley's short-lived peaceful interlude was shattered.[82]

The Northern Department in mid-October began receiving disturbing and conflicting intelligence reports that two enemy armies were on the march, one by way of Lake Champlain from Canada, and the other, originating at Oswego, approaching the Mohawk Valley by the traditional Oneida Lake route. The British military had deliberated on the significance of Washington's stripping the Hudson Highland defenses to initiate the Yorktown offensive in the South, leaving Gen. William Heath with only twenty-five hundred Continentals to contest any northward threat by Sir Henry Clinton's seventeen thousand regulars and Hessians.

Governor Sir Frederick Haldimand at once recognized the opportunity to again mount a three-pronged assault against the rebels. This latest renewal of the Burgoyne design of offense was an even more abysmal failure. Overcautious and lethargic Sir Henry in New York City, having lost whatever little talent he had for audacity, made no effort to act on Haldimand's directive. St. Leger and his column departed from Canada and reached Ticonderoga, where he made the tragic error of stopping too long. He became involved in puzzling, protracted negotiations with Ethan Allen, who headed a petty, unpatriotic Vermont clique that threatened to annex their territory to Canada (Vermont in 1777 had declared itself independent of the Continental Congress because of the long-standing territorial controversy with New York over the New Hampshire Grants).

Only the third and least important of the three armies, a diversionary offensive, managed to get under way. Maj. John Ross, with Walter Butler as his second in command, had departed from Fort Haldimand on Carleton Island (of which Ross was commandant) early in October with a mixed force of 570 Tories, Royal Greens, and regulars, and proceeded to Oswego. They waited there a few days for a large contingent of Indians. But only 130 Iroquois showed up instead of the 600 expected, indicative of how much Brant's influence was missed in his absence. On October 10 the force left Oswego, descended to Oneida Lake by boat and, at the mouth of Canaseraga Creek near Lakeport on the lake's south shore, secreted its watercraft and a reserve supply of provisions.

Ross and Butler made a wide circuit through the wilderness far to the south of abandoned Fort Stanwix to the Susquehanna River, then headed north and entered the Mohawk Valley by way of Otsego Lake and Cherry Valley. En route they took prisoners who gave exaggerated reports about the strength of Willett's Continental contingent and the Tyron County militia. Slowed down by heavy rains that turned Indian paths into wide ribbons of mud, the British force entered Warrenbush (Warren's Bush) on Schoharie Creek before daybreak on October 25. The raiders burned everything in a twenty-mile stretch of countryside, coming within a dozen miles of Schenectady before turning back. Ross and Butler by now had to acknowledge the bitter news that their army could not count on either Clinton or St. Leger for military support.

A small detachment of Willett's scouts, scouring the country in the direction of Sharon and Argusville, south of Canajoharie, on the morning of October 24, almost blundered into the Tory expedition. The startling sight of a host of the enemy sped the scouts northward to the Mohawk to raise the alarm. Ross and Butler marched their marauders through Currytown, Yatesville (today's Randall), Fultonville, and Auriesville, pillaging, burning, and taking prisoners (women and children taken in the Currytown settlement were apparently released at Yatesville). The destructives forded Schoharie Creek below Fort Hunter and established camp for the night. At dawn they forded the Mohawk below Amsterdam and marched for Johnstown.

As soon as he was apprised of the enemy's presence in the valley, Willett assembled a force of a small number of Continentals and nearly four hundred militia and made an all-night twenty-mile eastward march along the south side of the Mohawk. On reaching Schoharie Creek in the morning, he learned that the Tories had crossed the river and were proceeding along the road to Johnstown. The Patriot pursuers forded the river six miles higher up. The weather was abominable. Both the British and the American forces were exceedingly hampered by almost continuous heavy rains that turned country roads into ankle-deep mires; streams, usually easy to cross, became tempestuous torrents.

Ross and Butler entered Johnstown about mid-afternoon. Willett and his army, close on their heels, engaged the Tories near Johnson Hall.

Willett sent Col. Aaron Rowley with one hundred militia around the enemy to attack their rear. The battle was joined, however, before Rowley could reach position. The Patriot right flank, in possession of a small fieldpiece, broke and fled. Nearly a score of them became casualties as they attempted escape across Cayadutta Creek near Johnson Hall, while the rest continued their flight until they reached the refuge of Fort Johnstown on today's South Perry Street. The Patriots regrouped, rallied, and regained the gun and cart, but minus its ammunition.

A report to Gen. Stirling, dated the day after the action, merits repetition in part here:

> The evening coming on put an end to the action; part of Col. Willett's men, however, passed the hall all night. The enemy retreated about 6 miles back into the woods [west of Johnstown], where the last account just now comes leaves them. About thirty British have been taken during the action and in the morning before the action commenced yesterday in the afternoon. Col. Willett went in pursuit of them this morning with a force about equal to theirs. An account is also come to hand (altho not official) that a party is sent from Fort Herkimer to destroy their boats and provisions. There are 7 of the enemy found dead on the field of action this morning, and 3 of ours; between thirty and 40 wounded on both sides.[83]

Except for scouts left in the wilderness to check on the enemy's movements, Willett marched his men on Friday, October 26, the day after the battle, to Fort Paris at Stone Arabia and bivouacked overnight. The next morning they resumed the chase, crossing the river to the south side to march to Fort Herkimer, where Willet reassembled his pursuit force, and collected more militia, the service of sixty Oneidas, and several days' provisions.

Informed by his scouts that Ross and Butler were heading for the Jerseyfield Patent area, Willett left the fort with his augmented army on the evening of October 28 and recrossed the Mohawk to camp for the night in the woods. In the morning the Patriots headed up West Canada Creek to Middleville, then east to Fairfield, where they struck the Jerseyfield road and swiftly proceeded north.

The incessant rain, turning to sleet and snow on the twenty-ninth, did not raise the spirits of Ross and Butler. They learned that their Indians were deliberately misleading them in the direction of Fort Niagara instead of Oswego and the St. Lawrence, by which duplicity the frantic British retreat was retarded the best part of three days.

At 8 A.M. on October 30 Willett caught up with the tail end of the enemy column. Six hours later, at 2 P.M., the hot pursuit ended at West

Canada Creek when all of the British regulars, Tories, Hessian mercenaries, and Indians had crossed the stream. Walter Butler was commanding the rear guard. He and his men determined to make a stand to foil a crossing of the ford by the Patriots.

A spirited musket duel was waged for some minutes across the width of the stream. Several casualties had been suffered by each side by the time the firing ceased. The rest of the enemy's rear guard dissolved among the trees. The Patriots, with several Oneidas in the vanguard, hurriedly waded across the creek. Near the creek's bank[84] the archenemy of the Cherry Valley inhabitants, Walter Butler, lay mortally wounded with a musket ball through his head, and close by were the dead bodies of some of his Rangers. An Oneida Indian, knife in hand, bent over the stricken Tory leader. Three days later, on November 2 from Fort Rensselaer, Willett penned a graphic report to Governor Clinton:

> Dear Sir, I am just returned from a most fatiguing pursuit of the Enemy, and tho it has not been in my power to take or kill the whole of the Detachment that lately made their Appearance in this Quarter, yet I flatter myself they are very little better off As those that are not among the killed and taken, are in a famishing situation, scattered throughout the Wilderness on the rout to Buck [Carleton] Island, where any of them that may arrive will have tales of Horror only to Relate. After the Affair at Johnstown, which happened on the 25th ultimo, and which would at once have proved fatal to them had the Right Wing of the small number of Troops I had engaged, behaved half as well as the left, the enemy took to the wilderness and finding it out of their Power to pass us so as to get to the Oneida Creek where they left their Boats, they directed their Rout towards Buck Island keeping far back in the Wilderness; This Determined me to cut across from the German Flatts in order to Intercept them on that Rout. Accordingly on the evening of the 28th, having furnished near 400 men and sixty Indians who had just joined me with four days and a half Provisions, which was all I could procure, I Crossed the Mohawk from Fort Herkimer and Incamped in the Woods.
>
> The 29th we marched North upwards of Twenty Miles in a snow storm, and at Eight o'clock A.M. of the 30th we fell in with the enemy, who without making any Resistance worth mentioning fled from that time, untill night; we pursued them as closely and warmly as Possible Nor did they ever attempt to Check us in our Advance Except at one Difficult ford in Canada Creek, where they lost several of their men. Amongst those killed at that Place was Walter Butler, the Person who commanded the Massacre at Cherry Valley in November 1778. He was called Major, but by the Commission found in his Pocket appears to be no more than a Captain.
>
> A Number of Prisoners have been taken and many were killed in our Intercourse with those Gentry.
>
> To Pursue them any farther was thought Improper: many of the Troops as Well as the Indians had laid aside their Blankets and Provisions in order to pursue with Greater ease. And in the evening we

found ourselves at least Twenty miles from those packs. The woods was strewed with the packs of the Enemy; Provision they had none. The few horses they had amongst them when we first fell in with them, they were obliged to leave; except five, which were sent a Considerable way in front, with some of their Wounded and a few Prisoners. Their flight was performed in an Indian file upon a Constant trott, and one man's being Knocked in the head or falling off into the woods never stopped the Progress of his Neighbour, not even the fall of their favourite Butler, could attract their attention so much as to Induce them to take even the Money or anything Else out of his Pocket, altho he was not Dead when found by one of our Indians, who finished his business for him and got a Considerable Booty.

Strange it may appear, yet it is true, that notwithstanding the Enemy had been four days with only half a pound of horse flesh for each man per day, yet they did not halt from the time we began to Pursue them until they had Proceeded more than thirty miles: (and they Continued their Rout a Considerable part of the night). In this Situation to the Compassion of a starving Wilderness, we left them in a fair way of Receiving a Punishment better suited to their Merit than a muskquet ball, a Tomahawk or Captivity. . . .

I am sure the loss of the Enemy must be great. It is, however, out of my power to ascertain it. The man who sent such a fine Detachment of Troops upon such a Paltry Business, when they Return, will be best able to say how great their loss has been and to him I leave it. Upwards of Fifty Prisoners are Returned to me to be taken. Their Killed is by no means Trifling and many, very many, must be scattered about the Wilderness almost sure of Perishing there. I have not yet been able to procure an Exact Return of our Killed and Wounded but from my Present Accounts we must have had in the whole about Ten Killed and Thirty Wounded.[85]

What proved to be the war's last substantial Tory-Indian invasion of the northern frontier had been severely punished by the rebels. The beaten enemy destructives had discarded their packs and blankets, in some cases even their muskets, along the path of precipitate flight. Minus their reserve supply of provisions, cached on the southern bank of Oneida Lake, they were in desperate straits. It is not known how many of them, including their few prisoners, survived the retreat to Carleton Island (most of the British-allied Indians had elected to return to Niagara). During the two engagements—Johnstown and West Canada Creek—the Patriots had taken at least sixty British prisoners; the number of enemy dead and wounded is not known. The Patriots reported the loss of thirteen killed and twenty-four wounded. The death of Walter Butler was a serious blow to Tory morale. That loss, and the determined presence of Marinus Willett, served to convince the British that it was not advisable to plan any more large-scale forays against the New York Frontier.[86]

When Willett and his weary troops returned to Fort Rensselaer, they learned of the American-French victory at Yorktown. The Tryon County settlers, however, were decidedly more elated over the simultaneous news of the death of hated Walter Butler of Butlersbury (near Fonda).[87] The destructive operations of the Johnsons and the Butlers were over. By the Acts of Attainder enacted by the New York State Legislature, Sir John, his brother-in-law, Guy, the Butlers, and other Loyalists had their properties, both real and personal, forfeited to, and vested in the people of the state.[88]

End of War

The formal surrender of Cornwallis and his army on October 19 was almost coincident with the fourth anniversary of Burgoyne's surrender at Saratoga (October 17, 1777). Despite great rejoicing and celebration throughout the new nation, the war was far from over. Two more years of the Revolution had to run their historic course though Yorktown, which would be the last of the war's major military operations.[89]

During the remaining weeks of the 1781 fall season, the frontier war was still continued by small, fast-moving Indian raiding parties, most of them out to reap more scalps. On November 18 Lieut. Adam Crysler, [90] an exiled Fort Plains Tory, with twenty-eight Indians from Oquaga, raided the Schoharie Valley. One man was killed, two houses were set afire, and fifty cattle and a small number of horses were driven off. The militia came out in strength, pursued the raiders, and engaged them in two running battles. The militia suffered five men killed and an undetermined number wounded, but Crysler and his Indians had to surrender the seized cattle as they retreated toward their Susquehanna base.[91]

The winter of 1781/82 was so balmy that small Indian raiding parties resumed their marauding as early as February. The obstinate settlers, who still held on grimly, strengthened their existing forts and erected more blockhouses, though the border warfare had appreciably decreased in intensity and in number of raids. They sensed the near end of the frontier war, and their relatives and friends who had fled to larger fortified havens began in the months following to return to their blackened homesteads to rebuild their houses and replant their crops.[92]

During the spring months more Iroquois war parties left from Fort Niagara. Two Mohawk captains, John Deserontyon[93] and Isaac Hill, took a detachment of their tribesmen to Little Falls (east of Herkimer), burned a mill, and took some prisoners. Minor raids were carried out in the New York-Pennsylvania border areas. The noted Seneca war chief and orator Old King (Sayenqueraghta or Old Smoke), almost a septuagenarian at the beginning of the war, led about three hundred Indians in raids along the Ohio River.

During the summer Tories and Indians made lightning raids on German Flats south of the Mohawk and in the area around Fort Dayton on the north side of the river. Having great respect for Col. Willett and his alert Continentals and militia, the destructives burned what they could in the very limited time they set for themselves, and made no attempts against Forts Dayton and Herkimer. Tory Adam Crysler and a small detachment of Indians revisited the upper Schoharie, taking a few prisoners for Niagara. Roaming small bands of Indians attacked isolated settlers' homes in search of more scalps for their belts.[94]

Washington's Mohawk and Schoharie granaries suffered the most devastation and loss of life. By war's end in 1783 it was estimated that Tryon County counted among its inhabitants three hundred widows and two thousand orphans.[95]

[After the news of the British defeat at Yorktown had reached London], no one but the king thought of pursuing the war in America any further. Even the king gave up all hope of subduing the United States; but he insisted upon retaining the state of Georgia, with the cities of Charleston and New York; and he vowed that, rather than acknowledge the independence of the United States, he would abdicate the throne and retire to Hanover [upon later reflection, the avid hunter and amateur locksmith thought better of it]. Lord George Germain was dismissed from office, Sir Henry Clinton was superseded by Sir Guy Carleton, and the king began to dream of a new campaign.[96]

On March 22, 1782, Lord North resigned as prime minister, to be succeeded by Charles Rockingham (his second occupancy of the ministry). Rockingham, however, died suddenly on July 1, elevating the Earl of Shelburne to the post. The government sent delegates to Paris to negotiate peace with both the United States and France. Orders had been dispatched to the British military commanders in America to suspend all hostilities.[97]

The Patriots had largely destroyed Oswego's Fort Ontario in 1778, burning all the structures within its ramparts. Col. Guy Johnson and British-allied Iroquois urgently petitioned Haldimand to rehabilitate the fort, but the governor of Canada replied that the troops were needed much more elsewhere. Very soon after their application had been denied, the Onondagas saw their villages south of Syracuse invaded and burned down by a large force of men led by Colonels Marinus Willett and Gose Van Schaick.

fo. 32.   Oswego June 18th. 1782

Sir

I am very sorry to acquaint you the chiefs of the five nations who came with me find themselves much disapointed in not being properly fitted out for war as they were promised at Niagara, such as Mokosins and ammunition, Had they these necessarys they would not complain and meant to show themselves in this occasion, which they can not do for real want did they not show themselves if they were provided the blame must ly at their door but as that is not the case and that they are in real want any inactivity at present must not be imputed to the chiefs and warriors I also beg to leave to mention that I myself told to Col.ʳ Butler frequently this before I left Niagara nor did I imagine that no regard had been paid to my request untill my arrival here when scarce found anything I asked for The chiefs desire that you will write this to the General and beg he will let us know why, perhaps we are strangers to the reason —

— I am your most Humble Servant

To Major Ross   Jos. Brant/   A.L.S.

ff. 32 - 33 Blank.
p33 Addressed: To Major Ross
[Endorsed]

From   1782
Capt Joseph Brant to
Major Ross of 18.ᵗʰ June
inclosed in the Majors Letter
of the 18th D.ʳ

JOSEPH BRANT LETTER
Courtesy of Manuscript Division, Public Archives of Canada

In 1780 and 1781 decrepit Fort Ontario was occasionally used as a base for raids led by Sir John Johnson and Walter Butler. After long procrastination, and spurred by strong rumors of peace, Haldimand finally instructed Maj. John Ross on February 18, 1782, to go to Oswego with the object of reestablishing a garrison there. Ross made a couple of preliminary inspections to determine what rebuilding was necessary. In April a garrison, including Johnson's Royal Greens and Butler's Rangers, was transported from Carleton Island to reoccupy the important Lake Ontario site. The British occupied Oswego until July 15,

1796, when they evacuated the post according to the provisions of the Jay Treaty.[98]

On June 18, Brant, with about three hundred Indians, arrived at Oswego to make preparations for continuing his destructive war against the Americans. Completely dependent on the British for sustenance and war supplies, the Mohawk leader was much annoyed to learn that Oswego could not provide the ammunition and supplies to outfit his warriors.[99] The British proclivity for shortsightedness baffled Brant. Furthermore, he and the Iroquois were kept in the dark with respect to the impending cessation of hostilities. Fort Ontario was being rebuilt to some degree and, since he could not take to the warpath, Brant enjoined his Mohawks to work on the fortification they had been seeking to have reconstructed. They energetically labored on the fort with such devotion that Ross was impelled on June 27 to communicate his high regard for Joseph Brant to Haldimand.[100]

While his warriors were occupied with labors on Fort Ontario, Brant was putting on the pressure to obtain the wherewithal to allow him and his Indians to resume the warpath. Fort Haldimand on Carleton Island finally provided what Brant needed. On July 5, less than three weeks after his arrival, Brant departed from Oswego with about 460 Indians and a company of men from Ross's regiment. They were hardly out of Oswego's environs when they were recalled by Maj. Ross, who had received a dispatch from Haldimand advising a halt to all hostilities because peace negotiations among the principals had been initiated. Brant returned with his column at once. Needless to say, the Indians were much chagrined at this latest effort of the British to restrain their war-making activities and they evinced their anger in no uncertain terms. During the following weeks the Iroquois League chieftains became increasingly certain that whatever came out of the peace negotiations at Paris would be to their detriment. They were right.[101]

The news that Britain was throwing in the towel came as a great shock to Loyalists in British-held New York City. Gen. Washington, writing from Newburgh on August 14, welcomed the possibility of peace and commented on the bitterness of enemy citizenry:

> 'Ere this can have reached you, you will have seen the letter of Sir Guy Carleton and Adml. Digby to me, transmitted to Congress on the 5th. If this letter does not breathe a great deal of disengenuity [*sic*], there is a solid basis for our Commissioners to work upon. . . .
> One thing however, *is certain,* but how it came to pass, is not so well understood; and that is that their letter to me is published in New York and has spread universal consternation among the Refugees; who, actuated by different passions, or rather by the same passion in different degrees; are little better than a medley of confused, enraged,

and dejected people. Some are Swearing and some crying; while the greater part of them are almost speechless.[102]

Britain's tacit recognition of the independence of the Thirteen United States had initiated formal negotiations. On November 5 a second set of articles was agreed to by the commissioners, after John Adams and John Jay had convinced Benjamin Franklin to leave France out of the negotiations and work out a separate peace treaty with Great Britain. After a few minor changes the Preliminary Articles of Peace were signed by the American and British commissioners on November 30 and, with no further modifications, the pact was transmuted into the final Peace Treaty on September 3, 1783.[103]

When the Preliminary Articles were made known in America, those British officers who had served and lived almost side by side with the Iroquois were aghast at their government's disavowal of their Indian allies. Nowhere in the pact was there any proviso for the sanctity of Iroquois lands. Instead, the Indians, not only the Iroquois, were completely ignored. All their ancestral domains south of the Great Lakes and the St. Lawrence River as far west as the Mississippi were given *in toto* into the ownership of the United States.

Unsuccessful efforts were made to keep knowledge of the Preliminary Treaty's stipulations from the Indians, in overoptimistic trust that the ultimate articles of peace would provide the guarantees to safeguard the Indian's land from incursion by the whites.

Before the Iroquois became fully acquainted with the provisions, or rather omissions, of the Preliminary Articles, Joseph Brant at Niagara dictated a long, complaining letter to Sir John Johnson:

> We think the Rebels will ruin us at last if we go on as we do one year after another, doing nothing, only Destroying the government goods. . . . So we are in as it were between two Hells. I am sure you will assist all you can to Let us have an Expedition Early in the Spring. Let it be [a] great or small one, let us not hang our heads between our knees. . . . I am as much forward to go to war as I ever did but I am not so contented as I used to be formerly because the Warriors are in want; they are treated worse & worse instead of better. I shall tell you the particulars, if you should want to know why I write you so.[104]

When the full import of the final articles of peace was made known, the Iroquois were furious, and Brant charged England with delivering the Indians into American bondage. The century following the end of the Revolution witnessed sessions of frustrated Indian diplomacy and coercive white "forked-tongue" treaty-making, accompanied by intermittent wars.[105]

The last act of the war on New York's Revolutionary frontier properly belonged to Col. Marinus Willett, indomitable hero of Fort Stanwix and the savior of the Mohawk Valley. Willett reasoned, just as Haldimand belatedly had, that strategic Oswego was a vital portal to the corridor leading to vulnerable western and central New York. It seemed obvious to Willett that the site at the mouth of the Oswego River, in the possession of the British, could be rehabilitated and used for continued murderous Tory-Indian incursions.

Willett, overconfident and not averse to taking the main chance, wrote to Washington, and requested permission to take the fort by a surprise night assault.[106] The plan was ill-advised and a serious lapse of judgment, since there was certainly no indication at the time that the British would use Oswego as a springboard for harassment of New York's northern settlements. The commander-in-chief agreed with the plan and issued personal orders to "capture and hold Oswego."

On February 8, 1783, Willet assembled a force of 470 Continentals at Fort Herkimer, with Captain John, an Oneida Indian, to act as guide for the expedition. With the white mantle of full winter over the Mohawk Valley and the temperature hovering near zero, the force moved out the next evening. They marched to frozen Oneida Lake, trudged across the ice to the remains of old Fort Brewerton, and arrived at the Oswego River about four miles above the falls on February 12.

After spending several hours fashioning scaling-ladders, they continued to trek through the snow-buried woods. They emerged from the wilderness and marched on the river ice to a point where the ice began to give way beneath them. They returned to the woods, certain that they were then only several miles from the British-held fort. It was approximately one hour to midnight on February 12, with 4 A.M. set as the zero hour for the surprise attack. Captain John assured Willett that they were only a few miles from the fort.

With their objective now apparently about to loom up before them, Willett's men, confidently cheerful, pressed forward eagerly through the silent, snow-laden woodland. After an hour Willett was informed by his Oneida guide that they were about two miles from the British base. They trudged on for another hour. Captain John again assured the colonel that it was only two more miles. At intervals for the next several hours, Willett was given the same answer: *two more miles*. Willett was positive that they were lost. Suspecting duplicity, he had Captain John put under strict guard; the Oneida guide then reluctantly admitted that he had lost his way.

The cold had deepened to sub-zero. They kept on the move to prevent their limbs from freezing. Dawn of February 13 found them, by astonishing chance, on the edge of the forest, barely a mile from Fort Ontario.

The Continental Army's commander-in-chief had issued hard orders not to attack the fort unless there was indubitably present the element of surprise. After Willett conferred with his subordinates, it was decided to stay low in the woods during the daylight hours and make the assault that night. Just then, as luck would have it, five British soldiers, bent on gathering firewood, emerged from the fort and approached the Americans' position. Every effort was made to capture them quickly and quietly. Two of the soldiers were expertly tomahawked but the others effected their escape and made all haste back to the fort, yelling the alarm with all their might. There was at once the beat to arms, and troops appeared on the fort's ramparts.

Bitterly disappointed, Willett ordered the retreat. The men silently turned about and retraced the trail back to Fort Brewerton. When they arrived at Fort Herkimer a few days later, they learned that their expedition had been a useless exercise: during their absence news had reached the garrison there that a cessation of hostilities had been declared between the mother country and her rebellious offspring. Peace, at long last, had come to America's northern hinterland.[107]

Col. Willets, during the next month, received a commendatory letter from his commander-in-chief:

> Sir: I have been favoured with your Letter of the 19th of Febry. announcing the failure of your Attempt against Oswego.
> Unfortunate as the Circumstance is, I am happy in the persuasion that no Imputation or reflection can justly reach your Character, and that you are enabled to derive much Consolation from the animated Zeal, fortitude and Activity of the Officers and Soldiers who accompanied you. The failure, it seems, must be attributed to some of those unaccountable Events, which are not within the controul of human Means and which, tho' they often occur in military life, yet require not only the fortitude of the Soldier, but the calm reflection of the Philosopher, to bear.
> I cannot omit expressing to you the high Sense I entertain of your persevering Exertions and Zeal on this Expedition; and begging you to accept my warm Thanks on the Occasion; And that you will be pleased to communicate my Gratitude to the Officers and men under your Command, for the Share they have taken in that Service.[108]

Britain held on to her military posts in the Northwest, at Niagara, Fort Oswegatchie (Ogdensburg), and Fort Ontario (Oswego), because the United States had not complied with articles four and five of the Peace Treaty (recompense of pre-Revolutionary War obligations to British businessmen and compensation for dispossessed Loyalists). After the crisis in 1793 (British seizure of American merchantmen and crews) that threatened a resumption of war between the two nations after a decade of argumentive peace, John Jay negotiated a treaty the following year. Provisions stipulated Britain's evacuation of her military posts by June 1, 1796, and alliance with the United States should Indians wars erupt, with American debts to be resolved by joint commissions (the United States in 1802 paid a total of $13,009,200 to settle all claims).[109]

The westward expansion of settlement was very much influenced by British efforts to restrain their former Indian allies. Even while peace negotiations in Paris were still in progress, great numbers of whites were pouring into Indian ancestral domains to erect crude cabins and defoliate tracts of land for farming.

George Clinton's energetic enterprise to open up New York's central and western Indian lands to white settlement was accomplished by a series of treaties with the Iroquois between 1784 and 1790. New York State purchased almost all of the Indian domain between Fort Stanwix and the Genesee River. The secretary of the state's Land Board, scholarly Robert Harpur, sliced up the Indian lands into two plats, identifying them with such place names out of the classics as Ithaca, Rome, and Syracuse, and put them up for sale to land-hungry settlers.[110]

The remnants of the Iroquois nations, once lords of a beautiful and almost trackless primeval wilderness, had but two choices: settle on small restricted reservations in upstate New York, or emigrate to Canada, where the not unappreciative British bestowed upon their former allies generous tracts of land along the Grand River in Ontario.

The Mohawk Valley, for many decades a frontier battleground, became the great gateway to the peaceful settling of New York's western lands. The axe and the plow replaced the tomahawk and the torch.

The Forts

2

New York's Revolutionary Forts

alphabetically listed and discussed

Fort Alden
Cherry Valley, Otsego County

The inhabitants of Cherry Valley, even before the war's first hostilities, had demonstrated their partisanship for the Patriot cause. Contrary to the nearly equal division of sentiment in Tryon County, Cherry Valley was almost unanimous in its display of patriotism: out of a total population of only three hundred people, at least thirty-three men answered the call to arms in 1776. Early in the summer of that year the settlers raised a company of militia under the command of Capt. Robert McKean. When this ranger unit was ordered elsewhere, the village immediately petitioned for military replacements because of the community's situation, one of the most exposed in the Schoharie county.

Cherry Valley sits in the elongated depression of Cherry Valley Creek, a tributary of the Susquehanna, which was a major route for Tory-Indian invasions from the Iroquois base at Ouaquaga. The Provincial Congress answered their appeal by sending another company of militia. Up to the late summer of 1777, no fortified defenses had been erected in Cherry Valley since the destruction of the village's stockade during the French and Indian War.

The certainty that sooner or later Brant and his Indians would make a bloody incursion into the settlement convinced the inhabitants that a fortified refuge was needed at once. They selected the dwelling of Col. Samuel Campbell for its size and elevated position, and surrounded both the house and two barns with a breastwork of logs and earth. Duane H. Hurd, in his *History of Otsego County,* claims that two blockhouses were subsequently erected within the enclosure, but no other source confirms this. If a pair of blockhouses had been added to the Campbell compound, there would have been no need for the construction of Fort Alden the following year. The fortified refuge, reasonably enough, was called Fort Campbell.

After convincing solicitations were made to the Marquis de Lafayette, then at Johnstown in the spring of 1778, a strong fort was constructed at Cherry Valley. There is an unfortunate dearth of descriptive information concerning this fortification, with no details as to its size, construction, and armaments; all that could be learned was that its palisades enclosed two structures, probably blockhouses. It was named Fort Alden for its first commander, Col. Ichabod Alden, who arrived in July with Continental troops to garrison the new post. Additional measures were taken to further safeguard the village, such as stockading the community's church.

Several months later, on November 11, the long-feared enemy strike came. A force of two hundred Tories and more than five hundred Indians under the dual command of Capt. Walter Butler and Joseph Brant caught the settlement by surprise. The raiders almost at once directed their attention to Fort Alden, attempting to overwhelm it by a major initial assault, but the soldiers closed the gates in time and then withstood more than three hours of sniping and sneak attacks. Bands of Brant's Indians stole away from the siege and roamed through the settlement, killing, pillaging, and burning. Butler and Brant finally broke off the engagement and ordered a retreat, knowing full well that elements of the Tryon County militia were being congregated for a counterattack and inevitable pursuit. The gross inefficiency and stupid obstinacy of Col. Alden conspired in his own death and cost the lives of fifteen soldiers. Thirty-two noncombatants, and several women and children were killed; seventy-one prisoners were taken, but most of them were released the next day.

Grim-faced inhabitants, together with militiamen from Fort Plain who arrived two days later, buried the dead amid the blackened ruins of what was a prosperous farming village. With practically all their worldly possessions destroyed in the holocaust, it was determined to abandon the settlement in which nothing remained except Fort Alden, the stockaded church, and very few houses. The livestock had been slaughtered or driven away, the precious grain burned, and the vegetables destroyed by fire or frost. Most of the survivors departed and sought refuge in more secure settlements along the Mohawk River, where most of them stayed for the next three years. Fort Alden, however, was continuously garrisoned until the summer of 1779, when the regiment was ordered to join up with Gen. James Clinton's forces in the Sullivan expedition against the Iroquois towns.

Gradually recovering from the massacre and the terrible devastation, Cherry Valley remained peaceful throughout 1779. Those inhabitants who had elected to remain had begun to regain some confidence and hope when, without a hint of warning, on April 24, 1780, the settlement was struck again by a party of seventy-nine Indians and two Tories. Eight people were killed and fourteen taken into captivity. What structures remained after the 1778 raid—the fort, church, and a few dwellings—were now put to the torch, leaving the settlement a complete desolation.

Before the war was officially terminated, Cherry Valley's people, scattered from Fort Plain eastward to Schenectady, began to return to their ruined homesteads, to rebuild and regain their former prosperity. The settlers were still engaged in erecting new homes and renewing their fields when they were honored in October 1783 by a visit of Gen. Washington, accompanied by Gens. Clinton and Hand.

Fort Alden's site is within the Cherry Valley Cemetery, close by its gates, and quite near the old church's location. To commemorate the centennial of the massacre, the residents erected a memorial to the fallen inside the cemetery.

Fort Anne

Fort Ann, Washington County

A veteran of several wars and lesser military involvements, Fort Anne was strategically located on the Champlain-Hudson route, at present-day Fort Ann, a summer resort village about halfway between Whitehall and Fort Edward. The site is at the end of the mountain corridor through which thousands of soldiers and warring Indians moved along Wood Creek from the southern tip of Lake Champlain to emerge into the more pastoral country leading to the Hudson River.

Despite its participation in the colonial wars between England and France and in the War for American Independence, there is an unfortunate paucity of credible historical evidence on Fort Anne. For one thing, there is a controversy regarding the number of forts that occupied the site. Reason, however, suggests that most of the fortifications were rebuilds. There is also a sad lack of information concerning the structural features of most editions of the fort. Searches in the Library of Congress, National Map Collection of the Public Archives of Canada, and the Royal Archives at Windsor Castle failed to produce any plans.

The Fort Anne site, at the confluence of Wood Creek and Halfway Brook (formerly Cheshire's Brook), was first occupied as a fortified camp in 1690 by a motley army on its way to invade Canada. King William's War (corresponding to Europe's War of the Grand Alliance) was one year old. The American Colonies were shocked and furious over French invasions and brutal massacres, particularly the wholesale killing of noncombatants at Schenectady in February. A decision was made to deal the French a crushing blow on their own home ground in New France. Sir William Phipps sailed to take Quebec by sea assault and a land army, led by Governor Fitz-John Winthrop of Connecticut, marched up the Champlain route to seize Montreal. After several days of futile bombardment of Quebec's cliffs, Phipps sailed home; Winthrop's force of colonists and Indians, stricken with smallpox and dysentery, never got beyond the southern end of Lake Champlain.

Two years later Winthrop, leading another invasion of Canada that was also aborted, again camped on Fort Anne's site. At that time he erected the first of the series of forts at the junction of the two streams. This work, known as the "Old Stone Fort," was simply a rough earthwork.

Queen Anne's War (known in England as the War of the Spanish Succession) broke out in 1702. The Five Nations of the Iroquois abstained from participating actively in this conflict; their neutrality was formulated by an agreement with their Catholicized cousins in Canada. Although New York and the Iroquois country were unmolested throughout the war, the French and their Indian allies did not neglect Maine, New Hampshire, and Massachusetts. For a dozen terrible years fire and the sword ravaged New England, especially with the devastations of Deerfield in 1704 and Haverhill in 1708.

In 1709 the governors of four provinces—Connecticut, Massachusetts, New Jersey, and New York—agreed to pool their armed forces and invade Canada to avenge the bloody outrages. An armada was to again attack Quebec, while an army of about sixteen hundred English and Dutch, led by Gen. Francis Nicholson, was to capture

Montreal. The route of march was lined with forts. Fort Anne, the farthest north, was originally called the Queen's Fort or Fort Schuyler (for Col. Peter Schuyler), but was renamed for the queen two years later.

This expedition likewise ended in abysmal failure. The British fleet never got to the St. Lawrence and the army, stricken with a "malignant disease," probably smallpox, stagnated and died at Fort Anne, losing many more men by contagion than it would have if it had fought a calamitous battle with the French. While the costly expedition ended ingloriously, the campaign produced a noteworthy "first." Col. Schuyler and his Dutchmen cut through the wilderness the first military road in America, beginning at Old Saratoga on the east side of the Hudson, north through Fort Edward (the Great Carrying Place), to Fort Anne on Wood Creek.

Fort Anne was built by Gen. Nicholson. The palisades, surrounding a 140-foot square, were constructed of timber, standing on end outwardly and filled with earth on the inside to both support the stockade and form a platform for armament. Within were two large log buildings for the garrison. At each angle was a 20-foot-square bastion. The fort's water supply was obtained from Kane's Falls, one mile to the northwest, ingeniously piped through cedar pump logs with a three-inch-in-diameter hole. Archaeological explorations in the Fort Anne area have unearthed sections of the conduit, handsmithed iron bands still wrapped about the logs. The expense for all this construction was borne by both Queen Anne and the Province of New York. Before he withdrew with his decimated army, Nicholson burned the fort, but in 1711 he returned and rebuilt it.

During the next several decades, Fort Anne was allowed to deteriorate into total disrepair. Shortly after the outbreak of the French and Indian War, a fourth fort was erected here, with an addition consisting of an arsenal and powder house. The site of the arsenal is on the Fort Ann-West Fort Ann road, near the Mud Brook Bridge and west of Fort Ann's Union Cemetery. The stone from the arsenal was used as the foundation for the bridge after the site was marked.

In 1765 a large tract of land, consisting of most of the present village of Fort Ann, was divided and granted by royal decree to a group of army artillery officers. Within a short time a sawmill and a blockhouse, then known as Cheshire's, were constructed at what is now Kane's Falls, one mile up Halfway Brook. In 1769 another fort, known as the Mud Fort—nothing more than an earthwork and abandoned shortly after— was constructed at Needhamville, a suburb or extension of Fort Ann Village. In 1776 boards from the sawmill at Kane's Falls were used as planking for the first American fleet built at Skenesborough.

In 1777 Fort Anne served as a fortified refuge for the Patriot force,

under the command of Col. Pierce Long, on its retreat from Fort
Ticonderoga down the Champlain Valley before Burgoyne's invasion
army. Burgoyne, waiting in Skenesborough until his men built a road
through the wilderness for his heavy artillery, ordered Col. Hill and the
Ninth Regiment of Foot to proceed to Fort Anne. On the night of July 7
Col. Hill, with fewer than 200 men, entered a narrow gorge about a half
mile north of the fort. Long had with him at the fort 150 men, mostly sick
and wounded. Envisioning a disastrous confrontation with the enemy,
he sent for reinforcements. During the early dawn hours of July 8, Long
was reinforced by the arrival of Col. Henry Van Rensselaer with about
400 militia.

Shortly after Van Rensselaer's appearance, a Patriot soldier, claiming
to be a deserter, showed up in the enemy camp with the tale that one
thousand sick and thoroughly fear-stricken rebels were holed up in the
fort. Col. Hill apparently accepted the story as gospel and, not having
the force to attack, determined to stand his ground. He then sent for
reinforcement. The American "deserter" escaped the camp of the
British advance guard and reported to Col. Long the weakness of Hill's
detachment. At 10:30 that morning Long and Van Rensselaer, with all
their effectives, emerged from the fort and marched to attack the enemy.
Hill's men were camped in a narrow, thickly wooded defile between
Wood Creek and an almost precipitous high ridge (now known as Battle
Hill). The British frantically clambered up the steep slope and for two
hours fought off the Americans in one of the most spirited actions of the
war.

The Patriots, running low on powder, were forced to break off the
engagement. They burned the fort and, as they slowly withdrew to Fort
Edward, cut down hundreds of trees on the banks of Wood Creek and
along the military road beside it, creating an almost impenetrable
barricade behind them. Because of these obstacles placed in his line of
march, it took Burgoyne from the 9th to the 29th of July to reach Fort
Edward, only twenty miles from Skenesborough. This delay afforded
the Americans the benefit of three extra weeks in which to intrench and
reinforce their army at Saratoga, where Gen. Burgoyne was forced into
total capitulation only several weeks later.

After Saratoga the Patriots erected a fifth and final fort on Fort Anne's
site. Garrisoned by about seventy-five men under Capt. Adiel Sherwood, this post was surrendered to and burned by Maj. Christopher
Carleton in October 1780, during his large-scale raid toward Albany in
which he ravaged Fort George, Fort Anne, Fort Edward, and got as far
south as Ballston, only fourteen miles above Schenectady. The women
and children belonging to the soldiers of Fort Anne's garrison were

permitted to leave for their homes unmolested, but Sherwood and his men were taken prisoners.

In 1954, after one of the properties constituting part of the Fort Anne site was purchased, the Fort Anne Restoration Corporation was organized and archaeological excavations were begun. Reproductions of the blockhouse and the stockade were constructed. The blockhouse was utilized as a museum to house all of the fort's artifacts. Then, mysteriously, the museum collection disappeared. Eventually it was discovered intact in the home of one of the officers of the restoration group. The Fort Anne project soon after dissolved, the stockade fell down, and the blockhouse was purchased by a bank to house one of its branches.

Fort au Fer
near Rouses Point, Clinton County

Strategic Point au Fer, a tongue of land bending southeast from the New York shore of Lake Champlain, about a mile south of Rouses Point, was a fortified military post garrisoned first by Americans and then by the British. The name is probably derived from "Point au Fer de Cheval" or "Horseshoe Point." One 1899 newspaper chronicler suggested that, since "fer" is French for iron, it is very likely that Point au Fer was named for a seventeenth-century Iroquois chief of some note, Garistatsia ("The Iron"), who fell there mortally wounded by an Algonquin javelin.

William Gilliland, Irish land entrepreneur in the northern Champlain Valley, somehow persuaded the British authorities to permit him to erect on the point a large stone building which came to be known as the "White House." Construction took place prior to the Revolution, probably during the early 1770s. Gilliland had been influenced by the colonial turmoil to the southward, and he evidenced increasing pro-American sympathy. He joined in organizing a local company of minute men and became a menace to the British interest, to the point where the governor of Canada, Guy Carleton, put up one hundred pounds for his capture. To add to his difficulties, Gilliland earned the enmity of Benedict Arnold by his insistence that he, Gilliland, was the first to propose the plan to seize Ticonderoga and Crown Point, and thus take control of Lakes George and Champlain.

During the early days of the Continental invasion of Canada in 1775, Gen. John Sullivan ordered Gilliland's "White House" fortified with cannon and an intrenchment. Since a Patriot garrison was to occupy the point, Sullivan also had a strong barracks of brick built and surrounded by a continuously manned stockade.

The Canada invasion evolved into a tragic venture in futility before the cliffs of Quebec. Talented Richard Montgomery was killed and impetuous Benedict Arnold suffered a serious leg wound. The Patriots under Gen. Sullivan finally retreated southward in June 1776. Many of the disabled, racked by smallpox, were taken by boat to Fort au Fer, where Gilliland housed and fed them, and then by easy stages to Fort Ticonderoga. When the Patriots evacuated the works at Point au Fer, the redcoats moved in.

A year later Gen. John Burgoyne's invasion army took the traditional Champlain Valley route, marching through the wilderness on the west side of the lake. He occupied the fort at the point and constructed a crossway of logs over the impassable marshy flat southward from the mouth of the Chazy River. Documents in the Public Archives of Canada testify that the British thereafter kept the fortification in habitable condition. A report dated December 9, 1778, states:

> The House is in good repair, conveniently fitted up and surrounded with a strong double Abbates and Barriers. . . . The proposed Well is not yet sunk sufficiently deep for Water, but I have ordered a miner from the Isle aux Noix, who will certainly perform that service in a few days.

Another report, dated February 4, 1781, stipulates:

> The House at Point au Fer is very habitable [but that] the Cellar and Fireplaces are nevertheless in bad repair, and therefore I propose to lay before your Excellency a plan for a permanent floor over the Cellars, which shall be proof against small shells, to be executed in summer during which the Garrison is to live in Huts.

Throughout the remainder of the war Point au Fer was a rendezvous for passing armies and a temporary prison for rebels caught infiltrating to gain information. The site was visited by a host of military notables, including Benedict Arnold, John Sullivan, John Burgoyne, Philip Schuyler, Ethan Allen, Seth Warner, and Governor George Clinton; in addition, Benjamin Franklin and Charles Carroll, signers of the Declaration of Independence, came to inspect the historic place.

Though the conflict terminated in 1783 by the Treaty of Paris, the British stayed until 1796, when they had finally to relinquish their control of Lake Champlain according to the terms of the Jay Treaty. Capt. John Steel, during the early 1790s, kept his brig, H.M.S. *Maria,* in the channel between Point au Fer and Alburg on the Vermont shore, guarding the outlet to Lake Champlain. Every American vessel was required to lower its peak in obeisance to British sovereignty over the lake. Governor Carleton, to reinforce British claims over the territory, issued a proclamation to the effect that all male inhabitants residing in the area for ten miles south of the present-day border had to enroll in the Canadian militia.

The "White House" on Point au Fer was destroyed by fire sometime during the first years of the nineteenth century, probably in the year 1805. Today a private dwelling occupies the fort site. Archaeological explorations, carried on intermittently for years in this century, revealed that not far from the "White House" was a cemetery in which more than 160 Revolutionary War smallpox victims were buried in trenches four feet deep. Apparently the bodies of the soldiers, probably Patriots, were rolled in blankets for burial and their infected clothes were given a sulphur treatment to permit their use by others.

A trench ran northward from the fort toward the bay where the watercraft were anchored. Everywhere in the vicinity of the fort, which covered a sizable tract of land, pieces of brick were unearthed, and the lime kiln that produced the material for the fortification was located on the lake shore.

Fort Canaseraga
Sullivan, Madison County

Complying with an order from Gen. Van Rensselaer, an American detachment of fifty men from Fort Stanwix led by Capt. Walter Vrooman captured Fort Canaseraga on October 23, 1780, several miles south of Oneida Lake, from a guard of Tories and Indians who became their prisoners. The main body of Sir John Johnson's army was then engaged in devastating the Mohawk and Schoharie valleys.

In retaliation for the destruction wreaked in the Iroquois country by Sullivan's expedition (1779), an army of up to eight hundred men, Tories and Rangers under Johnson and Indians under Brant, descended from Canada to raid the settlements. With many bateaux filled with provisions, supplies, and ammunition, they took the traditional invasion route—up the St. Lawrence from Lachine, across Lake Ontario, then up the Oswego River to its Oneida River branch, and down to Oneida Lake. They crossed the lake and entered Chittenango Creek, proceeding up that waterway about six miles to land on its eastern shore, where an old palisaded fort was situated. The enemy spent some little time repairing the fort's works and left a strong guard to oversee the safety of the army's cache of supplies.

While the enemy was pillaging and burning the settlements to the east,

Vrooman's men destroyed Johnson's supply base, sinking all the boats but two, burning their supplies, and throwing most of their provisions into Chittenango Creek. Retreating from Klock's Field, where they had been engaged by Van Rensselaer's militia, Johnson sent ahead a large detachment of Butler's Rangers to Fort Canaseraga. They came on Vrooman's men in middle of dinner, their last meal before embarking with their prisoners for Fort Stanwix. Vrooman's entire party was taken without a shot being fired. In retribution for the ruination of their stores, four Americans were handed over to the Indians to be tortured and finally killed, while the remainder were marched off to Canada and imprisonment.

Located on Oneida land, Fort Canaseraga's site was originally in the old Tuscarora village of Canaseraga (not to be confused with the town of the same name in northern Alleghany County). The old Tuscarora village is now included in today's town of Sullivan. The fort's site is about a mile south of the juncture of Black Creek with Chittenango Creek, on a hill less than a hundred feet from the latter's bank.

It is not known when the fort was first constructed. At least one nineteenth-century chronicler has speculated that it may originally have been a French fortification. Another regional historian placed the site of the fort somewhere between the present-day towns of Kirkville and Bridgeport, on the south shore of Oneida Lake. The prevailing thought is that it was erected by Tuscarora Indians in imitation of white settlers' fortifications. In 1756, during the French and Indian War, Sir William Johnson ordered Jacob Vrooman and a party of men to add a blockhouse, construct a huge gate of three-inch oak plank, and make such repairs to the existing palisades as the Tuscarora chiefs might request. The blockhouse was constructed of hewn logs, with the first story twenty feet square, and the second story twenty-three feet square, with a sentry box on its roof.

Surviving their imprisonment, the members of Capt. Walter Vrooman's party returned to their homes along the Mohawk River. In March 1790 nine of these veterans, remembering the beautiful and fertile region south of Oneida Lake, came to Canseraga with their families and erected new homes. They selected adjoining farmlands, opened clearings, and planted and harvested fruitful crops. Unfortunately, they had located on Oneida property. The Oneidas, resenting the encroachment and, in many cases, the depredations of hundreds of whites who were streaming into the Genesee country, petitioned the New York governor through the good offices of their friend, the Rev. Samuel Kirkland. The governor ordered the settlers at Canaseraga to remove, which they refused to do. In 1791 the sheriff of Montgomery County (of which Madison County was then a part) came to Canaseraga with a party of sixty armed deputies. The Dutch settlers, unawed by this show of strength, still refused to surrender their new homes. The sheriff then ordered his men to remove all possessions from the dwellings to a safe distance, then had them burn down the houses and barns.

Many Oneidas, chiefs among them, had assembled to see justice done. But this brutal destruction of a tiny white pioneering community revived memories of their own misfortunes during the Revolution, when their own cousins, the Mohawks and Senecas, set fire to their homes and fields. While the settlement was still burning, the Oneida chiefs called a council and formally granted new farmlands to the dispossessed Vrooman veterans in the area surrounding present-day Chittenango.

Fort Caughnawaga
Fonda, Montgomery County

There is an unverified tradition that a small blockhouse, called Fort Caughnawaga, was built at Sand Flats just west of today's Fonda in 1779 and torn down after the end of the Revolution.

The name Caughnawaga has been applied to several localities, one of them far removed from Montgomery County: the Indian castle at Sand Flats; the early white pioneers' settlement in what is now the eastern portion of Fonda; the early Indian village of Ossernenon, on the south bank of the Mohawk, on the site of today's Auriesville Shrine; and the Christianized Iroquois settlement (Caughnawaga Mohawks who left their nation after Jesuit missionary proselytism in the seventeenth century) nine miles from Montreal.

The white pioneer settlement of Caughnawaga in eastern Fonda was destroyed by Sir John Johnson's army of destructives in the spring of 1780. The home of Douw Fonda, founder of the settlement, was burned down and its owner brutally murdered. His three sons, Adam, Maj. Jelles, and John served heroically throughout the war.

If indeed there was a Caughnawaga blockhouse at Sand Flats, isolated though it may have been, it is strange that Mohawk Valley historians did not jot down even a microscopic note of the fact.

Forts Clinton and Montgomery
Bear Mountain State Park, Orange County

To introduce the "Twin Forts of the Popolopen," Clinton and Montgomery, it is necessary to frame the region's strategic geography and to specify the crucial implications that impelled the Patriots to establish these defenses. The delineation also bears on the establishment of the other fortifications in the Highlands—Stony Point, Fort Lafayette, Fort Independence, Constitution Island, and West Point, the last-named bastion being the dramatic target of a treasonable conspiracy.

The Hudson River runs a particularly scenic route for some three hundred miles from its origin in Lake Tear of the Clouds high in the Adirondacks to New York Bay and the Atlantic. It seems that from the very moment when, on September 4, 1609, Henry Hudson sailed his *Halve Maen* up the estuary beyond today's Albany to a point near its confluence with the Mohawk, the river began to assume increasing strategic importance. Today, twentieth-century commerce takes advantage of 160 navigable miles of the Hudson, open to heavy tonnage shipping from the sea.

About forty miles north of New York City's Battery is King's Ferry, between Stony Point on the west shore and Verplanck's Point[1] on the east, the gateway to the twenty-mile-long tortuous Hudson gorge, banked by steep cliffs and hills more than a thousand feet high, called the Highlands of the Hudson—the "Key to the Continent"—a mountain range extending some fifty miles east and west. The fortifications, cantonments, and military engagements between Stony Point and Newburgh constitute a Revolutionary gazetteer of the Highlands.

Every approach by civilized road or Indian wilderness trail, from New England to all the other Colonies, crossed the Hudson River at some point. Continental troops, militia units, and supply trains had no other avenues but these paths for movement east to west or north to south. Furthermore, the transportation afforded by the waterways from the St. Lawrence through Lake Champlain and Lake George and from the Oneida Carry in central New York through the Mohawk River were subject to control of the Hudson Valley.

On May 25, 1775, the Continental Congress in Philadelphia instituted measures to secure the Hudson River to the interests of the American cause and resolved "that a post be also taken in the Highlands on each side of Hudson's River and batteries erected in such a manner as will most effectually prevent any vessels passing that may be sent to harass the inhabitants on the borders of said river. . . ."[2] The President of the Congress, John Hancock, forwarded the resolution to the New York Provincial Congress (later renamed Convention), meeting in the Exchange Building in New York City. Two members of that conclave, Col. James Clinton and Christopher Tappen, were much better acquainted with the area than any of their compatriots in the Convention, having been lifelong residents of the region just north of the Highlands.

Furthermore, giving assurance of harmony, the two men were brothers-in-law by virtue of the marriage of James Clinton's younger brother, George, to Cornelia Tappen.[3]

On May 30 the Convention ordered the two men "to go to the Highlands and view the banks of Hudson's River there, and report to this Congress the most proper place for erecting one or more fortifications; and likewise an estimate of the expense that will attend erecting the same. . . ."[4] Clinton and Tappen rented a boat and, in company with two militia captains, Samuel Bayard and Erasmus Williams, set sail up the Hudson on Friday, June 2. They made notes on likely sites, taking pains to accurately mark the places on a map for future inspection and consideration. They recorded the sites of Verplanck's Point and Stony Point, opposite each other, as possibilities for outposts, but discounted the rocky tor of Anthony's Nose as being too precipitous and too lofty for military use.

But across the Hudson, on the west bank and on either side of Popolopen Creek, were two rather promising prospects, affording a splendid view of the Hudson, but "Clinton was not enthusiastic . . . because he was looking for a place where works could be erected on both sides of the river." As their hired sloop sailed blithely before a good breeze, Clinton and Tappen gazed ahead and a little to the westward and noted with instant appreciation the elevated plateau known as the West Point and, almost hidden behind it by the S-curve in the river, Martelaer's Rock (Constitution Island) standing off the eastern shore.[5] They recommended the construction of a pair of defenses on the east and west sides of the river, designated as "A" and "B" on a map that they submitted, to be located at the bend of the river where West Point and Constitution Island face each other. To limit this description to the Popolopen forts, it is enough to say that West Point was not fortified until early 1778, and that Fort Constitution, the first Highlands defense, was condemned after several months of controversial strife over its merits (a separate section deals with these two Patriot defenses).

A Provincial Convention committee—Francis Nicoll, Joseph Drake, and Thomas Palmer—reported on December 14 that Fort Constitution should be condemned and that a strong battery be placed five miles to the south, on the river's west shore, opposite Anthony's Nose. On January 16, 1776, the Committee of Safety ordered "that the timber designed for the additional barracks at Martlyr's Rock and not yet erected, be removed by the first opportunity to Pooplopen's kill, there to be applied to use, pursuant to some future order."[6]

Commissioner Palmer was in need of an engineer. The Provinical Convention suggested that he approach Gen. Charles Lee, then assigned to the construction of New York City's fortifications. Lee generously provided Capt. William Smith, his chief engineer, to assist the commissioners. Smith departed from the city on February 27 and returned on Leap Year Day. His two days' sojourn in the Highlands was well spent: he laid out the lines for a new work east of Fort Constitution, marked the site for a battery on the east shore a mile south of the fort, and staked out the lines for the defense on the precipitous height just north of Popolopen Creek. The last-proposed fortification had already been named Fort Montgomery in memory of Brig. Gen. Richard Montgomery, commander of one of the two wings of the Patriot army sent into Canada in 1775, who was killed during a blinding snowstorm while unsuccessfully assaulting the Citadel of Quebec on December 31.

Several buildings were almost completed and work was begun on the battery itself, but under very trying circumstances. The militiamen were on the verge of mutiny because of insufficient supplies and accommodations, threatening to desert in a body if relief was not provided. In their dissatisfaction, they would take off and visit their homes and return when they chose, if at all.

With the ouster of the British from Boston, Continental Army headquarters were transferred to New York, where Gen. Washington gave his attention to the construction of defensive works in the city and in the Highlands. There was no doubt in his mind that New York's legislative body was unable to cope with the problems associated with defensive construction and the garrisoning of the new posts. The New York Provincial Convention recognized Washington's authority, allowing the Continental Army to assume the responsibilities. Washington began by appointing various officers to deeply probe the discouraging conditions in the Highlands, which resulted in the local commands being changed frequently.

On receipt of reports reflecting the inadequacy and neglect of the defenses already built and the utter disregard for the well-being of both military and civilian workers, Washington assembled a group of the best military experts available. Heading the investigative delegation was Lord Stirling (Brig. Gen. William Alexander), with Cols. Rufus Putnam and Henry Knox, representing respectively the Continental engineers and artillery, as assistants. For some reason—probably because of prior commitments—Knox was replaced by Capt. Winthrop Sargent, an experienced artillery officer. Washington instructed Stirling to inspect the forts and recommend "such alterations as shall be judg'd necessary for putting them into a fit and proper posture of defense."[7]

A brave, talented, and respected Continental officer, Stirling intended to be thorough in his inspection of every facet of the Highland defenses.

The committee's first approach to the Highlands was at its gateway between Stony Point and Verplanck's Point. They concluded that a small defensive work should be erected there. At Fort Montgomery, the next stop, they found Continentals and Tory prisoners working side by side.

Stirling and Capt. Sargent paced the fort's perimeter. From the river and along Popolopen Creek, sheer rock soared 125 feet to the fort's site. On the third side was a deep, precipitous ravine. The only deficiency was to the west, where unimpeded level ground had to be offset by defensive earthworks or barricades. Sargent's attention was suddenly focused on the rock formations across the creek. His experienced eyes lit on a sizable crag that certainly overlooked Fort Montgomery. There was no question in his mind but that enemy artillery mounted there would surely negate Fort Montgomery's defenses. Lord Stirling and the artillery officer crossed the creek. Striding across the plateau on the rocky tor, Stirling determined that a strong work, possibly "the grand post" of the Highlands, should be built there.

The committee then proceeded to Constitution Island. They found the works there incomplete, poorly planned, and criminally expensive to erect. At the West Point across the river, which they crossed by boat, Stirling could see that a strong work was required there for several obvious reasons. Back in New York City on June 1, he went to work and wrote a lengthy, precise report. Gen. Washington received an abridged version of the committee's findings and, unaccountably, there was not a word in it concerning the West Point. About Fort Constitution, Stirling acidly reported that "upon the whole, Mr. Romans had displayed his genius at a very great expense, and to very little public advantage." With reference to Fort Montgomery's vulnerability, Stirling recommended:

> The works begun and designed at Fort Montgomery are open lines, and all lie on the north side of a small creek called Pooplopen's Kill, on the south side of which is a point of land which projects more into the river, commands all the principal works, and is within two and three hundred yards of them. On top of this point is a level spot of ground, of near an acre, commanded by nothing but the high, inaccessible mountains, at about twelve hundred yards distance; this spot, I think, should by all means be fortified, as well for the annoyance of the enemy in their approach up the river, as for the protection of the works of Fort Montgomery. Indeed, this appears to me the most proper place I have seen on the river to be made the grand post; and in my opinion, should be a regular strong work, capable of resisting every kind of attack and containing a grand magazine of all kinds of warlike stores. The whole would then command the passage of the river with so formidable a cross fire as would deter any attempt to approach with shipping.[8]

On July 2 two coincidental developments, crucial to America's future, practically put to death diplomatic efforts for reconciliation between Britain and her rebellious children: the Continental Congress declared the Colonies independent, and Gen. William Howe, fresh from Halifax with 130 ships in New York's Lower Bay, began to land on Staten Island the first units of a thirty-four-thousand-man army. Ten days later, two British men-of-war, the *Phoenix* and the *Rose*, disproved the efficacy of New York City's artillery when they blithely ran the gauntlet of Patriot guns to emerge unharmed at Tappan Zee. To Gen. Washington, who was a flabbergasted spectator, it proved "the incompetency of batteries to stop a ship's passage with a brisk wind and strong tide where there are no obstructions in the Water to impede their motion."[9]

For a year the Patriots had speculated but accomplished nothing on how the Hudson River should be obstructed to bar enemy shipping. The feat by the *Phoenix* and the *Rose* spurred New York's Provincial Convention to resolve that "a Secret Committee be appointed to devise and carry into execution such measures as to them shall appear most effectual for obstructing the channel of Hudson's River . . .; and that this Convention pledge themselves for defraying the charges incident thereto. . . ."[10]

GENERAL GEORGE CLINTON
Courtesy of USMA Library

The importance of the project determined the impecunious Convention to furnish five thousand pounds to initiate the job, and it empowered its Secret Committee "to impress boats, vessels, teams, wagons, horses, and drivers when they shall find it necessary for the publick service, as well as to call out the militia, if occasion should require."[11]

After conferring with Gen. Washington, the six-member Secret Committee, which included John Jay and Robert R. Livingston (New York delegates to the Continental Congress), chose George Clinton to command the militia with the rank of brigadier general. On June 14 official assent confirmed his brother, Col. James Clinton, as overseer of the Highland defenses, a post he had assumed on May 20. The two Clintons made history at Forts Clinton and Montgomery. A New York delegate to the Continental Congress in 1775 and newly elected to the New York Provincial Convention on June 25, 1776, Gen. George Clinton was in command at Fort Montgomery. By his stimulating energy and incessant prodding, the works there began to take on the semblance of a fortification: a two-story, eighty-by-twenty-foot barracks, with a store of salt in a basement under the structure; an arched, eight-foot-thick powder magazine; gun platforms; the ground to the west or rear cleared, with a wall planned to guard that open side of the works.[12] In his letter of July 23 to Gen. Washington, Clinton shows his preoccupation with the commanding eminence on the south side of Popolopen Creek:

> The Hill on the South side Pouplopen's Kill & not above 1½ Miles of it overlooks our works, every Gun on our Battery lays in open view of it . . . this Fortress is by no means safe, unless that Hill is secured. Genl. [John] Fellows & other Officers from the Eastward are all of the same Oppinion. They advised me to begin some small Works there. I have laid out as well as I know how and the Militia are employed in making Facines & other Preparations. . . . A few Cannon will serve them & these I believe may be spared from our other Fortifications where they cannot be so serviceable.[13]

Gen. Washington replied on July 26, agreeing to Clinton's prognosis:

> I have sent up Lieut. [Thomas] Machin to lay out and oversee such Works as shall be tho't necessary by the Officers there, and from your representation of the Hill, which overlooks the Fort, I think it ought to be taken possession of Immediately.[14]

The first assignment undertaken by combat-experienced, 32-year-old engineer Thomas Machin was to lay out and build a battery on the tor just south of Fort Montgomery. Designated a "battery" on some British maps, the new defense came to be called Fort Clinton, certainly in honor of either one or both of the brothers Clinton.[15] Machin was kept busy. In

GENERAL JAMES CLINTON
Courtesy of USMA Library

addition to turning Fort Clinton into the "grand post," he also was given the task of implementing one of the most grandiose Patriot undertakings of the war, that of placing an iron chain across the Hudson to obstruct British shipping. In July the Secret Committee, to which body Gen. Washington had described the young engineer as "an ingenious, faithful hand," decided that the narrow part of the river at Popolopen was the most logical and proper position for the giant chain.[16]

James Clinton then sent Machin across the river to lay out and construct a fortification on a small eminence under Anthony's Nose at Roa's Hook to protect the mouth of Peekskill Creek on the northern rim of Peekskill Bay. For some weeks it was called Fort Constitution, then "Red-Hook," and, finally, Fort Independence; it played a minor role in subsequent engagements.[17]

By the end of August, though unusually wet weather shortened the work days, the twin forts bristled with cannon, ramparts were rising, bombproofs hid large quantities of powder, and several barracks were well along toward completion. On September 8 James Clinton, writing from Fort Montgomery, informed his brother of other construction progress:[18]

We have mounted four twelve Pounders on the south side of the Kill where you begun the Battery and Expect soon to have more; we turn out all hands on Duty Every Day to work on the Battery &c; we are Building three Barracks, one at Fort Constitution, one on the south side of the Kill, and the other at Red Hook [Roa's Hook] but Cant finish them for want of nails.[19]

Unproductive diplomatic moves at reconciliation meant only one thing to Gen. William Howe: while his army was killing time on Staten Island, the rebels were busy erecting fortifications all the way from the southern tip of Manhattan Island to the Hudson Highlands. Finally, in the last week of August, Howe put his ready army on the road toward dispossessing the Patriots of New York City and Long Island. For the next three months the war raged about the defenses in the city and its environs. It was a catastrophic defensive campaign for the Patriots. They were badly defeated in the Battle of Brooklyn, driven to evacuate New York City, beaten at Fort Washington, forced from Westchester, and compelled to seek a haven in New Jersey. Howe moved his headquarters to New York and his troops jubilantly occupied the city. Ten days after the King's troops had entered, much of the town, either by accident or design, was destroyed by fire. Trinity Church, despite heroic efforts to save it, burned to the ground.[20]

While the links of the great iron chain were still being laboriously forged, several members of the Secret Committee, having second thoughts, took another look at the Highlands. On October 9 they met in conference and concluded, after a lengthy debate, that the chain would serve to greater advantage if it were drawn across the river between West Point and Constitution Island, and "that a fortification be erected at West Point in order to defend the chain."[21]

The Committee's decision startled James Clinton and Thomas Machin. On October 11, at a conference on Constitution Island, they diplomatically informed the Committee that a fortification could not be erected at West Point in the little time remaining to them before Sir Guy Carleton's army, poised on the northern frontier, would launch its assault toward the Hudson Valley. Furthermore, the officers argued, Fort Constitution by itself could not guard the proposed chain. The Committee's members, persuaded, resolved then and there[22]

that Mr. Machin immediately prepare a place on each side of the River at Fort Montgomery to fasten the ends of the intended chain to. That he place two or three guns in a small work to be erected for that purpose on the flat place just under the north end of the grand battery, where the fire rafts now lay—also a small work, if time permit, near the water edge on the south side of Pooplopin's Kill.[23]

Finally, during the first days of November, the links of the chain were floated down to the fort. Despite Machin's practical ingenuity, one mishap after another occurred with drawing the chain eighteen hundred feet across the Hudson, and these failures, combined with the onset of foul winter weather, prevented completion of the project.[24] With regard to the *chevaux-de-frise,* planned for the wide but shallow depths of the river between Pollepel Island (now Bannerman's Island) off the east shore and Plum Point on the west bank, a shortage of tools and "extream bad" weather precluded its installation until spring.[25]

Fortune favored the Patriots. Benedict Arnold's Champlain navy upset Carleton's timetable at Valcour Bay, so that, with the imminence of the winter season, the British commander withdrew his forces into Canada, to try again in 1777.

During the winter and following spring, progress on Forts Clinton and Montgomery was maddeningly slow. George Clinton's reports and letters are replete with complaints regarding the delinquencies of the militia from the surrounding counties. With the threat of invasion postponed for a time, complacency had set in. But there was preparedness in the environs of the forts, with beacons, signal guns, and alarm posts planted at significant vantage points to give warning of the inevitable coming of the enemy.

With the onset of spring 1777, called "The Year of the Hangman," the British commenced their new campaign. Gen. John Burgoyne, full of expectations of conquering the rebels, sailed from England on April 3 for Canada, accompanied by several thousand reinforcements. To make a beginning, plans were made to reduce to rubble the rebel magazines and storehouses. On March 23 five hundred men landed at Peekskill, a major American supply collection center, easily drove out McDougall's small defensive force, and destroyed considerable amounts of armaments and stores. A month later a destructive expedition under Governor William Tryon raided Danbury, Connecticut, an important Patriot depot, destroyed vital army stores, and fired the town.

The days after the Peekskill raid were accompanied by warmer weather. Machin went to work again on the chain that was stored for the winter in Popolopen Creek. Men and boats took their stations in the river. The chain was floated across on log booms and fastened at each terminus where it was held down by anchors. Machin waited with bated breath. The tide came in, the great chain slowly lifted, pulled taut in an arc, and remained suspended—*unbroken.*[26] The Hudson was barred to enemy naval traffic. Receiving deserved plaudits for his feat, Machin went ahead with his work. He had the *chevaux-de-frise* installed as planned between Pollepel Island and Plum Point and had it guarded by his battery of fourteen guns (Machin's Battery or Fort Plum Point).

McDougall's delinquency at Peekskill alarmed Washington. The commander-in-chief could not abide either complacency or timorous behavior on the part of his generals. If the Hudson Highlands was going to be a battleground, an intrepid field commander was required. The need for such a man almost immediately focused his attention on Benedict Arnold. The combination of growing Patriot false security, militia inadequacies, and the British raids spurred Washington to definite action. On May 7 he wrote a pointedly urgent letter to McDougall:

> The imperfect state of the fortifications of Fort Montgomery, gives me great uneasiness, because I think from a concurrence of circumstances, that it begins to look as if the enemy intended to turn their view towards the North River, instead of the Delaware. I therefore, desire, that General George Clinton and yourself will fall upon every measure to put the fortifications in such a state, that they may at least resist a sudden attack, and keep the enemy employed, till reinforcements may arrive.[27]

It was at this time that Gen. Washington fully decided that his choice for a new commander in the Highlands was Benedict Arnold, but the "whirlwind hero" was unavailable: he had already left for Philadelphia, where he had a bone to pick with Congress over his rank. Washington then had to be satisfied with his second choice, Maj. Gen. Israel ("Old Put") Putnam, and he notified that doughty old soldier of his selection on May 12. "Gentleman Johnny" Burgoyne, during this time, was already congregating his assault forces on the Canadian border.

The strike for independence of the United States was nearly a year old in June when the British launched their grand military campaign, adhering in the main to Guy Carleton's aborted invasion plan of the preceding year. The objective was to win control of the entire valley of the Hudson, along with that of the Mohawk. Burgoyne's plan was to march his army from Canada to the Hudson, capturing Crown Point, Ticonderoga, and other American posts en route. Barry St. Leger was to enter the fertile Mohawk Valley, gain the cooperation of the Loyalists there, and subjugate the American farmers. William Howe, from New York, was to embark his army aboard men-of-war and transports, sail up the Hudson, reduce the Highland forts, and sail victoriously to Albany, the rendezvous for the three armies.

Burgoyne and St. Leger advanced as planned, but Lord Germain's negligence in not issuing a sufficient number of directives left Sir William Howe with his usual discretionary power and did not put upon him the onus of unconditional orders such as was received by the first-two-named commanders. Thus did the fortunes of an army, and perhaps a nation, turn on the oversight of one man in high position in England.[28]

Instead, Howe took by far the greater part of his army and sailed for the Chesapeake in an attempt to seize Philadelphia. Sir Henry Clinton was left with a force inadequate to both defend New York City and engage in any large-scale operation. He took over command in New York and had no recourse but to await reinforcements from Europe. Clinton was quite vehemently critical of Howe's ill-conceived strategy, contending that "Mr. Washington would move with everything he could collect either against General Burgoyne or me, and crush the one or the other."[29]

St. Leger was routed by the approach of Benedict Arnold's relief column, after an unsuccessful siege of Fort Stanwix. Burgoyne was brought to a halt at Saratoga where he formally surrendered his army on October 17 to Horatio Gates and ever-increasing Patriot forces. But not before immensely dramatic events took place to the south, in the Highlands of the Hudson.

On the last day of June, much to the amazement and mystification of Washington, Howe suddenly deserted New Jersey, taking his troops to Staten Island after his feint at Philadelphia failed to draw the Continentals into battle. The answer to the Americans' puzzlement over that maneuver came late in the afternoon of the next day, July 1. Specific news came from Lake Champlain that Burgoyne was about to besiege Fort Ticonderoga. The information led Washington to but one conclusion: Gen. Howe was planning to come up the Hudson to synchronize with Burgoyne's invasion march from the north. Washington and his generals met in a war council that lasted far into the night. Directives were issued to have two brigades march at dawn to reinforce the Highland forts; an express messenger was dispatched to alert Putnam; and Washington wrote an order to George Clinton, urging him "to call forth a respectable force of the militia" to take post in the Highlands until Continental forces should arrive by forced marches.[30]

During the first week of July, in the midst of frantic efforts to further advance the fortifications, strengthen their garrisons, and to either complete, crew, or arm new galleys built at Poughkeepsie, almost simultaneous news arrived that Ticonderoga had fallen to Burgoyne and that George Clinton had been elected governor of New York. Fort Ti had been evacuated by Gen. Arthur St. Clair when the British had the imagination to plant cannon on Patriot-neglected Mount Defiance, to directly threaten the fort's main works. George Clinton was informed by his brother-in-law, Christopher Tappen, that he, Clinton, had narrowly defeated Gen. Philip Schuyler, who had seemed the winner in early returns.[31]

The new governor, dedicated to giving all his energies to the defense of the Highlands, stubbornly stayed on. On July 11, four days after the news of his accession, he wrote Washington that Forts Clinton and Montgomery were "in as good Condition as could be expected," and that he had just enhanced the value of the great chain in the river by the addition of all the cabling stripped from the new Continental frigate *Montgomery*. On the 24th he was ordered by the Council of Safety to go to Kingston to assume his duties as chief executive of the new State. Two days later, from Fort Montgomery, he notified Gen. Putnam:

> As there seems to be no great Prospect of a sudden attempt against this Quarter I must ask you Leave of absence for an unlimited Times as it is impossible to determine when, if ever, I shall be able to return to Military Service.[32]

SIR HENRY CLINTON (1787)
Painting by Thomas Day (watercolor on ivory)
Courtesy of the R. W. Norton Art Gallery, Shreveport, La.

Gen. Howe took most of his troops off Staten Island and sailed for the Chesapeake. Despite his wrath over Howe's dereliction of obligation to the main strategy, and the nonappearance of early replacements, Sir Henry Clinton proceeded with plans for the expedition up the Hudson, hopefully in time to aid Burgoyne. Finally, late on Wednesday, September 24—five days after the first battle of Saratoga—an English fleet anchored in New York Bay and Sir Henry's decimated army were reinforced by seventeen hundred regulars and German mercenaries. Sir Henry dispatched large foraging parties into New Jersey and congregated units of his three thousand-man attack force in camps at King's Bridge on the northern end of Manhattan Island.

Washington's Highlands forces had been depleted by heavy withdrawals of troops to supplement Gates's army in the north and aid in the Philadelphia campaign. At his Peekskill headquarters, "Old Put" had scrounged up about 1,000 Continentals and 400 militia to face any enemy attack in that quarter. The combined garrisons at Forts Clinton and Montgomery amounted to around only 600 militia and a few Continentals, under the command of Gen. James Clinton. Fort Constitution was guarded by a minuscule thirty-man contingent, commanded by artillery Capt. Gershom Mott. Fort Independence, commanded by Maj. Israel Thompson, garrisoned only a couple of companies of men.

By week's end Gen. Putnam had received exaggerated reports of the number of men Britain had sent Sir Henry, and lost no time acquainting Governor Clinton with the news. The governor at once dispatched instructions to his militia colonels: three regiments were ordered to Peekskill and four were to take post at Fort Montgomery. He also wrote his brother James, counseling him to adopt all possible defensive measures at Popolopen Creek and empowering him to call up reinforcements from Orange and Ulster Counties. While expediting the movements of these men, he adjourned the Legislature and hurried to reassume command of Fort Montgomery's defenses.[33]

During the night and morning of October 3/4, Sir Henry (a distant cousin of the American Generals Clinton) embarked his three-division assault force of three thousand men on transports, moved up the river, and made a landing at Tarrytown. The next day Clinton's ships again moved upstream, to drop anchor off Verplanck's Point on the east bank, about five miles below Peekskill and ten below the Popolopen forts. To create a diversionary feint towards Putnam, Clinton landed large numbers of troops at Verplanck's during the evening hours, routing a small American outpost. Simultaneously, galleys commanded by Sir James Wallace sailed into Peekskill Bay. These maneuvers had the desired effect: "Old Put" was thoroughly convinced that Peekskill was the enemy's objective. And to keep that rebel illusion alive, Sir Henry kept several hundred Loyalists at Verplanck's while, early the next morning, he surreptitiously crossed the Hudson, fortuitously blanketed by a dense fog, to the opposite shore. The futile British attempt to relieve Burgoyne's burden at Saratoga is recounted by Sir Henry:

After having given the enemy every jealousy for the east side, [I]

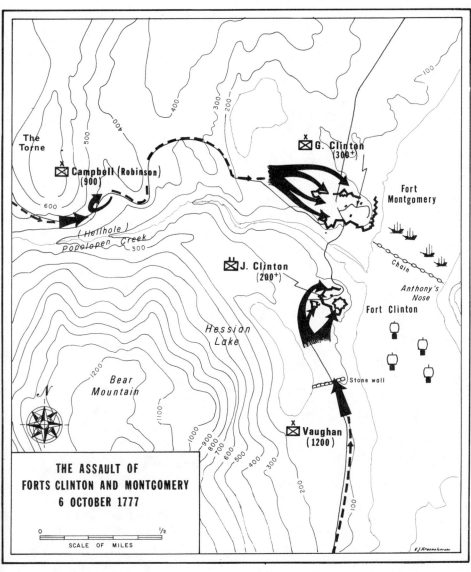

The Torne

Campbell (Robinson)
(900)

(Hellhole)
Popolopen Creek

G. Clinton
(300+)

Fort
Montgomery

Chain

Anthony's
Nose

J. Clinton
(200+)

Fort Clinton

Hessian
Lake

Stone wall

Bear
Mountain

N

Vaughan
(1200)

THE ASSAULT OF
FORTS CLINTON AND MONTGOMERY
6 OCTOBER 1777

0   ½
SCALE OF MILES

E. J. Krasnoborski

Infantry regiment   Ship at anchor

Infantry battalion   Ship under sail

From *The River and the Rock* (New York: Greenwood Press, 1969).
Courtesy of Dave Richard Palmer

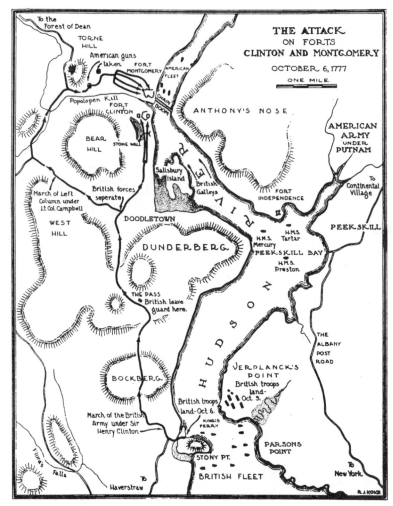

From *Twin Forts of the Popolopen: Forts Clinton and Montgomery, New York,*
1775-1777 by William H. Carr and Richard J. Koke (Bear Mountain, N.Y., 1937).
Courtesy of Palisades Interstate Park Commission.

landed the troops suddenly on the west, at Stony Point, the 6th of October at break of day. As soon as they were all on shore the *avant garde* . . . (under Lieutenant Colonel [Mungo] Campbell of the Fifth-second Regiment) directly began their march over the mountain with orders to secure pass of Thunder Hill [Dunderberg] and, having made a detour of seven miles round the hills, to form in the rear of Fort Montgomery. The main body . . . (under the command of Major General [John] Vaughan) followed immediately after and, continuing their march straight on to Fort Clinton, not only covered that of the *avant garde* but, by their attack of this fort, were expected to facilitate Colonel Campbell's attempt against the other. . . .

These two forts had been constructed by the rebels upon the high steep rocks which form the western border of the Hudson at its passage through the mountains, about sixty miles above New York, and were at that time their northern barrier of that river, being intended to cover a large chain, or boom, which they had run across it under them to obstruct the navigation. They had likewise another chain and a *chevaux-de-frise* higher up. The forts, which were called Montgomery and Clinton, were separated from each other by a creek that flowed from the mountains between them, and they communicated by means of a narrow bridge thrown across it. The approaches to them on the land side were rendered almost impracticable by steep, craggy mountains; and the high upright rocks on which they were placed made all access to them by water still more difficult, while the numerous redoubts that covered them had all the regular appendages of ditch, picket, fraise, and abatis, lined by an adequate proportion of troops for their defense and connected by an intrenchment.

The tremendous precipices and other natural impediments opposed to the progress of the King's troops over the mountain, with a circuit of about seventeen miles, prevented Colonel Campbell from getting to his ground before five o'clock in the afternoon. His arrival being that instant made known by signal, General Vaughan (who, by having a somewhat shorter route, had got to his [ground] earlier) was directed to dislodge the enemy from a stone breastwork that lay a little in front of their works, under the range of their cannon and covered for half a mile by a strong abatis. This the General very soon accomplished, and by my directions waited for a favorable moment in Colonel Campbell's attack on Montgomery before he began his on Fort Clinton. This latter was a circular height lined with musketry, having a battery of three guns in barbette in the center, a redoubt on each flank, and the approaches to it through a continued abatis of four hundred yards, every inch of which was defensible and exposed to the fire of ten pieces of cannon.

Agreeable to my wishes, General Vaughan seized a critical instant of the assault on Montgomery and advanced, trusting by order to the bayonet only. The order was punctually obeyed, the troops not firing a shot; and much about the same instant both redoubts were stormed and carried, the ardor of the assailants being greatly animated by seeing the galleys pressing forward with their oars and the frigates crowding every sail to support them. Unfortunately Colonel Campbell did not live to enjoy the glory of this success, as he was killed in the first of the assault. But the attack on his side was afterward conducted with very proper spirit and judgment by Colonel Beverly Robinson of the provincials, who was next in command, and to whose knowledge of the country and very useful information I must acknowledge myself to be indebted in the arrangement of my plan.

The rebels, finding we had succeeded against the forts, set fire about ten o'clock to their frigates, *Montgomery* and *Congress,* and some galleys and other armed vessels that lay a little higher up the river; and in the morning the Commodore [William Hotham] joined me in a summons to Fort Constitution. . . .

The loss of the King's troops sustained in the whole of this service was trifling when weighed against its possible importance and the strength of the works assaulted, as it did not exceed one hundred and ninety men in all—of which only forty-one lost their lives on the spot, though some valuable officers who fell in the attack cannot, certainly, be too much lamented. I had also the pleasure to find that the number of the enemy who were unavoidably sacrificed in the ardor of assault was comparatively small, their dead who lay within and without the works not exceeding one hundred, though I am credibly informed the two state regiments added to the militia engaged in the defense of them amounted to more than one thousand. It must, however, be confessed that only 263 were taken prisoners,[34] from whence it is presumed great numbers must have escaped under the darkness of the night.

Another letter was now dispatched to General Burgoyne, to inform him of our success and let him know that all the obstructions on the river between us and Albany were removed. But I told him likewise that I must still hold myself excused from either ordering or advising, though I should not relax in my exertions to facilitate his operations.[35] General [William] Tryon was afterward detached to Continental Village[36] on the east side of the river, where he burned a range of barracks for 1500 men and several storehouses and loaded wagons, this being the only establishment the rebels had in that part of the Highlands from whence their troops in the vicinage could draw their supplies.[37]

The first news of the British coming up the Hudson startled the Patriots, though they knew that sooner or later an assault would be made on the Highlands. The two Clintons and Gen. Putnam were kept informed by scouts of the progress of Sir Henry's waterborne army. Early on the morning of October 5, Governor Clinton set out downstream for the Popolopen forts. A mile north of Fort Constitution he heard the signal guns roar the alarm and saw the beacon lighted at the fort. He thereupon landed, issued orders to have the gun signals repeated, and then took off for Fort Montgomery, where he arrived in the middle of the afternoon.

Despite Sir Henry's inflated opinion of the defenses, the works above the Hudson were not complete. Fort Clinton was in its final phase of

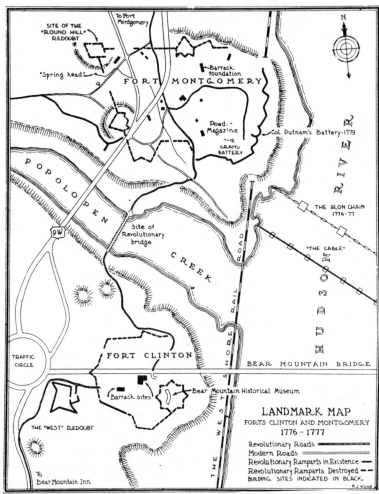

LANDMARK MAP
FORTS CLINTON AND MONTGOMERY
1776 – 1777

From *Twin Forts of the Popolopen: Forts Clinton and Montgomery, New York, 1775-1777* by William H. Carr and Richard J. Koke (Bear Mountain, N.Y., 1937). *Courtesy of Palisades Interstate Park Commission* construction, consisting of a circular line following the ground contour. On the heights was an eight-pointed-star redoubt commanding the river, while to the rear of the works lay a four-pointed redoubt, so massively constructed of stone and earth that it is still in existence today. Fort Montgomery's lines fronting the river were eminently defensible with their great complement of guns, but the rear was comparatively open, with incomplete works poorly positioned. Both forts were surrounded with abatis of felled trees, that of Fort Clinton running southward for four hundred yards and protected by the fire of ten cannon.

The two defenses, on that fatal day, were garrisoned by only five to six hundred men: two regiments of the line, the Fifth New York Regiment from Ulster County under Col. Lewis Dubois, and Col. John Lamb's Regiment of Continental Artillery, with the remainder consisting of militia and detached men from other commands. On the evening that the enemy landed at Verplanck's Point, Governor Clinton sent Maj. Samuel Logan and 100 men southward through the rugged country to reconnoiter.[38] Gen. Putnam contrived to have the Continental frigates *Congress* and *Montgomery,* two row galleys, and a privateer sloop sent downstream to positions just above the chain and boom. The fog on the morning of the sixth had convinced Sir Henry that his shift of troops across the Hudson to Stony Point was hidden from anxious rebel eyes. But Governor Clinton's scouts returned with information that the British had debarked "above & opposite to Kings Ferry, as they supposed, about two thousand men from upwards of forty flat bottomed boats & that they had reason to believe that a greater number were about to land."[39]

On receipt of the news during the time of the obfuscated sunrise, the governor hurriedly penned a report of it to his superior, Gen. Putnam. But before he could send off the dispatch, he received one from Putnam, already cognizant of the situation, who promised reinforcements should Fort Montgomery be attacked.[40] "Old Put's" assurance was the only message of support received from across the Hudson until late in the day, when any reinforcement was already of no avail.

Governor Clinton ordered the frigate *Congress* to return upstream and take position off Fort Constitution while he kept the *Montgomery* and naval auxiliaries to stand by in defense of the Popolopen forts. Maj. Logan returned about nine o'clock with the news that the enemy had disembarked a substantial force at Stony Point, the west landing of King's Ferry. The governor immediately dispatched thirty men under Lieut. Paton Jackson to check on the enemy's movements. About an hour later Jackson's party ran into the British columns at Doodletown, two miles south of Fort Clinton. A furious fire was exchanged and the

Patriot detachment managed to fight its way back. The governor heard the firing and sent a second request to Putnam for reinforcements, stressing the need of immediate assistance. Then reports started coming in that the British were marching around the rear of Bear Hill (Bear Mountain) and were about to cross Popolopen Creek to climb rock-strewn Torne Hill.

Desperate and in need of vital minutes to allow the expected men from the east bank to reinforce the American defenses, Governor Clinton dispatched Lieut. Col. Jacobus Bruyn, with 50 Continentals, and Lieut. Col. James McClaghry (future brother-in-law of George Clinton) with a like number of militia, to post themselve in the direction of Doodletown. Simultaneously, Col. John Lamb was directed to order the only field gun in Fort Montgomery out on the road to the iron works at the Forest of Dean Mine. This road intersected the route Col. Campbell's column was taking to ascend Torne Hill. Orders were to spike the gun and destroy the ammunition should the British win the confrontation. The brass fieldpiece, commanded by Capt. John Fenno, rumbled out of the fort, with 120 men to cover for the gunners.[41]

The assault on the south came soon after Bruyn and McClaghry had posted their men behind a stone wall on the edge of Hessian Lake, half a mile from Fort Clinton.[42] The Americans opened fire. The enemy under Maj. Gen. Vaughan forced the outnumbered defenders back to the main defense perimeter. The gallantry of the Patriots and the wild terrain checked the enemy only momentarily.

While this bitter skirmish was going on, Capt. Fenno's men had ascended Torne Hill, which drops precipitously to Popolopen Creek below.[43] Their fieldpiece was positioned among the rocks on the steep slope, more than a mile from Fort Montgomery. Hardly had the Americans set themselves when the British were observed advancing with "hasty strides." A well-aimed barrage of grape and spirited assistance by the covering party threw Campbell's men into startled confusion. "Great havoc" was caused among the enemy ranks, which were repeatedly driven back. Campbell finally deployed flanks into the woods on both sides of the road. The maneuver forced the prompt spiking and abandonment of the fieldpiece, and the artillerymen were driven from their position by fixed enemy bayonets.[44]

Governor Clinton had the foresight to send out a twelve-pounder to cover the retreat of the Patriots, who fell back in good order to the second position. Again they cannonaded the enemy with grapeshot. This gun was also soon abandoned and the Americans retreated to the fort with very few casualties. Capt. Fenno, obstinately trying to get off one more shot at the enemy, was unfortunately taken prisoner.

Governor Clinton, with every means at hand, was feverishly making preparations to withstand the impending assault. He wrote a third and last urgent appeal for reinforcements. Shortly thereafter, Campbell and Vaughan, joined by Sir Henry Clinton, closed in with their forces and "invested on all sides" Forts Clinton and Montgomery. The British, without cannon, pushed the attack, dodging from rock to rock, only to be driven back repeatedly by Patriot artillery. For three long hours, from two o'clock until dusk, the defenders fought off the enemy. The air was thick with gunpowder smoke as the guns roared continuously.[45]

Gen. Putnam remained with his troops at Peekskill. Unaware of the enemy's crossing to Stony Point ("owing to the morning being so exceedingly foggy") and confused regarding the number of the enemy on his side of the river, "Old Put" was deeply troubled by Governor Clinton's urgent plea for reinforcements, which he had solemnly promised on demand. Convinced that at least fifteen hundred enemy troops were posted at Verplanck's Point, Putnam was completely taken in by Sir Henry's ruse. The first reports of the proximity of the British panicked Peekskill's inhabitants, who evacuated their homes and fled either eastward toward Connecticut or northward in the direction of Newburgh.[46]

To deepen Putnam's dilemma, British naval craft had taken up positions in Peekskill Bay during the early afternoon. The general then became dead certain that a joint land and sea attack was about to be launched against him. He himself went to look at the enemy vessels anchored at his doorstep. Upon returning to his headquarters, he was "alarmed" to hear the roar of battle at the forts across the Hudson. Hours past their need, five hundred men were dispatched to reinforce the two Clintons.[47]

David Humphreys, with Putnam's troops, later wrote:

> The author of these memoires, then major of brigade to the first Connecticut Brigade, was alone at Headquarters when the firing began. He hastened to Col. Wyllys, the senior officer in camp, and advised him to dispatch all the men not on duty to Fort Montgomery, without waiting for orders. About five hundred men marched instantly under Colonel (Return J.) Meigs: and the author with Dr. Beardsleys, a surgeon in the brigade rode, at full speed, through a bye-path, to let the garrison know that a reinforcement was on its march. Notwithstanding all the efforts these officers made to and over the river, the fort was so completely invested on their arrival, that it was impossible to enter; they went on board the new frigate which lay near the fortress and had the misfortune to be idle, though not unconcerned, spectators of the storm.[48]

Col. Meigs arrived with the relief force at the ferry at Robinson's

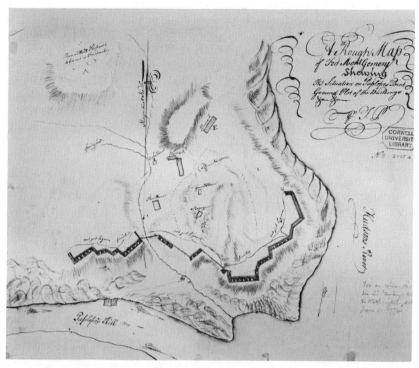

GROUND PLAN: FORT MONTGOMERY IN THE HIGHLANDS
Courtesy of Cornell University Library (Library of Jared Sparks)

Landing, just south of Fort Constitution, too late to be of any assistance
to the beleaguered defenders across the river.

At three o'clock units of the British man-of-war fleet fought their way
against an ebb tide to take up stations opposite the Popolopen forts. Two
hours later the naval craft commenced a bombardment, not only against
the American works on the heights, but also against the Patriot flotilla
north of the chain.

Shortly after five o'clock, Col. Campbell, under a flag of truce,
appeared from the British lines. An American officer of like rank, Lieut.
Col. William S. Livingston, accompanied by Thomas Machin, emerged
from the works to learn that the flag consisted of a demand for surrender
within five minutes "to prevent the effusion of blood" on the part of the
defenders. Livingston declined the offer but suggested that if the British
desired to "surrender themselves prisoners of war, they might depend
upon being well treated." It is not known what Campbell replied to this

rejoinder. Livingston's parting words closed the parley: "You may renew the attack as soon as I shall return within the fort." The two men turned about and walked in opposite directions, terminating a remarkably amicable exchange of offers.[49]

Ten minutes later the British mounted an all-out concentrated assault upon the fort. Campbell, leading his regiment, was killed in the first wave. The enemy overpowered all resistance. The tired American troops, at least half of whom had neither bayonet nor spear, fought gallantly and obstinately, but superior numbers clambered over the walls at almost every point and invaded the works to engage the defenders in fierce hand-to-hand combat.

As Campbell's command launched the final assault against Fort Montgomery, Gen. Vaughan was ordered to storm Fort Clinton. Directives were circulated that not a shot be fired and that the men depend only upon their bayoneted muskets. The soldiers surged forward in the face of a steady fire of round and grapeshot, scrambling over the rocky terrain to fight their way through the mesh of the abatis. At the base of the works they actually shoved one another up and over the walls. One after another they dropped, shot or bayoneted, with some killed in the embrasures. The outnumbered Patriots were overwhelmed by trained British and German soldiers who vaulted the parapets and made their way into Fort Clinton's works.

> On both heights there was a tumultuous melee of struggling men, savagely contesting the ground from redoubt to redoubt. The British crushed the garrisons everywhere. The fight was practically over; the defense crumpled like a deck of cards. It was no longer a struggle to retain the forts, but one of escape. Those of the garrisons who broke out of the works had to hack and slash their way through the opposition. Favored by the growing dusk, which spread its mantle over the scenes of strife and contention, many officers and men, well acquainted with the ground, managed to stumble out of the forts and lose themselves to pursuit in the gloom.[50]

Both Clinton brothers evaded the clutches of the British. James, wounded in the thigh by a bayonet, escaped into the ravine north of Fort Clinton, limped across the bridge, and up to Fort Montgomery's works. George, unhurt, was hurriedly escorted out of Fort Montgomery by a cordon of men drafted by brother James. The governor slid and scrambled his six-foot-four length down the face of the mountain to the water's edge. Clinton brushed off his pants and declared with spirit, "I would rather roast in hell to all eternity than be dependent on Great Britain or show mercy to a damned Tory." He had the additional good fortune of being picked up by a Patriot boat.[51]

There were many other wounded officers. Col. Lewis Dubois escaped with a bayonet wound in the neck. Col. John Lamb and Thomas Machin, the latter with a serious breast wound, escaped in the gathering darkness. Lieut. Col. McClaghry and Maj. Logan, both wounded, were among the prisoners taken. The Americans captured numbered 263, of whom 26 were commissioned officers. The British casualties, according to their own estimate, amounted to 41 dead and 142 wounded, while an undetermined number of Americans suffered death or wounds.[52]

By six o'clock all firing had ceased in the forts, the captured were taken in hand, and the wounded on both sides sought the ministrations of army surgeons. While the battle for the heights was over, the Hudson below became the stage for further American ignominy. In the river just above the chain, American vessels, manned by insufficient and inexperienced crews, were vainly straining to beat their way upstream against a strong ebb tide and an adverse breeze. The frigate *Montgomery* drifted downstream closer and closer to Machin's barrier. Her commander, Capt. John Hodge, "was constrained to set her on fire to prevent her from falling in the hands of the enemy." At ten o'clock that night, the *Montgomery* and the two galleys, the *Shark* and the *Camden,* all three aground and helpless, were deliberately set afire.

Charles Stedman delineated the beginning of the dramatic death of the Americans' Hudson River navy:

> The flames suddenly broke forth; and, as every sail was set, the vessels soon became magificent pyramids of fire. The reflection on the steep face of the opposite mountain [Anthony's Nose], and the long train of ruddy light that shone upon the water for a prodigious distance, had a wonderful effect; whilst the ear was awfully filled with the continued echoes from the rocky shores, as the flames gradually reached the cannon. The whole was sublimely terminated by the explosions, which again left all to darkness.[53]

The frigate *Congress* was manned by inept soldiers and convicts who allowed her to become grounded in the mud flats near Fort Constitution. Her captain, early on the morning of the seventh, put the torch to his vessel after the crew escaped to the shore.

By midnight Governor Clinton had entered Continental Village, the American military complex north of Peekskill. In a council there with Gen. Putnam and other staff officers, it was decided to evacuate the posts around Peekskill and retreat to the northern limits of the Highlands. The next morning the Patriot army, led by "Old Put," started its march out of the mountains, taking up positions on the Albany Post Road about three miles south of Fishkill.

The day after the battle, Fort Clinton was renamed Fort Vaughan in tribute to the British officer who led in its reduction. Fort Constitution was abandoned by a panic-stricken minuscule garrison under Capt. Gershom Mott after it had fired upon a flag of truce in a British demand for the fort's surrender. At eleven o'clock on the morning of October 8, Machin's great iron chain was severed by British artificers. In the afternoon, British naval craft went up the river to Fort Constitution and disembarked troops to occupy the deserted works. Sir Henry Clinton then penned the following message to embattled Burgoyne:

> *Nous y voici* [We are here], and nothing now between us but Gates. I sincerely hope this little success of ours may facilitate your operations. In answer to your letter of the 28th Sept. by C. C. I shall only say, I cannot presume to order or even advise, for reasons obvious. I heartily wish you success.[54]

The British commander's message was compacted into a silver bullet and given to Lieut. Daniel Taylor of the Ninth Regiment of Foot. He left Fort Montgomery that night and headed for Burgoyne's headquarters. The next day, however, he was captured by an American patrol near the village of Little Britain, about six miles west of Newburgh. The particulars subsequent to Taylor's capture make for interested reading as described in a report by Governor Clinton, written on October 11:

> The letter from Clinton to Burgoyne, taken from Danl. Taylor, was enclosed in a small silver ball of an oval form, about the size of a fusee bullet, and shut with a screw in the middle. When he was taken and brought before me he swallowed it. I mistrusted this to be [the] case from information I received, and administered him a very strong emetic, calculated to operate either way. This had the desired effect; it brought it from him; but though close watched, he had the art to conceal it a second time. I made him believe that I had taken one Capt. Campbell, another messenger who he knew was out on the same business; that I learned from him all I wanted to know, and demanded the ball on pain of being hung up instantly and cut open to search it. This brought it forth.[55]

Lieut. Taylor was arraigned before a general court-martial on October 14 and condemned to hang as a spy. The court's sentence, after some delay, was executed on October 18 in the village of Hurley, three miles from Kingston.

In the interim, on October 11, Sir James Wallace with four vessels maneuvered the *chevaux-de-frise* and proceeded unimpeded as far north as Poughkeepsie. Neither Governor Clinton and his shattered force near New Windsor, nor Gen. Putnam on the east bank, had the means to prevent the British reconnoitering expedition.

Sir Henry Clinton decided that former Fort Clinton should be the base for further operations in the Highlands. The letter by Commodore Hotham to William Howe, dated October 15, explains Clinton's judgment:

> I take the . . . opportunity to acquaint your Lordship that the number of men which would be necessary for the defense of the more extensive garrison of Fort Montgomery has induced Sir Henry to destroy it and to add some works to that of Fort Clinton which commanding the first effectually removes all apprehension from thence and reduces the force necessary to maintain it to about 800 men.[56]

A romanticized and exaggerated view of the captured Popolopen forts is contained in the following extract from a letter dated Fort Montgomery, October 13:

> No Place on Earth bears more visible Marks of the Divine Vengeance than this; indeed it baffles Description, and fills the Minds with the most shocking Ideas. Were a Plan of the Forts here (one of which is nearly demolished) taken, it would hardly gain Credit in future Ages, that so small a Number of Men, with so little Loss, reduced them:—were you to see them, you would not think 20,000 Men adequate to the Task.[57]

On the morning of October 15, a British fleet of some thirty vessels, with sixteen hundred troops aboard, commanded by Maj. Gen. Vaughan and Sir James Wallace, made its way through the *chevaux-de-frise* and took up stations that night about six miles below Kingston. The next day Vaughan debarked with his troops at Kingston Landing, wiped out two American batteries, and marched to Kingston. To accommodate his view that Kingston was "a Nursery for every Villan in the Country," Vaughan ordered the town burned down.

The next morning, October 17, about ninety-five miles to the north at Saratoga, Burgoyne's ambitious campaign came to an inglorious end when he ceremoniously surrendered his army to Gen. Gates and an ever-increasing force of Patriots. Vaughan and Wallace lingered in the Kingston area for several days, then returned southward. By the twenty-fifth Sir Henry had become convinced from reports that Burgoyne had indeed capitulated. On the same day, the British general received instructions from Howe to send reinforcements to Philadelphia (Gen. Washington's Germantown campaign, though an American failure, served to alarm Howe). On the twenty-sixth, Sir Henry issued orders to destroy Fort Clinton (Vaughan) and the bridge across

Popolopen Creek. The British forces pulled out and a short time later Sir James Wallace's fleet sailed back to New York City.

Sir Henry Clinton's expedition had been executed with brilliant finesse. John Martin Hammond holds the exaggerated and optimistic opinion that a greater effort by the general would have saved Burgoyne the embarrassment of surrender and put a different ending to the Revolution:

> Such a signal success . . . should have caused him to push quickly on to effect a junction with Burgoyne . . . but, having done this much, the English knight seemed to think that nothing more was expected of him, for, beyond sending a marauding expedition up the Hudson as far as Kingston, he made no further northern advance. . . . Had he joined Burgoyne in time to prevent the capitulation of the latter, it is probable that the whole history of this country would have been written in another fashion from that date.[58]

Sir Henry's mission dealt a severe blow to American morale. Forts Clinton, Montgomery, Constitution, and Independence were destroyed. Machin's great chain across the Hudson, the small American naval squadron, and considerable quantities of stores in Continental Village were destroyed. The Americans lost sixty-seven pieces of ordnance, along with great quantities of cannon shot, ammunition, and powder in the Twin Forts. The *chevaux-de-frise* proved to be a dismal failure, allowing the enemy to enter the Highlands and lay waste the country on both sides of the river, even to the burning of incomplete vessels still on their stocks. Kingston was a ruination, with only one structure left standing out of more than three hundred buildings in the town. Sir Henry's visitation of less than three weeks had accomplished the destruction of everything material produced by the Americans for the defense of the Hudson Valley in the last thirty months.[59]

Gen. Washington's remarkable stability in the face of adversity provided the stimulus in December for his staff officers and the Legislature once again to make plans for Highland defenses. Various people, military and government, again recommended Fort Clinton's strategic position rather than West Point.

On the 20th of the month Governor Clinton wrote Washington, recommending that the new works be constructed either at West Point or "on the opposite Side of the Creek from where Fort Montgomery stood."[60] A vehement proponent of the Popolopen site was Lieut. Col. Louis Deshaix de la Radière, a young French engineer. Despite his professional estimate, Governor Clinton, his brother, James, Gen. Putnam, and a committee of the New York Provincial Convention appointed on January 8, 1778, voted against the Fort Clinton location.[61]

The members of the committee were distinctly partial to West Point as the site for the new "grand" fortification. On January 20 a brigade of Connecticut Continentals under Gen. Samuel H. Parsons crossed the river and began the task of constructing the new defensive works that evolved eventually into the citadel of West Point.

The horrors of war in the aftermath of the British victory were revealed in April 1778 to one of Gen. Parsons's officers, Samuel Richards, who accompanied Timothy Dwight on his inspection tour of the sites where the two forts had stood:

> When the weather had become mild and pleasant in April I went one day with Doctor Dwight down to view the ruins of Fort Montgomery, distant about 8 or 10 miles. There was a pond just north of the fort, where we found the British had thrown in the bodies of their own and our men who fell in the assault of the fort.[62] The water had receded, leaving a number of the bodies entirely out of the water, while others lay covered at different depths. I saw many fine sets of teeth, bare and skeleton-like. Mournful and impressive reflections arose in my mind. There lie the youth who stood in the hour of their country's trial; they fought and fell to purchase the independence of their country; and there they lie without burial. I thought too, of the vicissitudes to which a soldier is subject. Had the fort held out a little longer, I very probably might had lain among them.[63]

Until the end of the war, the Americans frequently occupied Fort Montgomery's site and its near environs as a campground. Brig. Gen. Anthony Wayne, before and after his spectacular capture of Stony Point on July 16, 1779, dated letters and reports from the Popolopen fort. In August 1779 Col. Rufus Putnam constructed a small crescent-shaped battery on the lines of the fort's ramparts, to serve as a watchpost for West Point.[64]

To this day the remarkably well-preserved remains of Putnam's battery overlooks the strategic river pass. Where Machin's great iron chain was once drawn across the Hudson, there is now a great steel bridge, and not far from the western terminus of the span are the remains of one of Fort Clinton's redoubts.[65]

Fort Clyde
Freysbush, Montgomery County

The construction of Fort Clyde, probably in the spring of 1777, was on the property of Gen. George H. Nellis (Frothingham has his given name as Henry), about two miles southwest of Fort Plain. Its building was largely due to the energies of Col. Samuel Clyde, who was an officer in the Tryon County militia and who resided in Cherry Valley. The fortification was built to safeguard the inhabitants of Frey's Bush in the present township of Minden.

The fort, a blockhouse in the center of a strong rectangle of palisades, had enough room within the enclosure to provide refuge to the settlement's people should a Tory-Indian attack come. As with most of the other Mohawk Valley forts, Fort Clyde possessed a six-pounder signal gun, one firing of which announced the presence of the enemy in the area. Usually garrisoned by militia, the blockhouse stood on the farm's high ground and commanded a good view of the surrounding country.

It is very probable that Gen. Washington, on an inspection tour of the frontier posts in 1783, made a stop at Fort Clyde as he traveled from Fort Plain to Cherry Valley. Col. Clyde was rewarded for his valiant services throughout the Revolution by later being appointed sheriff of Montgomery County by Governor Clinton, who acted on Washington's suggestion that Clyde should receive recognition for his valued participation in the conflict.

Constitution Island and West Point
Putnam and Orange Counties

The site of Fort Constitution, the first Patriot defense in the Hudson Highlands, is on an island,[1] roughly triangular in shape and consisting of somewhat less than two hundred acres, opposite the United States Military Academy at West Point. Now part of the USMA complex, the island is detached from the mainland by a marsh approximately half-a-mile wide. Ten major eminences, 50 to 140 feet high, most of them bedrock, dominate the rugged island terrain—in fact, there are very few level spots more than a few paces across. Though the gravelly land abounds with glacial boulders, there is also a profusion of varieties of oak and maple, with some white ash, hickory, and pine.[2]

The island's proprietorial history is rather interesting. Part of a five thousand-acre grant by the Crown to Judge Frederick Philipse in 1697, Constitution Island remained in the possession of the Philipse family until November 1836, at which time it was sold by Samuel Gouverneur and his wife to Henry W. Warner, a Long Island lawyer. Henry Warner became interested in the property when he visited his brother Thomas, who, besides being a chaplain at West Point, was teaching history, geography, and ethics there. Henry Warner made his home on the island

THE S-CURVE OF WEST POINT AND CONSTITUTION ISLAND
Courtesy of New York State Department of Conservation

and his residence, "Wood Crag," formerly the caretaker's four-room cottage, still retained one outside wall dating back to the Revolution; to enlarge the family's living quarters, Warner added a wing to the cottage.

Financial reverses during the Panic of 1837 and the expenditure of much money on unsuccessful litigation to establish his right to build a road across the swamp to the Hudson, in time impoverished the family. After Henry Warner's death his two daughters, Anna and Susan, were besieged by enticing offers to sell the island for the purpose of converting it into an amusement park. Despite their financial straits they refused, feeling that the historical value of the island would be destroyed.

In 1908 Mrs. Russell Sage, widow of financier Russell Sage, became interested in the property while engaged in philanthropic enterprises. She was wholly in accord with the patriotic desires of Anna Warner, who still resided on the island after her sister's death. Mrs. Sage generously offered to purchase Constitution Island and present it as a joint gift from

Anna Warner and herself to the government. There was no change in proprietorship until the death of Anna Warner in 1915 when, by the terms of her will and the generosity of Mrs. Sage, the property was deeded to the United States. President Theodore Roosevelt accepted the property, which is now part of the United States Military Academy Reservation.[3]

> The story of Fort Constitution is a reflection in miniature of the Revolutionary War. It reveals the heroism and sacrifice, high motives and low motives, good leadership and bad leadership, efficiency coupled with disorder and chaos, the lack of responsible authority capable of quick and effective action, self-seeking, jealousy, hatreds, ambition for place and power, uncertainty, troops refusing to work in the cause they professed to espouse, lack of funds and the munitions of war, poverty, and hardships unspeakable. The record is full of these shortcomings and perplexities and difficulties. One conflict was no sooner adjusted than another emerged.[4]

The history of Fort Constitution bridged all the years of the war. The eight-year span can be better comprehended if contemplated as consisting of two periods:

> The first, when the responsibility of the construction of the fortifications in the Highlands was primarily left in the hands of civilians. This came to a fiery end with the destruction of the fortifications of Forts Constitution, Montgomery and Clinton in October of 1777. This period was followed by the erection of a new set of fortifications at West Point under military control and relying heavily on experienced foreign engineers. The fortifications eventually evolved into a vast complex of forts, redoubts and batteries on both sides of the River. Fort Constitution was refortified and this entire complex then became the main bastion in guarding the Hudson Highlands and the all-important Hudson River during the rest of the war.[5]

The civilian responsibility for erecting defenses on Constitution Island began with the New York Provincial Convention's assignment of Col. James Clinton and Christopher Tappen to inspect the Highlands and report on proper sites for the establishment of fortifications.[6] Their recommendation of two sites, the island and West Point, was followed by pressure by the Continental Congress to commence construction at once. The Convention, however, made no move until August 18, some two months later, when it appointed five commissioners (augmented to seven the next month) to oversee the construction of the new defenses.[7]

On September 7 the Committee of Safety received a letter from the Highlands commissioners requesting instructions regarding the plan of the defenses and construction costs of same. They were informed that it would be advisable to hold off until the arrival of Bernard Romans, who was then in Philadelphia seeking a colonel's commission as a Continental Army engineer. In 1775 engineers in the American Colonies were rarities, particularly those conversant with military science. Gen. Washington was fortunate in his search for just such a man, Lieut. Col. Rufus Putnam, a cousin of Gen. Israel Putnam, whose touch of engineering genius at Dorchester Heights contributed to the Patriot ouster of the British from Boston.

But the commissioners had to be content with Romans, a rather good Dutch botanist and cartographer, trained in England as an engineer. Some of his very limited experience was gained at Fort Ticonderoga when Benedict Arnold asked him to assist in the repair of the fortress after it was flamboyantly captured on May 10. The pressures and temper of the times dictated the unfortunate selection of "a Dutchman turned English and a botanist turned engineer" to plan and construct the ill-designed fortress on Constitution Island.[8]

Romans inspected Martelaer's Rock and wrote a long report, dated September 14, 1775, from "Martelaer's Rock, on Martyr's Reach." He also suggested a small battery at West Point, where a farm was then situated. On the 18th he submitted an estimate and expense account for the construction of his planned defenses. Romans' grand plan, transferred to paper with cartographic excellence, captivated the Convention, which approved on September 19 his scheme for transforming Constitution Island. His delineation provided for a "Grand Bastion," five blockhouses, batteries, barracks, and storehouses, plus a blockhouse on West Point, with the whole complex to be defended by sixty-one guns and twenty swivels. The "Grand Bastion," outlined as Plan No. 3 in his report, never materialized, and has been aptly described as "The Fort That Never Was."[9]

Work commenced before the end of September despite bitter contention between Romans and the Highlands commissioners regarding what defenses were to go where and who was to supervise construction. But progress was slow because of the insufficient number of workmen, who came and went as they pleased. In addition, reports began to filter through to the Provincial Convention that the laborers on the project were drinking to excess. A committee was dispatched to ascertain the truth of the rumors. They found "the workmen were appallingly drunk." And while they were there, the committeemen were almost instantly struck by the gross ineptitude displayed by Romans in his selection of the place for the fort, "at the bottom of a natural bowl, surrounded on three sides by high ground," and "lacking the advantage of an elevated site."[10]

The early history of the island's fortifications, soon to be called Fort

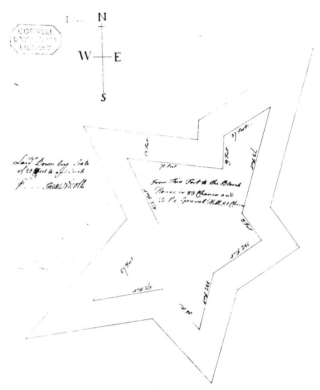

PLAN OF FORT CONSTITUTION THAT ACCOMPANIED LORD
STIRLING'S REPORT
Courtesy of Cornell University Library

Constitution,[11] is one of bitter disillusionment. Acrimony, verging on childishness, between Romans and the commissioners developed into a major controversy. Notwithstanding recurrent arguments, the commissioners reported to the Convention on November 11 that one blockhouse and an eighty-by-twenty-foot barracks had been completed; a one hundred-by-twenty-foot barracks was nearly completed; and Romans' Battery was well along the way, with a small magazine planned for the northwest corner of the work. A Congress-appointed committee, consisting of John Langdon, Robert R. Livingston, and Robert Treat Paine, reported on November 23, after its inspection of the crucial Highlands defenses, that Romans' Battery apparently had one more week of work for completion and that it would mount fourteen cannon; that the blockhouse was completed and held six four-pounders; and that fourteen barracks rooms, each large enough for thirty men, were finished except for brick chimneys.[12]

The Provincial Convention sent a committee composed of Francis Nicoll, Joseph Drake, and Thomas Palmer to settle the differences between the self-styled engineer and the commissioners. On December 14 the three men tendered their report, condemning Fort Constitution and recommending that a strong battery be constructed five miles downstream on the west bank and just north of Popolopen Creek. The committee believed "that the fortress now erecting will by no means be sufficient to secure Hudson's River, if it be attacked by any considerable force." In addition to advising a new survey of the river, the committee was strongly in favor of river obstructions.[13] In the middle of January 1776, orders were issued to transfer the stock of planks meant for Fort Constitution's second and third barracks to Fort Montgomery's site opposite Anthony's Nose.[14] One of the Highlands commissioners sent word on January 22 to the Committee of Safety that the foundation for "the intended battery" on Constitution Island was finished. Made of huge rocks, each a half ton or more, with its crevices filled with small stones and gravel, the base for the battery was 140 feet long, 12 feet wide at the bottom, 10 feet wide at the top, and 4 feet high.[15]

The beginning of 1776 saw Fort Constitution without an engineer: Bernard Romans was in Philadelphia, fighting to retain his "professional" engineering status. In February his services were terminated and in his place appeared, temporarily, Capt. William Smith.[16] Neither the Congress nor the New York Provincial Convention could come up with a replacement for Romans. Finally, the Convention settled on Thomas Palmer to be superintending commissioner, advising him to approach Maj. Gen. Charles Lee, who was then wrestling with the problems of erecting New York City defenses, for engineering assistance. Gen. Lee, surprisingly, volunteered the services of his chief engineer, Capt. Smith. Palmer relayed his orders from the Continental Congress to Smith: complete the already initiated defenses on Constitution Island and lay out the ground for the new fortification on the north side of Popolopen Creek (Fort Montgomery). In just two days the energetic Smith had laid out the lines for a new fort east of Fort Constitution, selected a site for another on the east shore about a mile south of the island, and staked out the ground for Fort Montgomery. Unfortunately, Capt. Smith had to return to New York to continue work on that city's defenses, leaving the Highlands still without permanent engineering talent.[17]

Isaac Nicoll, who won out over Thomas Palmer in a battle for complete authority over the troops at both Fort Constitution and Fort Montgomery, reported to the Convention on March 5 that the island's garrison had been without "fresh provisions" for two months and lacked many necessities.[18] A Congressional committee consisting of Benjamin Franklin, Charles Carroll, and Samuel Chase was dispatched to Canada in an attempt to solicit the sympathy of the people there with respect to the Continental invasion of the British stronghold. The men stopped off at Constitution Island on April 5 and there found only three companies of minutemen. Their report revealed that the blockhouse was defended by "eight double fortified four-pound guns, mounted;" the south bastion held thirteen six-pounders and one nine-pounder while the east bastion was defended by seven nine-pounders and one six-pounder. The committee's short inspection tour also found that "the fortifications ordered by Congress on the 15th of February and laid out by Engineer Smith remain wholly neglected."[19] A few days later, to justify why his garrison was in such a weak state and most of the men without arms, Isaac Nicoll reported that it was not possible to obtain well-equipped soldiers because of the low pay scale.[20]

After he had established his headquarters in New York City on April 13, Washington kept a close watch on the progress of the Highlands defenses. Reports from the commissioners were very discouraging. In a letter of May 21 to Gen. Putnam, Washington expressed his deep dissatisfaction: "I have great reason to think that the fortifications in the Highlands are in a bad situation, and the garrison on account of arms, worse." The commander-in-chief on May 26 dispatched Gen. (Lord) Stirling, Col. Rufus Putnam, and Capt. Winthrop Sargent, a competent artilleryman, up the Hudson to learn once and for all the military deficiencies in the Highlands.[21] This was the first time military experts were assigned to the task and they formulated plans that became the bases for defenses later projected.

On June 1 Stirling penned a painstakingly concise report to Washington. His graphic description of Constitution Island's defenses in the late spring of 1776 merits quoting:

> Fort Constitution is about six miles above Fort Montgomery, on an island near the east side of the river, and near the north end of the Highlands, which on the west and south sides is bounded by the river, and on the north and east sides by low marsh and small creeks running through it. The works here consist of four open lines or batteries, fronting the river; the two eastermost command the approach up the river very well; the next, or middle line, commands the approach from West Point upwards; the westermost battery is a straight line, constructed by Mr. Romans, at a very great expense; it has fifteen

embrasures which face the river at a right angle, and can only annoy a ship in going past; the embrasures are within twelve feet of each other; the merlons on the outside are but about two feet in the face, and about seven feet deep made of square timber covered with plank, and look very neat; he also built a loghouse or tower on the highest cliff, near the water, mounted with eight cannon (four-pounders) pointed out of the garret windows, and looks very picturesque. Upon the whole, Mr. Romans has displayed his genius at a very great expense, and to very little public advantage. The works in their present open condition and scattered situation are defenseless; nor is there one good place on the island on which a redoubt may be erected that will command the whole.

The garrison of Fort Constitution consists of two companies of Col. James Clinton's regiment, and Captain Wisner's company of minute men, in all about 160, rank and file. The garrison of Fort Montgomery consists of three companies of the same regiment, amounting to about 200 men, rank and file. The field officer of the regiment is Lieut. Col. Livingston, but the command of the whole of both the garrisons is still in the hands of Colonel Nicoll, who, it seems, last fall raised a regiment of minute men for the purpose of garrisoning Fort Constitution, which regiment is all dismissed except Captain Wisner's company of about 40 privates.[22]

Stirling's statistics accompanying his report pointed out the great deficiencies in men, armaments, and munitions.[23] On June 13 the Convention discharged all the commissioners, along with the minutemen.[24]

During the summer days of 1776, the inhabitants of New York were greatly disturbed by rampant rumors that the enemy had definite plans to invade the Hudson Valley.[25] The Continental Army's officers were likewise affected. Gen. Gates cautioned the Convention that he believed the British intended to "make a push up the river," and that he had been advised "that Fort Constitution is in a bad state of defence."[26] Washington was kept informed of the exposed condition of the Highlands and he pressed for greater vigor on the fortifications. He sent Lieut. (later Captain) Thomas Machin, "one of the truly unsung heroes of the Revolution," to apply his engineering genius toward improving the Highlands defenses.[27]

By the end of July major construction at Constitution Island was ended. The completed fortifications were Romans' Battery, Marine Battery, Hill Cliff Battery, Gravel Hill Battery, and Romans' Blockhouse. There was a large barracks (Romans' Barracks) behind the blockhouse and an adjacent building described as either a storehouse or another barracks. Stirling's Barracks was probably finished also, though no contemporaneous documentation of its existence has come to light. On Stirling's sketch two unidentified buildings are shown near Romans' Battery, one of them probably the smithy.[28]

With Gen. Howe's large army safely berthed on Staten Island, Washington took the initiative in August by going after the British men-of-war in the Hudson, first with four puny row-galleys and then threatening the enemy vessels with two fire ships primed with ''spirits of turpentine and salt petre.'' The enemy flotilla, including the *Phoenix* and the *Rose,* heeded the warning and retired down the river below Fort Washington, which shelled the ships ineffectively as they passed. American genius for invention, in the guise of Yale graduate David Bushnell, gave birth to the *American Turtle,* a one-man submarine with a piggyback timed torpedo. The underwater attack, the first in the history of naval warfare, was made on a dark night during the same month in New York Bay. The target was the *Asia,* Admiral Richard Howe's sixty-four-gun flagship. The attack was a failure because the *Asia's* hull was copper-sheathed and the *American Turtle's* auger for attaching the bomb was for wood-bottomed vessels.[29]

With the British navy quite free to pass up and down the wide lower Hudson, despite deliberately scuttled watercraft, other underwater obstructions, and Forts Washington and Lee, the commander-in-chief and his generals realized that only the Highlands, fully fortified and adequately defended, could give the Continentals custody of the rest of the estuary. During the autumn months, in response to renewed Continental anxiety over the state of military preparedness in the Highlands, labor forces from the adjoining counties were drafted to continue work on the fortifications; though there was the usual lack of orderly planning, additional barracks were constructed at Forts Constitution and Montgomery.[30]

Routed by the enemy in the Battle of Brooklyn, Washington took his beaten army to Manhattan. The Convention wisely removed to Fishkill above the Highlands and in the course of its journey left a committee to inspect the forts. Its appraisal—''to render Fort Constitution tenable, the West-Point, which commands it, ought to be fortified''—confirms James Clinton's and Lord Stirling's earlier findings. Beset by fears of an imminent British attack, James Clinton and Thomas Machin elected to fortify the tor on the south side of Popolopen Creek and run a gigantic chain across the Hudson from Fort Montgomery, rather than spend valuable months on a ''grand bastion'' at West Point.[31]

Fort Clinton, across the creek from its twin, Fort Montgomery, was begun. Benedict Arnold's amazing naval escapade on Lake Champlain stymied Gen. Carleton's invasion march from Canada. The Highlands' Continental command had been handed a year of grace on a silver platter. The spring of 1777—''The Year of the Hangman''—brought news of John Burgoyne's ascendancy in Britain's military hierarchy, displacing Carleton. The Americans were certain that the strategically critical Hudson Valley was a primary target in that year's British plan of operations to put down the colonial rebellion. The expectation of an enemy invasion, from either Canada or New York, or both simultaneously, found Continental generals faced with the dilemma of how best to defend the Highlands. Not one of the major fortifications—Constitution, Montgomery, Independence, or Clinton—was complete.

A hint of what to expect came later in the form of a raid on Peekskill, a major American munitions magazine, on March 23. This Continental depot held a goodly portion of Washington's powder and weapons. Gen. Alexander McDougall, later claiming that his garrison was too small to oppose the enemy, pulled his men out of the depot after burning some stores and sought refuge on the Post Road leading north into the Highlands. Washington, at his headquarters at Morristown, wrathfully denounced the inadequacy of the Americans at Peekskill, as to both their fewer numbers than ordered and their cowardly behavior.[32]

The expectancy of another British raid in April brought hurried orders to reinforce the Highlands. The Provincial Convention empowered George Clinton to call up militia from the four nearest counties—simply said but not easily done. The independence of militiamen, their innate distrust of authority and lack of discipline, worked contrary to their political convictions and varying degrees of patriotism. Their disinclination to bend to military authority was demonstrated by the inhabitants of Dutchess County, which had been asked to supply eight hundred men to garrison Forts Constitution and Montgomery; at the end of three weeks not one militiaman answered the call to arms from that county.[33]

On May 7 Gen. Washington informed McDougall, still at Peekskill, that he believed the enemy would make a thrust up the Hudson and that he was distressed by the inadequacy of the defenses. He ordered McDougall to work with George Clinton to put the fortifications in such a state of readiness as to resist a sudden assault or stall the enemy's forces until American reinforcements could arrive.[34] The commander of Peekskill sent word to Generals Greene, Knox, and Wayne to join Clinton in an inspection of the Highland forts. On the 17th they recommended a chain and a pair of cables across the Hudson at Fort Montgomery in addition to underwater wood obstructions, with a flotilla of American ships just above them to offer fire power as protection. The generals were "very confident" that, should the river barriers be effective, the British would "not attempt to operate by land" through the difficult mountain defiles.[35] Not five months later, the British disproved the American generals' hypothesis.

By the beginning of July, Washington was "almost certain" that John

Burgoyne from Canada and William Howe from New York had every intention of forming "a juncture of their two armies." If that was the British plan of strategy, the American commander-in-chief believed that Howe would "make a rapid and vigorous push to gain the Highland passes."[36] In expectation of the imminency of such a double-barreled assault, Washington on August 1 ordered Gen. Clinton to "immediately call in every man of the militia you possibly can to strengthen the Highlands" and at once take personal command of Fort Montgomery.[37]

More than two years of on-and-off frenetic labor, accompanied by inept, indecisive engineering and bitter recriminations, availed Fort Constitution nothing but utter destruction; the same fate awaited Forts Montgomery, Clinton, and Independence.

To complement Burgoyne's advance, Sir Henry Clinton, replacing Howe who went off on his Philadelphia campaign, made his move during the first week of October. The British force debarked at Verplanck's Point in a feint, crossed the Hudson in an early morning fog to Stony Point, marched through the rugged passes to the west of Dunderberg Mountain, and split into two columns at Doodletown—one passing to the west of Bear Mountain to attack Fort Montgomery, the other to the east or river side to assail Fort Clinton. On October 6 Popolopen's twin forts were invested on all sides but George Clinton disdained surrender. The battles at both forts raged till dusk when the British, without cannon but far outnumbering the defenders, bayoneted their way through embrasures and over ramparts to impose capitulation upon the Patriots.[38]

The next morning, while victorious British soldiery curiously inspected the river chain and boom, a small boat bearing an officer and a flag of truce went upriver to Constitution Island to request surrender from its garrison. A frightened trigger-happy sentry fired on the flag, inspiring the boat's rowers to back off apprehensively and return to Popolopen Creek. Sir Henry Clinton, beside himself with anger at this flagrant violation, at once ordered the seizure of Constitution Island.

Late the following morning, artificers cut the chain. Three British galleys and twenty-two flatboats laden with soldiers proceeded upriver by oar—there was hardly a whisper of a breeze—to land on the island's beach just before sunset. Bayoneted muskets in hand, the soldiers jumped into the water and charged ashore, only to find the works of Fort Constitution absolutely deserted.[39]

Long before the British assaults on the Popolopen forts, the commander of Constitution Island, Maj. Lewis Dubois[40] had little hope of ever being able to defend his post. For one thing, discounting Capt. Gershom Mott's artillerymen, Dubois had only about 130 men. For another, the officer realized all too clearly that the island was a sitting duck, dominated as it was by the high plain of the West Point opposite: enemy artillery from that vantage point could undoubtedly wreak tremendous havoc on both the works and the men of Fort Constitution.

After the enemy's truce boat had been fired on, Dubois felt that the island was about to be assaulted by greatly superior enemy numbers. In apparent hysteria, he immediately ordered the barracks burned, and evacuated the entire garrison. Not one gun on the island was spiked and very little of the military stores was either taken in the flight or destroyed. When the British landed, they found a bonanza awaiting them.[41] It was George Clinton's opinion that Fort Constitution was "demolished by our men without orders" but "I cannot as yet condemn the measure."[42]

Units of Sir Henry's invasion army went upriver to Kingston (also known as Esopus) and set fire to the town. News of Burgoyne's fate at Saratoga terminated Sir Henry's temporary occupation, only twenty days, of the Highlands. Before withdrawing to New York City, the British commander had the forts demolished. Fort Constitution, left almost whole by the fleeing garrison, was destroyed by enemy soldiers, who mined the works and completed the demolition by firing everything combustible.

The American disaster cost the Revolutionary cause more than two years of heartbreaking effort and labor at an estimated loss of $250,000, a treasure in those days.[43] Sir Henry's prize in American war matériel included seventy-seven guns, six tons of powder, and several thousand cannon balls.[44] But the American loss in weaponry was more than offset by the armaments taken at Saratoga when Burgoyne surrendered his entire army.[45]

The grand plan by Lord Germain and his executor, John Burgoyne, victorious in the first weeks of the campaign, had turned into a debacle of world-shaking political proportions. When the news reached London, utter consternation overwhelmed the Ministry of War while smiles of wonderment were displayed by Revolutionary partisans in Parliament. William Howe had taken Philadelphia, for what little it was worth militarily, but Sir Henry Clinton could not hold the strategic Highlands.

It had not been the Year of the Hangman; it was the year of salvation. France, for months a covert ally of America, was emboldened to side overtly with the rebels. Spain later declared war on George III, eventually the Dutch, too, became an active enemy of the British. England was no longer faced with suppressing a colonial uprising, but with waging a world-wide war of major proportions.[46]

The Continental Army and New York's new state government at once

VILLEFRANCHE'S PLAN OF WEST POINT AND CONSTITUTION
ISLAND
Courtesy of USMA Library

made plans for the refortification of the Highlands. Competent military
men, profiting by earlier lapses in judgment and inept engineering,
resurveyed the region and settled on the West Point as the nucleus of a
new system of defenses on both sides of the river. "But efficiency was
never the hallmark of our revolutionary ancestors; and nowhere was
that fact better evidenced than in the Hudson Highlands. American
fortification efforts in the five months following Henry Clinton's
withdrawal were half farce, half futile, wholly frustrating." What finally
evolved, however, was variously and grandiosely called "The Gibraltar
of America" and "The Key to the Continent."[47]

Through the efforts of Benjamin Franklin, Minister to France, four
French military engineers—Louis Duportail, Jean de Gouvion, Jean de
Laumoy, and Louis de la Radière—departed secretly from their
homeland to arrive in Philadelphia in July 1777. Franklin had agreed that
these four men would be commissioned into the Continental Army one

grade higher than the ranks they held when they left France. On July 8 the Congress conferred on Duportail the rank of colonel, Radière lieutenant colonel, and Gouvion major; Laumoy, because of illness, had not yet arrived in Philadelphia.

For many weeks Radière lobbied in Philadelphia for a full colonelship—he had been only a captain in the French army—threatening to leave at the end of the year if he did not get the promotion. He was assigned to the Highlands. The date of his arrival there is not known for certain, but apparently he made his appearance either during the destruction of the forts by the British or very soon thereafter. The French engineer's first task was a survey of the Highlands to ascertain where the new defenses should be placed to best advantage. In December Congress bowed to his insistence, conferring upon him the rank of full colonel.[48]

Fully committed to Vauban's ideas on defensive engineering, Radière was stubbornly alone in his contention for a new bastion on the blackened ruins of Fort Clinton, while the American officers held to the opinion that West Point's location was much more desirable for numerous reasons. Washington, disenchanted with Gates and Putnam, had but one man in mind for the job of refortifying the Highlands: George Clinton. The commander-in-chief, along with his men already suffering slow starvation and freezing temperatures at Valley Forge, penned a letter, delayed two weeks in transit, to the New York governor.

Writing from Poughkeepsie, Clinton declined the Highlands command, pleading that the duties of his office would prevent him from devoting the full time necessary for the task, but that he would give up "every leisure hour" to assist in the mounting of new defenses. The governor's long reply revealed that he too was in favor of the West Point site:

> I am clearly of opinion that a strong fortress ought to be erected on the opposite side of the creek from where Fort Montgomery stood or at the West Point opposite Fort Constitution. The latter I prefer as the most defensible ground and because the navigation of the river there is more difficult and uncertain and the river something narrower than it is at the former place. A new chain should be procured (if possible) and . . . stretched across the river.[49]

To settle the dispute, reminiscent of the Romans controversy two years earlier, a board of commissioners visited the Popolopen Creek and West Point sites. After hearing out Radière, the commissioners on January 12, 1778, voted unanimously in favor of West Point.[50] Washington had speculated whether these imported military engineers justified

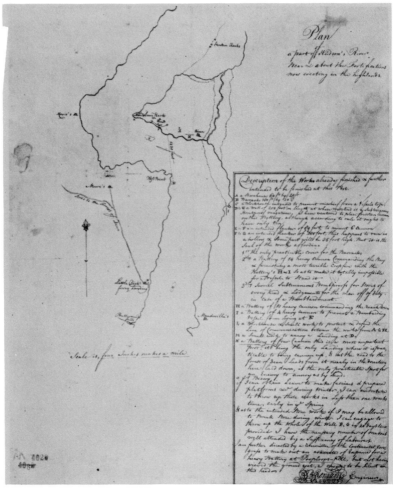

ROMANS'S MAP OF WEST POINT AND CONSTITUTION ISLAND
Courtesy of USMA Library

"GREAT CHAIN" LINKS
U.S. Army Photograph. Courtesy of USMA Library

PIN AND LINK OF THE "GREAT CHAIN" AT WEST POINT
U.S. Army Photograph. *Courtesy of USMA Library*

all the bother and controversy. He became convinced that plans for America's future should take into consideration the establishment of a military academy for the training of American engineers, forever eliminating dependence on foreign military experts.[51]

Fearful of a British movement up the river with the coming of spring, Washington deferred to absolute necessity and gave the Highlands command to Gen. Israel Putnam. But very soon "Old Put's" procrastinations were more than Washington could bear. The commander-in-chief took him to task in a scathing letter. On the same day, Washington sent a directive to Radière, urging him to devote his energies to fortifying West Point. Furious with the lack of initiative, Washington made West Point his personal responsibility.

Defending his efforts, Putnam overemphasized the work already accomplished under his direction. In essence, his reply to Washington showed that what had been completed were only a barracks and some huts for three hundred men and a road from West Point's plateau to a landing on the river. The old general dwelled on the "laid out" plans for water batteries and a large covering fort, Radière's planned fortress, with walls 14 feet high, 21 feet thick, and 600 feet in length, and a "contracted for" chain to span the river to Constitution Island. At the end of his apologia, Putnam reported that he was leaving West Point on the morrow for Connecticut, automatically devolving the command on Gen. Samuel Holden Parsons, who became superintendent of construction.[52]

Radière left West Point in March—"the Americans had forced West Point upon him and now they were trying to tell him how to build the fort as well"[53]—to vent his Gallic obstinacy on Washington and Congress. But he returned in April. Also present was thirty-two-year-old Col. Thaddeus Kosciuszko, the Polish engineer who had fortified Bemis Heights at Saratoga for Gen. Gates. But the man of the hour was Thomas Machin, whose genius put new heart into the West Point project. Again he was given the task of spanning the river with a giant chain, the massive links of which were fashioned at the Sterling Ironworks. On the last day of April, relying on his experiences at Fort Montgomery, Machin succeeded in floating the Great Chain across the Hudson on log rafts and anchoring it securely on the West Point and Constitution Island. Several of the Great Chain's links are memorialized on Trophy Point at the United State Military Academy.[54]

On July 16, 1778, the new defensive works at West Point were examined for the first time by George Washington, who was greeted by an unprofessionally timed thirteen-gun salute by Fort Arnold's artillerymen. Col. Kosciuszko had the honor of escorting the commander-

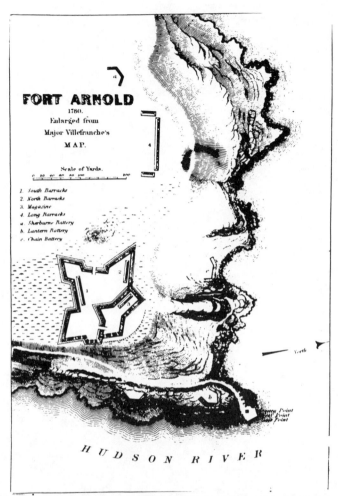

FORT ARNOLD (FORT CLINTON) PLAN. From Boynton's *History of West Point. Courtesy of USMA Library*

FORT PUTNAM, WEST POINT (LOOKING NORTHEAST)
Courtesy of National Archives

FORT PUTNAM, WEST POINT
U.S. Army Photograph. *Courtesy of USMA Library*

in-chief on the tour of inspection (Duportail, Washington's chief engineer, was absent). Washington was evidently pleased with what he saw and complimented the Polish engineer.

West Point became the grand citadel and the key position in the Hudson Highlands. Constitution Island, on the east shore, became the supporting defense, protecting the chain and boom (installed below the chain in late June) and offering the island's fire power against enemy naval forces.

All of West Point's works were initially constructed of a hodgepodge of materials since there was not enough time to have them built of masonry. Eventually, through the years, some of the defenses were reconstructed of masonry.[55]

The river's barriers were guarded by the Walter Battery and Battery Knox. Around the Point and lining the shore were Chain, Lanthorn, Green, and South Batteries. Above, on the Point's plain (still called the Plain) stood Fort Arnold (renamed Fort Clinton in 1780) and Sherburne's Redoubt. To the southwest, high amid the rocky crags, was Fort Putnam (named for Rufus Putnam) on Crown Hill, with fourteen pieces

FORT PUTNAM, WEST POINT
U.S. Army Photograph. *Courtesy of USMA Library*

of artillery, looming over Forts Webb, Wyllys, and Meigs, from north to south in that order, and protecting Fort Arnold from enemy assault from the south and west. West Point's artillery complement consisted of nearly sixty cannon, with about fifteen guns not yet mounted, most of them taken at Saratoga in 1777.[56]

The construction of Redoubts One, Two, Three, and Four was initiated during the week following Anthony Wayne's brilliant *coup de main* at Stony Point on July 16, 1779. Washington moved his headquarters from New Windsor to West Point; the citadel was to be protected by his entire army. He suspected that Sir Henry Clinton might attempt a retaliatory attack up the Hudson, in which case West Point could very well be in the thick of a crucial battle. During a critical inspection tour of the works, Washington saw the need for greater depth in the defenses, with particular emphasis on a long ridge to the west and southwest of and higher than Fort Putnam.[57] He ordered that overlooking elevation be fortified without delay, thus initiating the construction of the four additional redoubts.[58]

Thus within a week of Washington's arrival at West Point, the

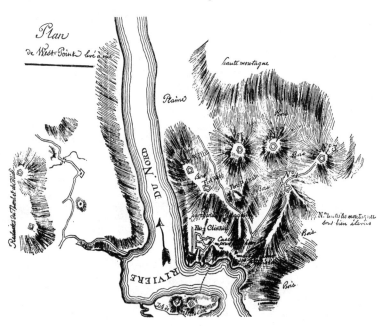

FRENCH PLAN OF WEST POINT DEFENSES
From *Magazine of American History* (April 1880).

fortress reached the greatest limit of its expansion. Every defensive position had been planned. From then until war's end those several works would be improved and maintained, but no new ones would be erected. Sixteen enclosed positions and ten major battery sites formed three roughly concentric defensive rings around the great chain. Each fort was capable both of defending itself and providing support by fire to its neighbors. No more formidable a position had ever been seen in the New World. . . . [In comparison with the European tradition of constructing single massive fortresses], West Point, the Gibraltar of America, was a prototype, a forerunner of things to come.[59]

The concentration of engineers on West Point's defenses precluded any attention to the refortification of Constitution Island, at least for a time. It was indeed ironical that nearly three years earlier the island had been considered the bulwark of the Highlands defense to the exclusion of West Point. In 1778 there was a complete reversal—Constitution Island was practically eclipsed by the intensive focus on West Point. A month after Capt. Thomas Machin and his crews successfully laid the Great Chain, Col. John Greaton's Massachusetts regiment was ordered by Gen. Parsons to begin new batteries on the island on May 31. There was, however, only one fortification built, Greaton's Battery on the site of the old Gravel Hill Battery.

Duportail proved to be a good engineer, despite his proclivity for needling Congress to advance himself and his compatriot engineers to higher ranks. In the autumn of 1778 he clearly perceived that West Point, without the refortification of Constitution Island, would be ineffectual as a guardian over the closing of the Hudson River—"together they were mutually reinforcing." He conceived the addition of three small redoubts and another battery on the island. One of the redoubts, to hold about sixty men, was constructed on the site of Romans' two-story blockhouse, to immediately defend both the chain and its eastern anchor.[60] North and South Redoubts, approximately two miles south-southeast of the island, on the way to Continental Village, were constructed on two sides of a hill, near today's town of Garrison.

The Hard Winter of 1779/80, the most severe in recorded American history, for many days froze almost all human activity to a standstill between Canada and Chesapeake Bay. As miserable as the weather had been in December—several heavy snowfalls, freezing rain, and gale winds—it became unbearable during the first seven weeks of 1780. On January 2, a Sunday, West Point and environs were suddenly enveloped by a furious blizzard raging down from the Arctic. Temperatures dropped so fast that even watercraft, caught in midstream, were iced into immobility and Hudson's River froze solid all the way to the Atlantic.

West Point's commissary began to run short. Bread, the army's staff of life, was not to be had; plentiful wheat could not be ground into flour because mill wheels were congealed into ice-sculptured stillness. Christmas for the men was a bleak holiday. Soldiers were jammed into the bombproofs of Forts Arnold and Putnam, unfinished barracks, and huts, and yet there were still many men in tents. First McDougall, then Gen. Heath grappled with the critical problems of extremely short rations, insufficient clothing, and the lack of winter shelters.

The horrible weather, foul living conditions, and impending starvation combined to foment a mutiny on New Year's Day. That morning about a hundred Massachusetts men, insisting that their enlistments had expired and ignoring the remonstrances of officers, set out for home. They did not get far. Two officers with a large body of loyal troops pursued the mutineers and marched them back. The punishment, tempered by knowledge of the causes that inspired the mutiny, was relatively light, with only the ringleaders meriting a hundred lashes while the others were absolved of all guilt. There were some few men, not among these mutineers, whose enlistments did expire, but they could not go home because they were inadequately clothed against the fierce elements.

Living conditions became an extreme cruelty after practically all the tents blew away. Men slept in shifts, in the same foul-smelling bunks. Clothing was swapped back and forth as the men took turns going out for rations or firewood. Fire within the shelters was an absolute necessity but the emergency-built chimneys were unable to withstand the demands of continuously roaring fireplaces. On January 9 a portion of North Redoubt burned and total destruction was averted only by the reckless bravery of the men who carried barrels of powder out of danger and labored to halt the spread of the flames. During the night of January 26, a large barracks on West Point's plain went up in flames. Gen. Heath instituted through-the-night inspection watches by officers and men to prevent recurrences. The last reported fire occurred later that winter: North Redoubt again caught fire and burned for two days before the flames were put out.

Apparently the spell of George Washington's steadfastness was over the Hudson Highlands on his birthday in 1780, when a thawing rain began to descend and the temperature started to rise precipitately. A week later, on March 1, the Hudson ice broke and the continuous cracking explosions reverberated among the hills. This portent of spring, unfortunately, was not witnessed by many of West Point's garrison. Starvation had nurtured the usual camp diseases and, with the men living in their own filth, contagion spread through all the barracks. The wasted bodies of the dead, denuded of all clothing to satisfy the needs of the living, were interred in the rock-hard earth of the small cemetery, the site of which is now, ironically enough, occupied by Washington Hall, today's Cadet Dining Hall.[61]

Inside the old Cadet Chapel at the Academy are black marble shields inscribed in gold letters with the name, rank, and dates of birth and death of the senior American generals in the Revolution. One shield has all of the inscription chiseled out except "Major General" and "1741." Maj. Gen. Benedict Arnold, great-grandson of a Benedict Arnold who had been a royal governor of Rhode Island, was born in Norwich, Connecticut on January 14, 1741.

There was no doubt about Arnold's ability: he was one of the best field commanders in the history of this nation's military forces. Though Washington went out of his way to see his "whirlwind hero" obtain the recognition he deserved, the Continental Congress continually kept him off promotion lists. Revolutionary generals were required to keep accounts, justifying every Continental dollar spent feeding their men and equipping them. Arnold, hating the demeaning job of "keeping books," was almost always unable to account to Congress for monies expended. Beset by personal financial problems brought on by his high living style, possessed by an avarice to get rich quickly, and for other reasons, Arnold determined to find his military destiny on the British side. He and the enemy's high command came to a tentative understanding through intermediaries: Arnold was to get twenty thousand British pounds for surrendering West Point. Command of the Hudson Highlands was the key to the conspiracy and in August 1780 Arnold won it. From that time until the dramatic exposure of his treachery, Arnold did all in his power to undermine first Kosciuszko's endeavors, then engineer Villefranche's efforts to strengthen Washington's "Key to America."

For fifteen months Arnold had been dealing through go-betweens with Maj. John André, Gen. Sir Henry Clinton's talented adjutant. During the British occupation of Philadelphia, André often visited the Shippen household. History hints at his romantic interest in teenager Margaret Shippen, youngest daughter of Tory Edward Shippen. Peggy Shippen in April 1779 became Arnold's second wife,[62] and her Tory sympathies undoubtedly influenced Arnold to finally seek his fortune with the enemy.

The time had come for a face-to-face meeting to settle final details and for Arnold to hand over the plans of West Point. André came up the river on the British armed sloop *Vulture*, anchoring off Teller's Point on September 17. After two aborted appointments, he met Arnold on the night of September 21/22 in the woods south of Stony Point. Toward dawn the two men rode to the home of Joshua Hett Smith, staunch Patriot and unsuspecting participant in the conspiracy, who lived near Haverstraw not far south of King's Ferry.

Lieut. Col. James Livingston, commander of the American battery on Teller's Point, had been waiting impatiently three days for a stilled wind. At first morning light on that day of the twenty-second, Livingston had his two four-pounders begin firing at the becalmed *Vulture*. Arnold and André, watching from a second-story window of the Smith house, were dismayed spectators of the action. The sloop, stalled in midstream and ineffectually responding with its own guns, was a fine sitting target for the American guns. After thirty minutes of allowing his ship to be splintered by enemy shot and shell, the *Vulture's* commander had his ship towed downstream by longboats.

With the *Vulture* now out of reach, Arnold made arrangements to have Smith guide André through the American lines on the east side of the river while he returned to his residence near West Point. Smith took André to a point fifteen miles north of White Plains, leaving the British officer to make it alone through the unfriendly countryside. Just north of Tarrytown André, using the alias of "John Anderson," was captured by three so-called volunteer militiamen, who searched him and found the incriminating evidence of the West Point plot. Arnold heard the astounding news over breakfast on Monday morning. He at once made his excuses to his meal companions, went to his Tory wife, related the disastrous news, ran to his barge, and headed downstream to the *Vulture*.

Washington, en route to West Point, arrived half an hour later. Not until about six hours after Arnold's escape did Washington and his officers learn the essential facts of the conspiracy. Arnold's treason was, by all odds, Washington's greatest disillusionment. Gathering his wits, he did not shirk his immediate duty. He at once ordered Alexander Hamilton and Maj. James McHenry to take up the pursuit of Arnold, on the possible chance that the traitor had been delayed in his flight. That night Washington, unaware that Sir Henry Clinton would not initiate an attack until André's return to New York City, ordered all West Point's defenses reinforced.

Despite Sir Henry's entreaties, André was tried, convicted, and hanged as a spy at Tappan, New York. In 1821 his remains were taken to Westminister Abbey, where George III had had a monument erected to his memory. Benedict Arnold, after serving briefly against his fellow Americans, took his family to England in 1781. He suffered disdain from the British and hatred from the Americans, penury, bitterness, and recurrent bouts of melancholia. He died in 1801 and was interred in a crypt in St. Mary's Church located on the Thames River waterfront in south London. In an effort to vindicate his memory, his four sons entered the British army, one of them earning the rank of lieutenant general.

The name of America's "whirlwind hero" of the Revolution, even a score of years before his death, was stricken from the official register of the officers in the United States Army. For five years Revolutionary Americans had taken Arnold into their hearts; in the space of one brief moment on the page of history, popular patriotic glorification of Arnold the Hero had turned into deep-dyed hatred of Arnold the Traitor. Today

WEST POINT ON THE HUDSON
Courtesy of New York State Department of Commerce

there is a group of six hundred Americans called the Arnold Society seeking to clear Arnold's name. On November 15, 1975, representatives of the society met a number of Arnold's English descendants at his tomb. A wreath was laid and the eulogy was delivered by the society's president.[63]

West Point remained inviolate. The Revolution's major battlegrounds shifted to Virginia and the Carolinas. The American-French victory over

Cornwallis at Yorktown spelled the beginning of the end of Britain's efforts to subjugate her rebellious colonial cousins in America.

> Many of the factors that fettered the Patriots throughout the War of Independence are nowhere better illustrated than in the painfully frustrating but eventually successful exertions to protect Henry Hudson's River. Inexperienced leadership, lack of military know-how, a shortage of funds and equipment, a dearth of professional engineers, and near-ruinous political interference are only some of the difficulties faced by those responsible for the prosecution of the defenses. Not surprisingly, many of the reasons for ultimate American victory are neatly evidenced in the story of the ultimately successful defense of the Hudson: the steadfastness of George Washington; British blunders; assistance from foreign powers; the difficulty of campaigning in eighteenth-century America; and a smile from Lady Luck. . . . The long travail and eventual success at West Point mirrored the larger struggle and the greater victory of the Thirteen Colonies.[64]

The evolution of the prestigious United States Military Academy from the Revolutionary fortress of West Point did not come about overnight. In October 1776 Congress had directed a group of men "to prepare a plan for establishing a Continental laboratory and a military academy," but, as with many inefficient Patriot committees, nothing was done about the idea. During the early throes of constructing West Point's battlements, Washington clearly saw the overpowering need for an American military academy. There was a lesson to be learned from Revolutionary America's abject solicitation of foreign military expertise. During those first months Washington initiated the innovation of "academic and practical research and study," though with unproductive results.[65]

In July 1777 Congress established what was called the Corps of Invalids, initially an organization to care for disabled veterans unfit for duty in the field but serviceable in a limited capacity, to become the nucleus of "a military school for young gentlemen." In reality, it was meant to be "a school for propagating military knowledge and discipline." After four years of caretaking-guard duties in the larger urban areas, these handicapped men were escorted to their permanent station at West Point in 1781. These invalids constituted West Point's first faculty.[66]

In 1790 West Point legally became a government property. Through the efforts of Henry Knox, Secretary of War, and Alexander Hamilton, Secretary of the Treasury, Congress appropriated $11,085 to be paid to Stephen Moore, the actual proprietor of the fortress of West Point. Time and again during the next decade proposals for a military academy were eliminated from the national budget by Congress, but concessions in

1794 were made for the provision of books and instruments and the selection of a small number of cadets from the few regular army companies to be housed at first in the old Revolutionary jail at West Point. At the same time engineers began the reconstruction of Forts Clinton (Arnold) and Putnam, heightening their walls and sinking their magazines even deeper; but the work was halted when Congress cut off funds. During the next eight years it was a verbal battle between the old military stalwarts and Congress.

VIEW OF HUDSON RIVER FROM FORT PUTNAM, WEST POINT
U.S. Army Photograph. *Courtesy of USMA Library.*

Finally, on March 16, 1802, Congress did authorize a Corps of Engineers, to include ten cadets with a provision for ten additional men. The act specified that the Corps "shall be stationed at West Point, in the State of New York, and shall constitute a military academy." Operations began, appropriately enough, on July 4, 1802. Three months later its first class of two men graduated. This slight beginning evolved into what is now the most honored military academy in the world.[67]

The landmark atop the granite eminence above the academy, Fort Putnam, was rebuilt in 1908/10. Now, in our era of the nation's bicentennial, reconstruction of the fort and a comprehensive plan to develop the site have been initiated.[68]

Continental Village
near Peekskill, Putnam County

To add to Washington's tribulations, the British twice during the year 1777 descended in force on his collection point and depot for munitions near the entrance to the Highlands. The Patriots late in 1776 had turned the Hudson River village of Peekskill, with more than fifty habitations, into a vast storehouse. Three miles to the north was Continental Village, an army community designed to hold two thousand troops that held much of the Americans' armaments, powder, and equipment. During the winter of 1776/77, Gen. William Howe made plans to capture and destroy the rebel arsenal to atone for his less-than-successful campaign of the past year.

Late on Friday night, March 21, Howe embarked a force of five hundred troops, under the command of Lieut. Col. Bird, aboard a frigate and transports. Late in the afternoon of the next day, the British destructives anchored their vessels near Teller's Point. On Sunday, shortly after daybreak, the flotilla resumed its course upriver, to arrive at Peekskill and debark its troops at about noontime.

Gen. Alexander McDougall, commandant of Peekskill and Continental Village, had been informed on Saturday of the approach of the enemy, estimated at about a thousand men by Patriot scouts. With only a small garrison, McDougall felt that he could not justify any kind of a defense. What munitions and supplies could not be speedily transported out were set afire, and the Americans evacuated the depot area to take shelter on the Albany Post Road to the north.

While the British raiders did not pursue, their derisive hoots followed the fleeting rebels. When Fort Constitution learned of the incursion some four hours later, the warning beacon was set ablaze. George Clinton, about to become New York's first governor under a new constitution, spotted the signal from his residence in New Windsor and hurriedly called up three regiments of militia to reinforce Constitution Island and Fort Montgomery. By midafternoon, however, it had become evident to the Patriots that the British had planned no more than a raid. Howe's troops, after completing the destruction of the depot, reboarded their transports and departed downriver.

At his Morristown headquarters Washington expressed his wrath over the lack of American opposition and was greatly puzzled as to why the depot's garrison was undermanned. He sent off a letter to the President of the Continental Congress, degrading in no uncertain terms the value of militia troops.

On October 9, after Sir Henry Clinton's capture of the principal Patriot forts in the Highlands, the British commander dispatched ex-Governor William Tryon with a force of regulars and Hessians to Peekskill (Fort Independence) to destroy the "rebel settlement" of Continental Village. To make certain the success of the mission, Clinton also had a British force sent up from Verplanck's Point to assist Tryon.

Upon their arrival they found the Patriot depot deserted. Instead of a stubborn rebel defense, they found a train of wagons loaded with valuable military stores, warehouses crammed to the rafters, and newly built barracks to accommodate about fifteen hundred men. Despite a heavy rain that slowed down demolition, the British put the torch to what public stores they could not take with them.

Crown Point and Ticonderoga
Lake Champlain, Essex County

In the year 1608, when the English had established a permanent settlement on the James River in Virginia and Samuel de Champlain had settled his tiny French colony at Quebec, the water corridor formed by Lake Champlain, Lake George, and the Hudson River was a strategic thoroughfare connecting the Algonquin wilderness of eastern Canada with the Iroquois domain to the south. For centuries the Champlain route was an Indian battleground and the rivalry for its control was greatly intensified when Europeans came to the New World. It is doubtful that any other territory of the same area in the world had so long been the stage for barbaric warfare and ambassadorial disputes.

European wars between England and France were reflected by their counterparts in North America: War of the Grand Alliance (1689-97) or King William's War; War of the Spanish Succession (1702-13) or Queen Anne's War; War of the Austrian Succession (1745-48) or King George's War; and the Seven Years' War (1754-60) or the French and Indian War. The first decade of the eighteenth century saw New France's and England's territorial expansion courses temporarily halted. The 1713 Treaty of Utrecht side stepped the touchy problem of establishing the boundary between New France and the American Colonies, with England and France claiming territorial rights to the same strategic area incorporating the water corridor.

During the comparatively peaceful years between Queen Anne's War and King George's War, both governments expanded their spheres of influence and settlement. New France pushed new settlements as far south as Crown Point and by the year 1732 had established twenty-five seigneuries along the shores of Lake Champlain, thus conceiving the need for a strong fortification in the Crown Point district. French military men had perceived that as one sailed up the lake, the first restriction in the course of the waterway was the ideal site for a fortress that would command the passage of all vessels. At this point the lake is only one-half mile wide.

Persistent requests for defenses on the lake finally bore fruit. Louis XV granted approval for a new fort at Pointe de la Chevelure, a tiny peninsula on the eastern or Vermont shore, opposite Crown Point. The English later knew this place as Chimney Point. The royal commission was received in the spring of 1731, with construction commencing at once; the fort was completed in September. Its first garrison consisted of two officers and twenty men, augmented during the summer. The semi-permanent fort was four-sided, about one hundred feet square, with the usual bastions in the four angles.

There was a revision in French military thinking. A joint letter, penned by New France's governor and the Intendant, requested a royal commission for a much stronger work, to be built on the western shore of the lake. The design recommended called for a four-storied stone machicolated tower or redoubt, loopholed for cannon, which they claimed would be more economical to construct and would have the advantage of protection for the armaments, which otherwise would be at the mercy of the elements on the ramparts of the conventional palisaded fort. In addition, a drawbridge and a portcullis were suggested.

The plan was approved and construction started in 1735. The move to the western bank, despite the much better military position at Pointe de la Chevelure, was apparently motivated by a virgin limestone quarry at Crown Point, providing the needed material for the tower. Almost from the very beginning, the original plan was amended to include stone walls, surrounded by a walled-in ditch or moat.[1]

Peter Kalm, during his visit to Crown Point in 1749, observed that the fort was erected on a huge limestock rock, and described it as being nearly square, with

> high thick walls made of the same limestone. . . . On the eastern part of the fort, is a high tower, which is proof against bombshells, provided with cannon from the bottom almost to the very top; and the governor [commandant] lives in the tower.[2]

The post was named Fort St. Frederic for Frederic Maurepas,

RUINS OF FORT ST. FREDERIC (1731-59), CROWN POINT
(North end [left] and west side)
Courtesy of National Park Service

Secretary of State. By 1737 the main work was completed, but the fort was still without parapets three years later. The men lived uncomfortably in the tower until a barracks was constructed about the year 1745 to house the increased garrison of nine officers and seventy-two men. In 1739 a fortified stone windmill was erected about three hundred yards east of the fort. Serving as a flanking outwork, its greatest asset was the fine view, which the fort lacked, of the southern sector of the lake. It was built on what is known today as Windmill Point, where the Champlain monument stands. Lossing describes this structure but mistakenly places it at Chimney Point.

The fort's ordnance in 1743 consisted of twelve four-pounders, an iron two-pounder, two mortars, and thirteen swivels mounted on the parapets, the last group of armament including at least several extremely obsolete guns. The windmill, according to Kalm, served as a redoubt as well as a watch point, and was armed with five or six cannon of small caliber. Apparently sixty-three artillery pieces were the greatest number ever mounted at Fort St. Frederic and the windmill. Kalm observed that the parapeted walls enclosed a barracks, officers' quarters, a hospital, a munitions warehouse, provision sheds, and a chapel to sustain the spiritual needs of the garrison.

Designed by Chaussegros de Lery, a usually competent engineer, the work was ill-conceived as to location and very badly constructed. The contractor was one Janson Lapoline, and most of the blame for the poor workmanship was laid at his door. The walls of the fort began to crumble away a few years after they were erected. French military men were highly critical and declared that the fort was useless as a defense. The consensus was that a new fortification should be erected rather than spending good money on the rapidly disintegrating Fort St. Frederic. Maj. Gen. Francois de Lévis asserted that the fort's inadequate position and its physical condition were responsible for the decision to begin construction of Fort Carillon at Ticonderoga, about twelve miles to the south, in 1755.[3]

The original name of the new fortress was Fort Vaudreuil, for the governor-general of Canada, but was soon renamed Fort Carillon ("a chime of bells") for the sound of the falls where Lake George (Lac St. Sacrement) runs into Lake Champlain.[4] It was erected on the classic lines laid down earlier by the celebrated French military engineer, Sebastien LePrestre de Vauban, in his *Traité des Sièges,* a treatise on military science first published at Paris in 1714. The works consisted of an ingenious system of redoubts, parapets, a terreplein, a glacis, two demilunes, and a *place d'armes,* constructed by Michel Cartier, who was afterwards honored as the Marquis de Lotbinìere. The fort, renamed Fort Ticonderoga in 1759, was later touted as "The Key to the Continent."

The French and Indian War began on July 4, 1754, when George Washington's tiny stockade, Fort Necessity, fell to the French. Official war, however, was not declared for another two years. Indeed, the American Colonies, had they been more amenable to cooperation among themselves, could have conquered Canada many years earlier. In 1754 the numerical superiority in population of the Colonies was twenty times that of French Canada, whose economy was primarily based on the fur trade.[6]

The northern provinces had daggers pointed at their hearts with the establishment of the French forts. The dilatory exercises in the high echelons of the colonial governments—petty differences and jealousy, the disorderly practice of making separate treaties with the Indians, and the fear of the home government's arming its colonial subjects—allowed the French to advance ever southward. Francis Parkman discusses the constriction of the Colonies in their little sphere:

In the interest of that practical independence which they had so much at heart, two conditions were essential to the colonists. The one was a field for expansion, and the other was mutual help. Their first necessity was to rid themselves of the French, who, by shutting them between the Alleghenies and the sea, would cramp them into perpetual littleness. With France on their backs, growing while they had no room to grow, they must remain in helpless wardship, dependent on England, whose aid they would always need; but with the West open before them, their future was their own. King and Parliament would respect perforce the will of a people spread from the ocean to the Mississippi, and united in action as in aims. But in the middle of the last century the vision of the ordinary colonist rarely reached so far. The immediate victory over a governor, however slight the point at issue, was more precious in his eyes than the remote though decisive advantage which he saw but dimly. . . . The Home Government, on its part, was but half-hearted in the wish that they should unite in opposition to the common enemy. It was very willing that the several provinces should give money and men, but not that they should acquire military habits and a dangerous capacity of acting together.[7]

Relegated to secondary importance and used as a depot after Fort Carillon was completed, Crown Point was the base that unleashed frequent little sorties against the northern Colonies. Raids on occasion were made by French-allied Indians alone, but more often led by Canadian officers accompanied by a small number of regulars. Despite this constant threat on the northern frontier, Fort St. Frederic was never assaulted or even seriously threatened by the English or the colonists. Because of conflicts among the provincial governments, no cooperation was possible, and no plan to take Crown Point was devised until the spring of 1755, months before Fort Carillon was started by Lotbinière. In a letter dated Alexandria, Virginia, April 19, 1755, Gen. Edward Braddock wrote to Robert Napier, Adjutant General, concerning an expedition against Fort St. Frederic:

I also settled with the Governors present a plan for the Reduction of Crown Point which is to be undertaken by provincial Troops alone, rais'd in the Northern Colonies to the Number of about four thousand four hundred to be commanded by Col. [William] Johnson a person particularly qualify'd for it by his Knowledge of those parts, his great Influence over the Six Nations and the universal opinion they have of him in the Northern Colonies: I am to supply him with an Engineer [William Eyre].[8]

Johnson's expedition stopped at the head of Lake George, defeated the French under Baron Dieskau, and built Fort William Henry. The French had had ample warning. Dieskau, a German veteran of European battlefields, with two hundred French regulars, seven hundred Canadians, and six hundred Indians, was sent to Crown Point, where he obtained provisions for his army. He then set out to attack Fort Lyman (Fort Edward) at the Great Carrying Place to head off Johnson, but got only as far as the southern end of Lake George where French scouts spotted elements of Johnson's provincial army.

Dieskau set up an ambush, taking the British by surprise. During this initial action of the Battle of Lake George, September 8, 1755, Chief Hendrick of the Mohawks and Col. Ephraim Williams were killed. Had the French and their allies been more effectively organized and cognizant of the situation, there is reason to believe that Johnson's troops would have suffered a disastrous defeat. While the French were busy congratulating themselves, Johnson had barricades erected and brought forward a number of cannon. Dieskau's Indians, having no stomach for canister and grape, vanished into the woods. The French were badly mauled and Gen. Dieskau, badly wounded, was taken prisoner.

Johnson neglected to take advantage of the victory by pursuing the remnants of the enemy force to Crown Point and taking Fort St. Frederic. The commander, shot through the thigh at the beginning of the fight, was resting in his tent at the height of the battle. He was afterwards highly complimented by the home government, made a baronet, and awarded five thousand pounds by Parliament.

As a substitute for the capture of Crown Point, Johnson built Fort William Henry on a bluff just outside the present town of Lake George, at the head of Lac St. Sacrement, which he promptly renamed Lake George. On September 10, two days after the battle, the soldiers were put to work throwing up earthworks and felling trees for the palisades. In orders for November 8, to mark the completion of the fortification, Gen. Johnson said that the new fort would be named in honor of a grandson of King George II, and that Fort Lyman thereafter would be called Fort Edward for another grandson of the king.

In the summer of 1756, another provincial force was congregated at the head of Lake George for assaults against Ticonderoga and Crown Point, but it never got started. During the early days of August 1757, Montcalm invested Fort William Henry and forced its capitulation. Lieut. Col. George Munro surrendered more than twenty-one hundred men who were attacked by French-allied Indians, eventuating in a massacre.

Early in June 1758 Gen. James Abercromby, after frustrating delays, had gathered at Lake George the mightiest military force ever seen on the continent. His adversary, the brilliant Marquis de Montcalm, was entrenched before Fort Carillon (almost completed), with only thirty-one hundred toops. Abercromby, a political appointee with little or no ability as a military commander, depended almost entirely on his talented second in command, Brig. Gen. Lord Howe, who was considered by Gen. James Wolfe to be "the noblest Englishman that has appeared in my time, and the best soldier in the British Army." The entire campaign, up to the point of the initial skirmish with the French, had been directed by Howe.[9]

On July 4 the army embarked in hundreds of whaleboats and bateaux upon Lake George—a brilliant line six miles long, the red coats of the regulars and the plaids of the Highlanders resplendent in the sun. Early in the morning, two days later, the army debarked at a point now known as Howe's Cove, about seven miles from Fort Carillon. At two o'clock they marched in four columns into the dense woods. A French scouting party, numbering about 350 regulars and Canadians, had become lost while endeavoring to return to the fort and encountered the principal column headed by Lord Howe.

In the sharp fighting that immediately erupted, Howe was killed instanteously. The other British columns wheeled about on hearing the firing. The French, surrounded, fought with desperate courage. They were almost wiped out—50 of them managed to escape, but 148 were captured and the remainder killed or drowned while attempting to cross the rapids. The British loss was numerically very small but catastrophic in the death of Lord Howe. As Francis Parkman neatly put it, "The death of one man was the ruin of fifteen thousand."[10]

Howe's death cast a self-defeating gloom over the entire army. Robert Rogers remarked, "The fall of this noble and brave officer seemed to produce an almost general languor and consternation through the whole army." Another contemporary, Maj. Thomas Mante, wrote that with the death of Howe, "the soul of General Abercrombie's army seemed to expire. From the unhappy moment the General was deprived of his advice, neither order nor discipline was observed, and a strange kind of infatuation usurped the place of resolution."[11] Abercromby, for no good reason, ordered the troops back to Howe's Cove.

The next day the British resumed the march and at nightfall camped on the present site of Ticonderoga village. Early on the morning of July 8, a black day in the history of the British Army, Abercromby's regulars and provincials were given the order to attack Montcalm's entrenched line.

Montcalm had debated with himself whether to retire to Crown Point, having been informed by scouts that up to twenty-five thousand British had assembled at the ruins of Fort William Henry. His officers advised against such a retreat. Montcalm, wise in the science of military strategy, then determined not to allow an investment of Fort Carillon by a vastly superior force and chose to fight it out on the point of land where the large numbers of British would have much less room in which to maneuver. Selecting a line about three-quarters of a mile from the fort, he had his men exerting every ounce of their physical powers to throw up earthworks across the whole Ticonderoga peninsula. The defense consisted of trenches, an embankment topped with logs embrasured for cannon, and a dense abatis about one hundred feet from the ditch. By the evening of July 7 the French had completed their defenses and were awaiting the onslaught.[12]

The next day the French magnificently rebuffed wave on wave of Highlanders, Black Watch, Royal Americans, and provincials, with six major attacks in the hours between one and seven o'clock. Comparatively few British penetrated the abatis. The slaughter was terrible that hot, sultry July day. In the final half hour before dusk, the British fired only from the edge of the woods to protect comrades who were dragging off their wounded. Twilight dropped its curtain of uncertain obscurity, the battlefield became strangely quiet, and only the dead were left between the lines of the two armies.[13]

In the gathering darkness, ineffectual and despondent Abercromby withdrew with 13,000 men, leaving the field of battle to the French. His losses totaled 1,944 killed, wounded, and missing, ''in one of the most incredible incidents of bravery and stupidity in the annals of the British army,'' while the French officially reported only 377 casualties.[14]

Montcalm, overjoyed and indulging in excusable overstatement, wrote his wife:

> Without Indians, almost without Canadians or colony troops—I had only four hundred—alone with Levis and Bourlamaque and the troops of the line, thirty-one hundred fighting men, I have beaten an army of twenty-five thousand. They repassed the lake precipitately, with a loss of at least five thousand.[15]

In the same vein of excitement, he wrote a friend:

> What a day for France! If I had had two hundred Indians to send out at the head of a thousand picked men under the Chevalier de Levis, not a man would have escaped. Ah, my dear Doreil, what soldiers are ours! I never saw the like. Why were they not at Louisbourg?[16]

William Pitt, from his seat of power in England, recalled comatose Abercromby and replaced him with energetic and imaginative Jeffrey Amherst. Pitt conceived the campaign for 1759, ordering an assault from all directions against Canada. While Quebec was being attacked by

Wolfe, a determined effort should be made to enter New France by way of Ticonderoga and Crown Point. Should the Lake George-Lake Champlain gateway be unattainable, it would still have the effect of a strong diversion and would no doubt enhance Wolfe's chances. Pitt also instructed Amherst to conjure an additional threat, without endangering the main objectives of the campaign. The new commander-in-chief conceived the capture of Fort Niagara by entrusting that venture to able Brig. Gen. John Prideaux. Simultaneously, Oswego and its battered bastion of Fort Ontario were to be reoccupied and serve as a base for the Niagara campaign. Amherst himself would lead the assault against the gateway to Montreal—Forts Carillon and St. Frederic.[17]

Late in June Amherst had congregated at Fort William Henry's ruins more than eleven thousand regulars and provincials. He served notice that he would not countenance abridgments of discipline, malingering, or attempted desertions. The provincials, mostly independent-minded backwoodsmen and farmers unaccustomed to restricted camp routine, were often insubordinate. Floggings were a daily occurrence and once in a while a recruit was shot as an example to others.

Amherst, never one to have his bridges burned behind him, had the sixteen-mile military road to Fort Edward widened and, for the whole distance, a broad band of woods on both sides cut down and burned, thus depriving the enemy of undercover. Several guard posts, at intervals of three or four miles, were erected along the road. Amherst's precautions included the construction of Fort George on the site of Sir William Johnson's entrenched camp after his victory over Dieskau four years earlier,[18] and Fort Gage (for Gen. Thomas Gage, serving under Lord Amherst) on a knoll facing east, in the present vicinity of Luzerne and Lake George Roads.

On July 21, a Saturday, Amherst's army of 5,743 regulars and about the same number of provincials embarked on its historic sail down Lake George. Intelligence reports did not reveal the fact that the French garrison at Ticonderoga had been much reduced. Montcalm had left to mount the defense of Quebec, leaving Gen. Bourlamaque in command of Fort Carillon.

On the morning of July 22, the British invested the French fort. The French commander soon realized that he would be starved out and captured within two weeks. He determined to evacuate the fort after a few days' show of spirited defense. Bourlamaque left Gen. Hebecourt with four hundred of the garrison to continue a semblance of resistance and, with the rest of his troops, retreated to Fort St. Frederic and, eventually, to Isle-aux-Noix.

Amherst, methodically advancing his parallels, was within six

FORT TICONDEROGA
Courtesy of New York State Department of Commerce

FORT TICONDEROGA
Courtesy of New York State Department of Commerce

hundred yards of Fort Carillon's ramparts when the command was relinquished to Hebecourt who, for almost three days, maintained a heavy artillery fire against the British lines. On the third night he evacuated the fort, set the works on fire, and left a lighted fuse directed toward the powder magazine located in the southeast bastion. The summer night sky soon became suffused with the red glow of Fort Carillon going up in flames. Then the magazine exploded with a tremendous roar, raining shattered rock on the British.

The French retreated to Crown Point, mined the works of Fort St. Frederic, and blew them up. The first to go was the fortified windmill, the explosion of which ruptured the fuse to the fort's powder magazine. A courageous French volunteer, whose identity has been lost in the mists of history, reentered the works to rekindle the fuse. Before he could make a precipitous exit from the immediate environs, the charge went off, raining debris all about him, but he escaped with only a few bruises. Hebecourt and his men made it to Isle-aux-Noix, where he joined

FORT TICONDEROGA
Courtesy of New York State Department of Commerce

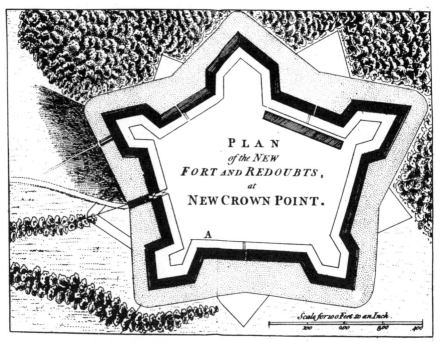

BRITISH PLAN OF FORT CROWN POINT
Courtesy of National Map Collection, Public Archives of Canada

Bourlamaque. Scarcely anything recognizable remains of the fort today, except the foundations of the walls and the base of the redoubt.

Amherst at once ordered the repair of Fort Carillon, which he renamed Fort Ticonderoga. Plans to take Crown Point were dropped immediately when he learned from his scouts on August 1 that the French had wrecked Fort St. Frederic.[19] The northern Colonies were jubilant. Their cup of joy was full to overflowing when Gen. Amherst delegated Maj. Robert Rogers to act out the last offensive of the 1759 campaign by attacking and massacring the French-allied St. Francis Indians sixteen days after Quebec capitulated.[20] The attack and historic retreat are memorialized in the popular *Northwest Passage* by Kenneth Roberts.

The French elsewhere also found 1759 to be a disastrous year in their fortunes. Their homeland was effectively blockaded by the English fleet, unable to succor Canada with men and arms. French posts in India and Guadeloupe in the West Indies were captured. They sustained severe losses on the battlefield at Minden, Germany, and in the decisive naval engagement near Brest, France. The French empire was fast slipping into oblivion.

Amherst was content to remain at Crown Point for the winter. Fort St. Frederic was deemed an irreparable loss. The Crown Point peninsula, with an average width of one mile, jutting out into Lake Champlain, had important strategic potentiality, and Gen. Amherst fully appreciated its position. He commenced the construction of a new and extensive fortification about two hundred yards southwest of the French fort's ruins, upon a site that afforded a much greater command of the lake.

The fort was immense, about the same size as historic Fort Pitt at the Forks of the Ohio. The home and colonial governments lavished the extraordinary sum of $10 million on its construction (never fully completed). It had been estimated that in the first two years nearly three thousand men were employed on the stone barracks and the walls. The truly impressive ramparts of solid masonry were 25 feet thick and nearly the same in height. The length of the curtains varied from 52 to 100 yards, and the whole circuit along the ramparts, including the bastions, was 853 yards, just under half a mile. A broad ditch, chiseled out of the solid limestone, circled the entire works. The limestone fragments excavated from the ditch were used to construct the revetting and the four rows of barracks within the walls. The north wall had a gate, with a covered way leading from the northeast bastion to the lake. Within this bastion a well was sunk, almost eight feet in diameter and ninety feety deep, thus furnishing the garrison with an ample supply of water. At the time of its conception, the fort was called Fort Amherst, but later the name was changed to Fort Crown Point. The fort was tremendous, three times the size of Fort Ticonderoga. British military men who visited the place gazed in wonderment at the circumferential extent of the works that enclosed the six-and-a-half-acre parade ground.[21]

After the evacuation of the civilian French, a new English settlement was established outside the towering walls of the fort and the land felt the teeth of the harrow again. The general store was run by one Hugh White, while the tavern was kept by a Mr. Lewis. The apothecary, Thomas Sparham, was married to the daughter of Adolphis Benzel, resident engineer at the fort. The blacksmith, a man named Gilfoil, was an ingenious character who occasionally strayed on the wrong side of the law. His most lucrative practice was counterfeiting, stamping out from brass trunk straps round discs called "Gilfoil's coppers," fourteen of them equal to one shilling and accepted locally as legal tender.[22]

For nearly sixteen years, from 1759 to 1775, life was tranquil at Forts Crown Point and Ticonderoga, except for an accidental catastrophe to the former. Though garrisons were maintained at both places, there is a sparsity of records reporting the activities during this period. Fort Ticonderoga was apparently used as a storehouse for military supplies while major activities were centered at Crown Point. Maj. Gavin Cochrane commanded for four years and was replaced by Maj. Thomas James who, in 1765, was dispatched to New York to assist in the enforcement of the Stamp Act. Detachments of the Sixtieth Regiment and the Royal American Regiment of Foot were stationed at both posts.

During the peaceful interlude, the works at Crown Point and Ticonderoga were allowed to deteriorate. On February 15, 1767, Sir Guy Carleton, lieutenant governor of Canada, wrote from Montreal to Gen. Thomas Gage: "The forts of Crown Point and Ticonderoga are in a very declining condition. . . . Should you approve of keeping up these posts, it will be best to repair them as soon as possible."[23]

In April 1773, two years before Lexington and Concord, disaster struck Crown Point. A fire broke out and the powder magazine exploded and seriously damaged the entire works, destroying the barracks. The garrison and the great guns were moved to Ticonderoga while an investigation was initiated to determine the cause of the fire and assess the damage. Simultaneously, military engineers went to work and drew up plans for rebuilding the fort.[24]

Early in 1775 Maj. Philip Skene of Skenesborough (now Whitehall, New York) was appointed lieutenant governor of Crown Point and Ticonderoga. His administrative post was short-lived for he was captured on his return from England after the beginning of hostilities and imprisoned as an active Loyalist. He was afterwards freed in a prisoner exchange and served with Burgoyne during his disastrous campaign in 1777.[25]

Initial clashes between the British military and the citizenry were preliminaries to the shooting incidents in two little Massachusetts villages in April 1775. For months some hope was held by both sides that a reconciliation could be effected. In May, three weeks after Lexington and Concord, when the New York Committee of One Hundred inquired what steps should be taken if British troops entered New York City, the Congress in Philadelphia replied that on no account should the people try to stop the entry of the redcoats; that the troops be permitted to occupy barracks but not be allowed to construct fortifications or impede the free passage of citizens; that force of arms should be exercised only if the military violated the people's rights. The Committee interpreted this to mean that on no account should the people take the law into their own hands and confiscate military property belonging to the Crown.[26]

The ink was hardly dry on the letter of instructions regarding civil behavior when two New England groups, one led by Ethan Allen, backwoodsman and hero of the New Hampshire Grants who had an activist following called the Green Mountain Boys, and the other commanded by Benedict Arnold, a Massachusetts-commissioned militia colonel, reluctantly combined their forces and captured Fort Ticonderoga on May 10 and Fort Crown Point two days later. Fort Ti, as the Americans called it, was garrisoned by only two officers and forty-eight men and was taken without a fight. On May 12 Allen sent a detachment under Seth Warner, his second in command, to capture Crown Point. The British garrison there had taken the precaution of damaging a part of the works before evacuating. Warner's men found only nine enlisted men and ten women and children there. The most precious prize was the huge amount of war matériel captured at both posts: a minimum of seventy-eight serviceable guns, six mortars, three howitzers, cannon balls in the thousands, more than thirty thousand flints, and a vast assortment of stores.

The successful expropriation gave the Americans two immensely strategic bases on the historic water route but instigated an intercolonial quarrel because the forts were within the boundaries of the Province of New York and were seized by "private citizens" from New England. During the early months of the Revolution, petty jealousies and feuding over land grants prevented the Colonies from uniting as a harmonious and effective fighting force.[27]

Though Ethan Allen and Benedict Arnold fought over who should get the glory, they were of one mind concerning the order to have the captured matériel moved to the head of Lake George and inventoried for possible surrender to the British—should a reconciliation be effected. They sent a strenuous letter to Philadelphia urging Congress to countermand the order, since it would leave the northern settlements without protection. They furthermore put it to Congress that Canada, which they considered unprepared, should be invaded at once.

Congress canceled the order to have the armaments moved but, with regard to aggression against Canada, passed a resolution that stated that "this Congress has nothing more in view than the defence of the Colonies." On June 27 the Philadelphia conclave reversed itself and called for the invasion across the northern borders, dispatching Gen. Philip Schuyler to Fort Ticonderoga to formulate plans for the assault. Three days later Congress adopted articles of war.[28]

The Massachusetts authorities at Watertown accused Arnold of mismanaging the funds allotted him for the expedition against the Lake Champlain forts, apparently suspecting him of padding the expense accounts. He left the lakes region in the first week of July and journeyed to Cambridge to defend himself against the charges, arriving there at the end of the month. He was cleared by the Massachusetts Legislature which, in addition, paid Arnold for expenses he personally incurred.[29]

Carl Van Doren's astute delineation of Arnold's character and personality merits repetition:

> This first chapter of Arnold's Revolutionary history was an epitome of the whole. As a soldier he was original and audacious, quick in forming plans, quick in putting them into vigorous execution. He led his soldiers, not drove them, and won and held the devotion of the rank and file. He had a gift for command when the objective was clear and his imperious will could be fully bent upon it. . . . But in the conflict of instructions and of officers of rank equal or nearly equal with his, Arnold was restive and arrogant. He could not turn philosopher and patiently endure small irritations day by day. He was

MAJOR GENERAL BENEDICT ARNOLD
Courtesy of USMA Library

passionate and personal in almost all his judgments. Whoever doubted that Arnold should have his way was a fool and an enemy. Arnold knew he was a better soldier than any other at Ticonderoga or Crown Point. . . . At the same time, Arnold was a whirlwind hero who could not be bothered with keeping track of small expenses. Spend what had to be spent, and figure the amount up later. Let civilians supply what soldiers needed. Here Arnold was bound to be at odds with civilian auditors. If he was reckless with public money, might he not be keeping some of it for himself? As long as Arnold served in the Continental army quarrels went with him and unsettled accounts trailed after him.[30]

The "whirlwind hero" was an exceedingly energetic man, approximately five feet seven inches tall, solidly built, almost squat, possessed of great strength and stamina. His black hair and swarthy complexion made his chilling gray eyes instantly noticeable. No authentic portrait of Arnold has ever been discovered. Pierre du Simitière, in July 1777, did a black lead sketch from life, depicting Arnold with a beaked nose, a heavy jutting jaw, and a sloping brow.[31] The most recent judgment of Benedict Arnold, from the British viewpoint, is that of Correlli Barnett: "The only soldier of genius in the conflict—and that of a demonic, erratic kind—emerged on the rebel side in Benedict Arnold."[32]

The Canadian invasion, an adventure of heroic proportions, was a failure for several reasons. Congress had authorized it but "the cooperation of Arnold through an advance on Quebec had been Washington's own design."[33] The American plan became a two-pronged assault: one column under Gen. Richard Montgomery (substituting for Gen. Schuyler, who was evacuated because of illness), leaving from Ticonderoga to proceed down the lake to enter the Sorel (Richelieu) River, exiting at the St. Lawrence and Montreal; the other, led by Col. Benedict Arnold, to take the much more hazardous route, marching from Cambridge to Newburyport at the mouth of the Merrimack River, then by boat to the Kennebec River and Fort Western (now Augusta, Maine), across the height of land and down the Chaudière to Quebec.[34]

The chances for success were indeed slim, considering the wild terrain that had to be traversed, the inevitable shortage of supplies and provisions, and the limited time available to complete the mission (most of the men's enlistments were up at the end of the year). Maj. Gen. Sir Guy Carleton, governor general of Canada, had about seven hundred regulars under his command. The Americans optimistically banked on the Canadians, mostly French, to transfer their allegiance from the Crown to the Continental Congress, a much hoped-for-consequence that did not materialize.

On August 28 the western invasion column of 2,000 men, without Schuyler, left Ticonderoga and embarked in a heterogeneous fleet of vessels. Before the army reached St. Johns on September 5, Schuyler had caught up.[35] On the 16th, however, Schuyler's condition worsened and he returned to Ticonderoga, leaving Montgomery in command. On the west side of the Sorel, twenty miles southeast of Montreal, St. Johns was a military strongpoint along the historic route between Lake Champlain and the St. Lawrence, defended by 200 regulars (later reinforced by 300 regulars and 225 militiamen and marines), a small Indian contingent, and several cannon. The British were still at work there constructing two sixty-foot, twelve-gun vessels. Maj. Charles Preston had the unenviable task of defending the fort against superior numbers, and a very creditable and heroic job he made of it. The British also had 90 officers and men posted at Fort Chambly, ten miles to the north on a promontory at the rapids of the Sorel River.

The stubborn defense of St. Johns was finally beaten on November 2. The success of the operation was assured by the fall of Fort Chambly two weeks earlier, with three hundred Canadian volunteers assisting. The surrender of Chambly gave Montgomery the stores and provisions necessary to continue the investment of St. Johns. Among the prisoners taken there was John André, who was first escorted to Fort Ticonderoga, and then released on a one-year parole in Pennsylvania.

During the last days of the siege of St. Johns, Montgomery sent Ethan Allen and John Brown ahead to recruit additional Canadians. Some little success was attained by convincing a small number of French that they should join the American standard. With no orders from his commander to do so, Allen on September 25 attempted an attack on Montreal. The town's defenders came out, scattered Allen's small force, and took him prisoner.

Allen was a courageous but foolhardy Patriot, and this, the latest of his irresponsible adventures, did a great deal of harm to the American cause, which needed the sympathy and arms of the Canadians. When the British learned that Allen was one of the leaders who had captured Ticonderoga, he was put in irons and shipped to England, where he languished in Pendennis Castle. In the spring of 1776, fearing reprisals if they hanged Allen, the British returned him to America, where he was placed under parole in New York City.

Eleven days after the fall of St. Johns, Montgomery took Montreal, with almost no opposition from the tiny garrison (Carleton escaped by boat to Quebec). By November 22 Montgomery had consolidated his position on the St. Lawrence and was ready to join Arnold before Quebec. The element of surprise for a combined operation against the Citadel of Quebec, however, was gone, because Montgomery's schedule, greatly delayed, did not coincide with Arnold's. The travails and misfortunes of these two commanders were such that other military leaders would have been utterly disheartened in similar circumstances.

In an operation that proved to be one of the epics in American military annals, Arnold's column of 1,050 men left Cambridge between September 11 and 13 and arrived at Fort Western, where 50 carpenters joined them. The army emerged at the mouth of the Chaudière River at Point Levis, opposite Quebec, on November 9, with 675 survivors of the terrible march, after covering 350 miles of almost trackless wilderness in forty-five days. Bateaux furnished by a Kennebec contractor leaked and spoiled a good part of the army's provisions, with the result that food supplies ran short; the Kennebec-Chaudière portage turned out to be far more difficult than anticipated. At the halfway mark, about 400 men called it quits and turned back, but the rest went on, near-starved, sick, and physically exhausted.[36]

Encamped at Point Levis, obstinately energetic Arnold rounded up an assortment of small watercraft for transport across the St. Lawrence, only a half-mile wide at this point. The crossing was delayed, however, by a violent storm that raged until the 13th. That night only three-quarters of his men managed to cross the icy waters, but the following night the remainder crossed with their stock of previously prepared scaling ladders. They climbed the precipitous cliffs to the Plains of Abraham to confront Quebec's twelve hundred defenders.

With unusual prudence, Arnold did not attempt an assault, realizing that his force, with practically no artillery to speak of and a limited amount of ammunition for their muskets, was not strong enough to batter through Quebec's barricades. He resorted to a short-lived siege from the land side, then retreated to Pointe aux Trembles (now Neuville), twenty miles upriver, made camp, and awaited the arrival of Montgomery.

In the meantime Montgomery's force had been seriously reduced by disease, desertions, and the expiration of enlistments. On November 13, the same day as Arnold's first crossing to Quebec, the Continentals took possession of Montreal. In the following few months they completely alienated the Canadians by looting and pillaging the churches and homes. Faced with a drastic reduction in his troop strength—the enlistments of almost all his Connecticut men had terminated—Montgomery offered a bounty to those who would reenlist for another five months: a watch, greatcoat, jacket and breeches, stockings and shoes, caps, mittens, and an English crown. Only two hundred of them accepted the offer, volunteering to stick it out with Montgomery. After leaving garrisons at St. Johns and Montreal, the commander had only three hundred men with which to join Arnold, bringing the combined forces before Quebec to about one thousand men. But Montgomery brought with him what Arnold needed above all else—artillery and ammunition, provisions, and a huge stockpile of clothing, all captured from the British.[37]

Gen. Schuyler, kept aware by messengers of what Arnold and Montgomery were suffering in Canada, received a letter dated Cambridge, December 24, 1775, from his commander-in-chief, Gen. Washington:

When is the time for brave men to exert themselves in the cause of liberty and their country, if this is not? Should any difficulties that they may have to encounter, at this important crisis, deter them? God knows, there is not a difficulty that you both [Schuyler and Montgomery] very justly complain of, that I have not in an eminent degree experienced, that I am not every day experiencing; but we must bear up against them, and make the best of mankind as they are, since we cannot have them as we wish.[38]

Despite reverses of every nature, Arnold and Montgomery refused to abort the campaign. On New Year's Eve, December 31/January 1, in the midst of a howling blizzard, they launched a furious assault, timed primarily to the expiration on New Year's Day of the enlistments of many of Arnold's men. The attack, made with desperate courage, was an unqualified failure. They had not the men to carry the redoubts and the barricades. Montgomery was killed, struck down by three bullets, while Arnold suffered a serious leg wound. Carleton's garrison suffered few casualties, only five killed and thirteen wounded. Of the eight hundred American effectives engaged in the assault, sixty were killed or wounded and 426 captured.[39]

A man of astounding perversity, apparently discounting the loss of his able joint commander, Arnold still refused to raise the investment of Quebec and issued orders from his sickbed. The siege lines were maintained despite brutal sub-zero weather; one bitter night the temperature dropped to twenty-eight degrees below zero.

The hopelessness of the Americans' situation did not penetrate the armor of Arnold's bitterness. The British and Canadians, eighteen hundred of them, safe and warm behind Quebec's walls, now outnumbered the Americans.[40] The citadel's battlements mounted 148 guns, most of them of much larger caliber than any the besiegers could boast. In addition, in the St. Lawrence were two British men-of-war, mounting 42 guns between them, four smaller armed vessels, and a couple of transports. Arnold's idiocy was further compounded by the certainty that once the ice thawed, transports from England would bring heavy reinforcements.

On April 2, having recovered from his wound, Arnold (promoted to brigadier general on January 10) relinquished the command to old, alcoholic Gen. David Wooster, and journeyed to Montreal to take over control of the occupied town. On May 1 Congress-appointed Maj. Gen. John Thomas arrived, deposing Wooster as commander of the troops, now numbering about twenty-five hundred men, less than half of them effectives (smallpox and the usual camp diseases had taken their toll). Thomas made a thorough examination of the situation and concluded that the siege should be lifted. During the initial preparations to remove the men from the siege lines, a large number of British transports sailed into view, bringing reinforcements led by John Burgoyne. Even before any of the new troops set foot on land, Carleton led a force of more than nine hundred men out of Quebec's walls and drove panic-stricken Americans all the way back to the Sorel River.

During May 1776 the Continental Congress awoke to the realization that portentous events were occurring in Canada, with damaging results to the American cause. Orders were issued to bolster the tattered and sick survivors of the Arnold-Montgomery expedition.

Gen. John Sullivan, imbued with traditional Irish hatred for the English, and Gen. William Thompson, on June 1 assembled their reinforcements at St. Johns where they found the tragic remnants of Gen. Thomas's retreating army. Thomas had contracted smallpox and died the next day at Sorel. Sullivan had arrived with orders to return to the siege lines. He delegated Thompson to take two thousand effectives and capture Toris Riviéres (Three Rivers) on the St. Lawrence's north shore, about halfway between Montreal and Quebec. Faulty intelligence deluded the Americans into believing that the town was being defended by only eight hundred men; they learned, too late, that the forces there numbered about six thousand of Burgoyne's regulars under Brig. Gen. Simon Fraser.

Thompson was staffed with such subordinate commanders as Anthony Wayne, Arthur St. Clair, William Irvine, and William Maxwell. The talent was wasted. The attack was launched on the morning of June 8, and despite momentary successes achieved early in the fighting, it was a fiasco. Thompson's men were beaten by vastly superior numbers into disorganized retreat and driven into the swamps and woods, with their avenue of escape by water foiled by their own boat guards, who made off with the bateaux. Hounded by British, Canadians, and Indians, the Americans, broken up into small parties, fought their way to Sorel. About 1,100 made it back, the last known survivor staggering in on the night of June 11. The seriousness of the debacle was reflected in the casualty figures: Thompson was captured, along with 236 other Americans, with total losses numbering at least 400 men; the British lost only eight killed and nine wounded.

Sullivan ordered Sorel evacuated. The men limped southward to St. Johns where, on June 17, they were joined by Arnold and his Montreal occupation garrison. The combined forces beat their way south by degrees, to Isle-aux-Noix, Crown Point and, finally, Ticonderoga. Their camps along the way were unmarked cemeteries for the men who sickened and died by the dozen of smallpox and dysentery. Sullivan left a regiment of Pennsylvania troops at Crown Point to keep watch on Lake

Champlain while the remainder took up quarters at Fort Ti in the early days of July.

A multitude of military strategists and historians have condemned the Quebec expedition as an out-and-out ill-advised, reckless adventure. But they cannot gainsay the audacity that instigated the assault and the great courage of the participants who carried the war to the very ramparts of the enemy's strongholds in Canada. There is no doubt that had Quebec fallen to the Americans, they could not have held it for any appreciable length of time. Britain's navy on the St. Lawrence and the inevitable reinforcements from England would have ousted the rebels from their seat of temporary success.

Though it proved to have been a terrible waste of men and supplies, the Canada invasion had three long-range effects on British military plans for conquering the rebellious Colonies: postponement of a spearhead southward along the traditional water invasion route; the inevitable delay in Howe's New York campaign; and British over-confidence, which prompted the fatal Burgoyne expedition in 1777.

The Continental Army, approximately 17,000 men, was besieging Boston (April 1775–March 17, 1776), but without heavy artillery it would be impossible to oust the British. The Americans' lack of such armament had prompted the capture of Ticonderoga and Crown Point. On November 16, 1775, Gen. Washington sent from Cambridge the following instructions to Henry Knox, who was on the seventeenth appointed Colonel of the gun-bankrupt Continental Regiment of Artillery:

> You are immediately to examine into the State of the Artillery of this Army, and take an account of the Cannon, Motors [mortars], Shells, Lead and Ammunition, that are wanting. When you have done that, you are to proceed in the most expeditious Manner to New York; there apply to the President of the provisional Congress, and learn of him whether Colonel [Joseph] Reed did any Thing, or left any Orders respecting these Articles, and get him to procure such of them as can possibly be had there [Lawyer Reed, at this time, was on leave from his military duties to attend to certain cases that were pending]. The President, if he can, will have them immediately sent hither: If he cannot you must put them in a proper Channel for being transported to this Camp with Dispatch, before you leave New York. After you have procured as many of these Necessaries as you can there, you must go to Major General Schuyler, and get the Remainder from Ticonderoga, Crown Point, or St. John's. If it should be necessary, from Quebec; if in our Hands. The Want of them is so great, that no Trouble or Expence must be spared to obtain them. I have wrote to General Schuyler, he will give every necessary assistance that they may be had and forwarded to this Place, with the utmost Dispatch. I have given you a Warrant to the Pay-Master General of the Continental Army, for

MAJOR GENERAL HENRY KNOX
Courtesy of West Point Museum Collection

a Thousand Dollars to defray the Expence attending your Journey, and procuring these Articles; an Account of which you are to keep and render upon your Return. Endeavour to procure what Flints you can.[41]

The Patriots were faced with an instantaneous shortage of war matériel, particularly armaments. For a hundred years the Colonies had relied on England for their goods, including cannon to protect their frontiers. Now that source was completely cut off and there was no immediate substitute. Shortages in the Continental Army ran the whole gamut of contemporary military stores—cannon, powder, muskets, bayonets, cartridge cases, cloth for uniforms, camp kettles and other utensils, and the very important condiment salt. The Continentals lost the Bunker Hill battle mainly because they ran out of powder and had no bayonets. In desperation, handmade spears were substituted for bayonets, and some soldiers, minus firearms, had only spears.

Col. Knox reached Ticonderoga on December 5. Within twenty-four hours he was busy dismantling more than fifty heavy cannon, mortars, and howitzers. Schuyler's garrison assisted in the construction of forty-two sledges to be hauled by eighty yoke of oxen. On January 7 the weapons, aboard gondolas, reached the head of Lake George, where the guns were loaded on the sledges. In the middle of a severe winter, Knox transported them across three hundred miles of murderous terrain: Fort Edward, Saratoga, Albany, Kinderhook, Claverack, the snow-laden Berkshires, to Framingham, only twenty miles from Washington's Cambridge headquarters.

The first gun of the "noble train of artillery" reached Cambridge on either the 24th or 25th of January. Though historians disagree on the number of guns (it was between fifty-two and fifty-nine), they are of one mind that the artillery weighed 119,900 pounds, and that the "train" also convoyed 2,300 pounds of lead and a barrel of flints. The superhuman efforts to cart the machines of war over poor or nonexistent roads constituted one of the truly great epics of the Revolution.

These siege guns, emplaced on Dorchester Heights, were the primary factor in the Continental Army's success at Boston. The redcoats were so effectively penned in that Gen. Sir William Howe came to the inevitable conclusion that the British position had become complete indefensible. On March 17, 1776, his army sailed off to Nova Scotia, abandoning 250 valuable cannon to the victorious rebels.[42]

Ever since the abysmal failure of the American invasion of Canada, Carleton planned a counteroffensive into New York by way of the lakes. The primary need was control of Lake Champlain, the critical link between the St. Lawrence and the Hudson River Valley. The major problem facing the British was how to get their gunboats, transports, and bateaux afloat on the 125-mile-long lake, which had navigation into it obstructed at both ends. Some of their watercraft came from England in frame, ready for planking. At St. Johns they constructed or reassembled their vessels.

By June Carleton had congregated about thirteen thousand troops, including five thousand Hessian mercenaries under Maj. Gen. Baron Friedrich Adolphus Riedesel. The British commander initiated land operations on September 10, although the fleet was not ready to sail until October 4 from St. Johns which, with Chambly, was garrisoned by more than four regiments with some artillery. Gen. Burgoyne, with six regiments, was stationed at Isle-aux-Noix, captured in August by the British and converted into a strongly fortified base. Gen. Simon Fraser (mortally wounded in the second battle of Saratoga) and his troops took up positions just north of the present border.

In the fall of 1775, the Continental Congress established an American navy and a marine corps. The coastal waters, however, were controlled by the all-powerful British navy. Practically all of the American navy's actions on the high seas consisted of individual engagements. The most memorable and vitally significant American naval battle of the Revolution was fought on an inland sea by soldiers under the command of a brigadier general, Benedict Arnold.

On June 17 Gen. Horatio Gates took command of the survivors of the Canada invasion, withdrew them from Crown Point, and garrisoned them at Fort Ti. When intelligence reports verified Carleton's preparations for an invasion fleet, Gates ordered Arnold to construct an opposing armada. Arnold had considerable knowledge of sailing, acquired as a successful West Indies trader during his more youthful years. With what tools were then available, soldiers were sent into the forests to fell trees. Within the next few weeks shipwrights with tools and vital naval supplies such as canvas, anchors, hawsers, caulking, and spikes began to arrive. The old abandoned sawmills at Ticonderoga, Crown Point, and Skenesborough were repaired, and soon planks were forthcoming at a steady rate. Boat ways built at Skenesborough were at first worked on by troops.

In answer to insistent demands for skilled artisans, more than two hundred shipwrights and carpenters started to arrive from Albany, Connecticut, Massachusetts, Rhode Island, and from as far south as Philadelphia. These craftsmen were not paid with Continental currency, backed by the Spanish milled dollar, but with hard money, five dollars a day and free food, extremely good pay for those days. The Skenesborough operation was supervised by Brig. Gen. David Waterbury, Jr., with Arnold as superintendent of the whole project. The fleet was ready more than a month before the enemy's, due to the desperate energy and driving leadership of Benedict Arnold.

During the last week of September, Arnold's fleet took station in a small bay west of Valcour Island, about seven miles south of what is now Plattsburgh. The channel between Valcour Island and the mainland is about three-quarters of a mile wide, divided by a prominent headland projecting from the west side of the island. Arnold's eighty-three-gun fleet of fifteen vessels formed a line south of the headland and awaited the enemy navy, which cautiously set out from St. Johns and headed south.

It was in this position, with the wings of his armada secured, that Arnold fought a seven-hour battle on October 11 with the superior eighty-seven-gun British fleet of more than twenty vessels, manned by seven hundred picked sailors and gunners, essential personnel prerequisites that Arnold lacked. Aboard his flagship, the galley *Congress,* he personally pointed some of the guns. The American fleet was badly damaged, and it was only with providential luck that he eluded the enemy that night, sneaking his fog-shrouded, battered armada, aided by a northeast breeze, along the lake's west shore and by the flank of the British fleet.

The schooner *Royal Savage* was lost, blown up after it grounded on the southwest tip of the island. Also lost on October 11 was the gondola

BATTLE OF VALCOUR BAY

Courtesy of Royal Library, Windsor Castle. Reproduced by gracious permission of Her Majesty, Queen Elizabeth II. Copyright reserved.

KEY

a — Cumberland Head

b — Cumberland Bay

c — Isle de Valcour

d — Petite Isle

e — Grande Isle

f — Rebel Fleet

g — *Carleton* Schooner

h — *Royal Savage* aground

i — Line of Gun Boats

k — *Inflexible*

l — *Maria*

m — *Royal Convert*

n — *Thunderer Radeau*

Philadelphia.[43] At dawn on October 12 the British discovered that Arnold had escaped them. Carleton took up the chase. One by one the American gunships were raked by broadsides and sunk. By the afternoon of October 13, Arnold was left with the *Congress* and four gondolas. He beached his battered surviving vessels on the Vermont shore at the edge of Buttonmould Bay. At his orders the men set fire to the wrecks, which went down with their flags still flying.

That night, after eluding an Indian ambush, Arnold and two hundred men reached Crown Point ten miles away. There he found four other naval survivors: the schooner *Revenge,* the galley *Trumbull,* and the sloops *Liberty* and *Enterprise.* It was apparent even to bold Arnold that Crown Point could not be held against the heavy odds that Carleton offered. He withdrew to Fort Ti with his surviving force and the small garrison of Pennsylvania troops, after everything combustible at Crown Point was burned to the ground.[44]

Doubtless the war's most controversial figure and undeniably the Continental Army's most talented field commander, Arnold, by his invaluable heroic efforts on Lake Champlain, had rescued the Revolution for the Americans he later betrayed. Carleton's plans were wrecked. He moved his army down the lake to Crown Point after the battle and went into garrison there on October 14. He concluded that it was then too far advanced in the season to continue the invasion; he had lost the race against time. On November 3 he withdrew all his troops to Canada. The invasion plan was recast the following year, with "Gentleman Johnny" Burgoyne the new protagonist. The Americans, having gained a valuable year's grace, had appreciated in men and arms, and were equal to the task of imposing capitulation on Burgoyne, in what was considered the turning point of the war.

While Arnold was helping plan a campaign to force the British out of Newport, Rhode Island, he was shocked to learn that on February 19 the Continental Congress had appointed five new major generals—William Alexander (Lord Stirling), Thomas Mifflin, Arthur St. Clair, Adam Stephen, and Benjamin Lincoln—passing over himself, who was the senior brigadier. Arnold took this to mean that Congress had invited him to resign his commission. Washington, holding Arnold in the highest esteem, persuaded him not to leave the service, and the commander-in-chief made an effort to have the outrage corrected.

Arnold's public image was further enhanced by his actions immediately subsequent to the British raid in late April on the Continental depot at Danbury, Connecticut. His leadership of the militia was very effective in dealing with the British raiders who did great damage to the storehouses and dwellings. This time Congress could not in conscience fail to recognize the popular acclaim that Arnold reaped from his latest exploit. He was promoted to major general on May 2 but Congress did not erase the stigma of rating him junior to the five men on the February list. The Congressional insult was another grievance that rankled with Arnold.

Gen. Gates succeeded Gen. Schuyler as commander of the northern army. Irascible Anthony Wayne, commandant of Ticonderoga—he called the fort "the last place in the world that God made"—learned how to deal with undisciplined troops, even having to deal with a mutiny. Congress appreciated his efforts by rewarding him with a promotion to brigadier on February 21, then shifting him on April 12 to Washington's command at Morristown, New Jersey. Two months later, on June 12, St. Clair took over at Ticonderoga, commanding 2,546 troops that included 10 Continental and 2 militia regiments, 250 artillerymen, 124 mechanics, and a small detachment of scouts. The garrison was reinforced by 900 additional militia prior to Burgoyne's attack. Additional militia were posted at Skenesborough, Fort Edward, Fort Anne, and Albany. The Mohawk Valley was guarded by a Continental regiment at Fort Stanwix and efforts were being made to marshal the militia in that region.[45]

GENERAL ARTHUR ST. CLAIR
Painting by C. W. Peale
Courtesy of National Archives

There was dire need for repairs on Fort Ticonderoga's works and the approaches to the fortress needed appreciable strengthening. The work plan was drawn up by John Trumbull, with the professional engineering skill furnished by Thaddeus Kosciuszko. Blockhouses were constructed and the old French earthworks that guarded the northwest approach were restored and augmented. Mount Hope, about a mile and a half west of the earthworks, was fortified with a barbette battery. Mount Independence, to the south in present-day Vermont, was fortified, and a floating bridge on boats was constructed across the quarter-mile channel between this new work and the fort. A water barricade of logs and iron chain was fashioned to the north of the boat bridge. Southwest of the fort was an eminence, nearly eight hundred feet high, named Sugar Hill, Sugarloaf, or, its much more popular name, Mount Defiance, which had never been fortified.

Despite Trumbull's demonstration of the hill's accessibility and warning that British artillery mounted there would certainly be a major threat to the fort's main works, no defenses were installed there. Gen. Gates did not see the need to fortify the hill. With only a fifth of the troops required to adequately man the original defenses, St. Clair had no choice but to concur with Gates, take the chance, and leave Mount Defiance bare of Continental defenses. Revolutionary authorities differed on the probable route the British offensive would take: the military held it more likely that Burgoyne's army would take the Mohawk Valley route; the Congress was of the opinion that the enemy would take the lakes route. When Burgoyne came down Lake Champlain, there was no doubt left.

During the winter of 1776/77, Carleton had very efficiently organized troops, supplies, and watercraft necessary for the thrust southward. When Burgoyne arrived in Canada on May 6 from England, almost everything was in readiness. He had got the nod for the invasion's command instead of Carleton, a much more likely candidate for the job. In fact, so effective was Carleton's homework that Burgoyne was able to begin operations within six weeks after his arrival.

Burgoyne's heterogeneous army was comprised of about 10,500 men—regulars, Hessian mercenaries, Canadian and Tory auxiliaries, 600 artillerymen to man at least 138 guns, and about 400 Six Nations Indians. His armada consisted of 9 ships, 28 gunboats, and hundreds of bateaux for the transport of the troops, supplies, and provisions.[47] In mid-June the colorful mile-long flotilla sailed out of St. Johns, entered Lake Champlain, and assembled off Cumberland Head, north of Valcour Island.

At the end of the third week in June, at his camp forty miles north of

Ticonderoga, Burgoyne committed two major blunders. He first issued a bombastic proclamation that soon became the butt of laughs on both sides of the Atlantic. Among other views, he indulged in the following verbose inanities:

> The Forces entrusted to my Command are designed to act in concert, and upon a common Principle, with the numerous Armies and Fleets which already display, in every Quarter of America, the Power, the Justice, and, when properly sought, the Mercy of the King.
>
> The Cause in which the British Arms are thus exerted, applied to the most affecting Interest of the human Heart: And the Military Servants of the Crown, at first called for the sole Purpose of restoring the Rights of the Constitution, now combine with the Love of their Country, and Duty to their Sovereign, the other extensive Incitements, which spring from a due Sense of the general Privileges of Mankind. To the Eyes and Ears of the temperate Part of the Public, and to the Breasts of suffering Thousands in the Provinces [Tories and Loyalists], be the melancholy Appeal—Whether the present unnatural Rebellion has not been made the Foundation of the compleatest System of Tyranny that ever God, in his Displeasure, suffered, for a Time, to be exercised over a froward [contrary] and stubborn Generation.
>
> Arbitrary Imprisonments, Confiscation of Property, Persecution and Torture, unprecedented in the Inquisitions of the Romish Church, are among the palpable Enormities that verify the Affirmative: These are inflicted by Assemblies and Committees, who dare to profess themselves Friends of Liberty, upon the most quiet Subject, without Distinction of Age or Sex, for the sole Crime, often the sole Suspicion, of having adhered in Principle to the Government under which they were born, and to which, by every Tie divine and human, they owe Allegiance. To consummate these shocking Proceedings the Profanation of Religion is added to the most profligate Prostitution of common Reason! The Consciences of Men are set at naught, and the Multitudes are compelled not only to bear Arms, but also to swear Subjection to an Usurpation they abhor.
>
> Animated by these Considerations, at the Head of Troops in the full Powers of Health, Disciplines and Valour, determined to strike where necessary, and anxious to save where possible, I, by these Presents, invite and exhort all Persons, in all Places where the Progress of this Army may point, and by the Blessing of God I will extend it FAR, to maintain such a Conduct as may justify me in protecting their Lands, Habitations, and Families. . . .
>
> If notwithstanding these Endeavors and sincere Inclination to assist them, the Phrenzy of Hostility should remain, I trust I shall stand acquitted in the Eyes of God and Men in denouncing and executing the Vengeance of the State against the wilful Outcast. The Messengers of Justice and of Wrath await them in the Field, and Devastation, Famine, and every concomitant Horror that a reluctant but indispensable Prosecution of Military Duty must occasion, will bar the Way to their Return.[48]

Then he convened a council of his Indians and proceeded to lay down the law regarding their conduct: "I positively forbid bloodshed, when you are not opposed in arms. Aged men, women, and children and prisoners must be held sacred from the knife or hatchet, even in the time of actual combat. . . ."[49] This admonition backfired when Jane McCrea, betrothed to a British officer, was taken by an advance contingent of allied Indians at Fort Edward on July 27. She was murdered, scalped, and her tresses brought to Fort Anne, where Burgoyne's headquarters were established at the time. Her fiancé, Lieut. David Jones, made the identification. The news of the manner of her death spread throughout the northern settlements. The tragic incident, combined with Burgoyne's ridiculous rhetoric, served to incense farmer-militiamen, who flocked to join the Revolutionary colors.

Burgoyne and his army departed from Cumberland Head and proceeded down the lake to Crown Point, where he lingered long enough to plant a garrison, a powder magazine, and a hospital. On the last day of June he moved his forces down to the perimeter of Ticonderoga's outer defenses.

On July 2 Gen. Fraser and his light infantry went up Mount Hope and captured the barbette battery there. The next day additional forces were placed on the hill, thus closing off American egress to Lake George to the westward. On July 4 the British set out to prove what John Trumbull had feared. Burgoyne's chief engineer was dispatched to explore the possibilities of Sugar Loaf Hill or Mount Defiance. His report revealed that the eminence could be made accessible and that the fort's works and Mount Independence were within its artillery range of 2,200 yards—too great for precision fire but there was no doubt that great havoc could be caused by making use of it.

Burgoyne's second in command, Maj. Gen. William Phillips, a highly skilled artillerist, agreed with the engineer: "Where a goat can go a man can go, and where a man can go he can drag a gun."[50] It took but one day to build a road to the top and on the next day four twelve-pounders were hauled up, with the prospect of having them set up in time to commence firing at noon on July 6. The Americans, on the 5th, watched the British proceedings with fascinated consternation. In mid-afternoon of the same day, St. Clair convened a council of war and all of the officers concurred that immediate evacuation was the only alternative.

As the summer sun began to descend below the horizon of trees, St. Clair ordered all of Ticonderoga's heavy guns to commence firing at will, to cover his troops' preparations for leave-taking. All the light fieldpieces and stores that could be loaded were carted down to the boats. Some minutes after midnight Col. Pierce Long, with about 450 of his troops and the sick and wounded, embarked and made for Skenesborough. Two hours later St. Clair led the balance of the fort's garrison across the boat bridge, with the last men taking the time to partially destroy the span. It was the commander's idea to take a forty-five mile circuitous route, by way of Castleton, Vermont (thirty miles from Ticonderoga), to meet up with Col. Long at Skenesborough.

What could have been a well-conceived, orderly evacuation was ruined by the dereliction of some of St. Clair's subordinates. Mount Independence was occupied by troops under Brig. Gen. Matthias Fermoy, a French Martinique-born soldier of fortune.[51] In extreme neglect of his men, he went to sleep, failing to issue orders for a general withdrawal of his command. To add to his criminality, at about 3 A.M., when he thought it was high time to make his exit, he set his quarters on fire. The flames were an invitation to Riedesel to send his Hessians to the scene. In addition, the hill's four artillerymen, who had orders to enfilade the boat bridge, had imbibed liberally of a cask of wine and lapsed into deep slumber.[52]

With the dawn Burgoyne discovered to his discomfiture that the fort was deserted. Troops were put to work repairing the bridge and destroying the boom from Willow Point to the Vermont shore. Ordering Gen. Fraser to go overland after the main body of rebels under St. Clair, Burgoyne and his troops took the water route in pursuit, leaving a garrison under Brig. Gen. Powell at Fort Ticonderoga.

Col. Long dallied along the lake, relying with overconfidence on the log-and-chain boom at Fort Ti to hold off pursuit. In addition he committed the serious error of failing to establish rear-guard stations along the shores of the lake. Burgoyne caught up with the American flotilla at Skenesborough. Long burned everything that was flammable and made all haste for Fort Anne, taking with him the 150 men who had been posted at Skenesborough. The British overran the place but failed to capture or even do any appreciable damage to Long's column. Of the five vessels, the remainder of Arnold's Champlain squadron, Long destroyed by fire the *Enterprise, Gates,* and *Liberty;* the British captured the *Revenge* and *Trumbull.* As a result, St. Clair was forced to make a costly seven-day detour to escape possible confrontation with Burgoyne's forces.

The British commander still had hopes of catching up with the retreating Americans and destroying them at Fort Anne. He sent Lieut. Col. Hill ahead with a detachment of 190 officers and men; though they failed to capture Long's rear guard of 150 men, they did take as prisoners several boatloads of sick and wounded attempting to flee up Wood

Creek. Hill's camp, a mile from Fort Anne, was attacked by Long and reinforcements of militia under Col. Henry Van Rensselaer. After a two-hour battle, the Americans fired Fort Anne and took off for Fort Edward.[53]

Early on the morning of the seventh, at the tiny village of Hubbardton, Vermont, Gen. Fraser overtook and surprised St. Clair's rear guard of about 1,000 men under Col. Seth Warner who failed to perform the elementary military duty of taking security measures to prevent just such an occurrence. There followed a bloody action in which the British were getting the worst of it until Gen. Riedesel and his Germans came and saved them. Warner broke off the engagement and ordered his men to scatter and regroup at Manchester. The casualty figures for both sides were greatly out of proportion, considering the number of men engaged: the Americans lost 40 dead, with 12 officers and 312 men, including wounded, captured; the British and Hessians lost 35 killed and 148 wounded.[54]

Patriot optimists had considered Fort Ti the "Gibraltar of America," and its abandonment caused consternation. Sectional jealously inspired the New Englanders to put the blame on Schuyler and St. Clair. In 1778 Congress instituted court-martial proceedings against St. Clair, but absolved him of all blame and acquitted him with honor. The army he had saved despite the serious lapses of his subordinates constituted the nucleus for the forces that defeated Burgoyne at Saratoga.

American plans to harass Burgoyne's long lines of communications assigned Maj. Gen. Benjamin Lincoln to the task of organizing militia forces in Vermont. His efforts during the late summer of 1777 resulted in the dispatching of three five hundred-man detachments to wreak havoc at the British posts and depots in the region. Col. John Brown was awarded the primary objective of retaking Fort Ticonderoga, with a planned assist by Col. Johnson's column in a strong diversionary attack against Mount Independence. The third detachment, commanded by Col. Woodbridge, was to occupy Skenesborough, abandoned by the British, and to scour southward to Forts Anne and Edward.

For two days in mid-September Brown and his men had an extraordinarily easy time reconnoitering Ticonderoga's environs. Gen. Powell, the fort's commander, had nine hundred men in his garrison but, lulled into complacency by Burgoyne's victories, failed to take proper security measures at the fort's outposts. At dawn on the eighteenth, Brown launched his assault, taking all the outposts between the landing place at the north end of Lake George and the fort's main works, capturing three hundred enemy troops and releasing more than one hundred American prisoners. Col. Johnson's effort against Mount Independence was ineffective because of his failure to synchronize his attack with Brown's. The Americans indulged in four days of cannonading the ramparts with light artillery. Powell was not cowed into surrendering and Brown withdrew to try his luck elsewhere.[55]

The rebels' booty included an armed sloop, several gunboats, and a fleet of bateaux. Brown embarked his men on the captured craft and sailed up Lake George. His plan was to surprise and capture the British post and depot on Diamond Island in Dunham Bay, about twenty-five miles south of Ticonderoga. The attack, timed for dawn on the twenty-third, was postponed because of adverse winds. The island's two-company garrison was already aware of the Americans' presence in the lake when Brown attacked the next morning. The defenders possessed heavy artillery that more than outmatched Brown's boat-borne light guns. After a short and useless bombardment of the enemy's works, Brown ordered the flotilla to the east shore, where the boats were beached and burned. The detachment marched south to Skenesborough and then to Pawlet, just east of the New York-Vermont border, to rejoin Lincoln.

Although the raid was a limited success, Brown had gathered enough information to reveal that Burgoyne's supply lines were drying up, with only about one month's provisions on hand to support his troops. The news reached the American camp at Saratoga. Jubilation inspired bursts of cheering and the firing of guns. Burgoyne's troops, checked by the Patriot lines, heard of it a few days later from a deliberately released prisoner.[56]

British deserters from the Saratoga battlefield showed up at Fort Ti and informed Gen. Powell of Burgoyne's desperate situation. The commandant immediately made preparations to retreat to Canada. He burned the barracks and houses at the fort and at Mount Independence and evacuated his troops. Crown Point's garrison left at the same time.

Fort Ticonderoga was occupied in 1780 by Carleton's replacement, Sir Frederick Haldimand, with a force of Canadian troops. In 1781 Col. Barry St. Leger and a small detachment joined the garrison. The purpose of his visit was twofold: to capture Gen. Philip Schuyler, and to meet with representatives from Vermont to treat on the possibility of bringing that region back under Crown control as a Canadian province. In neither case was he successful.

Resentment against civil and military control by New York and Schuyler's command over New England troops led Vermont's colonists in 1777 to declare their independence. They adopted a constitution (the first to give universal manhood suffrage without property qualifications) and elected a governor, Thomas Chittenden. Both New York and New

Hampshire made claims to Vermont's territory and Congress refused to intervene by taking Vermont in as the fourteenth state. Ethan and Ira Allen, and Governor Chittenden, rather than submit to division and loss of identity, entered into negotiations with Haldimand and St. Leger, the object being to bring pressure on Congress to act in their behalf. The Vermont partisans were successful: on March 4, 1791, Vermont became the nation's fourteenth state.[57]

In November 1781 Haldimand and St. Leger withdrew to Canada, and Fort Ticonderoga was never again occupied by a regular armed garrison. In July 1783 Gen. Washington, accompanied by Governor George Clinton, Alexander Hamilton, and other dignitaries, visited the fort on a tour of inspection, returning to Washington's headquarters at Newburgh on August 5.

Shortly after the Treaty of Paris was signed, the whole region began to be rapidly settled. There was no caretaking establishment at Ticonderoga and the fort provided a convenient treasure trove for the early settlers. All the furniture and other movable objects were taken first, then the doors and windows; floors were ripped up and the great beams removed, and in a short time the barracks collapsed. The abandoned cannon, most of them spiked, were removed to be melted down for the iron. The drawbridges and gun carriages were disassembled and used for firewood.

In 1796 the garrison grounds were granted, jointly with other state lands, to Columbia and Union Colleges as a possible source of income. William Ferris Pell, wealthy New York marble and mahogany importer and a great-grandson of the third Lord of the Manor of Pelham, Westchester County, whose branch of the family had settled in Canada after the Revolution, leased part of the garrison grounds and erected a small house that he called Bellevue. In 1820 he bought the property from the educational institutions as the site for a summer home. The deeds included all the land in a radius of fifteen hundred yards from the southwest bastion of the fort. Thus did the historic site, contrary to the usual practice, pass from the public domain into private hands, to remain in the possession of the Pell family for more than a century and a half.

The existence of the most faithfully restored Colonial fort in America is due to the remarkable dedication and work of the Pell family. William Pell at once took steps to stop the vandalism in the fort, but he had to contend with the settlers, who believed they had a vested right in the property that had belonged to New York State. He proceeded to buy up the habitations of the squatters, some of whom had repaired the old French lime kilns and were even burning the fort's walls for lime. To further the preservation of the historic ruins, he erected fences around the redoubts and made some rudimentary repairs on the main works.

William Pell's first house was destroyed by fire in 1825. The following year he built the Pavilion, named for the Regent's residence in Bath, England, and this edifice is still standing and continues to be occupied by William's descendants. In 1839 his son Archibald was killed by the explosion of a rusted old Revolutionary cannon that he attempted to fire as a welcome to his father on his arrival that spring. The tragedy saddened William Pell to the extent that he lost all interest in Fort Ticonderoga. For a number of years thereafter, the Pavilion was leased out as a hotel and subsequently occupied by a tenant farmer.

William Pell died intestate and the property was distributed in equal shares to his ten children. For the next half-century the fort property was owned in common by the children and their descendants. In 1909 Stephen Pell, a great-grandson of William, initiated steps to acquire control, with the express purpose of restoring Fort Ti. Some of his relatives gave him their shares without reservations; the other shares he acquired by purchase.

The whole world was searched for contemporary French and English cannon. The restoration was furthered by the assistance of half a dozen nations, their presidents and prime ministers, military officers and engineers, and many thousands of ordinary citizens. Pell had collected old prints of the fort executed by contemporary artists. These were carefully studied and compared with the outlines of the walls still standing. The design of the fort originated in the general plans delineated in Vauban's *Traité des Sièges*. Pell was successful in his efforts to obtain the original manuscript, the most valuable single item in the fort museum's library, which houses thousands of books, rare documents, maps, journals, and letters of the French and English periods.

The Fort Ticonderoga Museum of the French and Indian War and the Revolution contains thousands of exhibits relating to the long period of military occupancy, with displays of uniforms, equipment, muskets, swords, paintings, and engravings. John H. G. Pell, son of Stephen, now superintends the fort as a nonprofit historical and educational monument.[58]

After its destruction by fire in 1773, Fort Crown Point played a minor role during the Revolution and was used as an outpost of Fort Ticonderoga. Fort St. Frederic is in complete ruins. Only roofless shells remain of Crown Point's structures. In the middle of the last century Lossing reported that "there were four large buildings used for barracks within the fort, the walls and chimneys of which were built of limestone. One of them has been entirely removed, and another, 287 feet long, is almost demolished. The walls of the other two—one, 192, and the other,

RUINS OF FORT CROWN POINT
Courtesy of New York State Department of Commerce

FORT CROWN POINT (1760-73)
(Northeast Barracks [left]; Southeast Barracks [center];
Parade Ground [right]). *Courtesy of National Park Service*

216 feet long, and two stories high are quite perfect, and one of them was roofed and inhabited until two or three years [ago]. . . ."

Only the well-preserved ruins of Fort Crown Point and Fort St. Frederic remain. About the turn of this century the State of New York acquired the Crown Point forts from private ownership and purchased surrounding acreage that contains the sites of the early French and English settlements.

Fort Cummings
Honeoye, Ontario County

Established on September 11, 1779, this temporary fort incorporated an Indian blockhouse often used by Tory Rangers. Fort Cummings was a fortified supply base from which the troops on the Sullivan-Clinton Expedition advanced to Genesee Castle, leveled by fire the large Seneca town there, and crushed the power of the tribe for all time. Honeoye, an Indian village in 1779, was not settled by whites until 1789, when it was called Pittstown; in 1808 the pioneer village was renamed Honeoye.

Gen. John Sullivan's report of the campaign, dated "Teaogo [Tioga], September 30, 1779," was sent to John Jay, then president of the Continental Congress. An extract from it tells of the construction of the post named for Capt. John N. Cummings, who commanded it:

At Kanandaque [Canandaigua] we found twenty-three very elegant houses, mostly framed, and in general large. Here we also found very extensive fields of corn, which having been destroyed, we marched for Hannayaye [Honeoye], a small town of ten houses, which we also destroyed. At this place we established a post, leaving a strong garrison, our heavy stores and one field piece, and proceeded to Chinesee [Genesee], which, the prisoners informed, was the grand capital of the [Seneca] Indian country.

A diary, kept by Lieut. Obadiah Gore on the march to Genesee, describes the site of the Indian village:

[September] 11th Marched at 6 A.M. and went nearly a south-west course, over a good country of land 13½ miles, to an Indian town called Anwoughyawna [Honeoye], with great improvements about it. The Indians left some fires burning. This town is pleasantly situated near a small lake [Honeoye Lake]. Here we left the greatest part of our ammunition and provisions, together with our worst horses, under the care of a proper guard.

The journal of Lieut. Robert Parker, Second Continental Artillery.

reveals in lucid style his ecstatic vision for the future of the country the expedition traversed:

> September 12th.—Rain in the morning prevented our marching until 12—we then drew 4 days provision & leaving one piece of artillery, all our Baggage, pack horses, drivers & Invalids proceeded. . . .
>
> September 16th.—Thus had we advanced 140 miles in the Enemy's country from Tioga and carried fire, sword and destruction in every part, that we could possibly find out or approach, in the prosecution of which, we had to encounter many and almost insurmountable difficulties, such as forcing a march all the way, cutting a Road for the Artillery, in many places a continued swamp for several miles, want of provisions, hard marches, and fatigue.
>
> But here let us leave the busy army for a moment and suffer our imaginations to Run at large through these delightful wilds, & figure to ourselves the opening prospects of future greatness which we may reasonably suppose is not far distant, & that we may yet behold with a pleasing admiration those deserts that have so long been the habitation of beasts of prey & a safe asylum for our savage enemies, converted into fruitful fields, covered with all the richest productions of agriculture, amply rewarding the industrious husbandman by a golden harvest; the spacious plains abounding with flocks & herds to supply his necessary wants. These Lakes & Rivers that have for ages past rolled in sacred silence along their wonted course, unknown to Christian nations, produce spacious cities & guilded spires, rising in their banks, affording a safe retreat for the virtuous few that disdains to live in affluence at the expense of their liberties. The fish too, that have so long enjoyed a peaceful habitation in these transparent regions, may yet become subservient to the inhabitants of this delightful country.

In the 1930s archaeological diggings for Indian village sites accidentally unearthed what appeared to have been the log foundations of a large structure. A number of Continental uniform buttons were found in the debris. It was then established that the site of Fort Cummings had been discovered.

In the center of Honeoye, off Route 20A, there is a bronze commemorative tablet:

FORT CUMMINGS

Gen. John Sullivan and his army of Continental Troops encamped at the foot of Honeoye Lake Sept. 11, 1779. He left here stores, baggage and artillery, the "sick and lame and lazy" and 50 men under Capt. John N. Cummings, 300 men in all. The garrison strengthened an Indian blockhouse with kegs, boxes and bags of flour and held the fort till return of the expedition from Genesee Castle and the march eastward Sept. 18, 1779.

Fort Dayton
Herkimer, Herkimer County

The most important military post in the Herkimer County Settlements during the Revolution, Fort Dayton, at today's Herkimer on the north side of the Mohawk River, was strategically located to protect the inhabitants of German Flats (the name given the ten-mile stretch of Palatine villages on both sides of the river). The fort occupied the site of the first Fort Herkimer, a wooden blockhouse of the French and Indian War, which became a ruin through neglect (the site of the second Fort Herkimer, of Revolutionary fame, is located on the south side of the river). German Flats being exposed to the threat of Indian incursion from all directions, the settlers petitioned Maj. Gen. Philip Schuyler to provide them with a defensive work.

In the early fall of 1776, Schuyler sent Col. Elias Dayton to German Flats, where a fort was erected and named for him. Fort Dayton was a true fort, in that it possessed a stockade, blockhouse, bastions, curtains, barracks, an artillery park, and the rest of the appurtenances necessary for a complete fortification. It was constructed on ground now bounded by Main, Court, Washington, and German Streets.

It was from this fort, on August 4, 1777, that Gen. Nicholas Herkimer marched with about eight hundred undisciplined, sharpshooting men to the relief of Fort Stanwix at today's Rome. The fort was being besieged by Barry St. Leger's British regulars, Tory auxiliaries, and Indian allies. Herkimer's column never reached Fort Stanwix: it was ambushed at Oriskany and the roar of battle there could be plainly heard by the fort's garrison six miles away. About two hundred Patriots lost their lives in the battle, one of the bloodiest conflicts of the war, considering the relatively small number of men engaged. About an equal number were wounded, including the redoubtable Gen. Herkimer, who died ten days later.

In the late summer of 1778, rumors became a certainty that the celebrated Mohawk war chief, Joseph Brant (Thayendanegea), and Capt. William Caldwell, with about 300 Tories and 150 Mohawks, were planning to attack German Flats. Four scouts were dispatched by Fort Dayton's commandant, Col. Peter Bellinger, to range the country toward Unadilla, one of Brant's bases to the south. The scouts were stumbled upon or ambushed by a large number of Indians in the general area of Edmeston, southwest of Herkimer. The actual date is still a matter of historical controversy; some historians hold that the incursion happened on September 13, while others believe it occurred on September 17.

Three of the scouts were killed, but the fourth, Adam Helmer, who had the reputation of being the best cross-country runner in the whole Mohawk region, escaped. Helmer's twenty-odd-mile run, with pursuers constantly at his heels, became a legend in the Mohawk Valley. His feat has been graphically narrated in Walter D. Edmonds's *Drums Along the Mohawk* and vividly portrayed in the movie of the same name. Utterly exhausted and with his clothing in shreds, Helmer brought the news to Fort Herkimer, about two miles east of Fort Dayton, that an army of enemy destructives was fast approaching. At once the fort's signal gun was fired and the citizenry fled to the forts.

During the scout's heroic marathon run, Brant, with his main force, was coming up the Unadilla River. They came through Cedarville, at the head of the river, and reached the southern environs of German Flats about an hour after the signal gun was fired. Not realizing that the settlement had already been made cognizant of its danger, and with nightfall almost at hand, Brant camped close to Shoemaker's Tavern, at today's town of Mohawk, a notorious Tory hangout.

Before the first gray of dawn appeared, Brant's little army broke camp and silently invaded the settlement. The Tories and Indians had to be content with first plundering the unoccupied dwellings, then setting fire to them. Refugees, jammed in the two weakly garrisoned forts, had no recourse but to stay behind their stockades and watch with consternation while all their worldly possessions—homes and grain-stuffed barns, gristmills and sawmills—were consumed by fire. The ten-mile stretch of country from Little Falls to Frankfort was completely devastated. German Flats was a blackened ruin.

In the fall of 1780 German Flats was again raided, during Sir John Johnson's retreat following his expedition against the Schoharie Valley. Early in 1781 the Palatine settlements were revisited by small bands of Indians. On August 6, when Schell's Bush, five miles north of Herkimer, was attacked by sixty Tories and Indians, most of that village's inhabitants escaped to Fort Dayton. After the destruction of Fort Stanwix early in May 1781, Fort Dayton was more strongly garrisoned than ever before as it became the extreme western military outpost in New York State.

The end of the long war brought a declining need for fortifications. There was a gradual disappearance of forts, blockhouses, and stockades around dwellings. The people returned to their homesteads, removed the ravages of war, and took up once more the usual pursuits associated with peaceful times.

A quotation by Gen. F. E. Spinner, Treasurer of the United States (1860-73), a Herkimer County resident, was found in a newsclip (no source available). It reported that in 1874 the general wrote:

I recollect when a boy at school in Herkimer about the year 1813, the moat of the old fort could be easily traced. The area within which the Reform Church and Court House now stand was within the lines of the fort. The County Clerk's office occupies the site of the ditch that was outside of the southeast breastwork of old Fort Dayton.

The mid-Victorian mansion erected in 1884 by Dr. A. Walter Suiter and now owned by the Herkimer County Historical Society now occupies the Fort Dayton site. The mansion's first floor constitutes a library of history relating to the nation, the state, and, in particular, Herkimer County.

Dobbs Ferry Forts
Dobbs Ferry, Westchester County

The site of an important Hudson River crossing opposite present-day Tallman Mountain State Park on the west bank, Dobbs Ferry was first fortified by the Americans very early in 1776. When the British and Hessians ran the Patriots out of New York City and took over their defenses, the Dobbs Ferry crossing became too hazardous because of its proximity to the British lines. The Americans then relied on highly strategic King's Ferry, about fifteen miles to the north, which was protected by the fortifications at Verplanck's Point on the east bank and Stony Point on the opposite shore.

Robert Bolton, in his history of the county, delineates a bit of interesting background of Dobbs Ferry:

> The village . . . one mile north of Hastings, is prettily situated on the rising hills of Greenburgh, opposite the northern terminus of the Palisades and the village of Tappan. The Indian name of this place was Weec-quaes-guck, literally "the place of the bark kettle." Its present name [is derived] from the ancient family of the Dobbs, who have been long settled here, and also from the fact that they were the early ferrymen. In the year 1698, there was living in this vicinity "Jan Dobs en zyn huys vrou (and his wife)" Abigail, both members of the Dutch church, Sleepy Hollow. Thomas, their son, was born on the manor, A.D. 1712.

The remains of the fortification and at least two redoubts built in the vicinity were still plainly visible in 1850. Both Lossing and Bolton verified the ruins when they visited the place. Commanding a fine view of the Hudson in both directions, the main fort was situated on the horseshoe-shaped eminence overlooking the ferry landing (today the site looms over the railroad right of way). Commanding the ferry to old Paramus on the Jersey side (now included in the Palisades State Park), these forts often harrassed British shipping plying up and down the river.

Today's geography has Tappan (New York) and Old Tappan (New Jersey) as separate but adjoining communities, but during the Revolution it was one area known as Tappan. On August 8, 1780, Gen. Washington established his headquarters here for the primary purpose of formulating plans for an assault, in concert with the French, upon British-held New York City. The Continental Army's encampment occupied the countryside for several miles on either side of the old village.

The Dobbs Ferry crossing thus assumed much more importance. To further protect it, even before Washington came to Tappan, it was determined to construct on the heights of the Palisades, at the eastern end of the Continental camp, a large wood-and-stone blockhouse about fifteen hundred feet north of the road going down to the ferry at Sneden's Landing (today, just south of the Tallman Mountain State Park). With construction taking nearly all summer, the fortification, with an additional battery of three guns nearby, was generally called the Dobbs Ferry Blockhouse.

In early August a deserter slipped out of camp and swam out to the H.M.S. *Vulture,* anchored in the Hudson. He informed the enemy of the blockhouse, reporting that there were 350 Americans there, momentarily expecting two eighteen-pounders. Later, British intelligence determined that Baron von Steuben had 2,000 men there fashioning fascines and that the blockhouse's batteries included three eighteen-pounders and a number of howitzers. The Dobbs Ferry Blockhouse was finally completed in late September, and the works were inspected by Gen. Nathanael Greene and a French official. All those weeks of summer construction, however, went for naught: Washington was disappointed by the small number of men offered by the French and New York City was not invaded.

In early October 1776 Gen. William Heath had a strong garrison posted at Dobbs Ferry: five hundred infantry, forty light horse, and an artillery company with two twelve-pounders and a howitzer. Bolton reflected that "besides the two redoubts, there must have been a military blockhouse erected here; for, on the 17th of March, 1781, we find Major Graham ordered out with a detachment of 150 men for its relief."

After the battle of White Plains, the British retreated to Dobbs Ferry with Patriot scouting parties dogging their every step. The enemy held the place for a short period, during which time they foraged through the area for grain and hay and rounded up rebel cattle. On January 29, 1777, Gen. Benjamin Lincoln's Continentals were ordered to repossess Dobbs Ferry.

Benedict Arnold, commandant of West Point, was occupying the manor home of the notorious Tory, Beverley Robinson, situated opposite the Patriot citadel (the dwelling had been confiscated by the Continentals and used as American headquarters in the Highlands). The immediately prior occupant of the Robinson house was none other than Gen. William Howe.

By exchanges of secret correspondence through intermediaries, Dobbs Ferry was selected by Arnold and Maj. John André as the place for their first meeting on September 11, 1780. Arnold left headquarters on the afternoon of the 10th, sailed down the river on his barge to King's Ferry, and stayed the night at the home of Joshua Hett Smith, Arnold's secret service agent and unsuspecting accomplice, about two-and-a-half miles from the ferry landing. Early the next morning he proceeded toward Dobbs Ferry.

John André and Col. Robinson, under a flag of truce, came up from Kingsbridge and arrived at Dobbs Ferry on the morning of the 11th. The British, through an oversight, had failed to withdraw their gunboats stationed in that part of the river. When Arnold, under no flag, was approaching his destination by water, he was fired upon by the British naval patrol. Arnold ordered his eight bargemen to make for the west shore, and the meeting with André was aborted.

There is little doubt that had Arnold lost his life or been captured at that time, the treasonable conspiracy would have been discovered two weeks earlier than it was. After spending the remaining hours of daylight at the King's Ferry blockhouse on the west bank, he returned that night to the Robinson house. One may imagine the frustration that overcame him. In retrospect, it seems that predestination for Benedict Arnold was delayed a fortnight.

In reply to criticism that the Dobbs Ferry forts were vulnerable to enemy attack, Gen. Washington dictated the following letter, dated "Head Quarters, Dec. 16, 1782," to Lieut. Col. William S. Smith (words in brackets are in Washington's handwriting):

> I have myself seen the Work at Dobbs Ferry but cannot agree with you as to its indefensible State. It never was calculated to withstand a serious attack but has always been supposed equal to any small party that might attempt it by a Coup de Main; and as that Post is assigned for the only communication we have with the Enemy it appears [if not] the only [at least the best] place where the duties of your Office can be performed.

Fort Dubois
Cobleskill, Schoharie County

For a century and a half Schoharie Valley chroniclers and residents were under the impression that Fort Dubois at Cobleskill was erected in 1781, two years after its actual construction. Simms and Roscoe, the popular valley historians of the nineteenth century, were misled by the similarity of the names of two Cobleskill commanders—Col. Lewis Dubois and Capt. Benjamin Dubois, the first named being the man responsible for the fort's erection. Col. Dubois of New Marlboro (in modern Orange County) was the highest ranking officer in the Schoharie Valley during the fall, winter, and spring of 1778/79, while Capt. Dubois of Catskill, no relation to the colonel, was ordered to Schoharie on May 19, 1781, to take command of the levies coming from Dutchess County. Simms, in particular, overlooked the earlier garrisoning of Cobleskill and mistakenly assumed that Capt. Dubois' levies built the fort.

The publication of Governor Clinton's *Papers* and the discovery of other letters, reports, and orders have definitely narrowed down the time of the fort's construction to the three-month period between April 6 and July 11, 1779. Fort Dubois was located on a height of land then owned by Jacob Shaffer on present-day Main Street about a mile east of Cobleskill's center; in addition, Shaffer's house was also picketed. The fort covered nearly three acres and was commodious enough to accommodate all of the valley's inhabitants. The need for the defense was overpoweringly apparent after the devastating raid of the previous year. A natural stream fed water into the moat surrounding the fort's palisades. There is, unfortunately, no further description of the fortification.

In the last week of May 1778 Joseph Brant led a large party of Tories and Indians in a raid on Cobleskill. A skillfully laid ambush trapped a detachment of Continentals and militia and killed fourteen of them. The inhabitants fled just before the enemy set fire to the settlement's dwellings and barns.

In April 1779 the first of the expeditions against the Iroquois took place. Col. Gose Van Schaick marched his army of destructives into Onondaga country and laid waste three large villages, killing a dozen Indians and taking thirty-three others prisoners. The Onondagas, particularly their chiefs, had maintained a neutral attitude during the war; a small number of individual Onondagas, however, did participate in British forays against the settlements. The expedition merited the justifiable criticism levied against it. It was an ill-advised abrogation of the trust between the Americans and the officially neutral nation. The fact that the Onondagas were a member nation of the Iroquois Confederacy was no excuse.

Not much more than a month later, the now overtly hostile Onondagas, impoverished but not cowed, retaliated with unbridled fury. Three hundred of them, practically all of the nation's warriors, struck Cobleskill. A militia scout spotted them in the near environs and word was hurriedly sent to Schoharie.

A detachment of Continentals immediately set out from Schoharie to guard Cobleskill. There was no confrontation until the next day, when a small number of the Indians emerged from the woods and deliberately made their presence known. The Continentals surged to attack them but the Onondagas retreated precipitately, drawing the Americans into reckless pursuit. The lure was out and the Continentals swallowed it whole.

It was a replay of the Cobleskill raid the previous year. The Patriots were cleverly led into an ambush set by Onondagas ten times their number. The inhabitants wasted no time—they immediately fled along the road to Schoharie. About half of the Continentals managed to fight their way out of the trap and took refuge in a dwelling on the same road. They held off the Indian horde until their refuge was set afire. Only two soldiers survived to be taken prisoners, while twenty-two of their compatriots were killed, some of them burned to death. The settlement was pillaged and burned. Now Cobleskill was a total ruin.

The last reported raid against Cobleskill was a minor hit-and-run affair by a small band of Indians on August 26, 1781.

Fort Edward
Fort Edward, Washington County

During the eighteenth-century wars, Fort Edward was one of the most important military posts between Albany and Canada. The general area of the fort was called the "First," "Long," or "Great Carrying Place." It was the first and nearest point on the Hudson River where troops and military stores were landed for portage to and from the southern end of Lake Champlain (today's Whitehall), or, by the alternate route, to and from Ticonderoga and Lake George (Lac St. Sacrement).

British fortifications were constructed on the site in 1709, 1731, 1755, and 1757. The first, a stockaded affair erected by Gen. Francis Nicholson during his aborted march against Canada, was named for its builder. The second fort was built to protect the trading post settlement established by John Henry Lydius, an Albany Dutchman, the first white man to settle in what is now the village of Fort Edward; this defense, called Fort Lydius, was destroyed by the French and Indians in 1745. The third fort, a preliminary to Maj. Gen. William Johnson's expedition against Crown Point, was initiated by Gen. Phineas Lyman with six hundred men and completed by Capt. William Eyre, engineer, and named Fort Lyman; after the Battle of Lake George, Johnson renamed it Fort Edward "in Honour to Our Young Prince," the Duke of York and

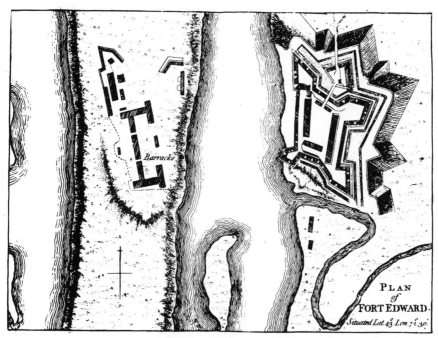

FORT EDWARD (1765)
Courtesy of National Map Collection, Public Archives of Canada

Albany, eldest son of George II and brother of the future George III. The fourth and last, in 1757, came as a result of the downgrading of the works by a British engineer and an accidental fire that destroyed the barracks in 1756.[1]

Gen. William Shirley, Governor of Massachusetts, had ordered army engineer Harry Gordon to inspect Forts Edward and William Henry and consider "what works are most necessary to be added for the Strengthening of them."[2] Gordon's report, accompanying a letter dated Albany, June 22, 1756, to Robert Napier, Adjutant General, was highly critical of Fort Edward's works. The thoroughness of his inspection is noteworthy:

Fort Edward is situated on Hudson River 14 miles below the other Fort above described [William Henry]. It is a Work of four Bastions as the other—that on the River below is rather a half Bastion, one Side is close to the River another to a small Rivulet which winds towards the third. The Gate is in the Curtain towards the Plain. There is a Gate likewise in the Side thats towards the Rivulet. There is a Ditch on the North and East Sides, and a Row of Pallisades (which has been the Preservation of the Fort) goes quite round between the Ditch & the Parapet, with their Points inclining towards the Country. There is no Rampart to the Fort and the Parapet is not above eight Foot thick in some Places it has washed to six a Top. The Parapet is from eight to ten Foot high reared up of Sand, without any regular Banquet, or any kind of facing. There is a Magazine in the East Bastion, which is only covered with one layer of Logs. The River Hudson divides itself a little above the Fort and forms a large Island [Rogers Island] opposite to it. The Branch of the River between the Fort and the Island is about sixty Yards across. The Island a hundred, and the other Branch seventy.

In order to strengthen this Fort the Parapets ought to be faced with Logs as at Fort William Henry, and made from 14 to 16 Foot thick; the Rampart on the East & South Sides ought to be raised so as to have Casemates under the Curtains, and proper Cover for 2 Magazines under the 2 Bastions. A Ravelin constructed before the Gate of the North Curtain, and a Redoubt detached before the East Curtain to discover the Banks of the Morass which are high; this Redout to communicate by a Sally Port under its Curtain and a covered Way well pallisaded. A covered Way may be carried from the Redout to the Ravelin and prolonged to the River. A Hornwork ought to be made in the Island with its Lunette across the Western Branch. This Work will secure the Passage of the River and cover Storehouses to lodge Provisions &ca. Care must be had to raise the Floors of the Storehouses as the River has been known to rise over the Island. Landing Places must be made for Boats in the Island. The Curtain towards the River must be secured against Floods as the Ground the Fort stands upon is rather lower than the Island. . . .

These Works as the Timber is nigh may be soon Constructed, and without them the Passage of the River (The Design of this Fort) cannot be covered properly for communication nor prevented our Enemies as they may goe along with any Number of Battoes or Canoes down the Western Branch without being discovered by the Fort. If it is supposed ever to be attacked the Out Works will add greatly to the Strength of it. Seeing, in such Case, it would have all the upper Inhabitants of the Province of New York to defend it, whose principal Frontier this Fort certainly is. And with the addition of these Works, it could with great Numbers & Risque only, be invested.[3]

An extract from a letter-report by Lord Loudoun to the first Duke of Cumberland (second son of George II and captain general of the British Army from 1745 to 1757), dated Albany, October 3, 1756, lists the armaments at the post, with an afterword that the fort was "far from being compleated":

> At Fort Edward, there are two 18:Pounders, four 9:Pounders, five 6:Pounders, one 4:Pounder; and Six field Pieces with the Regiments, 6:Pounders each, in an Intrenched Camp under the Forts. With the Americans, there are two Six pounders, and a 3:Pounder field Piece.[4]

Also in the Cumberland Papers at Windsor Castle is a letter in French, dated October 24, 1758, by Col. James Prevost to the Duke, in which "he encloses a plan of Fort Edward, a fort so badly placed that a Vauban could not make it tenable against four mortars."[5] In 1760 Prevost reported that Fort Edward could accommodate six hundred men, an indication that some improvements, at least with respect to barracks, had been made.[6]

In 1755, less than a year after Washington's surrender of Fort Necessity, the British determined to make an all-out attack against the French at Fort St. Frederic at Crown Point. William Johnson took his army of provincials and Indians to Fort Edward, from which place he had a military road cut through the wilderness to Lake George.[7]

Immediately after arriving at the head of the lake in the middle of the afternoon of August 28, the army was put to work clearing the land for a fortified camp. Col. Ephraim Williams, on Johnson's orders, set about laying out the lines for a new fortification on a height of land overlooking Lake George. One week later, on September 3, Johnson wrote to the Lords of Trade that:

> I am building a fort at this lake which the French call Lake St. Sacrement, but I have given it the name of Lake George, not only in honor to His Majesty but to ascertain his undoubted domain here. I have found it a mere wilderness not one foot cleared. I have made a good wagon road to it from Albany, distance about seventy miles; never was house or fort erected here before; we have cleared land enough to encamp men.[8]

During the evening of September 7 scouts brought in word that Baron Dieskau and a large force of French and Indians had left Crown Point and were advancing on their camp. September 8 was a day of three murderous battles—Bloody Morning Scout, Lake George, and Bloody Pond, collectively called the Battle of Lake George. Almost disastrous for the provincials in the beginning, the tide of battle later in the day proved to be a French debacle in the end. Col. Williams and King Hendrick of the Mohawks were killed in the first of the battles. Baron Dieskau, badly wounded, was taken prisoner. The flush of victory was upon the colonials—not a single British regular was involved. England, in her gratitude, conferred on Gen. Johnson a baronetcy and five thousand pounds.

Johnson, wounded in the thigh early in the day, wasted little time in strengthening the temporary defenses. He erected a fort that he named Fort William Henry, in honor of the first and second Dukes of Cumberland, William Augustus (1721-65) and Henry (1745-90). The new English fort was a distinct challenge to French control over Lakes George and Champlain.

In the winter of 1756 Ford Edward's barracks caught fire and served as the setting for one of Maj. Israel Putnam's daring feats. At that time the barracks were near the northwestern bastion and only twelve feet from the magazine, that contained three hundred barrels of powder. Lossing describes the ensuing action:

> Attempts were made to batter the barracks to the ground with heavy cannons, but without success. Putnam, who was stationed upon Rogers's Island, in the Hudson, opposite the fort, hurried thither, and, taking his station on the roof of the barracks, ordered a line of soldiers to hand him water. But, despite his efforts, the flames raged and approached nearer and nearer to the magazine. The commandant, Colonel Haviland, seeing his danger, ordered him down; but the brave major did not leave his perilous post until the fabric began to totter. He then leaped to the ground, placed himself between the falling building and the magazine, and poured on water with all his might. The external planks of the magazine were consumed, and there was only a thin partition between the flames and the powder. But Putnam succeeded in subduing the flames and saving the ammunition. His hands and face were dreadfully burned, his whole body was more or less blistered, and it was several weeks before he recovered from the effects of his daring conflict with the fire.[9]

The first French attack against Fort William Henry came on St. Patrick's Day 1757, in the midst of a snowstorm. The enemy force of fifteen hundred regulars, Canadians, and Indians could not capture the post, but they burned almost everything outside of its walls—bateaux, sloops, two warehouses full of provisions, barracks, and a sawmill. Nearly five months later, in early August, a much larger French army under Montcalm laid siege to the fort. Lieut. Col. George Munro defended the fort to the best of his ability, but the garrison was outnumbered four to one.

Fort William Henry was surrendered to the French, who offered liberal terms, including safe escort to Halfway Brook where the beaten defenders were to be met by a detachment from Fort Edward. Montcalm's Canadian Indians, however, despite Montcalm's assurances, fell upon the helpless prisoners, including women and children, in their temporary camp outside the fort. Montcalm, sword in hand, rushed to the scene and put a stop to the slaughter. Reports disagree widely on the number massacred, but the dead were in the hundreds. Montcalm ordered the fort torn down. The logs and the dead were collected in one huge pile and set afire. While the funeral pyre was burning, the survivors were marched under heavy guard in the direction of Fort Edward.

Throughout the war the French and their allied Indians conducted terror raids against the inhabitants in New York and New England, destroying homes, barns, and supply trains, and capturing civilian and military hostages. They had a favorite place for ambuscades: the military road between Fort Edward and Lake George. In early July 1758 a train of 60 ox-drawn carts, convoyed by troops, was dispatched from Fort Edward to the lake with supplies for Abercromby, camped there with his troops on their way to Ticonderoga. The supply train spent the night at Halfway Brook's little stockaded post. Almost immediately after resuming the journey in the morning, it was attacked by the French and their Indians. The culmination of the ambush was the slaughter of 250 oxen, horribly mangled soldiers, women, and teamsters, pillaged provisions and stores, and wrecked carts. Every corpse was scalped. In reprisal, the English and the provincials stalked the French posts. The Rangers under Robert Rogers, with the assistance of Israel Putnam and John Stark, scoured the woods, rivers, and lakes north of Fort Edward, their base of operations. They waylaid French patrols and disrupted the enemy's lines of communication.

In 1759 Amherst's successful expedition forced the abandonment of Ticonderoga and Crown Point, the preliminary to ultimate French defeat. Fort Edward was evacuated and abandoned in 1766, and its works were partially dismantled by pioneering settlers, who utilized the timbers for new homes in the environs of the fort.

In 1775 the ruins of old Fort Edward, approximately 250 feet wide and 500 feet long, were razed by the Americans upon orders of the Albany Committee of Safety, to prevent its use by the British. This was no great loss, even for the enemy, since the works were more or less dominated by the surrounding hills, one of which to the north held a small blockhouse in need of major repairs.

The fort's remains, however, were occupied during 1775-77 by Patriot forces and used as an ordance and supply depot, and as Gen. Schuyler's temporary headquarters, until surrendered to Burgoyne's army. Schuyler and his men attempted to hinder as much as possible Burgoyne's advance from Skenesborough. The Patriots labored mightily as they felled thousands of trees across the old military road, destroyed bridges, and toppled trees into all navigable waterways, thereby forming an almost natural *chevaux-de-frise*. Schuyler abandoned Fort Edward, leaving a rear guard there, before Burgoyne's advance units arrived.

On the approach of the enemy's invasion force, the hundred or so men posted in the fort's ruins were withdrawn southward to the mouth of Moses Kill. They destroyed what remained of the superstructure of the fort, reportedly on July 23. The tumbledown blockhouse on the hill to the north was held by some twenty men under Lieut. Tobias Van Vechten until July 27, when they were overpowered by a strong party of Burgoyne's Indians, the same detachment that a short time later captured and killed Jane McCrea.

In what would have been but a relatively minor incident during the bloody frontier war, the circumstances of the murder of Jane McCrea, daughter of a Presbyterian minister, became the crux of a cleverly manipulated and highly successful Patriot propaganda campaign. The major effect was the amazing concentration of thousands of militia and volunteers at Saratoga's Continental Army camp, sealing the fate of Burgoyne's army.

Jane McCrea was betrothed to Lieut. David Jones, a member of a Tory contingent in Burgoyne's army. She had been living with a brother at his home between Saratoga and Fort Edward, but when he took the precaution to move to Albany, Jane proceeded to Fort Edward with the intention of effecting a rendezvous with Jones. She stayed with a Mrs. McNeil, an elderly cousin of British Gen. Simon Fraser.

On July 27 Jane and Mrs. McNeil were taken in hand by Burgoyne's Indians. Tradition and hearsay have engendered a variety of versions of what subsequently occurred. The most acceptable story is that after the Indians took the two women they started back for Fort Anne, where Burgoyne had established temporary headquarters. While en route, two of the Indians, possibly rum-drunk, engaged in a furious quarrel over which of them should be the personal guard over the women. One of the Indians, Wyandot Panther by name, became enraged, shot and scalped young Jane, and stripped her body. The Indians arrived at Fort Anne with Mrs. McNeil and a scalp of long tresses that was immediately identified by Lieut. Jones.[10]

Even though Jane McCrea was a Tory sympathizer, Gen. Washington and his staff made the most of the propaganda value of the atrocity, sending out inflammatory communiqués to stir up the north country. Gen. Gates, having taken over the command of the Northern Department from Schuyler, was in receipt of a complaining letter from Burgoyne regarding the treatment of prisoners taken during the British debacle at Bennington. Gates replied with what he called his "Tickler upon Scalping:"

U.S. Headquarters, September 2, 1777

Last night I had the honor to receive your Excellencys letter of the 1st instant. I am astonished you should mention inhumanity, or threaten retaliation; nothing happened in the action at Bennington but what is common when works are carried by assault.

That the savages of America should in their warfare mangle and scalp the unhappy prisoners who fall into their hands, is neither new nor extraordinary; but that the famous Lieutenant General Burgoyne, in whom the fine Gentleman is united with the Soldier and the Scholar, should hire the savages of America to scalp Europeans and the descendants of Europeans, nay more, that he should pay a price for each scalp so barbarously taken, is more than will be believed in Europe, until authenticated facts shall, in every Gazette, convince mankind of the truth of the horrid fate.

Miss McCrea, a young lady lovely to the sight, of virtuous character and amiable disposition, engaged to be married to an officer in your Army, was with other women and children taken out of a house near Fort-Edward, carried into the woods, and there scalped and mangled in a most shocking manner. Two parents, with their six children, were all treated with the same inhumanity, while quietly residing in their once happy and peaceful dwelling. The miserable fate of Miss McCrea was particularly aggravated by her being dressed to receive her promised husband, but met her murderer employed by you."[11]

Fort Edward was occupied by Burgoyne's troops, but after his defeat at Saratoga, the Americans reoccupied the site for the remainder of the war, using it intermittently as a way station while passing up and down the Hudson-Champlain corridor. There never was, however, any subsequent reconstruction of the fort.

Chastellux visited Fort Edward on December 30, 1780. The following passage is his view of it:

As you approach Fort Edward the houses become more rare. This fort was built sixteen miles from Saratoga, in a little valley near the river, on the only spot which is not covered with woods and where you can see for as much as a gunshot around you. Formerly it consisted of a square, fortified by two bastions on the east side, and by two demi-bastions on the river side; but this old fortification has been abandoned, because it was too easily commanded from the heights, and a large redoubt, with a simple parapet and a wretched palisade, has been built on a more elevated spot: within are small barracks which can accommodate two hundred soldiers. Such is Fort Edward, so much spoken of in Europe, although it has never been in a state to resist five hundred men equipped with four pieces of cannon.[12]

There is no archival evidence to support Chastellux's statements. Apparently he was referring to the Americans' occupancy of the fort's earthworks, or possibly either a reconstruction of the blockhouses at old Fort Miller, farther down the river, or Fort Anne to the north, "either or both of which might have been construed as being in the vicinity of Fort Edward."[13]

Today, due to the changes made in the Hudson's course in the immediate area, most of the Colonial and Revolutionary camp and fort sites are located on Rogers Island, linked to the mainland by SR 197. The actual site of forty-acre Fort Edward, privately owned, is located approximately in the center of the island.[14] No recognizable remnants of Fort Edward can be seen except for perhaps the slight traces of the earthworks and the moat.[15]

Fort Ehle
Canajoharie, Montgomery County

Rev. John Ehle, a Palatine German emigrant, came in America in 1722 and married Johanna Van Slyke of Kinderhook the following year. The newly married couple left the Hudson Valley, going first to Schenectady, and then to the Schoharie Valley. His ministerial endeavors very soon brought him to Canajoharie, where he and his wife established permanent residence.

Their first home was a log house built in 1723, replaced in 1729, the year their son Peter was born, with a single-story stone house. In 1752 Peter erected a two-story addition to his parents' dwelling. In 1777 or 1778 the structure was loopholed, probably minimally fortified, and palisaded. There is no record of any attacks by the enemy.

In 1777 the Rev. Ehle, then ninety-two years old, died and was buried in the Frey cemetery in what is now the town of Palatine Bridge. The probable site of the Ehle house, now a pile of stones, is situated on Mapletown Road (R92), a few miles south of the Van Alstyne residence (Fort Rensselaer) in Canajoharie.

Fort Failing
Canajoharie, Montgomery County

The fortified stone Failing house occupied a site about a mile and a half west of Canajoharie on the south side of the Mohawk. The dwelling, about a mile west of Fort Rensselaer, was built by Nicholas Failing and occupied by his son, Henry N. Failing, during the Revolution. Simms's history gives a capsule description of the structure:

> The windows and doors were secured with oak plank, bullet proof, while along its southern or hill side a staging was erected, to which access was gained from second story windows. This staging, with an oak floor, was planked breast high, so that a few men, posted there, could protect the house against a strong invasion. This house was not palisaded nor was it ever invaded. It unfortunately took fire and burnt down about the year 1833 and it was the writer's fortune, as a Canajoharie fireman, to see it burn.

After the war the house became the residence of the Rev. John Daniel Gros, a pioneer clergymen, who subsequently exchanged it to Col. Henry Frey for property in Freysbush, where the minister erected a large brick dwelling in which he lived for many years until his death in 1812. Col. Frey took over the Failing house, next to which he owned a two hundred-acre farm; his entire landholdings south and west of Canajoharie at that time consisted of some thirty-two hundred acres. The colonel's suspected Tory sympathies and activities during the Revolution are chronicled in the histories of the Palatine settlement in which the first of the Frey family pioneered. Apparently, at an earlier date Col. Frey also owned a fortified house at Palatine Bridge.

In 1700 everything west of Schenectady was Iroquois country. Only one white person remained in the area at the beginning of the eighteenth century. The few homes of settlers were abandoned during King William's War (1689-97), for French raids from Canada made the valley a virtual no-man's-land. The one white survivor was Heinrich Frey, who operated a trading post at the present site of Palatine Bridge.

Fishkill Barracks
Fishkill, Dutchess County

An entire volume could be written about Fishkill during the War for American Independence. The largest of the Continental Army depots, Fishkill Barracks (Fishkill Supply Depot) operated from 1776 until sometime in 1782. It was more or less officially opened in the autumn of 1776, with magazines and provision storehouses initiated during August.

In November 1776 Gen. Washington requested the New York Provincial Convention to provide for the construction of enough barracks at Fishkill to accommodate 2,000 troops through the coming winter. A sergeant and 14 men were to be detailed from each militia regiment within Albany County to do the work. At the very outset, however, there were two serious deficiencies: lumber and men. To take care of the first problem, the Convention decided to erect mud-walled huts instead of barracks. Conscription was the answer to the second problem. The drafting of a labor force constituted the first known use of conscientious objectors for noncombat duty in American history.

The Convention determined that, because a number of Albany County militia regiments "either through want of zeal in, or disaffection to, the cause of American freedom," had not volunteered their share, it was "highly just and equitable . . . that such as, through enmity or cowardice, will not step forth as soldiers should contribute an equivalent in labour."

The mud huts came first. When lumber became more plentiful through a larger labor force, barracks were constructed. These housing facilities were located on both sides of today's Route 9, one mile below the village of Fishkill. Archaeological excavations several years ago uncovered the remains of some of these structures.

The Marquis de Chastellux wrote a highly interesting account of his travels in Revolutionary America. In November 1780 he visited Fishkill:

> These barracks are regular wooden houses, well built and well covered, having garrets and even cellars, so that we should form a very false idea were we to judge of them by what we see in our armies when our troops are "in barracks." The Americans sometimes make them like ours, but this is merely to shelter the soldiers when they are more within reach of the enemy. They call the latter "huts," and they are very expert in constructing both. They require only three days to build the barracks, reckoning from the moment they begin to cut down the trees; the huts are finished in twenty-four hours. They consist of little walls made of heaped-up stones, the intervals of which are filled with earth kneaded with water or simply with mud; a few planks form the roof; but what renders them very warm is that the chimney occupies the outer side, and that you can only enter by a small door, at the side of the chimney. The army has passed whole winters in such huts, without suffering and without sickness. As for the barracks, or rather the little military town of Fishkill, such ample provision is made for everything which the service and discipline of the army may require that a provostry and a prison, surrounded by palisades, have been built there. One gate only affords access to the enclosure of the provostry and in front of this is placed a guardhouse. Through the window bars of the prison I distinguished some prisoners in English uniforms; these were about thirty soldiers, or "Tories" enrolled in English regiments. These wretches had accompanied the Indians on the raids they had just made by way of Lake Ontario and the Mohawk River. They had burned upwards of two hundred houses, killed horses and cows, and destroyed above one hundred thousand bushels of wheat. The gallows should have been the reward for these exploits, but the enemy having also made some prisoners, reprisals were

dreaded, and so these brigands were only confined in rigorous and close imprisonment.

Fishkill (for the area's fish-filled streams) existed on the site of the depot as a village before 1716. The river port for the community five miles to the east was Fishkill Landing, now incorporated in today's river town of Beacon. The military complex consisted, in the main, of the administration headquarters for the Patriot troops on the east bank of the Hudson, the Continental Army supply depot, a hospital, a prison for both Loyalists and enemy captured, and the Corps of Invalids encampment.

The New York Provincial Convention, after the Patriots were ousted from New York City, met at the Reformed Dutch Church on Main Street (Route 52) from September 1776 to February 1777; after the Convention moved on to Kingston the church was pressed into service as a prison. Continental wounded of the Battle of White Plains were taken to Fishkill, and the Trinity Episcopal Church, also on Main Street, was pressed into service as an auxiliary hospital.

When the depot was started, Fishkill Clove or Wiccopee Pass, just south of the village, was fortified with three gun batteries that remained there for the duration of the war. It is believed that the camp for the Corps of Invalids was situated near the top of the pass. Benedict Arnold, during his treasonable plan to weaken and surrender the citadel of West Point to the enemy, very often sent soldiers to Fishkill to cut wood or mount excessive guard duty. Fishkill was deactivated as a supply depot late in 1782, when the Quartermaster Commissary Department removed the remainder of the munitions and general stores.

Fort Fox
near Nellistown, Montgomery County

The fortified and loopholed stone house of Philip Fox, Fort Fox was situated at the western end of Palatine Township, about a mile and a half north of Nelliston. It stood a short distance west of Fort Wagner and near Palatine Church. Fox's Mills was the name of this locality when Gen. Robert Van Rensselaer and his troops made camp there on the night of October 19, 1780, during their pursuit of Sir John Johnson's raiders. Fox operated a gristmill here, using the water power of Caroga Creek; Johnson's Tories and Indians burned the mill during the 1780 raid.

Fort Frey
Palatine Bridge, Montgomery County

Famous in Mohawk Valley history, Fort Frey still stands remarkably well preserved on SR 5, one mile west of its junction with SR 10 in Palatine Bridge on the north shore of the Mohawk, almost opposite the city of Canajoharie. Truly representative of Palatine construction, the long, stone story-and-a-half house with a gable roof was erected in 1739 on or near the site of the small, crude, log cabin and trading post built in 1689 by Heinrich Frey (most descendants with the same given name anglicized it to Hendrick or Henry). A native of Zurich, Switzerland, Heinrich came to America in 1688 and resided, however temporarily, in the Schoharie Valley. He possessed a "location ticket," entitling him to one hundred acres along Schoharie Creek, issued by Thomas Dongan, then the province's royal governor.

In 1689 Frey permanently settled himself in the Palatine district, when he purchased three hundred acres from the Mohawks and built his little cabin some forty miles west of Schenectady. He was the only white inhabitant in what was then Indian country. The Indians forgot the transaction and granted to Harmanus Van Slyke more than a score of years later a tract of about two thousand acres that included Frey's original purchase. The following conveyance, dated January 12, 1713, attests to the grant:

> In consideration of ye love, good will and affection which we have and do bear toward our loving cozen and friend Capt. Harmon Van Slyke of Schenectady, aforesaid, whose grandmother was a right Mohaugh [Mohawk] squaw and his father born with us in above said Kanajoree [Canajoharie]. . . . It being his the said Harmon Van Slyke's right of inheritance from his father.

The matter of conflicting ownership was amicably settled when Van Slyke deeded the three hundred acres back to Frey. This transaction is shown on the Van Slyke patent map now reposing in the Fort Johnson Museum.

The British palisaded Frey's cabin at the beginning of Queen Anne's War (1702-13) and used it as a military post until the end of the conflict. According to Dr. Charles K. Winne, Jr., of Albany, a direct Frey descendant:

> The present stone house was built in 1739 by the son of the original Heinrich, he too called Heinrich. This was never to our knowledge used as a fort though there may have been a stockade about it and there are portholes in the east and west walls. This house was

somewhat enlarged some years later. It has been almost continuously occupied as a dwelling since it was built and is at present [1946] so in use. . . . The house now occupied by the family is a few hundred yards to the north and west on rising ground and was built in 1808 by Henry I. Frey [my] great-grandfather . . . and the great-grandson of the original Heinrich. It is a large stone house of the Georgian type.

There is no record that the 1739 dwelling was ever stockaded, though the British again imposed on the Frey family and occupied the structure as a military post during most of the French and Indian War. The second Heinrich (or Hendrick) Frey married Elizabeth Herkimer, a sister of Gen. Nicholas Herkimer, and held the rank of colonel and served with Sir William Johnson; he died shortly before the start of the Revolution. His three sons, Henry (or Heinrich III), John, and Bernard took opposing views of the colonial turmoil over England's oppressive acts against the Americans.

Henry, the estate's main legatee, espoused the British position; he was arrested, imprisoned, and finally released on parole. He held his parole inviolate and did not participate actively in the war but his inherited property was confiscated by the Patriots. Bernard, the youngest of the three brothers, with his nephew Philip R., joined the Tories and went to Canada. Bernard was a member of Butler's Rangers, rose to the rank of captain in 1780, settled at Niagara after the war, and was killed during the War of 1812 by an American artillery barrage across the border. Philip was an ensign in the British Eighth Foot, served with St. Leger at the siege of Fort Stanwix, and returned after the war to the Mohawk Valley, where he took up the practice of law close to the place of his birth.

John Frey, the most noted of the three brothers, was born in the Frey house in 1740 and became chairman of the Tryon County Committee of Safety and a major in the Palatine Regiment of the Tryon County Militia. He was seriously wounded at Oriskany and taken prisoner to Canada. His former neighbor, Col. John Butler of Butlersbury, despite their opposing positions in the conflict, went out of his way to obtain the best treatment possible under the circumstances for Frey while the latter was a prisoner at Niagara. When Frey was finally freed in a prisoner exchange, Butler loaned him twenty guineas to ease his trip home.

When Montgomery County became one of ten counties formed from Tryon County in 1784, John Frey was its first sheriff. He won a seat in the State Senate, serving for twenty years, and later assisted in the compilation of the informative *Annals of Tryon County,* the first history of the Mohawk Valley. He died in 1833, two years after the *Annals* was published. One of the earliest communities in the region, the village of

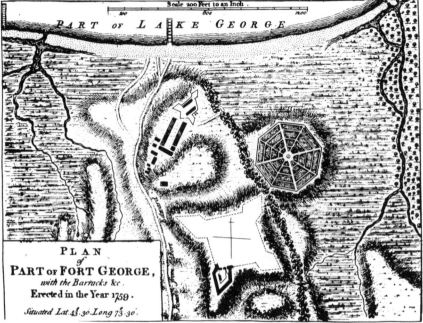

A. *Fort, shewing what was finished.* 1. *Officers Barracks.* 2. *Soldiers Barracks.* 3. *Powder Magazine.* B. *Stockaded Fort erected to serve during the time the other was Building.* *Guard Room* *the Kitchin* 6.6. *Store houses.* 7. *Saw Mill in the Swamp to the south westward.*

PLAN OF FORT GEORGE ON LAKE GEORGE
Courtesy of National Map Collection, Public Archives of Canada

Freysbush is in Minden Township, about three miles south of Fort Plain.

The old quadrangular stone house, beyond the replacement of exterior wood trim and porches during the past two-and-a-half centuries, remains to this day in excellent condition. At present a project is planned to enclose the noted Mohawk Valley landmark within a fifteen-acre park.

Fort George
Lake George, Warren County

A half mile southeast of tragic Fort William Henry (now reconstructed), Fort George's site at the head of Lake George served as a base for three colonial armies and as a hospital for a demoralized early Revolutionary War army. In June 1759 Gen. Jeffrey Amherst, with ten thousand troops on their way to victory at Ticonderoga, occupied the former fortified camp used by both Gen. William Johnson and Gen. James Abercromby.

In 1755 Johnson had established the complex at the time he defeated Baron Dieskau in the Battle of Lake George. In 1758 Abercromby arrived with the largest army ever assembled in North America up to that time. By the general's orders, more than three hundred buildings—barracks, storehouses, and hospitals—were constructed. Around the blackened ruins of Fort William Henry he had an earthwork thrown up and armed it with several small cannon. After his ignominious defeat before the French trenches stretched across Ticonderoga peninsula, the fortified camp site was converted into an oversize field hospital to accommodate the many sick and wounded of his army.

Gen. Amherst renovated the place and commenced building a new fort, which he called Fort George for George II. At the same time he ordered buried the burned remains of Fort William Henry, the scene of the infamous massacre of 1757. He also directed Col. Thomas Gage (Massachusetts governor in 1774) to build Fort Gage, merely an earthwork, on high ground a half mile to the south.

Fort George stood on a hill about a half mile from the lake, across which it had a commanding view to the north for at least ten miles. The quadrangular fort, with its long sides measuring about 100 feet, was built on a solid base of black limestone within William Johnson's old breastworks. Only the southwest bastion was ever completed. On July 21 Amherst and his army embarked upon Lake George and headed for Fort Ti. With the end of the last of the French and Indian wars, Fort Gage was abandoned and Fort George was allowed to fall into disrepair.

Shortly after the Revolution's first hostilities Fort George, garrisoned by a British caretaking detachment, was seized by the Patriots under Seth Warner. In 1776 a large hospital under Dr. Jonathan Potts was established here by Gen. Philip Schuyler for the smallpox-stricken remnants of the disastrous Canadian invasion commanded by Gen. Benedict Arnold and Richard Montgomery.

The Americans were forced to retire from the fortification before the might of Burgoyne's formidable force in 1777. For a time, while Burgoyne was marching south, Lake George's fort and environs were links in the chain of communication by which the British expedition received its supplies from Canada. After the Battle of Saratoga, Fort George was reoccupied by a small American garrison, which held it until the surprise arrival of Sir John Johnson's Tories and Indians in 1780, en route to raid the Mohawk Valley. For the remainder of the war and until 1787, a militia garrison was maintained at the fort. Fort George was then abandoned and allowed to fall into utter ruin.

A mound fifteen to twenty feet high and one hundred feet long, within which the fort's east wall was reconstructed about forty years ago,

FORT HALDIMAND ON CARLETON ISLAND
Courtesy of National Map Collection, Public Archives of Canada

symbolizes what was once a Colonial and Revolutionary War fort. The
ruins are located in Battleground Park just south of the village of Lake
George.

Fort Haldimand

Carleton Island, Jefferson County

Long recognized for its strategic military importance, Carleton Island
is situated in the south (American) channel of the St. Lawrence River,
one mile off Burnham Point State Park in Cape Vincent Township and at
the river's entrance into Lake Ontario. Composed entirely of stone, with
a sparse covering of fertile soil, the island is roughly three miles long and
a half mile wide. The peak of its occupation came during the Revolution,
when it was a major supply base and a springboard for Tory expeditions
into the Mohawk and Schoharie Valleys.

During French occupation of Canada, Carleton Island (then called Isle
aux Chevreuils—Buck or Deer Island) was not fortified and only

constituted a transient stopping place for fur voyageurs and small military detachments. The only temporary French military residency occurred in 1757, when a guard of a dozen men was posted there to observe any threat of incursion by the English.

About a year before the Revolution's first hostilities, the island was the site of an important trading post operated by Quebec fur entrepreneurs, who did a brisk business with Indians in the area. Soon after the outbreak of the war, Loyalists escaping from Whig harassment found a haven on the island and established a quasi-military occupation force. Because of its isolation from the main theater of war, the British in 1775/76 converted the island into a major military and naval supply depot to which large quantities of stores and armaments were transported from Lachine, near Montreal, and then forwarded to Oswego, Niagara, and the Old Northwest posts.

Barry St. Leger, graced with the temporary rank of brigadier general, departed from Montreal on June 23, 1777, and proceeded to Oswegatchie, where he assembled his arm of the Burgoyne expedition. Pursuant to orders, St. Leger and his force left Oswegatchie early in July and landed on Buck Island on the 8th.

They established themselves on a cleared area of the island's plateau and erected temporary bark huts. Three days later word came that Ticonderoga had fallen to Burgoyne's army. St. Leger thereupon put his men on instant alert. Provisions for forty days, ammunition, and general stores, plus his artillery of two six-pounders and two mortars, were loaded into waiting bateaux. On the 19th the armada of bateaux, preceded by an armed sloop, departed for Oswego, arriving there on the 25th. The next day St. Leger initiated his offensive against the Mohawk Valley, only to bitterly taste utter frustration and ultimate defeat before the ramparts of Fort Stanwix.

Sir Guy Carleton, one of the more talented military men on either side in the war and with an extraordinary flair for diplomacy, left Canada at the end of July 1778. Three factors had determined Sir Guy's decision to resign his dual position as governor general of Canada and commander-in-chief of the British forces therein: the unrelieved personal animosity between himself and Lord Germain, British Secretary of State; official disenchantment with Sir Guy's failure to take Ticonderoga in 1776 (the British military timetable was stalemated by the brilliant heroics of Benedict Arnold and his "navy" at Valcour Bay in October of that year); and the machinations of Burgoyne, while on leave in London, to the detriment of Sir Guy's active military role in North America (despite Gentleman Johnny's behind-the-scene politicking, Sir Guy unstintingly supported Burgoyne's ill-fated offensive to split the Colonies).

On June 27, 1778, Carleton was replaced by Sir Frederick Haldimand, Swiss soldier of fortune, who had a long record as a field commander in the French and Indian War. Sir Frederick was the antithesis of the former governor, accruing in the six years of his tenure (1778-84) both a reputation as an arbitrary administrator and several sustained official accusations for false imprisonments.

One month after replacing Carleton, Haldimand ordered Lieut. William Twiss, engineer, Lieut. (later Capt.) John Schank of the British navy, and Capt. Thomas Aubrey of the Forty-seventh Regiment to proceed to the upper St. Lawrence and there select a place best suited for a fort and shipyard. After examining several sites, Twiss was most impressed by the defensive potentialities of Buck Island. In compliment to the ex-governor general of Canada, Twiss named the island Carleton; after consultation with his two colleagues, the proposed fort was named for Gen. Haldimand.

Capt. Aubrey was commandant of the island while the fort was being built according to the plan designed by Twiss. On September 8, 1778, he reported to Haldimand that "all the lower logs for the works here will be laid this afternoon, [and] a general hospital is building." On the same day, a report by the engineer stated that the fort's parapet, eight feet high and eight feet thick at the bottom, was in the process of construction.

The head of Carleton Island is a low peninsula, connected to the mainland by an isthmus, on either side of which are two bays—North Bay and South Bay. To the rear the island rises swiftly to a steep bluff to a height of nearly sixty feet above the water. Upon this eminence stood Fort Haldimand.

Gen. Haddock, late nineteenth-century local historian, labeled the British post "Fort Carleton." His examination of the site revealed the following findings:

> A group of stone chimneys . . . stood within an elaborately fortified enclosure of which the outlines are not only distinct, but in a degree quite perfect, so that the plan is readily determined, the system identified, its armament approximately adjudged, its magazines and barracks located, and, in short, its whole scope, object and intent made reasonably plain. . . .
> The work occupied three-eighths of an octagon, extending from edge to edge of the cliff on which it was built, which faces to the southwest. The rear, or landward side, was protected by a strong earth-work, a ditch, an out-work and glacis of stone and a strong abatis. The ditch was cut in the limestone rock. In the center of each face of the ramparts, and midway between the salients, was a strong bastion, constructed for four guns, two of which in each bastion could enfilade corresponding angles of the ditch, which was cut to a depth of nearly five feet, with an average width of twenty-four feet. The scarp

was vertical and protected by a *chevaux-de-frise* of cedar logs, sharpened at the outer ends, and extending beyond the berme; these were held in place by the earth of the parapet. The counterscarp was also vertical, and beyond it extended a couvert [covered] way of about the same average width as the ditch. There were also bomb-proof magazines and barracks erected, and a well sunk to a level of or below the water in North Bay. On the 10th of June, 1793, there still remained in the fort ten eighteen-pounders, five twelve-pounders, two nine-pounders and two six-pounders. In 1783, ten years previous, six eighteens and five twelves had been taken from the armament of the fort and placed upon vessels; so that the complete armament must have been sixteen eighteens, ten twelves, two nines, and two sixes; in all, thirty guns. . . . The fort was never fully completed, work being discontinued by order of General Haldimand in 1783.[1]

A large detachment of Sir John Johnson's Royal Greens[2] was stationed for some time on the island. Later in the war, there was a detachment of the regiment known as the Royal Highland Immigrants, a Tory corps raised in 1775 by Lieut. Col. Allan MacLean in Canada. At Fort Haldimand plans for the organized raids against the fertile Mohawk Valley were formulated by Joseph Brant, Col. Daniel Claus, Tory leader and son-in-law of the late Sir William Johnson, Sir John Johnson, and John and Walter Butler. The last large-scale British incursion, October 1781, was led by Maj. John Ross, the fort's commandant.

A stronger-than-usual British Revolutionary War bastion of defense—and offense—Fort Haldimand was never assaulted by any American force. When it became known that an enemy fortification was building on Carleton Island, American scouts on the mainland established a watch on British activities in the area. This is not to say that the Patriots had no thoughts about taking the fort by a *coup de main*. One of the more nebulous ideas was delineated in an offering by Col. Robert Cockran, dated from Fort Schuyler (Stanwix), May 4, 1781, and directed to Governor George Clinton:

Sir, I am of the opinion that an expedition against Buck Island, if successful, might be attended with good consequences to our frontiers. I beg leave to lay before your Excellence my plan, as follows: if two or three hundred of our best regular troops, well officered, was to be sent to this post, with a number of boats sufficient to carry them, and to proceed down the Wood Creek, with one scaleing Ladder in each boat, and to enter the Onyda Lake in the night, the men to have their provision cooked, and not to make any fires, whilst advanceing; if this plan, was well conducted, I make no doubt but they might arrive undiscovered, and as the garrison is not strong, there would be the greatest probability of carrying it by surprise; in this case the oars must be muffled with green hides or old clothes; but no preparation of this kind ought to be made untill the boats arrived at this post; the only objection, to our arriveing undiscovered, is that we must pass the Osweago Falls in the daytime; but I think it would be ten chances to one if ever we was discovered, as no enemy resides near that place; if a plan of this kind should meet with your approbation, I wish you to solicite the Commander in Chief, for my haveing the Command; a good gide or two would be necessary, as I never was there.[3]

From the many hundreds of orders, reports, post returns, accounts, and receipts, it has been learned that during the Revolution and for many years afterward, Carleton Island was the principal British naval base on Lake Ontario.[4]

Fort Herkimer
near Little Falls, Herkimer County

The Mohawk Valley was made all the richer by the legacy left by Johann Yost Herscheimer and his eldest son, Gen. Nicholas Herkimer. Johann's original home, a log house erected about 1723, stood less than a half mile east of Herkimer Church Fort.

When "Jan Jost" built a large stone house in 1740 just to the east of the log dwelling, it was the only structure of its type in the western part of the valley. He ran a store and trading post and furnished the English at Oswego with such provisions and supplies as salt pork, corn meal, rum, and candles. In his trading with the Indians he bartered rum, powder and lead, rough cloth and duffel for their valuable furs, a highly profitable exchange for the Dutchman.

On the south bank of the Mohawk River across from the present city of Herkimer, the dwelling was called Fort Herkimer by the English when it was fortified by William Johnson. The Indians, however, called the establishment Fort Kouari ("bear"), for that was how old "Jan Jost" was known to them, in recognition of his great physical strength. The target of many attacks during the French and Indian War, the forted dwelling proved to be a sanctuary for the settlers.

The great house was truly a fort, forty feet wide and seventy feet long, two-storied, with its outer walls more than two feet thick. Each story was loopholed, as was the basement. The structure, with a roof of three-foot-long oak shingles, was surrounded by a ditch six feet deep and seven feet wide, at a distance of perhaps thirty feet. The crown of the ditch was planted with well-jointed palisades, set obliquely, behind which was a parapet of earth to facilitate firing over the pickets. The angles of the parapet were occupied by four small bastions that

Plan and Profile of Retrenched Work round Harkemeis house at ẙ German Flats 1756.

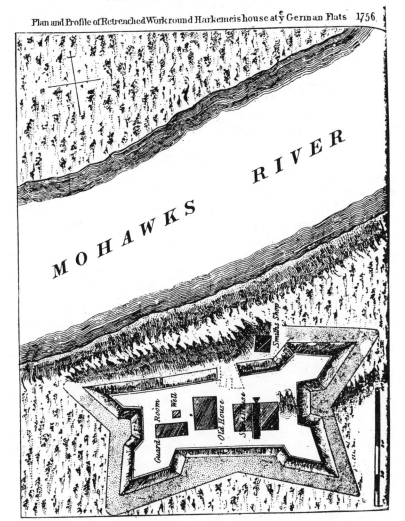

FORT HERKIMER
From Benton's *History of Herkimer County*

reciprocally flanked each other. On the west side, backed up against the parapet of the palisade, was a house apart that served as a barracks and guardhouse.

Fort Herkimer was destroyed during the construction of the Erie Canal (completed 1825). There are no traces of either the house or of the works in its fortified perimeter. The fort was rebuilt in 1756 around the stone Herkimer Dutch Reformed Church, a quarter of a mile or so west of its original site and two miles east of the village of Mohawk. A French report in 1757 confirms the transplanted fortification as "a stockaded work around the church and block-house, with a ditch and a parapet pallisadoed, thrown up by Sir William Johnson a year ago upon an alarm then given."

Palatine German settlers began the construction of the church in 1740 to replace their small log church built in 1723. Because of the French and Indian War and the impoverishment of the inhabitants during the conflict, construction was not completed until 1767. The one-story stone structure measured forty-eight by fifty-eight feet, with square buttresses at the corners and a swivel gun in its open tower.

During the Revolution's early days the church was refortified and surrounded by a strong palisade and earthworks. The fort, then known as Herkimer Church Fort, was one of the more important valley defenses. It was used as a secondary headquarters by Marinus Willett; Benedict Arnold stopped here in 1777; and Gen. Washington paid a visit in 1783 while on an inspection tour of the Mohawk Valley.

Tryon County had had no major Indian incursions for about two months during the summer of 1778. But the comparatively peaceful hiatus ended when Joseph Brant and a sizable force of Tories and Indians struck the area in mid-September from their bases at Unadilla and Ouaquaga. A patrol of four scouts from Fort Dayton was surprised by some of Brant's Indians in the environs of Edmeston on September 17. Three of the scouts were killed, while the fourth, Adam Helmer, escaped. Helmer was the courier who carried Gen. Herkimer's message to Col. Gansevoort at Fort Stanwix on the day of the Battle of Oriskany. Helmer had the reputation of being the swiftest cross-country runner in the valley and now he proved it. He outran his Indian pursuers in a highly dramatic twenty-odd-mile run to Herkimer Church Fort. The fort's signal gun was fired, the inhabitants fled to the forts, and a general massacre was averted.

In 1812 the church, one of the oldest in New York State, was renovated, altered, and enlarged, with the addition of a second story, a pitched roof, and a cupola. It is located on the bank of the Barge Canal, which replaced the old Erie Canal and was completed in 1918. The ramparts of the second Fort Herkimer were destroyed at that time. The old church is in a state of good repair and a recent grant will help in its preservation.

Gen. Herkimer's home, five miles east of the original Fort Herkimer site, overlooks the river in a 135-acre park maintained by New York State. The colonial brick house was built by Nicholas Herkimer in 1763, and it is here that the hero of Oriskany died after amputation of a shattered leg suffered ten days earlier in the battle. The general's burial place, an imposing monument, is close by.

Fort Hess
near Palatine Church, Montgomery County

Another refuge for Mohawk Valley inhabitants was Fort Hess, a small fortified stone dwelling of John Hess. It stood between Palatine Church and St. Johnsville, a mile west of Fort Fox and about three-quarters of a mile south of Fort Klock.

Fort Hill
St. Johnsville, Montgomery County

Very little is known about Fort Hill. Most Mohawk Valley histories do not even mention the place. Minuscule information rumors that the fortification, most probably a fortified dwelling, was built during the French and Indian War and was located on a hill in the western part of St. Johnsville, near or on East Canada Creek.

Tradition says that the fort was repaired subsequently and served as a haven during the Revolution. Reason suggests that Fort Hill was a stockaded home and may be the same as Fort House, also located in St. Johnsville.

Fort House
St. Johnsville, Montgomery County

Historians have been confused regarding the exact location of Fort House, due to an error in reporting by Jeptha Simms, valley historian, who placed the stone farmhouse at the eastern edge of St. Johnsville. Fort House stood at the *western* end of the village. It was home of George Klock, who fortified and stockaded it. Since there were other dwellings in the eastern end of the village owned by other members of the Klock family, including Fort Klock, George Klock called his home Fort House in honor of its builder, Christian House (Haus).

The structure, since somewhat remodeled, is one mile west of the town's center and six miles northwest of Nelliston. Fort House may be the same as Fort Hill.

Fort Hunter
Fort Hunter, Montgomery County

The major incentive for the settling by Germans and Dutch of the fertile Mohawk Valley was the establishment of Fort Hunter in 1711/12 at the confluence of the Mohawk River and Schoharie Creek. Capt. John Scott was the first commandant of the fort, garrisoned at the time by only twenty men.

A strategically placed defensive works that became significantly important in New York's colonial history, the fort was constructed at a cost of 1,000 pounds on the site of an old Mohawk village called Tienonderoga or Icanderoga. The fort was the first English fortified defense among the Five Nations of the Iroquois (the Tuscaroras, refugees from white Carolinian persecution, joined the Confederacy about the year 1716). It was erected principally to deal with French and Indian incursions from Canada and was often utilized as an assembling stage for retaliatory forays against the French.

In 1709 a delegation that included Albany's mayor, Peter Schuyler, and several Mohawk chiefs made the long journey to London and the court of Queen Anne to obtain the authority to construct fortifications in the Mohawk Valley. At the time there were living in London numerous Palatine Germans (Protestants), refugees from French wars and religious persecution. The Indian chiefs offered the queen a tract of land called Schoorie (Schoharie) as a haven for the displaced people. Queen Anne gratefully accepted the offer. Schuyler was successful in his mission, returning to America with orders to erect two forts—one at the mouth of Schoharie Creek, with the other, never constructed, in Onondaga Indian country.

Fort Hunter was named for Governor Robert Hunter who brought three thousand Palatines to America in 1709, the year he assumed the governorship of the province. The fortification was a square, 150 feet on each side, with a 12-foot-high palisade of one-foot square logs raised horizontally and pinned one on the other. At each of the four angles was a two-story, 24-foot-square, double-loopholed blockhouse or bastion, with the first story nine feet high, the second eight. The logs of the chimneyed blockhouses were nine inches square; the interiors were furnished with fixed bedsteads and benches to accommodate twenty men in each blockhouse. These bastions were armed with seven- and nine-pounder cannon. On the inner sides of the palisade were parapets, 5 feet wide along each curtain. The fort had no ditch or moat but there was a massive swing-gate at the entrance.

In the center of the fort was the famous Queen Anne's Chapel, ordered by Her Majesty for "my Mohawk Indians," a one-story, twenty-four-foot square limestone building with an attic. The chapel was well-floored, with a fifteen-foot square cellar lined with logs and apparently used as a powder magazine. Queen Anne furnished the communion set, the altar cloth, and other church appurtenances. She also periodically sent ministers to officiate at the services for the Indians, with Robert Barclay among the first to serve there.

Also within the enclosure were some thirty cabins for Mohawk residents. In 1733 the commandant of Fort Hunter was Capt. Walter Butler, father of the Tory leader John Butler and grandfather of Walter, Jr., equally notorious on the Revolutionary frontier. Shortly after assuming command of the fort's garrison, he gave a party for the Indians who, after imbibing more than liberally of the free rum and accepting gifts of blankets and knives, affixed their marks to a parchment document. In this way Butler secured for himself an Indian conveyance deeding to the officer eighty-six thousand acres along the south bank of the Mohawk River.

A two-story stone parsonage, built in 1734 and first occupied by the Rev. William Andrews, was substantially built and measured about twenty-five by thirty-five feet. During the Revolution the parsonage was fortified, palisaded, and garrisoned. New York City's Trinity Church supervised the chapel's affairs and some of the ministers who graced the chapel's pulpit later became rectors of the church. In 1769 Sir William Johnson established one of his free schools at Fort Hunter with a class of thirty pupils.

The fort was kept under constant repair through the years but, as with all similarly built fortifications, the ravages of time caught up. Decaying old Fort Hunter was torn down at the beginning of the Revolution and a new fort rose in its place, with Queen Anne's Chapel enclosed by strong palisades and cannon-mounted blockhouses at the four angles. During the war the fort was frequently garrisoned, with many Oneidas and Stockbridges using the chapel as a barracks.

The fort and the chapel were demolished in 1820 to make way for "Clinton's Ditch," the Erie Canal, but the old stone parsonage still remains and is one of the oldest structures in the Mohawk Valley. A good deal of the stone from Queen Anne's Chapel was used for the Schoharie Creek lock. At present there are markers placed near the site of the fort. A proposal has been made to New York State authorities for a major historical museum on an appropriate site in the village of Fort Hunter.

Fort Independence
Peekskill, Westchester County

Relatively short-lived and of minor significance, Fort Independence was constructed at Peekskill during August 1776 under the supervision of George Clinton. In September a barracks was begun to house the defense's garrison. The fort was situated on Tethard's Hill on Roa (Rahway) Hook on the Hudson's east bank, opposite Dunderberg Mountain. The site was often confused with Red Hook at Rhinebeck, New York. Initially called Fort Constitution for a short period, the fort had an entrenchment eighty yards long, ten feet wide, and three-and-a-half feet deep. Guarding the approaches to Peekskill Bay and ultimately Continental Village's munitions depot, this Patriot work was under the command of Maj. Israel Thompson.

Robert Bolton, just before the middle of the nineteenth century, described the fort's site and environs thus:

> Upon the highest ground of Rahway [Roa] Hook stands "Fort Independence Hotel," lately erected by Col. Pierre van Cortlandt. From its elevated position this spot commands a most extensive prospect of the Hudson River and adjacent country. To the north rise the majestic Highlands, on the west the race and towering Dunderbarrack. To the south the waters of the Peekskill bay resemble a vast lake bounded by the mountains of Rockland and Stony and Verplanck's Points, while on the east appears the village of Peekskill and the Cortlandt hills. . . . In the rear of the hotel are situated the remains of Fort Independence. . . . A small portion of its embankments and trenches are yet to be discerned. During the Revolutionary War two British vessels were sunk in the race opposite Fort Independence. About thirty years since, several cannon were raised from the vessels.

On March 23, 1777, a British force of about five hundred men raided Peekskill. The small garrison under Gen. McDougall evacuated the supply depot after removing all they could carry and destroying the remainder of the military stores.

Six months later Sir Henry Clinton led an expedition up the Hudson

River to capture the Highlands forts. The American forces on the east bank were under the immediate command of Maj. Gen. Israel Putnam who, at his headquarters at Peekskill, had a garrison of twelve hundred men. "Old Put" was deluded into believing that a major assault against Peekskill was imminent when Sir James Wallace, commanding a British flotilla, appeared in the bay and commenced a bombardment of Fort Independence.

At midnight of October 6, the day Forts Clinton and Montgomery fell to Sir Henry's forces, Governor Clinton reached Continental Village, three miles north of Peekskill. In a war council with Gen. Putnam and other staff officers, it was determined to evacuate the American defenses in and around Peekskill and retreat to the upper Highlands.

It is not known by whose direct authority Fort Independence was evacuated. The fort shared the same fate with the other Highlands forts—destruction by Sir Henry's regulars and Hessians. There was no rebuilding of Fort Independence, and its blackened ruins have served as a war reminder for decades to Peekskill's people.

On a hill to the east of Fort Independence and north of Peekskill Creek was located a smaller Patriot work called Fort Look Out. An adjoining eminence, Gallows Hill, was the site of the hanging of Edmund Palmer, a British spy, in the summer of 1780. A fine view of the river was commanded by these two hills. Fort Look Out was also destroyed when British and German troops pillaged and burned the depot, the whole village of Peekskill, and most of the homes and farms in the environs of the town.

Fort Johnstown
Johnstown, Fulton County

In 1772 Sir William Johnson decided that Johnstown (1760), the capital of his immense frontier empire, needed a jail and courthouse. Designing the first structure primarily as a gaol, prescient Sir William ordered that its construction throughout should be of stone, in case of Indian attack or outright war. When almost completed in 1773, the jail, with its massive stone walls and situation upon the highest ground in the village, was considered one of America's strongest buildings for defense, impervious to all weapons except perhaps heavy artillery. In 1774 the New York Provincial Legislature, no doubt at the urging of Sir William, appropriated sixteen hundred pounds to complete the work.

During the Revolution the jail was strongly palisaded with bastions or lookout towers at diagonal corners and named Fort Johnstown. The defensive measures were taken to protect the Sacandaga route from enemy infiltration from Canada. In the first of his two raids in 1780, Sir John Johnson, with about four hundred Tories and two hundred Indians, stealthily entered Johnstown's environs on the night of May 21, using the Sacandaga River road the Patriots were trying to safeguard. Two days later, detouring around Fort Johnstown, now the assembly point for mounting a militia pursuit, Sir John's raiders burned the settlement and headed for Mayfield a few miles to the northeast, taking with them forty prisoners.

The fort was a Patriot base during the Battle of Johnstown, October 25, 1781. An enemy army of destructives, about 570 Tories and 130 Indians led by Maj. John Ross, had been burning and plundering along the Mohawk to within a dozen miles of Schenectady. When Barry St. Leger failed to appear with promised assistance from Lake Champlain, Ross withdrew his force to Johnstown, closely pursued by Col. Marinus Willett and 400 militia.

The battle was not fought under the best of conditions. The men on both sides were bone-tired and wet through to the skin because of several days' heavy rains. Willett took over Fort Johnstown as the base from which the Patriots attacked the enemy strung along the general route of today's Johnson Avenue near Johnson Hall. Early in the battle Willett's right flank panicked and about twenty militiamen were killed attempting escape across Cayadutta Creek; others ran until they reached the sanctuaries of a church and Fort Johnstown's stockade. Willett regrouped his men and renewed the attack. The enemy had captured the Americans' only piece of artillery and stripped it of ammunition before the gun was retaken.

By the time darkness fell and put an end to the fighting, there was some doubt as to which side got the worst of it. Willett later reported that he believed his men had the upper hand until their only gun was seized and stripped. John Ross was positive that had darkness held off he would have surrounded the rebels with his numerically superior force and annihilated them. Willett also reported that a search of the battlefield found the bodies of only seven of the enemy and three of his men. He assessed the wounded at thirty to forty in each force, with thirty of the enemy as prisoners.

In 1783, some little time after the end of the war but before the jail was shorn of its palisades and bastions, Gen. Washington inspected the fort during a tour of the Mohawk Valley. The former fort is now the Fulton County Gaol on South Perry Street.

Fort Keyser
Stone Arabia, Montgomery County

Probably built during the decade preceding 1750 by Johannes Keyser (Kayser, Keisar) and his Palatine German family, Fort Keyser stood in the area then known as Stoneraby, one mile south of today's Stone Arabia. Primarily the farm house of the Keysers, the structure was all stone, approximately twenty by forty feet, with a wood frame roof through the center of which a stone chimney protruded.

Because of the exposed situation of the Mohawk Valley during the French and Indian War, the upper part of the first story was loopholed for musketry. During the first two years of the Revolution, Fort Keyser was fortified and served as a haven for Stone Arabia's inhabitants during enemy raids. It was abandoned when Fort Paris was built a half mile north in the spring of 1777.

Part of the fighting during the Battle of Stone Arabia, October 19, 1780, took place in the immediate vicinity of Fort Keyser. The scene of the battle and the site of the fort are pointed out by markers on SR 10, two miles north of Palatine Bridge. Bullets and cannonballs found through the years were evidence that Col. John Brown and his militiamen had been advancing west along the general route of today's SR 10 when they marched into an ambush set by Sir John Johnson's Indians. Col. Brown and about thirty of his men were killed; their bodies were interred in a common grave near Fort Paris. Johnson's raiders put the torch to Stone Arabia before they were cornered at Klock's Field during the afternoon of the same day.

Fort Keyser's site is about a quarter of a mile east of the junction of SR 10 and CR 43 (Dillenbeck Road). The building was torn down in the 1840s, with the surviving materials used in the construction of another farm house in the immediate neighborhood.

The King's Ferry Forts
Stony Point and Fort Lafayette
Rockland and Westchester Counties

Fifteen years after "Mad" Anthony Wayne's brilliant *coup de main* against British-occupied Stony Point on the night of July 15/16, 1779, a British historian wrote of the action: "The conduct of the Americans upon this occasion was highly meritorious: for they would have been fully justified in putting the garrison to the sword: not one man of which was put to death but in fair combat."[1]

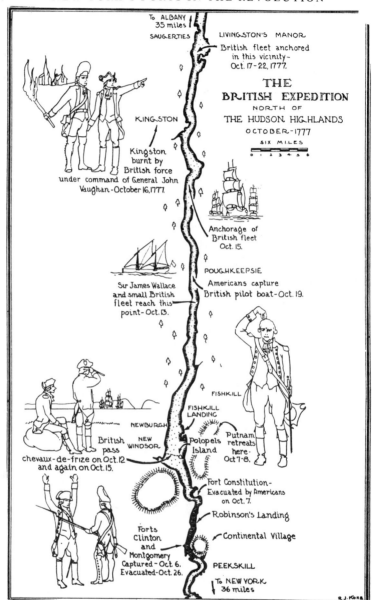

MAP OF THE BRITISH CAMPAIGN, STONY POINT TO KINGSTON
From *Twin Forts of the Popolopen: Forts Clinton and Montgomery, New York,
1775-1777* by William H. Carr and Richard J. Koke (Bear Mountain, N.Y., 1937).
Courtesy of Palisades Interstate Park Commission.

In 1779 the military situation in the northern theater of war had become stalemated after the Battle of Monmouth in 1778 and remained so until the end of the war. In late spring Sir Henry Clinton made his last important bid to lure Washington out of his fortifications centered around West Point and engage the rebels in open battle. Sir Henry's targets were Stony Point and Verplanck's Point (Fort Lafayette), respectively the western and eastern landings of King's Ferry, about twenty-five miles above New York City and half that distance below West Point.

The two Points are commanding promontories, with 150-foot-high rugged Stony Point jutting a half mile into the Hudson River. King's Ferry, the gateway to the Highlands, was crucial to the Patriots because it constituted the closest safe crossing of the river to British-held New York City, and the forts there were intended to be outposts of the Highlands defenses. The expedition up the Hudson was the last British effort to cut off New England from the southern Colonies.[2]

On May 30, a Sunday, Sir Henry personally led the effort to capture the gateway. His military force, consisting of six thousand British and Hessian regulars, boarded more than 120 frigates, galleys, gunboats, and flatboats at King's Bridge (Spuyten Duyvil Creek). The naval squadron was under the command of Sir George Collier "whose zealous assistance contributed very much to our subsequent success."[3] The next day Maj. Gen. John Vaughan landed with a force several miles below Verplanck's Point on the eastern bank, to come up behind Fort Lafayette; Sir Henry landed the rest of the troops three miles below the incomplete fortifications of Stony Point on the west shore.[4]

Sir Henry's report was more or less in agreement with the American version:

> As soon as our little fleet came in view, the enemy's troops [forty men] on the west side set fire to a large blockhouse at Stony Point and, evacuating their works, drew up on the hills with some show of an intended resistance. But, as the King's troops approached nearer, they fell back and left us the possession without a conflict. . . . We without molestation occupied the heights of Stony Point, which commanded it [Fort Lafayette]. The necessary ordnance being afterward landed and dragged up in the course of the night, a battery of cannon and mortars was mounted . . . on the summit of this difficult rock, and opened against Fort Lafayette by daybreak. The well directed and incessant fire from hence, which was also well supported by that of the galleys, had soon such an effect on the opposite works that the garrison, seeing themselves completely invested and their retreat cut off by General Vaughan in their rear, were obliged to surrender at discretion.[5]

After the bombardment of Fort Lafayette's works, garrisoned by

HENRY (LIGHT HORSE HARRY) LEE
Courtesy of National Archives

about seventy-five Carolinians, Capt. John André, bearing a flag, asked
for the fort's capitulation. Invested front and rear, the garrison had no
choice but to surrender. Verplanck's Point did not see the last of John
André: he had occasion to revisit the place some fifteen months later
under quite different circumstances. Benedict Arnold, at this time, was
already secretly in touch with Sir Henry Clinton.[6]

The loss of King's Ferry crossing meant costly detours for the
Americans. Sir Henry gloated over this inconvenience to the rebels:
"The loss of this pass obliged the enemy to pass and repass the
Highlands twice, and lengthened his communications between the east
and southern provinces at least sixty miles."[7]

To sweeten the lure for Washington and to severely chastise the
inhabitants of Connecticut's coastal towns for attacking British shipping
in Long Island Sound, Sir Henry followed his conquest of King's Ferry
with a series of destructive raids: New Haven, plundered, July 5/6;
Fairfield, briefly occupied and set afire, July 8; Green's Farms,
ransacked and burned, July 9; and Norwalk, plundered and utterly
devastated, July 11. Despite these heinous acts against colonial
citizenry, Washington would not take the bait but reinforced the Hudson
Valley in expectation of an attack against West Point and planned the
retaking of the King's Ferry landings.[8]

BARON VON STEUBEN
Courtesy of National Archives

After the British had "greatly enlarged and strengthened the two forts . . . well supplied them with ammunition and stores, and had them strongly garrisoned," Sir Henry dropped down the river and took up temporary headquarters at Phillipsburgh (now Yonkers) to await developments from the direction of West Point.[9]

Two weeks after the enemy's capture of Stony Point and Verplanck's Point, Washington requested the "boy-commander," Henry ("Light-Horse Harry") Lee, to learn the strength of the British garrison at Stony Point. On June 28 Washington ordered Anthony Wayne to look into the practicability of retaking both Points. On July 2 partisan leader Allen McLane, disguised as a local rustic, gained entrance into Stony Point's works and gathered much useful knowledge about its defenses, which he considered incomplete. Four days later Washington himself, accompanied by Wayne, scouted Stony Point from the crest of Buckberg Mountain, a mile to the northwest. The British had cleared the Point of all trees to forestall a secret approach by the rebels. Although only the north and west sides of the promontory could be seen, enough was revealed to the American officers to come up with an attack plan. It was determined, however, that to coordinate a simultaneous attack against Fort Lafayette would be inordinately difficult to put into practice. Washington ordered Wayne to immediately initiate plans for a surprise night assault.[10]

Stony Point's garrison "had been supplied with [fifteen] heavy guns, and strong defenses had been well advanced during the preceding six weeks of British occupation. Breastworks and batteries were built in advance of the fort, and two rows of abatis crossed the slope to the rear," separated from the mainland by a marsh flooded at high tide but bridged by a causeway.[11] On the rocky hill, beyond the second row of abatis, were seven batteries incompletely connected by trenches, but on the very top of the eminence was a semi-enclosed fort. Lieut. Col. Henry Johnson commanded Stony Point with about 625 men composed of regulars, Highlanders, and Royal Americans. In the river below were stationed several small British men-of-war, including the fourteen-gun sloop *Vulture,* within easy gun range of the forts.

Fort Lafayette had been begun sometime during the spring of 1778 and completed in May 1779. Occupying the highest ground on Verplanck's Point, it overlooked the ferry landing and the road leading to it. Originally defended by four guns while in Patriot hands, the British had substantially increased the number of cannon and the size of the garrison.[12]

Gen. Wayne had under his command twelve hundred light infantry and a reserve force of three hundred men under Gen. John Muhlenberg, with Henry Lee and his cavalry for scouting and securing the environs of Stony Point. Wayne initiated intensive training of his troops at Sandy Beach (near a tiny hamlet then called Swimtown, today's Highland Falls),[13] fourteen miles above Stony Point. Baron von Steuben was there to discipline and drill the men, and a remarkable job he made of it, in light of the short time allotted to him for the task.

There were only a couple of officers, other than Wayne, who had knowledge of the mission. On Thursday morning, July 15, the entire force was given the command to march south. The troops passed the ruins of Fort Montgomery, went along the north side of Popolopen Creek and around Torne Hill, and then south again between Black Mountain and West Mountain to a point a little more than a mile west of Stony Point, stopping at a place called Springsteel Farm.[14]

Wayne took no chances of discovery. According to Lossing, advance troops prepared the way by slaughtering every dog in the area and sequestering all inhabitants within their homes. The general's orders called for three assault columns: two groups to attack simultaneously from the north and the south (Wayne was to command the southern flank to attack the outer defenses nearest the fort's main works); the third group's men, the only ones allowed loaded muskets, were to go through the center as a diversion. The men in the flanks were strictly forbidden to fire their bayoneted weapons; violation of this order would have offenders instantly shot by their respective commanders. In order to obviate a mix-up in identities, all the men had pieces of white paper in their hats. An officer and twenty men, known as "Forlorn Hopes," were detached from each of the assault flanks to prepare the way by taking care of sentinels and hacking through the rows of abatis. To add to the ardor of the troops, there were prizes: the first man to enter the fort would merit a promotion and five hundred dollars; the second, four hundred dollars; the third, three hundred dollars; the fourth, two hundred dollars; and the fifth, one hundred dollars.[15]

MAJOR GENERAL ANTHONY WAYNE
Courtesy of USMA Library

Before commencing the attack, Wayne addressed his massed corps:

The distinguished honor conferred upon every officer and soldier who has been drafted into this corps by his Excellency, George Washington, the credit of the states they respectively belong to, and their own reputations, will be such powerful motives for each man to distinguish himself that the General cannot have the least doubt of a glorious victory. He hereby engages to reward the first man who enters the works. . . . But, should there be any soldier so lost to a feeling of honor as to retreat a single foot, or skulk in the face of danger, the officer next to him is immediately to put him to death that he may no longer disgrace the name of soldier, or the corps, or the state to which he belongs.[16]

It was an ideal dark night. At 11:30 the Americans moved out toward their target. At a few minutes after midnight they reached the flooded morass. The men waded through the neck-high water choked with weeds, their feet dragging through the bottom mud. Suddenly, a musket shot split the night silence: a British sentinel on shore duty had heard some movement in the darkness. The alarm spread swiftly up Stony Point's slopes to the main works.

The central column, consisting of Henry Lee's cavalry and Maj. Hardy Murfree's infantry, admirably performed its diversionary task by rushing along the causeway, yelling and shooting. It had the desired effect. Col. Johnson, the British commander, tumbled out of bed and pulled on his boots. The crash of musketry and shouting from the direction of the bridge over the marsh conveyed but one conclusion to him: the rebels were making their main effort through the center. With six companies, about three hundred half-dressed men, he charged toward the causeway. Too late he realized his mistake.

The Forlorn Hopes rushed forward to attack the first abatis with axes. Breaches were made in short order and the flanking columns crowded through the openings to begin their wild scramble up the nearly precipitous rocky hillside. The Americans fought their way through the second abatis where Wayne, in the vanguard of the south flank, received a musket ball across his scalp, temporarily knocking him out of action. His men rushed by him. The two flanking columns reached the center of the works almost simultaneously, bayoneting those defenders who refused to lay down their arms at once.

On the rocky slope within the second abatis, Wayne, with blood running down his forehead, recovered from the shock of the blow and, believing himself mortally wounded, begged to be taken to the top so that he could breathe his last on the scene of ultimate victory. Supported by two men, he was half-carried up into the fort.

A contemporary newspaper's rhetoric dwelled on American compassion versus British barbarity:

> And accordingly, in a little more than twenty minutes from the time the enemy first began to fire, our troops, overcoming all obstructions and resistance, entered the fort. Spurred on by their resentment of the former cruel bayoneting which many of them and others of our people had experienced and of the more recent and savage barbarity of plundering and burning unguarded towns, murdering old and unarmed men, abusing and forcing defenceless women, and reducing multitudes of innocent people from comfortable livings to the most distressful want of the means of subsistence—deeply affected by these cruel injuries, our people entered the fort with the resolution of putting every man to the sword. But the cry of "Mercy! mercy! Dear

Americans, mercy! Quarter! Brave Americans, quarter! Quarter!''
disarmed their resentment in an instant, insomuch that even Colonel
Johnson, the commandant, freely and candidly acknowledges that not
a drop of blood was spilled unnecessarily. Oh, Britain, turn thy eye
inward, behold and tremble at thyself.[17]

Wayne, only slightly wounded, and his men were overjoyed with their
victory, congratulating themselves on the swiftness and expertise of the
assault. For propaganda purposes the Americans grossly exaggerated
the British casualties, claiming 63 of the enemy killed. Col. Johnson, in
his official dispatch, reported only 20 of his men killed, a much more
truthful figure. A captain named Tew, impaled by an American bayonet
when he refused to surrender, was apparently the only British officer to
die on the heights of Stony Point.[18] In addition, the Americans reported
the enemy suffered 83 wounded; the British reported 74 in that category.
There were about 543 British taken as prisoners, including the wounded.
The Patriots' losses were given as 15 killed and 83 wounded.

The captured stores, supplies, and armaments (including fifteen
cannon) were valued at approximately $180,655, prize money divided
among Wayne, his officers, and men according to rank.[19] The appor-
tionment ranged from Gen. Wayne's share of $1,420.51 down to $78.92
for each private. The promise of rewards to the first five men who
entered the fort was eventually kept by the Continental Congress: Lieut.
Col. François Tessedre de Fleury, in Wayne's column, was the first
man to enter the enemy's main works, even tearing down the British
ensign with his own hands. He was awarded one of the only eight medals
dispensed by Congress during the Revolution. The medal was compara-
ble to today's Medal of Honor. Gen. Wayne and Maj. John Stewart, one
of the commanders in the south flank, were also awarded medals.[20]

The enemy on the *Vulture* and across the Hudson at Fort Lafayette
had become suddenly aware of a rebel assault against Stony Point. When
Wayne turned the captured British guns on the man-of-war and
Verplanck's Point, there was no doubt left which side was the victor.
The *Vulture* immediately lifted anchor and dropped down the river out of
range. At 2 A.M. Wayne wrote a note to his commander-in-chief: ''The
fort and garrison with Colonel Johnson are ours. Our officers and men
behaved like men who are determined to be free.''

Upon receipt of Wayne's message of victory, Washington at once
ordered troops to be ready should a decision be reached to attempt the
recapture of Fort Lafayette. To lead these men, he selected Robert
Howe—bachelor, woman-chaser, planter, and obscure politician—
who, as a major general, was quite beyond his depth in ability to
command. Washington, with his Inspector General, Baron von Steuben,

beside him, rode down to Stony Point to see for himself the fruits of victory. On the height Washington and Nathanael Greene surveyed the British-held bastion across the river. They determined that an attempt should be made immediately to retake the opposite Point. A message was drafted to Howe to "march down your troops and open a battery against their blockhouse."[21]

Howe did not have the foresight to requisition entrenching tools and coordinate his artillery and ammunition. He had the gall to notify Washington that, because of these deficiencies, he was unable to act upon his commander-in-chief's order. There was no limit to Washington's ire. The main chance was gone. Already Sir Henry Clinton was feverishly sending up light infantry, cavalry, and naval units to reinforce Verplanck's Point. Washington ordered Gen. William Heath to march the troops east of the Hudson into the country beyond Peekskill. The Patriots had to evacuate Stony Point. Orders were given to march off the prisoners, remove the big guns to West Point, and destroy the works. Among the prisoners were five American deserters. "They received revolutionary justice: a Saturday court-martial and a Sunday hanging."[22]

On Sunday the eighteenth, the British artillery was laboriously loaded on the gallant row-galley *Lady Washington,* which had come down from West Point. But the efforts of the short-handed crew came to naught. The heavily laden vessel slowly moved toward midriver. The British gunners at Fort Lafayette concentrated their artillery fire on the *Lady Washington.* Badly damaged by direct hits and listing badly, the vessel was beached near the Stony Point landing and set afire.[23]

The successful Stony Point adventure was a tremendous psychological boost to Continental morale. Propaganda artists among the Patriots exaggerated the dramatic capture. However blown up it became, the victory was still a glorious reflection of the indomitable spirit of George Washington and his closest generals. Anthony Wayne and Baron von Steuben were the real victors at Stony Point.

On the 19th Sir Henry reoccupied Stony Point with a force twice as large as the garrison he had lost there. He had the works rebuilt, even to completely enclosing the fort on the height. Fort Lafayette had its garrison augmented to more than seven hundred men. This concentration of British power on the lower Hudson, just to keep an eye on Washington and his Continentals upriver, necessitated the curtailment of Sir Henry's New England activities.

On July 26 Washington called a war council to determine whether it was again feasible to unseat Clinton from King's Ferry. His generals unanimously concurred that West Point was the main concern and that all efforts should be applied to defending it. With reference to Stony Point and Fort Lafayette, only Gen. Samuel Parsons was in favor of an attempt to take the two bastions. The commander-in-chief was in agreement with the majority advice. Almost every thought and effort thereafter were directed toward completing the planned additional West Point defenses. But in a corner of Washington's mind there was the nagging urge to annoy Sir Henry. As circumstances permitted, the Patriot commander planned surprise forays against isolated British posts in the perimeter around the enemy's headquarters in New York City.[24]

Sir Henry had received some four thousand replacements during the late summer. Most of the new men arrived "prostrated by a most virulent fever." New York City's inhabitants were already suffering fevers of their own, brought on by the excessive dampness of the summer season. Within several days the contagion spread by the new arrivals practically paralyzed the city's British garrisons, hospitalizing more than six thousand soldiers. The contagion held on right into the winter season. Crippled by the general invalidism of his troops, Sir Henry was unable to cope with "Mr. Washington's" thrusts at his outposts.[25]

Clinton could not see how he could possibly hold on to King's Ferry throughout the coming winter season. During the early fall days, he quite suddenly abandoned Stony Point and Fort Lafayette, much to Washington's gratification, withdrew his forces from Rhode Island, congregated all the elements of his army in New York City, and, in expectation of a French naval attack, sank many small watercraft to obstruct the Sandy Hook channel.[26]

It is to be conjectured that Clinton's utter frustration with Washington and the Highlands was only relieved by his expectation that soon West Point would be treasonably transferred from rebel ownership into the hands of the British. The Continental Army reoccupied the strategic King's Ferry forts and remained there during the last years of the War for American Independence.

Fort Klock

St. Johnsville, Montgomery County

A massive L-shaped, story-and-a-half stone building with two-foot-thick limestone walls, thoroughly loopholed, and resting on an eminence of solid rock, Fort Klock was built by Johannes Klock, Palatine German pioneer, in 1750 on the site of his former smaller home. On the east wall an inscription records the construction in that year by William Pick, apparently the master mason; a wing was added to the north wall of the structure in 1764. Distinctively superior in architecture, the fortified dwelling should not be confused with the home of George Klock (also called Fort Klock), brother of Johannes, about three-quarters of a mile to the northwest, no longer in existence.

Fort Klock stands on SR 10, on the north bank of the Mohawk, less than one mile east of St. Johnsville's center. One of the very few surviving fortified fur-trading posts in the Mohawk Valley, Fort Klock has been restored and is now a very charming museum. Its military and trading rooms feature interesting displays of skins, trade goods, and colonial military equipment. The large family dining room, a bedroom, and a room devoted to spinning and weaving have been restored and refurnished. The kitchen has an unusual sink constructed of native limestone. The cellar still has a spring flowing from fissures in the rock floor, no doubt an important benefit to the defenders of Fort Klock two centuries ago.

On October 19, 1780, on a battleground known as Klock's Field just to the east of Fort Klock, the militia under Gen. Robert Van Rensselaer attacked Sir Johnson's mixed force of raiders. During the dramatic action St. Johnsville's inhabitants ran for Fort Klock. The battle started in the fading light of a setting sun. Part of Sir John's force was routed and it seemed apparent that the Americans were getting the upper hand. Van Rensselaer, however, would not permit his militia to push the attack, a decision condemned by his subordinate officers. Charges were leveled against him, resulting in a court-martial that absolved him of all blame.

During the war John Klock, a member of the Tryon County Committee of Safety, lived in the fort and conducted the business of fur trading. Klock descendants held possession for almost two centuries and maintained the custom of annual family reunions at the old fort until recent years. Fort Klock was restored by the Tryon County Muzzle Loaders, Inc., and is now under the management of Fort Klock Historic Restoration, Inc.

Fort La Présentation

Ogdensburg, St. Lawrence County

There is no doubt that the original site of Fort La Présentation, today's Ogdensburg, was a wondrous slice of forest primeval, with majestic oaks, lofty maples, and graceful sycamores lining the banks of the *Swe-kat-si* (black water), right to its confluence with the St. Lawrence, opposite present-day Prescott, Ontario.

Recorded history reveals that the first party of white or Christian men to disembark on the peninsula extending into the St. Lawrence at the mouth of the Oswegatchie was the one led in the spring of 1626 by Father Gabriel Lalemant, a Jesuit priest martyred in 1649 by the Iroquois in Huron country. The expedition from Quebec, much enamored of the sylvan splendor, named the place La Galette (cake).

Settlement of the point of land, however, did not take place until more than a century later. Father François Picquet, a Sulpician Jesuit forty years old in 1748, and a group of companions left Villemarie (Montreal) and sailed along the St. Lawrence, studying its southern shore for a suitable spot to establish another New France outpost and a mission for the conversion of the Indians belonging to the Six Nations of the Iroquois.

On November 21 the party sailed through the mouth of the Oswegatchie and beheld Father Lalemant's La Galette. Father Picquet spent some days inspecting the area, reflecting on its merits as a site for a fortified French post to offset the influence of the English at Oswego and, more important to the Jesuit's interests, as a mission with good prospects for supportive farming. Greatly pleased, Father Picquet celebrated the day of their arrival by naming the place for the Feast of the Presentation of the Blessed Virgin in the Temple. The expedition returned to Montreal to initiate plans for their return with colonists, laborers, and supplies.

Father Picquet, glorified in history as "The Apostle to the Iroquois," was eminently qualified for his calling. He had arrived in Canada on July 6, 1734, after many years of careful schooling in France, completing theological studies at the Lyons Seminary and at the Petit Séminaire de Saint Sulpice at Paris, finally obtaining a doctorate at La Sorbonne. During the years he spent in Montreal, he learned the Algonquin, Huron, and Sioux tongues, which gave him a background for mastering the Iroquoian dialects.

Father Picquet was assigned to the Indian mission at Lac des Deux Montagnes on the Ottawa River, a site now occupied by the present village of Oka, some miles southwest of St. Eustache, Quebec. Here he spent almost ten unrewarding years among the lukewarm Christianized Indians who, nomadic by nature, could not adjust to settled lives in an organized community. This was further aggravated by the Indians' addiction to "firewater," which the avaricious traders sold them in return for valuable furs. In his eagerness to assure the Indians of their safety against incursions by tribal enemies, the abbé erected a stone fortress surrounded by a wide ditch and flanked by redoubts, all of the work financed by a French monetary grant and his own personal means.

During the War of the Austrian Succession, known in America as

King George's War, the governor of Canada outfitted an expedition in the fall of 1745, with the express purpose of raiding the New England settlements along the Connecticut River. The force was under the command of Sieur de Marin and consisted of 280 French and 229 Indians. The chaplain accompanying the expedition was Father Picquet.

They left Montreal November 4 and arrived at Crown Point nine days later. During the council of war there, the Indians took issue with the plan to go into the Connecticut Valley, saying that it was too late in the year to proceed over the mountains. Father Picquet thereupon displayed a map of the Hudson River Valley, pointing out alternate objectives worthy of assault. The destination agreed on was Saratoga, which was raided and burned on November 28.

His preparations completed at Montreal, Father Picquet set sail, arriving at La Présentation on May 30, 1747. The *Documentary History of New York* delineates the beginning of the settlement:

> Father Picquet arrived at the River de la Présentation (1749), called Soegatzy, with twenty-five Frenchmen and four Iroquois Indians. He set about building a stone house to secure his effects. He next had erected a small fort of pickets, and a small house constructed, to serve as a bastion. In due time, five cannon, of two-pound calibre, were sent to the Abbé for his little fort, so as to give confidence to his Indians, and persuade them that they would be in security.

The Sunday following Father Picquet's arrival, June 1, was the day of the Feast of the Blessed Trinity, and mass was celebrated for the first time in northern New York. The site selected was a hill now occupied by the Notre Dame Church. The first buildings and the fort were erected on the west bank of the Oswegatchie across the width of the peninsula, and the settlement was named Fort La Présentation. Contemporary historians have also called it Fort La Galette. By October 20 a palisaded fort with a flanking stone redoubt, the abbé's house, an oven, storehouse, and barn had been erected. In order to make the tiny colony self-sustaining, more than one hundred acres of wooded land had been cleared and prepared for cultivation.

The cornerstone that the abbé laid in his house was unearthed in 1831 from the ruins and is now enshrined in the entrance of Ogdensburg's City Hall. On it is inscribed the simple Latin legend: "*In nominee + Dei Omnipoentis, Huic habitations initia dedit, Frans Picquet, 1749,*" or translated, "François Picquet laid the foundation of this habitation, in the name of the Almighty God, in 1749."

Father Picquet's labors were devoted in some measure to effecting a prosperous community and a strong military establishment, but his most zealous efforts were in the direction of founding a successful mission. Having learned from bitter experience, he forbade the availability of liquor and banned any manner of promiscuity. French traders had no qualms about debauching Indian women, who were offered by their fathers and husbands in return for "firewater." In later years American fur traders in the West also engaged in this form of native degradation.

In the fall of 1749, while the abbé was visiting Montreal on matters of business, Fort La Présentation, guarded by only three soldiers, was attacked and burned on October 26 by a party of Iroquois, most probably Mohawks. The French knew that the instigation for the attack came from the English, who were quite upset by the establishment of an enemy fortified post in Iroquois country. The palisade and the barn were destroyed, but the stone redoubt survived repeated burnings. Father Picquet immediately commenced reconstruction. Foreseeing the possibility of further incursions, he applied to the authorities for permission to erect a permanent fortification. The governor of Canada, De la Jonquière, was in agreement and sent engineer Rocbert de la Morandière to draw the plans for the new fort and to oversee its construction.

In 1751, less than two years after the burning of the settlement, there were nearly four hundred families, mostly Indian, residing at La Présentation, a tribute to Father Picquet's zeal. There was the new palisaded fort, measuring seventy feet on each side, flanked with bastions, a powder house, chapel, ovens, provision warehouse, and the sawmill that had been one of the abbé's first desires ever since the mission started. Cultivation of the cleared land was eminently successful, for there were large fields of wheat and vegetables to sustain the community, which had three Iroquois villages consisting of forty-nine bark longhouses sixty to eighty feet in length, each capable of accommodating three or four families.

The fort's armaments included seven small stone guns and eleven four- and six-pounders. The original garrison consisted of thirty men, with Drouet de Beaudicourt as commandant. Pierre Joseph de Céleron de Blainville, stationed for a time at Detroit, was recalled from that post and succeeded Beaudicourt. After the death of Governor de la Jonquière on March 17, 1752, Lieut. Boucher de la Perière became the commandant of Fort La Présentation.

The fort had been described as a square, with tower-shaped bastions in the four angles, surrounded by a wide moat and an entrenchment. The palisades, Indian-fashioned, were higher than usual and were constructed of strong cedar posts. On the inner sides, near the top, was a parapet constructed of two thicknesses of timber, gun-proofed against

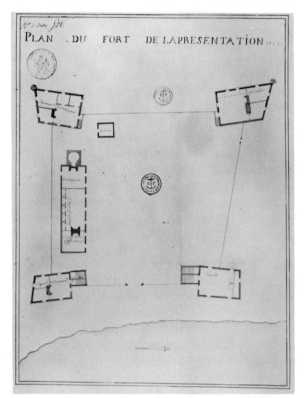

PLAN OF FORT LA PRESENTATION (1752)

Courtesy of Archives nationales de France, D. FC. Amérique septentrionale 526C and National Map Collection, Public Archives of Canada

small artillery fire. The main gate was in the north wall of the fort, fronting the confluence of the two rivers. Since the bay between the peninsula and the mainland was not very wide, all watercraft ascending or descending the Oswegatchie had to pass under the guns of the fort.

There assembled at Albany on June 19, 1754, a congress of representatives sent by several Colonies to devise a strategy against the encroachments of the French. The following is one of the statements that emanated from the conclave:

> That they [the French] are continually drawing off the Indians from the British interest, and have lately persuaded one-half of the Onondaga tribe, with many from the other nations along with them, to remove to a place called Oswegatchie, where they have built them a

church and fort; and many of the Senecas, the most numerous nation, appear wavering, and rather inclined to the French; and it is a melancholy consideration, that not more than 150 men of all the several nations have attended this treaty, though they had notice that all the Governments would be here by Commissioners, and that a large present would be given.

The French and Indian War brought to naught Father Picquet's labors to inculcate Christianity among the Indians. There are many historical commentators, mostly English, who have condemned the abbé's role in the barbarous war. He often accompanied his Indians into battles that many a time culminated in scenes of extreme barbarity and butchery, "encouraging their loyalty, forgiving their sins, administering the last rites of the Church, burying their dead bodies." A Canadian history of the area around Fort La Présentation offers this biting criticism of Father Picquet's conduct in the war:

In several other engagements the name of this indefatiable mission-ary is mentioned, the French authorities heaping upon him the highest encomiums; the English uniting in declaring that he was all that was vile, because he employed the Indians in making attacks upon defenceless settlements. That he was actuated by patriotic senti-ments, no one can doubt. With zeal unabated, and energy untiring, he labored in behalf of his religion and the cause of his King. The conversion of the savages was the ruling passion of his life; and to secure that end, he no doubt resorted to means which disregarded the common claims of humanity.

Indians from Fort La Présentation participated in Braddock's defeat near Fort Duquesne. Indeed, since the fort, mission, and trading post harbored more than three thousand people, the French sent out from that place large detachments to do battle with the English. It was the center from which the French dispatched scalping parties that harassed the settlements along the Mohawk River during the crucial years 1758–59. But the tide of battle had begun to turn against the French and their Indian allies, and the fortunes of war, bitterly fought for, were being won by the English. The French sun was going down in North America.

Early in 1759, the Apostle to the Iroquois went to Quebec for safety, knowing full well his fate should the English capture him. Before Quebec fell to the English later the same year, Father Picquet fled to New Orleans, where he spent three unhappy years, yearning to return to his mission on the Oswegatchie. When he finally knew in his heart that there was no hope of rejoining his Indians in the northern wilderness, he returned to France. He died at Verjon on July 15, 1781.

The downfall of New France was largely due to the failure of the Canadian French to successfully compete with the English for control of the continental trade routes, and to the overpowering efficiency of English manufactures. Canada's importation of goods and supplies from the homeland was cut to a bare minimum because of the effective English blockade of France's seaports. Expected troop reinforcements, military supplies, and provisions never arrived in the hour of New France's greatest need.

The English military strength was spread from the Great Lakes to the Atlantic. The plan for the ultimate reduction of Canada was centered on the capture of Montreal. The British stronghold at Oswego on Lake Ontario was the point from which the invasion army was to proceed to the entrance of the St. Lawrence, then up that estuary to Montreal, smashing and capturing all the French fortifications in the path.

Three expeditions were readied, the largest and most important one under the command of Maj. Gen. Jeffrey Amherst. On July 22, 1760, his force of more than ten thousand regulars and provincials was at Schenectady, where it was augmented by Sir William Johnson's six hundred Iroquois, increased later by a like number of Indians defecting from the French. The combined force then proceeded to Oswego.

On August 10 they set sail in an armada of four hundred open vessels, convoyed by two armed brigs, with an advance guard of one thousand men under Lieut. Col. Frederick Haldimand. It was an impressive display of English power. When the flotilla reached the mouth of the St. Lawrence, precautions were taken to fully reconnoiter both sides of the river. The land-and-sea army met no resistance until it reached the rapids above Fort La Présentation, where two armed French vessels appeared.

Gen. Amherst at once issued orders for a regiment to board them. One of the men-of-war, the *Outaouaise,* commanded by Capt. La Broquerie, was taken after a thrilling fight offered by five English row-galleys under Col. George Williamson. The second enemy vessel escaped in the direction of Fort La Présentation. The *Outaouaise* was sailed to a safe anchorage, manned by an English crew, and renamed the *Williamson.*

When the English flotilla approached Fort La Présentation on Lighthouse Point, there was the second man-of-war, in the company of another vessel, once again barring the passage of the river. The two ships were riding at anchor at the mouth of the Oswegatchie. Col. Israel Putnam, "Old Put" of Revolutionary War fame, was given the assignment of taking the two vessels, which he accomplished in short order. The capture of the ships was followed almost immediately by the evacuation of the fort's skeleton force.

To counteract Amherst, Maj. Gen. François Gaston de Lévis, second in command to Montcalm a year earlier, had sent Capt. François Pouchot, recent commandant of Fort Niagara and a British exchanged prisoner, to Fort La Présentation. It was a vain effort and almost the last gasp of a dying empire to hold on to the upper St. Lawrence.

A year earlier the French military had concluded that Fort La Présentation was not strategically effective enough to command the St. Lawrence and that another fortification should be erected in a more advantageous position. It was determined that Isle Royale, later known as Chimney Island, lying mid-river and three miles downstream from Fort La Présentation, should be the site of the new fort. The construction of the new works was begun on August 29, 1759, under the direction of de Lévis. The fort, named for the French commander, was a four-bastioned square and contained barracks, magazines, and officers' quarters, all built of wood. When captured, the ordnance consisted of twelve twelve-pounders, two sixes, thirteen fours, four ones, and four brass sixes. The surrendered garrison numbered two captains, six subalterns, and 291 men.

When news came of the British advance, Capt. Pouchot ordered the removal of guns, ammunition, and equipment from Fort La Présentation and had them transported downstream to Fort Lévis, leaving a very small force to manage as best it could. Amherst could safely have by-passed Fort Lévis but decided that it might be dangerous to leave an enemy fortification in his rear. He therefore had the fort besieged, and on August 23 began bombarding it from his vessels, from the mainland at a place now known as Adams or Wright's Point, and from two islands now called Spencer and Drummond. After almost three days of incessant heavy artillery fire, the fort was literally shredded into matchwood. Capt. Pouchot surrendered the remains of his fort and what was left of the garrison on August 25, thirteen months to the day after the surrender of his post of Fort Niagara. The garrison suffered terrible punishment: every officer was wounded, if not dead, and more than sixty other men were killed or wounded. Pouchot and his men, prisoners of war, were taken to New York City.

Sir William Johnson's Indians became highly incensed when they were not permitted to wreak their vengeance on the surrendered garrison, and became hysterical with rage when a few Mohawk scalps were discovered in the fort's barracks. To satisfy their lust, they disinterred fresh graves on the island and scalped the dead French soldiers. Most of Johnson's Iroquois force then absconded with a number of small craft and went home. Amherst was not at all amused by the Indians' temperamental antics. He spent several days rebuilding the fort, renamed Fort William Augustus, before continuing down the St. Lawrence. The site of the fort, Chimney Island, was later obliterated during the construction of the St. Lawrence Seaway.

The English occupied Fort La Présentation, renamed Fort Oswegatchie, from 1760 until their evacuation in 1796. Father Picquet's mission was gone, and the few remaining Indians were ordered to remove themselves from the precincts of the fort. What was once a highly touted French military post, with the promise of colonial status, became an English settlement important only to British fur and lumber interests. During the Revolution it was attacked once by an American militia detachment on April 1, 1779, but it retreated when the British garrison firmly repulsed the Patriots. The fort should have come under American control under the terms of the Treaty of Paris, but the British did not leave for another thirteen years.

According to a local magazine review of the history of Ogdensburg, a great deal of litigation resulted when the time came to establish legal ownership of what was by then known as Picquet's Folly:

> Meanwhile both the English at the fort and the Indians in the forest looked upon the countryside as their own and for a suitable consideration deeds of sale or leases were handed to all comers, practices which later gave rise to many suits and countersuits in establishing title to the land. . . . Then with the adoption of the New York State Constitution on April 20, 1777 . . . all treaties for land were reserved to the State Legislature, and all contracts made with the Indians after October of 1775 within the limits of the state were nullified.

In the course of establishing townships and of the legal sale of unappropriated lands, practically all of what is now Ogdensburg became the property of Alexander Macomb, a Detroit fur trader. In a subsequent sale and transfer of property, Samuel Ogden became the sole owner in 1792 and immediately took steps to clear his title to the land and to dispossess trespassers or squatters. The Jay Treaty included the evacuation of all English personnel from the fort and what was once French domain became Ogdensburg.

In celebration of the nation's two hundredth birthday, the American Revolution Bicentennial Administration granted the Ogdensburg Bicentennial Committee a sum of money to reconstruct Father Picquet's fort.

The Long Island Forts

Sag Harbor Fort, Fort Setauket, Oyster Bay Encampment
Fort Franklin, Fort St. George, Fort Slongo, Fort Golgotha
Nassau and Suffolk Counties

The majority of the inhabitants on New York's Long Island were Loyalists. The Church of England was strongly entrenched there and some of the largest church edifices and congregations were on the Island, with sizable estates belonging to officers of the Crown.

The menace of a "fifth column" so alarmed Gen. Washington that early in 1776 he ordered all British partisans on Long Island disarmed under the directive of the Tory Act. Many adherents to the Crown's cause either hid out in the boondocks or sought refuge on Staten Island under the protection of the British military.

In the midst of strong Loyalist centers were Patriot enclaves. The Huntington town meeting, on May 2, 1775, decided by vote that eighty men be chosen to drill and be ready to go into battle when called. The first five companies of militia were subsequently raised in Huntington and the command was given to Col. Josiah Smith of Brookhaven. On August 8, 1776, not quite three weeks before the Battle of Brooklyn, Smith was ordered to march his men to Gen. Nathanael Greene's camp in the extreme western part of Nassau Island, as Long Island was then often called.

The enemy finally made their move and invaded Brooklyn. The Americans, outnumbered and outmaneuvered, fled to Manhattan and left Long Island to the British, who quickly moved in. Enemy troops landed to the east of Huntington and seized cattle and stores of provisions. Long Island became an important granary and forage center for the British army in New York City. Though the Island was behind their lines, the redcoats never felt secure, and for several good reasons.

Martial law was declared. The British vindictively sought out the more outspoken Patriot activists. Rather than chance incarceration in a filthy British prison, many fled across Long Island Sound to Connecticut. Those who could not leave family and home took the oath of allegiance to the Crown with tongue in cheek and bided their time. Those who did not profess Loyalist sympathies were accorded the most grievous treatment. Their homes were commandeered as billets and, to add insult to injury, Hessian hirelings were lodged therein; their livestock was driven off and their hard-earned crops seized. In many cases the property of Patriots who fled was taken over by either the soldiery or Loyalists. The areas of Oyster Bay (in British possession for most of the war years), Huntington, Smithtown, and Sag Harbor, were the hardest hit.

Underground organizations were developed to harass and beleaguer the British occupation forces in their forts and cantonments. Whaleboat warfare was instituted, with Patriot refugees quartered in Connecticut assisting Continentals to cross Long Island Sound in the dead of night and set fire to the British forage centers. Privateers were commissioned by the Continental Congress to prey on British naval units in the Sound.

A spy network called the Culper Ring operated in the New York City-Long Island area and performed with distinction under the supervision of Maj. Benjamin Tallmadge, Washington's chief of intelligence. It was Tallmadge's perception and enterprise after the capture of John Anderson (John André) that led to the startling disclosure of Arnold's treason.

The Culper Ring is considered to have been the first American organization of espionage agents. Tallmadge, a Setauket native, enrolled home-town friends in his spy force. One of his recruits was Austin Roe, a farmer with an astounding insensitivity to danger, who many times made the 110-mile circuit between Setauket and New York.

Roe's role was to carry back to Setauket "a ½ ream of paper," a sheet of which was inscribed in Sympathetic Stain, an invisible ink developed by John Jay's brother, Sir James Jay. On his return to Setauket, Roe would amble out to Abraham Woodhull's pasture and drop the "blank" sheet into a box. Woodhull (alias Samuel Culper Senior) would retrieve the sheet of paper and, in the seclusion of his bedroom, apply the reagent to bring out the intelligence supplied in British-held New York by Robert Townsend (Samuel Culper Junior). At an appropriate time the transcription of the message would be handed to Caleb Brewster, who rowed across the Sound to Connecticut, where Tallmadge was waiting. Through a series of mounted dragoon relays, the message was carried to Washington's headquarters.

Later, after it was learned that British intelligence had discovered that American spies were using an invisible ink, and fearful that a highly important secret message would be intercepted, Washington had Maj. Tallmadge devise a cipher and numerical code as insurance. Only four people possessed a copy of the code book: Washington, Tallmadge, Townsend, and Woodhull.

The British occupation of Long Island was reinforced by seven forts and cantonments, all marked for destruction by Patriot guerrilla forces. The only post within the limits of today's Nassau County was the reigning British fort, the Oyster Bay Encampment, headquarters of the despised Queen's Rangers. To the east, along the north shore of the

Island, were Fort Franklin on Lloyd Neck, Fort Golgotha at Huntington, Fort Slongo on Treadwell Neck at today's Fort Salonga, and Fort Setauket. The south shore was not left unprotected. There Americans loyal to George III established Fort St. George at Mastic. The easternmost post was Sag Harbor Fort on Shelter Island Sound, 105 miles from New York. The only British fortifications to escape rebel wrath were the Oyster Bay Encampment, nerve center of British operations on the Island, and Fort Golgotha.

One of the most daring and brilliantly successful raids of the war was made against Sag Harbor Fort, an important British depot for military supplies, provisions, and forage on Long Island. Starting in 1770, Sag Harbor had established a profitable trade with the West Indies. About the same time, the Sag Harbor inhabitants instituted a lucrative shipbuilding industry. A year later a large wharf, 495 feet long, supplementing smaller docking facilities, was built to accommodate the larger coastal and West India trading vessels (the wharf in later years was appreciably extended and is now known as Long Wharf).

Before the Revolution, Sag Harbor was, next to New York City, the most important port in the province. In 1775 there were about three dozen resident families in the village. With the coming of the enemy in 1776, it did not take long before its population dwindled to only several diehards, and the prosperous trade was gone. Those maritime men who favored the Revolutionary cause took their vessels to Connecticut and, with the blessings of the Continental Congress, outfitted them as privateers to prey on British shipping. Their prizes were often converted into hard cash, which was contributed to the American cause to purchase arms and uniforms for the Continental Army.

By April 1777 the British had accumulated a very large stock of provisions, munitions, and forage at Sag Harbor. Intelligence reports inspired the Continental authorities to make plans for reducing the British arsenal. Gen. Samuel Holden Parsons, commanding the Patriot forces in Connecticut, selected a very competent field commander, Col. Return Jonathan Meigs, veteran of the Canada invasion, to head an assault party of 160 men in thirteen whaleboats.[1] Sachem's Head at Guilford, Connecticut, about ten miles east of New Haven, was the point of departure on May 23.[2] The whaleboats were convoyed across the Sound by two armed sloops, to land near Southold at about six o'clock in the evening. Leaving the sloops, Meigs's men hauled their whaleboats across a narrow isthmus and rowed across the bay to a point about three miles west of Sag Harbor.

Secreting their watercraft in some wild shrubbery and posting a guard, the Patriot raiders marched directly to Sag Harbor village, arriving at the

British post at about one o'clock in the morning. Two men on duty in the post hospital were compelled to lead the way to their commanding officer, who was quartered in Tory James Howell's dwelling. The commandant, found asleep in his bed, was taken prisoner. Seventy Tories, part of one of De Lancey's battalions, were taken at the point of the bayonet.

Gen. Parsons's letter to Connecticut's governor, Jonathan Trumbull (the only royal provincial governor to espouse the Patriot cause), dated "N. Haven, May 25, '77," reports the action with succinct clarity;

> [Having] made the proper dispositions for attacking the enemy in 5 different places, proceeded with the greatest order and silence till 20 rods of the enemy, when they rushed with fixed bayonets upon the different barracks, guards, and quarters of the enemy: whilst Capt. Troop, with a party under his command, at the same time took possession of the wharves and vessels lying there. The alarm soon became general, and an incessant fire of grape and round shot was kept up from an armed schooner of 12 guns, which lay within 120 yds. of the wharves, for near an hour; notwithstanding which the party burnt all the vessels at the wharf, killed and captivated all the men belonging to them, destroyed about 100 tons of hay, large quantities of grain, 10 hhds. of rum, and other W. Indian goods, and secured all the soldiers who were there stationed. 90 prisoners . . . not a man killed or wounded on our side. The officers and men behaved with the greatest order and bravery.[3]

Col. Meigs and his raiders returned to Guilford, arriving there at noon of the same day, having traveled a distance of almost one hundred miles in eighteen hours. Part of the Sag Harbor Fort site is now occupied by the Meigs Monument on Union Street.

Early in 1777 the central Island village of Setauket, originally settled by Boston Puritans, was occupied by the Third Battalion of De Lancey's Tories, numbering 260 men, under the command of Col. Richard Hewlett of Hempstead. They took possession of the Presbyterian Church on Strongs Neck Road and converted it into what became known as Setauket Fort, a comparatively short-lived post. Across the road is still standing the former Church of England Caroline Church, named in honor of George II's queen, Wilhemina-Karoline of Brandenburg-Anspach, inviolate in the eyes of the British military during the Revolution.

The Tories had mounted four swivels in the Presbyterian Church's gallery windows, with the horse stables directly below. The post was enclosed at a distance of thirty feet by an earthwork six feet high and five feet thick, surmounted by a palisade of pickets six feet high and three inches apart. Pickets were also set to project from the outer side of the ditch. The parapet consisted of two steps of earth inside the wall for the men to rise on and fire their muskets between the pickets. The only entry was through a heavy double gate in the south wall of the earthwork. Included within the palisaded area was the cemetery, with most of the monuments knocked down and the graves leveled.

To this day there is a controversy regarding when the first American attack against Setauket took place. In addition, there are varying estimates of the number of Americans in the assault force.[4] It was the Continental Army's desire to break up the Tory stronghold and capture its garrison.

Possibly stimulated by the success of Meigs's assault against Sag Harbor, Gen. Parsons undertook an expedition against Setauket. With a large party of hand-picked men (numbering between 150 and 500, depending on the authority researched) and three brass fieldpieces, Parsons embarked on August 21, 1777 (most probable correct date) from Black Rock (New Haven) in a sloop and an undetermined number of whaleboats.

The invasion force landed at Mt. Misery (now Belle Terre), about three miles east of Setauket, before break of day the next morning. Leaving their boats under sufficient guard, they marched to within hailing distance of the British garrison. A flag was at once sent to Col. Hewlett, demanding instant surrender. The British commander, hoping for reinforcements, asked for half an hour, but Parsons would allow him only ten minutes in which to decide. After consulting with his subordinates, Hewlett determined to defend his fort to the last man. The time was 5 A.M.

The Americans commenced the attack, with their artillery planted behind Tyler Rock about three hundred yards west of the fort. Some of the musket balls fired during the action are still lodged in the walls of Caroline Church, which was partly in the line of fire. After a warm engagement of two or three hours, with no apparent damage to either the fortified church or the besieged, Gen. Parsons received news that several British ships of war, which had been lying off Huntington, were proceeding eastward. Fear that his retreat might be cut off by the taking of his boats, Parsons abandoned the attack. The Americans hurriedly made their way to the boats and returned to Black Rock on the Connecticut shore. Four Patriots were killed and several others wounded. The British loss was less than that.

Toward the end of the same year, on December 10, Caleb Brewster led another American assault force against Setauket, and his attack was also successfully repulsed. Early in 1778, probably in January, the Tory garrison left Setauket and the fort was abandoned. The damaged and

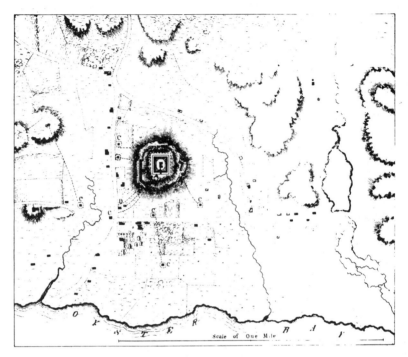

PLAN OF OYSTER BAY ENCAMPMENT, AS DRAWN BY LT. COL.
SIMCOE

desecrated parts of the Presbyterian Church were patched up. Some
years after the Revolution the edifice was struck by lightning and
burned. In 1811 a new church was erected on the same site.

The fortress that dominated the Oyster Bay Encampment was
situated at the present-day corner of Orchard and Prospect Streets. The
post was strategically placed; the harbor, sheltered by an island,
furnished a haven for small boats. In addition, the surrounding
countryside afforded abundant forage. The post was the headquarters of
Lieut. Col. John Graves Simcoe, one of Britain's ablest military men,
who arrived at the Oyster Bay village on November 19, 1778. Under his
command were hundreds of Queens Rangers, Americans who had
volunteered to serve George III.

Simcoe established himself in Raynham Hall (now a museum) and set
his Rangers to work felling trees for the stockade and fascines. A hill in
the western part of the village was the highest point in the area. A strong
redoubt was erected there, with a fine view of the entire bay. The

accessible ascents of the hill were fortified by flèches joined by abatis. The hill's summit held the square redoubt, which could be manned by as many as seventy men, with platforms for the cannon in the angles. The center of the redoubt was occupied by a guardhouse, cased and filled with sand, musket-proofed, and loopholed in a manner to command the platforms and parapets, with a twenty-man guard sufficient to defend it.

The Oyster Bay Encampment was always ready for an attack. Hundreds of rebel regulars were in Connecticut just waiting for orders and there were more than enough whaleboats to transport them across the Sound. Every possible avenue of approach around the village was fortified in one way or another. The New Light Meeting House was moved from its foundations to the beach area, where the Highland and Grenadier companies were quartered. Even civilian Tory sympathizers kept a nervous eye peeled for Patriot infiltrations.

The discipline and vigilance paid off. The Americans never made the expected assault. But another British fortification a dozen miles to the east was not so lucky. In 1779 Maj. Tallmadge was planning an assault on Fort Franklin, named for William Franklin, last royal governor of New Jersey and Tory son of Benjamin Franklin.[5] The fort was built in 1778 on Lloyd Neck, an elevated headland between Oyster Bay and Huntington Harbor (the site of the fort today is on the estate of Mrs. Willis D. Wood). This strongpoint, close to both New York City and Connecticut, was occupied by the British throughout the remainder of the war. Col. Benjamin Thompson, a Massachusetts Tory, designed Fort Franklin and resided in the Lloyd Manor House on the neck. The first Manor House was erected in 1711. The second one, still standing, was built in 1722 and, during the Revolution, the fort's officers were quartered there.[6] In 1782 Prince William Henry, Duke of Clarence (later known as the "Sailor King"), then seventeen, visited Lloyd Neck and was entertained at the Manor House.

Just before the war the Lloyd family had cleared about 100 acres of forest growth. That expanse became the fort's parade ground and on a slope to the south were the barracks and gardens of the soldiers. The fort was an irregular square surrounded by a ditch four feet deep and wide. Pickets, mostly of saddlewood, eight feet high and four inches thick, were placed in the center of the ditch, while an abatis surrounded the whole. Close to the center was a blockhouse made of four-inch planking. On the ramparts were mounted four twelve-pounders and two three-pounders. On the parade ground was a brass four-pounder fieldpiece.

On September 5, 1779, Tallmadge proceeded from Shipan Point, near Stamford, Connecticut, with 130 dismounted dragoons, and at ten o'clock that night attacked Lloyd Neck, where 500 Tories were holed up. The surprise was overwhelming. Before the morning light, Tallmadge returned to the Connecticut point of embarkation with almost the entire garrison as prisoners. He had not lost a single man in the daring enterprise.

In 1781 the fort was "bequeathed" to the Honourable Board of Associated Loyalists, organized December 28, 1780, with William Franklin as its president. The Board was founded at the suggestion of Lord Germain, with the purpose of collecting such Loyalists as did not desire to enter military ranks but were anxious to assist in the British war effort. They were licensed for indiscriminate plunder against Long Island rebels and the inhabitants on the Connecticut shore, and in the course of one year had collected in Oyster Bay a small navy of raiding vessels. Because of their often cruel methods, the Board was dissolved at the close of 1781 by the British high command.

On July 12, 1781, Fort Franklin was again attacked, this time by a force sent out from Newport, Rhode Island, by the Comte de Barras, consisting of three frigates and three whaleboats, with 250 men. After a landing in the early morning, it was learned that the place was too heavily garrisoned, being occupied at the time by about 800 Tories. The French assault force retreated to their boats but, saving the day from being a total loss, captured some British marines in Huntington Harbor.

No one is certain when the fort was dismantled. An old newspaper account reports that "when Fort Franklin was dismantled and abandoned, the work was done hurriedly and no one seems to know exactly what was done with the property. Tradition says that the guns were thrown to the bottom of an old well."

A little more than a year after his assault against Fort Franklin, Tallmadge was plotting another commando-style raid. The target was on the Island's south shore—Fort St. George at Mastic. The fort was situated on Smith Point, a promontory projecting into Great South Bay. In the autumn of 1780, a group of Rhode Island Tories took possession of Gen. John Smith's manor house on the point and built the fort nearby.

The triangular enclosure held several acres. At two angles were fortified houses, and at the third, a strong redoubt, ninety-six feet square, with bastions, a deep moat, and an abatis. Between the houses and the fort were twelve-foot palisades. The redoubt was embrasured for six guns, but only two were mounted. The fort was designed as a storehouse for the royalists in Suffolk County.

Tallmadge got the go-ahead from Washington and, on November 21, he and eighty dismounted dragoons assembled at Fairfield, Connecticut, where they embarked in eight whaleboats. They slipped across the Sound to land at Old Man's Harbor (now Mt. Sinai Harbor) at nine

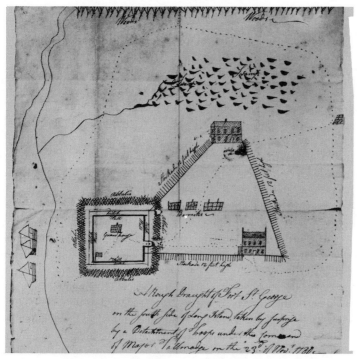

SKETCH OF FORT ST. GEORGE, LONG ISLAND, BY MAJOR
BENJAMIN TALLMADGE
Courtesy of Connecticut Historical Society

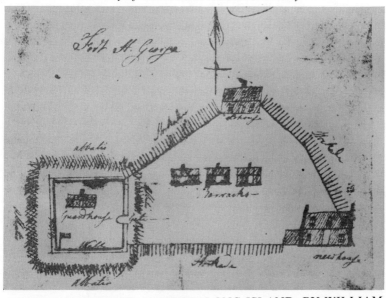

SKETCH OF FORT ST. GEORGE, LONG ISLAND, BY WILLIAM
BOOTH, CONTINENTAL ARMY SPY
Courtesy of the Museum, Manor of St. George, Shirley, L.I., New York

o'clock that night. Inclement weather delayed their march south to Mastic, but the following night the force proceeded toward Fort St. George.

At dawn on the twenty-third, the invaders rammed their way through the stockade on the southwest side. Shouting "Washington and Glory!" they ran across the parade ground and stormed the redoubt from three sides. The garrison, completely surprised, surrendered without a fight. There was a burst of musket fire from the upper windows of the manor house. The enraged Patriots splintered open the doors. If Tallmadge had not intervened, they would have killed every man in the house. More than three hundred prisoners were taken, the fort was destroyed, and the heavily laden vessels at the wharf were burned.

Today the manor house on William Floyd Parkway is open to the public as a museum, but not a trace of the nearby fort remains. In the foyer of the museum is a painting showing the American commandos pointing their muskets at the startled defenders in their nightshirts and caps.

Setting out on their return across the island, Tallmadge, leaving most of his force in the care of Capt. Edgar, proceeded with twelve men to Coram, midway between the north and south shores. There, after disposing of the guard, they destroyed three hundred tons of hay. They arrived at Fairfield early in the evening of the same day, their prisoners in tow, and without losing a single man of their own. Tallmadge's successful exploit earned him a very complimentary letter from Gen. Washington and the plaudits of Congress.

"The fortress at Treadwell's Neck, called Fort Slongo, seemed to demand attention as the next in course to Fort St. George, which we had already taken," wrote Tallmadge in his *Memoir*. Fort Slongo, corrupted to Fort Salonga by the inhabitants over the years, is not one of those quaint, archaic misspellings. The name originally was thought to have been of Indian derivation, but it is now known that the fort was named for a Philadelphia contractor named George Slongo, who constructed the defense for the British.

Fort Slongo was built just east of present-day Northport, in the area then known as Middleville, at the head of a small ravine on a farm then owned by William Arthur. It was an embankment forming a hollow square of perhaps fifty feet, constructed of trees set perpendicularly and filled with earth. The fort stood on a high point of land and commanded a view of hundreds of square miles of Long Island Sound. It became a notorious rendezvous for Tories and Loyalists, with a usual complement of 80 to 140 men who frequently raided neighboring farms, seizing stores of produce and making off with the cattle.

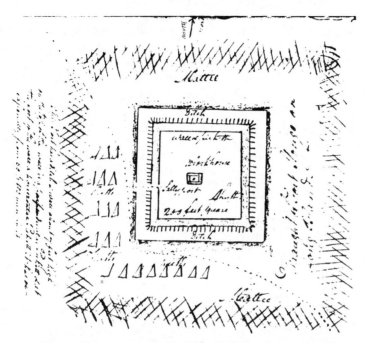

AMERICAN SPY PLAN OF FORT SLONGO, LONG ISLAND
"This Fort has a ditch & wall about 7 feet high; on the top of the wall is a
parpendicular Pickett & at the foot of the wall a horrizontal Pickett; it has
occasionally from 50 to 90 men in it." *Courtesy of Library of Congress*

Tallmadge was determined to get a plan of Fort Slongo. Lieut. Henry
Scudder, a native of Huntington who had fled to Connecticut, secretly
visited the area and was furnished with a plan of the fort by a neighbor.
This time Tallmadge did not lead the expedition, but he carefully
planned every move. He entrusted the mission to Maj. Lemuel Trescott,
with these instructions:

> I should recommend you to land your troops at least two miles to the
> east or west of the fort, to avoid any guards which may be advanced on
> the bank next to the sound. . . . If you find the garrison pretty much
> off their guard, from the draught of the works herewith given you, I
> should suppose you had better make two attacks at the same
> time—the one, directly against the sally port or gate, and the other
> against the huts within the abatis. . . . . You must by all means
> endeavor to accomplish your business so as to be ready to reembark
> your troops on or before daybreak, to avoid being cut off in the sound
> by any of the enemy's armed boats or guard ships.

The actual assault on the fort was made at dawn, October 3, 1781. On the previous night a small detachment under the command of Sgt. Elijah Churchill crossed the Sound in a whaleboat from the mouth of the Saugatuck River in Connecticut. They beached the boat at Crab Meadow, west of the British fort, and made their way to the nearby farm of Nathaniel Skidmore, who led them to Fort Slongo. The immediate neighborhood was studied carefully and the natural and man-made landmarks were memorized.

Tallmadge discusses the mission in his *Memoir:*

> On the 1st of October, I moved my detachment of light infantry into the neighborhood of Norwalk [Connecticut]. At the same time, I directed a suitable number of boats to assemble at the mouth of the Saugatuck River, east of the town of Norwalk, and on the evening of the 2nd of October, 1781, at 8 o'clock, I embarked a part of my detachment and placed Major Trescott at the head of it, with orders to assail the fort at a particular point. The troops landed on Long Island by 4 o'clock, and, at the dawn of day, the attack was made and the fortress subdued.

There was an element of luck in the assault on Fort Slongo. The commander of the post, Maj. Valanstine, was absent, apparently in New York City on military business. In addition, during the pre-dawn hours of that fateful Sunday morning, many of the fort's officers were making a night of it at Mulford House, a nearby inn. To cap the Patriots' good fortune, the post's sentry, completely confused by the suddenness of the attack, fired his musket in haste, beat a frantic retreat into the fort, and did not close the gate.

The fort was soon overwhelmed. Prior to the assault Tallmadge had estimated that there were 140 men in Fort Slongo. Despite precautions, most of the garrison escaped over the walls. The blockhouse and all other flammable materials were set afire. Two iron four-pounders were spiked, but the Patriots carted away two iron one-pounders, a brass one-pounder, and a quantity of small-caliber ammunition. Maj. Trescott's report shows that only 21 prisoners were taken, while two Tories were killed outright and two others left mortally wounded. The only Patriot wounded was Sgt. Churchill, who was later awarded the Purple Heart, then equivalent to today's Medal of Honor. The outline of the blockhouse can still be seen at the site, located in an area behind the dwelling at 46 Brookfield Road, Fort Salonga, about 100 yards from the Sound.

In the fall of 1782 the Patriots in Huntington were outraged when Col. Benjamin Thompson, commanding about five hundred men, dismantled the old First Presbyterian Church. The beams and planks were used to build a fort on Burying Hill on the present-day corner of Nassau Road and Main Street. The fort was called Fort Golgotha, after the biblical hill of the skulls, the place of Christ's crucifixion. The tombstones in the cemetery were removed and the graves leveled. An earthwork six feet high was thrown up around the fort, which covered two acres. The fortification faced north, overlooking Cold Spring Harbor, and was about eighty feet wide, with a large gate in the middle.

Over the bones of Huntington's early citizens the soldiers erected their barracks, with the tombstones used in the construction of tables, fireplaces, and ovens. When the bread loaves were taken out of the fire, one observer related, their bottom crusts were imprinted with words from epitaphs.

Thompson had his tent pitched in such a way that he would tread on a grave each time he entered or left his quarters. The grave thus desecrated was that of the old pastor of the First Presbyterian Church, Ebenezer Prime. When the British entered the town in 1776, they ousted the seventy-six-year-old pastor, destroyed his belongings, and quartered troops in the church. The elderly clergyman hid for three years in Long Swamp during that period, still performing marriages and holding services. When the British learned of his death, one of their officers was reported to have said, "Good! It will give me pleasure to dance on the old rebel's grave."

Fort Golgotha was used by Thompson's troops (Queen's Rangers) and the infamous Tarleton's Legion. With the war practically over, the fort was not involved in any military action. In 1784, after the British left, the fort was torn down by the townspeople, who restored the cemetery to its original condition.

At the time he built Fort Golgotha, Col. Thompson was commander of a regiment of Queen's Rangers. Born in Massachusetts in 1753, he became a Tory when he was refused a commission in the Continental Army. His vanity much hurt, in 1776 he went to England, where he finally won a commission as lieutenant colonel and returned to America to fight for the royalist cause.

Thompson was better known as Count von Rumford, receiving the title from the Elector of Bavaria, where he later served as a government administrator. The title came from the town of Rumford (now Concord), New Hampshire, where his wife was born. Thompson died an expatriate in 1814 at Auteuil, near Paris.

The Minisink Forts
Fort Martinus Decker and Fort Van Auken
Port Jervis, Orange County

The vulnerable Minisink settlements on and near the Delaware River suffered only small hit-and-run enemy incursions until Mohawk war chief Brant and a large force of his Indians and a detachment of Tories entered the area on the night of July 19/20, 1779. While the main body of his destructives stayed at Grassy Brook on the east bank of the Delaware, about two miles above the mouth of Lackawaxen Creek, Brant took about sixty Indians and twenty-seven Tories to attack old Minisink, today's Port Jervis.

Some of the farmhouses here were fortified and stockaded by their owners, among them Maj. Martinus Decker, whose rebuilt dwelling (1793) still stands on West Main Street. Another fortification, probably a blockhouse, was that built by Daniel Van Auken and situated behind his house and barn. The original Decker house, one of the strongest defenses in the settlement, had its lower story constructed of stone and the upper half-story of logs, covered with a roof of saplings chinked with gravel and overlaid with a thick clay coating.

Before the inhabitants awoke to their danger, the raiders had already set several dwellings and barns afire. The people, almost all of them still attired in their sleeping garments, fled their homes, some seeking refuge in fortified farmhouses, others finding a refuge in the hills. Brant kept his force in the area until eight o'clock in the morning, plundering and burning, killing and scalping four men, and taking three prisoners, one of them Jeremiah Van Auken. Brant left behind him a smoking ruination, his Indians carrying off considerable provisions and driving before them the inhabitants' livestock. Fort Decker's upper story was burned as was most of the stockade around the house.

Daniel Van Auken, his family, and some refugees, holed up in Fort Van Auken, withstood attacks for about an hour. An excerpt from Brant's official report reveals his exasperation:

> We had burnt all the settlement called Minnesink except one fort, which we lay before about an hour and had one man killed and one wounded. We destroyed several small stockades and forts and took four scalps and three prisoners, but did not in the least injure women and children. The reason we could not take any more of them was owing to the many forts about the place, into which they were always ready to run like ground-hogs.

The ensuing Battle of Minisink took place on July 22, very close to Brant's rendezvous of two days earlier. The aroused countryside had gathered up about 150 militiamen, most of them from the Goshen area, who went in pursuit of the raiders. The militiamen were outmaneuvered by Brant's generalship and lost at least forty-five killed.

Fort Nellis
near St. Johnsville, Montgomery County

A short distance from the better-known Fort Klock was the fortified dwelling of Christian Nellis. The wealthy farmer had six sons—Henry, Christian, Robert, Adam, George, and Theobald, with the first-named living with his father. The family was one of the most prominent in the Palatine settlements; the town of Nelliston southeast of the forted dwelling was named for the Nellis tribe.

The Nellis farm is one of the most remarkable illustrations of perpetuity in the Mohawk Valley. It has been occupied and operated by the male descendants of the family through a continuous chain of ten generations, dating from William Nellis, who first obtained title to the property on October 19, 1723.

Although the Nellis property faced on Klock's Field, where Van Rensselaer's militia battled with Tory and Indian raiders on October 19, 1780, it was not involved in the action. Most of the local inhabitants took refuge in Fort Klock. Sometime after the war, the elder Christian Nellis was killed when his horses became frightened and dragged him to his death.

New Petersburg Fort
East Schuyler, Herkimer County

About five miles west of Fort Dayton and on the same side of the Mohawk was the New Petersburg Fort, about which little is known, except that it consisted of three palisaded log houses. Its location was on the western boundary of white settlement before the Revolution. During the war the settlement's people suffered death and destruction at the hands of Tories and Indians. The settlement was founded by Peter Hasenclever in 1764. Its present name is East Schuyler.

New Windsor Cantonment
Vails Gate, Orange County

On May 8, 1965, muskets crackled in a *feu de joie* along a line of fifty men in Continental Army uniforms, and two three-pound cannons boomed across the parade ground. With 350 historians in attendance, fifes shrilled to the accompaniment of drums as musicians gave a rendition of "The World Turned Upside Down," the lively tune that tradition says was played by the British when they surrendered at Yorktown in October 1781. Almost midway between West Point and Newburgh, New Windsor Cantonment, Gen. Washington's last winter encampment, 1782/83, was opened to the American people as a museum, with the reconstruction in miniature of the original military village.

Though a peace treaty was in the works at Paris, the enemy still held New York City, Charleston, and Savannah. The new nation's French allies had their own problems in the West Indies and elsewhere. Washington had to hold his army together should attempts fail at a peace settlement.

Baron von Steuben, the commander-in-chief's indefatigable "drill sergeant," laid out the great military encampment that housed about seven thousand officers and men. Continental troops constructed about seven hundred huts, each accommodating two squads, using planks sawed from the felled trees that had forested the area. The entire camp was sectioned off into regular streets, an ultra-modern design for that era, with each regiment possessing its own district. The officers, of course, had their own quarters.

The largest structure in the camp, an all-purpose assembly hall measuring about 110 by 30 feet, was graced with a cupola and a flagpole. From the very first this building was called "The Temple of Virtue," and part of its name was given to the immediate ground, Temple Hill, the highest rise of ground in the cantonment. The noisy enthusiasm that attended its inauguration "disrobed it of its mantle of purity," according to historian Benson Lossing almost seventy years later.

It was at this camp that the Order of the Purple Heart, roughly equivalent to today's Medal of Honor, was created, and ultimately awarded to only eight Revolutionary military men. Here were held the first elections of the celebrated Society of the Cincinnati, the patriotic organization formed by Continental Army officers.

Somewhere in the camp's near environs Washington issued the final furloughs to his troops after the signing of the Paris treaty on September 3, 1783. The most dramatic occurrence in the cantonment's short-lived history was the distribution of the so-called Newburgh Addresses, the greatest threat to Washington's leadership during his military career, and the subsequent historic appearance of the general before an assemblage of his officers.

The intent of the Newburgh Addresses, also called the Newburgh Conspiracy, was a direct contravention of the principles for which the Revolution had been fought, and if allowed to progress beyond control could have resulted in the creation of a military dictatorship accompanied by bloody civil rioting. The conspiracy was the outgrowth of officers' grievances concerning arrears in pay, unresolved clothing and food allowances, and the neglect of Congress to provide half-pay life pensions beginning with October 21, 1780, the day of their promised final furloughs.

While the instigator of the plot was Col. Walter Stewart, the two Addresses were composed by Maj. John Armstrong, a member of Gen. Gates's staff. Among Washington's officers who subscribed in varying degrees, to the two anonymous, overtly hostile memorials to Congress were Gen. Alexander McDougall, Gen. Horatio Gates, and Alexander Hamilton. The inflammatory text in the first of the Addresses threatened, should Congress fail to meet their demands, to keep their arms after the war ended officially, or "retire to some unsettled country" should the war continue, leaving Washington and the Congress without an army.

On March 10 Washington received two documents: one was a request for a meeting of all officers set for the next day; the second was a copy of the first Newburgh Address. On March 11, in General Orders, Washington censured the Address. The same day he directed representative officers of all the regiments to assemble on March 15 to ascertain how "to attain the just and important object in view." The next day the second of the Addresses came into the hands of the commander-in-chief. The document cleverly intimated that the language used in the General Orders of the previous day supported the officers' complaints. It then became apparent to Washington that he had to confront his officers and put a stop to their machinations.

The officers assembled in the Temple. It was Saturday, March 15. The men were stunned when their leader entered. There was no doubt about the drama of the moment. Washington was obviously agitated, while his officers were tensely silent, some even sheepish. Washington then delivered a moving plea to their patriotism, to their consciences. In the course of his speech he required the use of his spectacles to read a letter from a Virginia congressman relating to officers' pay. He apologized while adjusting the eyeglasses on his face: "Gentlemen, you will permit me to put on my spectacles, for I have not only grown gray, but almost blind in the service of my country."

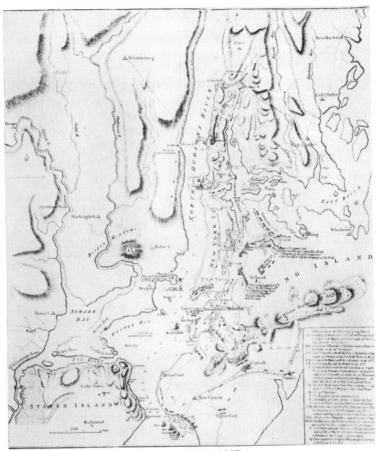

NEW YORK ISLAND
Courtesy of The Newberry Library, Chicago

Not many minutes after Washington had concluded his plea and left the Temple, leaving behind him more than a few officers weeping unashamed tears, a few of his most trusted subordinates took control of the assembly, and then and there the conspiracy died. Samuel Shaw, A.D.C. to Gen. Knox, penned valuable observations of the conspiracy in his *Journals*. He wrote of Washington: "On other occasions, he had been supported by the exertions of an Army and the countenance of his friends, but in this he stood single and alone." The quick and decisive handling of the conspiracy was testimony to Washington's monumental personal leadership.

In the middle of June 1783 almost all of the troops in New Windsor Cantonment departed for home after Congress granted them temporary furloughs pending the signing of the Paris Peace. On September 2 an auction was held in the Temple of Virtue. All of the camp's structures were sold for the lumber in them, with the exception of one officers' hut, which was moved a few miles away and used as a private dwelling. This one hut managed to survive 151 years of private ownership, to be finally saved and returned in 1934 to the site of the cantonment, where it now stands on exhibit among ten replicas.

New York City

In 1776 the tide of war washed northward from New York City to eventually engulf the whole state, which hosted a third of all the battles of the Revolution. The city then constituted only the southern end of today's Borough of Manhattan. Brooklyn, Staten Island, and Long Island were suburbs of the "metropolis."

In 1770 the most populated city in the Colonies was Philadelphia (34,000), followed by New York (22,000), and Boston (15,000), with the Province of New York ranking only seventh in colony population (162,920).[1] New York had the distinction of being one of the two most Loyalistic Colonies (North Carolina was the other), a fact that had little more than a microscopic effect on the outcome of the Battle of Brooklyn.[2]

Henry Knox visited New York on his way to Ticonderoga, where he obtained his "noble train of artillery" for the siege of Boston. In a letter to his wife, Lucy, he described the city in laudatory terms:

> New York is a place where I think in general the houses are better built than in Boston. They are generally of brick and three stories high with the largest kind of windows. Their churches are grand; their college, workhouse, and hospitals most excellently situated and also exceedingly commodious, their principal streets much wider than ours. The people—why, the people are magnificent: in their equipages which are numerous, in their house furniture which is fine, in their pride and conceit which are inimitable, in their profaneness which is intolerable, in the want of principle which is prevalent, in their Toryism which is insufferable, and for which they must repent in dust and ashes.[3]

Early in January 1776 Washington at Cambridge received news that the enemy had outfitted a new expedition, with Sir Henry Clinton as its commander. Washington believed that the expedition was destined for

New York. Fearing a surrender of the city by its preponderance of Loyalists, he agreed that Gen. Charles Lee and a column of Connecticut volunteers should march to New York.

Lee's entry into the city on February 4 coincided with the arrival of Clinton (bound for North Carolina) off Sandy Hook. The Patriots camped on the Fields (site of today's City Hall). Lee's presence alarmed the inhabitants, and many Tories and their families scurried to refuges afforded by Long Island and New Jersey. The Committee of Safety protested the "invasion" of Patriot troops because the commander of the enemy's sixty-gun man-of-war *Asia,* stationed in New York Bay, had threatened to bombard the city should the rebels make an appearance there.[4] But Lee was obdurate:

> I come to prevent the occupation of Long Island or the city by the enemies of liberty. If the ships of war are quiet, I shall be quiet; if they make my presence a pretext for firing on the town, the first house set in flames by their guns shall be the funeral pile [pyre] of some of their best friends.[5]

The threat of cannonading dissipated and those Tories who did not flee the city shrank into convenient shells of anonymity. Taking heart after the short-lived crisis, New York's Provincial Convention initiated plans to fortify the city against the inevitable coming of the enemy.

Gen. Lee assigned his engineer, William Smith, the task of surveying the salients to be fortified. In company with Lord Stirling, Lee roamed over the city and its environs; the more they inspected, the more they became convinced that a complete defense of the city was impractical. Surrounded by water on all sides, the island of Manhattan offered almost unlimited opportunities for enemy attack. Lee wrote of his frustration on February 19 to Washington: "What to do with the city, I own, puzzles me. It is so encircled with deep navigable waters, that whoever commands the sea must command the town." He came up with the proposal for a system of defenses that he believed would preclude the permanent occupation of the city by the British: New York would be "made a most advantageous field of battle . . . it might cost the enemy many thousands of men to get possession of it."[6]

Within the two weeks after his arrival, Lee could congregate only seventeen hundred Continentals and minute men from New York's Westchester and Dutchess Counties, New Jersey, and Connecticut. A month later, on March 7, he left the city to take command of the newly created Department of the South. He bequeathed to Stirling the monumental problem of fortifying an island city with open approaches on every hand. Promoted to brigadier general a month earlier by

Congress, Stirling spent every waking moment in planning and starting defenses, driving the troops to ever greater efforts.

The long Patriot siege of Boston finally forced the British to evacuate that city on March 17 and sail off to Halifax, Nova Scotia. Washington was positive that the enemy, once regrouped and reinforced, would next sail to New York. A council of war with his subordinates decided then to send units of his army there at once, and four regiments of riflemen were dispatched southward without delay. In the days that followed, more regiments departed from Boston by land and sea to garrison New York and work on that city's defenses. By the time Washington arrived on April 13, some defensive beginnings had been made in Manhattan, Brooklyn, and on Nutten (Governor's) Island.[7]

Before the war Manhattan Island was a wooded wonderland. In 1776 the primeval landscape was being shorn of trees at a tremendous rate. Some of the lumber was, of course, utilized in the construction of Patriot defenses, but most of the wood was burned by both American and British troops for cooking and heating. The soldiers, rank and file alike, had no compunction about chopping down orchards and destroying gardens that represented many years of hard labor, loving care, and great expense. The War for American Independence was no respecter of private property.[8]

When the British (delayed by the Arnold-Montgomery invasion of Canada) under Gen. Howe arrived off Sandy Hook on June 25, to begin the occupation of Staten Island with more than 31,000 troops, Washington had only 19,000 illy equipped and poorly armed raw Continentals and militia, a figure far below his authorized strength of 28,500 officers and men. With no naval support, no cavalry auxiliaries, and very little artillery to mount on his new defenses, Washington had to confront a professionally trained enemy army of men who were veterans of European battlefields.[9]

As at Boston in 1775, so here in 1776, we had the war at our doors and all about us. In what is now the heart of Brooklyn Revolutionary soldiers lay encamped for months, and in the heat of a trying summer surrounded themselves with lines of works. What have since been converted into spots of rare beauty—Greenwood Cemetery and Prospect Park—became, with the ground in their vicinity, a battlefield. New York, which was then taking its place as the most flourishing city on the continent, was transformed by the emergency into a fortified military base. Troops quartered in Broad Street and along the North [Hudson] and East rivers, and on the line of Grand Street permanent camps were established. Forts, redoubts, batteries, and intrenchments encircled the town. The streets were barricaded, the roads blocked, and efforts made to obstruct the navigation of both rivers. Where we have stores and warehouses, Washington fixed alarm and picket posts; and at points where costly residences stand, men fought, died, and were buried. In 1776 the cause had become general; soldiers gathered here from ten of the original thirteen States, and the contest assumed serious proportions. It was here around New York and Brooklyn that the War of the Revolution began in earnest.[10]

The Barrier Gate

In 1779 the British spent months, daily employing 160 to 200 horses, on the construction of a line of fortifications across Broadway, extending from Fort Tryon to Laurel Hill (Fort George). The system of defenses, never engaged in any action, was called the Barrier Gate. The works consisted of at least five redoubts and a number of stockades, with an armament of ten Swedish twelve-pounders.

Fort Bunker Hill

From Fort Pitt, a strong circular redoubt mounting eight guns, at the intersection of Grand and Pitt Streets in Manhattan's lower East Side, a string of strong Patriot defenses extended nearly on a line with today's Grand and Broome Streets to Broadway, from which point it diverged to the northwest, terminating at a redoubt near the intersection of Thompson and Spring Streets. Within this American line, on a rise of ground called Bayard's Mount or Hill, was the largest of all the works in lower Manhattan, with the exceptions of Fort George and the Grand Battery.

When first initiated it was called the Independent Battery; upon its completion by April 16, 1776, the Americans renamed it Fort Bunker Hill (Johnston, *Campaign of 1776,* 3: 88-89, says that "its proper name. . . . was Bayard's Hill Redoubt, this having been given to it officially in general orders.") This very extensive sod-banked earthworks covered the area now bounded by Centre, Broome, Mott, and Grand Streets. Its several batteries consisted of nine eight-pounders, four three-pounders, and six royal coehorns and mortars. Additional strengthening of the fort was begun on July 1, when a working party of 450 men was sent there.

The British line of defenses in lower Manhattan, erected in May 1780, went "by way of Bunker Hill." On May 16, 1782, all British work on New York City's defenses was terminated by orders of Gen. Guy Carleton. For many years after the Revolution, during which time Bayard's Hill was excavated, the brick lining of a well located within the fort reared up like a huge chimney and dominated the surrounding landscape.

Citizens Redoubt

Originally called Badlam's Redoubt, named for Capt. Stephen Badlam, Gen. Charles Lee's chief artillery officer, this Patriot defense, mounting eight guns, was constructed in the early spring of 1776. It stood on the high ground (Rutgers Hill) at Market and Madison Streets, just east of the old Jewish cemetery.

Garrisoned by Massachusetts Continentals before the Americans evacuated New York City, the redoubt was rebuilt by the town's inhabitants in 1780 and renamed Citizens Redoubt. Records reveal that in February 1780 its garrison consisted of elements of the Royal Navy—a captain, lieutenant, and one hundred seamen. The defense did not participate in any action.

Fort Cock Hill

Known contemporaneously by such names as Fort Cock Hill, Cock's Hill, Cox Hill, and New Battery, this earthwork defense was constructed by American troops in 1776. It was located on the summit of Inwood Hill, about in line with today's 207th Street, just south of Spuyten Duyvil Creek, which defines the northern boundary of Manhattan. The creek together with the Harlem River is a continuous waterway between the East River and the Hudson. The British took this route from the Hudson to assault Fort Washington.

The armament of this American defense cannot be determined from available records. It was designed both to defend the junction of the creek with the Hudson River and to guard the northern end of the ridge, which extended to Fort Washington. Ironically, the strategically important fortification did not participate in the battle for Manhattan because the Hessians by-passed it in their attack on Fort Washington, November 16, 1776. When the Patriots evacuated Manhattan, the enemy occupied the works.

In 1778 the British made extensive improvements on the defense, arming it with four twelve-pounders and surrounding the whole with an elaborate abatis. The following year two of the cannon were removed. On July 22, 1781, Gen. Washington noted after a reconnaisance of several British posts that ''the fort at Cox's Hill is in bad repair . . . there

is neither friezing nor ditch and the northeast corner appears quite easy
of access by a rock.''

Fort George at the Battery

In the year 1630 Johannes de Laet published *Beschryvinghe van
West-Indien,* a work of great interest and inspiration to seekers of new
worlds. The book included a new map on which were shown, for the first
time, the names ''Manhattes'' and ''N. Amsterdam.'' Four years earlier
the settlement of New Amsterdam had been created on the southern tip
of Manhattan Island, establishing the colony of New Netherland in the
New World, under the aegis of the Dutch West India Company,
chartered by Holland in 1621 and organized in 1623.

From 1626 until the outbreak of the Revolution, Fort George,
originally Fort Amsterdam, along with its subordinate batteries, was the
principal defensive work on Manhattan Island. During the century and a
half, the fort underwent several physical transformations and royal

FORT GEORGE AT THE BATTERY
Courtesy of National Archives

name changes. On the site now occupied by the United States Custom House, bounded by Whitehall, State, and Bridge Streets, and Bowling Green, the fortification was renamed Fort James in 1664, Fort Willem Hendrick in 1673, Fort James again in 1674, Fort William Henry in 1691, Fort Anne, or Queen's Fort, in 1703, and Fort George in 1714. Partially destroyed by fire in 1741, it was finally demolished in 1790.

The stunning news of Lexington and Concord reached New York at noon on Sunday, April 23, 1775. The Sons of Liberty and a host of other citizens wasted no time in getting to City Hall. After seizing the armaments there and distributing them, they formed themselves into a corps of volunteers and took over the reins of civil government. They also took possession of the custom house and all the public warehouses. Because of the chaotic manner in which decisions were being made, a Committee of One Hundred was formed on May 1. Delegates selected from the various counties to form a revolutionary congress met in New York early in June, at which time the enlistment of troops was authorized and plans were made for the establishment of fortifications on both sides of the Hudson River and at King's Bridge where the Boston Post Road crossed Spuyten Duyvil Creek.

On Sunday, June 25, two important personages arrived in New York. One was Governor Tryon, absent about fourteen months, who learned with great shock that the Province was being controlled by an independent government. The other was George Washington, who on June 15 had been appointed by the Continental Congress in Philadelphia to be "General and Commander in Chief of the United Colonies and of all the forces now raised or to be raised by them." He was passing through the city on his way to the Continental camp at Cambridge, Massachusetts.

The military efforts of the British were being concentrated on Boston, the nucleus of the American-rebellion movement. In June the British regulars stationed in New York and quartered in the Chambers Street barracks were ordered north to that port city.

The Provincial Convention issued orders to remove the guns from the Grand Battery just below Fort George. Shortly before midnight on August 23, Col. John Lasher's Independent Battalion and Capt. John Lamb's (captured December 31, 1775) New York Artillery Company, supported by a large body of citizens, proceeded to the Battery. A number of Patriot guards, one of whom was Lieut. Alexander Hamilton, watched for possible British interference.

The *Asia,* a sixty-four-gun British man-of-war, lying off the Battery, sent a sloop to observe the mysterious proceedings on shore. The sailors, as a signal to the *Asia,* opened fire. Lamb's men replied with a

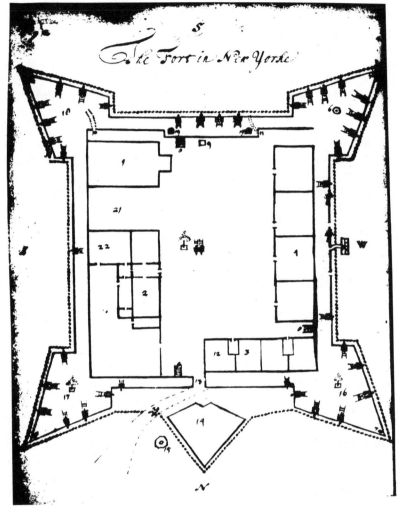

FORT GEORGE AT THE BATTERY (1695)
Courtesy of British Museum

KEY

1—Chapel
2—Governor's house
3—Officers' lodgings
4—Soldiers' lodgings
5—The "Necessary" house
6—Flagstaff
7—Lookouts
8—Wall ladders
9—Well inside the Fort
10—Magazine
11—Sallyport
12—Secretary's office

13—Fort's gate, facing what is now
    modern Broadway
14—Hornwork
15—Well and pump
16—"Stone" mount
17—"Iron" mount
18—"Town" mount
19—Two mortar pieces
20—Palisade gate and road
21—Open ground for additional
    buildings as needed
22—The armory over Governor's house

volley from their muskets, killing one and wounding several of the sloop's crew. Some minutes later the *Asia's* ordnance let loose with nine-, eighteen-, and twenty-four-pound shot. Some of the buildings on Whitehall Street, near Fort George, were holed in the upper stories, and one of the shots went through the roof of the tavern of Samuel Fraunces. Three men on shore were wounded. The Americans dragged a mixed assortment of twenty-one nine-pounders and eighteen-pounders up Broadway to the Commons (today's City Hall Park), to eventually be a part of the Hudson Highlands' defenses.

Early in January 1776 Washington suspected a British design to occupy New York. He ordered Gen. Charles Lee, who was to "earn" a court-martial conviction following the Battle of Monmouth, to gather an army as soon as possible and march to New York to put that city in the best possible condition for defense.

On February 4, the same day that Gen. Sir Henry Clinton arrived off Sandy Hook with his contingent on his way to North Carolina, Lee entered New York with four companies of New Jersey troops under Lord Stirling and a regiment of Connecticut men commanded by Col. Waterbury. Many inhabitants, fearing an all-out confrontation, left the city by boat and horse-drawn cart. The weather was bitterly cold and practically all business came to a standstill. Clinton crossed the harbor from Staten Island, conferred with Governor Tryon on the *Asia,* and was amazed to learn that he was not allowed to set foot on Manhattan soil.

Lee's arrival was met by deputations from the Committee of One Hundred, who opposed any military occupation of the city in their dread of a destructive bombardment from the British men-of-war lying offshore once it became known that the Patriots were in the process of erecting fortifications. But Lee brushed aside all objections. He had the troops working at a feverish pace, throwing up redoubts and barricades, and bordering the island with earthworks on which he mounted more than a hundred guns. Ruthless in his determination, he ordered the two bastions and ramparts on the north side of Fort George, facing Bowling Green, torn down. In a report to Congress, he gave his reasons for this seemingly reckless destruction:

> This fort cannot be defended, but as it is not possible in our hands to render it a fortification of offence against the enemy, it might in their possession be converted into a citadel to keep the town in subjection. These considerations have induced me to throw down the northeast and northwest bastions, with the communicating curtain, so that being entirely open behind, and a commanding traverse thrown across the Broad Way [two hundred yards from the fort] with three guns mounted, it is impossible for the enemy to lodge themselves in and repair the fort. . . . New York, from the circumstances, can with

difficulty be made a regular tenable fortification, but it may be a most disadvantageous field of battle.

Most of the heavy artillery at Fort George and the Grand Battery were transported up Broadway to the Commons and, shortly thereafter, to King's Bridge. The Continentals left a minimum of ordnance on Manhattan's southern tip: Fort George, two twelve-pounders and four thirty-two-pounders, though it could mount sixty guns; the Grand Battery, thirteen thirty-two-pounders, one twenty-four-pounder, two two-pounders, one brass and three iron mortars, though the battery could mount ninety guns; Whitehall Battery, two thirty-two-pounders; and Oyster Battery, two thirty-two-pounders and three twelve-pounders.

Lee's plan for the Patriot defense of New York called for preventing passage through Hellgate by a fort at the foot of present-day 88th Street, and by another redoubt on the opposite shore. Batteries were located at the intersection of Cherry and Catherine Streets, on Rutgers Hill, and at Coenties Slip, just below Wall Street. A battery was erected under the south wall of Fort George. Batteries were planned for both sides of the river at the harbor's entrance and at a number of points along the Hudson shore. All streets leading from the water were barricaded and a chain of forts was erected on Jones's, Bayard's, and Lispenard's Hills, to protect the city from the north.

Governor Tryon, writing to the home government in February, went into the reasons for the British fleet's failure to make an effort to prevent the Continentals from removing the guns, ammunition, and stores from Fort George. It was the opinion of Capt. Hyde Parker of the forty-gun frigate *Phoenix:*

> that he could not bring the ships under his command to lay off the Fort and Battery—where the chief part of the stores were deposited—without great risk to the King's ships from the ice at that severe season. The destruction therefore of the city, while there were so many friends to Government, with the loss of all their property, and the consideration of preserving the town for the King's army, was thought to be too great sacrifices to make for only retarding the removal of the artillery and stores.

When Lee was ordered south in early March, Lord Stirling was given the task of completing the fortifications. He was urged in a letter from Washington on March 14 to make all haste, since it was quite evident that the British were at the point of evacuating Boston, and it was his thought (no doubt based on intelligence reports) that they were planning to take New York. On the same day, the Continental Congress voted eight thousand men for the defense of the city and requested the authorities in New Jersey to have that province's militia ready to march to New York on short notice.

The British gave up Boston on March 17 and sailed off to Nova Scotia. Washington thereupon left Cambridge, accompanied by all but five regiments of his New England army, and made all possible speed for New York, arriving there on April 13. Gen. Israel Putnam had been sent to the city on April 4 to continue the work on the defenses. He fortified Red Hook and Governor's Island, and protected the heights of Brooklyn opposite the city by a chain of redoubts, stretching from Gowanus north to Wallabout Bay.

The British military plan began to develop. Intelligence reports verified that Gen. William Howe was to attack New York, ascend the Hudson, and rendezvous with an army from Canada. Sir Henry Clinton would meanwhile occupy the southern ports, pressing the Americans into the interior areas.

In the midst of hectic preparations to meet the British, Washington was faced with a treasonable conspiracy at his very door. Governor Tryon, on the *Asia,* had contrived, with the help of Loyalists in the city, to bribe several men who had admission to American headquarters. Some arrests were made in quick order. The charges—some of them overdrawn—against them were conspiracy to capture or assassinate Washington and his principal generals, blow up the magazines, and spike the guns stored at King's Bridge. A private in Washington's bodyguard, Thomas Hickey, was convicted of "mutiny and sedition and of holding treacherous correspondence with his country's enemies," and sentenced to death. A large crowd of citizens and hundreds of soldiers witnessed the hanging on June 28.

The *Asia* sailed through the Narrows, in expectation of Howe's fleet from Halifax. The first ships appeared off Sandy Hook on June 29 and were followed by many others until, on July 2, there were 130 vessels in the Upper and Lower Bays, the greatest aggregation of seapower ever seen in America. Gen. William Howe, on the *Greyhound,* arrived July 1 and conferred with Governor Tryon, who filled him in on Washington's defensive preparations. The troops, numbering between nine and ten thousand men, debarked and made camp on Staten Island. There the army awaited the arrival of Admiral Richard Howe, William's brother and senior by four years, who was coming from England with reinforcements. He arrived off Sandy Hook on July 12. During the first week of August, Gen. Clinton and Lord Cornwallis showed up with the army from South Carolina. These additional forces increased the British strength before New York to nearly thirty-three thousand men, including thirteen thousand Hessian mercenaries.

In contrast to Britain's army of trained troops and her fleet of men-of-war and transports, Washington commanded makeshift forces chiefly made up of untrained, untried, undisciplined farmers and working citizens completely devoid of knowledge regarding the accouterments of war. The Patriots' weakness was aggravated by their total lack of fighting ships to contest the British navy on the sea, rivers, and lakes. On August 8 Washington's army, stationed at posts in New York and Brooklyn, on Governor's Island, and at Paulus Hook, New Jersey, aggregated 17,225 men. The effective fighting force, however, numbered but 10,514 men, due to the usual camp diseases, a smallpox epidemic, and men given over to other duties.

After the Americans chased Howe out of Boston, Washington had dispatched Maj. Gen. John Thomas to the Canadian border, but his men had to retreat and fall back to Lake Champlain, where the troops were being decimated by a virulent smallpox epidemic. Thomas died of the fever on June 2 at Sorel on the St. Lawrence. Washington had to release sizable detachments to reinforce the fever-stricken camps on Lake Champlain.

While both sides were flexing their military muscles, the Continental Congress on July 4 proclaimed the Declaration of Independence, adopted two days earlier. The New York Provincial Convention ratified and adopted the Declaration on July 9. Washington saw to it that it was read to every unit of his army in the New York area. A large congregation of soldiers and citizens, in a burst of joyous patriotic enthusiasm, pulled down the gilded equestrian statue of George III that had been erected on Bowling Green six years before. Most of its four thousand pounds of lead was molded into more than forty-two thousand bullets for the muskets of Connecticut's troops. On July 12 there was a spirited artillery duel between the British men-of-war, the *Phoenix* and the *Rose,* and the American batteries located at Governor's Island, the Battery, Red Hook, and Paulus Hook.

Two months after the proclamation of the Declaration of Independence, the first American submarine attempted an underwater attack against an enemy vessel. The *American Turtle,* designed and built by David Bushnell of Connecticut, and operated by Sgt. Ezra Lee of the Connecticut line, attacked the British flagship *Asia* anchored in New York Bay. The armament of the manually operated submarine, built of oak and shaped like a coconut and standing on end, was a piggyback time bomb attached to an auger that was to be screwed into the hull of an enemy vessel. Sgt. Lee, however, could not pierce the *Asia's* copper sheathing and the bomb was set adrift to explode harmlessly.

On August 22 Howe's forces landed on the Brooklyn shore of Gravesend Bay. On the 27th the Battle of Brooklyn commenced. By two o'clock in the afternoon there was no doubt as to the outcome of the battle. On the night of the 29th, Washington removed the remnants of his army from Brooklyn Heights, with the blessing of a dense fog, across the river to Manhattan.

The Loyalists in the city belabored the British military for its failure to take advantage of the victory by capturing Governor's Island, where two thousand Patriots were virtually stranded. During the night of the 27th, Americans from the Manhattan shore ran a rowboat shuttle between the Battery and the island and removed the whole garrison, forty heavy guns, and a sizable quantity of supplies. When British troops finally took the island, they found the fortified positions deserted.

There was no question about the possibility of the Americans holding New York: the overwhelming British victory and their unimpaired strength obviated the practicability of such. That left the problem of what should be done about the city. Should the Americans sack and burn the town or leave it whole for the British to use as their winter headquarters? The Congress, in reply to Washington's plea for advice, said that by all means New York should not be damaged in any way because, in their thinking, the Patriots in due time would repossess the city. On September 7, at a conclave of Washington's generals, it was decided to abandon the city, with only Gen. Nathanael Greene and John Jay voting for the destruction of New York. On the 12th another meeting was held and it was decided ten to three that a withdrawal must be made to save the army, with Congress concurring in the decision.

The next day, September 13, four British men-of-war, with the assistance of Governor's Island's guns, hammered away in the direction of the Battery and Fort George. The Patriot shore batteries replied in kind. The only fatalities were three citizens who were killed by one cannon shot. Property damage was slight, with some buildings behind the Battery riddled by shot. On the next day the British, with a covering fire from their men-of-war, landed a large force at Kip's or Turtle Bay, on the east side of Manhattan, between present-day 32nd and 38th Streets. The southern half of Manhattan was relinquished to the British and the Americans began their retreat northward. At Fort George the rebels' flag was taken down and the British flag run up. The next day Governor Tryon and other royal officials, accompanied by British troops, entered the city from the south.

It was the Loyalists' turn to crow. Persons who were openly known to be Patriot activists were thrown into numerous makeshift prisons and their property confiscated. Those Americans whose sympathies were suspect were subjected to the same merciless indignities and mayhem as were the Tories and Loyalists before the Battle of Brooklyn.

The British military authorities had hardly had time to get settled when, on September 21, a fire broke out in Whitehall Street and spread north and west, flaring up Broadway and Broad Street as far north as City Hall and St. Paul's Church, and destroying practically all the structures between Broadway and the Hudson. The buildings within Fort George, and No. 1 Broadway (taken over by the British as military headquarters), escaped the flames. In spite of heroic efforts to save it, Trinity Church was completely destroyed; St. Paul's was saved only by superhuman efforts. In the path of the flames were hundreds of wooden structures.

In 1761 an ordinance had been passed banning the erection of wooden buildings after 1766, but the deadline was later extended to 1774. About five hundred houses were destroyed in the conflagration. The British, of course, laid the blame on rebel incendiaries. Several arrests were made, but those taken in were acquitted for lack of evidence. There is little doubt that the fire was purely accidental. A second great fire, not so disastrous, originated at Cruger's Wharf near Little Dock Street on August 3, 1778, and destroyed about sixty houses and stores. The following day, to add to the excitement, a munitions vessel anchored in the East River near Wall Street was apparently struck by lightning and blew up, damaging nearby buildings.

The British under Howe moved steadily northward. The American had to abandon the Harlem Heights fortifications in their retreat. Fort Washington, on the Hudson and opposite Fort Lee, New Jersey, was heavily garrisoned while Washington moved into his new headquarters at White Plains. On November 16 Fort Washington was assaulted and captured; the defense was renamed Fort Knyphausen for the commander of the Hessians. All of Manhattan Island was now in the hands of the enemy and remained so until the close of the war. The civil government was superseded by a military establishment and virtual martial law was instituted.

New York, under British military rule, was beset by many problems, all arising from the consequences of the war and the great fires of 1776 and 1778. There were a great many poor people who suffered throughout the war years, despite some alleviating measures adopted by the British. Many citizens had lost their homes and businesses in the fires; a majority of these people and others were unemployed because of the virtual nonexistence of business.

The American prisoners taken during the Battle of Brooklyn, the capture of Fort Washington, and in other actions in and around the city were suffering much worse fates. They were incarcerated in various buildings converted into prisons throughout the town. The most infamous military prisons were Rhinelander's (corner of William and Duane Streets), the Liberty Street Sugar House, Van Cortlandt's Sugar House (northwest corner of Trinity Church cemetery), and the Provost Jail (on the grounds of present City Hall Park). Other structures taken over as prisons were dissenting churches, a hospital, and King's College (Columbia University). There was little food dispensed to the prisoners because of the rampant dishonesty of the British commissaries, who often pocketed the money allocated for provisions. The notorious prison ships, pressed into service because of the dearth of housing within the city, were anchored in Wallabout Bay. They were crammed with diseased and dying men in stifling holds. About eleven thousand military and civilian Patriots died in these death traps under conditions worse than those accorded the blacks transported from Africa in slave ships.

Until the Hard Winter of 1779/80, New York was reasonably safe from any American attack. The Hudson River froze over solid from shore to shore. Maj. Gen. James Pattison, British commandant of the city, anticipated a Patriot assault across the ice. There also was the danger of an attack by the French fleet cruising off the coast. All the fortifications, including Fort George and its auxiliary batteries, were repaired and strengthened.

Pattison, who had instituted a local militia earlier and had been commended for that work by Sir Henry Clinton, called out members of this auxiliary and organized forty companies of citizens to stand by. The commandant was much relieved when Washington's army and the French fleet departed to engage Lord Cornwallis at Yorktown. After the American victory in the South, Washington returned to the environs of New York, but his men engaged only in local skirmishes.

The glorious news of Yorktown was a tremendous lift to the spirits of the Americans. During the following spring it was learned that Sir Guy Carleton and Admiral Robert Digby were on their way to conclude a peace with the Colonies, with the former to assume military command of the city. On May 5, 1782, Carleton landed at Whitehall, and while the guns boomed a salute from Fort George, the peace commissioners were received "by a party of horse and foot, the gentlemen of the Army, most of the respectable inhabitants of the city, and a numerous concourse of people." Carleton's conciliatory overtures to the Americans in New York and his reforms in the cause of justice were very helpful while plans were being formulated to establish peace. The following day Gen. Washington met the two British emissaries at Tappan to negotiate the evacuation of New York.

In August the newspapers published proclamations of peace. It was not until November 30, however, that provisional articles were agreed on in Paris and witnessed by the heads of the delegations representing Great Britain and the Colonies. King George's peace proclamation, delivered at St. James's Palace on February 14, 1783, reached New York on April 5. Congress issued its own proclamation on April 11, declaring a cessation of hostilities. On the 19th, the eighth anniversary of Lexington and Concord, the Congressional proclamation was read to the troops in camp at Newburgh and sent to all the outlying posts.

The definitive peace treaty, signed at Paris on September 3, 1783, declared the desires of Great Britain and the new nation "to forget all past misunderstandings and differences" and to "establish such a satisfactory and beneficial intercourse between the two countries, upon the ground of reciprocal advantages and mutual convenience, as may promote and secure to both perpetual peace and harmony." The American commissioners who negotiated and signed the peace treaty were John Adams, Benjamin Franklin, and John Jay. The peace pact had ended the war but the vexing problems remaining in the aftermath had to be resolved years later by Jay's Treaty of 1794 and Pinckney's Treaty of 1795.

On November 3 the Continental Army was disbanded by order of the Congress. Early on the morning of November 25, by prearrangement, eight hundred New York artillerymen, Massachusetts infantry, and militia from West Point, commanded by Bvt. Brig. Gen. Henry Jackson, accompanied by Generals Washington and Knox and Governor George Clinton (elected April, 1777), marched from Harlem to the Bowery. They remained there until early afternoon while the British evacuated the city. The troops then marched to Chatham Square, down to Queen (now Pearl) and Wall Streets, over to Broadway and Fort George, where Gen. Knox took command of the army.

The introductory rite was the raising of the American banner, but the fort's flagstaff had been soaped and the cleats and halyards removed by British practical jokers. A visit to Goelet's hardware store for the necessaries soon enabled an agile sailor to nail on cleats, reeve new halyards, and float the Stars and Stripes to the breeze, much to the amusement of the British military spectators on the transports in the harbor. A salute of thirteen guns was fired from the ramparts of Fort George. With the formal occupation of the city finalized by the Continental troops, Washington and Clinton on horseback made their public entrance, accompanied by many important military and civil authorities and an honor guard of the Westchester Light Horse.

With the end of the war Congress reduced the new nation's army to virtual nonexistence. It directed that "the commanding officer . . . discharge the troops now in the service of the United States, except twenty-five privates to guard the stores at Fort Pitt [at Pittsburgh], and twenty-five to guard the stores at West Point and other magazines." Congress gave its explanation for the drastic step: "Standing armies in time of peace are inconsistent with the principles of republican government, dangerous to the liberties of a free people, and generally converted into destructive engines for establishing despotism."

The Americans who had exiled themselves during the British occupation now returned to the city in droves. The population at the time of the British evacuation was about 12,000; by 1786, the number of inhabitants had risen to 23,614, with 3,340 houses; in 1790, the figure was a little more than 33,000, greater than that of either Boston or Philadelphia.

In 1783 the repatriates found the city in a deplorable condition. The destruction caused by the 1776 and 1778 fires had not been cleared away and many of the remaining structures were badly in need of repairs. Homes, churches, and public buildings converted into hospitals, barracks, prisons, and ordnance and munitions warehouses had to be returned to their former states. The land had been torn up in the course of erecting defensive fortifications. Breastworks and entrenchments lined both river fronts, rude barricades still profaned most of the important street intersections, and forts and redoubts crowned every hill of consequence.

All property and installations formerly owned by the British government became possessions of the State of New York, and these included Fort George and other fortifications. During the British occupation, King's College was closed as an educational institution, the enemy having converted it into a hospital. The State Legislature on May 1, 1784, passed an enactment to change its name to Columbia College, placing it under the State Board of Regents created by the same act. The first student to matriculate under its new name was De Witt Clinton, nephew of Governor George Clinton, who later became mayor of the city, senator, presidential candidate, and Governor of the State.

New York in 1785 was the seat of the government of the United States and of the state. In January of that year, Fort George's guns boomed a salute to the president of the Congress, Richard Henry Lee of Virginia, who came to open the session of that body in City Hall. Governor Clinton, at Whitehall, welcomed the delegates to New York, which remained the national capital until 1790 when it was moved to Philadelphia. On July 23, 1788, news arrived that New York State had ratified by unanimous vote the new Constitution. There were large public celebrations, accompanied by the ringing of bells and the firing of the fort's guns. Trinity Church, destroyed in the 1776 fire, had its new cornerstone laid August 21, 1788. The edifice, rebuilt in a year and a half, was consecrated in 1790. Within was a canopied pew for President Washington.

Washington and his Vice-President, John Adams, were inaugurated in New York. Adams arrived April 20, 1789, and was met at King's Bridge by members of Congress and an escort of light horse. When the entourage reached lower Manhattan, the Grand Battery guns fired a salute of welcome. President Washington, dressed in blue and buff, had come from Paulus Hook one week earlier, arriving on a decorated barge that was accompanied by many vessels on which enthusiastic people cheered and sang patriotic songs, and that came to rest at the gaily decorated landing-place at the foot of Wall Street. There was a universal ringing of the church bells, and the Grand Battery guns boomed thirteen times.

On the morning of April 30, the day of the inauguration, the festivities were opened by the firing of Fort George's guns. At noon an official cortege escorted Washington from his residence on Cherry Street, followed by a great civic and military procession on foot and mounted, to Federal Hall, where he entered the Senate chamber. He then stepped out on the balcony and, in full view of the Senators and Representatives within and of many of the new nation's most illustrious who were also on the balcony, and of most of the city's citizens, who jammed the streets and rooftops, he took the oath and kissed the Bible. With that, a flag was immediately hoisted up to the cupola of Federal Hall, and at this signal the guns at Fort George and on the Battery boomed again. The President delivered his inaugural address and returned to the Senate chamber. The United States of America had become a nation, fully organized on a permanent basis.

Old Fort George, kept in costly repair for 160 years, was at last condemned by an act of the State Legislature on March 16, 1790, specifying that the land beneath the fort should forever be reserved for the erection of public buildings. A board of commissioners was appointed to demolish the fort, level the ground, erect a new bulkhead at the Battery, and construct new buildings for the State Government, stipulating that the new structures be consigned to the temporary use of the President of the United States during such time as the Congress of the United States should hold its sessions in the City of New York.

Fort George was torn down. While leveling the ground, workmen discovered beneath the fort's ruins the leaden caskets containing the remains of Richard Coote, Lord Bellomont, and his wife, who had occupied the official governor's residence within the fort in 1698. They were removed and reinterred in St. Paul's churchyard. Broadway was lengthened to continue on a portion of the fort's site. A marble slab marking the site of Fort George's southwest bastion was originally set in place in 1818. In 1904 subway workers removed the marker, which was reset in the lawn of Battery Park in 1907.

Fort George, née Fort Amsterdam, never fully proved its strength and power against an enemy fleet. New York history began at this place and one should not agree with the cynic who wrote: "From the beginning to end of its long life, this strange fortress continued a picturesque cumberer of the ground, useless in war, worse than useless in peace; and at last when it succumbed before the march of commerce there were few to regret its fall."

Fort George on Laurel Hill

There still exist remnants of Revolutionary fortifications on the west bank of the Harlem River, on an eminence known today as Fort George Hill. The site, east of Broadway at 192nd Street and Audubon Avenue, is marked by a D.A.R. tablet that reads: "In grateful remembrance of the Patriot Volunteers of the Pennsylvania Flying Camp led by Colonel William Baxter of Bucks County, Pennsylvania, who, with many of his men, fell while defending this height, 16 November 1776, and was buried near this spot."

The hill was known as Round Meadow during Dutch colonization days and as Laurel Hill during the Revolution. The Patriots constructed two redoubts on the hill, one about halfway up, and the other on the crest, and armed them with several three-pounders. Bravely defended by Baxter and his Volunteers, the fortifications were overrun by superior numbers of troops of the famed Black Watch (Scotch Royal Highlanders) and Hessians during the British attack on Fort Washington a half mile to the west.

During the summer of 1778 the British expanded the redoubts to include a new blockhouse on the hill's crest. The armaments installed then and during the next few months consisted of two six-pounders, one ten-pounder, one twelve-pounder, and three eighteen-pounders, testifying to the strategic value of the hill. On July 24 the blockhouse was dismantled and carted up to Stony Point on the Hudson.

During the winter of 1779 Laurel Hill was connected to Fort Tryon. The following winter the British circumvallated Laurel Hill's redoubts. Repairs on the works were made on June 2, 1781. A French reconnaissance map shows a hexagonal fort with two surrounding walls and a third line lower down the hill reinforced with small batteries. The fortifications at this time were armed with a very respectable assortment of cannons and mortars.

The British had for a short time named the defenses Fort Clinton, then renamed it Fort George. The site of the fort is now occupied by George Washington High School.

Governors Island

One of New York's most historic landmarks, Governors Island lies in New York Bay approximately a half mile off Manhattan's Battery and opposite Brooklyn's Red Hook. The site was occupied by Fort Jay, First U.S. Army Headquarters from July 1946 to 1966. The island is now the headquarters of the Third Coast Guard District.

The island has been a regularly garrisoned American military post without interruption since 1794, but its ties with the history of the nation reach much deeper into the past. The first white European to see the island was most probably the explorer Giovanni da Verrazano, who sailed into the harbor in 1524. At that time Governors Island was thickly overgrown with oak, chestnut, and hickory trees. Its Indian name, "Pagganck" and Dutch name, "Nooten Eylandt" or "Nutten Island" referred, of course, to these groves of nut trees.

Soon after the Governor General of New Netherland, Wouter Van Twiller, had purchased Pagganck from the Indians, he was charged with malfeasance and incompetence. Before removal from office, however, he quietly arranged to have Nutten Island granted to him for his personal use. In 1638 he was sent home in disgrace and the West India Company annulled the grant, returning the island to public domain. From that time on, it was set aside as the official residence-estate for the Dutch governors, and later, for their English successors. Van Twiller was probably the only private owner of the island.

In 1664 the English captured New Amsterdam and promptly renamed it New York. They also took Nutten Island which, during the Dutch regime, had not been fortified despite its very strategic location. In 1673, during the third Anglo-Dutch War, the Hollanders regained their province, only to lose it again to England according to the provisions of the Treaty of Westminster a year later.

In 1698 the island was reserved by the Assembly as being "part of the Denizen of His Majestie's Fort [William Henry] at New York for the benefit and accommodation of His Majestie's Governors for the time being," and so it became known as "The Governor's Island." The island's name was changed officially from "Nutten" to "The Governor's" by an act of the Legislature, March 29, 1784. Gradually "The" and the apostrophe in "Governor's" were dropped, leaving the title as it is today.

GOVERNORS ISLAND, NEW YORK
(Aerial view with Brooklyn in the background)
U.S. Army Photograph

GOVERNORS ISLAND, NEW YORK
U.S. Army Photograph

From 1691 to 1702 New York's royal governors urged the fortification of New York's harbor. Despite their efforts, only 15,000 pounds were raised for defenses at the Narrows. In 1702 this sum of money was misappropriated by corrupt Lord Cornbury for the construction of a mansion on the island.

In 1710 the authorities designated Governors Island as a quarantine station, the first in New York's history, for the thousands of Palatine Germans who were arriving in America through the efforts of Queen Anne and Governor Robert Hunter. From seven to ten thousand of these émigrés were camped on the island at one time. Later they were sent up the Hudson River to pioneer new settlements, with many of them finally winding up in the Mohawk Valley. One of these refugees, John Peter Zenger, later became publisher of the *New-York Weekly Journal* and America's first defender of freedom of the press.

Troops were stationed on Governors Island for the first time in 1755. The initial garrison was the Fifty-first Regiment of British Colonial Militia under the command of an American-born major general, Sir William Pepperrell, who commanded the New England provincial forces that captured the French fortress of Louisbourg in June 1745. His regiment, combined with other units, came to be known as the Royal Americans (Loyalists), who fought the Patriots throughout the Revolution.

During the years between the last of the French and Indian wars and the beginning of the Revolution, there was very little military activity on the island. Its defenses were neglected until New York was threatened by British assault from the sea. During the Americans' frantic preparations for the city's defense, Gen. Israel Putnam was ordered to the island to assist Col. William Prescott's famed Bunker Hill regiment and Col. John Nixon's Fourth Massachusetts Continentals. On April 8, 1776, as soon as it became dark, Putnam and one thousand men crossed to the island, where they labored all night throwing up defenses against the possibility of attack by a small armada of British warships. The men-of-war had been anchored in New York Bay since the British withdrawal of the city's garrisons to the ships because of the arrival of Washington's Continentals and rising public hostility.

By May the island's fortifications were sufficiently completed to accommodate the mounting of thirty-two-pounders and four eighteen-pounders. By August the defenses had been enlarged to cover almost the entire island, and this work was accompanied by a substantial increase in the number of cannon. On May 9 Gen. Washington wrote Gen. Charles Lee: "We have done a great deal of work at this place. In a fortnight more I think the City will be in a very respectable posture of defense. . . . Governors Island has a large and strong work erected and a Regiment encamped there."

While Washington was establishing his headquarters in New York and planning its defense, three large British forces were converging on the city. Sir William Howe arrived from Halifax with nearly ten thousand men; then his brother, Admiral Lord Richard Howe, sailed into the harbor with a great fleet from England; and on August 4, Admiral Sir Peter Parker entered the Narrows with ten more ships carrying Sir Henry Clinton's beaten army from the South. All these forces, more than thirty-two thousand men, were landed unopposed on Staten Island.

Command of the sea was a decisive advantage for the British because it made any American defense of Manhattan or Long Island (Brooklyn) untenable from the start. On July 2, 1776, the Governors Island batteries engaged the British frigates *Phoenix* and the *Rose,* and three other warships. The vessels sailed up the Hudson, through and over the obstructions in the river between Fort Washington and Fort Lee, and returned practically untouched, although they received concentrated artillery fire from Red Hook, the Battery, and Governors Island.

The inevitable attack by the British finally began on August 22, when they landed on the Brooklyn shore. Skirmishes preceded the major battle on August 27, followed by the amazingly successful withdrawal of Washington's troops across the East River to Manhattan on the night of August 29/30. Governors Island was one of the last bases to be evacuated. During the night of August 30, without firing a shot, Col. Prescott and his men spiked all the island's guns and slipped out quietly, abandoning about forty cannon and a large store of ammunition and provisions. While the Americans were crossing to Manhattan, four warships anchored below the island cannonaded its fortifications, causing one Patriot to be wounded; he lost an arm by a shot just as he was embarking. Gen. Howe's lethargy allowed an extra day of grace for the former defenders. The next day many of them, without hindrance, went back to the island and removed all the stores.

When the British moved in to occupy the island two days later, Ambrose Serle, civilian secretary to Admiral Howe, was among them. He later wrote: "The entrenchments are as extensive as the Island itself and have been constructed with immense labor and some art. There are several forts cannon-proof[ed], with many platforms and embrasures, stockaded and entrenched at every side. To the Sound, in particular, they seem impregnable."

After the British occupation of New York on September 15, the war moved up the Hudson, and Governors Island, though fortified and garrisoned continuously, remained inactive. In November 1783, with peace and reoccupation by the Americans, Governors Island changed hands for the last time.

Washington Irving's words are a fitting memorial epitaph for the Battery and Governors Island:

In the year of our Lord one thousand eight hundred and four, on a fine afternoon in the glowing month of September, I took my customary walk upon the Battery, which is at once the pride and bulwark of this ancient and impregnable city of New York. The ground on which I trod was hallowed by recollections of the past; and as I slowly wandered through the long alley of poplars, which, like so many birch brooms standing on end, diffused a melancholy and lugubrious shade, my imagination drew a contrast between the surrounding scenery and what it was in the classic days of our forefathers. Where the government house by name, but the custom-house by occupation, proudly reared its brick walls and wooden pillars, there whilom stood the low, but substantial, red-tiled mansion of the renowned Wouter Van Twiller. Around it the mighty bulwarks of Fort Amsterdam frowned defiance to every absent foe; but, like many a whiskered warrior and gallant militia captain, confined their martial deeds to frowns alone. The mud breastworks had long been levelled with the earth, and their site converted into the green lawns and leafy alleys of the Battery. The capacious bay still presented the same expansive sheet of water, studded with islands, sprinkled with fishing-boats, and bounded by shores of picturesque beauty. But the dark forests which once clothed these shores had been violated by the savage hand of civilization, and their tangled mazes, and impenetrable thickets, had degenerated into teeming orchards and waving fields of grain. Even Governors Island, once a smiling garden, appertaining to the sovereigns of the province, was now covered with fortifications, inclosing a tremendous block-house, so that this once peaceful island resembled a fierce little warrior in a big cocked hat, breathing gunpowder and defiance to the world!

Grenadier's Battery

The "beautiful" circular battery, on the bank of the Hudson River at the intersection of today's Washington and Harrison Streets in lower Manhattan, was constructed by Capt. Abraham Van Dyck's Grenadier Company of New York Independents. Armed with three twelve-pounders and two mortars, with a line of breastworks extending along the river to Hubert Street, the defense was started while Gen. Lee was still in command. Gen. Washington, gratified by the excellence of its construction, thanked Capt. Van Dyck in general orders.

The Grenadier Company was organized by Lord Stirling a few years earlier when he resided in New York City. He often watched with understandable pride the construction of the battery as it progressed. Even so, he received the following letter, dated "New-York, April 27th, 1776," from Capt. Van Dyck after "compleating" the defensive work:

> My Lord, The Circular Battery which the Grenadiers under my Command, have for some Time past been employed about, is now compleated, and I am requested to acquaint your Lordship therewith. Whenever you happen to be in the Neighbourhood of it, they beg your Lordship will take a View of it.

Lord Stirling replied two days later, expressing his appreciation and stating that he had already visited the Circular Battery.

Horn's Hook Fort

Horn's (Hoorn's) Hook, a projection of land now partly hidden by the East River Drive and incorporated in Carl Schurz Park, was the immediate area of a strong Patriot work. It consisted of a battery of nine guns, six of which were mortars, breastworks, and entrenchments. The site of the fort itself is now occupied by the Gracie Mansion (1799), the official home of New York City's mayors, on the south side of 89th Street and East End Avenue.

Also known as Rhinelander's Observation and Gracie's Point some years after the war, Horn's Hook was selected as the place for a strong defense by Gen. Charles Lee during the one month, February 4 to March 7, 1776, that he spent in the city. The East River, at this point only seven hundred yards wide, is at the entrance to all-important Hell Gate, the gateway for British penetration into upper Manhattan by way of the Harlem River.

The property on which the fort was constructed was owned by Jacob Walton. He was obliged to sacrifice his beautiful lawn and gardens and move his family out of their mansion, which was converted into a barracks. The star-shaped defense, one of the earliest in the New York City area, was initiated early in February by Drake's Westchester minute men, who called it Thompson's Battery.

After the American retreat from Brooklyn, Washington recognized Horn's Hook as the anchor of the Patriot defense of Hell Gate, and had the fort immediately reinforced. The British also perceived the fort's strategic value. On September 1 Maj. Gen. James Robertson reconnoitered the position and at once determined to neutralize it. Three days later, from the Queens shore opposite, his batteries of two twenty-four-pounders, six twelve-pounders, and three mortars pounded Horn's Hook Fort and "greatly destroyed it." Artillery response from the fort, aimed by inexperienced gunners, inflicted few enemy casualties—only two men killed and one wounded by mortar fire. By the middle of the month all of Manhattan south of Fort Washington was surrendered to Gen. Howe's forces.

While the British held Horn's Hook, the fort, partially restored, was not involved in any other action. In July 1781 the French scouted the position as a possible target for a projected attack that never took place. During the same month the British renovated and strengthened the fort's works, erecting palisades around it. A little north of it they constructed a secondary defense without either a stockade or a ditch, and just beyond that, a palisaded blockhouse with additional batteries.

About ten years after the war, Archibald Gracie purchased Horn's Hook, which then became known as Gracie's Point. The author of a New York City guide book in 1807 delineated a little of the history of the historic spot:

> His [Gracie's] superb house and gardens stand upon the very spot called Hornshook, upon which a fort erected by the Americans in 1776 stood until about the year 1794, when the present proprietor caused the remains of the military works to be levelled at great expense, and erected on their rocky base his present elegant mansion and appurtenances.

Hospital Redoubt

By April 1, 1776, the hospital situated at West Broadway and Worth Street was fortified by a strong breastwork. A contemporary, John Varick, described the defense as "composed solely of dirt and sod. The thickness is about ten feet and about seven feet high, with a ditch twelve feet wide and seven feet deep surrounding the whole. This will afford a safe retreat from small arms." On April 16 an undetermined number of men from McDougall's New York regiment took post there.

The redoubt is not shown on any British map. It appears that the fortification was destroyed sometime during the fall or winter of 1776, when the Patriots lost New York City to the enemy. Henry P. Johnston places the fortified hospital on Duane Street, two short blocks to the south.

Fort Independence

The strongest Revolutionary fort in what is now Bronx County until the British reconstructed captured Fort Number Four, Fort Independence was located on the heights between the old Boston and the Albany Post Roads. In today's geography its site was on the west side of Giles Place, about a thousand feet north of where it intersects Sedgwick Avenue. Fort Independence Park at the south end of the Jerome Park Reservoir now contains the site of the Patriot fort.

The first effort in the immediate area to protect the Spuyten Duyvil crossing was a Patriot breastworks. This was in answer to the resolution of the Continental Congress, passed on May 25, 1775, "to prevent the communications of New York City being interrupted by land." Fort Independence was initiated only after a personal reconnaisance by Gen. Washington on June 20, 1776. Construction of the work was performed by the Pennsylvania Line of Continentals and units of the New York militia, under the supervision of Washington's chief engineer, Col. Rufus Putnam.

The earthen fort was a rough parallelogram with bastions in the northwest and southwest angles, with a square bulge flanking the eastern wall. The fort's enclosure included a stone-based barracks, officers' quarters, a stone powder magazine, and a number of tents. A 1778 military map shows an abatis on the fort's eastern face, but there is no documentary evidence available to establish whether this existed earlier than the British takeover. In 1777 two more bastions were planned by the British but never bulilt.

At three o'clock on the morning of October 28, 1776, Col. John Lasher and his New York Independent Battalion of Militia abandoned Fort Independence after burning the barracks and hurriedly retreated toward King's Bridge. They left behind "three hundred stands of arms, out of repair, five tons of bar iron, spears, shot, shell, and numerous additional valuable stores." Some hours later Capt. John Montresor arrived with three hundred Hessians, a column of dragoons, and a brass four-pounder in expectation of a fight, but found only a deserted Patriot fortification.

Prompted by his victories over the enemy at Trenton (December 26, 1776) and Princeton (January 3, 1777), and a desire to alleviate British pressure in the Jerseys, Washington on January 5 wrote an urgent letter to Gen. William Heath, then in the Hudson Highlands:

> The enemy are in great consternation; and as the present affords us a favourable opportunity to drive them out of the Jerseys. . . . You should move down towards New York with a considerable force, as if you had a design upon the city; that [place] being an object of great importance, the enemy will be reduced to the necessity of withdrawing a considerable part of their force from the Jerseys, if not the whole, to secure the city.

Washington's tired and bedraggled men entered Morristown on January 7, where log huts were built for their winter quarters. On the same day Washington sent several additional directives to Heath, to Gen. Benjamin Lincoln who had arrived at Peekskill with four thousand New England militia, and to other commanders to the north and south.

Preparations for the assault against the enemy in New York progressed so smoothly that by the night of January 17/18 Gen. Heath (who described himself as "of middling stature, light complexion, very corpulent, and bald-headed") was able to give the signal for three divisions to proceed toward King's Bridge. The movements of the separate forces were so well synchronized that they arived almost simultaneously at the first British outposts at dawn.

> As a demonstration toward New York it undoubtedly had a great effect upon General Howe's movements, and the plan itself was well conceived, well initiated. The divisions arrived at King's Bridge with remarkable concert of time; but there they stopped, and the chief objective was not realized.

Gen. Lincoln advanced from Tarrytown on the Albany Post Road; Gen. John Scott and his militia, forming the center column, came down from White Plains; and Gens. Daniel Wooster and Samuel Parsons marched from New Rochelle and East Chester. The troops easily took the enemy's outposts and appeared before Fort Independence. The fort's garrison of nearly two thousand Hessians and Queens Rangers were given only "twenty minutes in which to surrender or abide the consequences." Not only did the garrison's commander disregard the summons, he ordered the fort's gunners to fire on the rebels. Heath thereupon sacrificed "his one chance for distinction as a field commander" by failing to immediately assault the fort with his numerically superior forces. He chose instead the fatal alternative of ineffectually cannonading the fort's walls for several days with small fieldpieces, and indulging in unprofitable, aimless maneuvering.

Finally, on the 25th, the Hessians and Rangers, who had had enough of this tomfoolery, came out and put the Patriots to rout, driving them out of the Negro Fort and the Valentine-Varian House, which they had captured on the 18th. Heath and his forces dallied in the area above Fort Independence until the twenty-ninth, when signs of an impending snowstorm caused them to withdraw completely. The fiasco angered Gen. Washington, who penned a stinging rebuke to Gen. Heath on February 3:

> This letter is additional to my public one of this date. It is to hint to

you, and I do it with concern, that your conduct is censured (and by men of sense and judgment who have been with you on the expedition to Fort Independence) as being fraught with too much cautions: by which the army has been disappointed and in some degrees disgraced. Your summons, as you did not attempt to fulfill your threats, was not only idle but farcical, and will not fail of turning the laugh exceedingly upon us.

The neighborhood of the fort was raided again repeatedly by the Patriots, but these subsequent actions did not seriously involve Fort Independence. On September 12, 1779, the British began the destruction of the fort, but substantial ruins were still standing in 1781 when the Americans and their French allies were reconnoitering in force the enemy posts in New York.

The residence, built about the year 1860 by William O. Giles, stood on part of the fort's ramparts. The first excavation of the site in 1914 was prompted by the discovery of cannonballs by children, which led to the recovery of hundreds of balls, shells, and bar iron. The finds were stored in the Valentine-Varian House Museum.

In 1958 five amateur archaeologists, referring to an old British map, turned up sections of Fort Independence. The area explored was roughly bounded by Giles Place, Cannon Place, and 238th Street. They uncovered walls between sixteen and nineteen inches thick that apparently were part of the powder magazine and officers' quarters. In addition, the men unearthed six-pound cannon balls, musket balls, crockery and rum bottles, regimental buttons, and old coins. The work was instigated by the plan to construct a massive apartment house complex, Fort Independence Village, on part of the site, replacing the old Giles home.

One of the two plaques on the gateposts at the entrance to Fort Independence Park reads: "This Park, Dedicated to the Public Service 7 May 1916, was Included in the Exterior Works of Fort Independence, Constructed in 1776 at the Direction of General George Washington, Evacuated by the American Garrison October 27, 1776, and Finally Abandoned by the British Garrison August, 1779."

Jersey Battery

One of the stronger Revolutionary forts in what is now downtown Manhattan, the Jersey Battery was located very close to the Hudson River shore. To the left of Grenadier's Battery, on the present line of Reade Street west of Greenwich Street, the battery was begun very soon after Gen. Lee's orders of February 29, 1776; it was practically completed by May 22.

The work was a five-sided fortification, mounting two twelve- and three thirty-two pounders. A line of intrenchments connected this redoubt with the Grenadier's Battery and extended beyond both redoubts on either end. The position of the two batteries was a particularly effective one, with their guns able to range up and down the river's shore and enfilade any enemy attempt to land in the near environs.

In April 1776 three companies of Col. William Bond's Massachusetts regiment were posted at the battery. Together with the Oyster Battery and the Whitehall Battery, the redoubt engaged in a duel with the British men-of-war, the *Phoenix* and the *Rose*. In possession of the enemy, the battery was renovated and improved during the summer of 1782.

Jones Hill Fort

When the Dutch founded New Amsterdam, the promontory known today as Corlear's and jutting out into the East River, was known to the Indians as Nechtanc. The first owner of that land was Jacob Van Corlear in Governor-General Van Twiller's time (1639). Years after the unseating of Dutch rule by the English, Corlear's Hook came to be known as Crown Point.

In the spring of 1776 the point was fortified with the Crown Point Battery by the Patriots. After the Americans were ousted from Manhattan, the British refortified the line from Corlear's Hook to Bunker's Hill, with Gen. Knyphausen's Hessians camped on nearby Cherry Hill, which was at the time the finest residential district in New York.

A line of entrenchments extended around the top of the height of land above Corlear's Hook to a circular battery, embrasured for eight guns, on the north side of Jones Hill, a little north of the intersection of Broome and Pitt Streets (Cohn places the fort at Grand and Columbia Streets). During Lord Stirling's command of New York City's defense-building, consideration was given to the proposal to call this fort "Washington," but it became known as Jones Hill Fort.

From this fort the works continued along the line of Grand Street to the Bowery, including two more circular batteries—one at Grand Street and Norfolk Streets, and the other near the intersection of Grand and Eldridge Streets. Jones Hill Fort was one of the early defenses planned by Gen. Lee during his short stay in the city. It was built on the property of Thomas Jones, Loyalist historian, who authored the only history of the war from the viewpoint of a Loyalist. In 1762 he married Anne, daughter of Chief Justice James De Lancey. In 1765 he constructed "Mount Pitt" on a two-acre tract between the Bowery and the East River, considered to have been one of the most beautiful estates on Manhattan Island.

The fort was constructed by Col. Joseph Spencer and his Connecticut troops sometime between April 16 and May 22. After New York was evacuated by the Patriots, the defense was strengthened with fraises and pickets by the British on October 2. Despite continued sub-zero temperatures during the Hard Winter of 1779/80, Gen. James Pattison on January 23, 1780, ordered gun platforms constructed to accommodate eight twelve-pounders. In February the garrison consisted of 1 naval captain, 2 lieutenants, and 210 seamen. Three months later, on May 29, the fort was connected to other major defenses by a new line of small redoubts, generally along the same ground as the old Patriot works.

King's Bridge Redoubt

Highly strategic to both the Americans and the British, King's Bridge was located at the place where the old Post Road crossed Spuyten Duyvil Creek, separating Manhattan Island from the Bronx. The name Kingsbridge is still attached to that geographical area.

The first span to cross the creek was a toll bridge, called the King's Bridge by its owners, the wealthy Philipse family. Built in 1693 and rebuilt twenty years later, this exclusive privilege was anathema to travelers. Money raised in 1759 by public subscription funded the erection of the Free Bridge, several hundred yards away, to discredit the monopoly. By the time the Revolution started, both spans were free to public use.

On May 25, 1775, the Continental Congress passed several resolutions that at last signified the decision of the Thirteen Colonies to wage war against Britain. The first resolution was that the Province of New York should take possession of King's Bridge and erect a fortification there; the second was to fortify both sides of the Hudson in the Highlands. Five days later, the members of the New York Provincial Convention agreed to the proposal and appointed a committee to go to King's Bridge to pick a site for a redoubt. Coincidentally, on the same day, the *Cerberus*, a thirty-two-gun frigate, entered Boston Harbor. On board were three British major generals—John Burgoyne, Henry Clinton, and William

Howe—whose military leaderships had a great bearing on America's transition from colonial status to complete independence.

There is no documentation available describing the American work at King's Bridge. It may be reasonably assumed that at least a small redoubt was constructed, probably an earthwork affair.

The so-called Hickey Mutiny involved two Continental soldiers, one of them Thomas Hickey. The conspiracy, for certain, included the destruction of King's Bridge, a Patriot battery elsewhere, and the secret recruitment by Loyalists. The plot was exaggerated by the Americans to the extent where the conspirators were even accused of making plans to assassinate Gen. Washington. On June 26, 1776, Hickey was court-martialed and convicted of mutiny and sedition. Two days later, in the presence of thousands of New Yorkers, he was hanged near Bowery Lane.

With the American army ousted from Manhattan and in full retreat, the British on November 22 occupied King's Bridge and erected a semicircular earthwork in the form of a flèche on the south side of the creek and Broadway and garrisoned it with a captain and twenty men of the Seventy-first Highlanders.

On June 27, 1914, the Empire State Society of the Sons of the American Revolution mistakenly located an inscribed tablet on the front of the apartment house at 108 West 227th Street. It read:

NORTHWEST OF THIS TABLET
WITHIN A DISTANCE OF 600 FEET STOOD THE
ORIGINAL KING'S BRIDGE
AND ITS SUCCESSORS FROM 1693 UNTIL 1913
WHEN SPUYTEN DUYVIL CREEK WAS FILLED UP.
OVER IT MARCHED THE TROOPS OF BOTH ARMIES
DURING THE AMERICAN REVOLUTION AND ITS
POSSESSION CONTROLLED THE LAND APPROACH
TO THE CITY.
GEN. GEORGE WASHINGTON
"RESTED AT KING'S BRIDGE" ON THE NIGHT
OF JUNE 26-27, 1775, WHILE EN ROUTE
FROM PHILADELPHIA TO CAMBRIDGE TO
ASSUME COMMAND OF THE CONTINENTAL ARMY.

Years passed before it was realized that the tablet was wrongly placed. The proper location should have been the intersection of 230th Street and Broadway. On September 24, 1932, a correction was attached to the weather-beaten tablet.

Lispenard's Redoubt

Just above the city proper and standing on Lispenard's Hill, named for Leonard Lispenard, wealthy brewer and delegate to the Provincial Convention, these works were the western anchor of the line defending New York City. A double post with a redoubt covering the approach from the country to the north and a battery guarding the Hudson River side, Lispenard's Redoubt was located at today's intersection of Varick and Laight Streets.

The defensive complex had a change in names, instigated by enemy reconstructions. The original redoubt was circular, armed with two twelve-pounders and two mortars, and named Lispenard's Redoubt or Circular Redoubt. It was built soon after May 22, 1776, the date of a Patriot post list. The auxiliary battery bore the name of the Grenadier Battery and was the first defense on the hill, erected before May 22. The battery's artillery went into action against British frigates sailing up the Hudson on July 12, 1776.

In possession of the British, the battery was reconstructed into a redoubt and renamed the Foundry Redoubt. The landward fort was rebuilt into a star-shaped work and renamed the Star Redoubt, both occurring before 1780. Archival records reveal that in 1780 the Foundry Redoubt was armed with one twenty-four-pounder, two six-pounders, and a thirteen-in. mortar; the Star Redoubt had an undetermined number of guns plus three small mortars.

McGown's Pass Redoubt

A fortified redoubt was constructed on one of two small, steep hills within the northeast corner of today's Central Park, at about the intersection of Fifth Avenue and East 107th Street, just above the home of Andrew McGown (McGowan). The hill is now graced with the Fort Clinton Monument, a cannon surmounting a huge flat boulder, to which is attached a tablet: "This Eminence Commanding McGowan's Pass Was Occupied by British Troops Sept. 15, 1776 and Evacuated Nov. 21, 1783. Here Beginning Aug. 18, 1814, the Citizens of New York Built Fort Clinton to Protect the City in the Second War with Great Britain."

The old Post Road ran between the two hills of McGown's Pass before dropping sharply to what was known as the Harlem Plains. The pass was therefore regarded as highly "critical terrain" and was prominently involved in the Revolutionary battle for Manhattan.

Montresor's Island

Strategically located at the mouth of the Harlem River, Montresor's (now Randall's) Island was owned by Capt. John Montresor, the British army's chief of engineers in the Colonies. He purchased the island in 1772 and resided there with his wife and family until 1783, except for a period of several months when the Americans had control of the island.

The history of the island is interesting. Its original Indian name was Minnehanonck. Two Indian chiefs sold it, along with today's Ward Island, to Wouter Van Twiller, Governor-General of New Netherland. The first private Dutch owners were named Barent, and they named it Little Barent Island (Ward's Island was known as Greater Barent Island).

When the Dutch were ousted from New Amsterdam by the English in 1664, the island was granted to Thomas Delavall, the customs collector for New York. On his death the island was inherited by his daughter Frances, wife of James Carteret. Her daughter, Elizabeth, married as her second husband Philip Pepson, an Englishman, whose younger son inherited American properites including the island, on which he erected a residence; he renamed the island Belle Isle. In 1739 he became bankrupt and returned to England.

George Talbot was the next owner. He changed the island's name to Talbot Island and lived there until his death in 1765. He bequeathed the property to Britain's Society for Propagating the Gospel to Foreign Parts, which sold it in 1772 to John Montresor, who renamed it. At the end of the Revolution, New York City confiscated the island and sold it the following year to Samuel Ogden, a New York merchant, who transferred it the same year to Jonathan Randall, who purchased it for six thousand dollars. He lived and farmed there for nearly fifty years until his death in 1830. Five years later the city bought the island from his heirs for fifty thousand dollars. For many years thereafter it was utilized as a potter's field. An almshouse and a hospital for the feeble-minded were constructed there. For about the last five decades Randall's Island has been increasingly popular for its improved park and recreational facilities.

Soon after the beginning of the Revolution, the Patriots took possession of Montresor's Island and used it as an isolation area for American troops stricken with smallpox. British forces occupied the island on September 10, 1776, fortified it, and used it as a stepping stone in Howe's campaign to oust Washington's Continentals from Manhattan Island. "From that well-chosen advance post, they could land either on the plains of Harlem, south of Kings Bridge, or on the Morrisania estate, whence they could flank the position at Kings Bridge by a march of six or seven miles.''

Washington authorized Gen. William Heath to attempt a surprise takeover of the island when the latter learned that the British post was weakly garrisoned. Lieut. Col. Michael Jackson of the Massachusetts Sixteenth Continentals commanded 240 men in three boats in the attack at dawn on September 23. Jackson's boat hit the island beach first. But when the island's garrison attacked the landing parties, the men in the other two boats pulled away, deserting their commanding officers in the first craft. The fiasco resulted in fourteen Americans killed, wounded, and captured. Among the casualties were Jackson, wounded in the leg, and Heath's aid, Maj. Thomas Henley, who was killed. ''The delinquents in the other boats were arrested, and tried by court-martial, and one of the Captains cashiered.''

Fort Number One

Col. James Swartwout (Bliven, *Under the Guns,* p. 114, has ''Jacobus'' for the colonel's given name) and his Dutchess County minute men constructed Fort Number One on the southwest slope of Spuyten Duyvil Hill, just north of the Henry Hudson Monument, at today's West 230th Street and Sycamore Avenue. The small square fort, protected by an abatis, was abandoned by its garrison without a fight. Hessian troops then manned the fort as an outpost with two six-pounders until November 1778, when British Guard troops took over. The fort was abandoned, and probably demolished, in the fall of 1779, when the British defense line was withdrawn to Manhattan Island.

The Americans built a halfmoon earthwork battery at the mouth of Spuyten Duyvil Creek, just behind today's Spuyten Duyvil Station of the Penn-Central Railroad. The need to protect the entrance of the creek against British men-of-war was apparent to Gen. Washington, by whose orders the defense was erected on October 11, 1776. It was no doubt abandoned at the same time as the other redoubts in the area. The Spuyten Duyvil Battery was apparently never renamed by the British and, although it does not appear on any garrison listing of the King's Bridge salient, it still appeared on military maps as late as 1781.

Fort Number Two

During August-September 1776 Col. Swartwout and his minute men built this small, probably circular, abatised fort on the crest of Spuyten

Duyvil Hill. Cohn locates the site "200 feet south of 230th Street and 230 feet west of Arlington Avenue." During its construction, the men named the defense for their colonel.

Fort Number Two was abandoned by the Patriots on October 28, the same day the main forces of Washington and Howe battled at White Plains, about eleven miles to the north. During Hessian occupation a small redan with two six-pounders was constructed on the west side of the fort. In the course of Sir Henry Clinton's realignment and reduction of British defenses, Fort Number Two was demolished in November 1779.

Fort Number Three

Col. Swartwout's minute men also built this fort during the summer of 1776. It was a square abatised earthwork located on the eastern slope of Spuyten Duyvil Hill on a line with today's Netherland Avenue, between 227th and 231st Streets. The fort's position was designed to cover the valley and the main road to Phillipsburgh (now Yonkers).

The fort was evacuated by the Patriots on November 28 to the advancing British. In 1778 Hessian units, occupying the fort, built a connecting curtain to Fort Number Two. There is no documentation available on the fort's artillery. Just before its abandonment by the British in the fall of 1779, the fort was garrisoned by thirty-five rank and file of the Brigade of Guards. The works still existed, though in a ruined condition, in 1781.

Fort Number Four

A square palisaded earthwork redoubt, about seventy feet to a side and surrounded by a ditch, Fort Number Four was located at the south end of the Jerome Park Reservoir, seven hundred feet east of Sedgwick Avenue. On Reservoir Avenue, just west of University Avenue, a tablet was attached to an outcropping of rock by the D.A.R. in 1914: "Fort Number Four of the Exterior Defenses of Fort Washington and King's Bridge, Constructed by the American Army under General Washington, 1776."

The British twice assaulted the fort and finally captured it, occupying the works with a force of British and Hessians. The redoubt was reconstructed by British Provincials, beginning the work on July 19, 1777, but not completing it until October. For about two years the British utilized the fort to protect the Harlem River front.

Fort Number Four was one of the redoubts or forts demolished by Sir Henry Clinton in the fall of 1779 in order to obtain the needed manpower for his campaign in the South. Archaeological excavations in 1910 revealed the remains of the brick fireplaces of the officers' quarters and the guard house, along with numerous figured buttons and other military relics.

Fort Number Five

The British constructed this square abatised earthwork, probably during the late summer of 1777, and garrisoned it by the first week of October. Located on Kingsbridge Road, the fort's position was designed to cover the approach to the Farmers or Dyckman Bridge spanning the Harlem River. The site of Fort Number Five is on the grounds of the U.S. Veterans Hospital, formerly a Catholic orphan asylum.

There are no records available on the fort's artillery. First garrisoned by Hessians for a very short time, and then, in rotation, by provincials of the Prince of Wales Regiment and the King's American Regiment, the fort was never involved in any action. The works were destroyed by the British during their reduction of fortifications north of Manhattan Island.

Fort Number Six

Construction of this earthwork fort was initiated by the British on May 19, 1777. Also located on the present grounds of the U.S. Veterans Hospital, the site of Fort Number Six is at Kingsbridge Road and Sedgwick Avenue. There is no documentation available on its artillery or whether it was ever involved in any action. Originally garrisoned by Hessians, the fort was then posted by provincials until its destruction on September 11, 1779.

During excavations preparatory to the building of the Catholic orphan asylum (later the Veterans Hospital) in 1899, the ruins of Fort Number Six were unearthed, along with a number of artifacts including some George II coins.

Fort Number Seven

Earthworks were constructed by the British on November 15, 1776, at the present-day intersection of Fordham Road and Sedgwick Avenue. Maj. Gen. James Robertson, one of Gen. Howe's staff officers, noted that they were "raising battery in barbette for 20 field pieces and howitzers . . . to cover attack on York Island." After the attack on Fort Washington the next day, Fort Number Seven was not involved in any further artillery action.

Reconstruction of the work into a square abatised fort was started on July 19, 1777, at which time it was mentioned as "begun but not complete." On December 4, 1778, a new log structure (barracks?) was erected between the fort and the King's Redoubt directly west.

Under orders of the Royal Artillery the King's Redoubt, a circular earthwork, was also constructed to cover the attack on Fort Washington. Guns from the redoubt pounded the Patriot fort's outlying works. Sometime in 1778 an abatis was constructed around the redoubt, which remained under the jurisdiction of the Royal Artillery. The stone magazine within the work was dismantled on September 17, 1779, when the post was presumably abandoned. Fort Number Seven was torn down a week earlier.

Fort Number Eight

Unlike the other forts and redoubts of the so-called Exterior Defense Line, Fort Number Eight was built by the British. It stood on the east side of the Harlem River, on today's New York University's campus, on University Heights in the Fordham section of the Bronx. A boulder inscribed "The Site of Fort Number Eight, 1776-1783" stands on Battery Hill eighty yards south of N.Y.U.'s Hall of Chemistry. The massive Schwab mansion (1857), just beyond the marker, was built within the site.

The four-pointed star fort, surrounded by a very effective abatis, was somewhat larger than the other forts in the defense perimeter. As the southern anchor of the Fordham Heights line, Fort Number Eight covered the advance of the Hessians and Lord Percy's troops during their attack on Fort Washington, actively engaging in the bombardment of the Patriot defense.

On July 19, 1777, the fort was listed as incomplete, but by October it was complete enough to be occupied by a garrison. In October 1779 a work party of fifty men did some repairing and renovating of the works. In July 1781 Gen. Washington observed that "Fort Number Eight is also abatised and friezed on top and the gate is next to the Harlem River."

During the years following the loss of Manhattan and the Bronx to the enemy, American troops often penetrated the so-called Neutral Ground between the Hudson Highlands and British-held New York City, harassing British contingents, raiding their outposts, engaging in spirited skirmishes, and causing, at times, considerable damage to life and matériel. Fort Number Eight's guns protected the encampments of Col. Peter De Lancey's Westchester Light Horse Battalion posted at and around the Archer House, just southeast of the fort. These camps were raided by the Patriots in May 1780, and again on January 20, 1781. During the "Grand Reconnaissance" of the British defenses on July 20, 1781, De Lancey's camps were again struck. In each case the fort's guns limited the expansion of the American raids. The fort's complement of guns changed little in number, with at least two nine-pounders always mounted on the ramparts.

During the early months of 1779, with the northern theater of war at a stalemate, Sir Henry Clinton was coming to the conclusion that British military fortunes lay in a vigorous campaign in the South. He ordered all troops out of Newport, Rhode Island, and initiated preparations for the orderly withdrawal of large numbers of men from New York, but keeping in mind the safe British occupation of the city. He then began to rearrange the British defenses by striking a "line of circumvallation" across Manhattan from Laurel Hill's Fort George to the Hudson River.

Early in October Sir Henry ordered the demolition of Fort Independence and the other forts on the Bronx side of the Harlem River, except for Fort Number Eight opposite Fort George, and the strengthening of these two fortifications. This sharp reduction in defenses eliminated eleven forts, redoubts, and blockhouses, leaving Fort Number Eight as the only British post in what is now Bronx County.

On October 8, 1782, Fort Number Eight was abandoned. Twelve days later the British began the actual demolition of the works, which for years defied assault by the Patriots. In 1965 excavations for a new N.Y.U. campus building unearthed numerous Revolutionary artifacts, most of them now lodged in the Valentine-Varian House Museum, headquarters for the Bronx County Historical Society.

Just north of the N.Y.U. campus was another redoubt, a circular earthwork, presumably constructed by the Patriots to judge by its name—the Rebel Redoubt—and armed with two nine-pounders. After British provincials garrisoned it, an abatis was added. It was abandoned in the fall of 1779.

Oyster Battery

Sources are at odds on whether the Oyster Battery and McDougall's Battery were interchangeable names for the same Patriot defense. The first-named was initiated, as were the other fortifications in lower Manhattan, pursuant to Gen. Lee's orders of February 29, 1776, and was armed with two thirty-two-pounders and three twelve-pounders.

Cohn claims that the Oyster Battery and McDougall's Battery were one and the same, and that it was located behind Trinity Church.

Lossing says the Oyster Battery stood in the rear of No. 1 Broadway (Washington's short-term headquarters on the west side of the street) and that McDougall's Battery, with a complement of four guns, was located southwest of Trinity Church "on the high river bank."

Johnston is puzzled:

The works next below [the Jersey Battery] on the Hudson consisted of two batteries situated on the high ground in the rear and to the south of Trinity Church. The one on the bluff near the church, or on the line of the present Rector Street, a little east of Greenwich, was known under Stirling as McDougall's Battery; but this name does not appear in the return of June 10th, and in its place in the order of the works we have the "Oyster Battery." It is possible that this was the work a little south of McDougall's, at the intersection of the present Morris and Greenwich streets. Its location is described by [General] Putnam in May as "behind General Washington's head-quarters." It mounted two thirty-two pounders and three twelve-pounders. In March, McDougall's Battery was provided with six guns.

In a note to the foregoing, Johnston continues his argument:

Washington's Head-Quarters in New York: This reference creates some uncertainty as to the particular house occupied by Washington in New York during the first part of the campaign. If the site of the Oyster Battery were known exactly the house could be identified. On the other hand, if head-quarters, as generally supposed, were at the Kennedy Mansion, No. 1 Broadway, then the battery should have stood still lower down, at the corner of Battery Place and Greenwich Street; but the Grand Battery terminated there, and Hill's map shows no distinct battery there.

The historical turmoil over where Gen. Washington had his headquarters in New York City is suitably resolved by Lossing. When Washington arrived in the city on April 13, 1776, he established his headquarters at 180 Pearl Street on the east side of lower Manhattan. After his return from a visit to Philadelphia on June 6, he took up quarters at the Kennedy house, but his stay there was relatively short. Within the next two weeks he moved to the Mortier home at 6th Avenue and Spring Street, the site of which is now occupied by the Butterick Building, and he resided there for most of the summer months. Other dignitaries, before and after Washington, occupied the mansion: Lord (Jeffrey)

Amherst, Lord (Guy) Carleton, John Adams while Vice-President, and Aaron Burr.

Double identities for fortifications in American history are very common. It is therefore more than probable that the Oyster Battery and McDougall's Battery were one and the same defensive work.

Fort Prince Charles

According to Stokes, this earthwork redoubt was erected by the Patriots as Fort Number Nine in 1776, taken over by the enemy after the battle for Fort Washington on November 16, and renamed Fort Prince Charles or the Charles Redoubt. He locates the site of the fortification on Marble Hill, at Fort Charles (Corlear) Place and Kingsbridge Avenue. Other sources report the location as Marble Hill Avenue and 228th Street. The fort's position was meant to cover the King's Bridge and Fort Cock Hill.

Officially called Fort Number Nine until the Hessians began reconstruction of the redoubt on January 7, 1777, it was renamed Fort Prince Charles. Details, however, concerning the design of the new works and its complement of artillery are not documented. The site of the fort is commemorated by a tablet on Marble Hill's St. Stevens Church.

Robert Bolton writes that "Prince Charles's Redoubt, and the Negro fort, both well known fortifications, in the annals of the Revolution, lie on the south side of Valentine's [Marble] Hill. From the former, which commands a splendid view of the surrounding country, the morning and evening gun of the British was fired."

The Negro Fort, a small work so named because of its one-company garrison of Negroes, was located on the south side of the old Boston Post Road about a quarter of a mile west of the Valentine-Varian House. Both Fort Prince Charles and the Negro Fort were presumably destroyed by the British in the fall of 1779.

Fort Tryon

The site where Americans displayed their most stubborn opposition to overwhelming numbers of the enemy before Fort Washington fell is now memorialized high in the wooded hillsides on the northern end of Manhattan Island. The northern outpost of Fort Washington, a small redan appropriately named Forest Hill Redoubt by the Patriots, was located where the main observation platform, flagpole, and two commemorative plaques are situated in Fort Tryon Park.

On November 16, 1776, the earthen redan on the 250-foot-high hill overlooking Inwood village, between Fort Washington and Fort Cock Hill, was being held by Col. Moses Rawlings and 250 Maryland and Virginia riflemen, supported by two six-pounders and gunners of the Pennsylvania Artillery. Outnumbering the defenders more than ten to one, 3,000 Hessians commanded by Gen. Knyphausen crossed King's Bridge and attacked the American position in two columns. The very narrow front afforded by the heavily wooded, almost precipitous terrain would not permit the European soldiers to spread out in their usual extended formations. In the face of the strong Patriot defense and very effective sharpshooting from both within the redan and by others part way down the hillside firing from behind trees and rocks, the enemy suffered heavy casualties. But on they came, plodding higher and higher, forcing the gradual retreat of the hillside defenders to their post on the height.

John Corbin was one of the Pennsylvania gunners. His wife, Margaret, was assisting with the loading of his gun. A Hessian bullet toppled John and he fell mortally wounded at his wife's feet. Margaret Corbin became one of America's legendary heroines when she replaced her husband at the gun until she herself was very severely wounded by enemy grapeshot. Her remains are interred in the West Point cemetery.

Two-and-a-half hours after the Hessians mounted their assault, they finally clambered over the redan's ramparts and bayoneted those defenders who refused to lay down their rifles. Fort Washington fell the same day. The Patriots were forced off Manhattan Island, not to return for nearly seven years.

The British in 1778/79 erected sizable Fort Tryon and a barracks on the site of the earthen redoubt, naming the new fort for the last royal governor of New York. During 1779/80 the famous Coldstream Guards garrisoned the post.

In 1933 the historical site was presented as a gift to New York City through the generosity of John D. Rockefeller, Jr., who purchased the estate that shortly became Fort Tryon Park. A private residence on the height was dismantled and an observation platform replaced it, providing a wondrous panorama of the Hudson River, the East River, and the Island of Manhattan.

Turtle Bay Depot

The little rock-lined cove in the East River at the end of 47th Street, since filled in and now the plaza one block north of the United Nations

Assembly Building, was called Turtle Bay. It was the site of a British magazine and storehouse captured by a bold strike for liberty late on the night of July 20, 1775.

The daring amphibious raid was conducted by the Liberty Boys, led by Isaac Sears, Marinus Willett, John Lamb, and Alexander McDougall, Sons of Liberty activists, who later attained some additional fame. They had procured a sloop at Greenwich, Connecticut, sailed across Long Island Sound into the East River, sneaked through Hell Gate at twilight, and just before midnight surprised and took prisoner the guards. A part of the captured stores was shipped to Washington's army besieging Boston and the remainder was forwarded to Fort Ticonderoga, where Gen. Montgomery's troops were assembling for their role in the invasion of Canada.

In 1776 the Patriots built a redoubt at Turtle Bay, on a site between today's 44th and 46th Streets, just south of the British depot.

Fort Washington

Designed to protect all of upper Manhattan, Fort Washington was situated on the highest eminence on the island, on a 230-foot-high, mile-long hill, covering the ground between 181st and 186th Streets along Fort Washington Avenue. The fort commanded the Hudson to the west, the valley of Broadway and Laurel Hill to the east, and the country down to about today's 120th Street to the south. Only the ridge to the north, on which Fort Tryon (Forest Hill Redoubt) was located, offered an open approach. Fort Washington was the last holdout of the Americans in Manhattan after the British and Hessians had driven Washington's main army north to White Plains and beyond.

Laid out by Gen. Washington's engineer, Rufus Putnam, the fort's construction was initiated on June 20, 1776, by the Third and Fifth Pennsylvania Continental regiments of Cols. John Shee and Robert Magaw, with the assistance of some militia. Originally planned as a five-bastioned fortress, Fort Washington eventuated as an extensive, crude, pentagonal earthwork, without the improvements dictated by military science to withstand attack or siege. Haste had precluded the building of what could have been an eminently strong fortification.

The fort had neither ditch nor palisade, no barracks, casemates, or source of water supply, and suffered from weak outworks, with one of them located at Harlem Cove (Manhattanville) to impede a British approach from the river. Added were a lunette battery at Jeffrey's Hook below the fort on the shore of the Hudson and the inevitably ineffectual *chevaux-de-frise* in the river between Fort Washington and Fort Lee

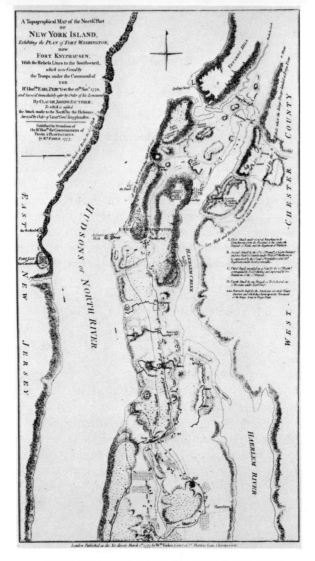

NORTH PART OF NEW YORK ISLAND
Courtesy of The Newberry Library, Chicago

LEGEND

"A Topographical Map of the North Part of New York Island Exhibiting the Plan of Fort Washington, now Fort Knyphausen, With the Rebel Lines to the Southward, which were Forced by the Troops under the Command of the R.ᵗ Hon.ᵇˡᵉ Earl Percy on the 16th Nov.ʳ 1776 . . . to which is added the Attack made to the North by the Hessians. Surveyed by Order of Lieut.ᵗ Gen.ˡ Knyphausen."

KEY

A.   First Attack under General Knyphausen by Detachments from the Hessians of his Corps.

B.   Second Attack.

C.   Third Attack intended as a Feint.

D.   Fourth Attack by one Brigade of British and one of Hessians under Earl Percy.

aaa.   Barracks built by the Americans for their Winter Quarters and which they burnt up in the Movement of the Kings Army to Frogs Point.

directly opposite on the Jersey shore, to barricade the waterway against British shipping.

The faults of the defense, which Gen. Putnam considered impregnable, were not recognized by either side. Col. Magaw, commandant, believed that he could successfully hold off the British until the end of the year, if need be. On September 20 general orders declared that "the heights we are now on may be defended against twice the force we now have to contend with." Washington was thus impressed at first by the fort's deceptive strength of position, only later to have an intuitive change of heart. Gen. Greene was all for keeping the fort, specifying that the garrison could be evacuated should the occasion arise to require it; Gen. Thomas Mifflin agreed, suggesting that Fort Washington be retained as winter quarters for the Patriot army. Gen. Charles Lee, writing to Joseph Reed, was not so impressed: "I cannot conceive what circumstances give Fort Washington so great a degree of value and importance as to counter-balance the probability or almost certainty of losing 1,400 of our best troops." Washington, however, bowed to his faith in Greene.

The treachery of English-born William Demont, promoted regimental adjutant to Col. Magaw on September 29, very possibly influenced Gen. Howe's decision to halt his chase of Washington's army, turn about, and take care of bypassed Fort Washington. Less than a week after the Battle of White Plains, Demont deserted on the night of November 2 and went directly to Earl Percy's camp at McGown's Pass. Carl Van Doren's excellently documented *Secret History* gives an extract of the deserter's justification for his action and the suspicions of a captured Patriot:

> I sacrificed all I was worth in the world . . . and brought in with [me] the plans of Fort Washington, by which plans that fortress was taken by his Majesty's troops the 16th instant, together with 2700 prisoners and stores and ammunition. . . . At the same time I may with justice affirm, from my knowledge of the works, I saved the lives of many of his Majesty's subjects.
>
> Captain [Alexander] Graydon, one of the prisoners taken, thought the British "must have had a perfect knowledge of the ground we occupied;" and he suspected Demont. The assault on Fort Washington was undertaken and carried out with great exactness. (Pp. 17-18)

The *chevaux-de-frise* in the Hudson proved to be a dismal failure; the British frigates *Phoenix* and *Rose* blithely sailed over and through the barrier, unscathed by the artillery fire from both river banks. During the night of November 14/15 the enemy, unseen by the Americans, convoyed a flotilla of loaded flatboats up the river into Spuyten Duyvil Creek and down the Harlem River to an assembly point that became the springboard for the British assaults westward. The individual enemy actions, contributing to the capture of the fortress, occurred at Forest Hill Redoubt (Fort Tryon), Laurel Hill (Fort George), Harlem Cove (Manhattanville), and Cock Hill Fort.

Fiske gloomily reviews the prelude to the American debacle:

> The officious interference of Congress, a venial error of judgment on the part of Greene, and gross insubordination on the part of Lee, occurring all together at this critical moment, brought about the greatest disaster of the war, and came within an ace of overwhelming the American cause in total and irretrievable ruin. Washington instructed Greene, who now commanded both fortresses, to withdraw the garrison and stores from Fort Washington, and to make arrangements for evacuating Fort Lee also. At the same time he did not give a positive order, but left the matter somewhat within Greene's discretion, in case military circumstances of an unforeseen kind should arise. When, while Washington had gone up to reconnoitre the site for the new fortress at West Point, there came a special order from Congress that Fort Washington should not be abandoned save under direst extremity [Greene] . . . believed that the fort could be held, and he did not like to take the responsibility of disregarding a message from Congress. In this dilemma he did the worst thing possible; he reinforced the doomed garrison, and awaited Washington's return.(1:229)

On the fifteenth a British officer hailed Fort Washington with a demand for surrender. Col. Magaw's answer was that if Gen. Howe wanted the fortress he would have to come and get it.

At seven o'clock on the morning of the sixteenth Howe mounted vicious assaults from three sides. His batteries on the east bank of the Harlem River opened fire, aided by cannonading from the frigate *Pearl* in the Hudson, which also served to cut off retreat across the river. The Bronx forts and Fort Washington's outer works were overcome one by one.

Col. Magaw's original garrison of about twelve hundred men had been reinforced on September 1 by Col. Israel Hutchinson's Twenty-seventh Massachusetts Continental Regiment, about seventeen hundred troops, on Greene's orders, but they were still outnumbered almost three to one. With bayoneted guns the enemy made a furious assault up the steep, rocky hill in the face of concentrated Patriot rifle fire. Cannonades from British artillery tore through the Patriot positions. Hessians scaled the ramparts of Fort Washington's earthworks and, as in the Battle of Brooklyn, the terror of the bayonet proved more efficacious than the musket. The American soldiers ran frantically for the fort's central redoubt, where they finally surrendered, but not before a number of them had been bayoneted. Gen. Washington at Fort Lee, with spyglass in hand, watched with horror and sadness the loss of some of his best troops.

The official British account of casualties reported 2,818 American rank and file captured, 53 dead, and 96 wounded. The combined British-Hessian loss was 452 killed and wounded. The British suffered 20 killed and 102 wounded, but the Hessians fared much worse, 58 killed and 272 wounded. [Snow, *American Heritage* (June 1973), p. 57, reports 2,837 Patriots captured, 59 dead, and 96 wounded, with the British and Hessians combined taking a loss of 136 killed and 646 wounded].

The blow to American morale was devastating; forebodings of ultimate disaster swept the Patriot ranks. Much more serious blows were the heavy losses of trained manpower and the great amount of almost priceless munitions. The approximate total of war matériel taken at Fort Washington and, four days later, Fort Lee was staggering: nearly 150 guns (almost all of the guns Col. Knox had laboriously congregated), 12,000 shot and shell, 2,800 muskets, 400,000 cartridges, besides tents, entrenching tools, and other accouterments. The capture of Fort Washington gave the British what they were striving for: New York and its great natural harbor.

On November 21 the captured American defense was renamed Fort Knyphausen for Hessian Gen. (Baron von) Knyphausen, who had captured Forest Hill Redoubt. Under British control it was occupied by Hessians for most of the remaining years of the war. They utilized it as a headquarters, with the additions of bakehouses, a hospital, and barracks. On May 18, 1779, a British and Hessian work party constructed a new six-gun battery. When Gen. Washington reconnoitered the fort on July 17, 1781, he perceived that it was "well friezed, ditched and abatissed," while Jeffrey's Hook below it on the Hudson shore had "a small work with a guard house in it."

More than fifty years ago, antiquarian and historian Reginald Pelham Bolton and colleagues began excavations on the site of Fort Washington in the vicinity of 183rd Street and Fort Washington Avenue. They unearthed cannonballs, bullets, regimental buttons, pieces of crockery, and many other items, all of which were carted over to the Heye Foundation's Museum of the American Indian. A monument with a Revolutionary cannon mounted on it was erected on Fort Washington Avenue to mark the site of the fort. Years later the landmark was demolished. Today the site is commemorated by a flagpole 265 feet high on Fort Washington Avenue in Gordon Bennett Park between 183rd and 185th Streets, the highest natural point on Manhattan Island.

Waterbury's Battery

Built by the Americans in the spring of 1776, Waterbury's Battery of seven guns (Cohn reports only two guns) was located at the foot of Catherine Street at its intersection with Cherry Street. At the beginning of the war the battery's site and environs were occupied by shipyards located along the shore at the narrowest point of the East River; during the mid-nineteenth-century years, the site was taken up by the Catherine Street Market. The actual site of the battery is now buried beneath the approaches to the Williamsburg Bridge.

Soon after the Battle of Brooklyn, the battery fired on British men-of-war proceeding up the river. On September 3, 1776, the twenty-gun frigate *Rose* came under the fire of Waterbury's Battery but no damage to the warship has been indicated. The British apparently made no effort to keep up the fortification after their occupation of the city.

Close by was another artillery position, the Shipyard Battery, armed with two guns of undetermined caliber. It was built in the early spring of 1776 and garrisoned by two companies of men. It too fired on the *Rose*, with no reported damage. Apparently this post also was not retained by the British.

Whitehall Battery

Located behind Washington's short-lived headquarters at No. 1 Broadway, on what was once known as the Whitehall Dock (now South Ferry), the Whitehall Battery was begun on orders of Gen. Lee on February 29, 1776. Standing a little to the east of the Grand Battery—practically a continuation of it—the battery was apparently completed by May 22.

Armed with two thirty-two-pounders, the battery, along with the Jersey Battery and the Oyster Battery, engaged the British warships *Phoenix* and *Rose* in an artillery duel. The British retained the battery position, repairing and improving the work in 1782.

Brooklyn

Beginning with Gen. Charles Lee, a succession of New York City commanders during the winter and spring of 1776 had come to the same inescapable conclusion. In order to safeguard New York City from enemy assault through Long Island (Brooklyn), a continuous line of entrenchments, strengthened by forts and redoubts in strategic places, would have to be constructed from Red Hook to Wallabout Bay. Most of the defense line was ready and garrisoned by May 30, with other fortified posts behind it. Improvements on the works continued right up to the moment when the British and Hessians swarmed out of Staten Island and launched attacks by way of Denyse Point and Gravesend Bay.

Washington and his staff determined to pull back the Patriot troops from Gowanus Bay through Prospect Park to Jamaica, with the purpose of resorting to their forts should enemy pressures become critical. Gen. Washington sent reinforcements across the river from New York during the night of August 26/27, and he himself arrived in Brooklyn at 8 A.M.

Gen. Howe's clever feints at the American west flank drew Washington's reserves to that sector, leaving the opposite flank exposed. Howe and Sir Henry Clinton with ten thousand men made a nine-mile, five-hour, forced night march without being detected by the Patriots, and they outflanked the entire rebel line by coming through the unfortified and unwatched Jamaica Pass while British troops feinted before the other hill passes.

At Flatbush Pass the Americans realized they were in a very precarious situation. They fled to their forts, covered by the brave, almost suicidal counterattacks of the Maryland and Delaware regiments against a pressuring horde of Hessians, with Gen. Cornwallis and his Fraser Highlanders as yet undiscovered behind the Americans. Soon it was all over, with all the fighting terminating at about two o'clock on the afternoon of August 27.

As is common with casualty reports released by opposing armies, Patriot figures varied greatly from those of the British. Reasonable estimates by historians have the Patriots suffering a loss of about 1,400 men, with 312 killed and the remainder wounded, captured, and missing. (Washington's figure was 800; Sir Henry Clinton's estimate was 6,000!). The British officially reported 89 American officers, including Gen. John Sullivan and Lord Stirling, and 1,097 others as prisoners. The British and Hessians engaged in the Battle of Brooklyn had a combined loss of a bit less than 400 killed and wounded.

It was a clear-cut enemy victory because of Gen. Howe's clever strategies, American ineptitude, and a numerical enemy superiority. The only serious flaw was Howe's characteristic failure to capitalize on his advantage over the rebels; a bolder general could have killed the rebellion then and there. To Howe the American forts appeared too formidable to take by storm and he initiated siege operations, no doubt recalling the slaughter of many Britons on Charlestown's Bunker Hill on June 17, 1775.

Fearful that Howe might mount an assault against New York City with fresh troops from Staten Island, Washington and his staff officers determined in a council of war on the afternoon of August 29 to evacuate Brooklyn Heights and reassemble his beaten army on Manhattan Island. That morning Washington had foreseen the possibility of an evacuation and had ordered Gen. Heath to congregate all available watercraft and move them to the East River by nightfall.

The secret extrication of nearly twelve thousand men from the Brooklyn forts was accomplished by the rare combination of extraordinary skill and courage, a feat that was destined to become one of the most memorable events of the war. With the loss of only three Patriot loiterers who remained behind to pillage and five heavy cannon mired in deep mud, Gen. Washington had the remainder of his troops, guns, supplies, and horses across the river and safe on Manhattan Island by seven o'clock on the morning of August 30. The entire evacuation took, almost unbelievably, only six hours.

Fort Box

Chroniclers a century ago had assigned various locations for this small, short-lived, diamond-shaped outpost. Since then it has been firmly established that Fort Box, constructed in 1776, was situated on Bergen's (Boerum's) Hill, on or very close to Pacific Street, a short distance above Bond Street and on the edge of the Gowanus Creek marshes.

Boerum Hill and today's Boerum Place were named for Simon Boerum, an influential resident of the area and a delegate to the first and second Continental Congresses. He was a great-grandson of William Jacobse Van Boerum, who emigrated from Holland with his family in 1649, when New York was still New Amsterdam. The progenitor of all the Brooklyn Boerums, Boorems, Booraems, Burams, and the like farmed in Flatbush and New Lots and is interred under the Flatbush Reformed Dutch Church (1796).

In his definitive history of Brooklyn's role in the Revolution, Henry Johnston reports:

> As to its name, we must assume that it was called Fort Box in honor of Major Daniel Box, [Gen. Nathanael] Greene's brigade-major . . . whose services were then highly appreciated. Box first appears as an old British soldier, who had been wounded in the French war, and

afterwards as an organizer and drill-master of Independent companies in Rhode Island. . . . That he was something of an engineer as well as an excellent brigade-major, is evident from the fact that he assisted in marking out the lines around Boston in 1775, and later superintended the construction of Fort Lee, on the Jersey side. (3:70-71)

Appearing on Continental lists of posts for May 30 and June 7, 1776, Fort Box possibly offered cover for Gen. Sullivan's retreat during the Battle of Brooklyn. Pursuant to Gen. Greene's order of June 1, five companies of Col. James Varnum's Ninth Rhode Island Continental Regiment were assigned to defend the fort and hold the trenches leading to Gowanus Creek.

Lossing (2:806n.) reports that the fort was a small redoubt with four guns, occupying a site between Smith Street and First Avenue, not far from the termination of Hoyt Street. The listing for June 7, 1776, shows that the post's garrison was defending the position with only thirty pikes, which appears to be an incomplete report of the garrison's actual possession of firearms.

After the Patriot evacuation of Brooklyn, British war maps do not show the fort, its function apparently having been taken over by Fort Corkscrew. During the War of 1812 the site of Fort Box, or ground very close to it, was occupied by Fort Fireman.

Fort Brooklyn

In May 1780 the recently appointed British military governor of New York, Gen. James Robertson, reported to London that "a large square fort is built on Brooklyn Heights: the season is late; not a blade of grass. The people within the lines begin to repair and rebuild houses, and manure and inclose lands."

The fort the general had reference to was Fort Brooklyn, otherwise known by the British as The Citadel. It was located at the intersection of Pierrepont and Henry Streets, about four blocks southwest of Fort Stirling. It was by far the most complete fortification built by the enemy during their occupation of Brooklyn. The land on which it stood had sustained herds of cattle grazing in the shade of several fine orchards ruthlessly destroyed by the army's engineers. Old inhabitants used to reminisce about watching from two to three thousand troops engaged on the works at one time, digging trenches and wheelbarrowing earth for the fort's walls.

Johnston, in his *Campaign of 1776,* writes that

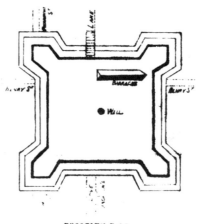

BPOOKLYN FORT

FORT BROOKLYN
Courtesy of Long Island Historical Society

the work, which was to be known as the Citadel, was in all probability
the "redoubte commencé," or unfinished fort, indicated on the
Hessian map in the rear and to the south of Fort Stirling. The site
corresponds with that of the British fort of 1780, corner of Henry and
Pierrepont sts., which was then, as it still is, the highest point on
Brooklyn Heights, and hence the natural position for a citadel or
commanding fortification. . . . The list of batteries, March 24th
[1776], contains a note to the effect that a citadel covering five acres,
called the Congress, was to be built in the rear of Fort Stirling. . . .
Work on the citadel was probably discontinued, because his [Stirl-
ing's] plan was so much enlarged as to make that fortification
unavailable. (3:77-78)

Brooklyn's inhabitants were assessed several days' labor, with
farmers cutting down acres of brushwood to be fashioned into twelve-
foot-long fascines to support the fort's earthen walls. A farmer with a
team of horses or oxen and a wagon was obliged to work for a week or
ten days in cutting and transporting these fascines, or timber and other
materials, for the barracks. Many mechanics were also employed in the
construction of a gate and drawbridge, a very substantial and costly
work so admirably built that it could be easily raised and lowered by only
one soldier. In addition, about forty men were put to work digging a deep
well in the exact center of the fort. In 1823 the well, not used since the
British evacuation, was fitted with a pump and a well-house.

The fort was 450 feet square, with ramparts soaring 40 to 50 feet above the bottom of the encircling ditch, itself 20 feet deep. The angles were occupied by bastions, on each of which was planted a buttonwood tree; within the enclosure was a substantial barracks and two bomb-proofed magazines. In front of the fort, on a line with today's Fulton Street, between Pierrepont and Clark Streets, stood a row of small sutler's mud huts. Construction on the fort was still in progress in July 1781, at which time it was garrisoned by two hundred Hessians and mounted eighteen cannon.

A diary kept by an inhabitant on Brooklyn Heights recorded under date of August 23, 1823 that "the frame of the first building erected on the site of the old British fort, through which Jackson's, alias Love Lane, passes, put up this day on Henry Street. A considerable part of the remains of the fort has been levelled within a year or two."

Fort Corkscrew

Erected in early 1776, the Patriot defense stood on a high conical hill (since drastically graded) on a site now bounded by Atlantic Avenue, Court, Pacific, and Clinton Streets. Its former location is now commemorated by a tablet on the corner of the first-two-named streets. The cone-shaped eminence was known as the Ponkiesbergh to seventeenth-century Dutch settlers and as Cobble Hill to the Massachusetts troops who garrisoned it. The soldiers first dubbed the redoubt Fort Cobble Hill, then the Spiral Fort, and finally Fort Corkscrew.

The crest of the hill commanded a very fine view of all the country between Gowanus Bay on the south and Brooklyn Heights on the north. During the Battle of Brooklyn it was this four-gun American position from which Gen. Washington, with Gen. Putnam beside him, watched his Maryland troops badly defeated by superior forces of the enemy. The commander-in-chief was overheard to exclaim: "Good God, what brave fellows I must this day lose!"

The British maintained the post until July 3, 1781, when they leveled off the hill somewhat so that the guns of captured Fort Stirling on Brooklyn Heights could adequately cover it. Shortly after the start of the War of 1812, the site of Fort Corkscrew was refortified and renamed Fort Swift for Gen. Joseph G. Swift, U.S. Army engineer, who built a new fort there.

In 1970 the fort's area, now known as Cobble Hill, was declared a historic district by the New York City Landmarks Preservation Commission. For most of its history, Cobble Hill was considered part of either Red Hook or Brooklyn Heights. A few blocks away, at 197 Amity Street, is the birthplace of Jennie Jerome, mother of the late Sir Winston Churchill.

Fort Defiance

On April 4, 1776, Gen. Israel Putnam arrived in New York City to take over the command from Gen. Stirling. "Old Put" quickly assessed what had been done so far and added to the already constructed or planned Patriot fortifications Governors Island and the peninsula opposite it on the Brooklyn shore, Red Hook (Roode Hoek), so named for the color of its earth.

On the same night of April 10, when one thousand Continentals took possession of Governors Island, a regiment occupied Red Hook, the northernmost point of land above Gowanus Bay. There they constructed a redoubt for one three-pounder and four eighteens *en barbette,* designed to prevent enemy shipping from proceeding through Buttermilk Channel behind Governors Island and entering the East River. The redoubt was named Fort Defiance by Col. Henry Knox's artillerymen stationed there.

GENERAL ISRAEL PUTNAM
Courtesy of USMA Library

Gen. Washington in May described Fort Defiance as being "small, but exceedingly strong." During the early summer months the fort was strengthened by additional works which, according to a Hessian military map, consisted of a second and larger redoubt, called Smith's Barbette, connected to the first by an enclosed way. On July 5 Gen. Greene wrote his commander-in-chief that he considered Fort Defiance "a post of vast importance," and he suggested the posting of a strong force there permanently; three days later Col. Varnum's regiment joined the Red Hook garrison.

Stiles places the fort's site near the intersection of today's Conover and Van Dyke Streets in the Erie Basin area of Red Hook. It has since been determined that the actual site is at Dwight and Beard Streets, several blocks to the southeast. There, in 1952, a bronze tablet was attached to a brick building to commemorate Fort Defiance. The attending ceremony was held on the 176th anniversary of the Battle of Brooklyn (August 27), during which a flotilla of six British men-of-war attempted to pass Fort Defiance and enter the East River to attack the Patriots' flank and rear. In the face of a stiff northeast breeze, five of the vessels had to drop down to New York Bay, but the frigate *Roebuck* managed to get as far as Red Hook. (Carrington, *Battles of the American Revolution,* p. 201, gives August 26 as the date when the *Roebuck* came under fire of Fort Defiance's guns). The fort's cannon, while not causing any damage, forced the *Roebuck* to retire out of range.

One month to the day later, September 27, the British destroyed the works of Fort Defiance.

Fort Greene

Occupying almost the center of the Americans' Brooklyn defense line, Fort Greene stood about three hundred yards to the left of Fort Box, a little distance above Bond Street, between State and Schermerhorn Streets. It was built on land then owned by two influential citizens, Van Brunt and De Bevoise, for whom two Brooklyn streets are named. The star-shaped fort, provided with an interior well and two magazines, mounted six guns, and possessed a stock of one hundred pikes. It occupied a strategic position on a small height, commanding the old Flatbush Road.

Completed by May 30, 1776, the fort was described by Col. Moses Little, its commander, as the largest of the Long Island defenses. His opinion was corroborated by the fact that its garrison consisted of a whole regiment, Col. Little's Twelfth Massachusetts Continentals, which was not the case with any of the other Brooklyn forts. Since it was the principal fortification on the defense line, the engineers, or possibly the garrison, named it after their brigade commander, Gen. Nathanael Greene.

There is some documentation that the British renamed the defense Fort Sutherland in November 1778 and that they "kept up and improved" it in 1782. During the War of 1812 the Americans named the defense Fort Masonic. The fort should not be confused with the Fort Greene of the War of 1812 (Fort Putnam during the Revolution), the site of which is in today's Fort Greene Park.

Narrows Fort

Erected in the spring of 1776, this Patriot redoubt, together with its companion defense opposite on the Staten Island shore, Flagstaff Fort, were designed to close off entry to New York's harbor by enemy ships. Armed with an undetermined number of guns and garrisoned by Col. Edward Hand with two hundred men of the First Pennsylvania Continentals, it was located very near strategic Denyse Point on the Narrows, the site of which was included in the future Fort Hamilton (1831).

On Thursday, August 22, 1776, British and Hessian troops were ferried from Staten Island across the Narrows to Denyse Point. Col. Hand withdrew his force to Prospect Hill, setting fire to all property and destroying supplies that might benefit the enemy. Other enemy troops followed to enter Gravesend Bay directly to the east and landed under the protection of men-of-war. They rapidly expanded their bridgehead to overrun South Brooklyn and occupy the Revolutionary villages of Gravesend, New Utrecht, and Flatlands, names still in use.

The Narrows Fort, kept up by the British, was still in existence in December 1778, with subsequent military maps continuing to show its location.

Oblong Redoubt

Constructed by the Americans in the spring of 1776 and destroyed by the British on September 27, the redoubt stood to the left of Fort Greene, on the other side of the Flatbush-Jamaica road. It was located on what was then a small hill at the intersection of today's De Kalb and Hudson Avenues.

Oddly enough, the Oblong Redoubt was circular in shape, and the reason for its misnomer has been lost in the mists of history. Gen. Greene's orders referred to the defense as the "Oblong Square" and the "Oblong Redoubt." On May 30 three companies of Col. Little's Massachusetts Continentals garrisoned the redoubt. There is no archival evidence of any armaments, except for twenty pikes. During the War of 1812, the Oblong Redoubt became Fort Cummings.

Fort Putnam

From the Oblong Redoubt the American defense line rose in a northeasterly direction to the crest of the hill now in Fort Greene Park, where the fourth in the chain of works was erected in the spring of 1776. Fort Putnam, star-shaped like Fort Greene, was somewhat smaller than the latter and mounted at least five guns. Its strong natural position made it the salient point of the line, thus to become one of the main objectives of the British attack during and after the Battle of Brooklyn, August 27-29, 1776.

The fort was named for Col. Rufus Putnam rather than Gen. Israel Putnam. Col. Putnam, Washington's chief engineer, marked out many of the defenses in Brooklyn as well as those in New York City, no doubt frequently crossing the East River to supervise the construction of the various works. On May 30 the fort's garrison consisted of five companies of Col. Daniel Hitchcock's Eleventh Rhode Island Continental Regiment.

At the eastern end of the hill, a short distance from Fort Putnam, was the last in the line of five works, identified in orders of the day as "redoubt on the left" or the Left Redoubt. It stood on Cumberland Street between Myrtle and Willoughby Avenues and covered the northern flank of the defense line. The redoubt was maintained by the British, at least until September 1779, when it was repaired.

Connecting the five works—Fort Box, Fort Greene, Oblong Redoubt, Fort Putnam, and the Left Redoubt—was a line of entrenchments, continuing on the right from Fort Box to the marshes, and on the left from Fort Putnam to the swamp at the edge of Wallabout Bay. Each work was a complete entity, surrounded with a wide ditch, and having a sally-port, sides lined with pointed stakes, and the garrison armed with pikes to resist assaults, and supplied with adequate water and provisions to endure an enemy siege. Most of the line was abatised, with the surrounding woods cut down to preclude cover for the enemy and allow a full sweep of the forts' guns.

Rather interesting information was brought out in 1779 when a parliamentary committee investigated Gen. Howe's conduct of the war in America. One of the witnesses was Capt. John Montresor, British

GENERAL NATHANAEL GREENE
Mezzotint by T. Green from painting by C. W. Peale
Courtesy of National Archives

engineer. Since he was sympathetic to the general, Montresor for the most part exaggerated the strength of the rebel defenses, but the essential points of his testimony should be accepted as historical fact. He was asked: "Can you give a particular account of the state of those [Brooklyn] lines?" Montresor elaborated as follows:

> Yes—the lines were constructed from Wallabout Bay, on one side to a swamp that intersects the land between the main land and Red Hook, which terminates the lines. The lines were about a mile and a half in extent, including the angles, cannon proof [ed], with a chain of five redoubts, or rather fortresses, with ditches, as had also the lines that formed the intervals, raised on the parapet and the counterscarp, and [the] whole surrounded with the most formidable abbaties.

There is some archival evidence that indicates that the British in 1782 erected a "new" square fort on Fort Putnam's site. It would seem more reasonable to believe, however, that Fort Putnam was *converted* into a square-shaped work.

During the War of 1812 Fort Putnam was renamed Fort Greene for Gen. Nathanael Greene. In 1826 the site was sold for $3,750 to two men who offered it to the city of Brooklyn as a location for a poor house. The

Brooklyn fathers accepted the offer and built an almshouse. On April 27, 1847, the New York State Legislature, over strong local objections, authorized the conversion of the site into a public park to be called Washington Park, a name changed years later to Fort Greene Park.

In the park, at Myrtle Avenue and Cumberland Street, is the imposing Prison Ship Martyrs' Monument, designed by Stanford White and dedicated in 1908 to the approximately 11,500 Patriots who died aboard disease-ridden British prison ships in nearby Wallabout Bay. The 145-foot fluted granite shaft, supporting a huge bronze urn, stands on a high plateau and is approached from the street level by a 100-foot-wide stone stariway.

The brutal treatment accorded the American prisoners, on such infamous prison ships as the *Jersey,* the worst one by reputation, the *Whitby, Hunter,* and *Stromboli,* commanded by the notorious Provost Marshal, William Cunningham, is recognized to this day as one of the most serious black marks in British colonial history. Prisoners died by the dozen each day from starvation and disease, floggings, and other brutal forms of punishment. Their bodies were buried, usually by their fellow prisoners, in the sands at the edge of Wallabout Bay, in the area now called the New York Naval Shipyard. Remains of about 11,500 bodies, located from time to time, were placed in the crypt beneath the monument.

Fort Stirling

In early March 1776 Lord Stirling (William Alexander) succeeded Gen. Charles Lee, to vigorously prosecute the construction of Patriot defenses planned and initiated by Lee. Shortly after Stirling had taken over the command with an army of about four thousand Continentals and militiamen, he received a dispatch from Gen. Washington at Cambridge to the effect that Gen. Howe appeared to be making preparations to abandon Boston, with New York as his next apparent objective.

The length of Stirling's command was even shorter than Lee's, less than a month, when he was replaced by Israel Putnam on April 4. But while he was in command, recurring bouts of rheumatism did not deter him from augmenting his efforts to get the job done.

The first American fort to be constructed in Brooklyn, Fort Stirling was located on the bluff at the very edge of Brooklyn (Columbia) Heights on today's Columbia Street, spanning the two-block distance between Clark and Orange Streets. Also known as Fort Half-Moon because of its open rear, Fort Stirling was designed to command the East River channel in front of it. Almost directly across the mouth of the river was Coenties Slip, also fortified, in downtown Manhattan. During the early decades of the nineteenth century, there was some confusion among writers and inhabitants who associated Fort Stirling with the remains of its British successor, Fort Brooklyn, four blocks to the southeast. A Hessian military map, however, distinguishes the two fortifications.

The construction of Fort Stirling, begun on March 1, was under the supervision of Col. (Artemus?) Ward who commanded 519 men. Kings County's inhabitants were ordered by Congress to assist the colonel, by "turning out for service at least one-half their male population (Negroes included) every day, with spades, hoes, and pick axes." The civilians were also required to furnish brushwood for fascines, wood for pickets, and other necessary timber. The fort was built on land then owned by Jacob Hicks, for whom Hicks Street is named, and others.

In his March 14 letter to the President of the Continental Congress, Gen. Stirling reported that "the work first begun on Long Island opposite to this city is almost completed, and the cannon carried over. The grand citadel there will be marked out to-morrow, and will be begun by the inhabitants of King's County and Colonel Ward's regiment."

A note on Stirling's "grand citadel" is contained in the March 24, 1776, Patriot list of batteries, to the effect that a citadel covering five acres, called The Congress, was to be constructed on the height (Henry and Pierrepont Streets) in the rear of Fort Stirling. "Work on the citadel was probably discontinued" because of the enormity of the task according to Stirling's plan. The British, however, appreciated this site and built Fort Brooklyn.

Fort Stirling was planned to mount eight heavy guns but on May 22 a report was issued showing that there were only six cannon, four thirty-two-pounders and two eighteen-pounders, manned by a garrison of a lieutenant and twelve men. On July 19 a work party was engaged on widening the fort's ditch.

After the Patriots were ousted from Brooklyn, the British posted a strong Hessian garrison at the fort, with every intention of keeping the fortification. In 1778 the German mercenaries were replaced by elements of a Grenadier Guards regiment. Despite the construction in 1780 of the larger and stronger Fort Brooklyn four blocks away, the British continued to make improvements on Fort Stirling because of its eminently strategic position at the mouth of the East River. There is some documentation, probably confusing this fort with Fort Brooklyn, that in 1782 the work mounted as many as thirty heavy guns and was garrisoned by one thousand men.

In 1924 the Fort Greene Chapter of the D.A.R. affixed a commemorative plaque to the iron fence at the foot of Clark Street:

THIS TABLET MARKS THE SITE OF FORT STIRLING. ON THIS BLUFF IN THE SPRING OF 1776 IT FORMED ONE OF A CHAIN OF REDOUBTS BUILT IN BROOKLYN OPPOSITE NEW YORK. THIS WORK FELL INTO THE HANDS OF THE BRITISH DURING THE BATTLE OF LONG ISLAND AND WAS THEREAFTER GARRISONED BY HESSIAN TROOPS UNTIL VICTORY BY THE AMERICAN ARMY LED TO THE EVACUATION OF NEW YORK NOVEMBER 25TH 1783.

Staten Island

This large island of fifty-seven square miles, bordered on the south and west by Upper and Lower New York Bays, and separated from New Jersey by Kill Van Kull and Arthur Kill, became the springboard for the massive invasion of Brooklyn by the British and their Hessian mercenaries in the fourth week of August 1776. It also served as an advanced base for British forays against Patriot posts in New Jersey. The island is approximately one mile across the Narrows from Brooklyn and seven miles across the Upper Bay from Manhattan's Battery.

On July 2, 1776, Gen. William Howe began an unopposed takeover of Staten Island, landing troops by the thousands; on the 13th his elder brother, Admiral Lord Howe, arrived with more troops from England, including thousands of Hessians. On August 12 Sir Henry Clinton returned from his Charleston campaign with more soldiers and joined the Howe brothers on the island, which supported a normal population of only two thousand farming and seafaring people. This was the greatest overseas expeditionary force ever congregated by the British, with the number of soldiers and seamen, rank and file, aggregating about forty-two thousand men.

On August 22 British and Hessians boarded boats to cross the Narrows, attack, and overcome the Patriots' Narrows Fort at Denyse Point on the Brooklyn shore. More troops were ferried over to enter Brooklyn by way of Gravesend Bay and fan out in all directions. During the ensuing week they won the Battle of Brooklyn, resulting in the brilliantly executed American retreat across the East River to Manhattan on the night of August 29/30.

One of the American officers captured during the battle was Gen. John Sullivan, who was held captive on Staten Island. He was deluded into believing that the Howe brothers were endowed with more power under their peace commissions than the Continental Congress realized. With Lord Howe's permission he traveled to Philadelphia, where he convinced Congress to send a committee to confer with the Howes. On September 11 the Congressional committee of Benjamin Franklin, John Adams, and Edward Rutledge arrived at Perth Amboy, New Jersey, where they were met by a British barge to carry them to Staten Island.

They met with Lord Howe at the ninety-year-old Billopp stone mansion in today's Tottenville (the Conference House opposite Perth Amboy); Gen. Howe begged to be excused because of pressing military duties, probably having to do with his planned invasion of Manhattan. The only offer Lord Howe was empowered to make was that if the Americans would drop the idea of independence, he would promise pardons for the Patriot leaders and the lifting of certain trade restrictions. Franklin told him there was no turning back. The meeting broke up with an exchange of polite expressions of good will and the Congressional ambassadors boarded the waiting barge to return to Perth Amboy.

The British completely occupied Staten Island, erecting forts and redoubts on all the strategically important heights and shore points, and converting almost every dwelling and tavern from Kill Van Kull to Raritan Bay into billets. And there the enemy stayed until the end of the Revolution.

At present there are no conclusive documentations to identify all the British fortification sites on the island. A map of the Revolutionary period in the Richmondtown Museum shows various tentative sites, but little if any actual work has been done to develop them.

Decker's Ferry Fort

This British strongpoint was located opposite Bayonne (New Jersey) Neck, facing today's Bayonne-Staten Island ferry landing in the town of Port Richmond on Kill van Kull. The ferry to Bergen Neck was also covered by the guns of the fort.

When the Patriots fled Staten Island in the face of Gen. Howe's landing of his troops, they burned the stone house belonging to a Tory named Decker. One week after the British arrived they took over the dwelling and converted it into a fort. A report in January 1779 described it as a "stone house fortified with loopholes and an abatis."

The fort was involved in the unsuccessful large-scale Patriot raid commanded by Gen. Sullivan on the first anniversary of the British invasion of Brooklyn, August 22, 1777. Sir Henry Clinton later reported that the Americans effected an almost total surprise of two provincial battalions belonging to [Brig. Gen. Cortlandt] Skinner's [Loyalist] Brigade, and after setting fire to the magazines at Decker's Ferry, were on their march to Richmond; while another corps, that had landed on the west part of the island for the purpose of cutting off three other provincial battalions, had taken Lt. Col. Lawrence, with a great part of his battalion, prisoners, and only missed the remainder by Lt. Cols. Dongan and Allen having the presence of mind to throw them into some old rebel works at Prince's Bay.

Brig. Gen. John Campbell's regiment and a Hessian Waldeck regiment put an end to Sullivan's march across Staten Island, with the Americans losing about 150 captured and 20 wounded men. Sir Henry, however, claims that the British, besides appropriating most of Sullivan's boats, had captured 259 officers and men. One consequence of the Patriot debacle was the court-martial and subsequent acquittal of Gen. Sullivan, who throughout his military career was beset by bad luck, some of it attributable to his own inadequacies.

On the night of January 14/15, 1780, with the whole Northeast in the relentless grip of the Hard Winter, Lord Stirling and three thousand men crossed frozen Arthur Kill from Elizabethtown to mount an ill-advised and poorly planned surprise raid against Staten Island's posts. Twenty-four hours of subzero cold and deep snow were enough for Stirling, and the Patriots withdrew with seventeen prisoners and some plunder, suffering six of his men killed and about five hundred frostbitten. New Jersey volunteers attached to Stirling's force indiscriminately looted a number of the island's farms. Ten days later the British retaliated with a raid of their own, entering Elizabethtown and Newark and setting fire to a number of public buildings and dwellings.

Flagstaff Fort

The Patriots had a redoubt called Flagstaff Fort, garrisoned by three to four hundred men in June 1776, on Signal Hill at the Narrows. This site has been continuously fortified for more than three hundred years, ever since 1663 when David Pietersen de Vries built a blockhouse there. Near today's town of Rosebank, this location and much more of the surrounding landscape is now occupied by Fort Wadsworth.

The Dutch built a lookout tower on the hill after they bought Staten Island from the Indians, the first of five such purchases. The first three Dutch settlements were destroyed by the Raritan and Hackensack Indians living on the island. The first fortification was the de Vries twenty-foot-square wooden blockhouse. The following year the English arrived to oust the Dutch from Manhattan and its environs.

The matter of which province—New York or New Jersey—owned Staten Island came up early in its history. According to tradition the Duke of York had had enough of the feuding among the influential landowners in the two colonies. He determined to deed the island to the province that had citizens capable of circumnavigating the island in twenty-four hours. Capt. Christopher Billopp accomplished the feat in a little over twenty-three. The grateful governor of New York, Sir Edmund Andros, granted him a couple of patents totaling nearly sixteen hundred acres on the southernmost end of Staten Island, where Tottenville now stands.

A kind of "telegraph" operated from a tall pole on Signal Hill, on which kegs or large balls painted black or white were utilized to signal to Manhattan the arrival of ships in the harbor; during the eighteenth century a semaphore device was contrived. In 1776 Gen. Washington used the lookout point to obtain information about the arrival of Gen. Howe's forces from Halifax, Nova Scotia.

The British wasted little time strengthening and rebuilding the Patriot defense, and constructing new ones. By July 1779 a redoubt and a line of gun platforms had been constructed to mount about twenty-six cannon; two months later there were six twenty-four-pounders and four eighteen-pounders, with thirty rounds of ammunition for each gun, and a hotshot oven. On October 8 a report claimed that the men "have lined the Narrows with cannon." In 1782 the fortification had five bastions and several barbette batteries. There is no record of any Patriot attack on the fortress. The British occupied this post and others on Staten Island until they evacuated New York in 1783.

Fort Richmond

This British post was situated on the top of the hill overlooking the present-day restored village of Richmondtown, located on the grounds of the La Tourette Country Club. The fort, consisting in the beginning of three earthen redoubts, was laid out by Gen. James Robertson on July 9, 1776, just one week after Gen. Howe arrived with his troops. The name Fort Izzard had been used on occasion during the British occupation, but there is no available archival evidence to indicate in whose honor the name was applied to the fort.

On October 3, 1779, there were three great redoubts covering both sides of the crest of the hill, with the garrison encamped between the works. The fort was renovated and strengthened in 1781, but in 1782 it appears that there were only two redoubts. In 1777, when Fort

Richmond was the headquarters of Hessian Maj. Gen. von Lossberg, two American raids, one in January and the other in August, were repulsed by the fort's garrison.

Extensive archaeological work, under the guidance of the Staten Island Historical Society, has been accomplished on the fort's site. Robert Bolton, the archaeologist, traced out one of the redoubts, about fifty feet square with a ditch and gun platforms, and found gun flints, bone buttons, scissors, and other artifacts.

Watering Place Redoubts

These fortifications at today's Tompkinsville were constructed at the spring on what was later called Pavillion Hill. The immediate area was also favored by the Patriots, who had built entrenchments there before the landing of the British, who added three redoubts between July 14 and July 27, 1776.

The two most important redoubts were described on December 3, 1780, as circular, double abatised, and picketed, with two hundred men in each of the three redoubts. A 1782 British military map not only delineates the forts but also notes that two thousand men could parade in order of battle in front of them, thus stressing the great extent of ground the works covered. Practically no documentation exists concerning the number of guns in the redoubts, with the exception of a note that one gun was mounted in the second redoubt built on July 23, 1776.

Other Staten Island Posts

The following British posts on Staten Island are not sufficiently documented to allow adequate descriptions of them:

AMBOY FERRY POST: On the southwestern shore of the island, it was garrisoned in 1777 by three companies under Col. von Wurmb.

DUTCH CHURCH FORT: This fortified stone church at Port Richmond was destroyed by Gen. Stirling and his troops during their raid on January 14/15, 1780.

ELIZABETH FERRY REDOUBTS: Three redoubts, armed with one eighteen-pounder and four twenty-four-pounders, were garrisoned by three Hessian companies under Col. Biedhausen in 1777.

FORT GEORGE: Located at St. George, this was considered "only an encampment."

FORT KNYPHAUSEN: Located at St. George, this earthen redoubt commanded the harbor from its position on an eminence known during the Revolution as the Watering Place and today as Fort Hill. Named for Hessian Gen. Wilhelm Baron von Knyphausen, the redoubt repelled the assault by Gen. Stirling during his twenty-four-hour raid in January 1780.

OLD BLAZING STAR POST: The fortified inn, garrisoned by Hessians, stood on the north bank of the mouth of Fresh Kills, west of Richmondtown.

New Jersey

New Jersey merited its title of "Cockpit of the Revolution" by virtue of the many military events that occurred in that state: Washington's retreat in 1776 after the Patriot disasters in Brooklyn and Manhattan; the British invasion northward by way of the Hudson and the Palisades; Washington's dramatic crossing of the Delaware and the battles of Trenton and Princeton; the Continental Army encampments at Morristown and Middlebrook; the battles of Monmouth, Springfield, Chestnut Neck, Powles Hook, and Red Bank; the march of the American and French armies in August 1781 down through the Ramapos into the heart of New Jersey and across the Delaware on their way to Yorktown.

The close proximity and strategic importance of Jersey's Hudson River military strongpoints to New York State's southern theater of war invites the inclusion of the delineations of three fortifications.

Bull's Ferry Fort

On April 30, 1780, a detachment of eighty to ninety Associated Loyalists began the construction of a blockhouse at Bull's Ferry on Jersey's Hudson River shore about four miles north of Hoboken. Almost straddling the Bergen-Hudson County line, the post was approximately opposite today's Manhattan's 89th Street. To protect the building of the blockhouse, Gen. James Pattison ordered one hundred men from Paulus Hook to cover the Loyalists.

Ostensibly a garrison house for woodcutting operations, the fortified blockhouse was a base for Loyalist destructives and plunderers. Strategically positioned on the brink of the Palisades, high above a ravine running inland from the river, the blockhouse was protectively screened on two sides by sheer precipices and in front by an abatis,

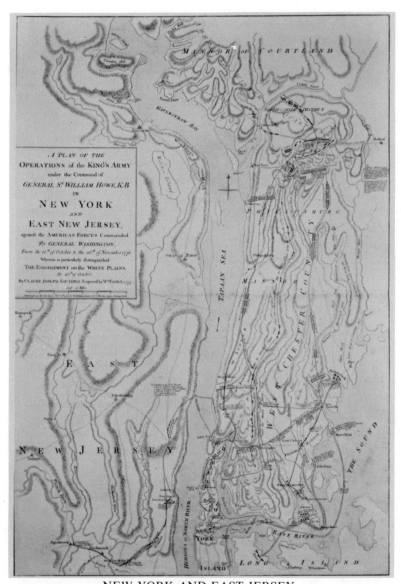

NEW YORK AND EAST JERSEY
Courtesy of Royal Library, Windsor Castle. Reproduced by gracious permission of Her Majesty, Queen Elizabeth II. Copyright reserved.

stockade, parapet, and ditch. Since the only entry was a covered way limiting admittance to one man at a time, there was obviously no escape route for the Loyalists in the event of a strong, well-planned American assault or even a siege.

Thomas Ward, a Continental Army deserter, was in charge of the Bull's Ferry contingent of so-called woodcutters, who terrorized the north Jersey countryside, plundering farmers and burning their dwellings. Continental prisoners and inhabitants in the area testified that the blockhouse was armed with two six-pounders and that its garrison usually numbered between one hundred and two hundred men, not "these poor people . . . only seventy in number," as Sir Henry Clinton later claimed.

In late May reports of the Loyalist base began filtering into Bergen County's militia headquarters. On the night of May 27/28, a combined force of about fifty militiamen from Closter and Hackensack stealthily gained the heights over Bull's Ferry. The obvious strength of the blockhouse convinced the militia captains that their force was inadequate to the task of reducing the enemy stronghold.

Shortly after the Americans left the precincts of the Loyalist base, they ran into a group of six of the enemy, of whom one was killed instantly, another mortally wounded, and two others taken prisoner. The man mortally wounded turned out to be the notorious Loyalist murderer John Berry, alias John the Regular, who claimed he had killed forty-eight persons by his own hand. The only militia casualty was one man wounded. The members of the militia detachment later learned, much to their joyous surprise, that they had merited the posted reward of one thousand dollars from the State of New Jersey for their killing of John the Regular.

The Patriots came to the conclusion by the middle of June that the woodcutting-plundering activities of the Bull's Ferry Loyalists had to be terminated as soon as possible. On July 20 Gen. Anthony Wayne, in a meeting with Washington, offered a particularized plan for mounting a Continental assault. Washington at once approved, with the stipulation that a horse patrol be detailed at once to cover the Bull's Ferry area through the night to give warning of any enemy concentration for the purpose of setting up an ambuscade in Wayne's rear.

Wayne lost no time assembling the nucleus of the attack force comprised of his First and Second Pennsylvania Brigades and Col. Stephen Moylan's Fourth Regiment of Light Dragoons. That night, at New Bridge, they were joined by the local militia, recently augmented by four officers and ninety militiamen from three counties farther to the west. After several hours' rest Wayne moved out and by break of day arrived in the neighborhood of Bull's Ferry. Units were deployed in all directions to intercept enemy reinforcements. With the remainder of his men, Wayne surrounded the blockhouse on three sides and took possession of the landing below where Loyalist watercraft were docked.

At about ten o'clock on the morning of July 21, the Americans commenced the attack with concentrated musket fire, while Wayne's four pieces of light artillery were brought up to within sixty yards or practically point-blank range of the blockhouse's covered way beyond which eighty-four Loyalists awaited the worst. At eleven o'clock the fieldpieces began a cannonading. It must have been a frustrating experience for Gen. Wayne to see what little effect his muskets and cannon were having on the blockhouse. In desperation, and contrary to orders, men of the First and Second Regiments fought their way through the abatis and attempted to force an entrance into the blockhouse. Many of them were cut down by Loyalist fire through the loopholes, which accounted for almost all of the American casualties. Fearing massive reinforcements from across the Hudson in Manhattan, where the sounds of the battle were heard, Wayne called for a withdrawal.

Worry that the American debacle would be greatly exaggerated in some quarters, Washington wrote a report of the action to the President of the Congress, dated from Bergen County Headquarters, July 26, 1780:

He [Wayne] for some time tried the effect of his fieldpieces upon it. But, though the fire was kept up for an hour, *they were found too light to penetrate the logs* of which it was constructed. The troops during this time being galled by a constant fire from the loopholes of the house, and seeing no chance of making a breach with cannon, those of the First and Second Regiments, notwithstanding the utmost efforts of the officers to restrain them, rushed through the abatis to the foot of the stockade with a view of forcing an entrance, which was found impracticable. This act of intemperate [*sic*] valor was the cause of the loss we sustained, and which amounted in the whole to three officers wounded, fifteen noncommissioned officers and privates killed, and forty-six noncommissioned officers and privates wounded. I have been thus particular lest the account of this affair should have reached Philadelphia much exaggerated.

Employing a remarkable mixture of understatement and exaggeration, Sir Henry Clinton's account of the Bull's Ferry affair gloried in the remarkable defense by the Loyalists in their "trifling work":

These poor people were only seventy in number (commanded by a Mr. Ward), who, being usually employed in cutting firewood for the inhabitants of New York for the support of their families, had erected this trifling work to protect them against such straggling parties of militia as might be disposed to molest them, not imagining they could ever become an object to a more formidable enemy. However, on the morning of the 21 July a select detachment from Mr. Washington's army, amounting to nearly 2,000 men, under Brigadier General Wayne, suddenly appeared before their post and opened against it a tremendous fire of musketry and cannon. But this gallant band defended themselves with activity and spirit; and, after sustaining the enemy's fire for some hours (by which one face of their little blockhouse was perforated by at least fifty cannon shot and twenty-one of their number killed and wounded) and repulsing an assault on their works, they sallied out and pursued their assilants to some distance, picking up stragglers and rescuing from them part of the cattle they were driving off. Such rare and exalted bravery merited every encouragement in my power, and I did not fail to distinguish it at the time by suitable commendations and rewards, to which I had soon after the satisfaction to add the fullest approbation of their sovereign.

The British immediately set about propagandizing the American defeat. For some weeks the Bull's Ferry commander, Thomas Ward, was feted in every coffeehouse in New York. His fame spanned the Atlantic to London, where his name was toasted in official circles. The talented John André was inspired to write *The Cow Chace,* a satirical poem in three cantos and seventy-two verses, and sent the epic to his friend James Rivington, the Tory publisher of New York's *The Royal Gazette.* Rivington serialized André's burlesque, with the final installment published the day André was captured near Tarrytown, September 23, 1780. André's last verse was indeed ironic:

> And now I've closed my epic strain,
> I tremble as I show it,
> Lest this same warrior-drover, Wayne,
> Should ever catch the poet.

Fort Lee

The mistaken reliance by the Americans on their *chevaux-de-frise* and other obstructions in the Hudson River fostered the construction of Fort Constitution on the Jersey side opposite Fort Washington on the Manhattan side, extensive and expensive undertakings to protect the river barriers. When the latter bastion fell to the British and Hessians on November 16, 1776, Fort Lee (Fort Constitution) became utterly useless.

Sometime durng the middle of July, Gen. Washington determined to have a fort laid out on the lofty Palisades, and wrote Gen. Hugh Mercer to that effect. Built by Gen. Mercer, the new Patriot defense, originally called Fort Constitution, was renamed Fort Lee on October 19 for Gen. Charles Lee in honor of his victory at Charleston. Gen. Washington personally superintended the beginnings of the fortification.

The site of the fort, at the western terminus of the George Washington Bridge in modern Fort Lee, was in Revolutionary days practically a natural fortification. Adrian Leiby, in his history of the Hackensack Valley during the war, graphically describes the terrain, and the building of the fort and barracks.

> A clove in the Palisades, where a farm road from English Neighbor-hood twisted its way from the heights down to a river landing, left a huge promontory standing out from the Palisades, inaccessible from three sides because of precipitous rocks, which fell off hundreds of feet to the river on one side and far enough on the other to discourage any assault. Ten acres were cleared, partly on this promontory and partly on the high land to the west, all rocky and heavily wooded wasteland on the farm of Peter Bourdet, whose farmhouse and cultivated land lay to the west, along the road to Bergen.
>
> At the northern entrance to the promontory an abatis of felled and pointed trees was built. Within this protected eminence heavy gun emplacements commanded the Hudson River below. To the west a square bastioned earthwork was built [centered at about today's Cedar and English Streets], and surrounding this, log huts for thousands of soldiers. . . .
>
> The garrison at the fort varied from a few hundred to more than two thousand, and it was commanded by the celebrated General Nathanael Greene. . . .
>
> The artillery at the fort soon proved to be less than effective against river traffic. . . . At eight o'clock in the morning of October 9, two British warships, the *Phoenix* and the *Roebuck,* sailed upstream despite the fort's heavy cannonading, without damage, so far as the Americans could see, although in fact there had been a good number of casualties aboard.

Below Fort Lee, at the base of the Palisades, was a strong gun emplacement called Burdette's (Bourdet's) Battery at the ferry landing, usually manned by at least 150 men. When the British frigates *Phoenix* and *Rose* sailed up the river on July 13, this battery fired at the ships, but without any apparent effect.

When Fort Washington fell on November 16, Washington and Greene determined to abandon Fort Lee, but not before the garrison had moved out all the stores. As it turned out, the Patriots had little more time than was necessary to save their skins.

On the morning of November 20, Gen. Howe dispatched Gen. Cornwallis with between five and six thousand troops across the river to capture Fort Lee. Cornwallis debarked at today's Alpine, about six miles by road above the fort. The enemy's movements did not go unnoticed. Gen. Greene hurriedly evacuated his two thousand men who had just enough time to take with them all the gunpowder. But they had to abandon a considerable amount of armaments, provisions, and equipment: three hundred tents, one thousand barrels of flour, their total stock of entrenching tools, and about fifty valuable cannon. In addition the British took in hand twelve drunken Patriots found in the fort and about 150 stragglers in the environs.

A letter dated November 25, 1776, probably written by young Francis, Lord Rawdon, a British officer, to Robert Auchmuty, an exiled Boston Tory then in London, tells of the evacuation of Fort Lee and forecasts the early dissolution of the Continental Army:

> This grand point [Fort Washington] being gained, by which York Island and a great part of the province was cleared from the rebels, General Howe, I think on the morning of the 20th instant, landed 5,000 men under the command of Lord Cornwallis up the North River on the Jersey shore, a few miles above the other famous fortification, called Fort Constitution or Fort Lee. His Lordship immediately marched to attack this place, and got to it by 1 o'clock the same day, but found it had been evacuated by the rebels so precipitately that the pots were left absolutely boiling on the fire, and the tables spread for dinner of some of their officers. In the fort they found but twelve men, who were all dead drunk. There were forty or fifty pieces of cannon found loaded, with two large iron sea mortars and one brass one, with a vast quantity of ammunition, provision and stores, with all their tents standing. . . .
>
> You see, my dear sir, that I have not been mistaken in my judgement of this people. The southern people will no more fight than the Yankees. The fact is that their army is broken all to pieces, and the spirits of their leaders and their abettors is also broken. However, I think one may venture to pronounce that it is well nigh over with them.

While Washington's army began its retreat across New Jersey, five battalions of the enemy were removing the valuable military stores from Fort Lee, and Gen. Cornwallis established a temporary camp for his troops alongside its works. Although the British partially dismantled Fort Lee during the winter of 1776/77, their troops continued to occupy it, finally abandoning it sometime in 1779. In 1781 a large contingent of Loyalists (Associated Refugees) moved into the fort sometime between May 15 and May 23 and reconstructed it to some extent, apparently enough to make it habitable.

During the early 1950s the Palisades Interstate Park Commission initiated plans to restore the Fort Lee redoubt. The plan called for the duplication of the original gun batteries, powder magazines, and barracks, with a small museum to delineate the fort's history. But the scheme fell through for various reasons.

In August 1974 the Commission began the preparation of the grounds for the reconstruction, with walkways and scenic overlooks commanding panoramic views of the lower Hudson River and the Manhattan sky line. From original maps the architects have designed historically accurate reconstructions of the three gun batteries and rifle parapet.

The eleven thousand square-foot Visitors Center, sheathed in redwood and modern in design, utilizes materials and character to fit the site. The Center contains a two-story exhibit area, a two hundred-seat auditorium, and towers at the corners topped by observation decks. The official opening day of Fort Lee Historic Park was May 15, 1976, just in time for the nation's two hundreth birthday.

Paulus Hook Fort

The strong British works of Paulus Hook Fort, opposite lower Manhattan, took up a fifteen-block area centered at about Sussex, Grand, and Washington Streets in modern-day Jersey City. The fort was the objective of the successful surprise assault by Maj. Henry (Light Horse Harry) Lee and three hundred men on August 19, 1779, an action that earned Lee one of the eight gold medals awarded by Congress during the Revolution. Coming close upon Wayne's victorious though temporary recapture of Stony Point in July, the British were shaken and had second thoughts about their control over the lower Hudson.

Paulus (Powle's) Hook was first occupied by the Americans on April 5, 1776, with the first fortifications initiated by them on about May 20; by June 10 there were mounted three thirty-two-pounders, three twelve-pounders, and two three-pounder fieldpieces. On July 10 some additional works were begun on Bergen Neck, to the rear of the point. When three British men-of-war, including the frigate *Roebuck,* threatened to bombard Paulus Hook on September 23, the Americans evacuated the works; within the next two weeks the British had cleared Bergen Neck of all Patriots.

The British moved in and greatly augmented the rebel defenses with formidable works: a circular redoubt mounting six heavy guns, protected by a ditch and an abatis; a second redoubt, oblong-shaped, a little northeast of the first, armed with three twelve-pounders and one eighteen-pounder; two blockhouses; five lines of breastworks fronting on the bay; and three barracks. The magazine was located in the oblong redoubt. A barred gate gave entrance across the deep-bridged abatised moat that was dug across the entire isthmus. In effect, the ditch and the marshes on all sides of it transformed the peninsula into an island. Paulus Hook Fort became, as Sir Henry Clinton put it, "the principal western outpost in the British defenses of New York."

While Sir Henry was camped on Harlem Heights, it was decided by Washington and his staff that an attempt should be made to take somewhat isolated Paulus Hook. Wayne's success at Stony Point no doubt had an influence on the decision. Henry Lee was given the command of four hundred men, half of them Virginians. Capt. Allen McLane, partisan leader, reconnoitered the objective's area and obtained information from a deserter that the British-Hessian garrison numbered little more than two hundred men. McLane was to lead the Patriot assault force through the maze of outer works. The timing was important since the deep ditch could be crossed only at low tide.

With two companies of Maryland troops, Lee moved out of Paramus late in the morning of Wednesday, August 18. At New Bridge, four miles away, the rest of the troops joined him; at about 4:30 P.M. they set out for Bergen sixteen miles away. Fort Paulus Hook was just two miles beyond Bergen. Lee had planned his schedule so that his men would penetrate the fort's perimeter in the darkness to eliminate detection by the enemy, and attack a half hour after midnight. High tide in the moat was 2 A.M.

Two unfortunate circumstances, either by design or accident, threw Lee's schedule off about three hours: a long, tiring detour, advised by Lee's guide to avoid enemy outposts, and news just before the attack of the defection, or genuine separation from their comrades in the dark, of about one hundred Virginians. Lee's immediate subordinate for the operation was Maj. Jonathan Clark, who was actually Lee's senior, an apparent violation of the military code of grades. This caused resentment among some of the Virginia and Maryland officers.

The men had been given hard orders not to fire their muskets, even by accident; officers were directed to kill any man disobeying the order. Capt. Levin Handy, in command of the Maryland troops, described the operation in a letter dated Paramus, August 22:

> Before this reaches you, I doubt not but you have heard of our success at Powles Hook, where the enemy had a very strong fort, within one and a quarter miles from New York. We started from this place on Wednesday last half after ten o'clock, taking our route by a place called New Bridge on Hackensac River, where my two companies were joined by three hundred Virginians and a company of dismounted Dragoons, commanded by Captain McLane. We took up our line of march about 5 o'clock in the evening from the bridge, the nearest route with safety, to Powles, distant then about twenty miles, with my detachment in front, the whole under command of the gallant

Major Lee. The works were to be carried by storm—the whole to advance in three columns, one of which I had the honour to command.

The attack was to commence at one half after 12 o'clock, but having been greatly embarrassed on our march, and having a number of difficulties to surmount, did not arrive at the point of attack till after four o'clock in the morning, when, after a small fire from them, we gained their works and put about fifty of them to the bayonet, took one hundred and fifty-seven prisoners, exclusive of seven commanding officers [actually, 158 prisoners, *including* seven officers]; this was completed in less than thirty minutes, and a retreat [was] ordered, as we had every reason to suppose unless timely it would be cut off. Our situation was so difficult that we could not bring off any stores. We had a morass to pass of upwards two miles, the greatest part of which we were obliged to pass by files, and several canals to ford up to our breast in water. We advanced with bayonets, pans open, cocks fallen, to prevent any fire from our side; and believe me when I assure you we did not fire a musket.

You will see a more particular account of it in the papers than it is in my power to give you at present. It is thought to be the greatest enterprise ever undertaken in America. Our loss is so inconsiderable that I do not mention it [two killed and three wounded].

After the successful operation, Lee was accused of having taken precedence over senior officers. Gen. Washington tried to head off an embarrassing trial but without success. Lee was court-martialed but the military court vindicated him. Alexander Hamilton's feeling in the matter was expressed in his letter to Lieut. Col. John Laurens, A.D.C. to Gen. Washington, dated September 11, 1779:

The Philadelphia papers will tell you of a handsome stroke by Lee at Powle's Hook. Some folks in the Virginia line, jealous of his glory, had the folly to get him arrested. He has been tried and acquitted with the highest honor. Lee unfolds himself more and more to be an officer of great capacity, and if he had not a little spice of the Julius Caesar or Cromwell in him, he would be a very clever fellow.

Sir Henry Clinton had some comments regarding the success of the surprise assault and its aftermath:

The enemy being mistaken by a careless guard for [Lt.] Colonel [Abram Van] Buskirk's corps [Loyalists] returning [from a foraging raid] entered without opposition. . . . As soon as the noise of firing reached New York some troops were thrown into boats as quickly as possible, enabling the commandant [Maj. William Sutherland] to pursue the enemy. He came up with their rear and made a captain and six privates prisoners but was not in time to recover some 40 invalids.

Gen. James Pattison of the Royal Artillery and commandant of New York City was more candid:

The strength of the garrison was 200 and by the return I have received there were killed 4 sergeants, 2 corporals, and 3 privates, wounded 2 sergeants and taken and missing 4 subalterns, 7 sergeants, and 97 privates. . . . The enemy, though in full possession of the fort, did not spike a gun, destroy the ammunition or do the least injury to any of the buildings.

Maj. Sutherland was court-martialed and acquitted; a sergeant who had abandoned his post was also court-martialed and sentenced to be executed, but apparently he was either reprieved or pardoned. By one o'clock Maj. Lee and his very tired men were back at New Bridge and beyond pursuit.

The British did not let the works at Paulus Hook fall into stagnation. They intermittently renovated and added new works, as evidenced by the report from Alexander Mercer, commanding engineer, to Maj. Oliver DeLancey, British Adjutant General, dated New York, July 3, 1781: "Paulus Hook: raising and thickening the fronts of the works; repairing and giving additional strength, and preparing additional materials for an intermediate battery of eight or ten guns."

Archival evidence reports that the last British garrison to occupy the fort consisted of the Forty-Second Highlanders, replacing the Hessian troops. The post was evacuated by the British and occupied by the Patriots on November 23, 1783.

Fort Niagara
Youngstown, Niagara County

Majestic, seemingly imperishable, Old Fort Niagara stands on a twenty-foot rise overlooking Lake Ontario, at the point where the impetuous waters of the Niagara River, after their plunge in breathtaking cataracts and frantic rushes through a gorge, at last find journey's end on the broad bosom of an inland sea. The three-hundred-year-old saga of the Niagara Frontier is part of the turbulent Colonial histories of France, England, and the United States, and incorporates the story of the ascendancy and downfall of the great Iroquois League. From the time of its construction the fort exercised an immense influence over a vast extent of territory, serving as a center of civilization from which all the commerce of that time radiated. It guarded the gateway to the West, prevented encroachments of rivals, and dispensed provisions and supplies for exploring expeditions or destructive raids.

The first accurate record of the white man on Niagara Frontier ground is that of Father Joseph de la Roche Dallion, a Franciscan priest. In 1626, while engaged in missionary and trading activities among the Hurons, he

determined to expand his work to the southward among the Attawan-
daronk or Neutral Indians (so-called by the French because of their
absolute neutrality in the Iroquois-Huron feud). Their principal village
was Onguiara, on the present site of Lewiston, New York, which name
was easily enough corrupted into *Niagara*.[1]

The next recorded visit was that of Father Jean Brébeuf and Father
Joseph Chaumonot, Jesuit priests, in November 1640.[2] No other white
men, it seems, visited the area during the next three decades. In the
interim, however, all of the Niagara Frontier and Huronia were
devastated by the genocidal wars waged by the Five Nations of the
Iroquois League. The great Indian confederation, founded about the
year 1570 by Dekanawida and Hiawatha, was formed for internal
preservation and external war. The story of the Iroquois is inseparably
linked with the history of Fort Niagara. Lewis Henry Morgan, the
celebrated ethnologist, discusses the evolvement of Iroquois power:

> After the formation of the League, the Iroquois rose rapidly in
> power and influence. It gave them additional strength by concentra-
> tion of effort; a constant increase of numbers by the unity of the race;
> and a firmer establishment, through their more ample means of
> self-protection and foreign conquest. One of the first results of their
> federal system was a universal spirit of aggression; a thirst for military
> glory and political aggrandizement, which made the old forests of
> America resound with human conflicts from New England to the
> Mississippi, and from the northern confines of the great lakes to the
> Tennessee and the hills of Carolina. Unrecorded, except by tradition,
> is the narrative of the warlike achievements of this gifted and
> progressive race, who raised themselves, through the vicissitudes of
> incessant strife, to a general and acknowledged supremacy over these
> boundless territories. Without considering the terrible and ferocious
> characteristics of Indian warfare, it must be admitted that the empire
> which they reared over Indian nations, furnishes no slight evidence of
> their hardihood, courage and sagacity.[3]

The next white men to visit the Niagara River region were Father
Fransçois Dollier de Casson and Father René Bréhant de Galinée,
Sulpician missionaries. They had left Montreal on July 6, 1669, for the
west with nine canoes. Accompanying them was a twenty-six-year-old
adventurer of Rouen named René Robert Cavalier de La Salle. The
small expedition sailed along the southern shore of Lake Ontario,
passing the mouth of the Niagara River and continuing to the head of the
lake, from which place they went overland and met Louis Joliet, joint
discoverer with Jacques Marquette of the upper Mississippi. La Salle
and Joliet returned to Montreal, while the missionaries continued their
westward journey.[4]

In 1673 La Salle erected Fort Frontenac on the present site of

Kingston, Ontario.[5] In May 1675 the French government granted to La Salle "privileges and concessions" for a period of five years, with the stipulation that he assume all the expenses; one of the "privileges" placed him in full charge of the fort. It was from this place, in 1678, that the explorer commenced his plan for the development of a fur trade to the west and south. In conjunction with this, a palisaded storehouse was built on the present site of Lewiston, the first building on the Niagara River.

La Salle, with his faithful lieutenant, Tonti, and Father Hennepin, established a shipyard on January 22, 1679, on the east bank of the Niagara, just south of Cayuga Creek, in the present city of Niagara Falls. After they had constructed cabins and a chapel, the initial laying of the *Griffon's* keel was commenced on January 26. During this same month, a party of men were at the river's mouth constructing a fort, the first white man's habitation on the barren, triangular point of land between the Niagara and Lake Ontario. La Salle named the post Fort Conti, in gratitude to the Prince of Conti for having recommended Tonti to him.

La Salle had realized the strategic importance of the fort at the river's mouth. He foresaw its use as a storehouse or depot for merchandise and, if fortified, as a defense against attacks by the Iroquois. The French, in addition, would be able to control all Indian trade passing down the river in the direction of the English and the Dutch.[6]

There is no record when Fort Conti was destroyed. La Salle, however, had summarized the brief history of the post in a letter from Fort Frontenac dated August 22, 1682:

> The Iroquois did not oppose the construction of the Fort commenced at the discharge of Lake Erie [the explorer considered the entire length of the Niagara as the "discharge"]. . . . I contented myself with making there two redoubts, 40 feet square, upon a point, made of great timbers one upon another, musket proof[ed] and joined by a palisade, where I put a sergeant and several men, who during my absence allowed all this work to burn through negligence; and not being in condition to restore it, there remains only a magazine.[7]

In 1683 Count Frontenac, La Salle's friend and patron, was recalled to France and Le Febvre La Barre took his place as governor of New France. La Barre, long an enemy of the explorer, withdrew most of the men from Fort Frontenac, which was a part of La Salle's seigneury. In this underhanded manner he provided the excuse for seizing the fortification: that it was not properly garrisoned, which called for automatic forfeiture. All of La Salle's property was seized, leaving him bereft of funds and supplies with which to carry on his explorations. He returned to France to seek support and additional finances. His star of destiny henceforth was to be found to the west and south of the Niagara Frontier, which he never saw again.[8]

Under La Barre, who devoted all his energies to increasing his personal treasury, neglect of his nation's interests in America brought a sharp decline in New France's influence. The rascally La Barre was replaced by Jacques René de Brisay, Marquis de Nonville, ex-colonel of dragoons, with thirty years' service in France's army. His instructions were to undo all the harm his predecessor had caused: renew alliances with the western tribes, call a halt to the bitter factionalism in the fur trade, and stop the English from enlarging their sphere of influence into the area south of the Great Lakes. De Nonville was already cognizant of English fur-trading penetration by the Hudson's Bay Company into the far north, in the regions of Hudson Bay and James Bay.

In 1683, the same year La Barre replaced Frontenac, Father Louis Hennepin's first book, *Description de la Louisiane,* was published in Paris.[9] The publication soon gained the interest of the English and French with regard to the Niagara Frontier's potential. Hennepin's assertions concerning the lucrative western fur trade and the strategic position of the Niagara River's mouth were so emphatic that two years later Thomas Dongan, Governor of New York, and de Nonville petitioned their respective home governments to establish a military post on the Niagara. Louis XIV, it seems, was easier to convince than James II. An exchange of a series of polite, though accusatory letters between the two governors deepened the crisis.

In 1687 de Nonville, having received the royal order to build a fort at Niagara's mouth, assembled a large force of French and Indians. At his request, Daniel Greysolon du Lhut (Duluth), Olivier de la Durantaye, an officer in the Carignan regiment, and Henri Tonti gathered a sizable party of French and Indians in the west. On July 4 both forces met on the south shore of Lake Ontario, with the intention of exterminating the Senecas. There was a pitched battle of short duration, but the most important result of the invasion of the Seneca villages was the destruction of more than one million bushels of corn, the loss of which infuriated the Iroquois.[10]

On the last day of July the French army began construction of a new fort on the site of Fort Conti. The work, described as a "fort of pales, with four bastions," was named Denonville, sometimes known merely as the "Fort at Niagara." When the work was near completion, de Nonville embarked his army on bateaux and set out for home, promising the garrison of one hundred men that provisions for the coming winter would arrive before the first snow.

The winter of 1687/88 in the north country was called the Winter of Starvation. Provisions in the fort ran low as winter approached. The men spent futile hours trying to take fish out of Lake Ontario. Seneca Indians constantly prowled the perimeter of the fort, preventing the garrison's soldiers from emerging, even for firewood. The men were at the point of starvation, with the scourge of scurvy already taking its toll, when a ship finally appeared. The vessel's crew unloaded the promised provisions, dumping them on the shore and, without as much as a salutation to the garrison, turned about and made for its haven at Fort Frontenac.

Chevalier de Tregay, the surviving commandant of Fort Denonville, related the story of that Winter of Starvation: "It was not until her sails had fall'n below the horizon that we fairly had sight or smell of what she had aboard." The food was rotten and unfit for human consumption. Instead of being a refuge and a bulwark of strength in the midst of a savage wilderness, with enemy Indians in almost constant attendance on the land side and the great empty expanse of Lake Ontario on the other, the fort became truly a prison for the beleaguered, dying garrison. By February 1688 at least sixty of the men were dead. De Tregay, weak with hunger and scurvy, had resigned himself to death in his last consciousness. He was brought back to stark awareness very suddenly, beholding the apparition of a painted Indian bending over him. It was a Miami from the distant Ohio Valley, who had raised the commandant's head with one hand and was offering him parched corn with the other.

A rescue party evacuated twelve survivors of the garrison on Good Friday. Father Pierre Millet, a member of the rescue team, had an eighteen-foot cross erected in the center of the fort's parade. On September 15, on orders from the Marquis de Nonville, the fort was abandoned, in compliance with the terms of a treaty between England and France.[11]

The history of the vast region encompassing the Niagara Frontier, New England, New York, and the Ohio and Mississippi Valleys, was remarkably influenced by the efforts of one man—Louis Thomas de Joncaire, Sieur de Chabert (more familiarly known as Chabert de Joncaire). His association with the numerous Senecas began about the year 1693, and from that time on it matured into a strong bond of friendship. His consummate skill in diplomacy with the Indians gained for New France her most profitable alliance. After Joncaire's death in 1739, his two sons, Philippe and Daniel, nurtured that alliance to the detriment of English interests. After William Johnson settled in the Mohawk Valley in 1738, eventually to be appointed British Superintendent for Indian Affairs, the Joncaires' sphere of influence gradually dissipated.

During the years of Chabert's power, when there was no open warfare between England and France in North America, there was a very tenuous peace, more in the nature of a cold war. There were numerous incidents between the two peoples, all hinging on control of the fur trade. The French, of course, endeavored to keep open their lines of communication between their string of forts in the west and their home bases at Montreal and Quebec, while the English strove to protect their fur-trading activities. Until Chabert's "love affair" with the Senecas, the Iroquois had been vacillating between the French and the English.

In 1720 Chabert, with the blessing of the Senecas, erected a new, palisaded trading store at Lewiston, initiating French control over the Niagara portage. In 1725 the French, who had carefully refrained from hinting that the structure was going to be fortified, were favored with Iroquois permission to erect a "stone house" on the Niagara. During a meeting with the Iroquois League at Onondaga, the Indians were informed that the Lewiston store had to be abandoned because of its condition. The Mohawks and the Oneidas objected, but Chabert's skillful diplomacy won them over.

The French Provincial Government made two appropriations—one for the building of the "stone house," and the other to provide the materials for the construction of two ships at Fort Frontenac. The vessels would transport the necessaries to the building site, and would eventually be used in the fur trade on the lake.

New France's lieutenant governor, Charles Le Moyne, Baron de Longueuil, planned to have the stone edifice erected in the immediate vicinity of Lewiston, but noted engineer Gaspard Chaussegros de Lery (designer of Quebec's citadel) determined that the most advantageous place for control of Lake Ontario and Niagara River traffic was the former site of Forts Conti and Denonville.

The "stone house" was indeed a fort, but not the traditional type of fortification. The structure, then called the "House of Peace" in consideration of the Iroquois, and now known as "The French Castle," was built in the likeness of a French provincial chateau that an affluent Frenchman would have erected on his seigneury. De Lery was particularly attentive as to materials, deciding that the granite found near Kingston would serve for the outer walls rather than the varicolored metamorphic rock in the Niagara area. Huge granite blocks were quarried and loaded on the ships as deck cargo. The stone used for flooring came from the Niagara escarpment. All the other materials, such as tools, beams and joists of seasoned oak, supplies and provisions, were also ferried across the lake.[12]

The House of Peace was not completed by the early fall of 1726 as

FORT NIAGARA: THE HOUSE OF PEACE ("THE CASTLE")
Courtesy of New York State Department of Commerce

expected, because of the unforeseen visitation of smallpox. De Lery, in his report to Quebec, described the work in progress and explained the delay:

I arrived, June 6th [1726], with a detachment of troops, at the entrance to the river Niagara. The same day I examined it, with the masters of the barques. We found it not navigable for the barques [the examination must have been superficial, for once past the bar at the mouth, they would have found a deep natural channel for seven miles]. I remarked, in beginning this house, that if I built it, like those in Canada, liable to fire, should war come and the savages invest it, as was the case formerly with Mons. Denonville's fort, if it caught fire the garrison and all the munitions would be wholly lost, and the [control of the] country as well. It was this which determined me to make a house proof against these accidents. Instead of wooden partitions I have had built bearing-walls, and paved all the floors with flat stones. . . . I have traced around a fort of four bastions; and in order that they may defend themselves in this house, I have made all the garret windows machicolated; the loft being paved with flat stones on a floor full of good oak joists, upon which cannon may be placed above this structure. Though large, it would have been entirely finished in September, had not some French voyageurs coming from the Miamis and Illinois, in passing this post, spread the fever here, so that nearly all the soldiers and workmen have had it. This has interfered with the construction so that it has not been completed in the time that I had expected. There remains about a fourth of it to do next year. This will not prevent the garrison or traders from lodging there this winter. I have the honor to inform you, Monseigneur, that my journeys to Niagara have occupied nearly five months.[13]

De Lery's creation, forty-eight by ninety-six feet, was two-storied, with a garret or attic to house the armament. With its four-foot-thick walls, tremendous arches to absorb the lateral sway caused by firing the cannon, an inside well as a prudent foresight in case of enemy investment, the House of Peace was a veritable fortress. The cannon, swathed in canvas, were transported across the lake in the spring of 1727. The installation of the guns was done in dark secrecy, between full night and dawn, might and brawn hauling the cannon up the two stories of stairs. Its first garrison of one hundred men was commanded by Capt. Charles Le Moyne, son of Baron de Longueuil.[14]

The English believed that the French fort at Niagara was a violation of the 1713 Treaty of Utrecht (the treaty had France ceding to Great Britain such important territories as Acadia, Newfoundland, and the Hudson's Bay region, and fully recognizing the Iroquois as subjects of the British Crown). Governor William Burnet of New York prevailed upon the Provincial Assembly to provide three hundred pounds for a stone fort at Oswego, in opposition to the House of Peace.

The French continued their building of forts and trading posts to the south and west, down the Allegheny River, on the Monongahela and the Ohio into the Mississippi, and on the shores of the Great Lakes, giving them control of the Midwest. A spear at the heart of New England was initially placed on the Vermont shore of Lake Champlain when the French built the semi-permanent fort at Pointe de la Chevelure in 1731, opposite Crown Point. French military minds envisioned a much stronger fortification at Crown Point and commenced the building of Fort St. Frederic at that place. As the French sphere of influence widened, bloody incidents and angry diplomatic thrusts became more frequent.

King George's War in America (1744) was the natural outgrowth of Europe's War of the Austrian Succession. The French thirsted for revenge after the English captured Louisbourg in April 1745. In November more than five hundred French and Indians raided Saratoga, plundering the village and burning the fort there. William Johnson and the Joncaires vied for the fidelity of the Iroquois, who throughout the war were divided in their fealty, with only the Onondagas and the Cayugas adhering to careful neutrality. The fort at Niagara, never garrisoned by more than one hundred officers and men during the conflict, was not threatened. The Treaty of Aix-la-Chapelle in 1748 ended the war, returning Louisbourg and Cape Breton to the French.

In the spring of 1749 the French took formal possession of the Ohio River "and of all those that therein fall, and of all the lands on both sides as far as the sources of the said rivers."[15] At the same time, Father François Picquet began the establishment of Fort La Présentation (Fort Oswegatchie) at present-day Ogdensburg. To this new bastion of French influence came the Cayugas, Onondagas, and Senecas, who listened to Father Picquet's orations and canticles glorifying Christ. William Johnson, in the Mohawk Valley, could not put on that good a show. In two years about four hundred Iroquois families were ensconced in the fort's environs.

The development of the Niagara portage was essential. The job was given to Daniel Joncaire, who in 1751 built Fort Little Niagara, otherwise more descriptively known as Fort du Portage, about a mile or so behind the falls of Niagara. By 1759 there was a village, with many large homes, a barn, a storehouse, and a couple of large sheds.

The English did not quite believe the rumors brought to them by the Iroquois in the spring of 1753. The French were invading the Ohio region with an army of artisans, accompanied by many soldiers and Indians. The expedition was headed by Sieur de Marin and Chevalier le Mercier. They had orders to erect fortifications in present Pennsylvania: Fort Le Boeuf, at today's Waterford, at the head of navigation on French Creek and the end of the portage from Presque Isle, fourteen miles to the north; Fort Presque Isle, on the south shore of Lake Erie; and Fort Machault, on the site of today's city of Franklin on the Allegheny River.

The French and English had been battling for nearly a century. The major focal point was that House of Peace on the triangular spit of land at Niagara. The fort was the one all-important link in the French line of communications. No waterborne enemy could proceed westward under the French guns. Conversely, however, it was a potential sword at New France's throat, for once in the possession of the English it would sever the link connecting the two halves of French America.

The French and Indian War started July 3, 1754, when George Washington and his Virginia militia surrendered Fort Necessity at Great

Meadows, Pennsylvania, but it took two years before formal declarations of war were made. The politicians in London fumbled away months of indecision until finally two regiments were dispatched to Virginia in the winter of 1754. Col. Edward Braddock of the Coldstream Guards was promoted to major general and given the command of the expeditionary force. His instructions were remarkably glib and optimistic, plainly evincing that the deskbound military minds in London had no conception of American geography and did not refer to various documents in the possession of the Duke of Cumberland that defined the wilderness distances between any two landmarks from Williamsburg to the Niagara Frontier.[16]

Braddock was to march to the point where the Allegheny and the Monongahela join to form the Ohio, capture Fort Duquesne at today's Pittsburgh; another force was to proceed to Niagara and occupy the vital portage and, as frosting on the cake, capture the Canadian posts of Forts Frontenac and Toronto. Braddock never reached the French post at the Forks of the Ohio. His army was ambushed and annihilated on July 9, only seven miles from Fort Duquesne, by Capt. Daniel de Beaujeu's 290 French and 600 Indians.

William Shirley, Governor of Massachusetts, was commander of the army slated to take Niagara. As late as July he was still in Albany, delaying the start of the campaign by his old-womanish fussing and fuming over provisions, troop enlistments, and Johnson's Indians. Finally, on July 29, his force of seventeen hundred regulars and militia got under way and headed for Oswego, the jumping-off place for Niagara. He had a promise from reluctant Johnson that he would have one hundred of his Indians at the Oswego base in time.

On July 23, six days before Shirley left Albany, France's new Governor-General at Quebec, Pierre Vaudreuil-Cavagnal, wrote Versailles that should the English attack Niagara there could be no doubt that they would take it easily. He reported that "I am informed that fort is so dilapidated, that it is impossible to put a peg in it without causing it to crumble. Stanchions have been obliged to be set up against it to support it. Its garrison consists of thirty men without any muskets."[17]

The first contingents of Shirley's army reached Oswego on August 18, with the rendezvous completed by September 2. New England carpenters and shipwrights had already built two vessels, the brig *Ontario* and the sloop *Oswego,* and were putting the finishing touches on a fleet of whaleboats that would transport his men up Lake Ontario. Oswego's artisans worked hard to make the expedition a success, but they did not reckon with the dilatory Shirley.

Intelligence reports informed Shirley that there were twelve hundred

French troops at Fort Frontenac, only fifty miles distant, poised to either reinforce Niagara or attempt an attack upon Oswego. He decided to delay his move against Fort Niagara and spent valuable time making the Oswego base defensively stronger. He set men to work on a second fort on the hill across the Oswego River, a log affair called Fort Ontario.

The Niagara campaign began to falter when heavy rains bogged down operations. A number of men became sick and the contagion spread. The last straw was the failure of promised provisions to arrive. A council of war on September 27 determined that the assault against Niagara should be postponed until spring. In late October Shirley departed from Oswego, leaving two regiments to garrison the pair of forts. It was reckoned that the aborted campaign cost 200,000 pounds or more.[18]

Now that a new war, greater and more far-reaching than the one ten years earlier, embroiled the two colonial powers, plans were formulated to implement the strengthening of Niagara. During the first week of October, while Shirley was fretting at Oswego, three vessels carrying Capt. François Pouchot and five regiments left Fort Frontenac and headed up the lake. Their purpose was to build at Niagara works worthy of the name *fort*. In the next four years, military engineer Pouchot converted Fort Niagara from a crumbling stone house and a few semi-permanent structures into an elaborate fortress of barracks, an ingenious system of earthworks and moats, a powder magazine, and complements of heavy artillery.

Of primary importance was the construction of barracks, and speed was essential since winter was almost upon the Niagara Frontier. Huts were constructed of round oaken logs, with a few windows and a planked roof. In the middle of each barrack was a chimney of horizontal logs laid inside a basketwork of four poles, with the interstices crammed with clay-impregnated straw or marsh grass; the whole was then thickly plastered with clay.[19]

The timber needed for these lodgings and the oak palisades came from the fort site's quarter-mile radial area, which was denuded of all wooded life. A deep moat came next. A visiting French officer reported in the spring of 1756 that Pouchot had redans constructed all around the fort, not neglecting the lake shore and the river banks. Several artillery pieces in barbette were installed atop the curtain and upon the demibastion overlooking the surrounding woods. Four cannon, designed to command the river, were placed in the river demibastion. In the rear of the House of Peace a battery of guns was placed to guard the entrance to the river.[20]

Still determined on an all-out offensive against the French, Shirley called a conference in December 1755 with the executives of New York,

Connecticut, Maryland, and Pennsylvania. He unfolded his plan for the spring campaign: a concentration of six thousand men at Oswego to attack Niagara; ten thousand men to proceed against Crown Point; three thousand men to reduce Fort Duquesne; and another undetermined number of men to make a feint at Quebec by way of the Kennebec River in Maine (Benedict Arnold's route twenty years later). This called for a minimum of twenty thousand troops and a tremendous outlay of colonial funds.

The petty jealousies among the provincial governors ran rampant and determined the outcome of the conference. Shirley was not to have his way. Undercover work influenced the home government to order Shirley to London in March 1756. He was forced to relinquish his command. The new commander-in-chief was John Campbell, the Earl of Loudoun, a Scot with long military experience, but a man who was devoid of imagination, ill-tempered, ill-mannered, and loud-mouthed. He, too, was ineffective in getting the Colonies to cooperate with one another.

The home government, reluctantly recognizing the lack of colonial cooperation in the prosecution of the war, sent two more regiments to America. To further augment the military forces, a plan was effected to raise four battalions of one thousand men each, who would be paid with Crown money. This regiment came to be known as the Royal Americans. This significant increase in numbers unfortunately was not met by a like increase in the quality of the officers. The ineffectual Loudoun was assisted by two mediocre major generals, James Abercromby and Daniel Webb. Shirley informed the new military hierarchy of Oswego's danger and suggested reinforcements. His advice, more in the nature of a warning, was rejected.

The French ministry of war, a great deal more imaginative than London, selected the Marquis de Montcalm to be the new commander of Canada's armed forces. The marquis and twelve hundred troops were dispatched to New France, reaching Quebec in mid-May. The brilliantly resourceful Montcalm lost no time planning his initial campaign. He went to Fort Frontenac, where he learned that Oswego was in a deplorably weak state, what with desertions, disease, and neglect by the Colonies. In two days, August 12 and 13, Oswego's forts (including the incomplete Fort George) capitulated to the French forces ferried across the lake from Fort Frontenac. Now there was no doubt that Lake Ontario was a French lake.

After the downfall of Oswego, several regiments, engineers, masons, and carpenters were sent to Niagara to continue work on the redoubts there. Two British schooners, captured in Oswego's harbor, were pressed into service as freighters, carrying granite blocks—facings for the redoubts—from the quarry near Fort Frontenac.

Loudoun came up with his plan for the 1757 campaign, with Quebec as the ultimate goal. While he was wrestling with the colonial governments over quotas of troops, the talented William Pitt became head of a coalition government in London. He instructed Loudoun to forget about Quebec for the time and concentrate on the taking of Louisbourg. The fortress on the Atlantic controlled the Cabot Strait entrance to the Gulf of St. Lawrence; in possession of the British, it would cut off almost all aid to Canada from France.

After some delay Loudoun and his regular troops embarked from New York on May 21, bound for Halifax, Nova Scotia. Two weeks earlier, ten regiments had departed from Ireland on Vice Admiral Francis Holburne's ships, bound for the same port. The rendezvous of the two forces was completed by June 30. The more punctual French, however, got to Louisbourg first, with twenty-two men-of-war and transports, greatly reinforcing the garrison of twenty-five hundred men. After more than a month of immobility due to bad weather, it was learned through capture of an enemy vessel that the French naval forces were superior in numbers to those of the English. Loudoun and Holburne conferred and decided to abort the campaign. It was, without a doubt, another disgraceful exhibition of British military ineptitude. Loudoun took his men back to New York. Holburne turned his fleet eastward, only to be overtaken a month later by a hurricane that wrecked his armada; only several vessels managed to make it back to England.

During that first week of August, when Loudoun at Halifax canceled the attack on Louisbourg, Montcalm assaulted Fort William Henry at the head of Lake George. His cannon mostly destroyed, and denied aid by the cowardly Gen. Webb at Fort Edward, Lieut. Col. George Munro, commander of the British garrison, had no alternative but to capitulate on August 9.

Fort Niagara's garrison experienced a period of roseate euphoria following the downfall of Oswego. A certain amount of permissiveness allowed officers' wives and girls of doubtful chastity to come to the fort. The House of Peace was turned into a festive social hall, with frequent receptions, dinners, and dances to take away the sting of being many miles away from home and civilization. Though New France had had two bad harvests, there was at first no dearth of food within the fort. Indian hunters brought in wild game, mostly turkey and deer, for which they were paid with well-diluted cognac. Soon the French and Indians, however, began to feel the pinch as essentials became scarcer and dearer. The British naval blockades of France's seaports and the St.

Lawrence River took a toll of French shipping, capturing in the summer of 1757 at least sixteen provision ships bound for New France.

Capt. Pouchot and most of the fort's garrison were ordered east in the fall of the year, with the command devolving to Capt. Jean Vassan.[21] If the British remained inactive on land at this time, the same could not be said about the French, who seemed constantly on the move, keeping northern New York in a perpetual state of nervous fear with raids into the Mohawk Valley.

At the head of a colony whose population was only one-twentieth of the number of the English to the south, Governor Vaudreuil may have had ambitious plans for 1758, but he was outdone by energetic William Pitt. Just before the new year began, Pitt recalled Loudoun and gave the command to Maj. Gen. James Abercromby. Pitt envisioned an invasion of Canada by way of Ticonderoga (Fort Carillon) and Crown Point (Fort St. Frederic), a land-and-sea assault against Louisbourg, and another attempt to take Fort Duquesne. His plans called for approximately fifty thousand men, divided equally between regulars and provincials.

Abercromby's campaign against Ticonderoga ended as a major British debacle in early July, even though his forces outnumbered the French five to one. The French entrenchments before Fort Carillon proved impregnable to repeated frontal assaults. In addition, to Great Britain's sorrow, the army lost their most popular officer, Brig. Gen. Lord George Howe, second in command.

French joy in Quebec and Montreal was short-lived, for on July 26 the fortress of Louisbourg fell to the British under the command of Brig. Gen. Jeffrey Amherst, with young James Wolfe as his second in command. Pitt's selections for this campaign were a vindication of his erroneous choice of Abercromby. The expedition, nine thousand regulars and only five hundred provincials, had started from Halifax on May 28. When Louisbourg capitulated two months later, most of the town had been battered into ruins by British artillery. In September Amherst, with most of his troops, sailed to Boston, from which place he marched to Lake George. From this time on the French fought a losing war. The capture of Louisbourg proved to be a tremendous psychological boost to British military morale.

One month later the French suffered another severe blow. Lieut. Col. John Bradstreet, with nearly three thousand men in a fleet of bateaux and whaleboats, left newly built Fort Stanwix and arrived at ruined Oswego on August 20. Bradstreet's instructions were to destroy Fort Frontenac, the great supply depot that fed the French posts to the west and south—Niagara, the Great Lakes, and the Ohio Valley. One week later the lightly defended fort was utterly destroyed; seven enemy vessels were burned, with two others used to transport the captured munitions, supplies, and furs across the lake to Oswego. By September 8 Bradstreet's army had returned to the Mohawk Valley, without the loss of a single man and much the richer.[22]

Fort Niagara, still unaware of the catastrophe to the east, was being held by only forty militiamen under Capt. Vassan. When word finally came of the disaster to Fort Frontenac, Vassan planned to burn all the structures outside the palisades. The contemplated destruction was averted when a relief force of one thousand five hundred men showed up in a fleet of bateaux. Iroquois Indians, attached to Fort La Présentation, had visited Montreal and reported the ruination of the depot. Within twenty-four hours, troops were gathered and sped toward Niagara.[23]

The fabric of the French empire in North America disintegrated even more as the upper Ohio Valley was lost when Fort Duquesne was abandoned. In the spring of 1758 Brig. Gen. John Forbes, with Lieut. Col. Henry Bouquet as his second in command, was handed the task of taking the French fort. Probably because of superstition, Braddock's road from Fort Cumberland was forsaken and a new military road was built, with two fortifications, Bedford and Ligonier, erected along its way. Capt. Marchand de Ligneris, commandant of Fort Duquesne, facing an acute shortage of provisions and the approach of a vastly superior force, was left with no alternative to destroying the fort. On the night of November 24 he ordered the powder kegs fused. The British, in camp several miles away, heard the tremendous blast. On the morning of the 25th, Forbes's men cautiously moved in on the smoking ruins of Fort Duquesne. The French had disappeared, having moved out under the cover of darkness, to retreat to Fort Machault.

While the fort at the Forks of the Ohio was being threatened, there was a tempestuous meeting between Montcalm and Vaudreuil. The governor was for rebuilding Fort Frontenac but Montcalm's engineers reported that the place was a total ruin and not worthy of any effort, and that Fort La Présentation was the only logical place to take over the roles of depot and shipyard. Montcalm felt that the Ohio Valley should be relinquished to the enemy and New France's arms concentrated on the borders much closer to home—the Niagara Frontier and the St. Lawrence Valley.[24]

With British arms accumulating successes in Europe, India, and Africa, William Pitt determined that the ultimate goal in North America was the capture of Canada. Abercromby was recalled and his command transferred to Amherst's direction. Pitt planned that Amherst should invade Canada by the Ticonderoga-Crown Point route, while Wolfe, honored with the rank of major general, was handed the task of assaulting New France by way of the St. Lawrence. In addition, he ordered Oswego rebuilt and insisted that, one way or another, an attack should be launched against Fort Niagara. He thought that May 1, 1759, was a suitable date for the simultaneous beginning of the two campaigns.

Wolfe, now with an independent command, and his naval partner, Vice Admiral Charles Saunders, reached Halifax on April 30 and Louisbourg two weeks later. The powerful squadron of 49 men-of-war, accompanied by 119 transports and supply ships, sailed up the St. Lawrence. On June 27, when they anchored at Ile d'Orléans, five miles from Quebec, Wolfe commenced one of the most dramatic sieges in the history of the continent. The end came on September 17, after Wolfe had drawn the French out of their fortified walls and beaten them on the Plains of Abraham. With the British victory, however, two valorous men, Wolfe and Montcalm, were mortally wounded on that battlefield.

By contrast, Amherst's campaign was a month and a half late in the starting. He spent a month building a new fortification, Fort George, on the site of William Johnson's entrenched camp at Lake George. On July 21 he finally had his seven thousand troops on the lake and headed for Ticonderoga. Only four hundred French held Fort Carillon while the main force, numbering twenty-five hundred, fell back to Fort St. Frederic at Crown Point. On July 26 the French commander blew up part of Ticonderoga's works and retreated to Crown Point. Five days later they mined and exploded Fort St. Frederic and retreated to the fort at Ile-aux-Noix (later Fort Lennox) on the Richelieu River. Amherst's original purpose, the invasion of Canada, was at first postponed, then abandoned, as he and his men spent two months reconstructing the works at Ticonderoga and building a new fortress at Crown Point.

The new campaign against Fort Niagara was masked as an operation to rebuild Oswego. It got under way in May 1759, leaving from Schenectady and following the Bradstreet route of the year before—the Mohawk River, Oneida Carrying Place, Wood Creek, Oneida Lake, and Oswego River—arriving at Oswego on June 27. Brig. Gen. John Prideaux, a strict disciplinarian, headed the expedition of thirty-one hundred regulars, exclusive of boatmen, with a Swiss military officer, Lieut. Col. Frederick Haldimand (Governor of Canada at a later date), as his second in command. Sir William Johnson led the large contingent of Iroquois, five hundred or so in number, many of whom had been former French allies. At Oswego the Indian force was augmented by some three hundred Hurons (Wyandots), Shawnees, and warriors from other tribes. The French reverses had caused sharp disaffection among the Indians, who sensed the outcome of the long conflict.[25]

About thirteen hundred troops under Haldimand remained to

safeguard Oswego and the line of communications and supply from Fort Stanwix. The shipyard was reactivated and orders were given to a company of carpenters to build three vessels. On Sunday, July 1, Prideaux's men boarded whaleboats, each of which carried several days' rations, and set out on their six-day *daylight* cruise. It was sheer luck that the two new armed French 160-ton schooners, *Iroquoise* and *Outaouaise,* built at Fort La Présentation the previous April, did not sight the British flotilla of whaleboats during their patrols on the lake. More amazing were the reports of the two French captains who informed Capt. Pouchot at Niagara that there were no English at Oswego or anywhere else on the lake's shore.[26]

A desperate and futile effort to destroy the expedition's base came on July 5. About twelve hundred French Canadians and Christianized Indians from Fort La Présentation, under the leadership of the notorious border raider St. Luc de la Corne and accompanied by Father Picquet, were sighted by vigilant scouts on the afternoon of July 4. There had been time to build barricades of bags of flour and kegs of pork in the midst of Fort Ontario's ruins before the French charged over the hill the next morning. Haldimand lost only two men killed and eleven wounded, while the French suffered more than one hundred casualties.[27]

Prideaux's forces made overnight camps at Great Sodus Bay, Irondequoit Bay, Braddock's Bay, Johnson's Creek, and late in the afternoon of July 6 they landed on the banks of Four Mile Creek, not quite two miles east of Fort Niagara. By nightfall the troops had shoveled a path through the clay bar across the mouth of the creek, and the first whaleboats entered the marshy pond on the other side. A mile of swamp, woods, and meadowland lay between them and the enemy's ramparts.[28]

Capt. Pouchot had left Montreal on March 27 to once again assume command of Niagara. Before he left he was informed by Montcalm that only 150 regulars and 300 militiamen could be spared to garrison the fort. On July 6 Pouchot commanded a garrison of 429 men. A British officer reported that the fort held 850 regulars and militia and about 350 Indians. It would appear then that the size of the garrison ranged from 429 to possibly 1,200 men, including Indians, and that the number of defenders increased as additional French and allied Indians were brought in during the eighteen-day siege.

The first indication that there were English and Indians anywhere in Niagara's environs was when a wounded French militiaman, lone survivor of a group of three, staggered to the fort's gate, hysterically screaming that the woods were full of Indians. A ten-man patrol, ordered out by Pouchot to find the other two militiamen, walked into an ambush. Pouchot then turned out the entire garrison to man the ramparts. In the first gray light of dawn another patrol returned to report that numerous English and Indians were in the immediate vicinity.[29]

To set up a battery on the river's side of the fort, Prideaux issued orders to have a dozen whaleboats and three cannon dragged five miles through the thick woodland to the Niagara River. Seneca guides led the boatmen to a ravine called La Belle Famille, about two miles southwest of the fort, that led down to the beach. By early morning the boats, laden with disassembled cannon, were afloat on the river and braving French artillery fire. The boats were beached on the Niagara's west shore, and while a number of men unloaded the guns, others went to work fashioning fascines to protect the weapons. At least a week was required to reassemble and mount the cannon that ultimately would attempt to breach the fort's walls from that sector.

Capt. Pouchot dispatched an officer to Fort Little Niagara, a mile and a half from the falls, with two messages. The first was to order the Joncaires, Daniel and Philippe, to evacuate their post at once and retreat to Grand Island; the second was to be relayed by runners to Capt . de Lignery, commandant of Fort Machault, urging that officer to come to his aid by attacking the British besiegers from behind, to "come down the west shore of the river. When you attack, we will sally out, too." The Joncaire brothers, however, elected to come to Fort Niagara. They led a party of about seventy people, several women and Indians among them, down the portage trail. Johnson's Indians wasted no time repairing to Fort Little Niagara. After rounding up all the livestock, they applied the torch to the Joncaires's fort. The Indians commercialized their windfall. A British officer reported on July 12 that the Indians "ran off all the horses and cattle there, and are now peddling the beef through our camp." The meat, to be sure, was a welcome respite, though hardly more than a toothsome morsel; the men had been subsisting on a daily diet of hardtack and beans. The country's wild game had normally deserted the Niagara Frontier and were in the mountains for the summer.[30]

Prideaux ordered trenches dug south and west of the fort's walls. Gun batteries, protected by fascines and gabions, commenced hammering away at Pouchot's fort. On July 16 a British officer wrote the following comments:

> The garrison and fort are much stronger than we expected. Our trenches are carried within 250 yards of the fort. Our batteries were opened yesterday—two brass 12's, four 6's and five royal howitz [ers] of eight inches. For three days past we have played upon them with eight pieces of cannon, and have set several of their buildings on fire.

. . . The enemy have already fired near 6,000 cannon ball, besides thousands of small arms, but as yet have killed only three men and wounded about 20; among the latter Captain Williams [Prideaux's chief engineer], dangerously. We now have 900 Indians with us, and more daily coming in.[31]

After receiving convincing dispatches from Haldimand that the line of communications was safe from French interruption, Prideaux sent one of his officers to the fort with a formal demand to capitulate. Capt. Pouchot's reply was humorously impertinent: "Before I make any terms, I wish an opportunity to gain your esteem."

On the morning of July 17 the British battery on the river's west bank began hurling hot shot at the fort's ramparts. The barrage was very effective. The barracks and storehouse were set on fire, holes were torn in the roof of the House of Peace, the palisades were holed here and there, and the fort's wharf was totally destroyed.

The grim war then laid a heavy hand on the command of the expedition. During the early evening of July 20, Gen. Prideaux and his aide, Col. John Johnstone, decided on an inspection tour of the siege lines. They were nearing a parallel only forty yards from the fort when an enemy musketball dropped Johnstone in his tracks, killing him instantly. Stifling his grief, the general assisted with the removal of the body to the rear lines and then returned to the same trench to continue the inspection. He halted to watch the loading and firing of a coehorn mortar. The gun blew up, sending a piece of its barrel into his head. He died soon after, without regaining consciousness.[32]

With Prideaux's death the Niagara command devolved on Sir William Johnson, who was the senior officer on the scene. British army ranking, however, passed the command to Col. Haldimand, who was far to the east at Oswego. The same night of the tragedies, Johnson sent a dispatch by boat to Haldimand, acquainting him with the sorrowful news and recommending that he hasten to Niagara. Within the siege lines a bitter controversy had begun, regulars against colonials, on the merits of Johnson, a provincial commander, versus Haldimand, a British army colonel. With resolute decisiveness, Sir William put an end to the dissension and determined to take the full responsibility until Brig. Gen. Thomas Gage, appointed by Amherst to take Prideaux's place, should make an appearance.[33]

Late in the evening of July 20, a couple of hours after Johnson had sent the dispatch to Haldimand, Indians brought news that a large flotilla of canoes and bateaux was entering the Niagara River from Lake Erie. The expectation of the arrival of French reinforcements was about to be fulfilled and events in the next forty-eight hours approached a crisis. Early the next morning Sir William sent another message to Haldimand, urging him to remain at Oswego. Ordering the mounting of three eighteen-pounders, Johnson sent Rangers and Indians to reconnoiter the area to the rear of Niagara's falls. Reports came in that the newcomers aggregated "a thousand French and twice as many Indians."[34]

Sometime during the morning of the 23rd, the two captains of the reinforcement army, François Le Marchand de Ligneris and Charles Aubry, had four Indians go under a flag of truce through the British lines with glowing messages of hope for Pouchot. De Ligneris had sped from Fort Machault with the four hundred-man remnant of the French Army of the Ohio and one thousand Indians to rendezvous at Presque Isle with Aubry's detachment of two hundred French, most of them trappers, and six hundred Indians from Detroit.

When the battle of La Belle Famille began, Pouchot was helpless behind the battered walls of his fort. He could not even muster a rudimentary sally force to assist his comrades. The arms of his garrison were in sad shape, with less than one hundred effective muskets, and his half-dozen gunsmiths working overtime. There was a great deal of havoc within the fort. The river battery and the newly positioned eighteen-pounders of the British had set off many fires, which forced Pouchot's artisans to spend hour after hour demolishing sections of buildings to prevent the flames from spreading. One bastion lost three of its five cannon through a direct hit. The chief of artillery was badly wounded and many of his men were killed or injured. The garrison's casualties numbered at least 109 dead and wounded.

Shortly after the four French Indians returned along the portage road, Johnson dispatched 150 infantrymen to La Belle Famille to erect a gabion-and-fascine breastwork or barricade across the road. He also issued orders to have an "all guns" bombardment of the fort commence at 4 A.M. (July 24). Meanwhile, Capt, James De Lancey, commander of the portage road detachment, directed a sergeant and 11 men to go upriver, cross by whaleboat, and bring back a six-pounder and ammunition from the west battery. His thought was to install the gun, loaded with deadly grape, behind the breastwork. The effectiveness of grapeshot was such that each round fired could kill or maim two dozen men at once.

The small detachment disappeared into the night. Some little time later, while De Lancey was preparing to take some rest until the bombardment hour, there was a sudden outburst of Indian yells, followed by gunfire, from down the ravine. He dispatched a messenger to the command post, requesting Johnson's attendance at once. A scout went upriver to ascertain the reason for the commotion. He returned to report that not only were all the whaleboats sunk, but also the sergeant and his men had been butchered, their heads severed, mounted on oar handles, and then rammed into the soft shore earth.

Johnson added six hundred men to De Lancey's force, while hundreds of Iroquois loped around the end of the barricade and entered the black forest. There was no sleep or rest. Aching eyes searched the darkness, seeking out the source of the tiniest sound. Time dragged by torturously. Then, at nine o'clock, the French attack began, with Huron, Mingo, and Shawnee warriors in the vanguard, right down the portage road, straight at the British breastwork. Capt. De Lancey reported later:

> They charged our breastwork with a very great noise and shouting. They began the attack on our right, and our men kept their ground and soon returned the fire. I ordered my men not to fire till they were sure of their mark, which they punctually obeyed. Part of the enemy then inclined to the left and gave us a very smart fire. We did not fire for some time, and then only about ten shots at some few of the enemy who came very near us. Very soon after this I found the enemy's fire slacken upon us, upon which I sent to Colonel Massey to desire he would let me leave the breastwork and rush in on the enemy, which he granted, desired I would move slow, and advanced with his party to the right. We jumped over the breastwork and rushed in on the enemy, who immediately gave way. They then endeavored to flank us on the left, but I ordered a party from the right to move to the left, which they did, and with them I pushed forwards to the enemy, who falling in with the party which was on my left, immediately ran away as fast as they could, and never offered to rally afterwards. A few of them remained behind and exchanged a few shots with us, and were either taken or killed. Our Indians, as soon as they saw the enemy give way, pursued them very briskly, and took and killed great numbers of them. We pursued about five miles and then returned.[35]

The number of casualties among the French and their Indians in this action can only be guessed at, with reports ranging from 225 to 500 slain. Sir William's journal for July 27 says, ''I divided among the several Nations, the prisoners and scalps amounting to 246, of which 96 were prisoners. The officers I released from them by ransom and good words.'' The toll among the French officers indicates the extent of the French defeat: De Lignery, mortally wounded, died some hours later in Johnson's tent, while his compatriots, Captains Aubry, Marin, Montigny, Vassan, and Villiers were prisoners. The survivors fled to their boats and canoes on the upper river beach above the falls. Their defeat on the Niagara Frontier forced the French to burn their Ohio forts, leaving that whole region in the undisputed possession of the English.[36]

At five o'clock, after one of his officers was allowed to see the prisoners and realize the seriousness of the French debacle in La Belle Famille, Pouchot had the white flag hoisted above Niagara's riddled ramparts. Even in his capitulation, the French commandant was gracious: he invited Sir William and his officers to dinner in the House of

Peace. The victorious officers helped themselves to expensive souvenirs, the personal possessions of the defeated, while Johnson's Iroquois, drunk on French wine, indulged in plundering and wrecking the interiors of the structures still standing after the heavy bombardments.

Col. Haldimand arrived from Oswego on July 26, two days after the fort's surrender. To fulfill guarantees of safe conduct for the garrison's officers and men, their women and children, a solid phalanx of officers of the militia and Royal Americans kept howling, inebriated Indians from harming any of the survivors, who were led to waiting boats. The women and children were escorted to Fort La Présentation, while the officers and men were taken first to Oswego, then to Albany, where they were exhibited at victory celebrations.

While soldiers spent a month cleaning up the wreckage inside Fort Niagara, Haldimand gave Capt. Schlosser the job of building a new fort to guard the upper reaches of the river, on the site of Little Fort Niagara. A shipbuilding facility was also established on an island in the river opposite Fort Schlosser.[37]

Fort Niagara was left in the care of five hundred militiamen. In the final months of the year, smallpox invaded the fort and killed the commandant, Lieut. Col. William Farquahar, and more than a dozen men in the garrison. In October 1760 Capt. Robert Rogers, with a company of his Rangers, arrived at the fort, on their way to Detroit to accept that post's surrender. Forts Niagara and Schlosser were not seriously threatened during Pontiac's War (1763-66), although not-too-distant Detroit, first attacked on May 9, 1763, was besieged for many months.[38]

In 1764, while Pontiac and his Indians were ravaging the English outposts, the Niagara Frontier defenses were strengthened by substantial construction. Capt. John Montresor, son of Gen. Amherst's leading military engineer, Col. James Montresor, was in charge of the building program. He arrived at Niagara on May 28, bringing with him a large force of militia and volunteers. He decided that the critical portage road should be guarded by five "redoubts with stockades"; by July 1 they were completed and manned.[39] The facilities at upriver Fort Schlosser were expanded by a substantial wharf and storehouse.

To insure protection for the Niagara River-Lake Erie cordelle haulway, Montresor on July 18 ordered battalions of New York and Connecticut militiamen to the "NW side of the Rapids at the Point of Lake Erie," opposite the present city of Buffalo. Maj. Israel Putnam, "Old Put" of Revolutionary War fame, supervised the Connecticut men who constructed Fort Erie, completed in just four weeks.[40]

While the work crews labored on Forts Schlosser and Erie, Montresor designed the still-standing North and South Redoubts, forming a triangular configuration with the House of Peace. The actual construction, however, did not commence for another two years, after Pontiac had made peace with the English. With stone walls five feet thick, each of the massive bastions could house and feed forty men. The top decks were armed with batteries of twelve-pounders. On August 14, while the finishing touches were applied to Fort Erie, Montresor left Niagara and accompanied Bradstreet's two thousand troops and three hundred Indians to Detroit.[41]

Sir William Johnson's influence over the Six Nations paid a handsome dividend to the English by depriving the Senecas of their absolute control over the Niagara portage. In return for a paltry gift of blankets, kettles, and knives, plus enough rum for a one-day spree, the Indians affixed their marks to a treaty that bestowed on "George III and his heirs forever" a four-mile-wide tract along the whole course of the Niagara River. At Fort Stanwix in 1768 Sir William presided over a great council of more than three thousand Indians, which eventuated in a new "permanent" boundary.

Old Fort Niagara was in the hands of the British when the first hostilities of the Revolution occurred at Lexington and Concord, and remained, heavily garrisoned, in their possession throughout the war. Names famous in the Mohawk Valley were connected with the fort during the long years of the conflict: Loyalist leader Maj. John Butler, and his son, Capt. Walter Butler, friends and neighbors of Sir William Johnson and his heirs; Sir John Johnson, Sir William's son; Col. Guy Johnson, Sir William's nephew and inheritor of the Superintendency of Indian Affairs (his uncle dying in July 1774); Molly Brant, Indian mistress of Sir William and mother of eight of his children; and her celebrated brother, Joseph Brant (Thayendanegea), war chief of the Mohawks.

Fort Niagara was the base from which some of the Tory-Indian expeditions operated to lay waste Cherry Valley, Wyoming Valley, and other settlements, killing and capturing, plundering and burning. Colonial records attest to the numerous protests of Fort Niagara's commandants against the use of Indian auxiliaries, who were often unpredictable and quite frequently uncontrollable. The British War Office felt that if the English did not avail themselves of Indian arms, the colonials would.[42]

Maj. Butler, accompanied by one hundred Mohawks, arrived at Fort Niagara on July 26, 1775 (his twenty-year-old son, Walter, arrived late in the fall of the year). He immediately set to work installing conveniences and stocking supplies, indicating that the British planned to use the fort as a springboard for forays against the rebellious colonists. He later converted one of the rooms in the House of Peace as the new headquarters for Guy Johnson who was to assume, with London's approval, the office of Superintendent of Indian Affairs. The extent of Butler's activities between the time of his arrival and May 1776 is disclosed in a report by the fort's commandant, Col. Mason Bolton. He wrote that he had drafted a bill of 14,760 pounds, about $75,000, for supplies issued the Indians by the Loyalist leader.

The Sullivan-Clinton Expedition in 1779 was primarily a punitive march of American destructives against the British-allied Six Nations (the Oneidas and Tuscaroras were either neutral or affiliated with the Patriots). The overriding purpose was to eradicate all future Indian threats against the vulnerable frontier settlements by destroying the Iroquois villages, cornfields, and orchards, thereby cutting off Indian food supplies to the British and Loyalists and forcing the Iroquois to seek succor from the British at Niagara.[43]

> It was a ruthless destruction of the greatest advance in civilization that the red men in this country have ever attained. . . . The Six Nations never recovered. Their organization was destroyed, their empire gone; they had to subsist during the following winter on British charity.[44]

But just as important, if not more so, was the part of the plan to take Niagara and Oswego. The calamitous blunder of the campaign was the expedition's armies to rendezvous at Genesee Castle, about eighty miles southeast of Niagara.[45] When Sullivan reached Chenussio on the Genesee River, his farthest point of advance, he could not attack Niagara without additional military support and had to turn about and retrace his steps for home. "In his official report of this expedition, General Sullivan stated that lack of 15 days' additional rations kept him from coming on and storming Fort Niagara, which he was confident he could have captured."[46]

The Iroquois somehow survived the terrible winter of 1779/80 at Fort Niagara, where they were refitted by the British. They returned to attack the frontier settlements with ever greater numbers of warriors. It was a whirlwind of red fury.

The end of the Revolution saw an undetermined line of demarcation between British Canada and the United Colonies. By the articles of the Treaty of Paris, Fort Niagara was termed the property of the United States, but the British held on to this fortification, with others along the border, for thirteen years, during which time they controlled the traffic of commerce on the Niagara River and Lake Ontario. The period

PRESENT PLAN OF FORT NIAGARA
Courtesy of Old Fort Niagara Association

KEY

1—Drawbridge and "Gate of the Five Nations"
2—South Redoubt (British, 1770)
3—Battery Dauphin
4—South Casemate Gallery
5—Sallyport
6—Carronade Battery
7—North Redoubt (British, 1770)
8—Millet Cross
9—Rush-Bagot Memorial
10—"The House of Peace"
11—French Bake House (1756?)
12—Hot-Shot Battery
13—Hot-Shot Furnace
14—Postern Gate (American, 1839)
15—Reconstruction, 18th-century log cabin
16—French Powder Magazine (1757)
17—French Storehouse (1754), now the Historical Institute

Three flags fly over the grounds: the golden fleurs-de-lis of France brought
by La Salle in 1679; the flag of King George II brought to Niagara by Sir
William Johnson in 1759; and the Stars and Stripes of 1796, first raised at
Niagara by a detachment of American artillerymen.

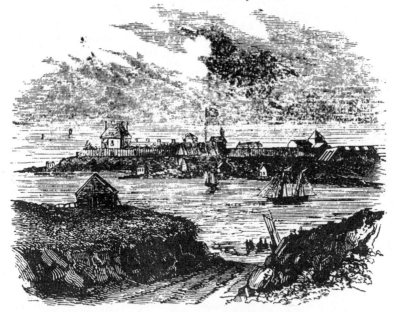

FORT NIAGARA
Courtesy of National Archives

FORT NIAGARA
Courtesy of New York State Department of Commerce

between 1783 and 1796 was called the "holdover," during which the British negotiated for a permanent boundary farther to the south and west than finally drawn. In 1796, by the Jay Treaty, Fort Niagara was finally turned over to a detachment of American artillerymen.

The first new of the declaration of the War of 1812, called the "Second War for Independence," did not reach Fort Niagara until June 26. Vigorous preparations were immediately undertaken to strengthen the fort's defenses.

After feeble and irresolute military actions on both sides for some months, Brig. Gen. George McClure, commanding the American militia, brutally burned the village of Newark in Ontario, evacuated nearby Fort George, and moved his headquarters to Buffalo. At this time Fort Niagara was garrisoned by 370 men under the command of Capt. Nathaniel Leonard of the artillery. On the night of December 19, 1813, during the absence of Leonard and several other officers, 500 British, led by Col. John Murray, crossed the river, captured the sentinels, and took the fort by surprise, losing only five men killed and six wounded. The Americans suffered 65 men killed, with nearly all of the remainder, among whom were numerous wounded, taken prisoners; twenty-seven cannon of large caliber, three thousand stand of small arms, and large amounts of munitions, provisions, and general stores were lost to the enemy. In addition the British, in retaliation for the burning of Newark, went on a rampage and destroyed the villages of Lewiston and Buffalo, and all the dwellings along the lake shore as far as Eighteen Mile Creek.[47] The British retained Fort Niagara until the end of the war. With the signing of the Treaty of Ghent in 1815, the fort again reverted to the United States.

After the war the American military constructed a number of permanent additions to Fort Niagara's works. The hot-shot battery, facing the lake, was built in 1839. During the same year, the stone wall and postern gate replaced the early rampart of earthwork and log palisades. The masonry in the north and south casemate galleries was constructed in 1861, in the manner of the nineteenth-century coastal fortifications.[48]

In 1817 the Rush-Bagot Treaty, simple in conception and language, fashioned an international agreement for the 3,500-mile boundary between Canada and the United States—a peaceful border without a single gun mounted anywhere along its entire length, a tribute to amicable relations between two civilized peoples.

The Oswego Forts
Fort Oswego–Fort George–Fort Ontario
Oswego County

From the first British toehold in the Great Lakes region to a training base for United States overseas troops, a succession of military installations has commanded the strategic mouth of the Oswego River on Lake Ontario. The importance of the location is reflected in the five battles fought in the immediate environs.

The designs of the various fortifications, both projected and actually constructed from 1727 through 1900, span the evolution of defensive works from the medieval concept in height, as seen in castlelike construction, to the modern concept in depth, as seen in underground coastal batteries. Included in these plans are two pentagonal five-bastioned forts, a square three-bastioned fort, an eight-pointed star-shaped fort, a rectangular four-bastioned fort, a temporary field fortification, a number of different redoubts, blockhouses, retrenched batteries, and other minor works.[1]

As one historian put it, "Oswego was the hinge upon which the fate of the Empire creaked."[2] Without Oswego, there possibly would have been a long delay in the captures of Fort Niagara, Fort Frontenac, Montreal, and Quebec. The story of Oswego is one of the epic dramas of North America. Occupied by the Iroquois as early as the fourteenth century, its first history was recorded in the travels of New France's Jesuit fathers in 1654. Strategically located near the eastern end of the Great Lakes chain, it was the gateway to central New York and the Hudson Valley.

The sites of two of the forts, and the location of the third, are placed in present-day Oswego geography: Fort Oswego's site, on the west side of the river, is marked by a plaque at West First and Lake Streets; Fort George's site is in Montcalm Park, at the junction of Montcalm and West Sixth Streets; Fort Ontario is at the foot of East Seventh Street, overlooking the juncture of the Oswego River and Lake Ontario.

One of the earliest mentions of Oswego in colonial history is that of the Onondaga Indians in 1687, when they presented a petition to Albany's mayor and council requesting them to establish a trading post there. The Albany fathers, however, thought such an undertaking too far afield. During the New York governorship of Lord Bellomont, some thought was given to such a project and token plans were made but not acted on. Governor William Burnet, assuming office in 1720, made great efforts to encourage the provincials to engage more vigorously in Indian trade. In 1722 he established the trading post at Oswego, for the first time planting

England's flag on the Great Lakes. Though this was not to the liking of the Iroquois League at the time, it was a very profitable venture for the English.

The French erected Fort Niagara in 1726 and secretly armed it in the spring of 1727, a direct violation of the terms of the Treaty of Utrecht. In a letter dated New York, December 4, 1726, addressed to the Duke of Newcastle, Governor Burnet recognized the threat:

> I am now to lay before your Grace a complaint in which the Indians of the Six Nations join with me against the French for having built a fort at Niagara on the land of one of the Six Nations, at the place through which they must pass to go to their own hunting country. . . . By means of this fort the French can hinder and molest these Indians when they please, which is directly contrary to the 15th Art[icle] of the Treaty of Utrecht. . . . I have likewise prevailed with the Assembly to raise 300 pounds in their last sessions in order to enable me to build a fort at the mouth of the Onondaga [Oswego] River, on the side of the lake, in the spring, in order to protect our trade.[3]

Burnet put on the pressure as incidents along the frontier became more serious. In his report of May 9, 1727, to the Lords of Trade, he gave details regarding the preparations for the building of Fort Oswego:

> I have this Spring sent up workmen to build a stone house of strength at a place called Oswego, at the mouth of the Onondaga River where our principal trade with the Far Nations is carried on. I have obtained the consent of the Six Nations to build it . . . and . . . sent up a detachment of sixty soldiers and a Captain and two Lieutenants to protect the building from any disturbance that any French and Indians may offer to it. There are besides, about two hundred traders now at the same place. . . . I have been obliged to lay out more than double that value [three hundred pounds] upon my own credit to furnish necessaries and provisions, and hire workmen, and make Battoes [bateaux] to carry up the men, for it is all water carriage [travel] from our utmost town called Schenectady, to this place, which is about two hundred miles, except five miles, where they must draw their Battoes over land [the Oneida Portage], which is easily enough done and this makes the communication much more convenient than by land.[4]

Fortifying Oswego, of course, was also a violation of the treaty, but it was the English response to the French fort at Niagara. The French usually referred to old Fort Oswego as Fort Chouaguen, as they called all the Oswego forts except when they described one of them specifically. New France's governor, Marquis de Beauharnais, disturbed by the threat to French navigation on the lake and to their fur trading activities, sent an indignant letter to Burnet. The New York governor answered by alluding to the establishment of Fort Niagara.

While Burnet pushed the work at Oswego, Maj. Begon, accompanied by a detachment of French troops, showed up at the fort and tendered the commanding officer an order demanding the evacuation and destruction of the post within fifteen days. The English officer, with infinite diplomacy, invited Maj. Begon and fellow officers into the fort and accorded them the hospitality of the garrison. Courteously but firmly, it was pointed out that the fort was not on French ground but rather on soil that belonged to the Iroquois, who had granted the English permission to build there. The commanding officer further informed them that he was under direct orders from Governor Burnet and could not entertain any notion of destroying the fort. The conference ended, apparently on an amicable note, and the French left. From time to time, however, the French sent harassing parties to disrupt the construction work.[5]

In 1731 the French constructed a semi-permanent post on the east side of Lake Champlain at Pointe de la Chevelure (later known as Chimney Point) in Addison County, Vermont. The post was shortly moved across the lake to Crown Point and named Fort St. Frederic. The northern Colonies, particularly New York, were embroiled in internecine squabbling and took no steps to offset this new threat.

The first fortification at Oswego, on occasion called Fort Burnet during its early history, was of simple design. The Marquis de Beauharnais complained that it was "a redoubt with galleries and full of loop-holes and other works belonging to fortifications." Burnet pointed out that it was merely a post with walls "four feet thick of large good stone." In 1741 the New York Assembly authorized the sum of six hundred pounds to "erect a sufficient stone wall at a proper distance around the trading house at Oswego, either in a triangular or quadrangular form, as the ground will best admit of, with a bastion or block-house in each corner to flank the curtain." The Assembly later received complaints that the contractors were lining their pockets by using clay instead of stone and skimping the work in general.

In 1744 a new conflict erupted in Europe, the War of the Austrian Succession, otherwise known as King George's War, which did not get into full swing in North America until the following year. Philippe and Daniel Joncaire, competent French *agent provocateurs,* spread the seeds of discontent throughout the Six Nations by disseminating such propaganda as "the English are organizing a great army to burn your castles and steal your land." Similar lies and half-truths served to arouse the Indians, who raided English wagon and bateau supply trains.[6]

During the first two years of the war, Fort Oswego was on the verge of closing shop, for it suffered from poor defenses and a chronically deficient commissary, even though its strategic position as watchdog on

French activities at Forts Niagara and Frontenac had to be protected. At the beginning of the conflict the fort and trading post had more than 150 traders operating in the area and were the fountainhead of the major share of New York's business. Fear of French and Indian raids drove away many traders, who took their business elsewhere.

The Assembly turned down requests to furnish funds to strengthen or even maintain the fort. Military supplies often could not get through because of the raiding activities of the French-allied Caughnawaga Indians (Mohawk émigrés). One company of provincial troops was sent to Oswego, the only reinforcement the province provided during the whole war. Fort Oswego was garrisoned from 1727 to 1755 by provincial troops—the so-called independent companies and by British regulars in 1755 and 1756.[7]

The only man who could provide the Lake Ontario post with the military necessaries, by reason of his success in sending goods there, was William Johnson, lord of the Mohawk Valley, mentor, friend, and "father" to the Six Nations. Johnson's energetic enterprise and tremendous influence over the Mohawks soon had the supply routes from the Mohawk River to Lake Ontario made safe, as the Iroquois tribe took up the tomahawk and fought their relatives the Caughnawagas.

The fort, enlarged between 1741 and 1743, was put in a condition for defense with minor rebuilding and no additional armaments. For a short time it was known as Fort Pepperrell for the conqueror of Louisbourg. By the end of the war, all the absent traders had returned and business at the post became even more lucrative.

The Treaty of Aix-la-Chapelle, as in earlier treaties, did nothing to resolve the dispute of territorial boundaries in North America. The English grew more and more exasperated as the French penetrated the Ohio Valley, basing their dubious claims to it on La Salle's explorations almost a century earlier.

The French were intent on strengthening the chain between Canada and New Orleans, inserting links of forts and missions, while the Colonies were embroiled in their mutually destructive jealousies. In 1749, a year after the war had ended, New France's governor sent Capt. Pierre Joseph Céleron de Blainville, at the head of a large party of soldiers, Indians, and a couple of missionaries, into the Ohio Valley to plant lead plates and erect signs, to demonstrate to all the world that the vast territory was indeed a French possession.[8]

At the same time a new post and mission, Fort La Présentation, was founded by Father Picquet at the mouth of the Oswegatchie River (Ogdensburg). This establishment was the French counterirritant to Oswego, about 120 miles to the west. While the French were shipping men, equipment, and supplies from Fort Frontenac, across the lake from Oswego, to their newly established posts, the English fort sat idly by, unable to put a stop to the busy French traffic. Fort Oswego had a garrison of less than one hundred provincials and no armed vessels to cripple the movement of French supplies.[9]

"A volley fired by a young Virginian in the backwoods of America set the world on fire," wrote Horace Walpole, contemporary British essayist.[10] George Washington's attack on the thirty-three-man French party at Jumonville Glen on Chestnut Ridge and the ensuing action at Fort Necessity, Pennsylvania, two events occurring five weeks apart (May 28 and July 3, 1754), initiated the last of the French and Indian wars in North America and embroiled Great Britain and France in Europe and throughout their colonial possessions. At the head of 120 men, young Washington had started out on April 2 with the purpose of unseating the French at the Forks of the Ohio, modern Pittsburgh.

The bloody conflict ultimately determined a new world order. When the formal peace was signed at Paris in 1763, all of Canada and the whole region east of the Mississippi River, with the exception of New Orleans, became an integral part of British Colonial America. Francis Parkman, the estimable historian, wrote that

the British victory crippled the commerce of her rivals, ruined France in two continents, and blighted her as a colonial power. It gave England control of the seas . . . made her the first of commercial nations, and prepared that vast colonial system that has planted New Englands in every quarter of the globe. . . . It supplied to the United States the indispensable condition of their greatness, if not of their national existence.[11]

After the Fort Necessity incident, the French were optimistic that further conflict in the trans-Allegheny region would be at an end, but the English would not have it so. After the aborted colonial attempt by Governor Robert Dinwiddie of Virginia to take Fort Duquesne in 1754, the English formulated an elaborate plan of attack on four fronts.

Expeditions were projected against the French strongholds of Fort Niagara, Fort St. Frederic at Crown Point, Fort Beausejour (Fort Cumberland) on the Acadian peninsula, and Fort Duquesne. The most powerful position in British Colonial America was that of Commander in Chief of His Majesty's Forces. The Duke of Cumberland, soldier son of George II and Captain General of the British Army, took over the reins of the major drive against the French. He appointed Maj. Gen. Edward Braddock, an officer with forty-five years' service, to be the commander of the Fort Duquesne expedition as well as of all the armed forces in

America. Braddock was chosen for this responsible position mainly because of his political and financial connections in London; he is more popularly remembered for his ignominious defeat on July 9, 1755. On his death in that action, his second in command, Maj. Gen. William Shirley, took over.

With Oswego as his base, Shirley commanded the expedition against Fort Niagara. Fort Frontenac, fifty miles away across the lake, was considered a threat; Shirley decided to strengthen Oswego before giving his whole attention to Niagara. The postponement turned out to be unlucky, because troubles came from all sides: continuous rain squalls, camp sicknesses, and the failure of promised provisions. On September 27 Shirley and his officers decided to forgo the Niagara venture, postponing it to the following spring. The commander and some of the militia left Oswego in late October and headed eastward toward home, leaving troops behind to continue their labors on the construction of vessels and the new works, Forts George and Ontario.

The first Fort Ontario, built on the bluff on the east side of the river's mouth, was on occasion called the Fort of the Six Nations and East Fort. Fort George, begun on a ridge about half a mile southwest of Fort Oswego, was sometimes known as New Fort Oswego, Fort Rascal, and West Fort, and, although never quite completed, was garrisoned by the New Jersey militia, the Jersey Blues. An idea of the undertaking to render Oswego impregnable to French attack was published in *Gentleman's Magazine* in 1756 and reprinted in *New York Colonial Documents:*

> When it was determined that the army at Oswego should go into winter quarters, they began a new fort upon the hill upon the east side of the river, about 470 yards from the old one; it is 800 feet in circumference and will command the harbor; it is built of logs from 20 to 30 inches thick; the wall is 14 feet high and is encompassed by a ditch 14 feet broad and 10 deep; it is to contain barracks for 300 men. On the other side of the river west from the old fort, another new fort is erecting; this is 170 feet square. A hospital of frame-work, 150 feet by 30, is already built, and may serve as a barrack for 200 men, and another barrack is preparing of 150 feet by 24.[12]

During Montcalm's short siege and capture of Oswego in August 1756, a French officer, probably an engineer, reported the following description of the three fortifications. Found in *Paris Documents* and reprinted in the *Documentary History of New York,* the report is more authoritative:

> Fort Ontario is situated on the right bank of the river, in the middle of a very high plateau. It consists of a square of 30 *toises* [a *toise* is

equal to 6.395 feet] a side, the faces of which, broken in the center, are flanked by a redan placed at the point of the break. It is constructed of pickets 18 inches in diameter, smooth on both sides, very well joined the one to the other, and rising 8 or 9 feet from the ground. The ditch that encircles the fort is 18 feet wide by 8 deep. The excavated earth had been thrown up *en glacis* [on the slope] on the counterscarp, with a very steep slope over the berm [covered way]. Loop-holes and embrasures are formed in the pickets on a level with the earth thrown up on the berm, and a scaffolding of carpenters' work extends all around so as to fire from above. It has eight guns, and four mortars with double grenades. The old fort, Chonaguen [Fort Oswego], situated on the left or west bank, consists of a house with galleries, with loop-holes on the ground-floor and principal story, the walls of which are 3 feet thick and encompassed, at a distance of 3 *toises,* by another wall 4 feet thick and 10 high, loop-holed, and flanked by two large square towers. It has likewise a trench encircling on the land side, where the enemy had placed eighteen pieces of cannon and fifteen mortars and howitzers. Fort George is situated 300 *toises* beyond that of Chonaguen [actually on a hill one-half mile southwest of Fort Oswego], on a hill that commanded it. It is of pickets, and badly enough entrenched with earth on two sides [Fort George's ramparts were designed to be 20 feet thick and 12 feet high, but they were never completed, and the cannon were still in their original packing].[13]

In order to keep open the supply routes to Oswego, Shirley in the autumn of 1755 ordered them fortified. In addition to fortifying his own home, which became known as Fort Johnson, William Johnson built Fort Canajoharie opposite the mouth of East Canada Creek, Fort Herkimer on the south side of the Mohawk opposite West Canada Creek, and Fort Hendrick in the immediate neighborhood of the Mohawk castle at Canajoharie. At the carrying place between the Mohawk and Oneida Lake, four new forts were constructed: Forts Craven and Williams on the Mohawk side; Fort Bull at the western terminus of the portage; and Fort Newport on Wood Creek, on the military road between Forts Bull and Williams. The waterways west of the carry were not fortified, in deference to the wishes of the Oneidas.[14]

Braddock's defeat on the Monongahela insured the existence of Fort Duquesne for another three years. William Johnson's victory at Lake George removed Gen. Dieskau, who was replaced by a great soldier and gentleman, Louis Joseph, Marquis de Montcalm. A master of strategy, Montcalm realized very soon after his arrival in Canada in May 1756 that Niagara was in jeopardy as long as Oswego remained a British strongpoint. Fort Niagara, controlling the portage from Lake Ontario to Lake Erie, and the navigation on the Allegheny and Ohio Rivers, had to be preserved in order to assure the safety of the French forts in the Ohio Valley and on the Great Lakes.

The French campaign of 1756 called for the isolation and ultimate capture of Oswego. All the British posts on the water route between the Great Carrying Place (Fort Edward) and Lake Ontario were destroyed by either British demolition or French capture. Fort Bull was taken on March 27 in a daring raid by de Lery's seventeen hundred winter-protected French and Indians from Fort La Présentation. Most of the garrison died by the sword and the tomahawk; the magazine was blown up; the fort set on fire and totally destroyed. The great loss in munitions and provisions, destined for Oswego, was a very costly one for the British.

In the fall of 1755 the French posts, particularly Niagara and Frontenac, were strengthened and their garrisons augmented. In February 1756 Capt. François Pouchot, the engineer who a year later converted Niagara's House of Peace into a fortress, sent a memorial to the authorities, setting forth the feasibility of capturing Oswego. Quebec, influenced by both Pouchot's and Montcalm's lucid arguments, set plans in motion to form an expedition for just such a purpose.

During the late spring and early summer, Capt. Coulon de Villiers and his nine hundred-man guerrilla force worked on throttling Oswego by systematically raiding its supply lines. They continued to scour the upper waters of the Oswego River, frequently capturing stores and provisions meant for Oswego's three forts, thus keeping the British post's garrisons in a constant state of alarm and starving its commissary.[16] While the French were scheming to obliterate Oswego, the British finally conceded that a state of war existed and so declared on May 15, almost two years after Fort Necessity, with the French replying in kind.

Patrick Mackellar, one of Britain's ablest engineers, inspected Fort Ontario. His report is contained in "A Journal of the Transactions at Oswego from the 16th of May to the 14th of August 1756." He wrote:

> The fort on the east Side of the River called Fort Ontario is stockaded with good Timber and the joints squared, but the Plan is bad, its other Defects are as follows: The Barracks for the Men and officers are mostly built against the Stockade which loses so much of the Fire, the Gate is placed in an Angle and flanked on neither Side, which must be the Case in a Star as all the Angles are dead; there is no Banquet [banquette], nor Loop holes cut, but for the Canon, however there is a Gallery carryd round the top where the Buildings do not interfere, which has a good Command and renders the Work capable of a tolerable Defence against small Arms. . . . The Repairs in Fort Ontario are soon done except that of removing the Buildings, which cannot be done without removing the Troops, it is besides too expensive a Work to go upon without a particular Order.[17]

Two letters, one in May and the other in June, verified the harassments the garrisons were enduring:

> There is continually Scalping Parties about this place. There was, the day before I got here, Eight of them Scalped and Four Carryed off Prisoners. The Day after I gott here, Lieut. Blair with a party of 25 men that was sent to protect the bateaus coming down here was attacked about a mile from this place. Blair and two of his men killed. We killed, it is imagined, five or six, two of which we got, the others were carried off.[18]
>
> We are yet much troubled with scalping parties, large bodies lying within 6 or 8 miles of us, and as our garrison is not sufficient to dislodge them, they do us much damage. We are obliged to have large parties to cover the carpenters, others to clear the woods around the garrison. . . . For these past 10 days, we have quitted the fort on the hill [Fort George], it not being tenable.[19]

During the first week in July, Bradstreet, now a colonel, brought reinforcements and additional armament from Schenectady—four hundred militiamen and sixteen heavy cannon. Two weeks later, on his return trip, thirty of his boatmen were killed in an ambush set by de Villiers' vigilant French and Indians on the portage between Oneida Lake and Wood Creek. With the remnants of his party, Bradstreet made all haste down the Mohawk to Fort Johnson, where he reported to Sir William on the state of affairs to the north. When he arrived at Albany, he warned the authorities of Oswego's danger and begged them to send a relief force at once.[20]

There was a change of leadership, but not for the better. Shirley's penchant for short-cutting or disregarding military spending accounts and paperwork, his feuding with William Johnson, and his short-tempered dealings with other colonial governors and assemblies brought about his replacement. John Campbell, Earl of Loudoun, was the new commander, arriving in New York City on July 23. He spent a week there, enjoying the social frivolities tendered in his honor. He finally sailed up the Hudson to Albany. He scoffed at Bradstreet's dire predictions until the second week of August, then belatedly ordered Col. Daniel Webb, a chronic dillydallier, to form a relief force for Oswego, a much-too-late and useless exercise. Loudoun was not the bundle of energy that Shirley personified. His procrastination and inability to get along with military unit commanders brought about the catastrophic downfall of Oswego.[21]

Montcalm hurried his preparations. On August 4 he was able to leave Fort Frontenac with a force of about five thousand French, Canadians, and Indians, amply supplied with artillery, some of which had been taken during the rout of Braddock's army. Two days earlier a pair of schooners were deliberately scuttled in the channel at Oswego River's mouth to prevent any escape by boat. On August 6 Montcalm landed at Four-Inch Point in Henderson Harbor, east of Oswego. De Villiers's guerrillas reconnoitered the approaches to the British post and captured a group of returning, unguarded carpenters only a few hundred yards from Oswego's ramparts, surely an indication of British dereliction. Oswego's garrisons were composed of two new and inexperienced regiments, with Col. James F. Mercer in command of the whole defense. His subordinate officers were Lieut. Col. Littlehales and Col. Peter Schuyler of the Jersey Blues militia.

Montcalm moved his camp along the lake's shore to the swamp in the rear of Fort Ontario on August 10 and delegated the engineering operations to the able Capt. Pouchot. A road was cut through the swamp during the night and a strong battery was positioned within a hundred yards of the fort. During the night of August 12, under a covering of French sharpshooters, parallels were dug on three sides of the fort, only 180 feet from the fort's walls. The French cannonading, now at almost point-blank range, began to take its toll of Fort Ontario's ramparts.

By nightfall of the 13th it appeared that the fort faced certain doom. Early the next morning Col. Mercer ordered the abandonment of the fort and the garrison fled in disorder across the river to old Fort Oswego, neglecting to spike the evacuated fort's guns. At the same time Fort George, untenable in its incomplete state, was also abandoned to the French and its small garrison scurried down the hill to the old fort.

Fort Ontario's guns were turned by the enemy against Fort Oswego, while sharpshooters occupied Fort George to snipe at the defenders below. Montcalm sent a strong force across the harbor above Fort Oswego to cut off all retreat. French artillery finally breached one of the walls. It was about this time that Col. Mercer was killed by a cannon shot. Littlhales, assuming command, surrendered just when the French were at the point of mounting an assault.

There are differing versions of the surrender and the events that transpired immediately afterward. Colonial newspapers printed stories that insinuated that Littlehales "sold out for French gold," a claim that was never substantiated. An Indian interpreter at Oswego, John Newkirk by name, later said that Oswego's defenders were hopelessly drunk, having raided the rum stores, and that the only English killed were Col. Mercer, a gunner, and eight others. To add to the furor, British publications printed "eyewitness accounts" that the French-allied Indians had "murthered several of our soldiers as they stood on the parade and scalped all our sick in the hospital."

The reports claimed that more than 150 men were massacred; the French countered this accusation by stating that Montcalm had "turned the guns of his troops on the Indians to prevent a massacre of the prisoners." The English claimed that a little more than 1,500 people survived Oswego; the French put the figure at 1,700, of whom 120 were women. Reports of casualties and prisoners released by warring nations, even in our modern era, never agree, and were used for purposes of propaganda.

Montcalm captured 120 cannon, nine men-of-war in process of construction, and a great quantity of munitions, stores, and provisions. Two days after the capitulation, the spoils were transported across the lake to Fort Frontenac, more than enough to see that French post and Fort Niagara through the following winter. The hundreds of prisoners were conveyed by captured bateaux to Montreal for either exchange or ransom.[22]

Montcalm had no idea of retaining Oswego, a position that would have preempted a great many men at extremely high risk. He ordered the forts and the outlying works destroyed. Displaying another facet of his genius, Montcalm told the Iroquois that Oswego was theirs again, to have and to hold. The Indians were very impressed by this show of magnanimity. So effective was the French leader's master stroke of diplomacy that for the next two years Sir William Johnson had the utmost difficulty in obtaining a modicum of Iroquoian cooperation, an indication of the low state of British prestige.[23]

The French victory transformed Niagara's House of Peace, now freed from the dread of attack, into a social center. In addition to formal receptions and dinners, attended by officers' wives, Indians from near and far—Shawnees, Ottawas, Hurons, Cayugas, Senecas, Sioux—came and offered their friendship and the power of their tomahawks. The French showed their gratitude by showering the Indians with gifts of guns, knives, blankets, and a great deal of brandy. The French had long realized the importance of weakening the chain of friendship between the British and the Six Nations.[24]

In December William Pitt came into power in England, but even this change in leadership did not stem British military losses. In 1757 the ineffectual Loudoun failed to take Louisbourg; Montcalm captured and destroyed Fort William Henry at Lake George; German Flats was pillaged and burned by the French and Indians. But in 1758 the tide of war turned, even though halfway through the year Gen. Abercromby was deservedly defeated by Montcalm at Ticonderoga. In the same month of July, Gen. Amherst took Louisbourg, the first British victory of note in two years. In August the French suffered a disastrous blow with the capture and destruction of Fort Frontenac by Bradstreet, with Lieut. Col. Charles Clinton, father of New York State's first governor, as his second in command.

The Bradstreet expedition, conceived in secrecy, was the most daring colonial venture of the war. So effective were the security precautions—only forty Mohawk and Oneida scouts were employed—that the French had not the slightest inkling until the provincials appeared very suddenly before the ramparts of Fort Frontenac on August 26. Even the watchful Senecas, faithful to the Joncaires, were completely unaware of the enemy's presence on the Oswego River.

The two primary objectives of the expedition were to utterly destroy Fort Frontenac, which distributed munitions and supplies to Niagara and the Ohio forts, and to regain British prestige in the councils of the Six Nations. A third objective, to be attained by a good measure of luck, was the crippling of the French supply fleet on Lake Ontario. The destruction of Fort Frontenac would certainly enhance the chances of Brig. Gen. John Forbes and his expedition against Fort Duquesne at the Forks of the Ohio.

Bradstreet's route was the one established by the construction of five forts between today's Utica on the Mohawk River and Fulton on the Oswego River. In response to urgent pleas for protection by Mohawk Valley inhabitants, Brig. Gen. Stanwix was dispatched in the spring of 1758 to the present site of Rome, at the Mohawk-Oneida carry, to construct a great four-bastioned fortress, named for the general. Simultaneously, another and smaller post, Fort Schuyler, was erected at today's Utica, sixteen miles to the east. To the west of Fort Stanwix, on Oneida Lake, two more forts were built: the Royal Blockhouse at the mouth of Wood Creek and Fort Brewerton at the entrance to the Oneida River. The fifth fort—apparently never officially named but identified as Fort Bradstreet by at least one historian—was built at today's Fulton to guard the Oswego Falls portage. In addition, a military road between Fort Stanwix and the Royal Blockhouse was sliced through the wilderness.

Bradstreet and fifty-six hundred New York, New Jersey, and Massachusetts provincials sped through the Mohawk Valley to Fort Stanwix's construction site. Gen. Stanwix kept two thousand of this force to work on his fort, allowing Bradstreet a force of a little more than thirty-six hundred men, including scouts and a couple of hundred armed oarsmen. Since speed was essential, Bradstreet hurried them down the new military road to Oneida Lake where they took to the boats.

Advance scouts arrived at Oswego's ruins on August 20 and their careful reconnaisance proved the area to be completely unoccupied.

The following morning the flotilla came through the mouth of the Oswego River and sailed into the little bay. The men spent the afternoon and early evening hours transferring five days' rations, cannon, and ammunition to whaleboats. At about eleven o'clock on the morning of August 22, the invasion fleet pushed out into the lake. Hiding out by day on islands and traveling by night, the force finally landed three days later on a small island in today's Kingston harbor, a mile from the fort. The men observed with great interest the loading of a schooner and a brig with supplies, no doubt meant for French forts to the west and south.

At dawn's light, the flotilla was again afloat. The boats approached the mainland beach unmolested. The cannon were at once unloaded and dragged to about 400 yards from the fort's ramparts. Despite bombardment throughout the day, with answering fire from the fort's guns, little or no damage was effected on either side. An examination of the terrain revealed an abandoned entrenchment on the fort's north side, only 160 yards from the fort's walls. During the night Bradstreet had some of the guns moved to that sector. The next morning the bombardment was resumed, but now with much greater effect, to the point where a serious breach was made in the fort's wall.

With only 110 men, sixty-year-old Capt. Pierre Jacques Payan de Noyan, commandant of Fort Frontenac, at the first sighting of the enemy, dispatched runners to Montreal with appeals for assistance. The square stone fort, about three hundred feet to each side, had a great bastion in each of the angles. About thirty cannon topped the walls. Within, in addition to the always-present French chapel, were the usual fixtures found in a large fortification: officers' quarters, soldiers' barracks, powder magazines, and storehouses for the garrison's commissary. The fort's inner and outer storage barns were crammed with munitions and provisions. Also stored here were the furs from the country to the west and Indian trade goods. This under-defended great storehouse was indeed a valuable prize.

With at least one wall breached, and outnumbered almost thirty to one, Capt. Payan had no choice but to capitulate. On August 27 he brought down France's colors. Bradstreet's terms were very lenient. He allowed the garrison to leave, no doubt for Montreal, with the stipulation that they be exchanged for a like number of English prisoners held captive in New France. The fort was destroyed by Bradstreet's orders. Seven French ships were beached and burned, and two more were loaded with captured munitions, provisions, and furs.

Lieut. Col. Clinton had kept a journal of the expedition:

The French took all their money, clothes and the best of everything they had in boats with them and were permitted to go to any of their own garrisons (under parole). They were not insulted or in any respect treated but with the greatest civility. . . . After we took out of the fort what we could carry of the best things, we broke the trunnions of their cannon, broke down the wall[s] of the fort and burned all the houses, barracks, buildings, a vast quantity of provisions, which were immediately to be sent to Niagara and other forts to the southward.[25]

They sailed back to Oswego, arriving there on August 29. After the two French ships were unloaded and the booty transferred to whaleboats and bateaux, the vessels were burned the next day. By September 8 the elated expedition was once again in the Mohawk Valley, without the loss of a single man. Bradstreet left about one thousand men with Gen. Stanwix and returned to Albany, where he was received with great admiration.[26]

Clinton, in his journal, commented on the great damage to French efforts in the continuing war:

The destruction of this place and of the shipping, artillery and stores is one of the greatest blows the French have met with in America, considering the consequence of it, as it was the store out of which all the forts to the southward were supplied. . . . It was concerted and agreed upon in an instant (tho looked upon by some as a chimerical wild undertaking) carried on so secretly that the French never heard of us coming until they saw us.[27]

This astounding success was the death blow to French aspirations in North America; it was no less than the turning point of the war. A tremendous quantity of war matériel and provisions was lost. The seriousness of the deprivation was aggravated by the British naval blockades of the Gulf of St. Lawrence and the French ports in Europe. The almost simultaneous loss of Louisburg to Amherst pointed up the inevitability of total French defeat. The surrender of Fort Frontenac proved to be the death knell for Fort Duquesne which, bereft of supplies, was blown up by the French while Forbes and his men were less than a day's march away. The ruins of the French fort at the Forks of the Ohio were later cleared away and the British erected on the site a great new fort, named Fort Pitt for the energetic English premier.

The lethargic Abercromby was recalled to London and the command of Britain's American forces was placed in the care of Jeffrey Amherst. While the new commander was at Albany at work on massing a large cohesive force, the Iroquois were being influenced by Sir William Johnson at a council at Canajoharie Castle to come in greater numbers and join with the British, their friends, to witness the final blow to French hopes in North America.

From Schenectady in June, Brig. Gen. John Prideaux led an army of five thousand men through the Mohawk Valley. Men were detached from his force to strengthen the garrisons of Fort Stanwix, the Royal Blockhouse, and Fort Brewerton. Arriving at Oswego, he was joined by Sir William with nearly one thousand Iroquois. About half the army was left at Oswego under Col. Frederick Haldimand, for the purpose of constructing temporary field fortifications to protect the lines of supply. On the first day of July, Prideaux with two thousand regulars and Johnson with his Iroquois boarded their watercraft and sailed west to assault the French bastion at Niagara.

Four days later St. Luc de la Corne, accompanied by Father Picquet, led a force of twelve hundred French Canadians and Indians from Fort La Présentation to appear before the battered fortifications of Oswego. While plans had been laid to build a new fort, Haldimand erected barricades of flourbags and pork barrels amid the ruins of Fort Ontario. The British withstood all the enemy's attacks, during which St. Luc was wounded, and finally emerged from their entrenchments and drove the French back to their boats in full retreat. The French suffered humiliating losses while the British sustained very light damage to life and limb.

After an eighteen-day siege, during which Gen. Prideaux was killed by the bursting of one of his own guns, Fort Niagara capitulated on July 25. The end of French dominance in Canada was hastened by the fall of Quebec on September 18.

In August the temporary barricades at Oswego were removed to permit the beginning of construction of the second Fort Ontario under the supervision of Brig. Gen. Thomas Gage. The new fort, much larger and stronger than the first, was utilized by the British during the final phases of the war, as well as during the 1760s, the Revolution, and right up to their evacuation in 1796.

In 1760 Fort Ontario was used as the base of operations against Montreal. Lord Amherst, with ten thousand regulars, accompanied by Johnson with thirteen hundred Iroquois, fitted up at the new fortress. A large force was left at Oswego to further strengthen the works and augment the garrison. The aggregation of resplendently uniformed troops and war-painted Indians was indeed the most astounding spectacle that the North American wilderness had ever seen. The surrender of Montreal signalized the complete surrender of all Canada by the French. The formal treaty of peace provided for the ceding to England of practically all the French overseas empire, with the exception of two small colonies in India.[30]

The Pontiac-led western Indian rebellion, coming only three months after the Treaty of Paris, was spawned by the insufferable treatment accorded the Indians by English traders and the settlers, who invaded Indian lands and largely denuded the forests that supported the game so necessary to the economic existence of the Indians.

For three years the forts and settlements in the old Northwest Territory were besieged and bloodied by the greatest Indian confederacy ever formed to oust the white usurpers. After his failure Pontiac was invited to Oswego to make obeisance to the Crown. The Ottawa Indian chief, by this time well on the way toward alcoholism, ran up a respectable bill for the rum he and his large retinue of allied tribal sachems consumed with unabashed avidity. The peace talks, emotionally heightened by the continuous imbibing of spirits, were held within sight of Fort Ontario's guns. The council ended on the last day of August 1766, at which time Sir William Johnson presented each chief with a silver medal inscribed "A pledge of peace and friendship with Great Britain." The chiefs, loaded with presents, got into their canoes and paddled their alcoholic way back toward the setting sun.[31]

The years following the end of the last French war in North America revealed the errant thinking of the British, who failed to discern the value of the prize they had won. In 1761 the Lords of Trade had arrived at the astonishing determination that Newfoundland was worth more than Canada and the Louisiana territory combined. Late in the same decade, this dim-witted standing committee of the Privy Council still adhered to the myopic, strictly commercial idea that, since the ultimate goal of colonization was to increase the dissemination of British home manufactures via navigation lanes, the colonial populations should be restricted to costal areas. No doubt this premise was inspired by the Hudson's Bay Company, the oldest commercial enterprise in North America, which had fought against Canadian settlement. The westward migration of the land-hungry, despite governmental frowns and Indian resistance, was the inevitable result of the population explosion in the ocean-bordering Colonies.[32]

The spirit of rebellion was spurred by the Fort Stanwix Treaty of 1768 and the Quebec Act of 1774, two British measures that were direct contraventions of colonial rights embraced in charters and grants and that closed the West to colonial expansion.[33] The sparks flared into flames in two small villages not far removed from Boston.

At the beginning of the Revolution, Oswego was deserted and Fort Ontario was well advanced toward decay. Because of its isolation, the British military in the spring of 1775 selected Oswego as an ideal place to formulate plans for war. Col. Guy Johnson moved his superintendency of Indian affairs from the Mohawk Valley and established himself for a time at Fort Stanwix. He arrived at Oswego on June 17 to meet with Capt. John Butler and the Mohawk chieftain, Joseph Brant.

Word was sent to the three westernmost Iroquois nations, calling them to a council set for the beginning of July. As many as one thousand warriors, with their wives and offspring, answered the request and the conference sat in the shadows cast by the dilapidated ramparts of Fort Ontario. The British were intent on cementing alliances with the Indians, who saw their unenviable position all too clearly: they were doomed to destruction whether they remained neutral or participated, on one side or the other, in a war that, in their understanding, had no other purpose than to determine which nation of white people would rule over a continent once occupied by only red men.[34]

The employment of savages as military auxiliaries was condemned by that master of rhetoric, Edmund Burke, when he delivered a three-and-a-half-hour Parliamentary speech in November 1777 on the immorality of his nation:[35]

The extremes of war and the desolation of a country, were sweet-sounding mutes and liquids; but their meaning was terrible. They meant the killing of man, woman, and child—burning their houses, and ravaging their lands, and annihilating humanity from the face of the earth, or rendering it so wretched that death was preferable. They exceeded all that the rights of war, as observed between civilised nations, would sanction; and, as no necessity could warrant them, so no argument could excuse them.[36]

In the late spring and summer of 1777 Oswego came to life again as the rendezvous for Col. Barry St. Leger's column, which was to support Gen. Burgoyne's drive for Albany. When the force began embarking for its march into the Mohawk Valley, the maneuver was observed by an alert Continental scout, Silas Towne, at his post on a small island (now known as Spy Island), a short distance east of Oswego. Towne waited until dark, then furiously paddled down the river some distance, to finally take the overland trail to Fort Stanwix, where he warned Col. Peter Gansevoort. The advance notice prompted Gansevoort to request reinforcements, which entered the fort just before the enemy's vanguard arrived.[37]

The turning point of the war was reflected in the double-barreled disaster that ruined the British campaign. A psychological stratagem compelled St. Leger's force into disorganized retreat after its siege of Fort Stanwix and the battle at nearby Oriskany on August 6. Six weeks later, on October 17, Burgoyne's army surrendered on Saratoga's farm fields. St. Leger's shattered army staggered back to Oswego, having abandoned all their artillery in the woods near Fort Stanwix. Pursued by

Continental units, the beaten British, Hessians, and Indians did not tarry long at Oswego but scattered to Niagara, Oswegatchie, and Montreal.

Abandoned by the British subsequent to Burgoyne's defeat, Oswego remained unoccupied throughout 1778. Fort Ontario became merely an overnight stopping place for military units in their movements between Montreal and Niagara. In order to make Oswego an unworthy place for even a rest stop, Col. Gansevoort in July dispatched a small force from Fort Stanwix to level and burn Fort Ontario and its auxiliary structures. They found the place deserted except for a lone woman and several children, who were moved to an isolated outbuilding and given a small supply of food. Though the instructions were to eradicate Oswego, the Americans did not completely destroy it.[38]

For a number of years after the Revolution, it was believed that Oswego had been continuously garrisoned by the British. In reality, the old military base remained quiescent until nearly the end of the war. Early in 1779 the Iroquois sought to have Oswego refortified and garrisoned in order to provide protection for their villages. Gen. Sir Frederick Haldimand, now governor of Canada, refused their request because his forces were required elsewhere. Hardly had the Iroquois been denied their application when the Onondaga villages south of today's Syracuse were raided and put to the torch by a large force of men under Gose Van Schaick and Marinus Willett.[39]

Although Col. Guy Johnson in the fall of 1779 urged the rehabilitation of Oswego the following spring, nothing was done. In 1780 and 1781 rickety Fort Ontario, partly burned out, was used on several occasions as a base for raiding forays led by Sir John Johnson and Walter Butler.

Finally, on February 18, 1782, Haldimand instructed Maj. John Ross, commandant of Carleton Island's Fort Haldimand, to proceed to Oswego as soon as the weather permitted, with the object of reestablishing a garrison there. Two preliminary inspections by Ross confirmed that the works there were indeed a shambles. Contrary to the claims of a few historians and a plaque erected outside the fort in 1905 by the Daughters of the American Revolution that the fort was rebuilt at this time, there is absolutely no evidence to support that conclusion. The British did construct a few buildings inside the fort to replace those burned by the Continentals in 1778, but there was no reconstruction of the main works, the ditch, or outer works.

The surrender of Cornwallis at Yorktown the previous October had depressed the British in Canada, with the border garrisons suffering a new low in morale. For this reason Ross issued instructions that the men, conveyed to Oswego by transport from Carleton Island, should not be informed of their destination. He furthermore requested that Brig.

Gen. Henry W. Powell, commandant of Fort Niagara, assign to Oswego duty all the men he could spare. Also stationed at Fort Ontario were Johnson's Royal Greens and Butler's Rangers.[40]

The following year Fort Ontario was almost surprised by a planned assault in the war's final action on the northern frontier. With the approval of Gen. Washington, Marinus Willett and a force of 470 Continentals slogged across frozen country in February to the very ramparts of the fort, but they had to abort the assault when they were discovered. During their unrewarding trek to and from Oswego, a cessation of hostilities had been declared between Britain and her rebellious offspring.

Despite provisions in the Treaty of Paris with respect to the national lines of demarcation, the British refused to evacuate the posts on the frontier until certain compensations were made by the victorious new nation. The Jay Treaty of 1794 definitely settled the argument, with the United States to occupy the disputed forts two years later. Fort Ontario was the last post evacuated by the British, surrendered to the Americans on July 15, 1796.

Oswego Falls Palisade
Fulton, Oswego County

Very little is known about this fortification. It had no name, at least none known to the Revolution's posterity. For want of a name it has been called the "Oswego Falls Palisade."

There is a dearth of archival evidence about it. It is known, however, that the defensive work was constructed by the British at the falls of Oswego (modern Fulton) in either 1758 or 1759, and was intended to guard the Oswego River route to Oswego on Lake Ontario.

Crisfield Johnson's history of the area has the most complete delineation of the stockade:

> Early in September [1758], the [British] army returned to Oswego. . . . A detachment (but whether detached before or after the expedition to [Fort] Frontenac is uncertain) built in that year (1758) a new fort, a short distance below Oswego falls. Its name, if it had one, is unknown. It was octagonal in form, with the sides curved inward, and the angles very acute, making it almost star-shaped. The west part of it was cut off where the Oswego canal was dug, but the remains of the rest could be traced down to a few years ago. Fifty rods below was also to be seen, within the recollection of the earliest settlers, the remains of another fortification, semicircular in form, situated on the high bank of the river; but this is supposed to have been built before

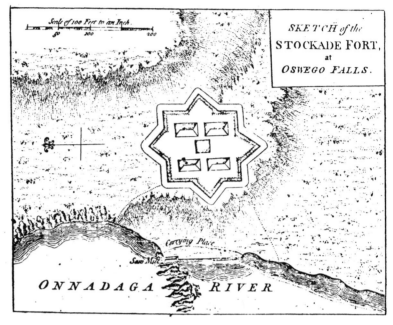

FORT BRADSTREET
Courtesy of Oswego County Historical Society

the coming of the white man, either by Indians or some still earlier race.

Minuscule hints say that the "fort" was still in existence into the 1770s, very possibly right into the early years of the Revolution, and that it was not normally garrisoned by either the British or the Patriots.

Fort Paris
Stone Arabia, Montgomery County

The site of Fort Paris is located about three-quarters of a mile east of SR 10, about midway between Hickory Hill Road (CR 33) and Stone Arabia Road (CR 34), in Stone Arabia. The fort was erected in early 1777 on land then owned by Isaac Paris (or his son of the same name), a native of the Alsatian city of Strasbourg.

Based on a combination of Mohawk Valley history, tradition, and hearsay, it would appear that Isaac Paris the elder came to the Palatine settlement of Stonearaby about the year 1737. Shortly after settling there, he opened a small store and trading post that included his living quarters.

When hostilities between the Colonies and the mother country seemed imminent, the Tryon County Committee of Safety was formed. Whether the original Isaac Paris, or his son, was a member of the Committee is not known. In any case, Paris was one of the twelve men who signed the minutes of the Committee's first meeting held on August 27, 1774, at the farm home of Adam Loucks in Stone Arabia. In December 1776 the Committee ordered the construction of a fort, incorporating Paris's home and trading store, and named the post for him.

A brief description of Fort Paris shows that it consisted of the Paris farm and outbuildings, the trading post, and a barracks for at least one hundred men, all surrounded by a strong palisade with a blockhouse on its western side. Unfortunately, no sketch or fort plan has ever been found.

The fort survived the Battle of Stone Arabia, October 19, 1780, though it was subjected to considerable attack by Sir John Johnson's destructives. About thirty dead, including Col. John Brown, commandant of Fort Paris, were found after the battle. According to an eyewitness, the bodies were interred in a common grave near the fort and the Trinity Lutheran Church (1792).

Revolutionary War records in the National Archives indicate that Fort Paris, during the years 1780 and 1781, was at times garrisoned by detachments of the Fourth Regiment of New York Continentals. Isaac Paris (father or son) was captured and killed by Brant's Indians sometime after August 6, 1777. Paris's widow was the first woman in New York State to be awarded a pension on the strength of her husband's service during the Revolution. Mrs. Paris later moved to Johnstown, where she lived out the rest of her years and then was buried in the Colonial Cemetery on Green Street.

Fort Plain
Fort Plain, Montgomery County

A plethora of distorted facts, based on exaggerated hearsay and erroneous traditions, was foisted on a gullible posterity by early Mohawk Valley chroniclers, notably Jeptha R. Simms. Even Benson Lossing, a much more astute historical reporter, was misled to some extent by the local gentry. Subsequent valley historians, including

Nelson Greene, were beguiled into accepting what was purported to be gospel, and they compounded the problem by repeating practically verbatim what had been written a century and a half ago.

The story of Fort Plain is a case in point. The strongest defense in the central region of the valley, situated near the confluence of Osquaga Creek and the Mohawk River, was never officially called Fort Plain, a name adopted by the inhabitants when a new fort was erected in the summer of 1780. The fort's official name was Fort Rensselaer.

Originally constructed in 1776 under the supervision of Gen. Robert Van Rensselaer, and occupying about a half acre of ground on the crest of a hill west of the village, the fort was an irregular quadrangle enclosing a small blockhouse and a barracks. The alchemy involved in changing the 1780 fort's name to Fort Plain is simple: the inhabitants heartily disliked Van Rensselaer and downgraded his debatable military talents. But the official name of Fort Rensselaer still held on, as evidenced by the reports and letters written by Marinus Willett, the so-called savior of the Mohawk Valley.

Historical data have recently been discovered to disprove the construction of an "octagonal" blockhouse in 1780/81. Archival evidence now establishes the certainty of a *square-shaped* three-story blockhouse, built in 1781/82 about five hundred feet to the northwest of the 1780 fortification while Col. Willett was in command of the Mohawk Valley. Sometime during the late summer of 1781, engineer Maj. Jean de Villefranche left Fort Herkimer (where he made some improvements) and came to Fort Plain, where he was requested by Willett to furnish a plan for a redoubt and a blockhouse to hold two hundred men and a large magazine. Willett approved the plan sketched by Villefranche, who sent a letter to Gen. Washington with a copy of the fort plan.

When Villefranche left Fort Plain in early October, no real work had been accomplished on the redoubt itself, but the two first stories of the blockhouse had been constructed. Washington's correspondence reveals that the blockhouse was still incomplete in May 1782 because of the lack of Continental funds to purchase the needed materials. Pleadings with the Continental high command finally produced an order to have the blockhouse and redoubt finished, which was done in the early fall.

Lossing, entranced by the "octagonal" blockhouse, describes the construction of the defensive work:

Ramparts of logs and earth were thrown up, and a strong block-house was erected. . . . It was octagonal in form, three stories in height, and composed of hewn timbers about fifteen inches square. There were numerous port-holes for musketry, and in the lower story

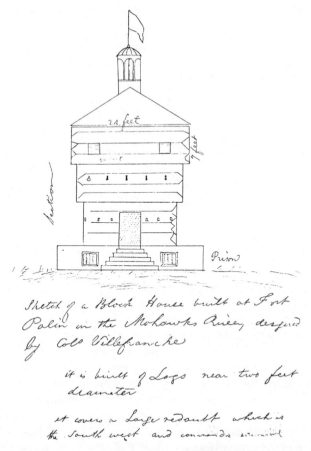

RECENTLY DISCOVERED CONTEMPORARY SKETCH BY
VILLEFRANCHE
OF THE FORT PLAIN BLOCKHOUSE
Courtesy of U.S. Revolution Papers, American Antiquarian Society

"Sketch of a Block House built at Fort Palin *(sic)* in the Mohawks River, desgned *(sic)* by Col. Villefranche. it is built of Logs near two feet diameter. it covers a Large redoubt which is the South west and commands extensively."

three or four cannons were placed. The first story was thirty feet in diameter, the second forty, and the third fifty. Each of the upper stories projected about five feet, and in the floor of each projection there were also port-holes, through which to fire perpendicularly upon an enemy below. The powder magazine of the fort was placed directly under the block-house for protection.

Some time after the completion of the work, doubts were expressed of its being cannon-ball proof. A trial was made with a six pounder placed at a proper distance. Its ball passed entirely *through* the block-house, crossed a broad ravine, and lodged in the hill on which the old parsonage stands, an eighth of a mile distant. This proved the inefficiency of the building, and its strength was increased by lining it with heavy planks. In order to form a protection for the magazine against hot shot, the little garrison that was stationed there in 1782 commenced throwing up a bank of earth around the block-house. Rumors of peace . . . caused the work to cease.

The village, in what was then known as the Canajoharie Settlements, was raided in August 1780 by about five hundred Indians and Tories commanded by Joseph Brant and Chief Cornplanter. Except for the fort, which was never directly assaulted, and the David Lipe homestead (on which site today's Nelson Greene House is located), all of Fort Plain was devastated. It was reported that fifty-three dwellings and a like number of barns were burned, sixteen settlers killed, and between fifty and sixty people, mostly women and children, taken prisoners. Hundreds of cattle and horses were driven off and the fields burnt to black ash.

The cries of supplication from the ruins of the Mohawk Valley finally had their effect. In the late spring of 1781 Col. Marinus Willett was prevailed upon by Governor George Clinton to undertake the defense of the valley. He could not have chosen a better man for the unenviable task. Willett made centrally located Fort Plain his headquarters. Shortly after he assumed command, Currytown was attacked. Willett led out his Continentals and militia and routed the enemy raiders in the battle at Sharon Springs, during which Capt. Robert McKean was mortally wounded. In honor of the slain officer, Fort Plain was renamed Fort McKean, but the new name was short-lived.

Four months later, in October, an army of Tories and Indians, under the joint command of Maj. John Ross and the notorious Capt. Walter Butler, again entered the Mohawk Valley. Willett's ready garrison caught up with the enemy at Johnstown. Following a sharp action, Ross and Butler retreated westward during the night. Willett took up the pursuit and engaged a part of the raiding force at a place now known as Butler's Ford on West Canada Creek. Capt. Butler, the "arch-fiend" of Cherry Valley, was shot through the head during the exchange of gunfire across the creek.

On July 31, 1783, during his tour of the Mohawk Valley, Gen. Washington spent some little time inspecting Fort Rensselaer and the exterior blockhouse. According to documentary evidence the fortifications at Fort Plain were still used for military purposes as late as 1786. The works were dismantled and the timbers helped in the reconstruction of the many houses and barns that had been burned by the enemy. Many of these rebuilt structures still exist, some of them in the village of Fort Plain.

In 1961 plans were begun for a reconstruction of the fort. But the project of restoration, despite the revelation of the three-story blockhouse, never got off the ground. Fort Plain Restoration, Inc., an organization of local businessmen, was dissolved two years later, to be replaced by the Fort Plain Museum, lodged in the Nelson Greene House. In 1975 there were no evidences of any regional desire to rconstruct the fort. Three years' research discovered the plan of the external three-story blockhouse but no contemporary plan of the fort itself. Archaeological programs begun in 1974 by the Fort Plain Museum reveal much more of the fort's general plan and outworks.

Fort Plank
Fort Plain, Montgomery County

Often confused with Fort Plain (Fort Rensselaer), two and a half miles to the northeast, Fort Plank was constructed in 1777 to strengthen the defenses of the Canajoharie Settlements. Frederick Plank, Patriot farmer, enclosed his house in a square of palisades with blockhouses at the angles. The fort often served as a refuge for numerous families during Indian incursions. Capt. Joseph House of the Tryon County militia lived with the Planks and commanded a small complement of men stationed in the blockhouses.

Fort Plank was attacked several times. One of the more serious assaults came in the first week of August 1780. Joseph Brant and a large force of his Indians entered the Canajoharie region (after most of the defensive forces were decoyed into going to Fort Stanwix to reinforce that post) and caused substantial damage, killing sixteen inhabitants and capturing many more who could not get to forted havens in time. In the midst of chaos Fort Plank successfully fought off a furious but short-lived enemy assault. The Plank house no longer exists.

Fort Plum Point
near New Windsor, Orange County

About three miles north of West Point, just beyond the Storm King and closely northeast of New Windsor, is Plum Point, the site of a Patriot battery called Fort Plum Point or Machin's Battery, named for the engineer who constructed it. During the Revolution, Plum Point, or Plum Island, was part of the large Nicoll family farm. Col. Isaac Nicoll, one of four sons, was for a time superintendent of the works on Constitution Island. In the Hudson opposite was Pollepel's (now Bannerman's) Island, the eastern anchor of Capt. Thomas Machin's *chevaux-de-frise* line.

Benson Lossing visited both New Windsor and Plum Point some little time before 1850, while researching Revolutionary sites for his history of the war:

> From New Windsor I rode to Plum Island, or Plum Point, the fine estate of Philip A. Verplanck, Esq. At high tide, this alluvial height, which rises about one hundred and twenty feet above the Hudson, is an island, approached by a narrow causeway from the main, which bridges a rivulet, with a heavy stone arch. Murderer's Creek [now the Moodna] washes its southwestern border, and a marsh and rivulet inclose it upon the land side. . . . I strolled down the winding pathway to the base of the steep river bank, where, overgrown by a new forest, are well-preserved remains of a fortification, erected there. . . . It was a redoubt, with a battery of fourteen guns, and was designed to cover strong *chevaux-de-frise* and other obstructions placed in the river, and extending from the flat below Murderer's Creek to Pollopel's Island. . . . The remains of this battery, the old Continental road, and the cinders of the forges, extend along the river bank several hundred feet. The embrasures are also very prominent.

Frantic suggestions came from all sides on how best to defend the Highlands and obstruct the passage of British naval craft up the Hudson River. George Clinton came up with the idea of sinking caissons and a *chevaux-de-frise* from Pollepel Island, standing off the eastern shore, to the west bank. The Committee of Safety, anxious to justify its responsibilities, seized on the plan. Apparently members of the Committee and the military had forgotten so soon the miserable failure of such devices between Fort Washington and New Jersey when the British drove the Continentals out of New York City.

Capt. Machin committed the plan to paper while George Clinton took five hundred men to Constitution Island to begin the building of the caissons. Although there was no want of energy, only a few caissons were constructed and submerged in a row from Pollepel Island to Plum

Point. Winter, an insufficiency of materials, and dimming interest put a temporary end to the project.

In January 1777 Machin returned. Two months later the *chevaux-de-frise* was completed and submerged, though anchors and cables for the readied chain were still not available and there were no cannon to protect the river obstructions. During the late summer more caissons had to be built and additional associated materials were required. While this project was progressing rather slowly, Machin built his battery on Plum Point. Available records reveal that the battery mounted fourteen guns at one time or another; there is some question what the battery's complement of guns was when some of Sir Henry Clinton's troops sailed up the river in mid-October, after they had captured the Highland forts, to sack and burn Kingston.

When Sir Henry's invasion armada of row-galleys and transports gingerly approached the river barrier, Plum Point's battery opened fire with five cannon. The crews of the transports successfully maneuvered their vessels over and through the *chevaux-de-frise* and caissons while three row-galleys engaged Fort Plum Point in a duel of shot and shell, with no reported major damage to either side. To confirm its uselessness, the barriers were even less of a problem when the enemy flotilla easily negotiated them on its return downriver.

Red Hook Barracks
Red Hook, Dutchess County

Located five miles north of Rhinebeck on the east side of the Hudson River, Red Hook was the site of an important American barracks.[1] The Patriot-built facility, continuously garrisoned, served several purposes.

The New York troops there guarded the area against Tory activists, provided protection for a Hudson River crossing, and maintained a protective guard around the Livingston family's powder mill located in Rhinebeck.[2] This mill was the largest producer of gunpowder in New York during the Revolution. The barracks was also often utilized as a rest area for Continental Army units moving from New England to the middle Atlantic Colonies.[3]

Fort Reid
Elmira, Chemung County

One of the forts erected by Gen. John Sullivan during his expedition against the Iroquois towns in the summer of 1779 was Fort Reid (also

Reed), named for its commander, Lieut. Col. George Reid. It was located at the junction of the Chemung (formerly Tioga) River and Newtown Creek, in present-day Elmira.

Built two days after the only battle of the campaign at New Town six miles away, the post was on the site of an Indian village named Canaweola, where twenty "good houses" and extensive fields of corn were set afire by Sullivan's destructives. The short-lived fort was erected on orders from Gen. Washington to Sullivan: "establish such intermediate posts, as you think necessary for the security of your communication and convoys."

Washington optimistically expected that among the primary rewards of the expedition would be the capture of the British strongholds at Niagara and Oswego:

> After you have very thoroughly completed the destruction of their settlements, if the Indians should show a disposition for peace, I would have you encourage it, on condition that they will give some decisive evidence of their sincerity, by delivering up some of the principal instigators of their past hostility into our hands: Butler, Brant, the most mischievous of the Tories, that have joined them, or any others they may have in their power, that we are interested to get into ours. They may possibly be engaged, by address, secrecy, and stratagem, to surprise the garrison of Niagara, and the shipping on the Lakes, and put them into our possession. They may be demanded, as a condition of our friendship, and would be a most important point gained.

But very few Indians were found in their mostly deserted villages. In addition, the expedition ran out of steam at Genesee Castle, the farthest point reached by the avenging army. On September 21 the first men of Sullivan's retreating forces began to arrive at Fort Reid, where they were greeted by a salute of thirteen guns; the elated, footsore soldiers answered with a like salute from their little six-pounder cannon.

For the next few days, as more veterans appeared at the fort, there was a great deal of rejoicing and carousing. The official celebration came on September 25 when five head of carefully selected cattle were barbecued and five gallons of spirits were issued to each brigade. Capping the festivities that evening, the whole line of men was drawn up and a salute of thirteen guns was fired as a preamble to the firing of a *feu de joie*,[1] which was repeated.

Even while the celebration was going on, detachments went up both sides of the Chemung and destroyed several more villages and additional large quantities of corn, with one of the columns going as far west as Painted Post. On September 29 the invasion army broke camp, destroyed the fort, and commenced the return to its original point of rendezvous.

Fort Rensselaer
Canajoharie, Montgomery County

In 1730 Marte Janse Van Alstyne and Hendrick Schrembling came to Canajoharie from a Hudson Valley Dutch settlement to inspect the lands they had purchased. They erected a log-and-stone house and mill on the east bank of Canajoharie Creek about half a mile from where the stream empties into the Mohawk River. In 1749 or 1750 Van Alstyne rebuilt the dwelling into a long one-and-a-half-story structure. It is located on present-day Moyer Street, named for John H. Moyer, who came into possession of the property some time after the war.

Because of its central location, the Van Alstyne home became the rendezvous for the Tryon County Committee of Safety, meeting there on sixteen occasions during the Revolution to direct the military and civil affairs in most of the Mohawk Valley. At the time of the Committee's meeting here on September 7, 1775, it had thirty-eight members. Early in the war the house was fortified, but Mohawk Valley historians are at odds on whether it was ever palisaded. It became known as Fort Rensselaer, though there is no record of Gen. Robert Van Rensselaer's ever stopping there.

Many distinguished people visited the Van Alstyne home during the Colonial and Revolutionary days. Gen. Washington was a guest there on August 1, 1783. Today the still structurally sound historic building is a private social club, owned and operated by the Fort Rensselaer Club, which restored and refurnished it some years ago.

Rheimensnyder's Fort
Dolgeville, Herkimer County

Henry Rheimensynder (Rheimensneider, Rhemensnyder) was one of the original settlers on what was known as Glen's Purchase, several miles north of Little Falls, included in the township of Manheim. He came there a few years before the beginning of the Revolution and, soon after hostilities began, built a blockhouse on his property now within the nearest environs of Dolgeville (called Snyder's Bush during the war). The inhabitants of this Palatine district came to the blockhouse on many nights for protection.

On April 3, 1780, a party of sixty to eighty Tories and Indians fell on the settlement. Strangely enough, the only structure they set fire to was the gristmill. They took nineteen men prisoner. So sudden was the incursion that most of the people fled to the woods instead of the blockhouse.

Col. Klock informed Governor Clinton of the raid in a report dated "Tryon County, Apr'l 5th 1780," in which he dwelled on the depopulating of the county:

> Honored Sir: Last Monday the 3d Instant a Party of the Enemie broot out here in a place Called Remersnyder's Bush, Consisting of Forty or Two & forty men; they have taken Nineteen of our men Prisoners; we have pursued them about Twenty five miles; Could not [go] further for want of Snow Shoes. This Remersnyder's Bush has been a Large settlement; now the People is all moaving away from there, Except a fue families that Lives in a Fort there, where I have kept a small guard. I am sorry that I must inform your Excellency that my oppinion is, if we are not very soon assisted with Troops, that this County will be Intirely destroyed, for the Regiments is but very small.

The raiders had come by way of Jerseyfield and they retreated by the same route, unsuccessfully pursued by the militia. There is no record of the blockhouse's ever being directly assaulted. A few years after the war's end, the blockhouse burned down, apparently through accident.

Sacandaga Blockhouse
Mayfield, Fulton County

Occasionally misnomered by nineteenth-century Mohawk Valley chroniclers as the "Mayfield Fort," the Sacandaga Blockhouse was probably built in the spring of 1777 as an outpost against enemy incursions. It was located about twenty miles north of the Mohawk in the old Mayfield Patent, just off Van Den Burgh Road near the point of the same name, and close to the southwestern edge of Sacandaga Lake.

There is no archival record of the blockhouse's dimensions, but no doubt it was constructed in the general style of frontier blockhouses. The defense was destroyed in June 1778 by a large band of Indians, most probably not directly connected with Joseph Brant's raiders, who entered the settlement, killed several men, burned some dwellings, and drove off a number of cattle. The site of the defense is memorialized by a New York State marker.

MAJOR GENERAL JOHN BURGOYNE
Courtesy of USMA Library

The Saratoga Battle Forts
Fort Neilson–Balcarres Redoubt
Breymann Redoubt–Great Redoubt
Schuylerville, Saratoga County

Old Saratoga was the place where a decisive Continental victory marked the startling turning point of the war. The Jane McCrea atrocity, propagandized by the Patriots, brought an outpouring of militia and volunteers to swell the ranks of the American army determined to stop Burgoyne above Albany. Most important, the Patriot success encouraged a hesitant France to come out openly on the side of the Colonies. Without the aid of the French it is indeed problematical whether the Revolutionary cause could have been fought to a successful conclusion.

The British campaign for 1777, the "Year of the Hangman," called for Gen. John Burgoyne's army to proceed from Canada along the Lake Champlain-Hudson River route; Barry St. Leger's troops were to march east from Oswego along the Mohawk River; and William Howe's forces were to move up the Hudson from New York. The plan was to unite all the armies at Albany, split the Colonies, and put an end to the American rebellion.

Unfortunately for Burgoyne, Gen. Howe failed to adhere to the original three-winged invasion plan. He instead took the bulk of his army and led a seaborne expedition against Philadelphia, leaving only a minuscule force under Sir Henry Clinton to invade the Hudson Highlands. It was Lord Germain's impractical hope that Howe would return to New York in time to fully cooperate with Burgoyne. A change of heart, in any case, would have been too late, because Howe was already at sea and committed to the Philadelphia campaign. Any hope of success of Burgoyne's invasion depended on simultaneous supportive action from the other two armies. As it turned out, because of British blundering Gentleman Johnny and his army found themselves isolated in a vast and hostile wilderness.

Burgoyne left St. Johns (St. Jean), Canada, on June 17, with a force of ninety-four hundred men consisting of British regulars, Hessian troops, Tory and Canadian auxiliaries, and hundreds of Indians.[1] On July 6, after a four-day siege, Fort Ticonderoga fell. Continuing southward through Skenesborough, Fort Anne, and Fort Edward, the British army was continuously hindered by wild terrain and the persistent delaying tactics of Gen. Philip Schuyler. The Patriots employed the scorched-earth policy as they toppled trees, destroyed bridges, and burned valuable crops in the barns and fields.

Both time and military adversities placed the British campaign in jeopardy. St. Leger halted his march down the Mohawk Valley to besiege Fort Stanwix in the first week of August. When, three weeks later, scouts informed him that strong reinforcements led by Benedict Arnold were on the way to the beleaguered fort, St. Leger was forced by his disorganized army into a frantic retreat back to Canada. Disaster befell the large detachment Burgoyne had sent to Bennington; on August 16 John Stark's and Seth Warner's forces practically annihilated the British column, inflicting about eight hundred casualties.

However portentous these military setbacks were, Burgoyne risked everything on the immediate future. On September 13 his army crossed to the west bank of the Hudson at Saratoga (Schuylerville) and headed for Albany. Four miles north of Stillwater they met the American forces under Gen. Horatio Gates, who had replaced Gen. Schuyler. The Patriots were dug in on Bemis Heights, a strong position where the road to Albany threaded through a narrow passage between the rugged hills and the river. Burgoyne had no choice but to pass through this defile. American artillery on the heights and in the redoubts that skirted the Hudson commanded both the road and the river. The British general was

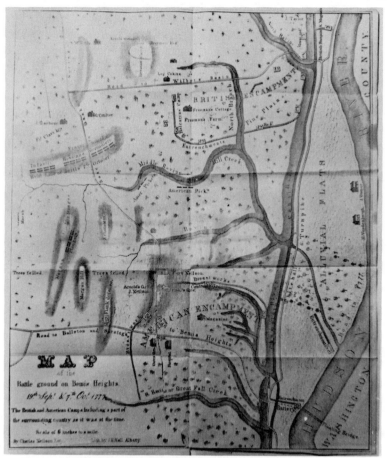

MAP OF THE BATTLES OF SARATOGA
Courtesy of Albany Institute of History and Art

faced with two alternatives: run the gauntlet, thus inviting certain
disaster, or attempt to force the rebels out of their fortifications.
Burgoyne elected to fight.

Thaddeus Kosciuszko, fervent disciple of the American cause, was a
colonel of engineers in the Continental Army. It was he who chose and
fortified the site for the Patriot defense. On the highest eminence of
Bemis Heights stood a barn, the property of farmer John Neilson. It was
strengthened by a double tier of logs on three sides. A circular form of
strong batteries extended about 150 feet south. In addition, the position

was encircled by a deep trench and a row of strong palisades. When it was completed, the defense was called Fort Neilson. About 800 feet south of it was another battery position, while in the rear, near the center of the American camp, was the bomb-proofed magazine. A deep ravine lay in front of the camp, with a dense woods on either side. Large trees were cut down some distance west of the fort and formed an almost impregnable abatis to challenge the enemy. Fort Neilson was considered a key point in the American line of defenses.

On September 19 the British advanced toward the Patriot lines in three separate columns, two of them through the dense woodland and the other, composed of Hessians, down the river road. It was Burgoyne's intention to consolidate a strong position from which he could besiege the Patriot fortifications. Col. Daniel Morgan was ordered to take his sharpshooting riflemen and reconnoiter the enemy's progress.[2] Some minutes past noon one of Morgan's detachments met and engaged the forward guard of the enemy center in a clearing known as the Freeman Farm, about a mile north of the American position.

A large-scale action ensued, and for more than three hours the fighting raged back and forth over the farmland. Again and again the British had to regroup and attempt charges with fixed bayonets, only to have their European-style battle tactics shattered by American riflemen, who fought Indian fashion, using natural cover.

Benedict Arnold skillfully placed American reinforcements where they could threaten to outflank the British right. At this point the Hessians on the river road entered the field and engaged the American right flank. There was a gradual Patriot withdrawal in good order, leaving the enemy badly mauled. For the time being Burgoyne had the field to himself, but still a mile from the American encampment. Burgoyne decided to wait for Clinton. He ordered his troops to entrench on the Freeman Farm.

The first battle of Saratoga was an Arnold-engineered victory. Even Burgoyne, later appearing before the House of Commons, testified that he owed his defeat to Arnold's bold generalship. Gen. Gates, as spiteful a man as any who appeared on the Continental stage, claimed all the credit, deliberately omitting any mention of the "whirlwind hero" in his messages to Congress. Arnold was for continuing the battle the next morning, while the enemy was still reeling, but Gates denied the plea for a renewal of the action. "A fierce quarrel ensued, in the course of which Gates told Arnold that as soon as [Gen. Benjamin] Lincoln should arrive he would have no further use for him." Except for the urging of fellow officers, Arnold would have ridden out of the American camp. He throttled his fury and "stayed in his quarters, awaiting the day of battle

. . . and Gates took no more notice of him than if he had been a dog."[3]

At the end of three weeks there was still no sign of supportive military aid from the south. Finally, in desperation, Burgoyne made his move on October 7. The next day, October 8, Sir Henry penned his *"Nous y voici"* note to Burgoyne from captured Fort Montgomery; Burgoyne never received it, Clinton's courier, Daniel Taylor, having been captured. Dr. James Thacher, Continental Army surgeon, had this entry in his *Journal* for October 14, 1777:

> After the capture of Fort Montgomery, Sir Henry Clinton despatched a messenger by the name of Daniel Taylor to Burgoyne with the intelligence; fortunately he was taken on his way as a spy, and finding himself in danger, he was seen to turn aside and take something from his pocket and swallow it. General George Clinton, into whose hands he had fallen, ordered a severe dose of emetic tartar to be administered. This produced the happiest effect as respects the prescriber; but it proved fatal to the patient. He discharged a small silver bullet, which being unscrewed, was found to enclose a letter from Sir Henry Clinton to Burgoyne.[4]

Patriot judgment was swift. Daniel Taylor was termed a spy, and as such, was tried, convicted, and executed.

Burgoyne's situation had become very critical. Opposed by a steadily growing American army (a Continental summons to the counties resulted in more than four thousand militiamen and volunteers showing up to swell the ranks), with no prospect of any aid from the south, and supplies rapidly dwindling, the British forces became weaker with each passing day; in addition, their Indian allies, tired of waiting for battle, had deserted. Burgoyne's dilemma was whether to advance or retreat. After suffering the throes of indecision, he finally determined to gamble on a second engagement with the enemy.

On October 7 Burgoyne ordered a reconnaissance-in-force to determine the strength of the American left flank. A force of fifteen hundred men, supported by ten cannon, moved out of the British encampment. After marching southwesterly about three-quarters of a mile, the troops deployed in a clearing. The greater part of the British front faced an open field, but both flanks rested in the woods, thus exposing them to surprise attack by the Patriots. American scouts reported the British move. In the middle of the afternoon, about three o'clock, the Americans attacked in three columns led by Col. Daniel Morgan, Gen. Ebenezer Learned, and Gen. Enoch Poor. The British line was repeatedly broken, with both flanks severely punished and driven back. It was during this action that Gen. Simon Fraser, commanding the British right wing, was mortally wounded and carried from the field.

Benedict Arnold, without a command because of the bitter altercation with Gates, acted on his own initiative and entered the field. He led Learned's brigade against the Hessians holding the British center. Under intense pressure from all sides, the entire British line retreated into their fortifications on the Freeman Farm. In the first hour of this engagement, Burgoyne lost more than four hundred officers and men, along with eight cannon.

The Patriots pushed their advantage. Again Arnold was in the forefront as he led relentless attacks on the Balcarres Redoubt, a very strong position 500 yards long and twelve to fourteen feet high, mounting eight guns. This position could not be carried, despite repeated assaults. Arnold wheeled his horse and, dashing through the crossfire of both armies, galloped northwest to the Breymann Redoubt, a single line of log breastworks 200 yards long. He arrived there just as the Patriots were assaulting both ends of the fortification. Hurdling the barrier to enter the works, Arnold suffered a serious leg wound. To memorialize Arnold's injury a controversial monument was erected in 1887 in the Saratoga National Historical Park. Without a doubt the most unusual piece of granite commemorating the War for American Independence, it is a likeness of Arnold's left boot.

Three days short of New Year's Day 1781, the Marquis Chastellux, accompanied by Gen. Schuyler, made a tour of the Saratoga battlefield:

General Burgoyne purchased dearly the frivolous honor of sleeping on the field of battle: he now encamped at Freeman's Farm, so near the American camp that it became impossible for him to maneuver, so that he found himself in the situation of a chess player who has allowed himself to be stalemated. In this position he remained until the 7th of October, when seeing his provisions expended, having no news of Clinton, and being too near the enemy to retreat without danger, he tried a second attack, and again wanted his advanced guard to turn the enemy's left. The Americans, with whom the woods were filled, penetrated his design, themselves turned the left flank of the corps which threatened theirs, put them to rout, and pursued them so far as to find themselves, without knowing it, opposite the camp of the Germans. This camp was situated at a right angle to, and a little in the rear of the line. Arnold and Lincoln, emboldened by success, attacked and carried the entrenchments: both of them bought the victory at the price of their blood; each of them had a leg shattered by a musket shot. I saw the spot where Arnold, uniting the boldness of a "jockey" with that of a soldier, leaped his horse over the entrenchment of the enemy. Like all those in this country, this was a sort of parapet, formed by trunks of trees piled one upon another. This action was very brisk, to which the fir trees, which are torn by musket and cannon shot, will long bear testimony.[5]

As night fell over the battlefield, Burgoyne withdrew his defeated troops behind the ramparts of the Great Redoubt, a system of fortifications erected to guard the hospital, the artillery park and supplies on the river flat, and the boat bridge crossing the Hudson. The next night, after interring Gen. Fraser's body within the redoubt, the beaten British started their retreat northward. They had suffered more than one thousand casualties, while the American loss was less than half that number.

Burgoyne took his decimated army to a fortified camp on the heights of Saratoga. They were now completely surrounded by the Patriot army, which by this time had grown to nearly twenty thousand men. Burgoyne now had no choice left him: he surrendered the remnants of his invasion force on October 17. By the terms of the Convention of Saratoga, some six thousand British and Hessians marched out of their camp and stacked their arms along the west bank of the Hudson River.[6] John Fiske wrote a fitting epitaph for Saratoga:

> The captured army was never sent home. The officers were treated as prisoners of war, and from time to time were exchanged. Burgoyne was allowed to go to England in the spring, and while still a prisoner on parole he took his seat in Parliament, and became conspicuous among the defenders of the American cause. The troops were detained in the neighbourhood of Boston until the autumn of 1778, when they were all transferred to Charlottesville in Virginia. Here a rude village was built on the brow of a pleasant ridge of hills, and gardens were laid out and planted. Much kind assistance was rendered in all this work by Thomas Jefferson, who was then living close by, on his estate at Monticello, and did everything in his power to make things comfortable for soldiers and officers. Two years afterward, when Virginia became the seat of war, some of them were removed to Winchester in the Shenandoah valley, to Frederick in Maryland, and to Lancaster in Pennsylvania. Those who wished to return to Europe were exchanged or allowed to escape. The greater number, especially of the Germans, preferred to stay in this country and become American citizens. Before the end of 1783 they had dispersed in all directions.
>
> Such was the strange sequel of a campaign which, whether we consider the picturesqueness of its incidents or the magnitude of its results, was one of the most memorable in the history of mankind. Its varied scenes, framed in landscapes of grand and stirring beauty, had brought together such types of manhood as the feathered Mohawk sachem, the helmeted Brunswick dragoon, and the blue-frocked yeoman of New England. . . . These men had mingled in a deadly struggle for the strategic centre of the Atlantic coast of North America, and now the fight had ended in the complete and overwhelming defeat of the forces of George III. . . . The triumph at Saratoga set in motion a train of events from which the winning of independence was destined surely to follow.[7]

When the news of the British debacle crossed the Atlantic, George III writhed in utter disbelief and Parliament was positively silenced in its astonishment.

Fort Schenectady
Schenectady, Schenectady County

Known in early colonial years by such names as Corlaer's Fort, the Royal or Queen's Fort (for Queen Anne), and Fort Cosby (for royal Governor William Cosby), this fort on the Mohawk River was all these things: fur trading center and northernmost fortified colonial outpost; major assembly point for English-Provincial and Revolutionary armies; Continental depot for armaments and supplies; and, in 1780, sanctuary for the persecuted Oneida and Tuscarora Indians.

For more than the first hundred years of its existence, it was considered absolutely essential to fortify Schenectady and post a garrison there. A very early petition by New York merchants pleaded "that a new fort be built at Schenectida which lyes twenty miles above Albany and is the utmost English settlement toward the Indians and French, and that fourteen guns and sixty men be placed there."

In early colonial days some settlements on the Hudson and Mohawk Rivers were protected by wooden walls or palisades. Because of the abundance of timber at their very doorsteps, the settlers depended on stockades for protection. In pre-colonial days, the Indians used this type of protection for their castles and villages. They almost universally utilized round poles and, to reduce the possibility of missiles passing through the narrow passages, two or more rows were fixed in quincunx order.

The Dutch were more practical. They employed poles of larger diameter, flattened on opposite sides so that all were fully in contact, with no interstice through which an arrow or bullet could enter. The stockade usually consisted of posts from twelve to eighteen feet long and a foot or more in thickness, sharpened at one end. After the planned line of the stockade was fixed, a trench three feet or more was dug, the poles set in perpendicularly, with flattened sides together, and the earth replaced and rammed against them. Strengthening the top of the stockade was effected by having two adjoining posts bored and fastened together with oaken treenails. Blockhouses or bastions were erected at the angles, with the usual insertion of only one gate in a palisade wall. The effectiveness of blockhouses was usually enhanced by armament.

Schenectady was planted in a strategic situation, surrounded by water and marshes on three sides, with only the southeast exposure open. The

THE WALLED TOWN OF SCHENECTADY (c.1750)
Courtesy of Schenectady County Historical Society

French and Indians knew the village as "Corlaer" for Arendt Van Curler who, with fourteen "freemen," founded the settlement in 1661 and immediately surrounded it with a palisade. These first Dutch settlers banded their homes together for their common protection, with their farms located outside the palisade. In today's geography the original plat started at State Street, with the line running along the east side of Ferry Street to about the old Episcopal Church, then straight to the north side of Front Street, just a little beyond Washington Street, then southerly and parallel to the same to State Street.

There was a blockhouse in one of the angles of the stockade that consisted of a double row of high palisades, with barracks, platforms, guns, and lookouts. Many years later, particularly during the Revolution, when the town became an important depot, barracks were constructed outside the walls. The south and west lines of the stockade remained substantially without change right up to the time of its removal soon after the end of the Revolution. The lines along Front and Washington Streets were moved north and west to the river bank, with the Ferry Street line, some time after 1765, carried southeasterly to the present-day Penn-Central depot and then north through the old Dutch Church burying ground to the river bank.

Hardly a year went by that the importance of having the outpost sufficiently fortified and garrisoned was not acknowledged by either the governor or the Assembly, or both. The period from 1688 to 1697 was the most critical in the history of Schenectady. During that time there came the destruction of the village by the French and their allied Jesuit-converted Indians, the massacre, and the captivity of many of the inhabitants, with the inevitable departure of almost all the survivors to Albany, New York City, and other havens of safety.

In anticipation of such an attack, Albany's mayor and civil and military officers met on September 4, 1689, and formed a Committee of Safety. After an anxious session it was resolved to express a message to Capt. Jacob Leisler, acting lieutenant governor in New York, requesting 100 more men, "a Recrute of six hundred weight of Powder and foure hundred Ball, viz. 200 Two pounders and 200 foure pounders with some match and one hundred hand Grenadoes."

Schenectady in 1690 was a village of eighty houses and about four hundred Dutch inhabitants, almost unanimously vehement Leislerian partisans. Jacob Leisler, Protestant leader, led an insurrection against the Council that had assumed a Catholic stand in support of James II, who was considered by the Protestants to be subservient to France's Louis XIV.

Leisler seized the fort in New York City and proclaimed Mary, James II's Protestant daughter, and her husband, William of Orange, the new rulers of England. Albany was governed by conservatives who adhered to the Stuart standard. The bitterness engendered by the royal controversy culminated in the destruction of Schenectady. When Albany's garrison sent a detachment to the Dutch village for its protection, the inhabitants there indignantly refused the soldiers and bade them return to their Catholic masters.

In defiance of repeated warnings by Albany's Committee of Safety, the Dutch at Schenectady foolishly removed the guards from the town's gates and, according to local legend, installed snowmen in the center of the gateways. The night of Saturday, February 8, 1690, is inscribed in the annals of Schenectady as the town's worst disaster. Peter Schuyler, mayor of Albany, was moved to write a few days after the murderous raid, "The cruelties committed at sd. Place no Penn can write nor Tongue expresse."

On that fateful night the Dutch were sound asleep in their houses while a blizzard raged. Just before midnight a force of 114 French and 96 Sault and Algonquin Indians, apparently on their way to attack Fort Orange

(Albany), arrived at the village and silently filed through the open gates. When all the homes were surrounded, the war whoop was raised. The night air was rent with hideous screams as the invaders battered down doors and attacked the half-wakened people with knife, club, and tomahawk.

Within an hour sixty inhabitants were slain, with no distinction made as to sex or age. The village was set aflame and seventy-eight houses were burned. Twenty-seven captives were taken and dragged through the snow-clad wilderness to Canada. At least forty horses were loaded with loot, much of it abandoned during the flight while the militia and an army of Mohawks pressed a close pursuit.

Schenectady, a ruination, was in danger of becoming completely depopulated. Albany issued stringent ordinances against removal and pleaded with the Mohawks to guard the remnants of the village. The inhabitants who had fled the butchery were loath to return. For seven years the village gained little or nothing in numbers until the 1697 Treaty of Ryswick (now Rijswijk), near The Hague, Netherlands.

According to a 1690 French account, there were two gates in the palisade—one at the north end of Church Street, and the other at the junction of State and Church streets. In later times there were other entrances, one at Front and Union streets. The foundations of the gates and guardhouses, where Ferry crossed State and Union streets, were unearthed when the town's engineers were laying water pipes in 1871. The first blockhouse, in the north angle of the stockade at or near the junction of Front and Washington streets, was destroyed in 1690. The second blockhouse was erected the same year between Washington Street and the river, opposite the west end of State Street.

Soon after the disastrous raid, the following order was issued by Leisler's commissioners: "Whereas it is judged necessary for to defend Schanechtede and to that purposed it is found requisite that a fort shall be erected to defend ye Inhabitants and oppugn the Enemy if should attack the same."

The second fortification was an extensive enclosure surrounded "by a triple stockade, a new blockhouse at every angle and in each blockhouse two great guns." Within were twenty-eight houses for the residents, two wigwams (more likely longhouses) for the Mohawk Indians, a large barn, and sties for the hogs. In 1698 the population of the township numbered 50 men, 41 women, and 133 children.

The Rev. John Miller's 1695 sketch of this fort is no doubt correct in all essentials. His plan shows that the fort extended across the west end of the village from State to Front Streets, and included much of the area between Washington Street and the *binne kil* (boat harbor). Miller was

chaplain to the British army stationed in New York City. He visited all
the upriver forts and returned to his native England the same year. His
manuscript is lodged in the British Museum.

The stockade shown on Miller's plan was probably erected on the site
of the original palisade. The first blockhouse erected after the massacre
was located at the foot of State Street, where it overlooked the farmlands
and Great Island, and is the southwest blockhouse of Miller's map. The
guardhouse of blockhouse design was at State and Ferry streets and
commanded the Albany road. Another blockhouse was at the angle
opposite the Episcopal Church, with the fourth blockhouse, larger than
the others, at about Washington and Front streets. Miller indicated two
entrance gates: one at the south end of South Street and the other on the
west side, which opened to the *binne kil,* the ferry, and the old river road.
The triple stockade was probably built by Indians and in their manner, of
light poles and not hewn logs; it had to be replaced five years later.

In 1698 the government sent one Col. Romer, a military engineer, to
inspect, report upon, and build certain forts needed on the coast and the
frontiers. After bewailing "It is a pity and even a shame, to behold a
frontier neglected as we not perceive this is," he strongly advised the
construction of stone forts.

On May 3, 1699, the governor downgraded the posts at Albany and
Schenectady, reporting that they "are so scandalous that I cannot give
your Lordships a low enough idea of them. They look more like pounds
to impound cattle than Forts." Letters and reports of all the civil and
military authorities combined to show England's reprehensible neglect
of the safety of the province. From the accounts, the condition of the
fortifications and barracks at Schenectady was indeed deplorable, with
the stockades completely rotted and the barracks practically uninhabit-
able. One critical comment said that "it was by no foresight or energy of
the Home government that Schenectady & its neighbors had been
preserved from a second attack & destruction."

New York's Governor Lord Cornbury, in his report of September 24,
1702, to the Lords of Trade, wrote that Schenectady was

> an open village, formerly stockaded round but since the peace they are
> all down, and that the stockaded fort is more like a pound than a Fort.
> There is eight Guns in it not above three for service, no garrison in it
> when I came but a serjeant & twelve men, no powder nor shot neither
> great nor small, nor no place to put them into.

The governor recommended that a stone fort be erected and garrisoned with "a captain and one hundred men." The following year
foundations were laid for a stone fort at Albany, and by the "advice of

Her Majesty's [Queen Anne] Council of this province repaired as well as possible the stockaded Fort at Schenectady."

By the year 1704 the Royal or Queen's New Fort had been built in the east corner of the village at the junction of Front, Ferry, and Green streets. This was the old fort around which all the traditions and legends of the Schenectady people are centered. Originally it was a double or triple stockade of 100 feet square, with bastions or blockhouses at all the angles. In 1735 it was substantially rebuilt of timbers on a stone foundation. The four curtains or ramparts were "about 76 ft. each and the four bastions or blockhouses 24 ft. square." While digging trenches for the installation of water pipes in 1871, the south wall and the fort's well were unearthed.

After the Peace of Utrecht, ending Queen Anne's War in America (1701-13), there was a long period of relative quiet, with no fear of war hanging over the heads of the frontier's inhabitants. The long peace, however, was shattered in 1745 with the outbreak of King George's War. Just before the war's end in 1748, marked by the Treaty of Aix-la-Chapelle, the Assembly in Albany passed an act to erect two new blockhouses at Schenectady.

Six years later, at the beginning of the last of the French and Indian wars, when the Schenectady fortification was called Fort Cosby, the Assembly voted to raise three thousand pounds "to be expended in fortifying" Schenectady. The appropriation was apparently made in answer to the following petition, dated August 31,1754:

To the Honorable James De Lancey, Lieut. Governor and Commander in Chief in and over the Province of New York and the Territories depending thereon.

The Humble petition of the Officers of the four Companies of Militia at Schonechtady and also the Magistrates and Principal Inhabitants thereof.

Most Humbly Sheweth that the security of this place as well as the preservation of the Lives of our Wives and children greatly depends on the strength of Fort Cosby as the only place of refuge in case of an Attack or surprize. The Hostilities committed by the Indians on our Neighbours and the Daily Expectation of their Attempts upon us also; Induces us most humbly to represent to your Honour the state of the said Garrison which Consists of 4 Curtains of about 76 feet each and four Bastions or block-houses 24 feet square, the superstructure built with timbers on a foundation of a stone wall about two feet above the surface of the earth.

On the Parade stands one Nine Pounder and one six pounder on carriages rotten and unfit for service. Nor is there any Embrasure or rather Port-Hole in the Curtains to fire them.

Above is a sort of Gallery Loophold but of little or no service. In each of the Bastions or Block houses Chambers stand of three or four pounder, mettle, very insignificant, Should the enemy make a lodgement in any part of the town; Nor is there Powder or any other Military Stores in the Garrison—Garrisoned with only an Officer, a corporal and sixteen Private men.

And we further beg leave to represent to your Honour the Ruinous and Defenceless condition of this town: the Block houses in Decay and the town open and exposed; and that the number of Indians passing and repassing is a daily burthen to us, too heavy to be borne to which add the Expenses of frequent Indian Expresses makes the weight still more grevious as there is no Allowance or Publick fund to Reimburse and we still groan our Losses, sufferings and fatigue in the Late War as well as heavy Debt then contracted.

To expatiate on the value of this town as a frontier of the Province would be troublesome, your Honour well knowing it to be the Key of a Large Country and of the greatest Consequence to the Metropolis as well as to the province in General you have the Honour to command.

Your Petitioners therefore most humbly entreat your Honour will be pleased to take the premises into your Serious Consideration and Grant us two Nine Pounders for each curtain and a Nine Pounder for each Bastion & that you would be pleased to give orders that the Port Holes be made to open and shut as in a Man of War, and to grant us a proper supply of Military stores, and such other assistance as you in Your great Wisdom shall think meet.

The Miller map of 1695 is the oldest and, though it lacks a scale and street lines, it is important in that it gives the historian a good perspective. The map of Schenectady made by British army topographers about 1750 appears in a book of thirty North American fortification plans published by Mary Anne Rocque at London in 1763. The line of palisades shown with blockhouses at the proper intervals and the Royal or Queen's Fort erected in 1704 in the northeast angle essentially represent the defensive works of Schenectady for more than half a century. The Vrooman map of 1768 depicts the fort, the marketplace, the two churches, all correctly placed.

Nicholas Veeder, who died in 1862 at the age of one hundred years at Glenville, a few miles north of Schenectady, had reported before his death that the fort was about twenty feet high and constructed of hewn timber, that it was dismantled at the end of the Revolution, and that the timber was used in the frame of the barracks erected at the south corner of Union and Lafayette streets.

The village during the Revolution boasted an armament of iron cannons and swivels, the largest of which were the "Lady Washington" and the "Long Nine-Pounder" placed in the streets to command the gates. Chastellux visited Schenectady on December 28, 1780. He reported that

this town stands at the foot of a small declivity, on your coming out of the woods; it is regularly built, and contains five hundred houses within the palisades, without counting some dwellings which form a suburb, and the Indian village [the Oneida and Tuscarora refugee camp] adjoining this suburb. Two families, and eight inhabitants, are reckoned to a house.

Today the Schenectady Stockade Historic District, established in 1962, encompasses the general area that was surrounded by the palisade erected by the settlement's founders. Within the district are some four hundred structures, about fifty of them with markers giving names of the early owners and the dates of construction before 1825. James Schmidt, President of the Stockade Association, stressed that "the Stockade is not a museum or a reconstructed area, but a community which had endured since 1661, despite time and tragedies."

Fort Schlosser
Niagara Falls, Niagara County

The only remnant of two old forts on the Niagara Frontier is a seemingly imperishable two-story double-flued chimney that has posed preservation and memorial problems for the city of Niagara Falls through most of the decades of this century.

The second oldest extant example of masonry construction in the region (Fort Niagara's House of Peace is the oldest), the chimney was first utilized in the two-story barracks and messhall of Fort Little Niagara (Fort du Portage). Built in the fall of 1750 by Robert de Clausonne, French army engineer, the fort stood at the head of the Niagara River's rapids a little more than a mile behind Niagara's Falls, and about a dozen miles south of old Fort Niagara.

Chabert Joncaire, whose influence shaped the history of the frontier, was Master of the Niagara Portage. His efforts during the next decade developed the village of Little Fort Niagara, which included log dwellings, a storehouse, a one-hundred-foot-long stable, a forty-two-foot barn, a forty-foot shed, a wharf on the river, and the fort's stockade that protected the blockhouse and barracks.

The French destroyed the fort in 1759 to prevent its use by the British then besieging Fort Niagara. The following year the British, needing a strong defense at the upper end of the portage, ordered Capt. Joseph Schlosser, a German officer in the Crown's service, to build a new fort. A much larger defense, an earthwork fort with four bastions, was constructed on the site of Fort du Portage, and called Fort Schlosser for its builder.

Capt. Schlosser, interestingly enough, made use of the chimney left intact after the French burned their fort. Since a strong garrison was to be posted at the new fort, a large barracks and messhouse were required. Peter A. Porter, descendant of the family that purchased the land on which the forts once stood, in his role of President of theNiagara Frontier Historical Society, wrote an article about the famous chimney in 1902:

> Just before their surrender of Fort Niagara the French had prepared the complete framework for a new chapel therein. This, the British carted over the portage and set up near and southeast of this chimney, even the belfry being placed on the roof. It was a two-story building, used as barracks above, and messhall below. Between it and the chimney they built a connecting two-story building. The first story of the chapel building, the messhall, evidently had a higher ceiling than that of the burned French barracks. For, in order to utilize the upper fireplace that existed in the chimney in the second story of this connecting building the British had to make the first story there of a less height than the lower story of the old chapel. In this addition or connecting building the first story was used as a kitchen, its upper story possibly as the sleeping-rooms for the soldier cooks, or more likely, as the sleeping-rooms of John Steadman, the master of the portage, after whom the whole house was always called, the Steadman House, and who occupied it for the greater part of a quarter of a century.

The Portage Road was the connecting link on the northern frontier between East and West, bridging the distance between Lake Ontario and Lake Erie. All the prominent actors in the history of the Niagara Frontier over a sixty-year span dined in the two messhalls, those of the French barracks and Fort Schlosser, both served by the same cooking fireplace.

During the Revolution the fort was garrisoned by a small force, serving as a guard on the portage, since the Patriot military never extended its operations that far. In 1796, according to the provisions of the Jay Treaty, the British evacuated all the posts on the northern frontier in American territory.

Fort Schlosser was garrisoned by a very small contingent, representing a caretaking crew, until the first hostilities of the War of 1812 required the posting of a larger force there. Early in the war the British occupied the fort for one day when a party of raiders went out to capture munitions and armaments. In December 1813 the British captured Fort Schlosser and burned it. All that was left was the stone chimney that had served the military needs of three nations.

Schuyler's Supply Depot
Stillwater, Saratoga County

The first of four forts at Stillwater, all approximately on the same site on the west bank of the Hudson River, was erected by Col. Peter Schuyler in 1709 and named Fort Ingoldsby in honor of Maj. Richard Ingoldsby, acting governor of the Province of New York at the time. The second was built in 1756 by Gen. John Winslow and called Fort Winslow in honor of himself. The third was constructed under the supervision of the Royal military engineer Col. James Montresor. These fortifications were stockaded and loopholed blockhouses erected for the express purpose of repelling Indian attacks and probably could not have held up against even the artillery of that era.

Continental Gen. Philip Schuyler, a descendant by marriage of Peter Schuyler, in an effort to stem the advance of Burgoyne's invasion army built a fortified supply depot at Stillwater during the first week of August 1777. In order to commemorate the place, with no vestige of any of these fortifications remaining, a New York State Historical Marker was placed at the approximate site:

> FORT INGOLDSBY BUILT 1709
> FORT WINSLOW BUILT 1756
> MONTRESSOR'S [*sic*] BLOCKHOUSE
> AND STOREHOUSE BARRACKS 1758
> SCHUYLER'S SUPPLY DEPOT 1777

Fort Skenesborough
Whitehall, Washington County

Fortifications involved in three wars were constructed at present-day Whitehall, in what was once Maj. Philip Skene's baronial wilderness empire of sixty thousand acres, with part of the domain spilling over into the disputed Hampshire Grants (now Vermont). The initial royal grant of thirty-four thousand acres (a tract later augmented by land purchases) on Lake Champlain in 1759 led the English-born Scotsman to establish Skenesborough (Whitehall after the Revolution) at the southern tip of the lake, the birthplace of the United States Navy.

The first structures in Skenesborough were the British blockhouse and barracks on a hill to the west of Wood Creek, erected during the French and Indian War. The hill has since been bisected by a road (SR 22). The site is between today's Presbyterian Church and the Masonic Temple.

The date of the fort's establishment is unknown, but reason suggests that the time was very nearly coincident with the awarding of the grant to Skene. At that time the garrison stationed there was the Fifty-ninth Regiment of Foot under the command of Col. John Wilkins. Archival sources do not reveal the name, if any, given the fort. Military tradition during that period leads one to believe that the fort was most likely named for Col. Wilkins, its builder.

In 1761 Skene brought thirty pioneering families to found Skenesborough, where the only marks of human occupation were the stockaded blockhouse and the garrison's barracks. By the time Ticonderoga was flamboyantly seized in May 1775, throttling a British plan to found a new political entity on Lake Champlain, unceasing energy and imaginative initiative had transformed the forest primeval into a very profitable far-flung barony.

With the labor of his black slaves, settlers, and a number of discharged soldiers whom he employed, Skene carved out a civilization, remarkable for that time, that included his mansion (Skenesborough House), settlers' dwellings, farms, gristmills, sawmills, iron foundries, and shipyards. His manor of limestone blocks stood on the east side of the harbor, in front of his oversize barn and facing the lake. It was opposite the fort and somewhat over two hundred yards from the falls of Wood Creek. The two-and-a-half-story edifice was fifty-six feet long and forty-six feet wide, with an attached wing thirty by twenty feet. Over the main entry was the famous keystone—"P K S–1770"—now enshrined in the town's Masonic Temple.

Skene had a sloop constructed for lake transportation and cut a road through the wilderness to Salem, nearly thirty miles to the south. He devoted special attention to the business of raising blooded horses and cattle, completing by late 1770 an immense barn and stables. The barn, 134 by 35 feet and built of native bluestone, was taken over by the British in 1777 and converted into a loopholed fort. One of Skene's early improvements was a sawmill with a mill dam on the east bank of Wood Creek's 20-foot falls. The sawmill was burned on July 6, 1777, by the Patriots, when they retreated before Burgoyne's offensive; the dam was destroyed by the pursuing British to allow passage of their boats up the creek.

In January 1775 Philip Skene was appointed Lieutenant Governor of Ticonderoga and Crown Point, but the proposed Province of Ticonderoga, with Skenesborough as its capital, was not meant to be. The Americans learned in April that Skenesborough's old fort was in a dilapidated condition, held by no more than fifty men armed with three or four small brass cannon and guarding a large stock of small arms, a great quantity of stores, and a forty-ton schooner. Left in the care of Andrew Skene, son of Philip, who was then in England, Skenesborough was a prize not to be ignored by the Patriots. Besides, the rebels had no liking for Philip Skene, an arch-Tory.

Ethan Allen and Benedict Arnold captured Fort Ti on May 10; two days later Seth Warner took Crown Point; and on May 13 a detachment under Capt. Samuel Herrick entered Skenesborough without opposition. Skene's schooner was captured and sent down the lake to Arnold who, renaming it *Liberty,* used it to raid St. Johns on May 17, where he seized the *Enterprise* (Gen. Richard Montgomery, in turn, employed these two vessels, and others, to attack St. Johns on November 2 during the Patriot invasion of Canada). Taken as prisoner were Andrew Skene, his two sisters and an aunt, fifty settlers, and a dozen blacks.

The family members were sent under military guard two hundred miles to Salisbury, Connecticut, where they were interned. When the elder Skene appeared in Philadelphia in June, he too was apprehended and sent into internment in Connecticut. Apparently both he and his son Andrew were released in October 1776 in a prisoner exchange. Philip went to New York to serve under Gen. Howe for a short spell and then attached himself as a Loyalist aide to Burgoyne during the latter's offensive. Andrew served with Gen. Fraser's troops during the same campaign. The two Skenes were surrendered along with Burgoyne's army at Saratoga.

Because of its strategic placement at the head of Lake Champlain and its value as a shipyard, Gen. Schuyler was ordered to occupy and fortify Skenesborough, by renovating and adding to the old entrenchments. While shipwrights and blacksmiths were building Benedict Arnold's Lake Champlain fleet, the first ships of the new United States Navy, a gang of Dutch carpenters was put to work producing the timbers needed for a two-story barracks, ninety-six by sixteen feet, with six rooms on each floor. The barracks, as planned, was not erected. Instead, upon the return of the commander of the Fourth New York Regiment, Col. Cornelius Wynkoop, from sick leave in early October, the men were put to work on a barracks only forty-five by twenty feet. The pressures of the time no doubt dictated the diminution.

By the 18th of October the barracks was completed and surrounded by a fortified stockade, built on or very close to the French and Indian War fort site. On November 8 Bernard Romans, engineer and cartographer, reported on the Skenesborough fortification. He described it as an irregular polygon that was "by its form indefensible with a vengence." He complained that the ground covered by the fort was so extensive that it required a minimum of three hundred men to defend it. Romans's criticisms cited a palisade constructed in the main of slabs, a flimsy pine gate only three inches thick, and the absence of a well within the large enclosure. When Romans suggested improvements, Col. Wynkoop rejected his advice and insisted that the fort would suffice as was, supposedly because his carpenters were very anxious to return home for the winter.[1]

Skenesborough had the reputation of being "a location of extreme unhealthfulness, which at that time, and for years afterwards, was undoubtedly true; for it is known the mortality here was very great among the soldiers of the garrison from 1775 to 1777, and was scarcely less in proportion, among the few inhabitants of the place, after the close of the war."[2] Exaggerated stories were related about the prevalence of giant mosquitoes. Isaac Weld, Jr., in 1795 toured the inhabited areas of the United States. He wrote that

Skenesborough is most dreadfully infested with mosquitoes. . . . These insects were of a much larger size than I ever saw elsewhere, and their bite was uncommonly venomous. General Washington told me that he never was so much annoyed by mosquitoes in any part of America as at Skenesborough, for they used to bite through the thickest boot![3]

Ticonderoga, the touted "Gibraltar of America," fell to Burgoyne's army during the night of July 5/6. The psychological spur to evacuate the fortress was the British preparations to fortify neglected Mount Defiance, the 800-foot eminence 2,200 yards from and overlooking the main works. While the fort's guns thundered a continuous cannonade, Americans stole out of Ticonderoga during the night and made for Skenesborough, the first group under Col. Pierce Long taking the water route, the second group, the main body of troops under Gen. Arthur St. Clair, going overland by way of Castleton. Burgoyne was not aware until dawn that the rebels were gone. Reacting with unusual decisiveness, he at once sent Gen. Simon Fraser after St. Clair, while he took up the pursuit of Long by water.

Relying on the boom and boat bridge between Fort Ti and Mount Independence to hold up pursuit (Burgoyne destroyed the undefended obstacles in half an hour), Long took his time, with the consequence that Burgoyne caught up with him at Skenesborough. To cut off Long's retreat to the south, three regiments were dispatched to effect an envelopment, while Burgoyne took the remainder of his men by way of Wood Creek to assault Skenesborough from the north. In his eagerness to entrap the fleeing Americans, the British commander did not give his overland forces enough time to get into position.

Skenesborough had been held by the Patriots for more than two years, during which time its harbor was the rendezvous for their Lake Champlain flotilla. In the harbor were five American vessels, the last of the fleet. The men crewing them put up a good fight but were soon overcome by greater numbers of the enemy.

The British captured the galley *Trumbull* and the schooner *Revenge,* but the sloop *Enterprise,* the galley *Gates,* and the schooner *Liberty* went down in flames amid explosions from their powder magazines. Other small craft, scows, and bateaux, loaded with valuable munitions, stores, and provisions, were destroyed. The rebels, escaping the enemy's trap, set afire every combustible, including the fort; the British quickly extinguished the flames and saved the fortification for their own use. The one hundred fifty surviving Americans of the Skenesborough garrison accompanied Long and his troops as they fled southward to Fort Anne. Because of Long's dereliction subsequent to the evacuation from Fort Ticonderoga, St. Clair was compelled to make a seven-day circuitous detour around now British-occupied Skenesborough.

Philip Skene was once again in his own home and hosted Burgoyne while the latter made the manor his temporary headquarters. The Second British Brigade garrisoned the fort. It was during this enemy occupation that Skene's barn was loopholed and fortified. In every direction there were encamped soldiers, including Gen. Riedesel's German dragoons.

Burgoyne occupied Skenesborough for three weeks while his engineers built roads through the wilderness and bridged swamps and creeks to allow his heavy artillery to proceed through ruined Fort Anne (burned by Long's troops) to Fort Edward. When the British commander was ready to move south once again, he posted 150 men—British, German, and loyalist provincials—in Skenesborough. Their stay was cut short by the British surrender at Saratoga.[4]

The Skene mansion was destroyed by fire, apparently set by the hand of Andrew Skene. In March 1780 Sir Frederick Haldimand ordered a raid on the American base at Skenesborough; selected to assist in the operation, Andrew assumed the sad task of destroying Skenesborough House.

During the War of 1812 the American military decided to reestablish fortifications at Whitehall (renamed from Skenesborough), in light of the vital shipyards there. A new blockhouse was constructed within the ruins of the old Revolutionary War fort. The barracks was erected on the site now located between a point just south of the Masonic Temple and the north end of the present-day railroad tunnel.

The Skenesborough Museum at Whitehall has an interesting model of the harbor as it appeared in 1776. Under a long shed outside the Museum are the well-preserved remains of the War of 1812 schooner U.S.S. *Ticonderoga* (1814), which was a participant in a naval victory over the British on Lake Champlain.

Fort Stanwix
Rome, Oneida County

The defiant defense of the American garrison at Fort Stanwix during that hot, critical month of August 1777 was substantially responsible for the turning back of St. Leger's army, the western wing of the ambitious Burgoyne offensive from Canada. St. Leger's march was aimed at fomenting a Loyalist uprising in Tryon County's Mohawk Valley, once Sir William Johnson's main sphere of influence. Its failure before Fort Stanwix contributed to Burgoyne's defeat at Saratoga in October.

Fort Stanwix was located at the Oneida Carrying Place, the one-mile portage between the head of navigation of the Mohawk River and Wood Creek, in modern Rome. It was a highly strategic spot on the water route between the Great Lakes and the upper Hudson River Valley. The importance of the site was recognized as early as the seventeenth century when the French, in 1689, built a fort, name unknown, on or near the position of Fort Stanwix to protect their trade route. There are also references to a nameless English fort built in 1728 at the same place.[1]

When the startling news of Montcalm's capture of the three Oswego forts arrived in the valley, the citizenry became very vocal and demanded protection; the outcry had its effect. In 1758 Abercromby ordered Gen. John Stanwix to take a force of men to the Oneida Carrying Place and there erect a very strong fortification. The cost of construction was estimated to have been approximately $266,000, a stupendous sum of money in those days of the French and Indian War. The fort, however, played a minor role during the remainder of the murderous conflict, and was allowed to fall into disrepair after 1760.

The Fort Stanwix Treaty of 1768, otherwise known as the Boundary Line Treaty, was a spectacular affair that lasted several weeks and marked one of the greatest triumphs in the career of that colorful Irishman Sir William Johnson. There were many barrels of rum and presents for the Indians and fine wines for the white dignitaries.

The treaty was negotiated by Sir William with more than two thousand members of the Six Nations of the Iroquois Confederacy. Millions of acres were bought from the Indians for the paltry sum of ten thousand pounds, and title to the lands was taken by Sir William in the name of

HUGUNINE'S CONCEPT OF FORT STANWIX

The view is from west southwest. The basic shape of the fort is correct. There are, however, some major mistakes: the pickets were on the glacis; there was an earthen redoubt in front of the main gate; the terreplein of the east and south walls were continuous over the main gate and sally port; the stream in the left center was much too large; and the barracks along the edge of the parade ground were not shown. No perspective drawings of Fort Stanwix have been found, so this late nineteenth-century rendition is the best available. *Courtesy of National Park Service*

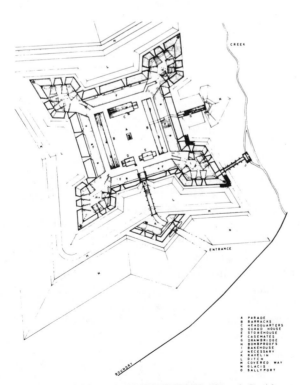

A PARADE
B BARRACKS
C HEADQUARTERS
D GUARD HOUSE
E STOREHOUSE
F CASEMATES
G DRAWBRIDGE
H BOMBPROOFS
I BAKEHOUSE
J NECESSARY
K RAVELIN
L DITCH
M COVERED WAY
N GLACIS
O SALLY PORT

FORT STANWIX NATIONAL MONUMENT (Wood Creek, upper right)
Courtesy of National Park Service

FORT STANWIX: AERIAL VIEW OF BICENTENNIAL
RECONSTRUCTION
Courtesy of Ed Miller, Rome (N.Y.) *Sentinel and National Park Service*

King George III. The immense tract lay in the rear of all colonies having
"ocean-to-ocean" grants in their charters. It meant, certainly, that King
George's possession of it effectively blocked all hope of expansion
accept on his terms.

The Six Nations ceded all land southeast of a line commencing at Fort
Stanwix and running to Fort Pitt at the Forks of the Ohio, along the south
bank of that river to the mouth of the Cherokee (Tennessee) River. The
Indians, by this treaty, surrendered all claims to lands lying roughly east
of this line, and their rights were to be protected to all else lying west of
the line. The pact made available for white settlement extensive tracts in
central New York, western Pennsylvania, and the regions now incorporated in West Virginia and Kentucky, erasing the old Proclamation Line
of 1763 now traced by the Blue Ridge Parkway. The Revolution, of
course, contravened the new demarcation line.[2]

In 1784 a new treaty, also effected at Fort Stanwix, between the

United States and the Iroquois (minus the Mohawks, who accepted a British offer of land in Canada, one hundred miles long on both sides of the Grand River), provided a new western boundary for the remaining five Indian nations. Four years later, in 1788, still another treaty was made at the same place, this time between New York State and the Iroquois, which threw open to settlement the major portion of western New York. The dignitaries present at this treaty included Governor George Clinton and Gen. Lafayette.[3]

In 1776, with the Lake Champlain forts, Ticonderoga and Crown Point, in the possession of the Americans, Gen. Philip Schuyler was ordered to repair and strengthen Fort Stanwix, then in a state of almost complete dilapidation. Col. Elias Dayton was charged with the task of rebuilding the fort, with the assistance of the Tryon County militia. The work, however, was not completed by the spring of 1777. In April Col. Peter Gansevoort of Albany, with the Third New York Continentals, numbering 550 men, took over the job. The twenty-eight-year-old colonel allowed no procrastination and the rebuilding went very well. The men went down into the Great Swamp to obtain cedar poles for the fort's palisades, and out beyond Fort Newport on Wood Creek to cut sod to cover the fort's embankments.[4]

The Patriots renamed the post Fort Schuyler, which caused no end of confusion among historians, for there was a Fort Schuyler, named for Col. Peter Schuyler, at Utica, built at the same time as the original Fort Stanwix. Official American dispatches often called it Fort Schuyler. Historians resolved the issue: they disregarded the change of name and called the fort Fort Stanwix.[5]

The fort had a perimeter of 1,450 feet, and in modern Rome's geography was bounded by Liberty, Spring, and Dominick streets, with the fort's parade spanning Willett Street. The stockade was about 14 feet high. The dry moat was immense, 40 feet wide at the top, 16 feet at the bottom, and 14 feet deep. On the outer wall of the ditch was a covert way or platform for the outguard. On the platform was a row of strong vertical pickets, and beyond was the glacis or embankment. The walls of the fort soared 17 feet above the parade and consisted of logs 2 feet square on the ends and flatted top and bottom, thus forming the barracks and storehouses. Against the walls all the earth excavated from the moat was thrown and then sodded, making for a strong earthwork that would accept cannon balls without doing damage to the main works. Out of the bottom of the moat and the covert way were tight rows of perpendicular palisades sharpened at the top. The parapet was embrasured to accept cannon.[6]

Between the southeast and northeast bastions the outworks were not

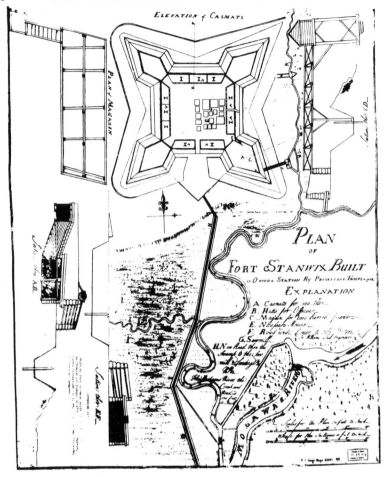

PLAN OF FORT STANWIX
Courtesy of Geography and Map Division, Library of Congress

"Plan of Fort Stanwix Built at Onieda *(sic)* Station By Provincial Troops.
EXPLANATION:

A. Casmats *(sic)* for 400 Men.
B. Hutts *(sic)* for Officers.
C. Magsin *(sic)* for 2000 Barrels Powder.
E. Necessary House.
F. Road under Cover to the Water.
G. Sawmill.
H. Road thro the Swamp, the Sawmill & Landing."

COLONEL BARRY ST. LEGER
Courtesy of USMA Library

so complete as on the three other sides because a nineteen-foot cliff and a swamp offered good protection for this sector. Two small streams traversed the swamp and ran out to the Mohawk River. Midway between the bastions on this side was a sallyport, out of which the soldiers proceeded to their chief water supply. On Sunday, August 3, 1777, the Stars and Stripes, improvised from a woman's skirt and a soldier's shirt, were unfurled above the fort's southwest bastion. Now, following our Bicentennial the controversy is still going strong over whether this flag was the first to be displayed by ground forces in battle.[7]

Lieut. Col. Barry St. Leger, veteran of frontier warfare during the French and Indian War, and graced with the temporary rank of brigadier general, left Montreal on June 23, 1777, with four hundred British regulars and went up the St. Lawrence to Carleton Island, which was used as a base for assembling a force of Indians under Col. Butler. On July 25 St. Leger arrived at Oswego, where he was joined by the two Butlers, John and Walter, Sir John Johnson, Col. Daniel Claus, and Joseph Brant.

John Butler had arrived from Niagara to exhort the Indians, promising them loot and downgrading the enemy's strength. St. Leger started his offensive the following day, three days before Burgoyne reached Fort

Edward on his march southward. St. Leger's heterogeneous force consisted of about two thousand men—half Indian (Mohawks, Senecas, and Cayugas), a third Tory and Canadian auxiliaries, and the rest regulars, Butler's Rangers, Johnson's Royal Greens, elements of Canadian militia, and German mercenaries.[8]

British intelligence misinformed St. Leger as to the condition of Fort Stanwix and the strength of its garrison. He was led to expect weak resistance on his march to Albany, where it was planned that the armies of the three-winged invasion would meet: his own Mohawk Valley column, Burgoyne's force, and Sir Henry Clinton's troops from New York. St. Leger's artillery support consisted of merely two three-pounders, two six-pounders, and four five-inch howitzers, inadequate both as to number and in fire power to reduce a strong fortification.

The supplies and provisions were boated up the Oswego River, across Oneida Lake, and up Wood Creek, while the army marched along the banks of the waterways. The vanguard of the column appeared before the ramparts of Fort Stanwix on August 2, just a bit too late to prevent reinforcements from entering the fort. This addition to the fort's garrison consisted of Lieut. Col. Mellon with two hundred men from Fort Dayton, accompanied by bateaux laden with sorely needed munitions, supplies, and provisions.[9]

Col. Gansevoort's garrison now numbered 750 men and the fort's defenses had been much improved. Friendly Oneida Indians kept the fort's commander aware of every St. Leger move. Fort Stanwix and its defenders were ready when the enemy's main force showed up the next day, August 3, a Sunday. Lieut. Col. Marinus Willett, the very competent second in command, wrote an account of St. Leger's arrival for the newspapers. His report was entitled "Narrative" and date-lined August 12:

> The enemy appeared in the edge of the woods, about a mile below the fort, where they took post, in order to invest it on that quarter and to cut off the communication with the country. . . . They sent in a flag, who told us of their great power, strength, and determination, in such a manner as gave us reason to suppose they were not possessed of great strength sufficient to take the fort. Our answer was a determination to support it.
> All day on Monday we were much annoyed by a sharp fire of musketry from the Indians and German riflemen, which, as our men were obliged to be exposed on the works, killed one and wounded seven. The day after, the firing was not so heavy, and our men under better cover, all the damage was, one man killed by a rifle ball. . . . Wednesday morning there was an unusual silence. We discovered some of the enemy marching along the edge of the woods downward. About eleven o'clock three men got into the fort, who brought a letter

from General Harkaman [Brig. Gen. Nicholas Herkimer] of the Tryon County Militia, advising us that he was at Oriska [Oriskany] (eight miles from the fort) [actually six miles] with part of his militia and proposed to force his way to the fort for our relief.[10]

In mid-July, when strong rumors of a British invasion had arrived at Fort Dayton, Gen. Herkimer put out a proclamation that ordered every able-bodied man between sixteen and sixty to be ready for duty when the call should come. He ordered the militia to convene at the fort when news came that St. Leger had appeared before Fort Stanwix. The Tryon County Militia was composed of four regiments, each numbering two hundred men. The First (Canajoharie) regiment was commanded by Col. Ebenezer Cox; the Second (Palatine) regiment, by Col. Jacob Klock; the Third (Mohawk) regiment, by Col. Frederick Fisher; and the Fourth (Kingsland and German Flats) regiment, by Col. Peter Bellinger.

Though the militiamen were green and undisciplined, a goodly number of them were sharpshooters. On August 4 they left Fort Dayton and headed west to reinforce Gansevoort's garrison, camping that night on Stirling Creek, east of Utica. There were heated debates among the militia's commanders as to which route should be taken. It was decided that the column and its long train of creaking ox-drawn wagons should ford the Mohawk and take the southern route. That night camp was made on the road between Sauquoit and Oriskany creeks, where they were joined by a small number of Oneida Indians.

Three scouts were sent by Herkimer to alert the fort of their approach and to advise it that a diversion on the part of the fort's defenders would assist the militia in gaining its objective. The plan was that Gansevoort should fire three cannon on receipt of the message, at which time Herkimer would start his advance. The scouts, however, had trouble penetrating the enemy lines and, instead of entering the fort at daybreak as planned, did not arrive until near noon.

As the morning hours slipped away and the signal was not given, Herkimer, against his innate sense of prudence, was argued into advancing by his hot-blooded, over-anxious officers, who foolishly accused him of Tory sympathies. Finally given the order to resume the march, the militiamen rushed ahead in great disorder and without any semblance of restraint.

In the meantime St. Leger had been made aware of Herkimer's expedition by a messenger from Molly Brant, sister of the Mohawk war chief and widow of Sir William Johnson. The British commander put scouts out in the countryside to advise him of Herkimer's progress. Early on the morning of August 6, a Wednesday, he sent most of the Indians under Brant, a large detachment of Royal Greens under Sir John

Johnson, and Rangers under Walter Butler, to waylay the relief column. Brant, sagacious in the ways of wilderness warfare, chose the place for the ambush, a ravine about six miles from the fort.

Herkimer and his noisy mile-long column entered the defile at about ten o'clock. His Indian allies, about sixty Oneidas, had not detected the enemy in the thick woods on either side of the ravine. Suddenly the ambuscade erupted, with the first firing directed at the ragged column's rear. Herkimer instantly reacted and turned his white horse in the direction of the initial burst of musketry. In the next moment Tories and Indians on both sides of him let loose. In the first firing from the woods nearest him, the general received a shattering musket ball through his leg. A wild melee ensued, with deadly hand-to-hand fighting.

For more than an hour the every-man-for-himself infighting raged up and down the ravine and in the woods. Then some order was restored as company commanders directed their men to a high knoll west of the defile and ordered them to form a defensive circle. At his request, badly wounded Herkimer was set in his saddle at the foot of a beech tree. Sword in hand, "Old Honikol" sat in the center of his men and directed the defense. Puffing on his old pipe, he ordered the militiamen to assign themselves two to a tree and to fire alternately.

During the height of the furious battle, the three-gun salute was heard from the fort. On this signal Marinus Willet led a sortie with 250 men and a cannon from the fort against the Tory and Indian camps, one of which was on the site of Fort Williams. This was the long-awaited diversion, but it came hours too late. Willett and his men destroyed what they could not carry back to the fort. Sir John Johnson's personal effects, plans, and orders, were part of the loot. Without losing a single man in the daring attack, they returned to the fort, escorting some prisoners who informed him and Gansevoort of Herkimer's plight. The garrison could do nothing except sit tight and anxiously await news of the outcome of the battle to the east.

The Tories and Indians, unable to make headway against the American militiamen on the hill above them, heard the sounds of firing to their west. Never for fighting endlessly against a strong position, the Indians decided to call it a day and evaporated among the trees. The Tories, deserted by their allies, and worried about what was transpiring in the Fort Stanwix sector, made a hasty retreat in that direction, leaving the bloody field of battle to the Patriots.

When the enemy returned to their camps, they found them a shambles. The Indians, practically naked in their breech-clout battle attire, found themselves completely beggared, with all their blankets, clothing, and cooking utensils having vanished. Instead of the rich spoils promised them by Col. Butler and St. Leger, they were now bereft of all their worldly possessions.

Herkimer and his decimated force took stock. The Dutchman was in serious condition from loss of blood. Most of his officers were either dead or wounded; among the ranks there were between 150 and 200 dead, with many other prisoners of the enemy. Gathering their wounded and putting Gen. Herkimer on a litter, the militiamen retraced their steps to Fort Dayton. That night they camped at old Fort Schuyler at Utica, and the next day "Old Honikol" was conveyed to his home near Little Falls, where he died ten days later.

St. Leger made additional overtures to the fort, pledging the garrison immunity from harm if they surrendered. The fort's officers were told that their position was quite hopeless since Herkimer's column was "defeated" and that they should not expect any aid from that quarter. In addition, Walter Butler, a member of the flag team, gave Gansevoort the big lie, that Burgoyne had already captured Albany. The offer of immunity was refused; Fort Stanwix would not surrender.

St. Leger then proposed a three-day truce, an idea with which Gansevoort was in full accord. Despite the tight cordon drawn about the fort, Willett and Lieut. Stockwell slipped out in the very early hours of August 9 and hid in the cedar swamp. Just before the light of dawn they worked their way through the enemy lines and headed for Stillwater and Gen. Schuyler's headquarters, about fifty miles to the east.

Already cognizant of St. Leger's presence before Fort Stanwix, Schuyler received the additional disturbing news of the bloody battle at Oriskany. He was confronted with the dilemma of how to deal with the danger to the Mohawk Valley, in light of the fact that Burgoyne and his army were at Fort Edward, only twenty-four miles from Stillwater.

Over the vehement objections of many of his officers, some of whom were New Englanders concerned only with their own home region, Schuyler decided to make the effort to save the Mohawk Valley. Throttling his fury at insinuations of recklessness and betrayal of trust, he declared that he would shoulder the responsibility for his decision. Apparently the only officer who wholeheartedly supported Schuyler was the hero of Valcour Bay, the dashing Benedict Arnold. He was given the assignment of taking 750 New York and Massachusetts Continentals to the beleaguered fort. Arnold left Stillwater the next night and arrived at Fort Dayton on August 21, at which time his force was augmented by 100 Tryon County militiamen. A plan to alarm St. Leger was devised.

A Tory prisoner, John Joost Schuyler, supposedly a nephew of Nicholas Herkimer, had been condemned to death for his part in a plot to start a Loyalist uprising in Tryon County. Arnold told "Hon-Yost" Schuyler that his life would be spared if he agreed to effect a ruse so that St. Leger's forces would raise the siege of Fort Stanwix.

Timothy Dwight, during his meanderings through the Mohawk Valley, heard this historical anecdote and incorporated it in his *Travels:*

> Arnold proposed to him a scheme for alarming the enemy, particularly the savages, by announcing to them that a formidable army was in full march to destroy them, and assured him of his life and estate if he would faithfully execute a mission of this nature. Schuyler, who was shrewd, resolute, versed in the language and manners of the Indians, readily engaged in the enterprise. His father and brother, were, in the meantime, kept as hostages and were both to be hung without mercy if he proved unfaithful. One of the Sachems of the Six Nations, a friend of the Americans and of Schuyler also, was let into the secret and cheerfully embarked in the design. . . .
>
> Colonel St. Leger had pushed the siege and advanced his works within one hundred and fifty yards of the fort. Upon Schuyler's arrival he told [St. Leger's Indians] of his being taken by Arnold, his escape [from] hanging, and flight. He declared that a formidable army of Americans was marching with full speed to attack the British. The Indians, being thus alarmed, the chief, who was in the secret, arrived, as if by mere accident, and began to insinuate to his countrymen that a bird had brought him intelligence of great moment concerning warriors in great numbers, marching with utmost rapidity and already far advanced. . . . The Indians, already disgusted with the service, which they found a mere contrast to the promises of the British commanders and their own expectations, and sore with the loss which they had sustained in the battle with General Herkimer, were now so completely alarmed that they determined upon an immediate retreat. . . .
>
> They reproached him [St. Leger] with having violated all his former promises. He attempted to get them drunk, but they refused to drink. When he found all his efforts fruitless and saw they were determined to go, he urged them to move in the rear of his army, but they charged him with a design to sacrifice them for his own safety. In a mixture of rage and despair, he broke up his encampment with such haste that he left his tents, cannon, and stores to the besieged. The flight of his army (for it could not be called a retreat) was not a little embarrassed and distressing. After much fatigue, they finally reached the Oneida Lake; and there, probably, felt themselves for the first time secure from the pursuit of their enemies.[11]

After the fort's garrison had made repeated refusals to surrender, St. Leger instituted formal siege operations and had advanced his works to within 150 yards of the fort's walls when the news came of Arnold's approach. Bitterly disappointed with the disaffection of his Indian allies, the British commander could do no other than abandon the siege. On August 23 he gave the order to march—not for Albany, but for Canada.

On the same day that St. Leger's army deserted its camps around Fort Stanwix, "Hon Yost" Schuyler took off to the east and met Arnold's column. Apparently with a great deal of satisfaction, the Tory informed Arnold that his mission was successful. The relief reached the fort that night and was greeted with open arms. The next morning Arnold dispatched a column after the fleeing enemy, who had taken to their boats on reaching Oneida Lake, getting out of range of their pursuers just in time.[12]

Arnold left part of his force at the fort to strengthen the guard on the Mohawk Valley and retraced his steps with the remainder to rejoin the main army, which was soon to have a fateful meeting with Burgoyne's forces at Saratoga. Benedict Arnold may have missed his chance to do battle against St. Leger, but destiny saw to it that he should not miss the opportunity to cross swords with Burgoyne's Grenadiers and Hessians on October 7.

In 1781 Fort Stanwix, sentinel of the Oneida portage and the Mohawk Valley, was destroyed by fire and flood. The fortification was substantially rebuilt; the Patriots' name for it, Fort Schuyler, was dropped, and the renovated fortress regained its original name. The fort was never again engaged in any military action.

During the War of 1812 an emergency fortified blockhouse was constructed on the parade ground because the whole works had fallen into ruin through neglect and had become utterly useless as a defense. The fury of that war, however, left the place unmolested. Beginning in the year 1828, the blockhouse and the surrounding dilapidated works were dismantled bit by bit as settlers and traders moved into the area. The site of Fort Stanwix in the course of years was buried under the homes and business edifices that eventually formed the city of Rome.

The National Park Service has undertaken the reconstruction of the fort, at an estimated cost of nine million dollars, part of a fifty-million-dollar combined urban renewal and Department of the Interior project. Archaeological excavations began in 1970 to unearth the foundations of the earth-and-log fortification. The reconstruction was the focal point in an eighteen-acre National Park completed by August 1977, the bicentennial of St. Leger's siege of Fort Stanwix.[13]

Fort Wagner
near Nelliston, Montgomery County

Originally a two-story all-stone farmhouse and fort, later lengthened by the addition of an unattractive frame house, Fort Wagner still stands a short distance from SR5, less than two miles north of Nelliston (the Mohawk River flows north and south here). One of the pioneer couples to settle in the Mohawk Valley district was Johan Peter Wagner (Waggoner) and his wife Margaretha Loucks. They had come, with some three thousand others, from the Lower Palatinate of the Rhine to settle in the Saugerties-Newburgh area, on lands offered the émigrés by Governor Robert Hunter.

The Wagners lived for a short time in West Camp, a few miles north of present-day Saugerties, then removed to the Schoharie Valley, where they remained for ten years. In 1722 they moved with about three hundred others to lands in the Mohawk Valley. This group of Palatines had had problems with securing titles to Schoharie Valley lands already patented to others.

The Wagners lived until about the year 1750. They left five or six children, apparently only one of them a son, Johan Peter II, who was born just about the time his parents took up residence in the Mohawk Valley. The second Johan Peter built the stone house in 1750. Soon after the start of the Revolution, he fortified and palisaded his dwelling, with a blockhouse inside the enclosure to billet troops and provide a refuge for the local inhabitants. Tories and Indians under Sir John Johnson, during their invasion in the fall of 1780, attacked the fort but were repulsed.

Johan Peter the younger was a lieutenant colonel in Tryon County's Palatine Regiment of militia and participated, with three sons, in the Battle of Oriskany. The old stone house, still fairly sound structurally but thoroughly neglected, is unoccupied.

Fort Walrath
St. Johnsville, Montgomery County

An unmanned blockhouse on the land of Henry Walrath, some little distance from his farmhouse dwelling, Fort Walrath was burned to the ground by Sir John Johnson's Indian auxiliaries during their destructive October, 1780 invasion. Simms says that the blockhouse was destroyed in "the August invasion of 1780," but it is more likely it was burned two months later. Fort Walrath stood near Fort Willett (one mile south of St. Johnsville), which was erected in 1780/81.

Fort Willett
St. Johnsville, Montgomery County

The devastation of the Mohawk Valley's Palatine strip by Sir John Johnson's raiders in the fall of 1780 pointed up the urgent need for additional defenses. After the Tory and Indian incursion a new fortification, named for Marinus Willett, was started on the rising ground south of the Mohawk, about one mile below St. Johnsville and four miles northwest of Fort Plain. It probably was not completed until the spring of 1781.

The fort's palisades, mostly of oak and contributed by farmers in the area, were fifteen feet high, with blockhouses at the northeast and southwest angles. The east palisade had a wagon entrance and the north palisade had a small gateway leading to a well. It was reported that the enclosure could hold a thousand people. Because of this ample accommodation, the fort was provided with a huge oven, the debris of which remained on the site for many years. Outside the fort's walls were log stables to shelter the inhabitants' livestock. The Montgomery County Department of History and Archives, contrary to the writings of Mohawk Valley chroniclers, says that Fort Willett was a "fortified wooden farm house, since taken down in mid-19th century."

When notified that the fort was completed, Col. Marinus Willett rode out from his headquarters at Fort Plain to inspect the defense. He was very pleased with the results and said so. "You have a nice little fort here. What do you call it?" He was told that "it has no name yet. Won't you give it one?" With that, Willett replied, "Well, this is one of the nicest little forts on the frontier, and you may call it after me, if you please."

After the war each farming family that had contributed the stockade took home its share of the pickets and the fort was torn down, just as many other frontier posts were demolished when their usefulness was at an end.

Fort Williams
Salem, Washington County

Originally Salem's first Presbyterian Church, started in 1774, the structure was never fully completed when it was taken over by the Patriot military at the beginning of the Revolution. At first it was occupied as a barracks, then it was fortified as the settlement's only defense, commanded by Col. Joseph McCracken.

For a short time the transformed church was called Salem Fort; then, in deference to Gen. (Doctor) John Williams, it was renamed Fort Williams. The church-fort had a short life. The inhabitants of the settlement were compelled to flee before the advance of Burgoyne's army and the fort was put to the torch by the enemy, probably during the last days of August 1777.

Fort Windecker
Minden, Montgomery County

The stockaded and fortified farm dwelling of Johannes Windecker stood on the river road, south of the Mohawk in the village of Minden, at the western edge of today's Montgomery County. Located one-and-a-half miles south of St. Johnsville (on the north side of the river) and about eight miles northwest of Fort Plain, Fort Windecker was one of the better fortified Mohawk Valley homes, with a blockhouse in one of the palisade's angles.

It is believed that the Windecker dwelling was stockaded in the spring of 1777, when the valley's inhabitants became increasingly apprehensive as the war became progressively more violent. Although there is no record of its having ever been attacked, it is probable that the defense, in the path of Iroquois war parties, underwent some minor assaults. The stockade was removed after the Revolution.

Fort Zimmerman
St. Johnsville, Montgomery County

From extracts of various records in the Montgomery County Department of History and Archives it is evident that the Mohawk Valley's prolific Zimmermans and Timmermans are genealogically branches of the same family tree. More than two hundred years ago local German and Dutch chroniclers, careless and inefficient in their chores, mistakenly and frequently substituted a T for the Z in the family's surname, thereby causing endless confusion for posterity's historians and genealogists. Nineteenth-century scribes carried forward the deception. Geographers, apparently in an effort at impartiality, named two parallel streams, less than a mile apart in St. Johnsville's environs, Zimmerman Creek and Timmerman Creek.

Records indicate that when Jacob Zimmerman, an émigré from the German Palatinate, left Holland, he had with him a *vrouw* (wife) and three children. Sometime during the first decade of his settlement as a trader in the valley (he was the first white man to permanently occupy land in what is now St. Johnsville), he wedded Anna Margareth, daughter of Tiyanoga, sachem of Fort Hunter's Mohawk castle, thereby indicating that he had lost his first wife. Tiyanoga was the celebrated Hendrick, one of four chiefs who accompanied Peter Schuyler to London in 1710 and were presented to Queen Anne. Staunch friend and aid to William Johnson, he was killed in the Battle of Lake George, September 8, 1755.

During the early years of the Revolution, two of Jacob Zimmerman's descendants, the brothers Conrad and David, fortified and palisaded their dwelling, which stood near their gristmill on Zimmerman Creek, about a mile above Fort Nellis. The fort was assaulted without success a number of times by bands of Tories and Indians.

The numerous family served conspicuously in the Revolutionary cause. Conrad Zimmerman was wounded at Oriskany but was able to return home under his own power. A 1971 Revolutionary roster, considered by its compiler by no means definitive or complete, of the Zimmermans and Timmermans, shows that at least fifteen members of the clan served in the Tryon County Militia; two of them were killed in action, while another was wounded and taken prisoner to Canada.

Notes

1 Frontier War

1. John Fiske, *The American Revolution,* 2 vols. (Boston, 1891), 1:1-2.

2. Frank B. Sarles and Charles E. Shedd, *Colonials and Patriots: Historic Places Commemorating Our Forebears, 1700-1783* (Washington, D.C., 1964):

> In 1700, settlements dotted the seaboard from Penobscot Bay, in present Maine, southward to the Edisto River in South Carolina. They were not continuous, and only in the valley of the Hudson River had they penetrated inland more than 100 miles. Seventy years later, however, settlement had spread down the coast another 150 miles, to the St. Marys River, and inland 200 miles and more, to the crest of the Appalachians. At intervals the restless frontier had swept beyond the Appalachian crest: in the south, to the headwaters of the Clinch and Holston; in the north, up the eastern shore of Lake Champlain and west along the Mohawk Valley, with the lonely outpost of Fort Ontario, on Lake Ontario; in the center—most significantly—past the former French post of Fort Duquesne, and thence 150 miles down the Ohio River.
>
> The westward movement flowed continuously but not evenly. Before 1754 it was slowed by the hostility of Indian tribes angered by the English invasion and incited by French and Spanish agents. In western Pennsylvania, where Indian resistance was weaker than elsewhere, settlement had crossed the mountains before the outbreak of the French and Indian War. But during the next 9 years the frontier line receded to the east side of the Appalachians, and in 1763, with French power crushed, England sought to reserve the trans-Appalachian country to the Indians. The colonists were not to be stopped. Before the outbreak of the Revolution they were firmly established in the upper Ohio Valley. P. 7

3. William R. Brock, *The Evolution of American Democracy* (New York, 1970), p. 22.

4. Irving Kristol, "The American Revolution as a Successful Revolution," Lecture, St. John's Church, October 12, 1973 (Washington, D.C., 1973), pp. 4, 8-9. Kristol delivered the lecture as part of the Distinguished Lecture Series on the Bicentennial. Quoted by permission of the American Enterprise Institute for Public Policy Research, which published the lecture the same year.

5. Randolph G. Adams and Howard H. Peckham, *Lexington to Fallen Timbers, 1775-1794: Episodes from the Earliest History of our Military Forces. Illustrated by Original Maps and Papers in the Clements Library of the University of Michigan* (Ann Arbor, Mich., 1942), pp. 1-2. Quoted by permission of Howard H. Peckham, Director.

6. Headquarters, Department of the Army, *American Military History, 1607-1958* (Washington, D.C., 1959), p. 47.

7. Ibid., pp. 47, 49; Mark Mayo Boatner, III, *Encyclopedia of the American Revolution* (New York, 1966), p. 412.

8. *American Military History,* p. 53.

9. Ibid., p. 49.

10. Erected in 1705 by Governor Claude de Ramezay, the chateau served as the official residence of French governors and the West India Company, and as the short-lived headquarters of the American occupation army in 1775 and 1776. After the Revolution, Benjamin Franklin stayed there as a guest of the Canadian government, which utilized the structure as its administrative offices. The chateau subsequently became an educational facility for Laval University's faculty. In 1895 the imposing building was relinquished by the university and converted into a museum. *Boston Globe,* June 9, 1974.

11. The publication of the Declaration of Independence appeared successively in the following colonial newspapers: first in the *Pennsylvania Evening Post,* July 6, then in *Dunlap's Maryland Gazette,* Baltimore, July 9, followed by the *Constitutional Gazette,* New York, July 10, the *Connecticut Gazette,* New London, July 12, the *Providence Gazette,* Rhode Island, July 13, the *New England Chronicle,* Boston, July 18, and the *Freeman's Journal,* Portsmouth, N.H., July 22. *Miami Herald,* February 10, 1974.

12. Various dates, from May 15 to 19, have been given for the post's surrender. Peter Force, ed., *American Archives,* 5th series (Washington, D.C., 1837-53), 1:158-61; Fred Anderson Berg, *Encyclopedia of Continental Army Units* (Harrisburg, Pa., 1972), pp. 78-79; Boatner, *Encyclopedia,* p. 191; Barbara Graymont, *The Iroquois in the American Revolution* (Syracuse, N.Y., 1972), p. 94; Howard Swiggett, *War out of Niagara* (New York, 1933), p. 71.

13. Fiske, *Revolution,* 2:83.

14. The fort's site is at River and Fort streets in the town of Forty Fort. The defense, begun in 1770, was so named for the forty Connecticut pioneers sent by the Susquehanna Company to take possession of the land.

15. Graymont, *Iroquois,* p. 168.

16. "In mid-April of 1778, possibly April 18, Walter Butler, who had been captured at German Flats the previous year, escaped from Albany with the help of Richard Cartwright, in whose house he had been confined on his parole." Ibid., pp. 164-65.

17. Ibid., pp. 167-68; Dale Van Every, *A Company of Heroes: The American Frontier, 1775-1783* (New York, 1962), p. 156.

18. Van Every, *Company of Heroes,* p. 155.

19. Jack M. Sosin, *The Revolutionary Frontier 1763-1783* (New York, 1967), p. 115.

20. Graymont, *Iroquois,* p. 174.

21. Boatner, *Encyclopedia,* p. 424; Swiggett, *War,* p. 143.

22. Boatner, *Encyclopedia,* pp. 221-25; William W. Campbell, *Annals of Tryon County* (New York, 1924), p. 112; William Leete Stone, *Border Wars of the American Revolution,* reprint ed. (New York, 1900), 1:346; Swiggett, *War,* p. 156.

23. Charles P. Whittemore, *A General of the Revolution: John Sullivan of New Hampshire* (New York, 1961), pp. 115-16.

24. Richard M. Ketchum, "Men of the Revolution," *American Heritage* (August 1974), pp. 30-31, 85.

25. Boatner, *Encyclopedia,* pp. 708-9, reporting on the raid and the subsequent battle, relied on Benson J. Lossing's *Pictorial Field-Book of the Revolution,* 2:101 n. for verification of the location of the devastated village, placing it about ten miles northwest of Goshen. Research and a careful study of Orange County maps have convinced this writer that Lossing was incorrect. Accounts of the movements of the militia and Brant's own

official report place the village within today's precincts of Port Jervis. This is supported by Donald F. Clark's article on the raid and battle: "A Look at Orange County History" in the *Orange County Government News Report* (September 1972).

26. Graymont, *Iroquois*, p. 215.

27. Graymont writes that the Americans killed twelve and took thirty-three prisoners, while "the Onondagas made homeless by Van Schaick's expedition went to live among the Senecas" (ibid., p. 196).

28. New York State Division of Archives and History, *The Sullivan-Clinton Campaign in 1779* (Albany, N.Y., 1929), pp. 132-33.

29. Ibid., p. 137.

30. Ibid., 138-39.

31. Richard M. Ketchum, ed., *The American Heritage Book of the Revolution* (New York, 1958), p. 310.

32. N.Y. State, *Sullivan-Clinton Campaign*, p. 149.

33. Swiggett, *War*, p. 204.

34. John R. Brodhead, *Documents Relative to the Colonial History of the State of New York*, E. B. O'Callaghan, ed., 15 vols. (Albany, N.Y., 1857), 8:797.

35. David M. Ludlum, *Early American Winters 1604-1820* (Boston 1966), p. 111.

36. Samuel Lane, *A Journal for the Years 1739-1803* (Concord, N.H., 1937), pp. 84-85.

37. Dave Richard Palmer, *The River and the Rock: The History of Fortress West Point, 1775-1783* (New York, 1969), p. 221.

38. Ludlum, *Winters*, p. 114; James Thacher, *A Military Journal during the American Revolutionary War from 1775 to 1783* (Boston, 1823), p. 221; Daniel Brodhead to George Washington, February 11, 1780, in *Pennsylvania Archives* (1855), 12:206.

39. Ludlum, *Winters*, p. 115.

40. George Clinton to the President of Congress, February 5, 1781, *Papers of the Continental Congress* (Library of Congress, Washington, D.C.), item 67, 2:348; Graymont, *Iroquois*, pp. 223-24; Van Every, *Company of Heroes*, p. 219.

41. The Oneidas' principal castle. The site of the village is near today's Sherrill, a few miles east of the city of Oneida. Barbara Graymont to the author, March 19, 1974.

42. Boatner, *Encyclopedia*, p. 88; Graymont, *Iroquois*, map, p. xii.; Robert West Howard, *Thundergate: The Forts of Niagara* (Englewood Cliffs, N.J., 1968), p. 14; Stone, *Border Wars*, 2:52.

43. J. K. Bloomfield, *The Oneidas* (New York, 1907), pp. 24, 117; Graymont, *Iroquois*, pp. 233-34; Van Every, *Company of Heroes*, pp. 34, 59; Anthony F. C. Wallace, *The Death and Rebirth of the Seneca* (New York, 1970), p. 126.

44. Bloomfield, *Oneidas*, pp. 94-95.

45. Ibid., p. 91; Graymont, *Iroquois*, p. 114.

46. T. Wood Clarke, *The Bloody Mohawk* (New York, 1940), p. 202; Graymont, *Iroquois*, p. 11.

47. Boatner, *Encyclopedia*, p. 562; Graymont, *Iroquois*, p. 111.

48. Boatner, *Encyclopedia*, p. 88; Henry B. Carrington, *Battles of the American Revolution, 1775-1781* (New York, 1877; reprint ed. 1974), p. 524; Clarke, *Bloody Mohawk*, pp. 275-76; Graymont, *Iroquois*, pp. 111, 223; Wallace, *Death and Rebirth*, pp. 126, 144.

49. Graymont, *Iroquois*, pp. 234-35; Wallace, *Death and Rebirth*, p. 131.

50. Carrington, *Battles*, p. 524; Fiske, *Revolution*, 2:97; Graymont, *Iroquois*, p. 235; Van Every, *Company of Heroes*, p. 236; Wallace, *Death and Rebirth*, p. 144.

51. Boatner, *Encyclopedia*, p. 992; Draper MSS. 11U200-201, Historical Society of Wisconsin; Graymont, *Iroquois*, p. 242.

52. Schuyler to Glen, November 6, 1780, Glen Papers, New York Public Library.

53. Marquis de Chastellux, *Travels in North America, in the Years 1780, 1781, and 1782*, ed. Howard C. Rice, Jr., 2 vols. (Chapel Hill, N.C., 1963), 2:208.

54. During the summer of 1780 this wretched "Continental" currency fell into contempt. As Washington said, it took a wagon-load of money to buy a wagon-load of provisions. At the end of the year 1778, the paper dollar was worth sixteen cents in the northern states and twelve cents in the south. Early in 1780 its value had fallen to two cents, and before the end of the year it took ten paper dollars to make a cent. In October, Indian corn sold wholesale in Boston for $150 a bushel, butter was $12 a pound, tea $90, sugar $10, beef $8, coffee $12, and a barrel of flour cost $1,575. Samuel Adams paid $2,000 for a hat and a suit of clothes. The money soon ceased to circulate, debts could not be collected, and there was a general prostration of credit. To say that a thing was "not worth a Continental" became the strongest possible expression of contempt. . . . Save for the scanty pittance of gold which came in from the French alliance, from the little foreign commerce that was left, and from trade with the British army itself, the country was without any circulating medium. In making its requisitions upon the states, Congress resorted to the measure which reminds one of the barbaric ages of barter. Instead of asking for money, it requested the states to send in their "specific supplies" of beef and pork, flour and rice, salt and hay, tobacco and rum. Fiske, *Revolution*, 2:201-3.

55. Graymont, *Iroquois*, pp. 243-44.

56. Boatner, *Encyclopedia*, pp. 83, 274-75, 488; Graymont, *Iroquois*, pp. 146, 242-44; Wallace, *Death and Rebirth*, pp. 153, 218.

57. Boatner, *Encyclopedia*, p. 492; Campbell, *Annals*, p. 151; Graymont, *Iroquois*, p. 230; Swiggett, *War*, p. 212.

58. Clarke, *Bloody Mohawk*, p. 239, mistakenly reports that the Snyder's Bush raid occurred on April 3, 1778, two years to the day earlier. Benton's *History of Herkimer County*, p. 90, says that the incident took place in 1780. Col. Jacob Klock, in his April 5, 1780, report to Governor Clinton, stipulates that the attack took place two days earlier, adding that "we pursued them about twenty-five miles; could not [go] further for want of Snow Shoes." On May 10, 1902, John B. Koetteritz of Little Falls read a paper before the Herkimer County Historical Society. He stated that the attack on Snyder's Bush took place in 1778. Not long after his address, the fifth volume of Governor Clinton's *Public Papers* was published, proving to the contrary. Mr. Koetteritz's paper was published in the Herkimer County Society *Historical Collections* without correction. Apparently, T. Wood Clarke obtained his information from this source.

59. Clarke, *Bloody Mohawk*, pp. 273-74; Sosin, *Frontier*, p. 133.

60. Boatner, *Encyclopedia*, pp. 88-89; Clarke, *Bloody Mohawk*, pp. 274-75.

61. Boatner, *Encyclopedia*, pp. 89, 180; Clarke, *Bloody Mohawk*, pp. 276-77; Graymont, *Iroquois*, p. 236; Sosin, *Frontier*, p. 134; Stone, *Border Wars*, 2:99; Van Every, *Company of Heroes*, p. 237.

62. Clarke, *Bloody Mohawk*, p. 277; Graymont, *Iroquois*, p. 237.

63. Herbert Aptheker, *The American Revolution* (New York, 1960), p. 133; Boatner, *Encyclopedia*, p. 89; Don Higginbotham, *The War of American Independence: Military Attitudes, Policies, and Practice, 1763-1789* (New York, 1971), p. 402; Van Every, *Company of Heroes*, p. 237; Russell F. Weigley, *History of the United States Army* (New York, 1967), p. 65.

64. Howard H. Peckham, *The War for Independence: A Military History* (Chicago, 1958), p. 61.

65. Participant in the capture of Fort Ticonderoga in 1775 and veteran of the Continental invasion of Canada the same year.

66. William M. Beauchamp, "Indian Raids in the Mohawk Valley," in New York State Historical Association *Proceedings* (Cooperstown, N.Y., 1915), 14:202-3; Boatner, *Encyclopedia*, pp. 89-90, 181-82, 191, 284, 389, 392, 445, 585-86, 990-91, 1130-31; Mark Mayo Boatner, III (*Landmarks of the American Revolution* (Harrisburg, Pa., 1973), pp. 292, 304, 309-10; Clarke, *Bloody Mohawk*, pp. 277-85; Graymont, *Iroquois*, pp. 237-39;

Howard, *Thundergate*, p. 142; Sosin, *Frontier*, p. 34; Stone, *Border Wars*, 2:216; Van Every, *Company of Heroes*, pp. 237-38.

67. Graymont, *Iroquois*, pp. 238-39.

68. Ibid.; Van Every, *Company of Heroes*, p. 238.

69. Hugh P. Donlon, in his *Montgomery County*, p. 46, reports that the Tryon County Board of Supervisors, just before Christmas 1780, had also assessed the damage suffered by Mohawk Valley settlers: approximately twelve hundred separate farmland units lay uncultivated; about 197 people were killed and 121 inhabitants carried off into captivity; 364 families had evacuated their farms to seek safety far removed from the flaming frontier; and "613 residents had defected and left for Canada to support the Loyalists"; Graymont, *Iroquois*, p. 240; Van Every, *Company of Heroes*, p. 258.

70. George Clinton to President of Congress, February 5, 1781, *Papers of the Continental Congress*, item 67, 2:351-52.

71. Boatner, *Encyclopedia*, p. 90; Clarke, *Bloody Mohawk*, p. 287; Graymont, *Iroquois*, p. 246; Van Every, *Company of Heroes*, pp. 259-60.

72. Ibid.

73. George Clinton to Col. Marinus Willett, Poughkeepsie, April 28, 1781, in George Clinton, *Public Papers*, 6:807.

74. To this day there is some confusion regarding the location of Willett's Mohawk Valley headquarters. The colonel's reports were dated from "Fort Rensselaer," a name used for both Van Alstyne's fortified stone dwelling in present-day Canajoharie and the Fort Plain blockhouse and stockade. Colonel Boatner is contradictory, but only by inference. In his *Encyclopedia*, p. 90, he writes: "His [Willett's] 'main body' . . . comprised 120 men at Canajoharie, where he established his headquarters." In his *Landmarks*, p. 246, he reports that "Col. Marinus Willett had his valley headquarters here ['Fort Plain (Fort Rensselaer) Site'] in 1781-83, when the place was called Fort Rensselaer." Other historians have similarly confused the two posts by failing to differentiate between the present-day towns of Fort Plain and Canajoharie. Even George Washington, touring the Mohawk Valley in 1783, mixed them up. Fort Plain's Fort Rensselaer for some little time was called Fort McKean, to honor Capt. Robert McKean, who was killed in the Sharon Springs Swamp battle.

75. Boatner, *Encyclopedia*, pp. 90, 103-4, 174, 962, 1207-8; *Landmarks*, p. 246; Clarke, *Bloody Mohawk*, p. 290; Marinus Willett to George Washington, July 6, 1781, *George Washington Papers*, Library of Congress, S-4, P-8, Microfilm no. 79; Van Every, *Company of Heroes*, p. 260.

76. Donlon, in *Montgomery County*, p. 47, estimates that Doxtader's force numbered about five hundred men, mostly Indians.

77. Beauchamp, "Indian Raids," p. 204; Boatner, *Encyclopedia*, pp. 90, 331, 998-99; Clarke, *Bloody Mohawk*, pp. 290-91; Hugh P. Donlon, *Outlines of History: Montgomery County, State of New York* (Amsterdam, N.Y., 1973), p. 47; Benson J. Lossing, *The Pictorial Field-Book of the Revolution*, 2 vols. (New York, 1851), 1:284-95; Col. James Bruyn to Governor George Clinton, Kingston, July 23, 1781, in Clinton, *Public Papers*, 7:105.

78. Boatner, *Encyclopedia*, pp. 90, 690, 1002; Clarke, *Bloody Mohawk*, p. 291; Lossing, *Revolution*, 1:299-300.

79. Boatner, *Encyclopedia*, pp. 90, 1172; Alf Evers, *The Catskills: From Wilderness to Woodstock* (Garden City, N.Y., 1972), p. 743 n.; John Mylod, *Biography of a River: The People & Legends of the Hudson Valley* (New York, 1969), p. 2.

80. Clarke, *Bloody Mohawk*, p. 288, erroneously reports this bloody incident as having occurred on July 2, more than two months earlier. According to his account, Lieut. Woodworth's column was sent to scour the "Royal Grant" territory between the East and

West Canada Creeks, but was caught in an ambuscade a few miles north of Herkimer, at least twenty miles to the west of Fort Plain.

81. According to U.S. pension records, the honor of "the last surviving soldier of the Revolution" went to Bakeman, who died April 5, 1869, at the remarkable age of 109 years, 5 months, and 26 days. "Appropriately, this veteran of the War of Independence spent his final years and is buried in a town named Freedom, in Cattaraugus County, New York. Bakeman was probably of Dutch ancestry. (His surname appears in records and local histories as Bakeman or Beekman, with at least five additional variant spellings recorded.) According to family tradition, he was born near the Delaware River in New Jersey, but his parents emigrated to the Mohawk Valley when he was still a child. And it was in the Mohawk Valley that Bakeman apparently enlisted and saw military service from 1779 to 1783. . . . Bakeman stated that he entered the Revolutionary Army in the militia in Captain [William] Van Arnum's company in Colonel Willett's regiment. It is possible, as alleged, that Bakeman participated in the skirmish at Fort Plain in which a company of this regiment is known to have been ambushed on September 7, 1781. He apparently also served as a teamster, possibly hauling farm produce from the Mohawk Valley to supply Washington's army on the lower Hudson" (*The Correspondent* [New York State American Revolution Bicentennial Commission] 1, no. 2 [Autumn 1970].

82. Beauchamp, "Indian Raids," p. 204; Clarke, *Bloody Mohawk*, pp. 291-92; Van Every, *Company of Heroes*, p. 264.

83. Col. Marinus Willett to Maj. Gen. Lord Stirling, October 26, 1781, in Clinton, *Public Papers*, 7:443-44.

84. The site where Walter Butler met his death was called Butler's Ford for many years. The West Canada Creek ford or crossing is now covered by the waters of the Hinckley Reservoir. Boatner, *Landmarks*, p. 327.

85. Marinus Willett to George Clinton, in Clinton, *Public Papers*, 7:472-74; Willett later estimated that the enemy force numbered 607 men.

86. Beauchamp, "Indian Raids," pp. 204-5; Boatner, *Encyclopedia*, pp. 90-91, 558-59, 564; *Landmarks*, pp. 256-57; Clarke, *Bloody Mohawk*, pp. 292-96; George Clinton, *Public Papers of George Clinton, First Governor of New York*, ed. Hugh Hastings. 10 vols. (New York and Albany, 1899-1914), 7:472-74, 482; Graymont, *Iroquois*, pp. 246-50; Howard, *Thundergate*, pp. 143-44; Van Every, *Company of Heroes*, pp. 265-66; Charles B. Briggs, Johnson Hall, N.Y., to author, May 22, 1974.

87. On November 16, 1781, Willett reported to Governor Clinton that the destruction caused by the latest enemy incursion in Tryon County consisted of twenty-two dwellings, twenty-eight barns, and one grist mill, 1500 bushels of wheat, 105 of rye, 1,875 of oats, 967 of peas, 964 of corn, and 109 tons of hay. The livestock losses were thirty-three horses, seventy-seven cattle, thirty-one sheep, and sixty-four hogs. Willett, in his preface to the foregoing losses, considered the damage "trifling." Clinton, *Public Papers*, 7:504-5.

88. New York State Historic Trust and New York State Parks and Recreation, *The Mohawk Valley and the American Revolution* (Albany, N.Y., 1972), pp. 26-27.

89. Without a doubt the greatest contribution to the winning of the Revolution was the military, naval, and small monetary support by the French. The alliance with the Americans was prompted by two ulterior motives: to dispossess England of her American Colonies and to avenge France's territorial losses in the battle for empire a score of years earlier. The besiegers of Yorktown consisted of nearly forty thousand ground and naval men, but of this number only nine thousand were American, with a little more than a third of them ineffective militiamen. Van Every, *Company of Heroes*, pp. 268-69.

"On the very same day that Cornwallis surrendered, Sir Henry Clinton, having received naval reinforcements, sailed from New York with twenty-five ships-of-the-line and ten frigates, and 7,000 of his best troops. Five days brought him to the mouth of the

Chesapeake, where he learned that he was too late, as had been the case four years before, when he tried to relieve Burgoyne'' (Fiske, *Revolution*, 2:297-98).

90. Clarke, *Bloody Mohawk*, p. 277, gives "Chrysler" as the spelling of the name of the notorious Mohawk Valley Tory.

91. Graymont, *Iroquois*, p. 251.

92. Van Every, *Company of Heroes*, p. 282.

93. One of the relatively few educated members of Brant's nation.

94. Clarke, *Bloody Mohawk*, pp. 296-97; Graymont, *Iroquois*, pp. 92, 123, 254.

95. Wallace, *Death and Rebirth*, p. 146.

96. Fiske, *Revolution*, 2:303.

97. Boatner, *Encyclopedia*, pp. 940-41; Graymont, *Iroquois*, p. 254.

98. Ibid.; Francis Paul Prucha, *Guide to the Military Posts of the United States* (Madison, Wis., 1964), p. 96; Wallace F. Workmaster, Central N.Y. State Parks Commission, Jamesville, N.Y., March 1, 1973, to the author.

99. Brant's letter to Major Ross was justifiably indignant: "I am very sorry to acquaint you the chiefs of the five nations who came with me find themselves much disappointed in not being properly fitted out for war as they were promised at Niagara, such as Makosins and ammunition. . . . I also beg to leave to mention that I myself told to Col'l Butler frequently this before I left Niagara nor did I imagine that no regard had been paid to my request untill my arrival here" (Joseph Brant to Major John Ross, June 18, 1782, in Public Archives of Canada, *Haldimand Papers*, M.G. 21, B 125).

100. Graymont, *Iroquois*, pp. 254-55; John Ross to Frederick Haldimand, June 27, 1782, in Public Archives of Canada, *Haldimand Papers*, M.G. 21, B 124.

101. Graymont, *Iroquois*, p. 255.

102. John C. Fitzpatrick, ed., *The Writings of George Washington*, 39 vols. (Washington, D.C., 1931-44), 25:16-17.

103. Boatner, *Encyclopedia*, p. 848.

104. Joseph Brant to Sir John Johnson, December 25, 1782, in Public Archives of Canada, *Haldimand Papers*, M.G. 21, B 115.

105. Boatner, *Encyclopedia*, p. 849; Graymont, *Iroquois*, p. 259; Wallace, *Birth and Death*, pp. 151-52.

106. Fitzpatrick, *Writings of Washington*, 25:449-51.

107. Graymont, *Iroquois*, pp. 256-58; Howard, *Thundergate*, p. 145; Marinus Willett to Henry Glen, February 19, 1783, Glen Papers, New York Public Library; Clarke, *Bloody Mohawk*, p. 297, holds that troops departed from Fort Dayton, while some other historians believe that Fort Stanwix was Willett's base.

108. Letter dated "Head Quarters, March 5, 1783," Fitzpatrick, *Writings of Washington*, 26:190.

109. Boatner, *Encyclopedia*, p. 553; Thomas D. Clark, *Frontier America: The Story of the Westward Movement* (New York, 1959), p. 166; Robert G. Ferris, ed., *Founders and Frontiersmen* (Washington, D.C., 1967), pp. 241, 292, 301.

110. Seymour Freedgood, *The Gateway States* (New York, 1967), pp. 35-39.

2   New York's Revolutionary Forts

FORT ALDEN

Boatner, *Encyclopedia*, pp. 221-25; *Landmarks*, p. 233; Clarke, *Bloody Mohawk*, pp. 204, 252-58; Donlon, *Montgomery County*, pp. 42-43. Donlon reports that the enemy took forty prisoners in the November 1778 raid and spent *two days* in futile attacks against

Cherry Valley's fort; Graymont, *Iroquois,* p. 185; Duane Hamilton Hurd, *History of Otsego County, New York* (Philadelphia, 1878), pp. 16-17; John Sawyer, *History of Cherry Valley, New York* (Cherry Valley, N.Y., 1898), pp. 9-11, 13, 29-30, 41-43.

FORT ANNE

Boatner, *Encyclopedia,* pp. 90, 181, 374-75; *Landmarks,* pp. 236-37; John Henry Brandow, *The Story of Old Saratoga and History of Schuylerville* (Albany, N.Y., 1900), pp. 23-26, 77; Clarke, *Bloody Mohawk,* pp. 99-100; Rutherford Hayner, *Troy and Rensselaer County, New York: A History* (New York and Chicago, 1925), p. 58; William Leete Stone, *Washington County History* (New York, 1901), p. 457; *New York Times,* May 6, 1956; Richard S. Allen, New York State American Revolution Bicentennial Commission, Albany, N.Y., May 22, 1974, to the author; James R. Cronkhite, Hudson Falls, N.Y., September 4, 1974, to the author.

FORT AU FER

Duane Hamilton Hurd, *History of Clinton and Franklin Counties, New York* (Philadelphia, 1880), p. 18; Peter Palmer, *History of Lake Champlain* (Albany, N.Y., 1866), pp. 9-10, 134-36; Frederic Franklyn Van De Water, *Lake Champlain and Lake George* (Indianapolis, Ind., 1946), pp. 133-34, 194-95, 237, 245-46; Plattsburgh (N.Y.) *Press-Republican,* October 10, 1960; Plattsburgh (N.Y.) *Republican,* February 12, 1898; Clinton County Historical Association, August 6, 1960, and February 4, 1974, to the author.

FORT CANASERAGA

(Mrs.) L. M. Hammond, *History of Madison County, New York* (Syracuse, N.Y., 1872), pp. 654-59; Karl H. Lehman, *Madison County Today* (Oneida Castle, N.Y., 1943), pp. 8-10.

FORT CAUGHNAWAGA

Washington Frothingham, *History of Montgomery County, N.Y.* (Syracuse, N.Y., 1892), pp. 262-67; Graymont, *Iroquois,* p. 59; Waldemar S. Raymond, Montgomery County Historian, December 28, 1973, to the author.

FORTS CLINTON and MONTGOMERY

1. The site of Fort Lafayette, erected in 1778.
2. *Journals of the Continental Congress, 1744-1789,* ed. Gaillard Hunt, 34 vols. (Washington, D.C., 1904-37), 2:60.
3. Palmer, *River and the Rock,* p. 25.
4. Force, *American Archives,* 4th ser., 2:1261-66.
5. Palmer, *River and the Rock,* pp. 25, 27.
6. *Journals of the New York Provincial Congress of New York, 1775-1777,* ed. John E. Wilmot, 2 vols. (Albany, N.Y., 1842), 1:253.
7. Fitzpatrick, *Writings of Washington,* 5:69.
8. William H. Carr and Richard J. Koke, *Twin Forts of the Popolopen: Forts Clinton and Montgomery, New York 1775-1777* (Bear Mountain, N.Y., 1937), pp. 13-14; Force, *American Archives,* 4th ser., 6:672.
9. Fitzpatrick, *Writings of Washington,* 5:265, 313.
10. Force, *American Archives,* 5th ser., 1:1409.
11. Ibid., 1:1411.

12. Palmer, *River and the Rock*, p. 59.

13. Clinton, *Public Papers*, 1:284-85.

14. Ibid., pp. 275-76.

15. Another "Fort Clinton," originally called Fort Arnold, was not erected until 1778 at West Point. The name was changed after Arnold's treason in 1780.

16. Carr and Koke, *Twin Forts*, pp. 18-19; Fitzpatrick, *Writings of Washington*, 5:318-19. A brief biography, Paul B. Mattice, "Captain Thomas Machin," will be found in the Schoharie County *Historical Review* (October 1955), pp. 5-13.

17. Palmer, *River and the Rock*, p. 66. Fort Independence was built under the supervision of George Clinton; construction started sometime in the middle of August 1776; in September a barracks was begun there (USMA Library to the author, January 9, 1975). See section on Fort Independence.

18. Palmer, *River and the Rock*, p. 66.

19. Clinton, *Public Papers*, 1:337.

20. John William Leonard, *History of the City of New York, 1609-1909* (New York, 1910), p. 280.

21. Palmer, *River and the Rock*, p. 67.

22. Ibid.

23. *Minutes of the Secret Committee*, Washington's Headquarters Museum, Newburgh, N.Y., October 9 and October 11, 1776.

24. A graphic description of Machin's problems will be found in Palmer's *River and the Rock*, pp. 68-69.

25. Carr and Koke, *Twin Forts*, p. 20; Palmer, *River and the Rock*, pp. 70-71. This system of obstructions consisted of several immense wood-frame caissons, filled with stone, to serve as immovable foundations for a series of long, iron-tipped logs designed to tear the wooden hull of any trespassing vessel. The defensive device proved to be a miserable failure, as was the one sunk in the Hudson at Fort Washington.

26. Links from the chains that spanned the Hudson at both Fort Montgomery and West Point may be seen in the historical museums at West Point, Newburgh, and Morristown National Historical Park. Robert Bolton, Jr., in his history of Westchester County, offers the stupendous figure of 70,000 pounds sterling as the cost of fabricating the chain and boom at Fort Montgomery.

27. Clinton, *Public Papers*, 1:808.

28. Fiske, *Revolution*, 1:271, 276-77.

29. Troyer Anderson, *The Command of the Howe Brothers during the American Revolution* (New York and London, 1936), p. 264, quoting Sir Henry Clinton, "Historical Detail," pp. 76-77, MS title for the general's *American Rebellion*.

30. Palmer, *River and the Rock*, p. 92; Fitzpatrick, *Writings of Washington*, 8:328-31.

31. Palmer, *River and the Rock*, p. 93; Alexander C. Flick, *The American Revolution in New York* (Albany, N. Y., 1926), pp. 93-94.

32. Clinton, *Public Papers*, 2:103, 105-6; Palmer, *River and the Rock*, p. 93.

33. Clinton, *Public Papers*, 2:348-49, 352; Palmer, *River and the Rock*, p. 97.

34. "One colonel, three lieutenant colonels, three majors, four captains, nine lieutenants, three ensigns, one assistant deputy quartermaster general, one director of ordnance, one quartermaster, and two hundred and thirty-seven privates" (Sir Henry Clinton, *American Rebellion*, p. 77 n. 39).

35. This was the famous dispatch of October 8, sent in a silver bullet and intercepted.

36. Continental Village was located at Canopus Creek, just above Peekskill. See section on this cantonment.

37. Clinton, *American Rebellion*, pp. 75-78.

38. Clinton, *Public Papers*, 2:287, 391.

39. "Governor Clinton to the Council of Inquiry, 1778," *Quarterly Journal,* New York State Historical Association (April 1931), p. 169.

40. Clinton, *Public Papers,* 2:375.

41. Ibid., 2:381, 392.

42. The site of this skirmish is marked by a boulder near today's Bear Mountain Inn. Hessian Lake was formerly called Bloody Pond, Lake Sinnipink, and Highland Lake.

43. Today this deep wild gorge is called, appropriately, the Hellhole.

44. Clinton, *Public Papers,* 2:381, 392.

45. Ibid., 2:381, 392-93; Palmer, *River and the Rock,* p. 111.

46. Carl Carmer, "This Hallowed-Out Ground," *American Heritage* 18, no. 4 (June 1967): 93.

47. Carr and Koke, *Twin Forts,* pp. 35-36.

48. Humphreys, *The Life . . . of Israel Putnam,* pp. 153-54 n.5, quoted from Carr and Koke, *Twin Forts,* p. 36.

49. Clinton, *Public Papers,* 2:393; Palmer, *River and the Rock,* pp. 112-13.

50. Carr and Koke, *Twin Forts,* pp. 38-39.

51. Brooks Atkinson, *New York Times,* October 20, 1964; Palmer, *River and the Rock,* p. 115.

52. Warring armies are traditionally inclined to minimize their own casualties and exaggerate losses suffered by the enemy. It has never been ascertained, with any degree of reasonable accuracy, how many men on both sides died that day. The day after the battle, October 7, it is believed that the victorious British had either interred or thrown into ponds more than 150 bodies. Six months later, during an investigation of the American defeat, the opinion was offered that about 70 Patriots were killed in the fight. Palmer, *River and the Rock,* p. 118 n. Carrington, *Battles,* pp. 359-60, says that "the American loss was not far from" 300 killed, wounded, and missing. He reports that Eager's *History of Orange County* lists 237 men as prisoners of the British.

53. Charles Stedman, *The History of the Origin, Progress and Termination of the American War,* 2 vols. (London, 1794), 1:405-6.

54. Clinton, *Public Papers,* 2:414.

55. Ibid., p. 413.

56. Dutchess County Historical Society, *Year Book, 1935,* p. 93.

57. *New York Gazette and Weekly Mercury,* October 27, 1777.

58. John Martin Hammond, *Quaint and Historic Forts of North America* (Philadelphia and London, 1915), p. 150.

59. Carr and Koke, *Twin Forts,* pp. 45-46.

60. Clinton, *Publc Papers,* 2:591.

61. Edward C. Boynton, *History of West Point,* pp. 53-54.

62. On the morning of October 7, the British were faced with the inevitable grisly ordeal of burying the dead found in and around the fort, but they were slowed down by the nature of the terrain. The shallow earth and hard rock beneath prevented decent burial of the corpses. The soldiers tired of digging and took the bodies from Fort Montgomery to a small pond, weighted them with stone, and unceremoniously threw them into the water. Fort Clinton's dead were accorded the same treatment, being deposited in Hessian Lake, just to the west or rear of the fort. Evidence of attempts at cremation, apparently for sanitary reasons, was found later.

63. United States Military Academy, *The Centennial of the United States Military Academy at West Point, New York,* 2 vols. (Washington, D.C., 1904), 1:156.

64. Carr and Koke, *Twin Forts,* p. 52.

65. During the summer of 1779 John André wrote a letter, never sent, to Benedict Arnold. Subsequently, from time to time, André added observations to the document.

Some of his speculations were startling, particularly in light of his having little knowledge "of the characters of the patriots he thought of as possible renegades." One of his observations relates to West Point's watchdog batteries above Popolopen Creek: "[Philip] Schuyler should be encouraged, as the people near Albany begin to show signs of impatience under the present rulers and as Indians are threatening in that quarter. Could he negotiate the purchase of [Forts] Montgomery and Clinton, spike their guns at a certain time?" (Carl Van Doren, *Secret History of the American Revolution: An Account of the Conspiracies of Benedict Arnold and Numerous Others drawn from the Secret Service Papers of the British Headquarters in North America* [New York, 1941; reprint ed., n.d.], pp. 231, 446-47).

FORT CLYDE

Frothingham, *Montgomery County,* p. 223; Nelson Greene, *The Story of Old Fort Plain and Middle Mohawk Valley* (Fort Plain, N.Y., 1915), p. 34; Lossing, *Revolution,* 1:262; Jeptha Root, *The Frontiersmen of New York,* 2 vols (Albany, N.Y., 1882), 1:575; New York State Historical Association, Cooperstown, N.Y., December 28, 1973, to the author.

CONSTITUTION ISLAND AND WEST POINT

1. At the beginning of the war it was known as Martelaer's Rock, a name corrupted in military correspondence to Martyr's Cliff, Matyr's Reach, Martland's Rock, etc. Carr and Koke, *Twin Forts of the Popolopen,* Appendix B, p. 58.

2. Edward B. Jelks, *Archaeological Excavations at Constitution Island, 1971* (West Point, N.Y., 1972), p. 5.

3. Constitution Island Association, *Constitution Island and West Point in the Revolutionary War* (West Point, N.Y., 1965), introduction.

4. Alexander C. Flick, "The Construction and History of Fort Constitution," in ibid., p. 20.

5. John H. Mead, "History Beneath Our Feet," address delivered September 29, 1969, at a joint meeting of the Constitution Island Association and Putnam County Historical Society.

6. See section on Forts Clinton and Montgomery.

7. Palmer, *River and the Rock,* pp. 31-32. The author is greatly indebted to this excellent work for much of the information in this chapter.

8. Ibid., pp. 32-33. The 55-year-old Romans was a rather adventurous and enterprising man with a talent for cartography. He had come to America some little time before Lexington and Concord and tried his hand at various pursuits. He went to East Florida, at the time a British territory, sketched the native Indians, and did pioneer work in charting some of the untracked Florida wilderness. His last job in Florida was as a botanist in the employ of the British. He was in New England when the war broke out, seeking a publisher for a book he had authored on Florida's natural history. His venturesome spirit led him to become a participant in the Allen-Arnold expedition against Ticonderoga. Whereas Palmer believes that Romans was a recent émigré to America, Boynton, *History of West Point,* p. 21 n., says that the artist-cartographer was employed as a civil engineer by the British in the Colonies, in 1755 and for some years before the Revolution, and that, from 1760 to 1771, he resided near St. Augustine, engaged in botanical studies. According to Force's *American Archives,* 4th ser., 3:1367, Romans left Florida in 1772 and went north, apparently to New England.

9. Merle G. Sheffield, *The Fort That Never Was: Constitution Island in the Revolutionary War* (West Point, N.Y., 1969), pp. 2-4; Jelks, *Excavations,* p. 12. Romans described Martelaer's Rock as a triangular piece of ground with three hills on the south side of the

island; he proposed to erect a bastioned fort on the highest of these hills. See Force, *American Archives,* 4th ser., 3:733-38, for Romans's detailed plans and cost accounts for the defenses.

10. Bruce Bliven, *Under the Guns, New York: 1775-1776* (New York, 1972), pp. 77-78.

11. Palmer, *River and the Rock,* p. 33: "At that point in the war Americans were fighting for their rights, as Englishmen, under the British Constitution. An 'iniquitous' Parliament, not George III, was their enemy. The Declaration of Independence was almost a year in the future. Discussing this one evening around the fireplace of the small house [an abandoned farmhouse on the island] they had taken over, the Commissioners decided to christen the fortress they were to build, Fort Constitution. The name stuck; to this day the island remains Constitution Island—a constant reminder that Americans once swore allegiance to English monarchs and the British Constitution." Flick, "The Construction and History of Fort Constitution," writes that the first mention of "Fort Constitution" appeared in official correspondence in a letter dated September 25, 1775, written by the Highlands commissioners.

12. Jelks, *Excavations,* p. 13.

13. *Journals of the Continental Congress,* 3:446.

14. *Journals of the New York Provincial Congress,* 1:253.

15. Flick, "Fort Constitution," 18.

16. Jelks, *Excavations,* p. 13; Palmer, *River and the Rock,* p. 51.

17. Force, *American Archives,* 4th ser., 4:1155-56; 5:297-99, 316, 321-22, 325-26; Palmer, *River and the Rock,* p. 51.

18. Force, *American Archives,* 4th ser., 5:76.

19. Boynton, *West Point,* pp. 27-28.

20. *Journals of the New York Provincial Congress,* 1:402.

21. Force, *American Archives,* 4th ser., 6:534.

22. Ibid., 6:672.

23. Boynton, *West Point,* pp. 35-38.

24. *Journals of the New York Provincial Congress,* 1:484, 493.

25. Clinton, *Public Papers,* 1:249.

26. *Journals of the New York Provincial Congress,* 1:488.

27. Palmer, *River and the Rock,* p. 62.

28. Jelks, *Excavations,* p. 15.

29. Boatner, *Encyclopedia,* pp. 147-48, says the *Turtle's* target was the man-of-war *Eagle.* Sgt. Lee, the volunteer pilot of the submarine, should know better; in his letter to David Humphreys, February 20, 1815 (*Magazine of American History,* March 1893, pp. 264-65), Lee states that his target was the *Asia.* Palmer, *River and the Rock,* follows Lee's lead.

30. Flick, "Fort Constitution," p. 24; Palmer, *River and the Rock,* p. 65.

31. Palmer, *River and the Rock,* p. 67.

32. Boatner, *Encyclopedia,* p. 850; Palmer, *River and the Rock,* p. 85.

33. Clinton, *Public Papers,* 1:589-94; Palmer, *River and the Rock,* p. 85.

34. Fitzpatrick, *Washington's Writings,* 4:409.

35. Ibid., 4:416; Flick, "Fort Constitution," pp. 27-28.

36. Fitzpatrick, *Washington's Writings,* 4:476.

37. *Journals of the New York Provincial Congress,* 1:1021.

38. See section on Forts Clinton and Montgomery.

39. Flick, "Constitution Island," p. 28; Palmer, *River and the Rock,* p. 119.

40. Not to be confused with the colonel of the same name in Fort Montgomery's garrison.

41. Palmer, *River and the Rock,* p. 119.

42. *Journals of the New York Provincial Congress,* 1:1064-65.

43. Boynton, *West Point,* p. 47.

44. Donald F. Clark, *Fort Montgomery and Fort Clinton* (Highlands, N.Y., 1952), p. 15, gives the complete report of captured and destroyed munitions, guns, and equipment.

45. Palmer, *River and the Rock,* p. 131.

46. Ibid., p. 127.

47. Ibid., p. 132.

48. Ibid., pp. 132-33, 137.

49. Clinton, *Public Papers,* 2:589-94.

50. Palmer, *River and the Rock,* pp. 138-39.

51. Fitzpatrick, *Washington's Writings,* 12:376-77.

52. Palmer, *River and the Rock,* pp. 140-42.

53. Ibid., p. 145.

54. Ibid., pp. 147-53; Adam E. Potts, "Constitution Island—Historical Sketch," in *Constitution Island and West Point in the Revolutionary War* (West Point, N.Y., 1965), p. 35.

55. Sol Stember, *Bicentennial Guide to the American Revolution,* 3 vols. (New York, 1974), 1:135, believes that Fort Putnam, considered a "last-ditch position," was not originally constructed of earth and logs as were the other works.

56. Palmer, *River and the Rock,* p. 168; Potts, "Constitution Island," p. 35.

57. Palmer, *River and the Rock,* p. 172. While inspecting Fort Putnam sometime in August 1778, Kosciuszko had also made note of the ridge, particularly Rocky Hill, two hundred feet higher than and less than a half-mile west of Fort Putnam. Rocky Hill became the site for Redoubt Number Four.

58. Palmer, *River and the Rock,* pp. 203-6.

59. Ibid., p. 206.

60. Ibid., p. 175.

61. Ibid., pp. 221-27.

62. Boatner, *Encyclopedia,* pp. 25-26; Van Doren, *Secret History,* pp. 145, 149. Arnold married Margaret Mansfield in 1767. She bore him three sons in five years and died on June 19, 1775.

63. Boatner, *Landmarks,* pp. 328-29; Palmer, *River and the Rock,* pp. 239-88; Van Doren, *Secret History,* pp. 145, 289; Fort Myers (Fla.) *News-Press,* November 16, 1975. The story of the American turncoat is admirably detailed in Carl Van Doren's superior *Secret History of the American Revolution;* Palmer's chapters on Arnold and Willard M. Wallace's *Traitorous Hero* are excellent reading.

64. Palmer, *River and the Rock,* preface, pp. xi-xii.

65. Ibid., pp. 172, 352.

66. Boatner, *Encyclopedia,* p. 289; Palmer, *River and the Rock,* pp. 351-52.

67. Palmer, *River and the Rock,* pp. 355-58.

68. Boatner, *Landmarks,* p. 327; Stember is of the opinion that the work done on Fort Putnam in 1907 (date ?) was accomplished "without sufficient research" and that "its present reconstructed appearance leaves much to be desired in historical accuarcy" (*The Bicentennial Guide to the American Revolution* [New York, 1974], 1:135).

Archaeologists have been at work for some years on the fortifications at West Point and on Constitution Island. Reports of their findings, delineated in a number of monographs, are being carefully studied so that reconstruction of a few of the more important redoubts will be faithfully executed. The author is very grateful to Lieut. Col. John H. Bradley, Director of Bicentennial Activities at USMA, for generously preparing and submitting capsule reports (June 13 and August 20, 1975) of USMA's commemorative plans. Accompanying the latest report is a chronological listing of the individual forts and redoubts constructed by the Patriots in the two face-to-face Hudson Highlands defenses. Col. Bradley writes:

> To the best of my knowledge, our present refurbishing and restoration of Fort Putnam is the first to be done since the 1908-1910 restoration.
>
> At the present time we have contracted for the construction of a small interpretive museum building. It should be built by August. We also have a contract for an audio-electronic terrain model for the museum. This is virtually complete. Pending are four other contracts: one for the refurbishment of the casemates, improvement of one to three, construction of gun platforms, and installation of safety railings; a second for the construction of a new gate, entrance steps, and landings; a third for clearing of trees and brush around the fort; and a fourth for the improvement of the footpath to the fort. Replica cannons and carriages have been ordered also. All the cannon barrels and mortars are on hand. Only one, however, is complete. We are waiting for the carriages and mortar beds. Fort Putnam is scheduled to open to the public in June 1976.
>
> By December I expect to have the final contracts awarded for the general landscaping and possibly for the development of archaeological displays.
>
> Action will begin in August to partially explore, stabilize, and partially restore Redoubt #4 on the west side of the river. A contract has been awarded for this work. Redoubt #4 will be opened to the public when completed. It will be connected to Fort Putnam by an existing trail.
>
> Only improved maintenance is planned for the batteries and redoubts on Constitution Island. In the past years, however, Romans' Battery's powder magazine was excavated and archaeological surveys were made on the island. Crews have already cleared out the areas near the fortifications, and action is continuing to upgrade, clear, and protect all the fortifications. . . .
>
> Attached is a summary of key dates pertaining to the various forts and redoubts in the West Point area. I believe that the information is fairly correct. . . . I can only find information about mortared masonry in the data collected for Putnam and Romans' Battery (and powder magazine). As you can see, Gravel Hill Battery, Sherburne's Redoubt, and Fort Clinton were apparently all log or earth works.

CONTINENTAL VILLAGE

Boatner, *Encyclopedia,* pp. 235, 275, 850; *Landmarks,* p. 234; Carrington, *Battles,* p. 360; Palmer, *River and the Rock,* pp. 84-85, 120.

FORTS CROWN POINT and TICONDEROGA

1. Fort Ticonderoga Museum *Bulletin* (October 1970), pp. 393-405.

2. Peter Kalm, *Travels in North America,* 2 vols. (New York, 1937), 2:391.

3. Fort Ticonderoga Museum *Bulletin* (October 1970), p. 396.

4. Stephen H. P. Pell, *Fort Ticonderoga: A Short History* (Ticonderoga, N.Y., 1935), p. 19.

5. John Maloney, "He Wouldn't Give Up the Fort," *Saturday Evening Post,* August 10, 1946; *New York Times,* May 10, 1959.

6. Walter D. Edmonds, *The Musket and the Cross* (Boston, 1968), pp. 3-4.

7. Francis Parkman, *Montcalm and Wolfe* (Boston, 1884), 1:170-71.

8. Stanley Pargellis, ed., *Military Affairs in North America, 1748-1765,* reprint ed. (Hamden, Conn., 1969), pp. 81-82.

9. Parkman, *Montcalm and Wolfe,* 2:89.

10. Ibid., 2:97.

11. Ibid.

12. Ibid., 2:100-103;

13. Ibid., 2:107.

14. Ibid., 2:110; Fort Ticonderoga Museum *Bulletin,* p. 77.

15. Parkman, *Montcalm and Wolfe,* 2:111.

16. Ibid., 2:111-12.

REVOLUTIONARY WAR FORTIFICATIONS
WEST POINT, NEW YORK

Fortification	Location	Date Started (Rebuilt)	Dry Stone Masonry	Masonry w/ Mortar	Comments
Roman's Battery	Constitution Island	1775	1775 (Scarp)	1775 (Bomb-proof)	Destroyed 1777 Good condition
Blockhouse	Constitution Island				Destroyed 1777 Virtually no trace
Marine Battery	Constitution Island	1775 (1778)	1775 (Scarp)		Destroyed 1777 Good condition
Hill Cliff Battery	Constitution Island	1776	1776 (Scarp)		Destroyed 1777 Fair condition
Gravel Hill Battery (Greaton's Battery)	Constitution Island	1776 (1778)			Destroyed 1777 Fair condition Possible stone scarp
Fort (Arnold) Clinton	West Point	1778	Partly		First and main fortification at West Point. Restored C1857 Good condition
Chain Battery	West Point	1778	1778 (Scarp)		Part of exterior parapet face is stone. Good condition
Lanthorn Battery (Lantern Battery)	West Point	1778	1778 (Scarp)		Poor condition

Fortification	Location	Date Started (Rebuilt)	Dry Stone Masonry	Masonry w/ Mortar	Comments
Water Battery (Green Battery?)	West Point	1778	1778 (Scarp)		Part of exterior parapet face is stone. Poor condition
Knox Battery (South Battery?)	West Point	1778	1778 (Scarp)		No trace remains
Sherburne's Redoubt	West Point	1778	No data		No trace remains
Fort Putnam	West Point	1778	by 1780	1794	Key fortification in the western defenses of West Point. Restored 1908-10. Excellent condition
Fort Webb	West Point	1778	No data		Virtually no traces remain
Fort Wyllys and Battery	West Point	1778	1778 (Scarp)	1778 (interior of magazine)	Excellent condition
Fort Meigs	West Point	1778	1778 (Scarp)		Good condition
Redoubt #1 and Batteries 1 and 2	West Point	1779	1779 (Scarp)		Cood condition
Redoubt #2 and Battery	West Point	1779	1779 (Scarp)		Excellent condition
Redoubt #3	West Point	1779	1779 (Scarp)		Poor condition
Redoubt #4	West Point	1779	1779 (Scarp)		Being stabilized and partially restored

Fortification	Location	Date Started (Rebuilt)	Dry Stone Masonry	Masonry w/ Mortar	Comments
Redoubt #5	Constitution Island	1778	1778 (Scarp)		Possibly contained a blockhouse. Good condition
Redoubt #6	Constitution	1779	1779 (Scarp)		Good condition
Redoubt #7	Constitution Island	1778	1778 (Entire ramparts)		Excellent condition
North Redoubt	VIC Garrison NY	1779	1779 (Scarp)		Evidence of a ditch. Good condition
South Redoubt	VIC Garrison NY	1779	1779 (Scarp)		Ditch. Good condition

NOTES:

1. Parapets were built of logs and fascines, logs and earth, logs and gravel, or something similar.

2. Inner revetments of ramparts have dry masonry walls. Inner revetments of parapets of most batteries exhibit some stone. Inner revetments of parapets of redoubts do not show stone.

3. The bases (ramparts or scarps) of all fortifications were generally of dry stone masonry.

SOURCES:

Personal Inspections, 1973-1975.

Mead, John, *Archaeological Survey of Fort Putnam and Fortifications at West Point, 1967-1968.*

Mead, John. *Archaeological Survey of Constitution Island and Adjoining Fortifications 1967-1968.*

Jelks, Edward, *Archaeological Excavations at Constitution Island* (1971).

Boynton, Edward, *History of West Point* (New York, 1863).

Palmer, Dave R. *The River and the Rock, The History of Fortress West Point, 1775-1783* (New York, 1969).

Prepared by: LtColonel John H. Bradley
Director, Bicentennial Activities
United States Military Academy
West Point, NY 10996
AC (914) 938-2272
17 Aug 1975

17. Ibid., 2:235-36.

18. Ibid., 2:236-37.

19. Ibid., 2:240.

20. Howard H. Peckham, *Colonial Wars: 1689-1762* (Chicago, 1964), pp. 193-94.

21. Hammond, *Quaint and Historic Forts*, p. 70; Alfred Procter James and Charles Morse Stotz, *Drums in the Forest* (Pittsburgh, Pa., 1958), pp. 68, 161; Lossing, *Revolution*, 1:150 ff.

22. Crown Point Foundation, "Crown Point and Lake Champlain, 1609-1783" (New York, n.d.).

23. Pell, *Fort Ticonderoga*, p. 55.

24. Ibid.

25. Ibid.

26. Merrill Jensen, *The Founding of a Nation: A History of the American Revolution* (New York, 1968), pp. 605-6.

27. Ibid., pp. 606-7.

28. Ibid., pp. 608, 616.

29. Van Doren, *Secret History*, p. 149.

30. Ibid., p. 150.

31. Ibid., p. 160.

32. Correlli Barnett, *Britain and Her Army, 1509-1970* (New York, 1970), p. 218.

33. Fitzpatrick, *Washington's Writings*, 4:10; Higginbotham, *War of American Independence*, p. 110.

34. Boatner, *Encyclopedia*, pp. 31-35.

35. Ibid., p. 174.

36. A summary of the expedition will be found in Boatner's *Encyclopedia*, pp. 31-34, 174-79, 906-9, 1116-17. For details, the authorities to be consulted regarding the extraordinary trek through the Maine wilderness are: Justin H. Smith, John Codman, Kenneth Roberts, and Brian Boylan. See bibliography.

37. Boatner, *Encyclopedia*, pp. 176-77.

38. Fitzpatrick, *Washington's Writings*, 4:179.

39. Boatner, *Encyclopedia*, p. 908.

40. Ibid.

41. Fitzpatrick, *Washington's Writings*, 4:93-94.

42. Boatner, *Encyclopedia*, pp. 586-88.

43. "In 1934 the wreck of the *Royal Savage* was recovered and the pieces saved. In the following year the *Philadelphia*, remarkably well preserved by the cold water, was identified and salvaged from the sandy lake bottom near the midchannel of Valcour Bay. After her guns were lifted, a 12-pounder and two 9-pounders, the hull was raised 57 feet to the surface and towed to the beach. In addition to her guns, hundreds of other relics were found on the vessel—shot, cooking utensils, tools, buttons, buckles, and human bones. The vessel was exhibited at various places on Lake Champlain and the Hudson River and finally, in 1960, was placed in the Smithsonian Institution." The gondola's present appearance shows that its hull "is 54 feet in length, 15 feet in beam, and approximately 5 feet deep. Construction was almost entirely of oak. The mast, nearly 36 feet high, ws found intact except for the top section, and the oaken hull timers were still in place. Three shotholes were visible in the hull, and in one of them a cannonball remained lodged" (Sarles and Shedd, *Colonials and Patriots*, p. 186).

44. Boatner, *Encyclopedia*, pp. 1133-36.

45. Ibid., pp. 1103-4.

46. Ibid., map, p. 1105.

47. Ibid., p. 135.

48. Ibid., p. 142; Massachusetts Historical Society *Proceedings* 12:189-90, quoted by permission of the Society.

49. Boatner, *Encyclopedia*, p. 142.

50. Ibid., p. 1106; Brian Richard Boylan, *Benedict Arnold, The Dark Eagle* (New York, 1973), p. 101.

51. Boatner, *Landmarks*, p. 319. His full name was Chevalier Matthias Alexis de Rochefermoy, but in America he was known only as Fermoy.

52. Boatner, *Encyclopedia*, p. 1106.

53. Ibid., pp. 374-75.

54. Ibid., pp. 526-28.

55. Ibid., pp. 1107-8.

56. Hoffman Nickerson, *The Turning Point of the Revolution* (Boston, 1928) pp. 322-26.

57. Boatner, *Encyclopedia*, p. 1147.

58. Data regarding the rebuilding of Fort Ticonderoga are based on various sources, including Boatner's *Landmarks of the American Revolution*, John Maloney's *Saturday Evening Post*, August 10, 1946, article, and Stephen Pell's *Fort Ticonderoga: A Short History*.

FORT CUMMINGS

Sullivan-Clinton Campaign, pp. 163, 186, 203, 205; Mrs. R. O. Stratton, Curator, Ontario County Historical Society, Canandaigua, N.Y., August 12, 1960, to author; J. Sheldon Fisher, Ontario County Historian, Fishers, N.Y., August 24, 1960, to author.

FORT DAYTON

A veteran who served under Gen. James Wolfe in the taking of Quebec, Col. Dayton served meritoriously throughout the Revolution, participating in the battles of Springfield, Monmouth, Brandywine, and Yorktown. Boatner, *Encyclopedia*, pp. 90, 376; *Landmarks*, pp. 237-38, 249-50; Clarke, *Bloody Mohawk*, pp. 248-51; Crouse, "Forts and Block Houses in the Mohawk Valley" (New York State Historical Association *Proceedings*), 14:88; Simms, *Frontiersmen*, 2:177; Herkimer County Historical Society, Herkimer, N.Y., April 18, 1974, to author.

DOBBS FERRY FORTS

Boatner, *Encyclopedia*, pp. 334, 575, 1015; *Landmarks*, p. 235; Robert Bolton, Jr., *History of the County of Westchester*, 3d ed. (New York, 1905), pp. 264-70, 273-80; Fitzpatrick, *Washington's Writings*, 25:438; Lossing, *Revolution*, 2:194-95; Van Doren, *Secret History*, pp. 285, 309-10, 482. Bergen County Historical Society, River Edge, N.J., November 17, 1976, to author.

FORT DUBOIS

Clarke, *Bloody Mohawk*, pp. 241, 262, 291; Clinton, *Public Papers*, 3:377-78; 408, 413, 506; Graymont, *Iroquois*, pp. 165-66; George S. Van Schaick, "Fort Dubois and the Revolutionary Officer for Whom It Was Named," *Schoharie County Historical Review* (November 1948), p. 6; Wallace, *Death and Rebirth*, pp. 141-42; Marinus Willett to Governor Clinton, September 2, 1781, in Clinton, *Public Papers*, 7:291.

FORT EDWARD

1. At this time the fort was located in Albany County, in what was known as the "Fort Edward District." In 1772 part of Albany County was constituted as Charlotte County, a

designation that was changed in 1784 to Washington, the first county in the United States so named. Fort Edward Historical Association.

2. Pargellis, *Military Affairs*, p. 177.

3. Ibid., pp. 179-80; Lossing, *Revolution*, 1:95-96, reports that the fort "was built of logs and earth, sixteen feet high and twenty-two feet thick, and stood at the junction of Fort Edward Creek and the Hudson River. From the creek, around the fort to the river, was a deep fosse or ditch." He does not indicate when the major improvements were made.

4. Pargellis, *Military Affairs*, p. 240.

5. Ibid., p. 477.

6. Ibid.

7. Today this road is roughly equivalent to Routes 4 and 9N from Fort Edward through Glens Falls to Lake George.

8. Stanley M. Gifford, *Fort William Henry: A History* (Glens Falls, N.Y., 1955), p. 15.

9. Lossing, *Revolution*, 1:95-96.

10. Boatner, *Encyclopedia*, pp. 688-90; *Landmarks*, p. 240; Graymont, *Iroquois*, pp. 151-52; Mylod, *Biography of a River*, pp. 29-32; Sosin, *Frontier*, p. 114.

11. Henry Steele Commager and Richard B. Morris, *The Spirit of 'Seventy-Six: The Story of the American Revolution as Told by Participants*, 2d ed. (New York, 1967), p. 560. Taken from Gates Papers in New-York Historical Society, Box 21b.

12. Chastellux, *Travels*, 1:215. W. H. Hill, *Old Fort Edward Before 1800* (Fort Edward, N.Y., 1929), p. 374, is of the opinion that the replaced fortification was the blockhouse and associated works on the hill "just north of what is now Case Street, near today's high school." He stresses that Chastellux's account is "the only description of its kind" that he has located.

13. Richard S. Allen, New York State American Revolution Bicentennial Commission, Albany, N.Y., November 3, 1975, to the author.

14. Boatner, *Landmarks*, p. 238.

15. *New York Times*, May 10, 1959.

FORT EHLE

Frothingham, *Montgomery County*, p. 243; Simms, *Frontiersmen*, 2:381; John J. Vrooman, *Forts and Firesides of the Mohawk Country* (Philadelphia, 1943), pp. 205-6. Vrooman's history, inaccurate but regionally popular, places the site of the Ehle house as "just east of Nelliston," on the *north* side of the Mohawk. He also gives the minister's name as Jacobus Ehle. The confusion is extended by Nelson Greene who, in his *Mohawk Turnpike*, places it "about one-third mile east of the Fort Plain Station," but the picture caption reads, "Ehle House, Nelliston." In another reference he locates the structure on Prospect Hill in Fort Plain.

FORT FAILING

Clarke, *Bloody Mohawk*, pp. 11-12, 175; Frothingham, *Montgomery County*, p. 243; Simms, *Frontiersmen*, 2:381.

FISHKILL BARRACKS

Force, *American Archives*, 5th ser., 3:302; Boatner, *Landmarks*, pp. 235-36; Chastellux, *Travels*, 1:88, 266 n. 71; Frank Hasbrouck, *History of the County of Dutchess* (Poughkeepsie, N.Y., 1900), p. 173; Palmer, *River and the Rock*, pp. 69-70; Stember, *Bicentennial Guide*, 1:211; Mrs. Ivan Skinner, Fishkill, N.Y., May 1, 1971, to the author.

FORT FOX

Simms, *Frontiersmen,* 2:382; Douglas Ayres, Jr., Fort Plain, N.Y., April 20, 1970, to the author; Charles B. Briggs, Johnson Hall, Johnstown, N.Y., March 25, 1970, to the author.

FORT FREY

Boatner, *Landmarks,* p. 242, has Philip Frey as one of Heinrich II's sons and omits Heinrich III (Henry), the eldest of the sons. The only "Philip Frey" listed on the available Frey family genealogy chart (incomplete) was the great-grandson of Heinrich II, born after the Revolution, and dying at the age of eighteen or nineteen.

Frothingham, *Montgomery County,* p. 320, has "Philip R." as Bernard's nephew. According to the Frey genealogy, John Frey had but one son, Heinrich III. Therefore, if indeed "Philip R.'s" surname was Frey, he must have been a son of Heinrich III (Bernard's brother). It then appears that Philip R. Frey, as a British participant in St. Leger's siege of Fort Stanwix in 1777, may have been fighting at Oriskany, six miles away, against his uncle John Frey.

Boatner, *Encyclopedia,* p. 1127; *Landmarks,* p. 242; Donlon, *Montgomery County,* pp. 64, 76, 80; Frothingham, *Montgomery County,* pp. 318-20; Vrooman, *Forts and Firesides,* pp. 201-2. Dr. Charles K. Winne, Jr., Albany, N.Y., May 12, 1946, to the author; Frey genealogy chart, Montgomery County Department of History and Archives, Fonda, N.Y., September 25, 1974, to the author.

FORT GEORGE

Boatner, *Landmarks,* p. 263; Gifford, *Fort William Henry,* p. 53; Lossing, *Revolution,* 1:112.

FORT HALDIMAND

1. John A. Haddock, *The Picturesque St. Lawrence River* (Watertown, N.Y., 1895), pp. 52-53. Franklin B. Hough examined the fort's site in mid-nineteenth century. Calling the island post "Fort Carleton," he gives some additional details: "Traces occur, showing that cannon were planted on conspicuous points, and the trace of a submerged wharf is still seen, as are also wrecks of vessels in the bottom of the river adjacent. In the rear of the works may be seen the cemetery. . . . Near the brow of the hill is a circular well about ten feet in diameter. . . . The plan of the fort shows it to have been after the system of Vauban, and formed three-eighths of a circle of about 800 feet in diameter" (*A History of Jefferson County in the State of New York* [Watertown, N.Y., 1854], pp. 21-23.

2. Later known as the Royal Yorkers, when their green uniforms were replaced by scarlet coats with blue facings.

3. Clinton, *Public Papers,* 6:832-33.

4. The General Electric Company owned Carleton Island for many years, with the intention of turning it into a vacation retreat for its employees. According to the town assessor's records, however, John C. McFarlane is now (November 1975) the proprietor of the major share of the 1,350-acre island, owning 1,343 acres. McFarlane's manager, Robert Kittle of Clayton, N.Y., in a letter of November 25, 1975, to the author, writes that the remains of the fort consist of two stone chimneys, a thirty-foot-deep well that is gradually being filled with rubbish deposited by nearby "cottagers," and a well-defined limestone ditch on the east side of the fort's site. He also reports that the "west side of the fort is a steep cliff overlooking North Bay where many artifacts have been found (cannon, bottles, cannon balls, old ships, etc.)." Kittle closes with: "At the present time the island is up for sale. I had hoped the State of New York would be interested in [purchasing] the island, especially to preserve the fort area."

Boatner, *Encyclopedia,* pp. 182-84, 474-75, 950, 961; Edgar C. Emerson, *Our County and Its People* (Boston, 1898), pp. 511-13; Franklin B. Hough, *The Thousand Islands of the St. Lawrence* (Syracuse, N.Y., 1880), pp. 52-53; Harry F. Landon, *The North Country* (Indianapolis, Ind., 1932), pp. 77-85, Office of the Historian, Town of Cape Vincent, N.Y., August 19 and 25, 1959, to the author; Jefferson County Historical Society, Watertown, N.Y., December 20, 1973, to the author; Public Archives of Canada, Ottawa, Ont., August 20, 1974, to the author; Ralph W. Kilborn, Cape Vincent, N.Y., October 9, 1975, to the author.

FORT HERKIMER

Nathaniel S. Benton, *A History of Herkimer County, Including the Upper Mohawk Valley* (Albany, N.Y., 1856), p. 54; Boatner, *Landmarks,* p. 243; Clarke, *Bloody Mohawk,* pp. 153, 159-60, 202-3; Graymont, *Iroquois,* pp. 178-89; Sarles and Shedd, *Colonials and Patriots,* p. 214; Vrooman, *Forts and Firesides,* pp. 240-55; Herkimer County Historical Society, Herkimer, N.Y., November 13, 1974, and August 28, 1975, to the author.

FORT HESS

Simms, *Frontiersmen,* 2:382; Douglas Ayres, Jr., Fort Plain, N.Y., April 20, 1970, to the author.

FORT HILL

Elizabeth Bilobrowka, St. Johnsville, N.Y., January 7, 1974, to the author; Fort Plain Museum, Fort Plain, N.Y., April 30, 1974, to the author.

FORT HOUSE

Margaret Reaney Memorial Library, St. Johnsville, N.Y., January 15, 1974, to the author; Montgomery County Department of History and Archives, Fonda, N.Y., March 15, 1974, to the author.

FORT HUNTER

Boatner, *Encyclopedia,* p. 378; *Landmarks,* p. 243; Crouse, "Forts and Block Houses," New York State Historical Association *Proceedings,* 14:81-82; Donlon, *Montgomery County,* p. 8, cites only one blockhouse for the original fort and gives John Scott, the fort's first commander, the rank of lieutenant; James Thomas Flexner, *Mohawk Baronet: Sir William Johnson of New York* (New York, 1959), pp. 10-11, 301; Simms, *Frontiersmen,* 1:70-71; Vrooman, *Forts and Firesides,* pp. 101-3, 192.

FORT INDEPENDENCE

Bolton, *County of Westchester,* 1:160; 2:528, 614; Carr and Koke, *Twin Forts,* pp. 18, 20, 24, 40; Carrington, *Battles,* p. 360; Palmer, *River and the Rock,* pp. 82-83; Emma Lillie Patterson, *Peekskill in the American Revolution* (Peekskill, N.Y., 1944), pp. 17, 21, 40, 64, 66, 72, 93; Chester A. Smith, *Peekskill, A Friendly Town: A Pictorial History of the City from 1654 to 1952* (Peekskill, N.Y., 1952), p. 122; Stember, *Bicentennial Guide,* 1:117; USMA Library, West Point, N.Y., January 9, 1975, to the author.

FORT JOHNSTOWN

Boatner, *Encyclopedia,* pp. 88, 564; *Landmarks,* pp. 256-58; Clarke, *Bloody Mohawk,* pp. 202, 294; Commager and Morris, *Spirit of 'Seventy-Six,* p. 1031; Washington

Frothingham, *History of Fulton County, N.Y.* (Syracuse, N.Y., 1892), pp. 237-38; Swiggett, *War*, p. 240.

FORT KEYSER

Boatner, *Encyclopedia*, p. 379; *Landmarks*, p. 310; paper by Charles B. Briggs, Johnson Hall, Johnstown, N.Y., "Fort Kayser," March 1970, presented to Montgomery County Department of History and Archives, Fonda, N.Y.; Donlon, *Montgomery County*, p. 45.

THE KING'S FERRY FORTS

1. Stedman, *History of the American War*, 2:145.
2. *American Military History*, pp. 83-84; Boatner, *Encyclopedia*, pp. 575, 1062.
3. Clinton, *American Rebellion*, p. 124.
4. Ibid., p. 125.
5. Ibid.
6. Palmer, *River and the Rock*, p. 191; Stember, *Bicentennial Guide*, 1:182.
7. Clinton, *American Rebellion*, p. 125.
8. Boatner, *Encyclopedia*, pp. 260-61, 359, 457, 782, 812; Stember, *Bicentennial Guide*, 1:183.
9. Lossing, *Revolution*, 2:174-75.
10. Boatner, *Encyclopedia*, pp. 608, 695, 1063.
11. Carrington, *Battles*, p. 472.
12. Stember, *Bicentennial Guide*, 1:155, 197.
13. Palisades Interstate Park Commission, *Stony Point Battlefield Reservation* (Bear Mountain, N.Y., 1968), p. 3.
14. Ibid.
15. Stember, *Bicentennial Guide*, 1:190-91.
16. Charles J. Stillé, *Major-General Anthony Wayne and the Pennsylvania Line in the Continental Army* (Philadelphia, 1893), p. 181.
17. *New York Journal*, August 2, 1779, quoted in George Clinton's *Public Papers*, 5:154 n.
18. Stember, *Bicentennial Guide*, 1:196.
19. Palmer, *River and the Rock*, p. 202, reports that the value was set at "some $160,000."
20. Boatner, *Encyclopedia*, p. 697. Apparently de Fleury was initially voted a *silver* medal but four years later he received a *gold* medal sent to him by Benjamin Franklin.
21. Palmer, *River and the Rock*, p. 200-201; Fitzpatrick, *Washington's Writings*, 15:433-34.
22. Palmer, *River and the Rock*, p. 201.
23. Ibid., p. 202.
24. Ibid., pp. 208-9; George F. Scheer and Hugh F. Rankin, *Rebels and Redcoats*, reprint ed. (New York, 1963), p. 418; Stember, *Bicentennial Guide*, 1:197.
25. Palmer, *River and the Rock*, p. 209.
26. Ibid., p. 215.

FORT KLOCK

Boatner, *Encyclopedia*, pp. 585-86; *Landmarks*, pp. 244-45; Donlon, *Montgomery County*, p. 198; Vrooman, *Forts and Firesides*, pp. 159-61; Douglas Ayres, Jr., Fort Plain, N.Y., April 20, 1970, to the author.

FORT LA PRÉSENTATION

Robert C. Alberts, *The Most Extraordinary Adventures of Major Robert Stobo* (Boston, 1965), pp. 282-83; Brandow, *Old Saratoga,* p. 31; Clarke, *Bloody Mohawk,* p. 176; Gates Curtis, *Our County and Its People: A Memorial Record of St. Lawrence County, New York* (Syracuse, N.Y., 1894), p. 42; Philias S. Garand, *The History of the City of Ogdensburg* (Ogdensburg, N.Y., 1927), pp. 18-30; Frederick Webb Hodge, *Handbook of American Indians, North of Mexico,* reprinted. (New York, 1960), 2:162; Harold A. Innis, *The Fur Trade in Canada,* reprint ed. (New Haven, Conn., 1962), p. 386; Thad. W. H. Leavitt, *History of Leeds and Grenville* (Brockville, Ont., 1879), pp. 6-7; Lossing, *Revolution,* 1:212-13; Peckham, *Colonial Wars,* pp. 197-99; *Watertown* (N.Y.) *Times,* March 26, 1961. Mary H. Biondi, St. Lawrence County History Center, Canton, N.Y., January 15, 1972, to the author; Ogdensburg Public Library, March 31, 1972, to the author; Public Archives of Canada, Ottawa, Ont., May 10, 1972, to the author; St. Lawrence County Historical Association, Canton, N.Y., November 22, 1960, to the author.

THE LONG ISLAND FORTS

1. According to the *Connecticut Bicentennial Gazette* (Winter 1972) Meigs commanded a force of 400 men. Boatner, *Landmarks,* pp. 295-96, puts the figure at 170 men. Parsons to Trumbull, dated "N. Haven, May, 25, '77," stipulates that only 160 men were with Meigs.

2. A century ago Richard M. Bayles wrote that Meigs and about two hundred men left New Haven on May 21 but that "foul weather detained them at Guilford a day or two" (*Historical and Descriptive Sketches of Suffolk County, New York* [Port Jefferson, N.Y., 1874], p. 342).

3 Henry Onderdonk, Jr., ed., *Revolutionary Incidents of Suffolk and Kings Counties: With an Account of the Battle of Long Island and the British Prisons and Prison-Ships at New-York* (New York, 1849), p. 64.

4. Boatner, *Landmarks,* pp. 305-6, says the attack by 500 Patriots took place on August 22. Bayles, *Historical Sketches,* pp. 98-99, stipulates 150 men but does not give date. Onderdonk says attack was launched by 500 men on August 25.

5. According to Boatner, *Encyclopedia,* p. 395, the Provincial Congress of New Jersey on June 15, 1776, declared William Franklin an enemy and ordered his arrest. The Tory son of Benjamin Franklin suffered "severe treatment" as a prisoner at East Windsor, Connecticut, being released in October 1778 in a prisoner exchange. Van Doren, *Secret History,* p. 114, says he was exchanged for John McKinley, American "president" of Delaware. According to the *Connecticut Bicentennial Gazette* (Winter 1972), Franklin, on July 5, 1776, was "sent first to Wallingford, subsequently to Middletown, and later to Litchfield for imprisonment."

6. Huntington Historical Society, September 10, 1974, to the author, reports that the original Lloyd Manor House, often claimed in history books to have been burned, is still standing and "restoration work will begin on it next week."

Bayles, *Historical Sketches,* pp. 96-97, 342; Boatner, *Encyclopedia,* pp. 376-77, 395; *Landmarks,* pp. 48-49, 243, 247, 295-96, 305-6; Clinton, *Public Papers,* 7:374-75; William R. Donaldson, *The Fort Salonga Story* (Fort Salonga, N.Y., n.d.); Allen Dulles, ed., *Great True Spy Stories* (New York, 1968), pp. 101-10; C. Russell Irwin, "Fort Slongo and Its Environs in the Revolutionary War," MS of address to the Smithtown (N.Y.) Historical Society, April 10, 1959; Lossing, *Revolution,* 2:833-34; W. W. Munsell, *History of Suffolk County, New York, 1683-1882* (New York, 1882), p. 16; Henry Onderdonk, Jr., ed., *Documents and Letters Intended to Illustrate the Revolutionary Incidents of Queens County,* (New York, 1846), pp. 211-13; *Suffolk and Kings Counties,* pp. 64, 104-5; Robert B. Roberts, "The British Were Here!" in Long Island *Newsday,* July 1, 1973; Harry D.

Sleight, *Sag Harbor in Earlier Days* (Bridgehampton, N.Y., 1930), pp. 37, 69-70, 72, 174, 196; *Brooklyn* (N.Y.) *Standard Union,* October 2, 1921; Kings Park (N.Y.) *The Independent,* August 8, 1961; Long Island (N.Y.) *Forum,* December 1948 and July 1961; Long Island (N.Y.) *Newsday,* January 28, 1973, February 19, 1968, July 1, 1973, and February 9, 1974; New York *Herald Tribune,* May 2, 1965; *New York Times,* September 22, 1959.

THE MINISINK FORTS

Boatner, *Encyclopedia,* pp. 708-9; Clark, "A Look at Orange County History," *Orange County Government News Report,* September 1972; Bruce Grant, *American Forts, Yesterday and Today* (New York, 1965), p. 53, reports that Decker's fort was built in 1779; Stone, *Border Wars,* 1:376.

FORT NELLIS

Boatner, *Encyclopedia,* p. 585; Donlon, *Montgomery County,* p. 177; Simms, *Frontiersmen,* 2:383-84; Elizabeth Bilobrowka, St. Johnsville, N.Y., January 7, 1974, to the author.

NEW PETERSBURG FORT

W. N. P. Dailey, "Mohawk Valley Forts: Historical Sketch," address delivered before Caughnawaga Chapter, D.A.R., Fonda, N.Y., June 14, 1917, n.p.

NEW WINDSOR CANTONMENT

Boatner, *Encyclopedia,* pp. 780-82, 999; *Landmarks,* pp. 267-68; Commager and Morris, *Spirit of 'Seventy-Six,* pp. 1245-46; Fitzpatrick, *Washington's Writings,* 26:76 n.; Stember, *Bicentennial Guide,* 1:203-6; Justin Winsor, *The American Revolution: A Narrative, Critical and Bibliographical History,* reprint ed. (New York, 1972), pp. 745-46; *New York Times,* May 9, 1965, and May 26, 1968.

NEW YORK CITY

1. U.S. Bureau of the Census, *Historical Statistics of the United States* (Washington, D.C., 1960). These 1770 population figures should be incremented by perhaps ten percent to reach approximations for the year 1776.

2. Boatner, *Encyclopedia,* p. 882; Donald Barr Chidsey, *The War in the South* (New York, 1969), p. 15.

3. Henry Knox to Lucy Knox, January 5, 1776, Society of the Cincinnati, Massachusetts, Francis S. Drake's *Memorials* (Boston, 1873), pp. 108-9.

4. Lossing, *Revolution,* 2:798.

5. Ibid.

6. Boatner, *Encyclopedia,* p. 797; Henry P. Johnston, *The Campaign of 1776 Around New York and Brooklyn* (Brooklyn, N.Y., 1878), 3:54.

7. Johnston, *Campaign of 1776,* 3:57-58, 61.

8. Bliven, *Under the Guns,* p. 151.

9. Boatner, *Encyclopedia,* pp. 797-98.

10. Johnston, *Campaign of 1776,* preface. More than adequate summaries of both the Battle of (Long Island) Brooklyn and the New York campaign will be found in Boatner's *Encyclopedia.* The most complete accounts of the campaigns in Brooklyn and New York are found in Henry P. Johnston's *The Campaign of 1776.*

The opposing armies were unlike in numbers as well as quality, with the British forces appearing from the outset the inevitable victors. Johnston, *Campaign of 1776,* 3:124, 132-33, discusses the obvious differences:

Washington's army, at the opening of the campaign on August 27th, consisted of 71 regiments or parts of regiments, 25 of which were Continental, aggregating in round numbers 28,500 officers and men. . . . Between eight and nine thousand were on the sick-list or not available for duty, leaving on the rolls not far from 19,000 effectives, most of them levies and militia, on the day of the battle of Long Island. . . .

A far more perfect and formidable army was that which lay encamped on Staten Island, seven miles down the bay. It was the best officered, disciplined, and equipped that Great Britain could then have mustered for any service. The fact that she found it difficult to raise new troops to conquer America only made it necessary to send forward all her available old soldiers. The greater part of Howe's army, accordingly, consisted of experienced regulars. He had with him 27 regiments of the line, four battalions of light infantry and four of grenadiers, two battalions of the king's guards, three brigades of artillery, and a regiment of light dragoons, numbering in the aggregate about 23,000 officers and men. The 6,000 or more that came from Halifax were the Boston "veterans." These had been joined by regiments from the West Indies; and among the reinforcements from Britain were troops that had garrisoned Gibraltar and posts in Ireland and England, with men from Scotland who had won a name in the Seven Years' War. Howe's generals were men who showed their fitness to command by their subsequent conduct during the war. . . .

The Hessians or "foreigners" formed more than one fourth of the enemy's strength. They numbered 8,000 officers and men, which, added to the distinctively British force, raised Howe's total to over 31,000. His total effectives on the 27th of August was something more than 24,000. To the British force should be added two or three companies of New York loyalists.

American Heritage (June 1974), p. 57; Berg, *Continental Army Units,* pp. 35, 59, 69. Bruce Bliven, Jr., *Battle for Manhattan* (New York, 1955), pp. 19-20, 54; *Under the Guns,* pp. 5, 35-38, 101-2, 104, 127, 131, 141, 150-51; Boatner, *Encyclopedia,* pp. 375, 377, 386, 388, 499, 568-69, 575, 729-30, 758, 835, 1044, 1048, 1130, 1200; *Landmarks,* pp. 272, 275, 277-78, 286-87; Bolton, *County of Westchester,* 2:336-37; Carrington, *Battles,* pp. 242, 292; Michael Cohn, "The Fortifications of New York City During the Revolution" (Brooklyn, N.Y., 1962); Kenneth Holcomb Dunshee, *As You Pass By* (New York, 1952), pp. 162, 164, 253; Fiske, *Revolution,* 1:129; Douglas S. Freeman, *George Washington, A Biography* (New York, 1948-52), 4:187; Rodman Gilder, *The Battery* (Boston, 1936), pp. 1-9, 15, 24-27, 30-32, 47, 50-90, 92-97, 100-116, 278; Hammond, *Quaint and Historic Forts,* pp. 36-42; William Heath, *Memoirs of the American War* (New York, 1904), pp. 15, 55, 73-76, 117; Otto Hufeland, *Westchester County During the American Revolution* (New York, 1926), pp. 104, 316, 398; Washington Irving, *Knickerbocker's History of New York,* reprint ed. (New York, 1959), pp. 116-17; Johnston, *Campaign of 1776,* 3:41, 55, 57, 85-90; Thomas Jones, *History of New York During the Revolution* (New York, 1879), 1:630; Leonard, *City of New York,* pp. 263, 266, 268; Lossing, *Revolution,* 2:799, 800, 816; (New York City) Municipal Reference Library *Notes* (June 1962), pp. 100-102; Palmer, *River and the Rock,* pp. 23, 25; Scheer and Rankin, *Rebels and Redcoats,* p. 166; Charles G. Shaw, *New York—Oddly Enough* (New York, 1938), p. 190; Stember, *Bicentennial Guide,* 1:231; I. N. Phelps Stokes, *The Iconography of Manhattan Island, 1498-1909* (New York, 1915-28), 1:317-20, 3:944-46; William A. Tieck, *Riverdale, Kingsbridge, Spuyten Duyvil: New York* (Old Tappan, N.J., 1968), p. 205; Albert Ulmann, *A Landmark History of New York* (New York, 1939), pp. 113-19, 330-31, 345, 366-69; Van Doren, *Secret History,* pp. 17-18; *New-York Gazette and Weekly Mercury,* April 15, 1776, and May 6, 1776; *New York Post,* January 2, 1966; *New York Times,* July 18, 1958 and October 6, 1964; Center of Military History, Department of the Army, Washington, D.C., September 23, 1975, to the author; New-York Historical Society, September 14, 1967, to the author.

BROOKLYN

Berg, *Continental Army Units*, p. 33; Boatner, *Encyclopedia*, pp. 647-55; 895; *Landmarks*, pp. 284-85; Carrington, *Battles*, pp. 201, 207-11; Cohn, "Fortifications"; Johnston, *Campaign of 1776*, 3:68-73, 75-78; Lossing, *Revolution*, 2:806 n. and map; Scheer and Rankin, *Rebels and Redcoats*, p. 163; Stember, *Bicentennial Gude*, 1:226-28; Henry R. Stiles, *A History of the City of Brooklyn* (New York, 1867), 1:62, 247-49, 252, 272, 278-79, 313-16; *History of Kings County, New York* (New York, 1884), 1:61, map; Ulmann, *Landmark History*, p. 385; *Brooklyn Daily Eagle*, March 17, 1939; *New York Times*, January 15, 1970, and June 25, 1975.

STATEN ISLAND

Boatner, *Encyclopedia*, pp. 847, 1012, 1054-55; *Landmarks*, pp. 288-89; Clinton, *American Rebellion*, p. 68 n.; Cohn, "Fortifications"; Emanuel Raymond Lewis, *Seacoast Fortifications of the United States: An Introductory History* (Washington, D.C., 1970), p. 27; Prucha, *Guide to the Military Posts*, p. 114; *Range Finder* (December 1944), Fort Wadsworth, N.Y.; Stember, *Bicentennial Guide*, 1:218-26; Staten Island Historical Society, Richmondtown, N.Y., August 12, 1960, and January 2, 1970.

NEW JERSEY

Boatner, *Encyclopedia*, pp. 119-20, 381, 836-41; *Landmarks*, p. 191; Clinton, *American Rebellion*, pp. 200-201, 538; Cohn, "Fortifications"; Commager and Morris, *Spirit of 'Seventy-Six*, p. 704; Fitzpatrick, *Washington's Writings*, 9:260-62; Grant, *American Forts*, pp. 75-76; Johnston, *Campaign of 1776*, 3:89; Adrian C. Leiby, *The Revolutionary War in the Hackensack Valley* (New Brunswick, N.J., 1962), pp. 50-52, 68, 253-60; Lossing, *Revolution*, 2:828; William B. Reed, *Life and Correspondence of Joseph Reed* (Philadelphia, 1847), 2:125-26; Royal Historical Manuscripts Commission, *Report on the Manuscripts of the Late Reginald Rawdon Hastings* (London, 1930-47), 3:190-92; Elswyth Thane, *The Fighting Quaker: Nathanael Greene* (New York, 1972), p. 67; New Jersey Historical Commission *Newsletter* (May 1973 and January 1975); *New York Times*, June 22, 1956.

FORT NIAGARA

1. Claud H. Hultzén, *Old Fort Niagara: The Story of an Ancient Gateway to the West* (Buffalo, N.Y., 1939), p. 11.
2. Ibid., p. 12.
3. Lewis Henry Morgan, *League of the Iroquois*, reprint ed. (New York, 1962), p. 8.
4. Hultzén, *Old Fort Niagara*, p. 15.
5. The location of Fort Frontenac was on the site of the old Indian village of Cadaraqui, a name sometimes applied to the fort.
6. Hultzén, *Old Fort Niagara*, pp. 16-17.
7. Ibid., p. 20.
8. Ibid., p. 21.
9. Ibid., p. 24.
10. Ibid.
11. Ibid., pp. 25, 27.
12. Ibid., pp. 29-31.
13. Frank H. Severance, *An Old Frontier of France* (New York, 1917), 1:237-38.
14. From the first day it opened its doors to trading, the House of Peace was eminently successful. The tremendous number of furs brought into the post during the years of

French control is incredible. Just for the 1977 season alone, with the fort-trading post just about completed, records reveal that beaver, called *castor* by the French, accounted for 2,580 pelts, with 4,096 of other animal species, including buck, red deer, bear, marten, otter, moose, polecat, mink, and fisher. Lloyd Graham, *Niagara Country* (New York, 1949), p. 38.

During the following three decades, the French constructed additional facilities and instituted military improvements. "It had its ravines, its ditches and pickets, its curtains and counterscarps, its covered way, drawbridge, and raking batteries, laboratory, and magazine; its mess-house, barracks, and bakery, and blacksmith shop; consistent with French practice, a chapel was constructed, with a large ancient dial over the front door to mark the course of the sun. For years it was the largest habitation, a city in itself, south of Montreal and west of Albany. Originally, the fortifications covered an area of eight acres" (U.S. War Department, Surgeon General's Office, Circular no. 4, *A Report on Barracks and Hospitals, with Descriptions of Military Posts* [Washington, D.C., 1870]).

The House of Peace (The Castle) itself included the council chamber, trading room, sleeping quarters, kitchen, prison, dungeon, chapel, and the gun deck. Boatner, *Landmarks*, p. 245.

15. Howard, *Thundergate*, p. 61.
16. These papers are in the Royal Archives, Windsor Castle.
17. Howard, *Thundergate*, p. 72.
18. Ibid., pp. 73-74.
19. Ibid., p. 75.
20. Ibid.
21. Ibid., p. 81.
22. Ibid., pp. 81-83.
23. Ibid., pp. 83-84.
24. Ibid., p. 84.
25. Ibid., p. 88; Arthur Pound, *Lake Ontario* (Indianapolis, Ind., 1945), p. 81.
26. Howard, *Thundergate*, pp. 89-90.
27. Pound, *Lake Ontario*, p. 81.
28. Howard, *Thundergate*, p. 90.
29. Ibid., p. 91.
30. Ibid., pp. 91-92.
31. Ibid., p. 93.
32. Ibid., p. 95; Pound, *Lake Ontario*, p. 81.
33. Pound, *Lake Ontario*, p. 82.
34. Howard, *Thundergate*, p. 96.
35. Ibid., p. 99.
36. Ibid., pp. 99-100; Pound, *Lake Ontario*, p. 83.
37. Navy Island, seized by William Lyon Mackenzie's Patriots in the late 1830s.
38. Howard, *Thundergate*, pp. 105.
39. Ibid., p. 111; "Blockhouses were built along the portage road; it was the best protected highway in all North America" (Edward T. Williams, *Scenic and Historic Niagara Falls* [Niagara Falls, N.Y., 1925], p. 101).
40. Howard, *Thundergate*, p. 113.
41. Ibid., pp. 113-14.
42. Hultzén, *Old Fort Niagara*, p. 37.
43. The Expedition against the Six Nations and their British and Loyalist leaders captured the imagination of the Americans. It awakened tremendous interest and was the theme of conversation all along the Atlantic seaboard. The newspapers of the day discussed it at great length. The novelty and uniqueness of this campaign against the red men in the wilderness with the strange sights and new experiences produced one result

which did not characterize any other movement in the Revolution to so great a degree. Officers and chaplains and privates kept diaries and journals of the happenings. About thirty of these personal observations have survived and most of them have been printed. Although a few letters written by men on the expedition have survived—it may be that owing to conditions few were written—yet these diaries and journals give us today a remarkable picture of the occurrences (Alexander C. Flick, *Sullivan-Clinton Campaign*, pp. 12-13).

44. Sydney G. Fisher, *The Struggle for American Independence* (Philadelphia and London, 1908), 2:245.

45. Chenussio, a major Seneca village; Graymont, *Iroquois*, p. 110.

46. Hultzén, *Old Fort Niagara*, p. 38.

47. U.S. War Department, *A Report on Barracks*.

48. Old Fort Niagara Association, Youngstown, N.Y., October 25, 1973, to the author.

THE OSWEGO FORTS

1. "Reference Bibliography," Fort Ontario Museum, p. 1.

2. Arthur Pound, former New York State Historian and author of *Lake Ontario*.

3. Vrooman, *Forts and Firesides*, pp. 279-80.

4. Ibid., pp. 280-81.

5. Clarke, *Bloody Mohawk*, p. 121.

6. Howard, *Thundergate*, p. 57.

7. Ibid., p. 60.

8. Ibid., pp. 61-62.

9. Ibid., p. 66.

10. Frederick Tilberg, *Fort Necessity National Battlefield Site, Pennsylvania*, National Park Service Historical Handbook Series, no. 19, rev. ed. (Washington, D. C., 1956), p. 1.

11. Ibid.

12. Hammond, *Quaint and Historic Forts*, p. 126.

13. "Fort Ontario," *Report on Barracks*.

14. Clarke, *Bloody Mohawk*, p. 153.

15. Ibid., pp. 154-55; Pound, *Lake Ontario*, p. 77.

16. Pound, *Lake Ontario*, p. 78.

17. Pargellis, *Military Affairs*, pp. 191-92.

18. Howard, *Thundergate*, p. 76.

19. Ibid.

20. Ibid., p. 77.

21. Ibid.

22. Clarke, *Bloody Mohawk*, pp. 156-58; Howard, *Thundergate*, pp. 77-78; Pound, *Lake Ontario*, pp. 78-79.

23. Pound, *Lake Ontario*, p. 79.

24. Howard, *Thundergate*, p. 79.

25. Ibid., p. 83.

26. Clarke, *Bloody Mohawk*, pp. 167-68; Howard, *Thundergate*, 81-83; Pound, *Lake Ontario*, pp. 79-80.

27. Pound, *Lake Ontario*, p. 80.

28. Clarke, *Bloody Mohawk*, p. 168; Pound, *Lake Ontario*, pp. 80-81.

29. Clarke, *Bloody Mohawk*, pp. 169-71; Pound, *Lake Ontario*, pp. 81-83.

30. Clarke, *Bloody Mohawk*, pp. 173-78; Pound, *Lake Ontario*, p. 84.

31. Clarke, *Bloody Mohawk*, pp. 184-85; Pound, *Lake Ontario*, pp. 85-87.

32. Pound, *Lake Ontario*, p. 91.

33. Ibid., p. 92.

34. Ibid., pp. 94-95.

35. Graymont, *Iroquois*, p. 161.
36. *Parliamentary History of England*, 19:1400.
37. Pound, *Lake Ontario*, p. 100.
38. Ibid., p. 102.
39. Ibid., p. 103.
40. Ibid., pp. 104-5.
Boatner, *Landmarks*, pp. 245-46; James and Stotz, *Drums in the Forest*, pp. 37-38, 47, 68-69; Prucha, *Guide to the Military Posts*, p. 96. Johnson G. Cooper, Teachers College, State University of New York, Oswego, N.Y., August 24, 1960, to the author; Wallace F. Workmaster, Central N.Y. State Parks Commission, Jamesville, N.Y., Mary 27, 1971, and January 8 and March 1, 1973, to the author.

OSWEGO FALLS PALISADE

Crisfield Johnson, *History of Oswego County, New York* (Philadelphia, 1877), pp. 32-33; Wallace F. Workmaster, Jamesville, N.Y., May 27, 1971, to the author.

FORT PARIS

Boatner, *Landmarks*, pp. 309-10; Charles B. Briggs, monograph, "Paris Blockhouse" (n.d.); Crouse, "Forts and Block Houses," p. 88; Donlon, *Montgomery County*, p. 199; Greene, *Old Fort Plain*, p. 34; Simms, *Frontiersmen*, 1:574, erroneously reports that Fort Paris was "a palisaded enclosure of strong block-houses"; Charles B. Briggs, Johnson Hall, Johnstown, N.Y., May 22, 1974, to the author.

FORT PLAIN

Boatner, *Landmarks*, p. 246; Crouse, "Forts and Block Houses," p. 88; Donlon, *Montgomery County*, pp. 75, 198-99; Nelson Greene, *History of the Mohawk Valley: Gateway to the West, 1614-1925* (Chicago, 1925), 2:1041; *Old Fort Plain*, pp. 32-35; Lossing, *Revolution*, 1:261-63, 294-95; Simms, *Frontiersmen*, 1:571-75; Fort Plain (N.Y.) *Courier-Standard*, February 1, 1945; St. Johnsville (N.Y.) *Courier-Standard-Enterprise*, August 2 and 9, 1972; *New York Times*, May 5, 1963; American Antiquarian Society, Worcester, Mass., August 28, 1974, to the author; Fort Plain Museum, April 30, 1974, to the author.

FORT PLANK

Boatner, *Encyclopedia*, p. 180; Greene, *Old Fort Plain*, p. 34, says the fort was erected in 1776; Lossing, *Revolution*, 1:262; Stone, *Border Wars*, 1:98-99; Elizabeth Bilobrowka, St. Johnsville, N.Y., January 7, 1974, to the author.

FORT PLUM POINT

Lossing, *Revolution*, 2:113-14; Palmer, *River and the Rock*, pp. 28, 70-71, 79, 83, 99, 127; USMA Library, West Point, N.Y., June 20, 1974, to the author.

RED HOOK BARRACKS

1. Red Hook was often confused by early historians with Roa Hook at Peekskill, the site of Fort Independence.
2. See Boatner, *Encyclopedia*, pp. 639-44, for summarized histories of members of the Livingston family and their descendants.
3. USMA Library, West Point, N.Y., January 8, 1975, to the author.

FORT REID

1. Literally, "fire of joy." According to the *Random House Dictionary of the English Language,* the original French term meant a "public bonfire, as in celebration of an event." During the Revolution, the term was applied to the "firing of guns in rapid succession, as along a line of troops, to mark a victory." Freeman, *George Washington,* 5:2, describes a similar ceremony at Valley Forge on May 6, 1778, to commemorate the French Alliance.

Boatner, *Encyclopedia,* p. 1075; Worthington Chauncey Ford, ed., *Writings of George Washington* (New York, 1889-93), 7:460-63; *Sullivan-Clinton Campaign,* pp. 90-93; Ausburn Towner, *Our County and Its People: A History of the Valley and County of Chemung, New York* (Syracuse, N.Y., 1892), pp. 35-37.

FORT RENSSELAER

Boatner, *Landmarks,* p. 325; Donlon, *Montgomery County,* p. 36; Frothingham, *Montgomery County,* p. 243; Simms, *Frontiersmen,* 2:381; Canajoharie (N.Y.) Library and Art Gallery, July 10, 1958, to the author.

RHEIMENSNYDER'S FORT

Benton, *Herkimer County,* pp. 90, 434, 436; Clinton, *Public Papers,* 5:589-90; John Homer French, *Gazetteer of the State of New York* (Syracuse, N.Y., 1860), p. 346; John B. Koetteritz, address, "The Town of Manheim," before the Herkimer County Historical Society, May 10, 1902; Hazel C. Patrick, Herkimer, N.Y., November 5 and 15, 1973, to the author.

SACANDAGA BLOCKHOUSE

Graymont, *Iroquois,* p. 167; Simms, *Frontiersmen,* 2:311-14, erroneously reports that the blockhouse was built in 1779 and was still in existence on April 1, 1780, when a few defenders successfully repulsed an Indian raid; Fulton County Historian, Gloversville, N.Y., May 17, 1974, to the author; Montgomery County Department of History and Archives, Fonda, N.Y., April 10, 1974, to the author.

THE SARATOGA FORTS

1. More than thirty thousand German soldiers, two-thirds of them from Hesse-Cassel, fought for the British in America. More than six thousand remained to start new lives.

2. Morgan's Rifle Corps (Eleventh Regiment of Virginia, Continental Line), largely consisting of men from the Morristown encampment, 1776/77, is credited with the Patriot victory at Saratoga. Morgan's men served at Valley Forge, Trenton, and Princeton, and were the last to engage the enemy at the Battle of Monmouth. New Jersey Historical Commission *Newsletter,* April 1973.

3. Fiske, *Revolution,* 1:335-37.

4. James Thacher, *A Military Journal during the American Revolutionary War from 1775 to 1783* (Boston, 1823), p. 106.

5. Chastellux, *Travels,* 1:213.

6. Particulars of the Saratoga Convention are more than adequately covered in Boatner, *Encyclopedia,* pp. 275-76, 978-80, and in Fiske, *American Revolution,* 1:343-47.

7. Fiske, *Revolution,* 1:350-51.

Boatner, *Encyclopedia,* pp. 275-76, 971-80; Chastellux, *Travels,* 1:210-13; Fiske, *Revolution,* 1:308-51; Lossing, *Revolution,* 1:48-49, 51, 57-58; *New York Times,* June 24, 1962, and October 31, 1965.

FORT SCHENECTADY

Boatner, *Landmarks,* p. 302; *Bicentennial Bulletin* (ARBA), June 26, 1973; Chastellux, *Travels,* 1:207; Clarke, *Bloody Mohawk,* pp. 68-69, 97-99; John Miller, *Description of the Province and City of New York, with Plans of the City and Several Forts as They Existed in the Year 1695* (London, 1696); U.S. Works Progress Administration (WPA), *New York: A Guide to the Empire State* (New York, 1940), pp. 318-19, 325; Jonathan Pearson, *History of the Schenectady Patent* (Albany, N.Y., 1883), pp. 304-33; *New York Times,* December 10, 1939, and September 14, 1969.

FORT SCHLOSSER

Graham, *Niagara Country,* p. 32; Grant, *American Forts,* p. 52; Howard, *Thundergate,* p. 63; Peter A. Porter, "The Old Stone Chimney at Schlosser," *Niagara Falls Gazette,* August 18, 1902; Donald E. Loker, Niagara Falls Public Library, December 26, 1973, and August 18, 1975, to the author.

SCHUYLER'S SUPPLY DEPOT

Brandow, *Story of Old Saratoga,* p. 86; Nathaniel B. Sylvester, *History of Saratoga County, New York* (Philadelphia, 1878), p. 286; Mrs. J. B. Vanderwerker, *Early Days in Eastern Saratoga County* (n.d.), p. 6.

FORT SKENESBOROUGH

1. Force, *American Archives,* 3d ser., pp. 606-7.
2. Crisfield Johnson, *History of Washington County, New York* (Philadelphia, 1878), p. 474.
3. Ibid., p. 474 n.
4. Sir Henry Clinton reports on how he "watched" from afar Burgoyne's progress. "And I had accordingly written to General Burgoyne about the 10th of August, to apprise him of my present inability to make a diversion in his favor, but assuring him that I should not neglect to attempt something the first moment it was in my power. . . . Besides, I did not perceive any possibility of my ever being in a condition to escort supplies to him from New York. I was at last relieved from my suspense by a letter from General Burgoyne dated from Fort Edward on the 6th of August, wherein was described his march thither from Skenesboro and his expectation of reaching Albany by the 23d at farthest" (*American Rebellion,* p. 70).
   Doris Begor Morton's *Philip Skene of Skenesborough* (Granville, N.Y., 1959) should be consulted for much more detailed information on the Skene family and Philip Skene's extraordinary settlement. There are some minor errors in fact and typography, but the little book is noteworthy for its genealogical scholarship.
   Berg, *Continental Army Units,* p. 85; Boatner, *Encyclopedia,* pp. 195, 1010-12, 1103; *Landmarks,* pp. 329-30; Johnson, *Washington County,* pp. 473-74; Morton, *Philip Skene,* pp. 28-30, 46-47, 49-60; Bernard Romans to Gen. Horatio Gates, November 8, 1776, in Force's *American Archives,* 3d ser., pp. 606-7; Mrs. Doris B. Morton, Whitehall, N.Y., April 13 and June 4, 1974, to the author.

FORT STANWIX

1. New York State, Department of Education, *The American Flag* (Albany, N.Y., 1927 [?]), p. 18; Boatner, *Landmarks,* p. 248, reports that the English first fortified the site in 1725.
2. Boatner, *Landmarks,* p. 248; Sarles and Shedd, *Colonials and Patriots,* pp. 125-26.

3. John Albert Scott, *Rome, N.Y.: A Short History* (Rome, N.Y., 1945), p. 6.
4. Ibid., pp. 10-11.
5. Boatner, *Encyclopedia*, p. 385; Clarke, *Bloody Mohawk*, p. 202; Scott, *Rome*, p. 10.
6. Scott, *Rome*, p. 31.
7. Ibid.; Boatner, *Landmarks*, p. 248.
8. Boatner, *Encyclopedia*, pp. 960-64.
9. Ibid., p. 961; Clarke, *Bloody Mohawk*, p. 210.
10. *Continental Journal and Weekly Advertiser* (Boston), September 4, 1777.
11. Dwight, *Travels*, 3:196-98. To enhance reader comprehension, the author has edited the passages for narrative continuity without changing a word of Dwight's anecdote.
12. Scheer and Rankin, *Rebels and Redcoats*, pp. 305-10.
13. *New York Times*, August 2, 1970.

FORT WAGNER

Boatner, *Landmarks*, p. 249; Simms, *Frontiersmen*, 2:381-82; Vrooman, *Forts and Friesides*, p. 145.

FORT WALRATH

Simms, *Frontiersmen*, 1:576.

FORT WILLETT

The talented Revolutionary War frontier field commander Col. Marinus Willett is well remembered in the village of Fort Plain, with one of its thoroughfares named for him.

Frothingham, *Montgomery County*, pp. 223-24; Greene, *Old Fort Plain*, pp. 33-34; Simms, *Frontiersmen*, 1:575; Montgomery County Department of History and Archives, Fonda, N.Y., December 4, 1973, to the author.

FORT WILLIAMS

Salem Press (N.Y.), August 9, 1945.

FORT WINDECKER

Greene, *Old Fort Plain*, p. 33; Simms, *Frontiersmen*, 1:575; Montgomery County Department of History and Archives, Fonda, N.Y., December 4, 1973, to the author.

FORT ZIMMERMAN

Donlon, *Montgomery County*, p. 85, suggests that Jacob Zimmerman was a Swiss. Definite clues, however, establish that the émigré was a Palatine German who, with many thousand others, fled their native land because of religious persecution, wars, and burdensome taxes. Most of these people came to America, at the invitation of Queen Anne, by way of Holland and England.

David Kendall Martin, "A Revolutionary Roster of Mohawk Valley Zimmermans-Timmermans" (June 1971), pp. 1-2; Charles and Belle King Mead, "The Timmerman Family," microfilm (1925); Simms, *Frontiersmen*, 2:384; Emma S. Timmerman, "Homestead Notes" (1971), pp. 1-2; "The Lawrence Zimmerman Papers," St. Johnsville (N.Y.) *Enterprise and News*, 1937, pp. 1-3; Douglas Ayres, Jr., Fort Plain, N.Y., April 20, 1970, to the author; Waldemar S. Raymond, County Historian, Fonda, N.Y., August 12, 1975, to the author.

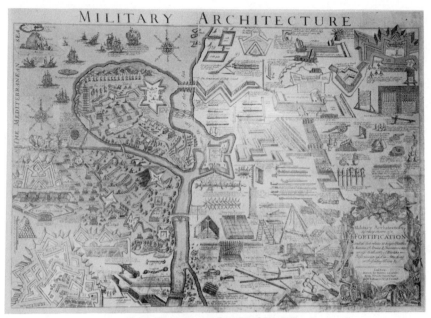

MILITARY ARCHITECTURE

Rare English print illustrates the wide variety of military techniques and tools of the mid-eighteenth century. At lower left is a town fortified according to Vauban's principles. Top left shows method of defense against attack from the sea, and at right are the tools necessary for construction and gunnery. *Courtesy of Fort Ticonderoga Museum*

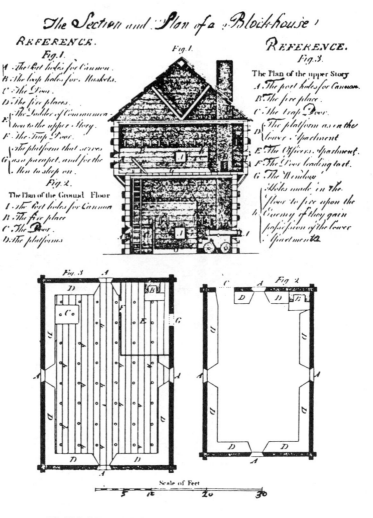

PLAN OF A FRONTIER BLOCKHOUSE (1789)
Drawn by Thomas Anburey, it shows cannon ports and musket loopholes on
both floors.

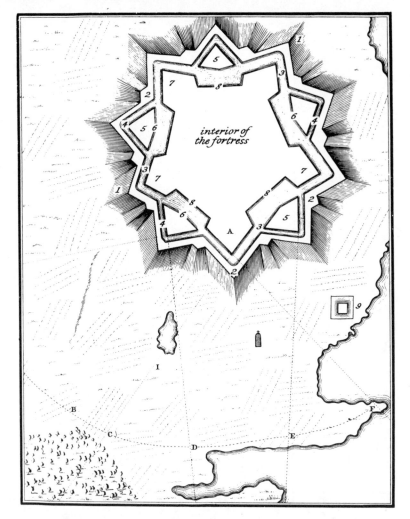

EIGHTEENTH-CENTURY FORTRESS (WITH SIGHT LINES) BY
VAUGAN

(Sebastien LePrestre de Vauban, *A Manual of Siegecraft and Fortification*,
translated by George A. Rothrock. Copyright 1968, University of Michigan
Press)

LEGEND

1. Glacis
2. Covered way
3. Main ditch
4. Ditches of the demilunes
5. Demilunes
6. Throats of the Demilunes
7. Bastions
8. Curtain walls
9. Redoubt
A. Fortress
B. Position of reference for attack force
C—I. Lines of prolongation (sight lines)

(Sebastien LePrestre de Vauban, *A Manual of Siegecraft and Fortification*,
trans. by George A. Rothrock. Copyright 1968, University of Michigan Press)

Cross Section of Simple Fortification

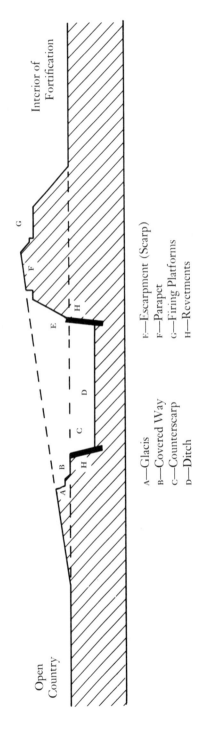

Interior of
Fortification

Open
Country

G   F   E   H   D   C   B   A

A—Glacis   E—Escarpment (Scarp)
B—Covered Way   F—Parapet
C—Counterscarp   G—Firing Platforms
D—Ditch   H—Revetments

Cross Section of Fortification with Outworks

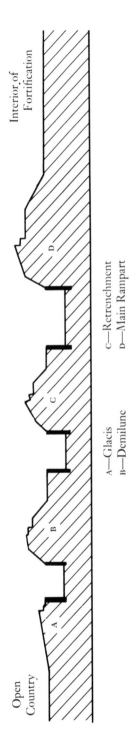

Interior of
Fortification

Open
Country

D   C   B   A

A—Glacis   C—Retrenchment
B—Demilune   D—Main Rampart

Glossary of Eighteenth-Century Fortification Terms

ABATIS: Barricade of felled trees with branches directed toward the enemy.

ARTIFICER: Soldier mechanic.

BANQUETTE: Platform for riflemen inside of parapet.

BARBETTE: Wooden or earthen platform inside a fortification, on which cannons were mounted to permit firing over the rampart instead of through embrasures.

BASTION: Projecting work or blockhouse, usually in angle of fort, to allow enfilading of the enemy along the wall or curtain.

BERME: Horizontal surface between the ditch and the base of the rampart.

BLOCKHOUSE: Traditional frontier defense, either detached or used as a bastion in a fort. Constructed of either rounded or squared logs, with an overhanging second story, the structure was loopholed for musketry or embrasured for cannon, or both.

BROWN BESS: Familiar name for a short, light musket first used by the British Army at the beginning of the eighteenth century, replaced by the rifle more than a century later. "Brown" was derived from the color of the gun's stock, while "Bess" was apparently a corruption of "buss" in the outmoded blunderbuss.

CALIBER or CALIBRE: Measurement applied to the bore of a gun.

CANISTER or CASE SHOT: Bagged or cased small metal pellets, loaded in cannon on top of gunpowder charge. Devastating at close quarters.

CARCASS: Sieved metal can, loaded with rags soaked in a flammable liquid, that was set afire when shot from a cannon; a firebomb.

CASEMATE: Bombproofed vault in fortification wall.

CAUSEWAY: Elevated roadway, usually over a ditch or moat, or occasionally a marsh or morass, leading to the fort's entrance.

CHEVAUX-DE-FRISE: A barricade used on land or in the water, it was constructed of massive timbers with protruding iron-tipped poles. Its use by the Americans during the Revolution was a dismal failure.

COHORN or COEHORN: Originally of Dutch derivation *(coehoorn),* it was a small short-barreled howitzer.

COUNTERSCARP: Outer wall or slope of moat or ditch.

COVERED WAY or COVERT: Depressed platform in outer wall of ditch (counterscarp) for riflemen thus protected by an earthen breastwork.

CURTAIN:The wall of a fortification between bastions.

DEFILADE: A natural or man-made shield to protect either troops or a gun position in face of the enemy.

DEMILUNE: A crescent-or half-moon-shaped gorged outwork to protect the fort's curtain or a bastion.

DRAWBRIDGE: Bridge across a ditch or moat at the fort's entrance, manually raised or lowered.

EMBRASURE: Aperture or slot in curtain or rampart with the sides of the opening slanted outward to increase the angle of cannon fire.

ENFILADE: Position of fortified works or soldiers subjected to a sweeping fire from a line of troops or gun batteries.

ENVELOPMENT: Assault directed against an enemy's flank. In case of attack against two flanks, a double envelopment.

EPAULEMENT: Immediate area where the curtain and a bastion meet.

FASCINE: Bound bundle of long branches or twigs, used in construction of a rampart or an earthworks.

FIELD GUN: Cannon mounted on a mobile carriage for use in the field.

FLÈCHE: (French for arrow). A defensive outwork with two walls or faces forming a salient angle with an open ditch or gorge.

FLINTLOCK or FIRELOCK: A gun with a mechanism for firing the priming charge by a piece of flint striking on steel to produce sparks.

FORT: An enclosed defensive work, with walls or palisades, blockhouses or bastions, armed with cannons, howitzers, etc., and manned by soldiers.

FORTALICE: A small fort or outwork of same.

FOSSE: Ditch or moat.

FRAISE: Pointed stakes in rampart or berme, either horizontal or inclined.

FRONTAL ASSAULT: Equally distributed forces attacking along the whole front.

GABION: Wickerwork filled with earth and stone, used to protect gun batteries, Revolutionary equivalent of today's sandbag.

GLACIS: Sloping earthwork from either the covered way or counterscrap.

GRAPE or GRAPESHOT: The same as CANISTER, except that the balls are much smaller and more plentiful.

GRASSHOPPER: Nickname for the small three-pounder field gun, mounted on legs instead of the normal wheeled carriage. Name derived from the action of the gun when fired. The "grasshopper" was the usual artillery piece carried during field operations.

HORNWORK: An outwork of a pair of demi-bastions joined by a wall or curtain.

HOT SHOT: Cannonballs heated red-hot in a hot-shot oven and utilized for setting fire to wooden fortifications or enemy vessels.

HOWITZER: In use today, it is a short-barreled gun with the ability to fire shells at a high angle of elevation, particularly effective against targets within fortified enclosures or trenches.

LINSTOCK: A cannoner's forked rod or stick that held the slow-burning match to be applied to the prime charge in the touchhole of a muzzle-loading cannon.

LOOPHOLES: Apertures or slots in defenses through which the fire of small arms or cannon can be directed at an outside enemy.

LUNETTE: Same as demilune.

MAGAZINE: Storage facility, usually bombproofed, for ammunition and armaments.

MAHAM TOWER: Devised by Col. Hezekiah Maham, it was first used during the successful siege of Fort Watson, South Carolina, April 1781. Made of logs, the tower had a parapeted superstructure higher than the walls of the fort being besieged.

MANTELET: A mobile bulletproof screen to protect gunners.

MARTELLO TOWER: Separate masonry tower defense, usually erected along the coast to fight off invasion by sea.

MERLON: Section of fortification wall located between any two embrasures.

MORTAR: In use today, it is a short-barreled gun with a large caliber bore, able to propel shells at high angles.

MUSKET: The heavy smoothbore handgun of large caliber, used universally throughout the Revolution.

PALISADE: Wall or curtain constructed of logs or stakes set perpendicularly in the ground, forming a defensive enclosure.

PARADE: Level area of interior of fortification where troops are assembled or reviewed while marching or drilling.

PARALLEL: Trench in the ground, parallel to the lines of the besieged fortification, for covering attacking force.

PARAPET: Earthen or stone defensive platform on wall of fort.

PORTCULLIS: Reinforced grating, raised or lowered on vertical channels, to prevent entrance through a fort's gateway.

POUNDAGE: Term applied to guns that fired solid balls (four-pounder, ten-pounder, etc.).

RAVELIN: V-shaped outwork outside main moat or ditch.

REDAN: V-shaped outwork, with its angle projected toward the enemy.

REDOUBT: A defensive outwork, usually square or polygonal, minus defensive flanks.

REVETMENT: Support facing, masonry or earthen, of a rampart between the fort's wall and the ditch.

ROYAL: Name for a small mortar.

SALIENT ANGLE: Projecting angle, opposite of recessed angle or reentrant.

SALLY PORT: Gateway or postern of a fortification.

SAP: A deep, narrow trench, protected by gabions, used as an approach to a besieged enemy's position or fortification.

SAPPER: British nomenclature for a military engineer.

SAUCISSON: A large fascine.

SCARP or ESCARP: Inner wall of ditch surrounding a fort's ramparts.

SHELL: Explosive missile or bomb fired from a cannon.

SLOW MATCH: Slow-burning fuse or match, consisting of a cord or rope usually soaked in saltpeter.

SPIKING A GUN: Rendering a muzzle-loading cannon useless by driving a spike deep into the gun's touchhole.

STOCKADE: Palisade or barricade, usually loopholed, for entrenchments, blockhouses, and bastions.

SWIVEL GUN: A small cannon mounted on a swivel support to permit wide movement of the weapon on a horizontal plane; usually mounted on a fort's parapet or in a blockhouse.

TENAILLE: A fieldwork with one or two reentering angles, planted in a ditch or moat between two blockhouses or bastions, immediately in front of the fort's curtain.

TERREPLEIN: Platform for cannon on rampart behind the parapet.

TRAVERSE: Defensive barrier placed across the terreplein to minimize enfilading by an attacking enemy.

TRUNNION: One of the two cylindrical projections on a cannon, one on each side to support the gun on its carriage.

Bibliography

Abbott, Wilbur C. *New York in the American Revolution*. New York, 1929.

Adams, James Truslow, ed. *Album of American History*. 5 vols. New York, 1944-49.

———. *Atlas of American History*. New York, 1943.

Adams, Randolph G., and Peckham, Howard H., eds. *Lexington to Fallen Timbers, 1775-1794: Episodes from the Earliest History of our Military Froces*. Ann Arbor, Mich., 1942.

Alberts, Robert C. *The Most Extraordinary Adventures of Major Robert Stobo*. Boston, 1965.

Alden, John Richard. *General Charles Lee: Traitor or Patriot?* Baton Rouge, La., 1951.

Aldrich, Lewis Cass. *History of Ontario County*. Syracuse, N.Y., 1893.

Anderson, George Baker. *Landmarks of Rensselaer County, New York*. Syracuse, N.Y., 1897.

Anderson, Troyer. *The Command of the Howe Brothers during the American Revolution*. New York and London, 1936.

Aptheker, Herbert. *The American Revolution*. New York, 1960.

Ayling, Stanley, *George the Third*. New York, 1972.

Bagg, Moses M. *Pioneers of Utica*. Utica, N.Y., 1877.

Bakeless, John. *Turncoats, Traitors, and Heroes*. Philadelphia, 1959.

Bancroft, George. *The History of the United States*. 12 vols. (vol. 3). New York, 1834-82.

Barnett, Correlli. *Britain and Her Army, 1509-1970*. New York, 1970.

Bayles, Richard M. *Historical and Descriptive Sketches of Suffolk County, New York*. Port Jefferson, N.Y., 1874.

Beauchamp, William M. *A History of the New York Iroquois*. Albany, N.Y., 1905.

————. "Indian Raids in the Mohawk Valley," New York State Historical Association *Proceedings,* vol. 14. Cooperstown, N.Y., 1915.

Beers, F. W. *History of Herkimer County.* New York, 1879.

Belcher, Henry. *The First American Civil War.* 2 vols. London, 1911.

Benton, Nathaniel S. *A History of Herkimer County, Including the Upper Mohawk Valley.* Albany, N.Y., 1856.

Berg, Fred Anderson. *Encyclopedia of Continental Army Units: Battalions, Regiments and Independent Corps.* Harrisburg, Pa., 1972.

Bird, Harrison. *Attack on Quebec.* New York, 1968.

Bliven, Bruce, Jr. *Battle for Manhattan.* New York, 1955.

————. *Under the Guns, New York: 1775-1776.* New York, 1972.

Bloomfield, J. K. *The Oneidas.* New York, 1907.

Boatner, Mark Mayo, III. *Encyclopedia of the American Revolution.* New York, 1966.

————. *Landmarks of the American Revolution.* Harrisburg, Pa., 1973.

Bolton, Robert, Jr. *The History of the Several Towns, Manors, and Patents of the County of Westchester.* 3d ed. New York, 1905.

Boorstin, Daniel J. *The Americans: The Colonial Experience.* New York, 1958.

Boylan, Brian Richard. *Benedict Arnold, The Dark Eagle.* New York, 1973.

Boynton, Edward C. *History of West Point.* New York, 1863.

Brandow, John Henry. *The Story of Old Saratoga and History of Schuylersville.* Albany, N.Y., 1900.

Brock, William R. *The Evolution of American Democracy.* New York, 1970.

Brodhead, John R. *Documents Relative to the Colonial History of the State of New-York,* edited by Edmund B. O'Callaghan. 15 vols. Albany, N.Y., 1853-87.

Callahan, North. *Flight from the Republic: The Tories of the American Revolution.* Indianapolis, Ind., 1967.

————. *Royal Raiders: The Tories of the American Revolution.* Indianapolis, Ind., 1963.

Callan, Estella Folts. "Fort Herkimer Church." New York State Historical Association *Proceedings.* vol. 14. Cooperstown, N.Y., 1915.

Campbell, William W. *Annals of Tryon County.* 4th ed. New York, 1924.

Carmer, Carl. "This Hollowed-Out Ground." *American Heritage* (June 1967).

Carr, William H., and Koke, Richard J. *Twin Forts of the Popolopen:* Forts *Clinton and Montgomery, New York, 1775-1777.* Bear Mountain, N.Y., 1937.

Carrington, Henry B. *Battles of the American Revolution, 1775-1781.* 1877; reprint ed. New York, 1974.

Casler, Nellie Horton. *Cape Vincent and Its History.* Watertown, N.Y., 1906.

Chastellux, Marquis de. *Travels in North America, in the Years 1780, 1781, and 1782.* Edited by Howard C. Rice, Jr. Chapel Hill, N.C., 1963.

Chidsey, Donald Barr. *The War in the South.* New York, 1969.

Clark, Donald F. "A Look at Orange County History." *Orange County Government News Report* (September 1972).

————, ed. *Fort Montgomery and Fort Clinton*. Highlands, N.Y., 1952.

Clark, Thomas D. *Frontier America: The Story of the Westward Movement*. New York, 1959.

Clarke, T. Wood. *The Bloody Mohawk*. New York, 1940.

Clinton, George. *Public Papers of George Clinton, First Governor of New York*, edited by Hugh Hastings. 10 vols. New York and Albany, 1899-1914.

Clinton, Sir Henry. *The American Rebellion: Sir Henry Clinton's Narrative of His Campaigns, 1775-1782*, edited by William B. Willcox. New Haven, Conn., 1954.

Cobleskill High School. *History of Cobleskill*. Cobleskill, N.Y., 1912.

Codman, John. *Arnold's Expedition to Quebec*. New York, 1902.

Cohn, Michael. "The Fortifications of New York City during the Revolution." Thesis in New-York Historical Society. Brooklyn, N.Y., 1962.

Colden, Cadwallader. *The History of the Five Indian Nations*. New York, 1904.

Cole, David. *History of Rockland County*. New York, 1884.

Commager, Henry Steele, and Morris, Richard B., eds. *The Spirit of 'Seventy-Six: The Story of the American Revolution as Told by Participants*. 2d ed. New York, 1967.

Constitution Island Association. *Constitution Island and West Point in the Revolutionary War*. Reprints from annual reports. West Point, N.Y., 1965.
   Dorothy C. Barck. "Constitution Island the Secret Committee."
   John R. Elting. "West Point during the Revolution."
   Alexander C. Flick. "The Construction and History of Fort Constitution."
   Adam E. Potts. "Constitution Island—Historical Sketch."

Cook, Frederick, ed. *Journals of the Military Expedition of Major General John Sullivan Against the Six Nations of Indians in 1779*. Auburn, N.Y., 1887.

Cookinham, Henry J. *History of Oneida County, New York*. vol. 1, pt. 2. Chicago, 1912.

Crouse, Nellis M. "Forts and Block Houses in the Mohawk Valley." New York State Historical Association *Proceedings* 14. Cooperstown, N.Y., 1915.

Crown Point Foundation. *Crown Point on Lake Champlain, 1609-1783*. New York, n.d.

Curtis, Gates. *Our County and Its People: A Memorial Record of St. Lawrence County, New York*. Syracuse, N.Y., 1894.

Dailey, W. N. P. "Mohawk Valley Forts: Historical Sketch." Address delivered before Caughnawaga Chapter, D.A.R., Fonda, N.Y., June 14, 1917.

Dawson, Henry B. *Battles of the United States, by Sea and Land: Embracing Those of the Revolutionary and Indian Wars*. 2 vols. New York, 1858.

Diefendorf, Mary Riggs. *The Historic Mohawk*. New York, 1910.

Donaldson, William R. *The Fort Salonga Story*. Fort Salonga, N.Y., n.d.

Donlon, Hugh P. *Outlines of History: Montgomery County, New York*. Amsterdam, N.Y., 1972.

Draper MSS. Historical Society of Wisconsin.

Dulles, Allen, ed. *Great True Spy Stories*. New York, 1968.

Dunshee, Kenneth Holcomb. *As You Pass By*. New York, 1952.

Durham, J. H. *Carleton Island in the Revolution*. Syracuse, N.Y. 1889.

Dutchess County Historical Society. *Year Book, 1935*.

Dwight, Timothy. *Travels in New England and New York*. 4 vols. Cambridge, Mass., 1969.

Eager, Samuel W. *An Outline History of Orange County*. Newburgh, N.Y., 1846-47.

Edmonds, Walter D. *The Musket and the Cross*. Boston, 1968.

Emerson, Edgar C. *Our County and Its People*. Boston, 1898.

Evers, Alf. *The Catskills: From Wilderness to Woodstock*. Garden City, N.Y., 1972.

Fernow, Berthold, ed. *New York in the Revolution*. Albany, N.Y., 1887.

Ferris, Robert G., ed. *Founders and Frontiersmen*. Washington, D.C., 1967.

Firch, Asa. *A Historical, Topographical and Agricultural Survey of the County of Washington, New York*. Albany, N.Y., 1849.

Fisher, Sydney G. *The Struggle for American Independence*. 2 vols. Philadelphia and London, 1908.

Fiske, John. *The American Revolution*. 2 vols. Boston, 1891.

Fitzpatrick, John C., ed. *The Writings of George Washington*. 39 vols. Washington, D.C., 1931-44.

Flexner, James Thomas. *Mohawk Baronet: Sir William Johnson of New York*. New York, 1959.

————. *The Traitor and the Spy: Benedict Arnold and John André*. New York, 1953.

Flick, Alexander C. *The American Revolution in New York*. Albany, N.Y., 1926.

————. *History of the State of New York*. 5 vols. New York, 1934.

Force, Peter, ed. *American Archives*. 4th and 5th ser. Washington, D.C., 1837-53.

Ford, Corey. *A Peculiar Service*. Boston, 1965.

Ford, Worthington Chauncey, ed. *Writings of George Washington*. 14 vols. New York, 1889-93.

Freedgood, Seymour. *The Gateway States*. New York, 1967.

Freeman, Douglas S. *George Washington, A Biography*. 5 vols. New York, 1948-52.

French, Allen. *The First Year of the American Revolution*. Boston and New York, 1934.

French, John Homer. *Gazetteer of the State of New York*. Syracuse, N.Y., 1860.

Frothingham, Washington. *History of Fulton County, N.Y.* Syracuse, N.Y., 1892.

————. *History of Montgomery County, N.Y.* Syracuse, N.Y., 1892.

Galvin, John R. *The Minute Men: A Compact History of the Defenders of the American Colonies, 1645-1775.* New York, 1967.

Garand, Philias S. *The History of the City of Ogdensburg.* Ogdensburg, N.Y., 1927.

Garden, Alexander. *Anecdotes of the American Revolution.* 3 vols. Brooklyn, N.Y., 1865.

Gates Papers. New-York Historical Society.

George Washington Papers. Library of Congress.

Gifford, Stanley M. *Fort William Henry: A History.* Glens Falls, N.Y., 1955.

Gilder, Rodman. *The Battery.* Boston, 1936.

Gipson, Lawrence Henry. *The British Empire Before the American Revolution.* 13 vols. New York, 1954-67.

Glen Papers. New York Public Library, Manuscript Division.

Goldstone, Harmon H., and Dalrymple, Martha. *History Preserved: A Guide to New York City Landmarks and Historic Districts.* New York, 1974.

Governors Island, The Story of. Headquarters, First U.S. Army. Governors Island, N.Y., 1960.

Graham, Lloyd. *Niagara Country.* New York, 1949.

Grant, Bruce. *American Forts, Yesterday and Today.* New York, 1965.

Graymont, Barbara. *The Iroquois in the American Revolution.* Syracuse, N.Y., 1972.

Greene, Nelson. *History of the Mohawk Valley: Gateway to the West, 1614-1925.* 4 vols. Chicago, 1925.

————. *The Story of Old Fort Plain and Middle Mohawk Valley.* Fort Plain, N.Y., 1915.

Haddock, John A. *The Growth of a Century: As Illustrated in the History of Jefferson County, New York, 1793-1894.* Albany, N.Y., 1895.

————. *The Picturesque St. Lawrence River.* Watertown, N.Y., 1895.

Haldimand Papers. Public Archives of Canada.

Hall, Edward Hagaman. *McGowan's Pass and Vicinity.* New York, 1905.

Halsey, Francis Whiting. *The Old New York Frontier: Its Wars with Indians and Tories. . . . 1614-1800.* New York, 1912.

Hamilton, Edward P. "The French Colonial Forts at Crown Point Strait." Fort Ticonderoga Museum *Bulletin* (October 1970).

Hammond, John Martin. *Quaint and Historic Forts of North America.* Philadelphia and London, 1915.

Hammond, Mrs. L. M. *History of Madison County, New York.* Syracuse, N.Y., 1872.

Hardin, G. A., and Willard, F. H. *History of Herkimer County,* Syracuse, N.Y., 1893.

Hasbrouck, Frank. *History of the County of Dutchess.* Poughkeepsie, N.Y., 1900.

Hayner, Rutherford. *Troy and Rensselaer County, New York: A History*. New York and Chicago, 1925.

Heath, Major General William. *Memoirs of the American War*. New York, 1904.

Heitman, Francis B. *Historical Register and Dictionary of the United States Army from Its Organization, September 29, 1789, to March 2, 1903*. 2 vols. Washington, D.C., 1903.

Higginbotham, Don. *The War for American Independence: Military Attitudes, Policies, and Practice, 1763-1789*. New York, 1971.

Hill, William H. *Old Fort Edward before 1800*. Fort Edward, N.Y., 1929.

Hodge, Frederick Webb, ed. *Handbook of American Indians North of Mexico*. 2 vols. Washington, D.C., 1907-10; reprint ed. New York, 1960.

Hough, Franklin B. *A History of Jefferson County in the State of New York*. Watertown, N.Y., 1854.

——. *The Thousand Islands of the St. Lawrence*. Syracuse, N.Y., 1880.

Howard, Robert West. *Thundergate: The Forts of Niagara*. Englewood Cliffs, N.J., 1968.

Hufeland, Otto. *Westchester County during the American Revolution*. New York, 1926.

Hultzén, Claud H. *Old Fort Niagara: The Story of an Ancient Gateway to the West*. Buffalo, N.Y., 1939.

Hunt, Gaillard, ed. *Journals of the Continental Congress, 1774-1789*. 34 vols. Washington, D.C., 1904-37.

Hurd, Duane Hamilton. *History of Clinton and Franklin Counties, New York*. Philadelphia, 1880.

——. *A History of Otsego County, New York*. Philadelphia, 1878.

Innis, Harold A. *The Fur Trade in Canada*. 1930; reprint ed. New Haven, Conn., 1962.

Irving, Washington. *Knickerbocker's History of New York*. 1809; reprint ed. New York, 1959.

Irwin, C. Russell. "Fort Slongo and Its Environs in the Revolutionary War." MS of address to the Smithtown (N.Y.) Historical Society, April 10, 1959.

James, Alfred Procter, and Stotz, Charles Morse. *Drums in the Forest*. Pittsburg, Pa., 1958.

Jelks, Edward B. *Archaeological Excavations at Constitution Island, 1971*. West Point, N.Y., 1972.

Jensen, Merrill. *The Founding of a Nation: A History of the American Revolution, 1763-1776*. New York, 1968.

Johnson, Crisfield. *History of Oswego County, New York*. Philadelphia, 1877.

——. *History of Washington County, New York*. Philadelphia, 1878.

Johnston, Henry P. *The Battle of Harlem Heights, September 16, 1776, With a Review of the Events of the Campaign*. New York, 1897.

——. *Campaign of 1776 Around New York and Brooklyn*. 3 vols. Brooklyn, N.Y., 1878.

——. *The Storming of Stony Point on the Hudson, Midnight, July 15, 1779: Its Importance in the Light of Unpublished Documents*. New York, 1900.

Jones, Pomeroy. *Annals of Oneida County, New York.* Rome, N.Y., 1851.

Jones, Thomas. *History of New York during the Revolutionary War.* 2 vols. New York, 1879.

Kalm, Peter. *Peter Kalm's Travels in North America.* 2 vols. Translated and edited by Adolph B. Benson. New York, 1937.

Kappler, Charles J. *Indian Affairs: Laws and Treaties.* 3 vols. Washington, D.C., 1904.

Ketchum, Richard M., ed. *American Heritage Book of the Revolution.* New York, 1958.

——. "Men of the Revolution." *American Heritage* (August 1974).

——. *The Winter Soldiers.* Garden City, N.Y., 1973.

Knittle, W. A. *Early Eighteenth-Century Palatine Emigration.* Philadelphia, 1937.

Knollenberg, Bernhard. *The Origin of the American Revolution: 1759-1766.* New York, 1960.

Koetteritz, John B. "The Town of Mannheim." MS of an address to the Herkimer County Historical Society, May 10, 1902. Also in Society's *Collections,* vol. 2.

Kristol, Irving. "The American Revolution as a Successful Revolution." Lecture, St. John's Church, Washington, D.C., October 12, 1973. Washington, D.C., 1973.

Landon, Harry F. *The North Country.* Indianapolis, Ind., 1932.

Lane, Samuel. *A Journal for the Years 1739-1803.* Concord, N.H., 1937.

Leavitt, Thad. W. H. *History of Leeds and Grenville.* Brockville, Ont., 1879.

Lehman, Karl H. *Madison County Today.* Oneida Castle, N.Y., 1943.

Leiby, Adrian C. *The Revolutionary War in the Hackensack Valley.* New Brunswick, N.J., 1962.

Leonard, John William. *History of the City of New York, 1609-1909.* New York, 1910.

Lewis, Emanuel Raymond. *Seacoast Fortifications of the United States: An Introductory History.* Washington, D.C., 1970.

Lewis, Theodore Burnham, Jr. "The Crown Point Campaign 1755." Fort Ticonderoga Museum *Bulletin* (October, December 1970).

Lossing, Benson J. *The Pictorial Field-Book of the Revolution.* 2 vols. New York, 1851.

——. *The Pictorial Field-Book of the War of 1812.* New York, 1868.

Lowell, Edward J. *The Hessians in the Revolution.* Williamstown, Mass., 1970.

Ludlum, David M. *Early American Winters, 1604-1820.* Boston, 1966.

Mackesy, Piers. *The War for America, 1775-1783.* Cambridge, Mass., 1965.

Maloney, John. "He Wouldn't Give Up the Fort." *Saturday Evening Post,* August 10, 1946.

Martin, David Kendall. "A Revolutionary Roster of Mohawk Valley Zimmermans-Timmermans." MS in Montgomery County Department of History and Archives, Fonda, N.Y., 1971.

Mead, Charles, and Mead, Belle King. "The Timmerman Family." Microfilm and MS in Montgomery County Department of Archives and History, Fonda, New York, 1925.

Mead, John H. "History Beneath Our Feet." Address delivered September 29, 1969, at a joint meeting of the Constitution Island Association and the Putnam County Historical Society.

Miller, John. *Description of the Province and City of New York, with Plans of the City and Several Forts as They Existed in the Year 1695.* London, 1696 (?)

Miller, John C. *Origins of the American Revolution.* Boston, 1943.

———. *Triumph of Freedom, 1775-1783.* Boston, 1948.

Minutes of the Secret Committee. Washington's Headquarters Museum, Newburgh, N.Y.

Morgan, Lewis Henry. *League of the Iroquois.* Rochester, N.Y., 1851, reprint ed. New York, 1962.

Morton, Doris Begor. *Philip Skene of Skenesborough.* Granville, N.Y., 1959.

Munsell, W. W. *History of Suffolk County, New York, 1683-1882.* New York, 1882.

Mylod, John. *Biography of a River: The People & Legends of the Hudson Valley.* New York, 1969.

Nevins, Allan. *The American States During and After Revolution, 1775-1789.* New York, 1924.

Newell, W. Allan. "Eight Forts of the Upper St. Lawrence River." Address delivered at a joint meeting of the Historical Societies of St. Lawrence, Jefferson, Oswego, and Lewis Counties, at Canton, N.Y., August 18, 1951.

New York City. Municipal Reference Library *Notes* 36, no. 6 (June 1962).

New York State American Revolution Bicentennial Commission. *The Correspondent.* Autumn 1970– . Albany, N.Y.

New York State, Division of Archives and History. *Sullivan-Clinton Campaign in 1779.* Albany, N.Y., 1929.

New York State Historic Trust and New York State Parks and Recreation. *The Mohawk Valley and the American Revolution.* Albany, N.Y., 1972.

Nickerson, Hoffman. *The Turning Point of the Revolution.* Boston, 1928.

Norris, Major. "Journal of Sullivan's Expedition." Buffalo Historical Society *Publications* 1 (1879): 217-52.

Onderdonk, Henry, Jr., ed. *Documents and Letters Intended to Illustrate the Revolutionary Incidents of Queens County.* New York, 1846.

———. *Revolutionary Incidents of Suffolk and Kings Counties: With an Account of the Battle of Long Island and the British Prisons and Prison-Ships at New-York.* New York, 1849.

Oneida Historical Society. *The American Flag.* Utica, N.Y., 1927.

Palisades Interstate Park Commission. *Stony Point Battlefield Reservation.* Bear Mountain, N.Y., 1968.

Palmer, Dave Richard. *The River and the Rock: The History of Fortress West Point, 1775-1783.* New York, 1969.

Palmer, Peter. *History of Lake Champlain*. Albany, N.Y., 1866.

Papers of the Continental Congress. Library of Congress.

Pargellis, Stanley, ed. *Military Affairs in North America, 1748-1763: Selected Documents from the Cumberland Papers in Windsor Castle*. 1936, reprint ed. Hamden, Conn., 1969.

Parliamentary History of England from the Earliest Period of the Year 1803. vol. 19. London, 1814.

Patterson, Emma Lillie. *Peekskill in the American Revolution*. Peekskill, N.Y., 1944.

Pearson, Johnathan. *History of the Schenectady Patent*. Albany, N.Y., 1883.

Peckham, Howard H. *The Colonial Wars: 1689-1762*. Chicago, 1964.

———. *The War for Independence: A Military History*. Chicago, 1958.

Pell, Stephen H. P. *Fort Ticonderoga: A Short History*. Ticonderoga, N.Y., 1935.

Peterson, A. Everett. *Landmarks of New York*. New York, 1923.

Porter, Peter A. "The Old Stone Chimney at Schlosser." *Niagara Falls Gazette*, August 18, 1902.

Pound, Arthur. *Lake Ontario*. Indianapolis, Ind., 1945.

Prucha, Francis Paul. *Guide to the Military Posts of the United States*. Madison, Wis., 1964.

Queen's County, New York, History of. Compiled by the publisher. New York, 1882.

Quinlan, James E. *History of Sullivan County, New York*. Liberty, N.Y., 1873.

Range Finder. (Fort Wadsworth, N.Y.) Holiday issue, December 1944.

Reed, William B. *Life and Correspondence of Joseph Reed*. 2 vols. Philadelphia, 1847.

Reid, William Maxwell. *Lake George and Lake Champlain*. New York, 1910.

———. *The Mohawk Valley*. New York, 1901.

———. *The Story of Old Fort Johnson*. New York, 1906.

Roberts, James A. *New York in the Revolution as Colony and State*. Albany, N.Y., 1897.

Roberts, Kenneth. *March to Quebec*. New York, 1938; rev. ed. 1940.

Roberts, Robert B. "The British Were Here! The British Were Here!" Long Island *Newsday*, July 1, 1973.

Roscoe, William E. *History of Schoharie County, New York*. Syracuse, N.Y., 1882.

Royal Historical Manuscripts Commission. *Report on the Manuscripts of the Late Reginald Rawdon Hastings*. 4 vols. London, 1930-47.

Russell, Carl P. *Guns on the Early Frontiers: A History of Firearms from Colonial Times through the Years of the Western Fur Trade*. Berkeley, Calif., 1957; reprint ed. New York, n.d.

Ruttenber, E. M., and Clark, L. M. *History of Orange County, New York*. Philadelphia, 1881.

Sarles, Frank B., and Shedd, Charles E. *Colonials and Patriots: Historic Places Commemorating Our Forebears, 1700-1783*. Washington, D.C., 1964.

Sawyer, John. *History of Cherry Valley, New York*. Cherry Valley, N.Y., 1898.

Scharf, J. Thomas, ed. *The History of Westchester County, New York, Including Morrisania, Kings Bridge, and West Farms*. 2 vols. Philadelphia, 1886.

Scheer, George F., and Rankin, Hugh F. *Rebels and Redcoats*. 1957; reprint ed. New York, 1963.

Schoonmaker, Marius. *History of Kingston, New York: From Its Earliest Settlement to 1820*. New York, 1888.

Scott, John Albert. *Fort Stanwix and Oriskany*. Rome, N.Y., 1927.

———. *Rome, N.Y.: A Short History*. Rome, N.Y., 1945.

Severance, Frank H. *An Old Frontier of France*. 2 vols. New York, 1917.

Shaw, Charles G. *New York—Oddly Enough*. New York, 1938.

Sheffield, Lieut. Col. Merle G. *The Fort That Never Was: Constitution Island in the Revolutionary War*. West Point, N.Y., 1969.

Shonnard, Frederick, and Spooner, W. W. *History of Westchester County, New York*. New York, 1900.

Simms, Jeptha Root. *The Frontiersmen of New York*. 2 vols. Albany, N.Y., 1882.

———. *History of Schoharie County, New York*. Albany, N.Y., 1845.

Sleight, Harry D. *Sag Harbor in Earlier Days*. Bridgehampton, N.Y., 1930.

Smith, Chester A. *Peekskill, A Friendly Town: A Pictorial History of the City from 1654 to 1952*. Peekskill, N.Y., 1952.

Smith, James H. *General History of Duchess (sic) County from 1609 to 1876 Inclusive*. Pawling, N.Y., 1877.

Smith, Justin H. *Arnold's March to Quebec*. New York, 1903.

———. *Our Struggle for the Fourteenth Colony*. 2 vols. New York, 1907.

Snyder, Charles M. *Oswego: From Buckskin to Bustles*. Port Washington, N.Y., 1968.

Society of the Cincinnati, Massachusetts. *Francis S. Drake's Memorials*. Boston, 1873.

Sosin, Jack. *The Revolutionary Frontier, 1763-1783*. New York, 1967.

Sparks, Jared. *The Writings of George Washington*. 12 vols. Boston, 1858.

Stedman, Charles. *The History of the Origin, Progress and Termination of the American War*. 2 vols. London, 1794.

Stember, Sol. *The Bicentennial Guide to the American Revolution*. 3 vols. Vol. 1: "The War in the North." New York, 1974.

Stiles, Henry R. *A History of the City of Brooklyn*. 3 vols. Brooklyn, N.Y., 1867.

———. *History of Kings County, New York*. 2 vols. New York, 1884.

Stillé, Charles J. *Major-General Anthony Wayne and the Pennsylvania Line in the Continental Army*. Philadelphia, 1893.

Stokes, I. N. Phelps. *The Iconography of Manhattan Island, 1498-1909*. 6 vols. New York, 1915-28.

Stone, William Leete. *Border Wars of the American Revolution.* 2 vols. New York, 1843, 1864; reprint ed. 1900.

————. *The Campaign of Lieut. Gen. John Burgoyne, and the Expedition of Lieut. Col. Barry St. Leger.* Albany, N.Y., 1877.

————. *Life of Joseph Brant–Thayendanegea.* New York, 1838.

————. *Washington County History.* New York, 1901.

Sullivan, James, ed. *The Papers of Sir William Johnson.* 14 vols. Albany, N.Y., 1921-65.

Sutherland, Stella H. *Population Distribution in Colonial America.* New York, 1956.

Swiggett, Howard. *War Out of Niagara.* New York, 1933.

Sylvester, Nathaniel B. *History of Saratoga County, New York.* Philadelphia, 1878.

Tallmadge, Benjamin. *Memoir of Col. Benj. Tallmadge, Prepared by Himself, at the Request of His Children.* New York, 1858.

Thacher, James. *A Military Journal during the American Revolutionary War from 1775 to 1783.* Boston, 1823.

Thane, Elswyth. *The Fighting Quaker: Nathanael Greene.* New York, 1972.

Thompson, Benjamin F. *History of Long Island.* 3d ed. vol. 1. New York, 1918.

Thwaites, Reuben Gold. *France in America, 1497-1763.* New York, 1905.

Tieck, William A. *Riverdale, Kingsbridge, Spuyten Duyvil: New York.* Old Tappan, N.J., 1968.

Tilberg, Frederick. *Fort Necessity National Battlefield Site, Pennsylvania.* rev. ed. Washington, D. C., 1956.

Timmerman, Emma S. "Homestead Notes" (1971). MS in Montgomery County Department of History and Archives, Fonda, N.Y.

Towner, Ausburn. *Our County and Its People: A History of the Valley and County of Chemung, New York.* Syracuse, N.Y., 1892.

Trevelyan, George Otto. *The American Revolution.* 1 vol. condensation of original 6 vols. Edited, arranged, and with an introduction and notes by Richard B. Morris. New York, 1965.

Ulmann, Albert. *A Landmark History of New York.* New York, 1939.

United States Bureau of the Census. *Historical Statistics of the United States.* Washington, D.C., 1960.

United States, Department of the Army. *American Military History* (extracts). Army Historical Series, Office of the Chief of Military History. Washington, D.C., 1969.

United States, Department of the Army Headquarters. *American Military History, 1607-1958.* Washington, D.C., 1959.

United States Military Academy. *The Centennial of the United States Military Academy at West Point, New York.* 2 vols. Washington, D.C., 1904.

United States War Department, Surgeon General's Office. *A Report on Barracks and Hospitals with Descriptions of Military Posts.* Washington, D.C., 1870.

United States Works Projects Administration (WPA). *New York: A Guide to the Empire State*. New York, 1940.

Vanderwerker, Mrs. J. B. *Early Days in EasternSaratoga County,* n.p., n.d.

Van De Water, Frederic Franklyn. *Lake Champlain and Lake George.* Indianapolis, Ind., 1946.

Van Doren, Carl. *Secret History of the American Revolution: An Account of the Conspiracies of Benedict Arnold and Numerous Others.* 1941; reprint ed. New York, 1969.

Van Every, Dale. *A Company of Heroes: The American Frontier, 1775-1783.* New York, 1962.

Van Schaick, George S. "Fort Dubois and the Revolutionary Officer for Whom It Was Named." *Schoharie County Historical Review* (November 1948).

Van Tyne, C. H. *The Loyalists in the American Revolution.* 2d ed. New York, 1929.

Vauban, Sebastien LePrestre de. *A Manual of Siegecraft and Fortification.* Translated, with an Introduction, by George A. Rothrock. Ann Arbor, Mich., 1968.

Vrooman, John J. *Forts and Firesides of the Mohawk Country.* Philadelphia, 1943.

Wager, D. E. "Forts Stanwix and Bull and Other Forts at Rome." Oneida Historical Society *Transactions,* no. 3 (1885-86).

Wallace, Anthony F.C. *The Death and Rebirth of the Seneca.* New York, 1970.

Wallace, Willard M. *Appeal to Arms: A Military History of the American Revolution.* New York, 1951.

———. *Traitorous Hero.* New York, 1954.

Ward, Christopher. *The War of the Revolution.* 2 vols. New York, 1952.

Weigley, Russell F. *History of the United States Army.* New York, 1967.

Whittemore, Charles P. *A General of the Revolution: John Sullivan of New Hampshire.* New York, 1961.

Wildes, Harry Emerson. *Anthony Wayne, Trouble Shooter of the American Revolution.* New York, 1941.

Willett, Marinus. *A Narrative of the Military Actions of Colonel Marinus Willett, Taken Chiefly from his Own Manuscript.* Prepared by his son, William M. Willett. New York, 1831.

Williams, Edward T. *Scenic and Historic Niagara Falls.* Niagara Falls, N.Y., 1925.

Wilmot, John E., ed. *Journals of the Provincial Congress of the State of New York, 1775-1777.* 2 vols. Albany, N.Y., 1842.

Winsor, Justin. *The American Revolution: A Narrative, Critical and Bibliographical History.* 8 vols. Boston, 1884-89; reprint ed. New York, 1972.

Wood, Gordon S. *The Creation of the American Republic, 1776-1787.* Chapel Hill, N.C., 1969.

Revolutionary Newspapers

Connecticut Gazette. New London, July 12, 1776.
Constitutional Gazette. New York, July 10, 1776.
Continental Journal and Weekly Advertiser. Boston, September 4, 1777.
Dunlap's Maryland Gazette. Baltimore, July 9, 1776.
Freeman's Journal. Portsmouth, N.H., July 22, 1776.
New England Chronicle. Boston, July 18, 1776.
New York Gazette and Weekly Mercury. April 15 and May 6, 1776; October 27, 1777.
New York Journal. August 2, 1779.
Pennsylvania Evening Post. Philadelphia, July 6, 1776.
Providence Gazette. Rhode Island, July 13, 1776.

Modern Newspapers

Boston Globe. June 9, 1974.
Brooklyn Daily Eagle. March 29, 1896, and March 17, 1939.
Brooklyn Standard Union. October 2, 1921.
Fort Myers (Fla.) *News-Press*. November 16, 1975.
Fort Plain (N.Y.) *Courier-Standard*. February 1, 1945.
Kings Park (Long Island, N.Y.) *Independent*. August 8, 1961.
Long Island (N.Y.) *Forum*. December 1948 and July 1961.
Long Island (N.Y.) *Newsday*. December 12, 1964; February 19, 1968; January 28, 1973; July 1, 1973; and February 9, 1974.
Miami (Fla.) *Herald*. February 10, 1974.
New York Herald Tribune. May 2, 1965.
New York Post. January 2, 1966.
New York Times. December 10, 1939; May 6, 1956; June 22, 1956; July 11, 1958; July 18, 1958; May 10, 1959; September 22, 1959; June 24, 1962; May 5, 1963; October 6, 1964; October 20, 1964; November 22, 1964; May 9, 1965; October 31, 1965; May 26, 1968; September 14, 1969; January 15, 1970; August 2, 1970; August 15, 1971; and June 25, 1975.
Niagara Falls (N.Y.) *Gazette*. August 18, 1902.
Plattsburgh (N.Y.) *Press-Republican*. October 10, 1960.
Plattsburgh (N.Y.) *Republican*. February 12, 1898, and August 5, 1899.
St. Johnsville (N.Y.) *Courier-Standard-Enterprise*. August 2 and 9, 1972.
Salem (N.Y.) *Press*. August 9, 1945.
Watertown (N.Y.) *Times*. March 25, 1961.

Index

485